AF845219

Security and Privacy of Cyber-physical Systems

Emerging Trends, Technologies, and Applications

RIVER PUBLISHERS SERIES IN DIGITAL SECURITY AND FORENSICS

Series Editors

ANAND R. PRASAD
Deloitte Tohmatsu Cyber LLC,
Japan

R. CHANDRAMOULI
Stevens Institute of Technology,
USA

ABDERRAHIM BENSLIMANE
University of Avignon,
France

PETER LANGENDÖRFER
IHP,
Germany

The "River Publishers Series in Security and Digital Forensics" is a series of comprehensive academic and professional books which focus on the theory and applications of Cyber Security, including Data Security, Mobile and Network Security, Cryptography and Digital Forensics. Topics in Prevention and Threat Management are also included in the scope of the book series, as are general business Standards in this domain.

Books published in the series include research monographs, edited volumes, handbooks and textbooks. The books provide professionals, researchers, educators, and advanced students in the field with an invaluable insight into the latest research and developments.

Topics covered in the series include:-

- Blockchain for secure transactions
- Cryptography
- Cyber Security
- Data and App Security
- Digital Forensics
- Hardware Security
- IoT Security
- Mobile Security
- Network Security
- Privacy
- Software Security
- Standardization
- Threat Management

For a list of other books in this series, visit www.riverpublishers.com

Security and Privacy of Cyber-physical Systems

Emerging Trends, Technologies, and Applications

Editors

Agbotiname Lucky Imoize
Department of Electrical and Electronics Engineering,
Faculty of Engineering, University of Lagos, Nigeria

Webert Montlouis
Applied Physics Laboratory (APL) and
Electrical and Computer Engineering Department,
Johns Hopkins University, United States

Segun I. Popoola
School of Computing and Information Science,
Anglia Ruskin University, United Kingdom

Mohammad Hammoudeh
Department of Information and Computer Science,
King Fahd University of Petroleum and Minerals, Saudi Arabia

River Publishers

Routledge
Taylor & Francis Group
NEW YORK AND LONDON

Published 2025 by River Publishers
River Publishers
Broagervej 10, 9260 Gistrup, Denmark
www.riverpublishers.com

Distributed exclusively by Routledge
605 Third Avenue, New York, NY 10017, USA
4 Park Square, Milton Park, Abingdon, Oxon OX14 4RN

Security and Privacy of Cyber-physical Systems: Emerging Trends, Technologies, and Applications / Agbotiname Lucky Imoize, Webert Montlouis, Segun I. Popoola, and Mohammad Hammoudeh.

©2025 River Publishers. All rights reserved. No part of this publication may be reproduced, stored in a retrieval systems, or transmitted in any form or by any means, mechanical, photocopying, recording or otherwise, without prior written permission of the publishers.

Routledge is an imprint of the Taylor & Francis Group, an informa business

ISBN 978-87-4380-129-0 (hardback)
ISBN 978-87-4380-673-8 (paperback)
ISBN 978-87-4380-131-3 (online)
ISBN 978-8-743-80130-6 (ebook master)
DOI: 10.1201/9788743801306

While every effort is made to provide dependable information, the publisher, authors, and editors cannot be held responsible for any errors or omissions.

Contents

Preface

The rapid advancement of cutting-edge technologies such as the Internet of Things (IoT), ubiquitous computing, and super intelligent networks has led to the design and development of innovative cyber-physical systems (CPS) that can drive developmental change in modern society. However, the benefits of these systems come with new concerns and challenges, particularly the security and privacy of critical user information. Therefore, the need to address the growing security and privacy concerns in modern cyber-physical systems cannot be overstated. While several works of literature have proposed various security measures to address the escalating security and privacy issues in cyber-physical systems, most existing schemes cannot withstand sophisticated vulnerability attacks in practical settings. To address this problem, this book proposes emerging ideas and trends in security and privacy issues in cyber-physical systems.

The book covers critical security and privacy concerns, including theoretical analysis, vulnerability discovery and mitigation, novel system architecture design and implementation, emerging application scenarios, experimental frameworks, and ethics and social impacts of cyber-physical systems. Additionally, the book examines the legal requirements, regulatory frameworks, and policies for enabling the security and privacy of cyber-physical systems. Lastly, it provides researchers and academics with new insights into the real-world scenarios of deploying, applying, and managing security and privacy in modern cyber-physical systems. The book is well structured into 20 chapters outlined as follows.

Chapter 1 presents an overview of security and privacy in cyber-physical systems, focusing on emerging trends and attack detection and mitigation strategies. Chapter 2 examines protection and fault diagnostics in legacy cyber-physical systems. Chapter 3 focuses on explainable artificial intelligence for intrusion detection in cyber-physical systems. Chapter 4 addresses security and privacy issues in cyber-physical systems. Chapter 5 examines the physical layer security of 6G vehicle visible light communications for cyber-physical systems. Chapter 6 presents hardware security and privacy for cyber-physical systems. Chapter 7 investigates a secure biometric authentication architecture for blockchain-driven cyber-physical systems.

Chapter 8 explores a secure IoT-based smart wheelchair system, highlighting the implementation of a security enhancement strategy.

Chapter 9 considers statistical estimation of user location distribution via anonymized dummy data transmission. Chapter 10 explores the emerging security and privacy schemes for cyber-physical systems. Chapter 11 critically examines security and privacy concerns and risks in modern cyber-physical systems. Chapter 12 presents the ethics of security and privacy of cyber-physical systems, considering emerging trends, technology, and applications. Chapter 13 focuses on intrusion detection techniques for cyber-physical systems. Chapter 14 reviews the application of cyber-physical systems, considering strategies for enhancing availability, recovery, and auditing for optimal performance. Chapter 15 delves into the intricate legal framework and regulatory policies for cyber-physical systems.

Chapter 16 offers an in-depth examination of blockchain-based security and privacy solutions for cyber-physical systems. Chapter 17 investigates privacy-utility trade-offs in IoT networks, exploring a comparative analysis of differential privacy mechanisms for sensor data aggregation. Chapter 18 sheds light on enhancing cyber-physical systems through artificial intelligence and machine learning. Chapter 19 highlights the case studies on the security and privacy of cyber-physical systems. Lastly, Chapter 20 concludes the book, highlighting recent advances and the future of cyber-physical systems.

The book is an ideal reference for practitioners and researchers in cyber-physical systems, security and privacy, the Internet of Things, cryptography, defensive walls, industrial systems, and cyber threats. It is also a good textbook for graduate and senior undergraduate courses in these subjects.

We would like to thank the reviewers of the original book proposal for their constructive suggestions, all the authors of the chapters for their insightful contributions, and the editors and editorial assistants for their cooperation and support.

Agbotiname Lucky Imoize
Gelsenkirchen, North Rhine-Westphalia, Germany

Webert Montlouis
Columbia, Maryland, United States

Segun I. Popoola
Cambridge, United Kingdom

Mohammad Hammoudeh
Saudi Arabia, United Arab Emirate

List of Contributors

Adeniyi, Abidemi Emmanuel, *Department of Computer Science, College of Computing and Communication Studies, Bowen University, Nigeria*

Adetola, Abdulfattah Sogbesan, *Centre for Cyberspace, Nasarawa State University, Nigeria*

Ahmad, Hasnain, *Department of Computer Science, COMSATS University, Islamabad-Lahore Campus, Pakistan*

Ajiboye, Grace Oluwamayowa, *Department of Computer Sciences, Precious Cornerstone University, Nigeria*

Akinyemi, Lateef Adesola, *Department of Electronic and Computer Engineering, Faculty of Engineering, Lagos State University, Nigeria; Centre for Augmented Intelligence and Data Science (CAIDS), School of Computing, CSET University of South Africa, South Africa*

Aliu, Opeyemi Habeeb, *IoT Africa Networks, Tranter IT Infrastructure Services Limited, Nigeria*

Aliyu, Abubakar, *Department of Computer Science, Faculty of Science, Federal University Lokoja, Nigeria*

Arnesano, Marco, *Department of Theoretical and Applied Sciences, eCampus University, Italy*

Atzeni, Gianluca, *Department of Theoretical and Applied Sciences, eCampus University, Italy*

Awotunde, Joseph Bamidele, *Department of Computer Science, Faculty of Communication and Information Sciences, University of Ilorin, Nigeria*

Delmonte, Nicola, *Department of Engineering and Architecture, University of Parma, Italy*

Ding, Jupeng, *College of Technology and Data, Yantai Nanshan University, China; Key Laboratory of Signal Detection and Processing in Xinjiang Uygur Autonomous Region, School of Computer Science and Technology (School of Cyberspace Security), Xinjiang University, China*

Ebute, Mercy Oka, *Department of Accounting, Anderson School of Management, University of New Mexico, USA*

Falola, Peace Busola, *Computer Science Unit, Distance Learning Center, University of Ibadan, Nigeria*

Folorunso, Comfort Oluwaseyi, *Department of Systems Engineering, Faculty of Engineering, University of Lagos, Nigeria*

Frontoni, Emanuele, *Department of Political Sciences, Communication and International Relations, University of Macerata, Italy*

Gbadega, Peter Anuoluwapo, *Department of Electrical and Electronic Engineering Science, University of Johannesburg, South Africa*

I, Chih-Lin, *China Mobile Research Institute, China*

Imoize, Agbotiname Lucky, *Department of Electrical and Electronics Engineering, Faculty of Engineering, University of Lagos, Nigeria; Department of Electrical Engineering and Information Technology, Institute of Digital Communication, Ruhr University, Germany*

Ipinnimo, Oluwafemi, *Department of Systems Engineering, Faculty of Engineering, University of Lagos, Nigeria*

Isiaka, Dauda Olorunkemi, *Department of Computer Science, Faculty of Science, Federal University Lokoja, Nigeria*

Jadon, Rahul, *CarGurus Inc., USA*

Jimoh, Rasheed Gbenga, *Department of Computer Science, University of Ilorin, Nigeria*

Joshua, Richard Govada, *Comprobase Inc, United States*

Kara, Ilker, *Department of Computer Engineering, Faculty of Engineering, Çankırı Karatekin University, Turkey; Department of Medical Services and Techniques, Çankırı Karatekin University, Turkey*

Khandan, Shokooh, *Department of Computing and Mathematics, Manchester Metropolitan University, UK*

Kuznetsov, Oleksandr, *Department of Theoretical and Applied Sciences, eCampus University, Italy*

Kuznetsova, Kateryna, *Department of Political Sciences, Communication and International Relations, University of Macerata, Italy; Vision, Robotics and Artificial Intelligence Lab, Italy*

Kuznetsova, Tatyana, *Department of Information and Communication Systems Security, V. N. Karazin Kharkiv National University, Ukraine*

Mbanaso, Uche M., *Centre for Cyberspace Studies, Nasarawa State University, Nigeria*

Noor, Kinzah, *Office of Research Innovation and Commercialization, University of Management and Technology, Pakistan*

Odeyinka, Olumide Francis, *Department of Systems Engineering, Faculty of Engineering, University of Lagos, Nigeria*

Ogbuju, Emeka, *Department of Computer Science, Faculty of Science, Federal University Lokoja, Nigeria*

Ohsuga, Akihiko, *Department of Informatics, Graduate School of Informatics and Engineering, The University of Electro-Communications, Japan*

Oladipo, Francisca, *Department of Computer Science, Faculty of Computing and Applied Science, Thomas Adewumi University, Nigeria*

Olaleye, Eniola Sodiq, *Department of Systems Engineering, Faculty of Engineering, University of Lagos, Nigeria*

Olusola Kareem, Yunus, *Department of Cybersecurity, College of Engineering, University of West England, United Kingdom*

Oluwatobi, Blessing Olorunfemi, *Department of Computer Science, Redeemer's University, Nigeria*

Popoola, Segun I., *School of Computing and Information Science, Anglia Ruskin University, UK*

Quadri, Habeeb, *University of Kent, United Kingdom*

Raheem, Wasiu Adewale, *Department of Systems Engineering, Faculty of Engineering, University of Lagos, Nigeria*

Randieri, Cristian, *Department of Theoretical and Applied Sciences, eCampus University, Italy*

Sani, Godwin, *Directorate of Information and Communication Technology, Federal University Lokoja, Nigeria*

Sei, Yuichi, *Department of Informatics, Graduate School of Informatics and Engineering, The University of Electro-Communications, Japan*

Shaikhanova, Aigul, *Department of Information Security, L.N. Gumilyov Eurasian National University, Republic of Kazakhstan*

Simonazzi, Marco, *Department of Engineering and Architecture, University of Parma, Italy*

Singh, Chauhan Guman, *John Tesla Inc., USA*

Smirnov, Oleksii, *Department of cyber security and software, Central Ukrainian National Technical University, Ukraine*

Srinivasan, Kannan, *Saiana Technologies Inc., USA*

Svatowsky, Igor, *Department of Information and Communication Systems Security, V. N. Karazin Kharkiv National University, Ukraine*

Tofade, Samuel Oluwatobi, *CleanTech Renewable Energy, Nigeria*

Tomazzoli, Claudio, *Department of Computer Science, University of Verona, Italy*

Tsado, Yakubu, *Department of Computing and Mathematics, Manchester Metropolitan University, UK*

Wang, Jintao, *Department of Electronic Engineering, Beijing National Research Center for Information Science and Technology, Tsinghua University, China*

Yang, Hui, *Department of Electronic Engineering, Beijing National Research Center for Information Science and Technology, Tsinghua University, China*

Yemi-Peters, Victoria, *Department of Computer Science, Faculty of Science, Federal University Lokoja, Nigeria*

List of Figures

List of Tables

List of Abbreviations

A.L.B.A.	Advanced Light Body Assistance
AADL	Architecture analysis and design language
AAS	Asset Administration Shell
ABGT	Agent-based game theory
ACE	Area control error
ACL	Access control list
ACSC	Australian Cyber Security Centre
ADC	Analog-to-digital conversion
ADF	Application development framework
ADN	Active distribution network
AE	Autoencoder
AI	Artificial intelligence
AKA	Authenticated key agreement
AMCBA	Attention Meditation Cost–Benefit Analysis
AMI	Advanced metering infrastructure
ANWS	Actuator networks & wireless sensor
API	Application programming interface
APS	Autonomous passenger ship
APT	Advanced persistent threat
AR	Augmented reality
AUC	Area under the curve
AVM	Average value model
BAN	Body area network
BCI	Brain–computer interface
BEM	Building energy model
BESS	Battery energy storage system
BLCS	Brain-like control security
BLS	Brain-like security
CAN	Controller area network
CCES	Consumer-centered energy system
CF	Cybersecurity framework
CFD	Computational fluid dynamics

CI	Computational intelligence
CIA	Confidentiality, integrity, and availability
CIP	Critical infrastructure protection
CISA	Cybersecurity Information Sharing Act
CNIIO	China National Internet Information Office
CNN	Convolutional neural network
COA	Coyote optimization algorithm
COP	Center of pressure
CPS	Cyber-physical system
CPSS	Cyber–physical social system
CPST	Cyber–physical–social thinking
CTL	Computation tree logic
CVE	Common vulnerabilities and exposures
CVSS	Common vulnerability scoring system
CYPREMS	Cyber-physical resistant energy management systems
D2D	Device-to-device
DAGA	Detecting attacks to in-vehicle networks via N-gram analysis
DBN	Deep belief network
DCS	Distributed control system
DDoS	Distributed denial of service
DER	Distributed energy resource
DES	Discrete event systems
DFD	Data flow diagram
DM	Data mining
DNN	Deep neural network
DOE	Department of Energy
DORA	Digital Operational Resilience Act
DoS	Denial of service
DP	Differentiated privacy
DREAD	Damage, reproducibility, exploitability, affected users, and discoverability
DSSoT	Dynamic social structure of things
DT	Decision tree
DVAE	Dirichlet variational autoencoder
EDPB	European Data Protection Board
EGTO	Enhanced Artificial Gorilla Troops Optimizer
EHR	Electronic health record
EIS	Electrochemical impedance spectroscopy
ELE	Enhanced living environment

EMG	Electromyography
EMS	Energy management system
ETB	Example-based technique
EV	Electric vehicle
FA	Factory automation
FAA	Federal Aviation Administration
FDA	Food and Drug Administration
FFNN	Feedforward neural network
FMEA	Failure mode and effects analysis
FN	False negative
FOV	Field of view
FP	False positive
FPR	False positive rate
F-RON	Fog radio and optical network
FSM	Finite state machine
FTA	Fault tree analysis
GDPR	General Data Protection Regulation
GME	Generic modeling environment
GPS	Global positioning system
GPSEnv	Gait and posture smart environment
GPSJack	Gait and posture smart jacket
GSHP	Geothermal source heat pump
HAI	HIL-based augmented ICS
HCI	Human–computer interaction
HE	Homomorphic encryption
HER	Electronic health record
HIL	Hardware-in-the-loop
HIPAA	Health Insurance Portability and Accountability Act
HITL	Human-in-the-loop
HMI	human–machine interface
HPC	High probability concept
HSE	Health and safety executive
HSM	Hardware security modules
ICE	Individual conditional expectation
ICO	Information Commissioner's office
ICPS	Integrated cyber-physical system
ICS	Industrial control system
ICT	Information and communication technologies
IDS	Intrusion detection system
IEC	International Electrotechnical Commission

IEEE	Institute of Electrical and Electronics Engineers
IF	Isolation forest
IIoT	Industrial Internet of Things
ILP	Interledger protocol
IoDT	Internet of digital twins
IoT	Internet of Things
IoV	Internet of vehicles
IP	Internet protocol
IPS	Intrusion prevention system
IR	InfraRed
ISMS	Information security management system
ISO	International Standards Organisation
IT	Information technology
ITS	Intelligent transportation systems
ITU	International Telecommunication Union
IWMCPS	Improved wireless medical cyber-physical system
IWSN	Industrial wireless sensor network
KNN	K-nearest neighbor
LAN	Local area network
LED	Light-emitting diode
LFW	Labeled Faces in the Wild
LIME	Local interpretable model-agnostic explanations
LOPA	Loss of protection analysis
LOS	Line of sight
LPASA	Lightweight privacy-aware secure authentication
LQ	Linear quadratic
LR	Linear regression
LTL	Linear temporal logic
LZIA	Lightweight zero-knowledge authentication
M2M	Machine-to-machine
MAC	Mandatory access control
MDA	Multi dimensional analysis
MDE	Model-driven engineering
MEC	Multi-access edge computing
MFA	Multi-factor authentication
MICS	Medical implant communication service
MIIT	Ministry of Industry and Information Technology
MitM	Man-in-the-middle
ML	Machine learning
MLP	Multilayer perceptron

MQTT	Message queuing telemetry transport
MSE	Mean squared error
NATO	North Atlantic Treaty Organization
NCSC	National Cyber Security Centre
NERC	North American Electric Reliability Corporation
NILM	Non-intrusive load monitoring
NIST	National Institute of Standards and Technology
NLOS	Non-line of sight
NQT	Negative Quad Tree
nZED	Near-zero energy district
OAIC	Office of the Australian Information Commissioner
OECD	Organization for Economic Cooperation and Development
OoT	Out-of-time
OT	Operational technology
P2P	Peer-to-peer
PA	Process automation
PASTA	Process for attack simulation and threat analysis
PBFT	Practical byzantine fault tolerant
PD	Photodetector
PDA	Pole dynamics attack
PDP	Partial dependence plot
PET	Privacy-enhancing technology
PFI	Permutation feature importance
PII	Personally identifiable information
PIPL	Personal Information Protection Law
PKI	Public key infrastructure
PLA	People's Liberation Army
PLC	Programmable logic controller
PLS	Physical layer security
PoLP	Principle of least privilege
POMDP	Partially observable Markov decision process
PoS	Proof of stake
PoW	Proof of work
PSST	Privacy, security, safety, and trust
QoS	Quality of service
R2L	Remote-to-local
RBAC	Role-based access control
RCE	Remote code execution
ReLU	Rectified linear unit
RER	Renewable energy resources

RF	Radio frequency
RFE	Recursive feature elimination
RFID	Radio frequency identification
RIS	Railway interlocking system
RMF	Risk management framework
RNN	Recurrent neural network
ROC	Receiver operating characteristic
RTU	Remote terminal unit
SC	Secrecy capacity
SCADA	Supervisory control and data acquisition
SDAE-DLM	Staked denoising autoencoders extreme learning machine
SDN	Software-defined network
SHAP	Shapley additive explanations
SI	Spark ignition
SIEM	Security information and event management
SMC	Secure multiparty computation
SMPC	Secure multi-party computation
SMV	Symbolic model checker
SNR	Signal-to-noise ratio
SoC	Systems on chips
SoH	State of health
SOM	Self-organizing map
SSH	Secure socket shell
STL	Self-taught learning
STRIDE	Spoofing, tampering, repudiation, information disclosure, denial of service, and elevation of privileges
SVM	Support vector machine
SVPL	Standard vulnerability profiling library
SVR	Support vector regression
SWAF	Smart wheelchair for fall risk assessment
TIA	Trans-impedance amplifier
TLS	Transport layer security
TN	True negative
TP	True positive
TPM	Trusted platform module
TPR	True positive rate
U2R	User-to-root
UWCPMS	Updated wireless cyber-physical medical system
V2I	Vehicle-to-infrastructure
V2V	Vehicle-to-vehicle

VC	Verifiable computation
VLAN	Virtual local area network
VLC	Visible light communication
VMS	Vulnerability management systems
VR	Virtual reality
XAI	Explainable AI
XSS	Cross-site scripting
ZDA	Zero dynamics attack
ZKP	Zero-knowledge proof

1

An Overview of Security and Privacy in Cyber-physical Systems: Emerging Trends and Strategies

Opeyemi Habeeb Aliu[1], Agbotiname Lucky Imoize[2], Kinzah Noor[3], Hasnain Ahmad[4] and Mercy Oka Ebute[5]

[1]IoT Africa Networks, Tranter IT Infrastructure Services Limited, Nigeria
[2]Department of Electrical and Electronics Engineering, Faculty of Engineering, University of Lagos, Nigeria
[3]Office of Research Innovation and Commercialization, University of Management and Technology, Pakistan
[4]Department of Computer Science, COMSATS University, Islamabad-Lahore Campus, Pakistan
[5]Department of Accounting, Anderson School of Management, University of New Mexico, USA

Email: habeeb.aliu@tranter-it.com; aimoize@unilag.edu.ng; kinzah.noor@umt.edu.pk; sp22-bcs-140@cuilahore.edu.pk; mercyebute02@gmail.com

Abstract

Cyber-physical systems (CPS) integrate networked digital technologies with analog physical processes, enabling process optimization and unlocking previously unattainable functionalities. These systems introduce unique dynamics that reshape traditional security frameworks due to their interconnected nature. Neither cyber security principles nor physical security strategies alone are sufficient to protect CPS. Instead, the convergence of cyber and physical domains creates complex interdependencies that can lead to unforeseen vulnerabilities. For instance, a physical attack on critical infrastructure may grant unauthorized access to sensitive assets, compromising the digital data

DOI: 10.1201/9788743801306-1

of the system. Conversely, a cyberattack could exploit digital vulnerabilities to cause physical malfunctions, resulting in real-world consequences. These interwoven threats highlight the need for a holistic approach to CPS security and privacy that addresses both domains simultaneously. Therefore, ensuring robust security and privacy is a foundational requirement for the design, development, and operation of CPS. This chapter explores the unique challenges of securing CPS and discusses how their security and privacy considerations differ from standalone cyber or physical systems. Strategies and best practices for protecting CPS are explored, offering guidance to system designers on developing secure and privacy-conscious solutions for future deployments.

1.1 Introduction

The term CPS emerged approximately two decades ago to describe the integration of embedded computing and communication technologies with various physical domains, including household appliances, automotive systems, the electrical power grid, energy infrastructure, healthcare, manufacturing, materials, and transportation. Today, many of these systems are integral to critical infrastructure (CI), life-support devices, and essential daily operations. Over the past decade, CPS has increasingly become a target for security breaches due to its complex and interconnected nature [1]. The combination of cyber and physical domains in CPS introduces unique vulnerabilities that cannot be addressed by traditional cyber or physical security alone. Physical attacks, for example, can compromise information systems of device, while cyberattacks can disrupt or damage physical processes, leading to system failures. When CPS is deployed in critical applications, such attacks can have far-reaching, real-world consequences that impact safety, operations, and public trust [2].

The principles of security and privacy are relevant to both the cyber and physical components of CPS, with overlapping terms such as cybersecurity, information security, and information assurance underscoring these concepts. Defensive measures, such as deterrence, avoidance, prevention, detection, recovery, and correction, play a critical role and should be integrated into the overall risk management strategy of an organization. These measures ensure resilience and continuity, even under adverse conditions. Information security is anchored by core principles, research [3] outlined key goals that influence the overall effectiveness of a system.

Traditional information technology (IT) security measures often prove inadequate for CPS, particularly when data transmission occurs through exposed or unprotected networks. A major source of vulnerability arises at the interfaces of sensors and actuators, where attackers can exploit physical entry points to compromise system integrity without the need to bypass the entire control mechanism. Supervisory control and data acquisition (SCADA) systems, which form the backbone of modern industrial infrastructure, are a prime example of CPS. The increasing interconnectivity of SCADA systems through cyberspace, however, has made them attractive targets for cyberattacks, thereby exposing them to significant security vulnerabilities.

In CPS, the availability of critical resources is of paramount importance, often surpassing the challenges faced by purely digital systems. Attacks such as denial of service (DoS) and distributed denial of service (DDoS) [4] can disrupt communication networks, delay operations, and cause substantial losses. For instance, in power grids, the unavailability of resources caused by such attacks can result in widespread outages and significant economic losses due to interruptions in electricity supply. This unique convergence of cyber and physical domains necessitates specialized security strategies to address the vulnerabilities and operational requirements of CPS.

The integration of CPS into smart grids has revolutionized power distribution networks, fostering advanced functionalities and enhanced efficiency. The extensive reliance on communication and information exchange in smart grids, while enabling greater operational capabilities, has also introduced significant security vulnerabilities. These vulnerabilities stem from the high dependence of the grid on cyber information, which exposes it to potential cyberattacks. A key challenge lies in harnessing the capabilities of communication and information technology infrastructures while mitigating these risks to ensure resilient and secure operations. To address the evolving objectives of future smart grids, it is imperative to develop comprehensive testbeds that facilitate interoperability assessments and enable the identification of cybersecurity weaknesses [5].

Personal CPS have been developed to generate economic value by automating routine tasks, with the cyber component serving as the core element and the physical counterpart enhancing the overall functionality of these systems. The pervasive adoption of personal CPS often obscures their underlying computational nature and the associated risks. These devices frequently store sensitive personally identifiable information (PII) and possess the capability to capture intricate details of the daily lives of users. While such observations once required close physical proximity, the integration of Internet connectivity now enables remote monitoring from virtually anywhere in the world. Consequently, privacy emerges as the foremost concern in personal CPS. However, in the case of personal medical devices [6], safety takes precedence, with privacy becoming a secondary consideration. Security also plays a critical role, as personal CPS often maintains trusting relationships with office or industrial systems, including industrial control systems (ICS). This interconnectivity introduces potential vulnerabilities, creating pathways for cyber threats to propagate across interconnected networks.

Smart devices in our homes, including smart refrigerators, TVs, and light bulbs, are increasingly connected to the Internet. This connectivity enables them to perform tasks like ordering groceries or monitoring home activity. However, this also exposes personal information and habits to potential risks, as these devices often communicate with their manufacturers, sharing data that could be used for targeted advertising or even malicious purposes. The interconnected nature of these systems creates vulnerabilities that can be exploited by attackers. For instance, gaining physical access to a device could allow an attacker to bypass digital security measures. The interconnectedness of CPS means that a vulnerability in one component can impact the entire system. This makes it challenging to secure these systems completely. Nonetheless, by understanding the potential risks and implementing robust security measures, research [7] can mitigate these threats and protect devices and data.

This chapter explores the security and privacy challenges inherent to CPS. The foundational principles of classical information security and physical security are introduced, with their relevance examined in the context of CPS. The composability and heterogeneity of CPS – spanning multiple application domains – are highlighted as factors that can lead to unforeseen vulnerabilities, magnified impacts, and cascading failures.

Given the emergent properties of CPS, the security and privacy considerations are highlighted as significantly different from those of purely cyber or purely physical systems; strategies for addressing these challenges and ensuring the robustness of CPS against evolving threats are discussed. Furthermore, the intricacies of security and privacy at the intersection of personal and infrastructural CPS are explored. Raising awareness about existing risks in current CPS products is crucial, but the primary aim is to guide future CPS designers toward building more secure and privacy-aware systems. By learning from past and present challenges, improved security practices can be implemented to ensure that next-generation CPS are resilient, reliable, and better equipped to address emerging threats.

1.1.1 Key contributions of the chapter

The following are the significant contributions of this chapter:

i. This chapter delves into the critical intersection of cyber and physical security within cyber-physical systems (CPS), emphasizing the profound implications of security breaches. It offers a comprehensive exploration of how cyberattacks can lead to physical malfunctions with real-world consequences and, conversely, how physical breaches can undermine the integrity of critical information systems. The discussion highlights the bidirectional vulnerabilities inherent to CPS, where disruptions in one domain can cascade into the other, leading to significant operational and safety challenges.

ii. Building upon classical security paradigms, this study extends these foundational concepts to the CPS domain. Traditional cyber and physical security frameworks often operate in silos, which are insufficient for addressing the intricate interdependencies of CPS. To overcome these limitations, the chapter proposes integrated security approaches tailored to safeguard these complex and interconnected systems. These approaches are designed to provide holistic protection by recognizing and mitigating the dynamic threats emerging at the intersection of cyber and physical domains.

iii. The chapter further illustrates these concepts through practical examples that reveal how CPS vulnerabilities often arise from unforeseen interactions between their cyber and physical components. These case studies underscore the importance of considering CPS as unified entities rather than isolated systems. By examining real-world scenarios, readers gain insights into the diverse pathways through which adversaries can exploit these vulnerabilities, leading to both operational disruptions and potential societal harm.

iv. Moreover, the chapter addresses the evolving role of CPS designers in anticipating and countering emerging threats. By analyzing current risks and vulnerabilities, this study provides actionable recommendations for adapting to the rapid pace of technological advancements in CPS. These insights empower designers to proactively incorporate resilience and adaptability into CPS architectures, ensuring that these systems remain secure and reliable in an increasingly interconnected and dynamic landscape.

v. In essence, this chapter bridges the gap between theoretical security principles and practical application, equipping researchers, practitioners, and policymakers with the knowledge and tools to enhance the security and resilience of CPS. The discussion is both forward-looking and grounded in present challenges, aiming to foster a deeper understanding of how to protect these systems against the complex and multifaceted threats of the modern era.

1.1.2 Chapter organization

The organization of this chapter is as follows: Section 1.2 provides a review of previous work on the security and privacy of cyber-physical systems, highlighting their limitations and challenges. Section 1.3 discusses the fundamental principles of privacy and security as they apply to both the cyber and physical components of CPS. It also addresses the inherent ambiguities of cyber-physical systems, contrasts them with traditional information systems, and underscores the rationale for transitioning from purely cyber or physical systems to integrated cyber-physical systems. Furthermore, this section explores key approaches to securing these systems. Section 1.4 outlines the current security and privacy challenges facing cyber-physical systems, identifies the limitations of this study, and summarizes the lessons learned. Finally, Section 1.5 concludes the chapter and provides recommendations for future research and development in this domain.

1.2 Related Work

Previously, embedded computers were primarily used to control and monitor physical processes through feedback loop control mechanisms. Over time, the integration of computational technologies with traditional embedded physical systems laid the foundation for a new class of systems known as CPS. Advances in CPS have garnered significant attention over the past decade [8]. In recent years, CPS has become increasingly integral to critical domains such as medical devices, smart vehicles, industrial systems, and the energy grid. Given their reliance on the Internet, ensuring their security – distinct from the security requirements of conventional information technology systems – has emerged as a crucial research area. However, the field remains underdeveloped, lacking a well-structured framework. The research [9] presents a systematic literature review focusing on core issues in CPS security, including defense mechanisms for system recovery, risk/threat assessments, and the ethical and societal implications of CPS.

Advancements in information and communication technologies (ICT) have enabled the widespread deployment of CPSs, offering numerous benefits and introducing growing security and privacy threats, particularly from passive attacks that compromise sensitive information. Strategies like encryption and k-anonymity have been proposed to address these challenges, but they often require adaptation to the evolving architecture of CPSs. Differential privacy has emerged as an effective technique for protecting CPS data privacy. The research [10] provides an in-depth survey of differential privacy techniques across key CPS applications, including energy systems, transportation systems, healthcare, and the industrial Internet of Things (IIoT). It discusses challenges, open issues, and future research directions, serving as a foundation for the development of advanced differential privacy techniques tailored to CPS environments.

CPS integrates physical processes with computational and communication technologies, forming a foundational component of Industry 4.0. To support CPS services, fog radio and optical networks (F-RON) have emerged as a critical infrastructure, leveraging the ubiquity of wireless technologies alongside the high capacity of optical networks. However, ensuring cybersecurity in CPS environments presents significant challenges, particularly due to the tradeoff between security controls and privacy preservation in F-RON. To address these challenges, the research [11] proposes a brain-like control security (BLCS) architecture for F-RON in CPS, which incorporates a brain-like security (BLS) scheme. The BLCS architecture enables secure cross-domain control through tripartite controller verification in decentralized F-RON environments for distributed computing and communication without requiring the disclosure of private domain-specific information. The BLS scheme leverages partial information for control identification using relational networks and deep learning techniques applied to a behavioral library.

Existing approaches to CPS privacy often lack a robust vulnerability characterization model and fail to account for the data preferences of providers. They also rely on uniform privacy mechanisms, leading to inadequate protection for some and overprotection for others while lacking comprehensive privacy quantification frameworks. To address these challenges, research [12] proposes a personalized privacy framework that integrates a standard vulnerability profiling library (SVPL) to rank nodes by privacy loss and a personalized privacy preference (PDP) framework that applies Laplace noise based on individual preferences. This approach effectively balances privacy, utility, and information risk, offering a novel solution for privacy preservation in CPS. With the proliferation of low-cost, smart, and interconnected IoT devices, the field of cyber-physical security has garnered significant attention. Prior research has unveiled novel threat vectors that exploit vulnerabilities in the interface between cyber and physical domains. Specifically, attackers have targeted sensing systems as an attack surface, enabling signal injection or the extraction of private information. Recent efforts have attempted to abstractly model signal injection attacks; however, these studies predominantly focus on the signal processing pathway. The research [13] provides a comprehensive systematization of existing research on security and privacy challenges arising from the interplay between the cyber and physical domains, encompassing a wide range of CPS applications.

The research [14] examines CPS security modeling, with a focus on distinguishing between threat modeling and attack modeling – two often conflated but distinct concepts. The study evaluates existing security modeling approaches, analyzing their effectiveness in addressing real-world CPS-specific threats and attacker capabilities over extended lifecycles, which are typically longer than those of traditional IT systems. Despite advancements, the research reveals significant limitations in current security models, which often employ overly simplistic approaches. These models fail to adequately account for the dynamic, multi-layered, multi-path, and multi-agent nature of real-world CPS attacks. Table 1.1 describes the background and future directions in CPS.

1.3 Cyber-physical Systems

Figure 1.1 illustrates a general architecture for CPSs, where computational processes (depicted at the top) interface with physical processes (depicted at the bottom) through a network layer. This architecture underscores the seamless integration of cyber and physical components, a defining characteristic of CPSs. Since the introduction of the term CPS, numerous research communities have actively sought to define and understand the unique challenges of CPS security, which differ significantly from conventional IT systems. This interdisciplinary approach set CPS security research apart from prior efforts that primarily focused on securing specific CPS applications, such as supervisory control and data acquisition (SCADA) systems in the power grid [15].

1.3.1 Cybersecurity and privacy

The interconnected nature of CPSs inherently introduces interdependencies and complex interactions that may not be immediately evident, even under meticulous examination. CPSs, by their very design, present both cyber and physical attack surfaces, thereby significantly expanding the range of potential adversarial strategies. The vulnerabilities inherent to the cyber and physical domains do not merely accumulate; they compound one another. For instance, physical access to a cyber system may enable certain attack vectors that would otherwise be infeasible. Conversely, integrating a networked cyber dimension into a physical system amplifies system complexity, enlarges the attack surface, and extends the range from which adversaries can launch an attack. True system protection requires simultaneous defense across both cyber and physical domains. While essential, isolated protections in either

Table 1.1 Background and future direction in CPS.

Research focus	Methodology	Key findings	Identified gaps	Research contribution	Future directions
Survey of security and privacy issues in CPS	Systematic literature review	Identified attack patterns and defense mechanisms in CPS	Lack of comprehensive models for emerging CPS threats	Provided a taxonomy of attacks and defenses in CPS	Development of holistic security models for emerging CPS threats
Review of security modeling methods for CPS	Systematic literature review	Categorized security modeling methods into attack modeling	Simplistic approaches, lack of consideration for dynamic, multi-layer attacks	Current security models and need for comprehensive approaches	Development of dynamic, multi-layered security models for CPS
Distributed control security in CPS using brain-like systems	Proposed a brain-like security (BLS) scheme; experimental verification	Achieved secure cross-domain control without disclosing private information	Need for real-world implementation and testing	Introduced a novel BLS scheme for distributed control security in CPS	Real-world deployment and evaluation of BLS in various CPS scenarios
Privacy protection in CPS data sharing	Developed a standard vulnerability profiling library (SVPL); proposed a personalized privacy framework	Improved privacy preservation by eliminating trade-offs between privacy, utility, and risk	Lack of consideration for dynamic CPS environments	Introduced SVPL and personalized privacy framework for CPS	Adaptation of framework to dynamic and real-time CPS environments

(Continued)

Table 1.1 *Continued.*

Research focus	Methodology	Key findings	Identified gaps	Research contribution	Future directions
Systematic review of CPS security	Comprehensive literature review	Identified key security challenges and solutions in CPS	Need for integration of emerging technologies in CPS security	Provided an overview of CPS security landscape	Exploration of emerging technologies (e.g., AI, blockchain) in enhancing CPS security
In-depth overview of safety, security, and privacy in CPS	Compilation of recent research and case studies	Highlighted interdisciplinary approaches to CPS security	Need for standardized frameworks and guidelines	Offered insights into interdisciplinary approaches for CPS security	Development of standardized frameworks and guidelines for CPS safety, security, and privacy
Analysis of CPS security challenges and proposed solutions	Discussion of current challenges and potential solutions	Identified privacy protection technologies for user information security	Lack of comprehensive solutions addressing all CPS security challenges	Provided an analysis of CPS security challenges and potential solutions	Development of comprehensive security solutions encompassing all aspects of CPS
Research on security problems in CPS implementations	Researching security, trust, and resilience in CPS	Developing mechanisms to address security in various CPS applications	Need for practical implementation of research findings	Contributing to the body of knowledge on CPS security	Application of research findings to real-world CPS

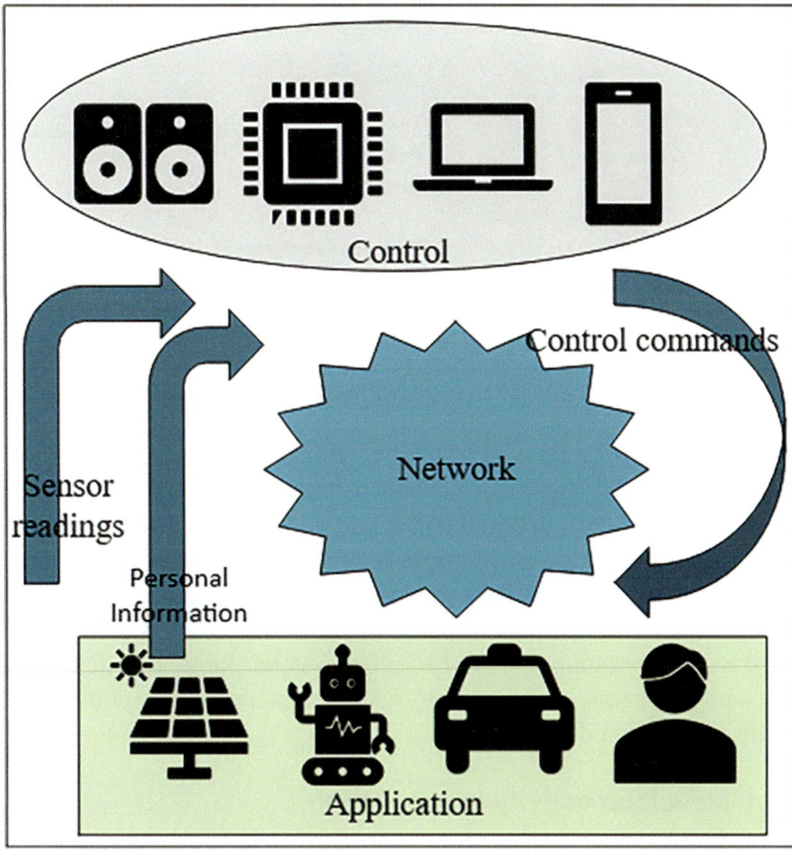

Figure 1.1 General CPS highlighting security risks from false sensor data.

domain are insufficient to safeguard the entire CPS. However, this duality also allows for cross-domain defensive strategies, where security measures in one domain can enhance the protection of the other. For example, computerized skid detection systems mitigate the physical hazard of icy roads through cyber-driven mechanisms. This interplay underscores the increased difficulty in assessing the security of CPSs, as the integration of the two domains introduces new challenges and dimensions of complexity [16].

Security and privacy vulnerabilities in CPSs can arise at various points, including device interfaces, the devices themselves, supporting infrastructures, the Internet, and even malicious actors within the user ecosystem. Figure 1.2 illustrates several potential attack points. Adversaries may exploit ambiguities in communication protocols to penetrate interfaces, leverage

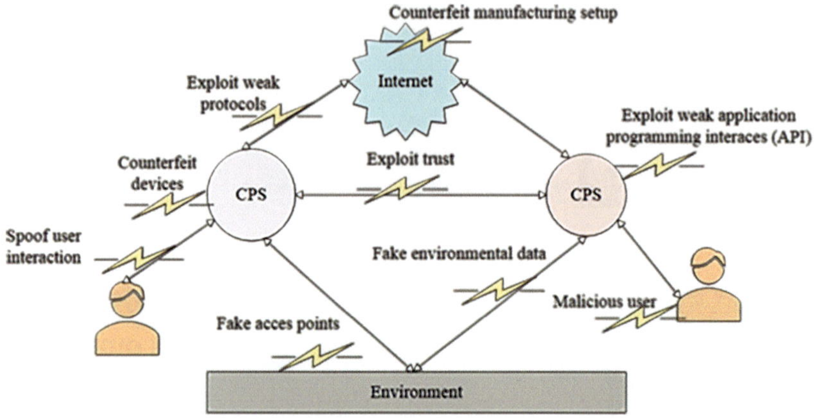

Figure 1.2 Possible security attack points in CPSs.

weaknesses in poorly implemented application programming interfaces to compromise components or manipulate trust relationships among devices, infrastructure, clients, and users. Each of these vulnerability points necessitates comprehensive security measures and must be treated as potential attack vectors from the standpoint of the entire system. Table 1.2 highlights the core security principles for cyber-physical systems, including confidentiality, integrity, and availability.

1.3.1.1 Malicious activity identification

The complexity of CPS introduces unique vulnerabilities that attackers can exploit. Figure 1.3 provides an overview of threats facing CPS, encompassing both direct cyber intrusions and indirect physical compromises that may propagate across interconnected components. The diverse and intricate nature of CPS elements presents substantial challenges to ensuring security and privacy. The interdependence between cyber and physical domains complicates threat evaluation and vulnerability assessment, resulting in the emergence of novel security concerns. Moreover, identifying, tracing, and analyzing attacks is increasingly challenging, as these attacks often originate from, traverse through, and target multiple CPS components [17].

Attack detection in CPS focuses on identifying and mitigating disruptions caused by adversaries using advanced techniques. Detection mechanisms often employ tools such as intrusion detection systems (IDS) and mathematical models to monitor system behavior and isolate anomalies. For instance, graph-theoretic approaches optimize resource allocation by minimizing the number of observer nodes required for effective detection in

Table 1.2 Core security principles for cyber-physical systems.

Principle	Detailed description	Examples and applications	Key features and benefits
Confidentiality	Ensures that sensitive data and information within a CPS can only be accessed by authorized parties	Secure communication protocols like TLS limit unauthorized usage and secure login systems	Prevents data exposure to unauthorized users and protects intellectual property or operational data
Integrity	Safeguards data, signals, and operations from unauthorized modifications or corruption	Cryptographic hash functions to verify data authenticity, and digital signatures to secure firmware updates	Maintains data accuracy and prevents system manipulation
Availability	Ensures that the system and its components remain operational and accessible whenever needed	Redundant power supplies, Backup communication channels, and protections against DoS attacks	Guarantees continuous system operation, reduces downtime, and ensures critical infrastructure

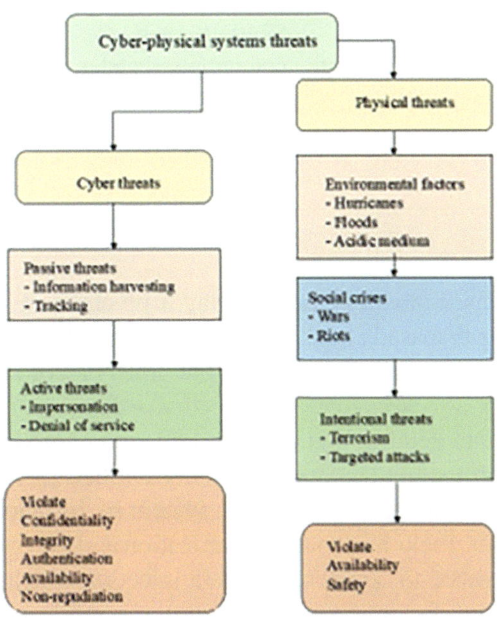

Figure 1.3 Threats associated with CPS.

Table 1.3 Attack types.

Principle	**Description**	**Examples/ Applications**	**Key features**
Deterrence	Discourages potential attackers by showcasing visible security measures and credible consequences	Warning signs, visible cameras, or tamper-proof designs in CPS systems	Focus on preventing malicious attempts before they happen
Detection	Identifies potential breaches or suspicious activities in real-time	Intrusion detection systems (IDS), anomaly detection algorithms, or security alarms	Enables proactive responses to potential threats
Delay	Creates obstacles to slow attackers and allows time for security responses	Physical locks, firewalls, or network segmentation in CPS infrastructure	Increases response time for neutralizing threats
Response	Implements immediate actions to stop or mitigate ongoing attacks	Automatic system lockdown, notifying authorities, or triggering countermeasures	Requires predefined strategies and quick execution
Neutralization	Eliminates threats completely to ensure system safety	Shutting down compromised nodes or deploying active countermeasures in networked environments	Involves multi-layered defenses for comprehensive security

distributed systems. Statistical models play a pivotal role in enhancing the detection of integrity-based attacks and other system vulnerabilities. Specific scenarios, such as replay attacks – where previously recorded legitimate data is retransmitted by attackers to evade detection – demand sophisticated strategies to differentiate genuine signals from replayed ones.

Optimization techniques are commonly applied to improve detection accuracy while minimizing the impact on system performance. Furthermore, innovative methods, including sparse optimization and low-rank matrix recovery, have been utilized to counter false data injection attacks, compromising state estimation and disrupting system operations. Table 1.3 categorizes the

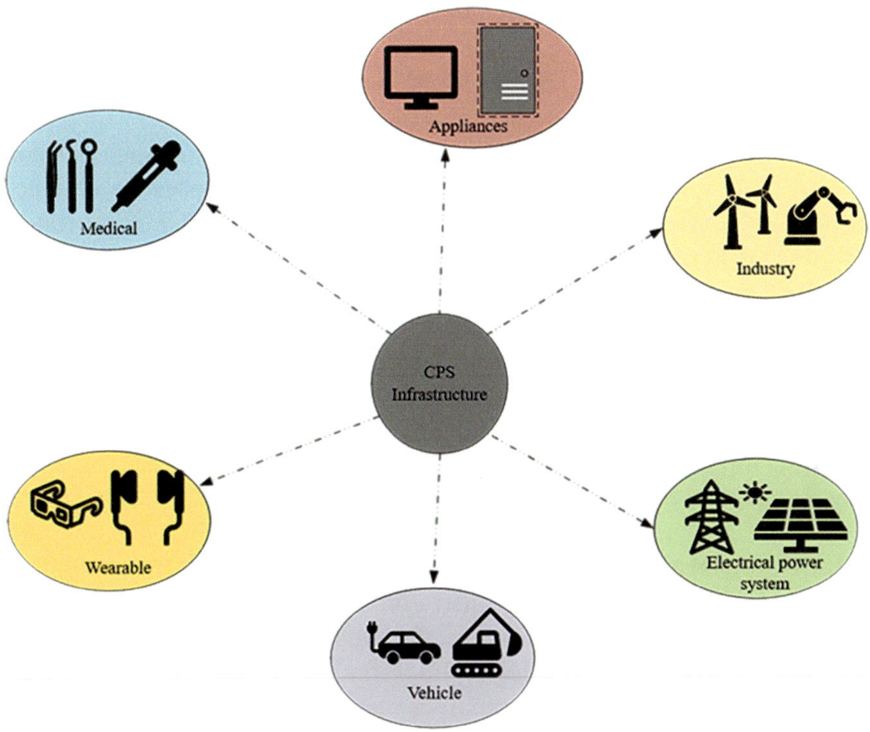

Figure 1.4 CPS infrastructure.

various types of attacks that CPS may encounter, ranging from design-level vulnerabilities to user interaction flaws, offering insights into common attack vectors and associated risks.

1.3.2 CPS infrastructure

CPS, such as ICS, is employed in factories and refineries and prioritizes physical operations while integrating cyber components for remote monitoring and control. These systems are often characterized by intricate, undocumented network structures, rendering them susceptible to cyberattacks. Key concerns for infrastructural CPS include safeguarding against property damage, economic losses, and physical harm. However, in critical infrastructure systems such as power grids and water supply networks, ensuring continuous availability is paramount due to their essential role in sustaining modern society [18]. CPS infrastructure is shown in Figure 1.4.

1.3.2.1 Illustrative example: Electrical power systems

Over the past decade, the emergence of the smart grid has accelerated the automation of networked devices in the power sector. The primary objectives include improving grid efficiency, reducing the burden on existing infrastructure, and minimizing future expansion costs. Innovations such as smart meters, home energy management tools, and smart appliances are designed to optimize energy usage. However, the involvement of human operators introduces additional security complexities. Human interactions with the system may deviate from anticipated behaviors, potentially exposing sensitive data or creating unforeseen risks. The integration of smart grids into personal environments, such as homes, further amplifies these risks. It can lead to service interruptions, energy theft, or privacy breaches through the analysis of personal behavior patterns. These challenges underscore the critical need for robust security measures to protect both the infrastructure and the individuals relying on these systems [19].

1.3.2.2 Vulnerability in smart grids

The integration of CPS into the smart grid has revolutionized power distribution networks. Figure 1.5 illustrates the dynamic interaction between CPS components within the grid, highlighting both their interconnected nature and the potential security vulnerabilities that arise. The advent of the smart grid, with its extensive reliance on communication networks, has introduced significant security risks, primarily due to its heavy dependence on cyber information. The core challenge lies in harnessing the potential of communication and information technology infrastructure while minimizing exposure to cyberattacks, ensuring a resilient security framework. To align with the evolving objectives of future smart grids, it is crucial to establish comprehensive testbeds for assessing interoperability and identifying cybersecurity vulnerabilities [20].

1.3.3 Personalized CPS

Personal CPS are designed to generate economic value by automating routine tasks. In these systems, the cyber component plays a central role, while the physical aspect is integrated to enhance the overall functionality of the information system. The widespread deployment of personal CPS can obscure their computational nature and the risks they introduce. These devices often store sensitive personally identifiable information (PII) and have the capacity to capture intimate details about the lives of individuals. While such information once required physical proximity to access, these devices now facilitate

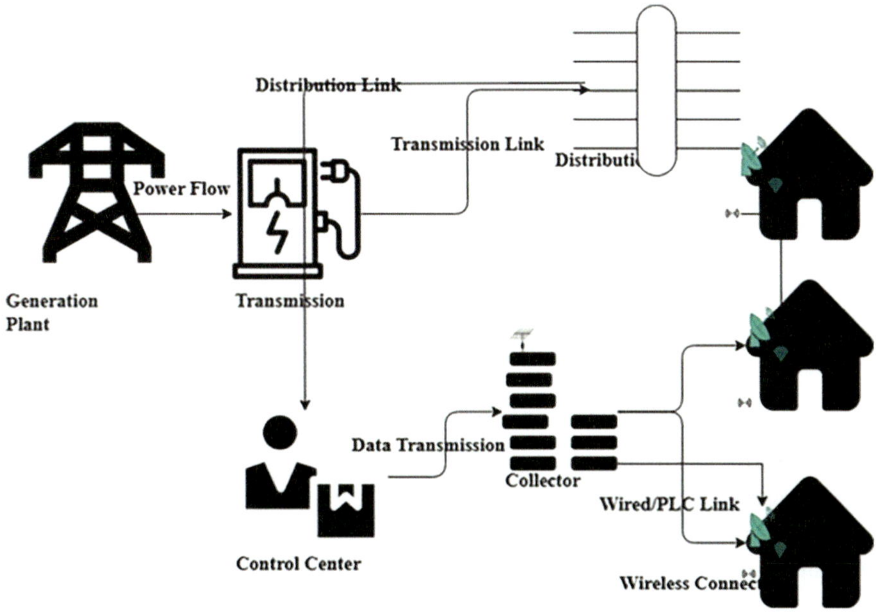

Figure 1.5 CPS in smart grid networks.

remote monitoring from anywhere in the world due to their Internet connectivity. Consequently, privacy becomes the primary concern for personal CPS. However, safety takes precedence for personal medical devices [21], with privacy considered a secondary issue. Security remains critical, especially since personal CPS often share trust relationships with office or industrial systems, including ICS, potentially exposing vulnerabilities across interconnected networks.

1.3.3.1 Smart appliances in practice

Personal CPS, such as smart appliances, wearable technologies, medical devices, and tracking tags, are designed to automate tasks and enhance user convenience. Despite their numerous advantages, these systems present significant privacy and security challenges due to their inherent reliance on collecting, processing, and storing personal information. The increasing interconnectedness of personal CPS with industrial systems further complicates the security landscape, necessitating comprehensive strategies to address privacy and security concerns.

Smart devices commonly found in modern households, such as smart refrigerators, televisions, and light bulbs, are frequently connected to the

Internet. This connectivity enables them to perform advanced functions, such as ordering groceries automatically or monitoring household activities. However, it also exposes sensitive personal information and behavioral patterns to potential security risks. These devices often transmit data to their manufacturers, which can be utilized for purposes such as targeted advertising or, in some cases, malicious activities.

The integration of personal devices within larger systems introduces vulnerabilities that attackers can exploit. For instance, physical access to a smart device can allow an attacker to circumvent digital security protocols. Moreover, the interconnected nature of CPS implies that a vulnerability in one component can compromise the security of the entire system. This interdependence increases the complexity of securing CPS, as the exploitation of a single weakness can have cascading effects across the system. Despite these challenges, understanding the potential risks associated with CPS and implementing robust security measures can mitigate these threats. By prioritizing data protection and adopting stringent cybersecurity protocols, individuals and organizations can safeguard their devices and sensitive information from potential adversaries [22]. As outlined in Table 1.4, the attack points in CPS are heterogeneous and multifaceted, encompassing cyber and physical vulnerabilities.

1.3.4 Privacy challenges in CPS

Understanding cybersecurity in CPS necessitates addressing both the physical and cyber dimensions. Similarly, ensuring privacy within CPS involves navigating the complexities of interconnected systems. Privacy risks are exacerbated by the often concealed links between CPS devices and larger networks, including the Internet. As highlighted by [23], consumers express significant concern regarding the collection and use of their personal data. In the era of the IoT, data is frequently collected and shared surreptitiously. Unlike earlier periods when data entry required manual input, modern devices such as wearables, smartphones, smart appliances, connected cars, and smart home systems autonomously gather and transmit vast amounts of information without explicit user consent. Many users remain unaware of the extent of these devices' communication with online networks, and even those who are aware often fail to fully comprehend the associated privacy risks.

The architecture of smart home systems, as illustrated in Figure 1.6, demonstrates the interconnections between personal CPS devices and broader networks. While this connectivity enables enhanced convenience, it also introduces significant privacy and security vulnerabilities. These links

Table 1.4 Attack locations in CPS.

Level	Threat	Type of attack
System design	Unforeseen vulnerabilities due to the integration of cyber and physical components	Replay attacks, false data injection, covert attacks, DoS, and DDoS
Infrastructure	Vulnerabilities in critical systems such as power grids, ICS	Physical manipulation of sensors, cyberattacks exploiting networked SCADA systems
Personal CPS	Privacy breaches, exposure of sensitive personal data	Exploiting wearable devices, malicious use of smart appliance data, unprotected app connections
Physical interfaces	Direct access to physical devices leading to compromised operations	Tampering, bypassing security locks, inserting malware via USBs
Network communication	Exploiting weak protocols and insecure communication channels	Man-in-the-middle attacks, traffic analysis, eavesdropping
Monitoring systems	Gaps in surveillance and alert systems	Disabling alarms, manipulating camera feeds, circumventing intrusion detection systems
User interaction	Human errors and insufficient training	Phishing, social engineering, abuse of user trust and credentials

may unintentionally expose sensitive information, rendering it susceptible to unauthorized sharing, harvesting, or theft without the user's knowledge.

1.3.4.1 Illustration: Wearable devices

Wearable devices exemplify significant privacy challenges. These devices frequently interact with data collection points in various environments, such as stores, restaurants, or public spaces, often without the explicit of user awareness. For instance, tools like active cell site simulators, commonly referred to as GSM interceptors, compel nearby cellular devices to disclose their identities and connect to these collection points [24]. Such mechanisms enable the collection of data without the consent of the user, underscoring the risks associated with ambiguous control mechanisms and unexpected data-sharing practices.

To mitigate such privacy risks, system designers must adopt a privacy-by-design approach. Devices should be configured to default to non-disclosure of user data and provide clear notifications whenever specific

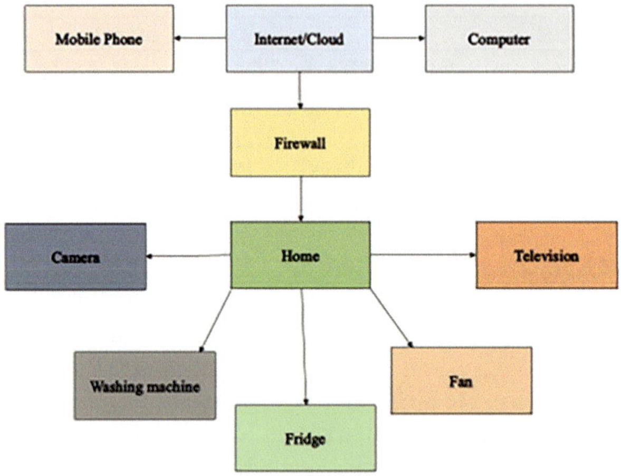

Figure 1.6 Networked architecture of smart home devices.

information is shared. Furthermore, all collected data should be encrypted to maintain confidentiality and require robust authentication mechanisms for access. Anonymizing user data through techniques such as pseudonymization can further reduce the risks of direct identification and enhance privacy protections.

1.3.5 Strategies for enhancing the security of CPSs

Securing CPS necessitates the application of principles that are specifically designed for their evaluation and design, emphasizing mitigations and controls that are unique to CPS rather than relying on generic cybersecurity practices such as the use of strong passwords. This discussion intentionally refrains from revisiting fundamental cybersecurity concepts and instead directs readers interested in the basics to reference resources [25]. The interplay between various security mechanisms and fundamental principles yields valuable insights. For instance, while highly effective for deterrence, barriers may inadvertently compromise system availability. These interactions underscore the inherent challenge of effectively implementing principles of availability and responsiveness within CPS. Figure 1.7 illustrates the fundamental noise addition mechanism employed in differential privacy. The discussion surrounding differential privacy can be broadly categorized into two key areas: existing differential privacy methodologies and noise addition mechanisms.

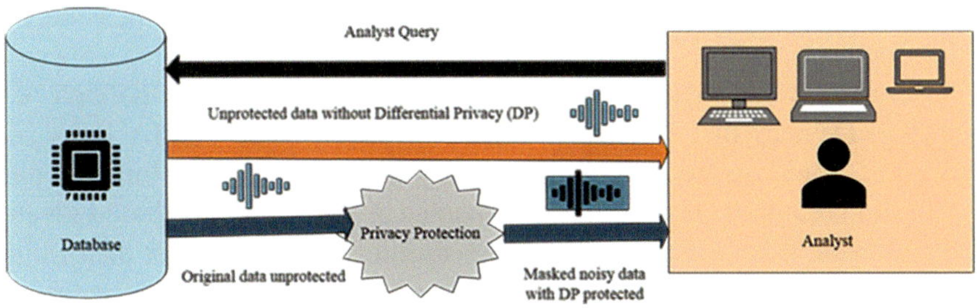

Figure 1.7 Data query evaluation: Protected vs. unprotected output with DP.

1.3.5.1 Minimal authorization principle

The principle of least privilege (PoLP) ensures that users or systems are granted access only to the resources necessary for their specific roles. For example, a word-processing application on a smartphone may require occasional access to the device's camera for embedding images into documents. Under PoLP, such access would be granted exclusively when the specific functionality is invoked, even after proper authentication. This principle is typically enforced through mechanisms like mandatory access control (MAC), which restricts resource access based on the sensitivity of the information and the clearance level of the user. Examples of such enforcement include application firewalls and proxy systems. However, accurately determining the sensitivity of certain types of information in advance poses significant challenges. Rigorous testing and analysis are often required to identify scenarios where ostensibly minor access permissions might necessitate additional safeguards [26].

1.3.5.2 Core insights

The core insights principle imposes stringent restrictions on access by ensuring that users or system components can access resources only when such access is essential for executing a specific task within their role. For instance, even if a word-processing application has permission to use a smartphone's camera, the need-to-know principle would prevent the app from activating the camera while the user is typing, as image capture is unnecessary for this activity. This principle enhances operational security and serves as a cornerstone for many privacy frameworks. Organizations often implement the need-to-know principle by sharing personal data exclusively when it directly benefits the individual whose information is being disclosed [27].

1.3.5.3 Classification

Segmentation enhances cyber-physical security by creating physical or logical barriers that separate device groups based on their communication needs, functions, criticality, and risk profiles. In cyber systems, this can be achieved using methods such as subnetting, encryption, virtual local area networks (VLANs), firewalls, access control lists (ACLs), and software-defined networking. Devices that frequently communicate or share similar risks and functions should be grouped, while those with distinct roles or limited communication requirements should be isolated. Critical functions should ideally be distributed across separate machines to minimize the impact of a single failure or attack.

Despite the convenience of sharing a common IT network, segmentation principles advocate for the construction of barriers between different layers and functions. Without regulating access between segments with varying risk profiles, less critical systems could serve as entry points for attacks on more sensitive ones. For example, automotive hacking has demonstrated how vulnerabilities in entertainment systems can provide access to critical real-time controls, such as brakes or throttles. This risk is exacerbated by the Controller Area Network CAN)-bus protocol, which prioritizes real-time communication over security. The lack of authentication protocols in CAN-bus means that any connected component can act with high privileges, making segmentation essential to mitigate such risks.

Segmentation should focus on separating components by function, criticality, and risk rather than physical proximity. Secure connections between segments must be limited and monitored, employing application firewalls or proxies to control devices, protocols, and messages. In addition, segmentation can account for factors such as access time and user roles. For instance, apps on devices like smartphones often require explicit permission to access certain features, such as the camera, although this access may persist beyond the immediate need. Temporal segmentation, where access is granted for a specific duration, adds another layer of security. Role-based access control (RBAC) also plays a key role in segmentation, restricting access to only the necessary functions for a specific role. For example, a machine functioning as both a workstation and a server should have its applications segmented and accessed via separate user accounts, ensuring that resources are utilized only for their intended purposes [28].

1.3.5.4 Defensive aspects

Effective security strategies are essential in addressing the sophisticated threats faced by CPS, requiring a combination of flexibility and robustness. Two foundational approaches, defense-in-depth and defense-in-breadth, work synergistically to provide comprehensive protection. Defense-in-depth implements multiple security layers within a single system, creating a progressive barrier that slows or halts potential intruders. Meanwhile, defense-in-breadth emphasizes collaboration among interconnected systems, ensuring mutual support to mitigate attacks targeting various vulnerabilities. Together, these strategies form a holistic defense framework, safeguarding today's complex and interconnected systems [29].

Defense-in-depth involves implementing multiple layers of security measures akin to concentric walls surrounding a castle to protect its central keep. This strategy integrates deterrence, detection, and delay as key security controls to safeguard systems. For instance, a device storing a private key should employ encryption to protect the key, enforce access restrictions through software barriers, and incorporate physical tamper-resistant features. In the event of a breach in one layer, subsequent defenses act to slow the attacker, while integrated alarms in each layer enhance both detection and deterrence [30].

While defense-in-depth is primarily concerned with securing individual systems, defense-in-breadth focuses on fostering collaboration across systems, similar to coordinating the defenses of multiple interconnected fortresses. This strategy ensures that various components work in unison to thwart divide-and-conquer attacks. By implementing principles of least-privilege access and need-to-know across devices and users, defense-in-breadth reduces the attack surface, even as the number of interconnected devices continues to grow. Resilient, edge-based defenses, such as Digital Ants [31], empower smart devices to utilize adaptive pattern recognition for collective detection and response to attacks. This approach aims to mitigate cascading failures, in which a single vulnerability could compromise the entire system.

1.3.5.5 Personalized data capture and logging

Data collection, particularly from personal cyber-physical systems (CPS), holds significant value for both individual users and broader insights into group dynamics. However, this utility must be carefully balanced with considerations regarding user privacy. For instance, Fitbit's initial data collection policy enabled users to compare their fitness metrics with group activities but lacked robust privacy controls. This oversight resulted in the unintended exposure of sensitive information, including private user activities, leading to a costly and embarrassing scandal. To mitigate such risks, it is crucial to implement stricter, user-centric policies. Data collection should be opt-in by default, with the presumption that all user data is private unless explicitly shared. Users must be provided with clear visibility regarding the information being collected and the entities with whom it is shared. For example, if Fitbit had transparently disclosed the data-sharing practices and offered user-configurable privacy settings, the scandal could have been avoided. Implementing these controls aligns with the principle of confidentiality, ensuring that users retain full control over their personal data [32].

1.3.5.6 Pattern encryption

An effective yet subtle approach to safeguarding CPS involves the obfuscation of usage patterns. For example, energy consumption patterns in ICS can inadvertently disclose the status of critical processes, providing attackers with valuable reconnaissance data. Similarly, malicious actors can replicate communication patterns in network traffic to evade detection by intrusion detection systems or exploit patterns in physical site visits to identify vulnerable moments for attack. By obfuscating these patterns, the principle of confidentiality is upheld in less overt ways. In the case of personal medical devices, for instance, data shared with healthcare providers or central repositories for analysis can be resampled rather than transmitted in its raw form, maintaining statistical accuracy while protecting individual identities [33]. These privacy-preserving techniques protect sensitive data, mitigate legal liabilities, and prevent the exploitation of personal information.

1.3.5.7 Total security coverage

End-to-end security ensures that data remains protected throughout its entire lifecycle, from transmission to reception and storage. This involves maintaining authentication, integrity, and encryption at the application level. For instance, a Fitbit device securely stores user data, transmits it via a protected internet connection, and subsequently transfers it to the manufacturer‘s servers. Each phase – ranging from device-level encryption to secure transmission protocols and safeguarded server infrastructure – must be robustly secured to maintain end-to-end security. However, encrypting all data with a single key introduces vulnerabilities if the key is compromised. Effective encryption, therefore, necessitates advanced key management systems, a complex subject extensively discussed in research [34].

1.3.5.8 Securing against tampering and attacks

A c`ombination of deterrence and detection measures is essential to protect equipment, especially in remote or unmonitored locations. These techniques include the use of tamper-resistant locks, code-based locks, security cameras, alarms, and other physical security tools. Additionally, authentication systems and access logging play a critical role in preventing unauthorized access, enabling the detection of intrusions, and ensuring accountability

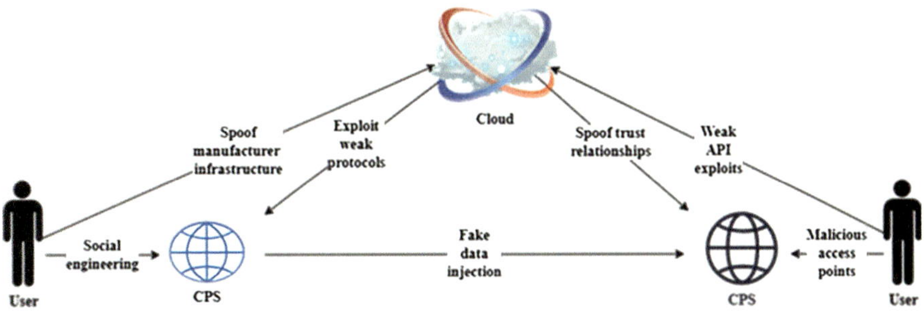

Figure 1.8 Security attack points in CPSs.

through non-repudiation mechanisms [35]. Figure 1.8 highlights critical security vulnerabilities, emphasizing areas that demand robust protective measures. Security flaws may arise from weak application programming interfaces (APIs) implementations, potentially disrupting system components. Additionally, vulnerabilities can exploit the trust relationships between devices, infrastructures, clients, and users. To mitigate these risks, the identified vulnerabilities must be addressed through comprehensive security measures or treated as potentially compromised system components from the perspective of other system elements.

Table 1.5 outlines various strategies for enhancing the security of CPSs, detailing the focus areas, techniques, benefits, and challenges of each approach. It serves as a comprehensive overview of current security measures and their potential impact on protecting CPSs from cyber and physical threats.

1.4 Challenges, Future Research Directions, and Lessons Learned

This section explores the key challenges, future research directions, and lessons learned in the security and privacy realm within CPS. Despite the growing integration of CPS in critical infrastructures, significant security and privacy concerns persist, including vulnerabilities to cyberattacks, data breaches, and unauthorized access to sensitive information. These challenges present opportunities for further research to develop advanced mechanisms that can safeguard both the physical and cyber components of CPS. Future investigations must focus on enhancing the resilience of CPS against emerging threats, improving data privacy protection, and optimizing trust management frameworks. Additionally, the lessons learned from ongoing studies provide valuable insights into best practices, helping to shape the evolution of security strategies in CPS.

Table 1.5 Strategies for enhancing the security of CPSs.

Strategy	Focus area	Techniques	Benefits	Challenges
Access control	Authentication and authorization	Role-based access control (RBAC), multi-factor authentication (MFA), biometrics, encryption	Prevent unauthorized access, secure sensitive data	Complexity in managing large user bases, performance overhead
Intrusion detection systems	Attack detection	Anomaly detection, signature-based detection, machine learning-based IDS	Early detection of malicious activity, real-time monitoring	False positives, high computational load
Secure communication protocols	Data integrity and confidentiality	TLS/SSL, IPsec, quantum cryptography, end-to-end encryption	Protect data in transit, ensure privacy and integrity	Key management complexity, potential performance degradation
Physical layer security	Device and sensor protection	Jamming-resistant signals, encryption at the physical layer, secure hardware (TPM, HSM)	Resilience against physical attacks, tamper resistance	Cost of implementation, compatibility with existing systems
Fault tolerant systems	System reliability	Redundancy, failover mechanisms, watchdog timers, diversity coding	High availability, resilience to component failure	Increased resource consumption, system complexity
Secure software development	Software integrity	Code review, static/dynamic analysis, fuzz testing, secure coding practices, software hardening	Prevention of vulnerabilities, reduction of software bugs	Time and resource intensive, expertise required
Blockchain for CPS security	Data integrity and auditing	Distributed ledgers, smart contracts, consensus algorithms	Immutable logs, transparency, decentralized trust management	Scalability, performance, energy consumption
Behavioral-based authentication	User and device authentication	Continuous authentication, behavioral biometrics, gait recognition	Continuous user verification, low friction for end users	Privacy concerns, accuracy, resistance to spoofing
Physical tamper detection	Device security	Tamper-proof enclosures, physical layer security sensors, environmental monitoring	Protect devices from tampering, alert on physical breaches	Cost of physical security measures, maintenance
Resilient control systems	System recovery and resilience	Adaptive control systems, robust control theory, cyber-physical feedback loops	Stability under attack, ability to recover from faults	High complexity and tuning difficulty in dynamic environments

1.4.1 Challenges

The security and privacy challenges in CPS are multifaceted, arising from the complex interplay between physical devices, networks, and software. These challenges include vulnerabilities to cyberattacks, data privacy concerns, and the difficulty of ensuring system integrity in dynamic and distributed environments.

1.4.1.1 Focus constraints

The research predominantly focused on specific case studies, which, while valuable, may not fully capture the diverse range of challenges encountered across various industries or applications. For instance, insights gained from a smart grid implementation may not directly apply to healthcare systems, where privacy concerns and operational priorities differ considerably. This limitation highlights the need for more comprehensive studies that span multiple sectors, environments, and scales of operation. Expanding the scope in future research could lead to more universally applicable findings, facilitating the identification of cross-industry best practices and innovative solutions.

1.4.1.2 Integration challenges

Integrating the diverse components of CPS presents significant challenges. For example, aligning communication protocols with physical infrastructure and ensuring robust cybersecurity often leads to interoperability issues. These integration difficulties are further exacerbated by the absence of standardized frameworks across industries, resulting in inefficiencies and security gaps. Overcoming this limitation requires the development of comprehensive guidelines or modular approaches that facilitate integration and enable seamless interaction among heterogeneous components.

1.4.1.3 Constraints on resources

Limited access to advanced resources, including cutting-edge software, sophisticated hardware, and comprehensive datasets, significantly constrained the capacity of research to fully explore and validate innovative ideas. For example, simulations conducted on resource-limited hardware may fail to accurately represent real-world conditions. Furthermore, the absence of large-scale datasets hindered the ability to rigorously test machine learning models and other computational methodologies. Future research efforts should prioritize securing access to state-of-the-art facilities or establishing collaborations with institutions equipped to provide the requisite resources.

1.4.1.4 Adapting to technological advancements

The rapid evolution of technologies such as IoT, machine learning, and blockchain fosters an environment where innovations quickly become obsolete. Although the research aimed to address current challenges, certain methods and frameworks discussed may already require updates to integrate recent advancements. This limitation highlights the importance of adopting dynamic and iterative research methodologies capable of incorporating continuous developments to maintain relevance over time.

1.4.1.5 Limitations of assumed parameters

The reliance on assumptions, such as predictable user behavior or controlled system interactions, poses a potential limitation to the real-world applicability of the research findings. For instance, assumptions regarding consistent network connectivity or strict adherence to security protocols may not hold in dynamic or high-risk environments. To address this limitation, future research should aim to minimize dependence on static assumptions by integrating adaptive, real-time analysis methodologies that account for variability and unpredictability in system behaviors.

1.4.2 Future research directions

Future research in the security and privacy of CPS should focus on developing resilient frameworks that can adapt to the evolving threats in interconnected environments. This includes integrating advanced AI techniques, real-time threat detection, and robust data protection mechanisms to safeguard critical infrastructures while ensuring user privacy.

1.4.2.1 Challenges in designing privacy regulations

Privacy regulations are struggling to keep pace with technological advancements despite growing concerns about privacy. While these regulations are essential, they must be carefully designed to avoid undermining the value of CPS [37]. IoT devices, for instance, provide significant benefits tied to the data they exchange. The integration of cyber capabilities into physical products has transformed ownership, with manufacturers often retaining control. Poorly conceived privacy regulations could undermine CPS adoption and benefits, often driven by anecdotal fears about data exchange. Effective regulation must balance privacy protection with CPS functionality, informed by economic and social studies. Overly restrictive regulations, such as those advocating for "security by design" or "data minimization," could increase costs and reduce functionality, harming consumers. Achieving the right balance between privacy protection and technological innovation is crucial for continued advancement.

1.4.2.2 Managing legacy systems in CPS

Legacy systems, typically defined as those over a decade old with diminishing capabilities [37], present unique challenges to the security and reliability of CPS. These systems often remain in operation for various reasons. They continue to function adequately, but their replacement is costly or introduces undesirable features or constant availability is required, as is the case with power grids. However, legacy systems are frequently plagued by unpatched vulnerabilities, outdated operating systems, and reliance on insecure protocols like Telnet or FTP. Integrating new functionality into legacy infrastructure can inadvertently inherit these vulnerabilities or introduce new insecurities, particularly through undefined states caused by compatibility issues.

Undefined states often arise when new functions built on older systems deviate from the original design of the legacy software or hardware. Early system components tend to be simpler, while newer, more complex functionalities may bypass or misuse these foundational elements in ways that disrupt modularity. Documented and undocumented interdependencies within the system further complicate integration efforts. Research into automated methods for securely integrating legacy and modern CPS remains a critical area of focus. One effective approach to managing legacy systems is to test their behavior under abnormal conditions, such as unexpected, delayed, or improperly formatted inputs. Additionally, planning for failures and enhancing system availability through redundancy, such as implementing backup systems, can help mitigate risks.

1.4.2.3 Distributed credential management and authentication

Identity management involves the maintenance of credentials to identify individuals, components, and systems, while authentication ensures that these entities are indeed who they claim to be, thereby enabling the appropriate granting of access rights. Traditional identity and authentication models typically rely on centralized authorities for credential validation and communication. However, in distributed CPS, maintaining a centralized authority is often impractical or unfeasible due to constraints such as connectivity limitations or the inherent architecture of the system. These challenges necessitate the development of novel models for identity management and authentication that are specifically designed for distributed environments. In this context, research [38] explored authentication methods and secure protocols utilizing lightweight cryptographic techniques to prevent cyber-physical attacks.

To effectively secure these systems, innovative approaches are required, ensuring that authentication processes remain robust even in the absence of a central governing authority. This continues to be a critical area of research, essential for the advancement of secure and scalable distributed CPS.

1.4.3 Lesson learned

An Overview of Security and Privacy in CPS focuses on the critical challenges and solutions in safeguarding these interconnected systems. CPS integrates physical processes with computational and networking elements, making them susceptible to a wide range of cyber and physical threats. This section explores foundational concepts, emerging vulnerabilities, and state-of-the-art techniques for ensuring robust security and preserving privacy within CPS, emphasizing their implications across domains such as smart grids, healthcare, transportation, and industrial automation.

Lesson 1: Leveraging interdisciplinary collaboration for enhanced innovation
The research emphasized the transformative impact of interdisciplinary collaboration. By integrating insights from engineering, computer science, behavioral studies, and data analytics, the team was able to address challenges from multiple perspectives. For instance, cybersecurity experts collaborated with systems engineers to develop more resilient defenses, while data scientists offered valuable insights into patterns and vulnerabilities. This collaborative approach not only enhanced the effectiveness of the solutions but also fostered innovation by leveraging diverse areas of expertise.

Lesson 2: Embracing flexibility is key to overcome unforeseen challenges
Unforeseen challenges emerged during the research, including resource limitations and integration issues. The ability to remain flexible in the methodologies – whether through adopting alternative approaches, refining experimental setups, or revising underlying assumptions – was critical in overcoming these obstacles. This adaptability underscores the importance of cultivating an agile mindset and maintaining a readiness to pivot strategies when confronted with unexpected difficulties.

Lesson 3: Real-world testing highlights the limits of theoretical models, requiring iterative validation
Theoretical models have provided a robust foundation; however, their limitations became evident during real-world testing. For instance, scalability challenges and operational constraints, such as unpredictable network

conditions or human error, often emerged only during practical implementation. These tests uncovered nuances that theoretical models could not account for, thereby underscoring the necessity for iterative development cycles that integrate real-world validation at each stage.

Lesson 4: Continuous learning keeps research relevant in evolving fields like CPS and IoT
The rapid evolution of CPS and the IoT underscores the necessity of continuous learning. Staying abreast of the latest advancements, including emerging security protocols and innovative communication frameworks, is essential for maintaining the relevance and impact of research. Regular engagement with industry developments, academic literature, and conferences ensures that the research remains at the forefront of technological progress and maintains its academic and practical significance.

Lesson 5: The necessity of comprehensive security measures
The interconnected nature of CPS exposes the cascading risks associated with even minor vulnerabilities. For example, a single compromised device can trigger widespread disruptions across a network. This realization highlights the imperative for multi-layered security strategies that address threats across all levels – physical, cyber, and human. The research underscores that an integrated security approach is not merely optional but a fundamental necessity for safeguarding these complex systems.

Lesson 6: User feedback is key to designing secure, user-friendly CPSs
Engaging with end-users provided invaluable insights into the real-world application of CPS systems. For instance, understanding user behavior and preferences facilitated the development of solutions that were not only secure but also intuitive and user-friendly. This experience underscored the importance of incorporating user feedback throughout the design process to ensure systems effectively address practical needs while upholding safety and security.

Lesson 7: Prioritize scalability and sustainability for long-term CPS success
Designing systems that scale without compromising performance or security presented significant challenges. For instance, a solution effective in a small network may struggle under the demands of a larger deployment. This research highlights the importance of adopting forward-thinking designs that account for long-term considerations, such as increased user loads and evolving threat landscapes. Planning for scalability and sustainability from the outset is essential to ensuring the long-term success of CPS implementations.

1.5 Conclusions and Future Scope

This chapter explores the intersection of security and privacy in CPS, applying established definitions from both cyber and physical domains to this emerging field. It highlights the unique requirements for infrastructural and personal CPS while emphasizing the need for comprehensive security and privacy measures across interconnected systems. The consequences of neglecting these critical elements are demonstrated through real-world examples, along with best practices for securely designing and managing CPS. As the adoption of CPS grows exponentially, addressing their associated security and privacy challenges becomes increasingly critical. The intricate interplay between cyber and physical dimensions necessitates a holistic approach to risk management. While CPS offers significant benefits, their widespread implementation raises concerns about misuse, system failures, and malicious exploitation. Policymakers and system designers must carefully balance these risks against the advantages when formulating regulations and design principles.

CPS is now an integral part of modern life, influencing the daily experiences of billions worldwide. Consequently, prioritizing security and privacy throughout their lifecycle – from initial design and deployment to eventual decommissioning – is paramount. Robust privacy and security frameworks should be incorporated from the outset, leveraging advanced encryption techniques and secure authentication protocols to safeguard sensitive data. Regular vulnerability assessments are essential to identify weaknesses in both physical and digital components, with tools such as intrusion detection systems and network segmentation playing critical roles in mitigating risks. Integrating artificial intelligence and machine learning can enhance the ability of CPS to detect and respond to threats in real time. Prior to deployment, CPS should undergo rigorous testing in simulated environments that replicate real-world conditions. Smart testbeds enable the evaluation of system performance, the identification of vulnerabilities, and the optimization of systems to address practical challenges effectively.

References

[1] J. Giraldo, E. Sarkar, A. A. Cardenas, M. Maniatakos, and M. Kantarcioglu, “Security and privacy in cyber-physical systems: A survey of surveys,” *IEEE Design and Test*, vol. 34, no. 4, pp. 7–17, Aug. 2017, doi: 10.1109/MDAT.2017.2709310

[2] A. Humayed, J. Lin, F. Li, and B. Luo, “Cyber-physical systems security - A survey,” *IEEE Internet of Things Journal*, vol. 4, no. 6, pp. 1802–1831, Dec. 2017, doi: 10.1109/JIOT.2017.2703172.

[3] W. Duo, M. C. Zhou, and A. Abusorrah, “A survey of cyber attacks on cyber physical systems: Recent advances and challenges,” *IEEE/CAA Journal of Automatica Sinica*, vol. 9, no. 5, pp. 784–800, May 2022, doi: 10.1109/JAS.2022.105548.

[4] M. Wankhade and S. V. Kottur, “Security facets of cyber physical system,” in *proceedings of the Third International Conference on Smart Systems and Inventive Technology (ICSSIT),* Tirunelveli, India, *2020*, , pp. 359–363, doi: 10.1109/ICSSIT48917.2020.921407.

[5] M. H. Cintuglu, O. A. Mohammed, K. Akkaya, and A. S. Uluagac, “A survey on smart grid cyber-physical system testbeds,” *IEEE Communications Surveys & Tutorials*, vol. 19, no. 1, pp. 446–464, Jan. 2017, doi: 10.1109/COMST.2016.2627399.

[6] R. Altawy and A. M. Youssef, “Security tradeoffs in cyber physical systems: A case study survey on implantable medical devices,” *IEEE Access*, vol. 4, pp. 959–979, 2016, doi: 10.1109/ACCESS.2016.2521727.

[7] R. Atat, L. Liu, H. Chen, J. Wu, H. Li, and Y. Yi, “Enabling cyber-physical communication in 5G cellular networks: challenges, spatial spectrum sensing, and cyber-security,” *IET Cyber-Physical Systems: Theory & Applications*, vol. 1, no. 1, pp. 1–11, Apr. 2017, doi: 10.1049/iet-cps.2017.0010.

[8] T. Zhu, P. Xiong, G. Li, W. Zhou, and P. S. Yu, “Differentially private model publishing in cyber physical systems,” *Future Generation Computer Systems,* vol. 108, pp. 1297–1306, Jul. 2020, doi:10.1016/j.future.2018.04.016.

[9] H. Harkat, L. M. Camarinha-Matos, J. Goes, and H. F. T. Ahmed, “Cyber-physical systems security: A systematic review,” *Computers in Industry*, Feb.2024, doi: 10.1016/j.cie.2024.109891.

[10] M. Ul Hassan, M. H. Rehmani, and J. Chen, “Differential Privacy Techniques for Cyber Physical Systems: A Survey,” IEEE Communications Surveys & Tutorials, vol. 22, no. 1, pp. 509–541, First Quarter .2020. DOI: 10.1109/COMST.2020.2982757.

[11] H. Yang, K. Zhan, M. Kadoch, Y. Liang, and M. Cheriet, “BLCS: Brain-Like Distributed Control Security in Cyber Physical Systems,” *IEEE Network*, vol. 34, no. 3, pp. 8–15, June 2020, doi: 10.1109/MNET.011.1900275.

[12] A. Bhattacharjee, S. Badsha, M. T. Hossain, C. Konstantinou, and X. Liang, “Vulnerability Characterization and Privacy Quantification for Cyber-Physical Systems,” in *proceedings of the IEEE International Conferences on Internet of Things (iThings), IEEE Green Computing & Communications (GreenCom), IEEE Cyber, Physical & Social Computing (CPSCom), IEEE Smart Data (SmartData), and IEEE Congress on*

Cybermatics (Cybermatics), Melbourne, Australia, 2021, doi: 10.1109/iThings-GreenCom-CPSCom-SmartData-Cybermatics53846.2021.00045.

[13] Z.Yu, Z. Kaplan, Q. Yan, and N. Zhang, "Security and Privacy in the Emerging Cyber-Physical World: A Survey," *IEEE Communications Surveys & Tutorials,* vol. 23, no. 3, pp. 1889–1926, May.2021. doi: 10.1109/COMST.2021.3081450.

[14] S. Huang, C. M. Poskitt, and L. K. Shar, "Security Modelling for Cyber-Physical Systems: A Systematic Literature Review," *arXiv preprint arXiv:2404.07527*, Apr. 2024, doi:10.48550/arXiv.2404.07527.

[15] H. He and J. Yan, "Cyber-physical attacks and defences in the smart grid: A survey," *IET Cyber-Physical Systems: Theory & Applications*, vol. 1, no. 1, pp. 13–27, 2016, doi: 10.1049/iet-cps.2015.0019.

[16] Y. Cherdantseva and J. Hilton, "A Reference Model of Information Assurance & Security," *in proceedings of the International Conference on Availability, Reliability and Security*, IEEE, 2013, pp. 546–555. doi: 10.1109/ARES.2013.72.

[17] H. Song, G. A. Fink, and S. Jeschke, Eds, *Overview of Security and Privacy in Cyber-Physical Systems,* Security and Privacy in Cyber-Physical Systems: Foundations, Principles, and Applications. Hoboken, NJ, USA: John Wiley & Sons Ltd, 1st ed, 2017. doi: 10.1002/9781119226079.

[18] C. Konstantinou, M. Maniatakos, F. Saqib, S. Hu, J. Plusquellic, and Y. Jin, "Cyber-physical systems: A security perspective," in *Proceedings of the European Test Symposiumn (ETS)*, June 2015, doi: 10.1109/ETS.2015.7138763.

[19] E. McCary and Y. Xiao, "Smart Grid Attacks and Countermeasures," *EAI Endorsed Transactions on Industrial Networks and Intelligent Systems*, vol. 2, no. 2, Feb. 2015, doi: 10.4108/inis.2.2.e4.

[20] H. Zhang, B. Liu, and H. Wu, "Smart grid cyber-physical attack and defense: A review," *IEEE Access*, vol. 9, pp. 1–1, Feb. 2021, doi: 10.1109/ACCESS.2021.3058628.

[21] H. I. Olagunju, E. Alozie, A. L. Imoize, N. Faruk, S. Garba, and B. A. Baba, *Cybersecurity in the Internet of Medical Things for healthcare applications*, in Cybersecurity in Emerging Healthcare Systems, 2024, doi: 10.1049/PBHE064E_ch2.

[22] S. Sullivan, A. Brighente, S. A. P. Kumar, and M. Conti, "5G Security Challenges and Solutions: A Review by OSI Layers," *IEEE Access*, vol. 9, pp. 116294–116314, Aug. 2021, doi: 10.1109/ACCESS.2021.3105396.

[23] G. P. Pinto, P. K. Donta, S. Dustdar, and C. Prazeres, "A Systematic Review on Privacy-Aware IoT Personal Data Stores," *Sensors (Basel)*, vol. 24, no. 7, p. 2197, Mar. 2024, doi: 10.3390/s24072197.

[24] P. Kitsos and P. Pappa, "Privacy in the era of new surveillance technologies: An E.U law mission impossible?" in *Proceedings of the 6th International Conference on Information Law and Ethics (ICIL 2014): Lifting Barriers to Empower the Future of Information Law and Ethics*, Thessaloniki, Greece, May 2014.

[25] D. Gollmann, *Computer Security*, 3rd ed. Hoboken, NJ: Wiley, 2010.

[26] L. Tandon, P. W. L. Fong, and R. Safavi-Naini, "HCAP: A History-Based Capability System for IoT Devices," *arXiv preprint*, arXiv:1804.00086, Apr. 2018, doi: 10.48550/arXiv.1804.00086.

[27] A. K. Y. S. Mohamed, D. Auer, D. Hofer, and J. Küng, "A systematic literature review for authorization and access control: definitions, strategies and models," *International Journal of Web Information Systems*, vol. 18, no. 4, Oct. 2022, doi: 10.1108/IJWIS-08-2022-0048.

[28] Z. Yu, H. Gao, X. Cong, and N. Wu, "A Survey on Cyber-Physical Systems Security," *IEEE Internet of Things Journal*, vol. PP, no. 99, Jun. 2023, doi: 10.1109/JIOT.2023.3289625.

[29] U. Tariq, I. Ahmed, A. K. Bashir, and K. Shaukat, "A Critical Cybersecurity Analysis and Future Research Directions for the Internet of Things: A Comprehensive Review," *Sensors*, vol. 23, no. 8, p. 4117, Apr. 2023, doi: 10.3390/s23084117.

[30] M. Coole, "Defence in depth, protection in depth and security in depth: A comparative analysis towards a common usage language," *in the Proceedings of the 5th Australian Security and Intelligence Conference*, Perth, Western Australia, Dec. 2012.

[31] G. A. Fink, J. N. Haack, A. D. McKinnon, and E. W. Fulp, "Defense on the Move: Ant-Based Cyber Defense," *IEEE Security and Privacy Magazine*, vol. 12, no. 2, pp. 36–43, Mar. 2014, doi: 10.1109/MSP.2014.21.

[32] H. J. Smith, T. Dinev, and H. Xu, "Information Privacy Research: An Interdisciplinary Review," *MIS Quarterly*, vol. 35, no. 4, pp. 989–1015, Dec. 2011, doi: 10.2307/41409970.

[33] C. Dwork and A. Roth, "The Algorithmic Foundations of Differential Privacy," *FNT in Theoretical Computer Science*, vol. 9, no. 3–4, pp. 211–407, 2013, doi: 10.1561/0400000042.

[34] J. Kim, "A Study on the Development of IT System Emergency Recovery - Focused on IT System Security," *Security, Reliability, and Safety 2015*, vol. 109, no. 6, pp. 38–42, Aug. 2015, doi: 10.14257/astl.2015.109.06.

[35] M. Adam, M. Hammoudeh, R. Alrawashdeh, and B. Alsulaimy, "A Survey on Security, Privacy, Trust, and Architectural Challenges in IoT Systems," *IEEE Access*, vol. 12, pp. 12345–12357, Feb. 2024, doi: 10.1109/ACCESS.2024.3382709.

[36] A. Jeyabose and J. Karthikeyan, "Privacy-preserving Internet of Things: Techniques and Applications," *International Journal of Engineering and Advanced Technology*, vol. 8, no. 6, pp. 3229–3234, Aug. 2019, doi: 10.35940/ijeat.F8830.088619.

[37] P. Van Vliet, T. Kechadi, and N.-A. Le-Khac, "Forensics in Industrial Control System: A Case Study," in *Lecture Notes in Computer Science*, vol. 9588, pp. 147–156, Nov. 2016, doi: 10.1007/978-3-319-40385-4_10.

[38] Ö. Aslan, S. S. Aktug, M. Ozkan, and A. A. Yılmaz, "A Comprehensive Review of Cyber Security Vulnerabilities, Threats, Attacks, and Solutions," *Electronics*, vol. 12, no. 6, pp. 1–42, Mar. 2023, doi: 10.3390/electronics12061333.

2

Protection and Fault Diagnostics in Legacy Cyber-physical Systems

Kinzah Noor[1], Agbotiname Lucky Imoize[2], Hasnain Ahmad[3] and Mercy Oka Ebute[4]

[1]Office of Research Innovation and Commercialization, University of Management and Technology, Pakistan
[2]Department of Electrical and Electronics Engineering, Faculty of Engineering, University of Lagos, Nigeria
[3]Department of Computer Science, COMSATS University, Pakistan
[4]Department of Accounting, Anderson School of Management, University of New Mexico, USA

Email: kinzah.noor@umt.edu.pk; aimoize@unilag.edu.ng; sp22-bcs-140@cuilahore.edu.pk; mercyebute02@gmail.com

Abstract

Cyber-physical systems (CPS) integrate software and physical components and are increasingly prevalent in industries like smart manufacturing, telemedicine, autonomous vehicles, IoT, industrial control systems, and smart grids. As CPS becomes more interconnected, cyberattacks on critical infrastructure, such as oil pipelines and power grids, are becoming more frequent. Since CPS has limited computing and communication capabilities, traditional security solutions for embedded systems are insufficient, even though CPS is frequently safeguarding and critically important. Security must be considered from the beginning of CPS design to reduce these difficulties. This chapter addresses platform-aware control design, techniques, and frameworks. The increased prevalence of external connectivity in contemporary automobiles has raised concerns in academia and industry about communication interface vulnerabilities that expose internal networks. The development of cellular connectivity has made remote car takeovers possible, exposing the vehicle's

DOI: 10.1201/9788743801306-2

controller area network (CAN) to threats previously deemed low risk due to physical access requirements. This chapter presents a multidisciplinary approach to anomaly detection utilizing a model of an internal combustion engine and a speed controller that communicates over CAN to safeguard a vehicle's powertrain system. The study assesses four detection techniques derived from control theory and computer security against diverse cyberattack scenarios, stressing the advantages and disadvantages of each approach.

2.1 Introduction

A cyber-physical system (CPS) is a computer network that can stay in touch with the physical system in which it functions. CPSs have applications in multiple domains like medical equipment, intelligent factories, transport networks, cities, buildings, and grids. These structures are now collectively referred to as cyber-physical systems [1]. The path toward Industry 4.0 [2], sometimes called the Fourth Industrial Revolution, is characterized by significant and highly influential technical advancements within the industrial context. In [3], Industry 4.0 refers to the innovative industrial framework in which conventional control approaches have replaced fresh technologies that enable distributive and remote digital control. Broadband and distributed computation become crucial features of contemporary automation technologies with Industry 4.0.

Because edge devices can improve work efficiency, they are becoming increasingly frequent in factories. Examples of such equipment are connected to the Internet of Things (IoT) with a restricted memory and CPU. Cyber-physical manufacturing systems facilitate the merging of physical and virtual environments, opening up new possibilities for the industrial Internet of Things (IIoT). Input from the real world informs virtual actions for continual optimization, while virtual choices impact actual processes. Security is frequently neglected in favor of effectiveness and security in ICS development. Recent CPS and IIoT safety initiatives focus on using techniques from adjacent domains such as actuator networks and wireless sensor (ANWS) and SCADA control systems. However, detection and prevention approaches were originally established for ANWS and SCADA. However, these techniques might not entirely fulfill IIoT safety requirements since they were not particularly created for CPS. No technology can be totally resistant to every attack vector, especially zero-day attacks, even if they are applicable [4].

Nonetheless, CPS operators frequently see the growing access to potentially dangerous networks as a barrier to system availability. A general observation of anomalies framework is not feasible because of their heterogeneity; a flexible arrangement that can accommodate customized extensions is ideal for particular CPS features. CPS frequently lacks accessibility by layout, and the variety of actuators, sensors, and protocols for communication limits the effectiveness of conventional detection using signatures compared to regular corporate networks. The unpredictability of CPS behavior, such as variations in power grid demand from repair or storms, presents difficulties for behavior-based detection techniques, such as heuristic analysis and AI/ML. Effective implementation of threshold-based identification, which compares power grid usage to predetermined limitations, is challenging because CPSs are constantly changing and frequently vary during the course of their lifetime [5].

In the past, the focus of IT safety has been on safeguarding the accessibility, security, and reliability of information while it is in use for private computations and while en route. The major objectives of cyber-physical systems (CPS) are now accessibility for the sake of operational reliability and network reliability to verify correct operation. Cybersecurity has three operational stages: detection of attacks, crisis reimbursement, and safeguarding against threats. The goal of resilience is to keep the framework stable even when malfunctions aren't the outcome of effective assaults. Furthermore, resilience also entails correcting unintentional errors, [6] focusing on improving durability toward purposeful intrusions. CPS are becoming more and more open and dynamic, and as Industry 4.0 and IIoT expand in popularity, there is a requirement for improved security for both new and old CPSs. Initially, cybersecurity concentrated on the IT aspect while frequently ignoring the physical aspect, which is normally only protected by physical means. Author in [7] suggests adding an extra layer of protection where both physical and IT parts meet, enabling CPS to continue operating even in the event of an assault and enabling incremental upgrades for older systems.

Integrated cyber-physical systems (ICPSs) are used by critical infrastructures (CIs) to handle industrial operations in difficult situations. Increased connectivity, a wider threat, and a varied architecture are the primary causes of the problems. In [8], identifying anomalies, encrypted navigation, game theory, and watermarking are examples of conventional CPS security protection techniques that are not readily helpful for ICPSs because of their particular needs. Since ICS (industrial control system), ICPS, IIoT, and IWSNs (industrial wireless sensor networks) are interrelated and cannot be addressed independently, security solutions for ICPSs must consider the challenging industrial environments. Despite their shared features, authors in [9] contend that because industrial settings have unique features from information technology (IT) and operational technology (OT), CPS and ICPS safety ought to be treated as distinct research fields. In these environments, cyber events might result in disastrous consequences. Because of this, it focuses on ICPS security and is structured with these particular characteristics

The goal of the research [10] is to improve the resilience of CPS by developing a new energy management system (EMS) called cyber-physical resistant energy management systems (CYPREMS). It highlights that thorough modeling and tracking throughout all layers are essential to guarantee avoidance, early identification, and anticipatory danger evaluation. The CYPREMS establishes a safe data transfer channel that connects field instruments to actuators and control hubs by fusing physical and cyber components. This novel strategy aims to increase the safety and durability of power systems in the face of changing challenges.

Wide area monitoring, protection, and control (WAMPAC) systems [11] focus on three primary contributions that have improved cybersecurity and resilience. It starts by outlining a thorough cybersecurity framework that is resistant to attacks and covers every stage of the protection phases, encompassing risk evaluation, prevention, identification, and resilience. Second, it suggests a deep defense design that combines conventional IT protections with domain-dependent safety measures to integrate threat resilience at both the platform and application levels. Lastly, using case studies as examples, it introduces many attack-resistant WAMPAC methods that use measurement layout and model-based recognition of anomalies and prevention.

Existing legacy systems, or older CPSs, present unique issues even though the most recent CPS incorporate better security and diagnostic features. For their modern infrastructure, industrial sectors such as transportation, energy, manufacturing, and healthcare depend on CPSs. Legacy systems lack fault tolerance and contemporary security and rely on antiquated software and hardware components. Plenty of organizations tend to rely on them despite their shortcomings since upgrading or replacing them comes with expenses and hazards.

Cyberattacks and natural disasters are two unforeseen dangers that CPS must contend with. This chapter emphasizes the importance of considering threats that can affect the physical resources necessary for CPS operations, including non-IT and cyber threats. It highlights the significance of creating robust CPS and reevaluating approaches, instruments, and systems to guarantee CPS behaves consistently, regardless of pressure. The case study of a unified, safe data flow pipeline for powertrain engines and automotive systems is discussed. This approach ensures secure and reliable control from handheld devices to executive platforms.

2.1.1 Key contributions of the chapter

The following are the significant contributions of this chapter:

i. This chapter explores the integration of modern protocols into legacy systems and their implementation in industry. It examines the cybersecurity threats during these upgrades and highlights the protective measures to mitigate them. It also provides insights into the challenges faced by legacy systems in adapting to new security standards.

ii. This chapter discusses the generic internal combustion engine, focusing on its dynamic modeling and analysis. It covers various cyberattack scenarios that could target the engine and outlines detection strategies for identifying these attacks. It also gives insights into safeguarding the engine's functionality in cyber-physical systems; and

iii. This chapter emphasizes the importance of integrating security measures early in the design process. It introduces a CPS framework for automotive applications, provides detailed results, and discusses the effectiveness of these security measures. It highlights how early-stage security incorporation can enhance system resilience.

2.1.2 Chapter organization

Section 2.2 presents related works on legacy systems and their applicability to emerging technology. Section 2.3 contributes to industrial CPS, security challenges, and protection strategies. Section 2.4 analyses the case studies of generic internal combustion engines in detail with attack detection and the CPS framework for automotive applications. Section 2.5 gives the results and discussion. Section 2.6 concludes the chapter and provides future perspectives.

2.2 Related Work

The CPS facilitates production, data collection, and decision-making by trustworthy and secure tasks. The results of [12] have practical ramifications for the manufacturing security sector since they offer fresh insights into the CPS attack detection dilemma by considering immune-inspired solutions and implementing cost-effective protection through system layout. The research evidence indicates that the suggested approach is capable of recognizing network assaults, improving application durability, and significantly decreasing programming and design complications without adversely affecting the CPS Edge devices' functionality. However, further research includes host data, which should be analyzed alongside network data to enhance recognition because the cyber and physical worlds are strongly intertwined. It is necessary to consider the distributed structure of CPS and provide industrial verification. Dynamic reconfiguration must be supported by the framework to respond to changing risks.

The authors in [13] investigates the most recent developments in anomaly detection methods for detecting security risks in CPS. It offers an innovative contribution to the area by outlining the major obstacles still facing industrial control networks, such as limited resources, an absence of industry-wide standards for communication, excessive diversity impeding industry collaboration, and disparate security-related targets between networks for OT and IT. Integrating telemetry into the CPS framework makes further research in a more reliable AI-based anomaly identification system possible. A hybrid approach that combines threshold-based identification for trivial hazards, signature-based for identified risks, and behavior-based for unknown dangers is proposed as a workaround for the impracticality of costly detection of attacks. Over time, despite its challenges, AI/ML may enhance the reliability of behavior-based identification.

The research [14] presents a CPS method for intralogistics that monitors performance via conveyor belt experimentation. On a tiny scale, the IoT-driven technology streamlines data gathering, processing, and visualization, facilitating the conversion of old manufacturing settings into networked CPS. The primary benefit is obtaining complete openness in corporate logistics, which improves performance optimization and surveillance. It's still difficult to coordinate and work together effectively with manufacturing resources. Adoption of these technical advancements still faces significant obstacles, especially in handling complicated data and establishing compatibility between physical, handle, and commercial levels. Context-aware techniques that improve internal logistics input value chains require more study.

A Dempster-Shafer (DS) foundation [15] is used by the inter-domain empirical theory method for intelligence to boost identification by lowering false alerts. This approach is showcased on a CPS power testbed using classifiers trained on man-in-the-middle attack scenarios within an artificial electricity grid. However, research lacks resilience under enhanced threats and integration with advanced technology. The research [16] creates a method to combine physical and actual time cyber information, improving contextual awareness and lowering the number of false positives. A CPS power prototype incorporates the hybrid engine, which uses data from several sensors to identify cyberattacks. These are combined to create attributes that algorithms use to find cyber breaches. Nevertheless, efficiency did not increase when models were trained using multiple learning embedded data, suggesting that multidimensional training is better suited for visualization than improving detection accuracy. Cyberattacks have the potential to undermine critical safety, so it is imperative to integrate cybersecurity with safety and health protocols. These issues must be addressed from system layout to execution [17]. Further research needs from existing standards tend to approach them in isolation, underscoring the necessity of comprehensive, collaborative initiatives. By creating automated control and threat designs, authors in [18] investigates CPS subjected to DoS attacks. A resilient observer-based control layout is presented to improve structure durability, and a linear quadratic (LQ) forecast controller is constructed to reduce data loss. Comparative simulations demonstrate that the method guarantees an asymptotically stable control system behavior under DoS assaults. Research lacks optimal strategy adoption.

IIoT-connected devices are typically left accessible via the Internet; safety and privacy are major concerns. Encrypted data sometimes requires sacrificing accessibility for security. To protect the levels below, efficient encryption must be performed at higher levels [19]. Massive networks with limited resources find that existing protections are insufficient due to their elevated computation and storage expenses. Current cryptographic techniques that have been legally confirmed must be included in quick and compact encryption. Furthermore, more investigation is needed to develop robust IIoT security measures that can fend off a range of cyberattacks, including distributed DoS attacks, eavesdropping, side-channel analysis, node capture, and man-in-the-middle attacks.

A recent study [20] has shown it to be a successful communication tool in the automobile sector, but it does not provide the necessary security assurances for contemporary applications. Researchers and manufacturers are investigating various security methods, such as intrusion detection devices, encryption, and authentication, to safeguard the CAN concerns about automobile safety increase. However, instead of considering the system as a whole, these solutions usually concentrate on certain vehicle domains.

A model with an internal combustion engine and speed controller coupled with a CAN bus is presented for investigating cyberattacks on a vehicle's powertrain [21]. Three attack scenarios are investigated: one involves CAN message injection, while the others target sensors and CAN communication. This is the first model that mimics how a car's engine would respond to a real-world cyberattack. Subsequent research endeavors will examine cutting-edge defenses against the assessed threat model to construct a framework that leverages both situations to surmount mutual constraints. Table 2.1 provides a summary of related work on legacy CPS.

Table 2.1 Related work on legacy CPS.

Research domain	Current state	Approach	Research gap	Future recommendation
IoT and CPS	Introduce IoT to unlock new designs and improve intralogistics efficiency and complete openness	Carries out a basic data processing chain in a conveyor test bed	Adoption in practical application and management of complex data	A flexible CPS that can be applied to a conveyor system and improve comprehension of the internal logistics system is produced by webcams
IoT security and privacy	Identifying the importance of data encryption and a secure and balanced system is required	Encryption that is quick and lightweight is required to achieve IIoT-adapted safety	Lightweight encryption considers new formally verified methods, and AKC protocols are in a new customization for the IIoT context	Develop appropriate IIoT security mechanisms that are resilient to the current IIoT cyberattacks
Attack detection in-vehicle network	The balance between detection performance and hardware requirements	Detecting Attacks to In-Vehicle Networks via N-Gram Analysis (DAGA) anomaly finding algorithm for vehicle network	Cannot support the vast majority of IDS approaches	Integration of multi-layer security measures and real-time anomaly detection
CPS design and attack detection in edge devices	Recognizing network assaults, decreasing code and design complexity, and improving reliability	CPS design based on the IEC 61499 standard	Dynamic reconfiguration needs to be supported	Host data deserves to be analyzed alongside the data network; consider the distributed structure of CPS

Security in industrial control networks	Anomaly detection methods for detecting risks in CPS	An innovation to the area by major obstacles by industrial control networks	AI-based anomaly identification system by integrating telemetry into the CPS	A hybrid approach combines threshold-based identification for trivial hazards
CPS power system	A Dempster-Shafer (DS) foundation, inter-domain empirical theory method for intelligence	CPS power testbed man-in-the-middle attack scenarios within an artificial electricity grid	Resilience under enhanced threats and integration with advanced technology	Improved identification precision and real-time application
CPS power prototype	Uses data from several sensors to identify cyberattacks by hybrid in cybersecurity and physical domain	Incorporates the hybrid engine and algorithm toidentify attacks	Situations with more data and equal records result in higher efficiency	Multidimensional training is better suited for visualization than for improving accuracy in detection
Safety and cybersecurity by design	Integrate cybersecurity with safety and health protocols	Address issues from layout to execution	Lack of proper guidelines to address cyber and physical attacks	Developing policies integrate safety and cybersecurity measures
CPS under DOS attacks	Comparative simulations demonstrate guarantees of an asymptotically stable control system behavior	A resilient observer-based control layout is presented, and a linear quadratic (LQ) forecast controller	Research lacks optimal strategy adoption	Integration with other security attacks and intelligent controller
Cyber-attacks on power CPS	Three attack scenarios: CAN message injection, target sensors, and CAN communication	CAN bus is used for cyberattacks on a vehicle's powertrain	Examining cutting-edge defenses against the assessed threat model	Construct framework leverages both situations to surmount mutual constraints

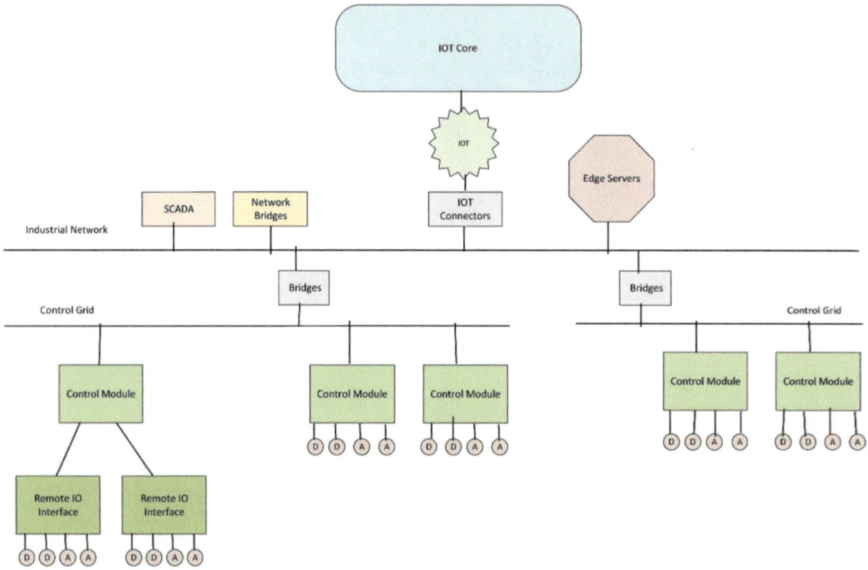

Figure 2.1 Industrial CPS.

2.3 Cyber-physical System

An industrial control and automation system [22] is an example of a CPS that tracks and regulates technical operations. Examples include automation of processes, machine control, power automation, and cloud robotics. Automation components can be connected directly to automation equipment or using remote input/output modules if the equipment is outfitted with detectors (D) and actuators (A). The system manages the operation by using detectors to measure the process's present state and produce actuator pulses in response.

Figure 2.1 shows an industrial automation framework with multiple control networks connected to a plant network and a cloud backend. Network isolation is frequently used to implement particular privacy regulations within manufacturing units or to create separate control networks with stringent actual time needs for sensor–actuator interactions. These systems find widespread use in several automation areas, such as building, energy, railway, factory, and process automation.

2.3.1 Autonomous CPS

Computer and physical elements are smoothly integrated in CPS. One of the most important requirements for CPS to cope with variable operational

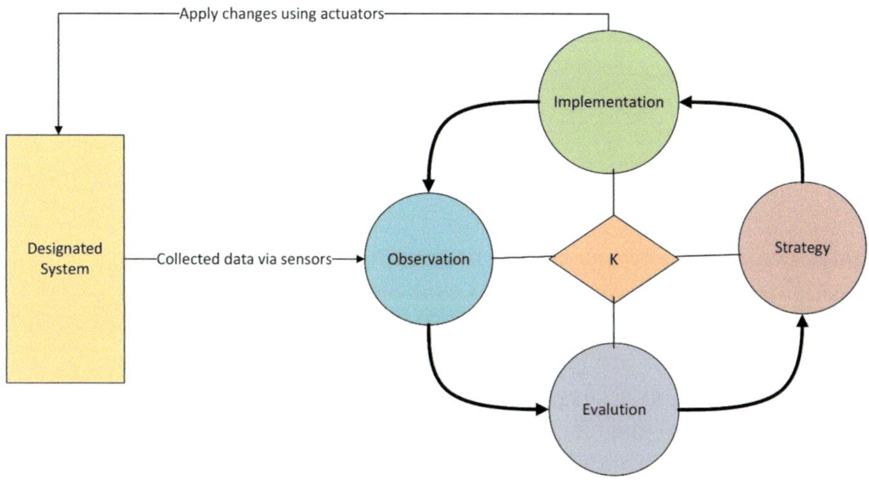

Figure 2.2 Control cycle.

circumstances is flexibility, which is realized with feedback cycles. The MAPE-K feedback cycle serves as the most prominent conventional control framework for centralized and self-adaptive systems as presented in Figure 2.2 [23]. Data about the designated system and its surroundings, evolving objectives, and other pertinent details exchanged by all Monitor, Analyze, Plan, and Execute (MAPE) stages are kept up to date in the database of knowledge (K). The observation (O) function obtains certain information from the core designated system and the operating environment, using detectors put in the structure. The gathered information is kept in the common knowledge base. The evaluation (E) function examines the information to determine whether a modification is required. If so, it initiates the strategy (S) function, which creates the sequence of adjustments required to meet the framework's objectives based on predetermined policies. The implementation (I) function then uses inhibitors, also known as actuators, installed on the controlled system to carry out these activities. All these processes can link directly or indirectly by exchanging data in the knowledge base.

2.3.2 Enabling self-adaptation through anomaly detection

Monitoring events within the CPS to obtain vital data, identify any unusual behavior, reduce threat levels, and ensure the system's security and safety is imperative. The best viewpoint locations for CPS monitoring with the least redundancy must be chosen. Typically, monitoring is keeping an eye on

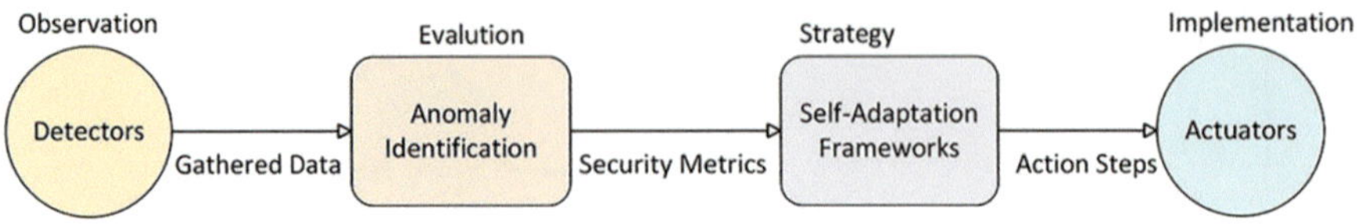

Figure 2.3 Anomaly identification to enhance observation and evaluation.

traffic across the network. During monitoring, data are gathered from devices positioned across the network and evaluated to identify potential risks and initiate a modification process. Next, the CPS protection state is evaluated, and harmful actions are identified using anomaly detection systems. A suitable self-adaptation strategy is chosen through the scheduling stage of an alteration proposal that emerges if security indicators uncover flaws. The data collected during the monitoring stage can be analyzed using various techniques. Relevant strategies involve correlation between events tools, anomaly detection techniques that use machine learning and/or clustering algorithms, rule-driven connection, and host attack detection systems [24].

2.3.2.1 Adaptive security metrics and policy frameworks

In detecting an anomalous data instance, an event known as a security incident sets off an alarm. In contrast, a security metric considers the probability of security incidents to assess the status of a framework's protection. As seen in Figure 2.3, abnormality detection systems can examine the information gathered throughout the observation stage, and warnings are subsequently deciphered, taking specified security metrics into account. The metrics related to safety are therefore assessed, and if required, specific steps are determined by the self-adaptation regulations in place at the time. During the planning stage, a self-adaptation strategy reduction approach is chosen to allow an appropriate response in the designated system. Depending on the data received from the assessment phase a transition strategy is developed, comprised of a series of required modifications, and provided to the implementation stage. The determined security metrics are the necessary inputs to make self-adaptation strategies possible.

2.3.2.2 Implementing response strategies

Ultimately, the implementation stage implements the preventative measures established during the organizing stage by deploying actuators on the designated system. The autonomy administrator will implement customized preventative measures to alter the safety status of the CPS [25] and counteract the detected attack after choosing a self-adaptation strategy that matches the modification request from a security metric. The reaction steps could be sending control messages to reactivate system processes, beginning the password-updating process, and setting firewall rules to prevent bogus links.

2.3.3 IT and CPS integration: Key challenges

As inexpensive Internet protocol (IP) technology grew popular, ICS operators switched to networked equipment with IP-based IT, allowing remote access using a TCP/IP stack. This technique uses reasonably priced serial-to-Ethernet adapters to incorporate older equipment and protocols – like the Modbus protocol, which is based on serial connections – into a fresh network firewall to stop shady links, and so forth. This method made it easier for users to establish links to and supervise dispersed systems. Coupling IT and CPS has an unexpected impact. However, it increases the danger of attack by providing new avenues for attacks to enter formerly separate control system networks through flaws in IT-related systems.

According to Sharma et al. [26], four main distinctions in CPS and IT platforms call for adjustments to the effectiveness of frameworks and metrics that are developed for protection and actions. The vital specifications of CPS require a disciplined engineering methodology distinct from that of IT applications due to its significant connection with cyber components and the physical environment through feedback loops. It is also difficult to determine state shift locations because CPS has several more modes of operation than IT networks. IT analysts can assess efficiency using typical machine learning approaches. However, as CPS uses inexpensive sensors, it has to be selective about which variables to analyze, how often to analyze them, and what adjustments are needed.

According to Hayes and El-Khatib [27], typical IT safety precautions like antivirus programs and firewalls are inadequate and unworkable because they influence accessibility when legacy CPS interfaces with IT systems. In CPS, execution on time is essential for the correct operation of the actual system, whereas, in IT systems, efficiency delays impact productivity. Environmental and individual safety might be jeopardized by inadequate CPS security. Piggin and Boyes [28] described a comprehensive safety and protection strategy to mitigate these hazards. This strategy prohibits malevolent or illegal activity while avoiding dangerous states that could result in harm, death, or environmental damage.

2.3.4 Challenges in securing CPSs

It's critical to consider the many kinds of assaults to comprehend the security problems that CPS architects and users must overcome.

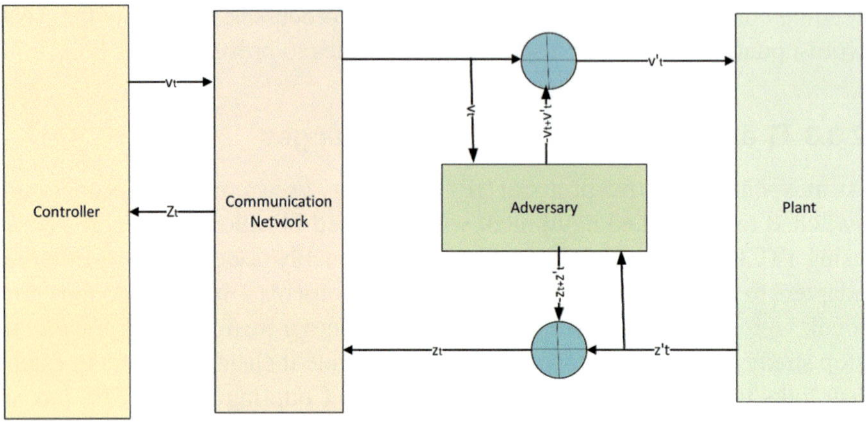

Figure 2.4 An adversarial-attacked CPS framework.

2.3.4.1 Kinds of attackers

The work by Rubio-Hernan et al. [29] distinguished between two kinds of attackers based on their capacity to break into a cyber network, comprehend the internal functioning of the infrastructure, and develop a framework of performance for exploitation, as seen in Figure 2.4.

A “cyber adversary,” the first kind of attacker described, can grab detector signals zt over communication connections, alter them to $z't$, and launch an assault. At this level of understanding a cyber adversary retains the ability to threaten CPS function state regardless of their complete lack of understanding of underlying control algorithms.

A more advanced “cyber-physical adversary” might exist, possessing all the traits of a cyber adversary plus the capacity to track communication from the actual controller output vt to gain a complete grasp of the entire system and launch more complex assaults. Equipped with such an ability, an attacker operating remotely may examine control inputs, network reactions, and sensor data to create a model of CPS efficiency. Once the model is created, the cyber-physical adversary can create assault scenarios that breach the control network and harm the physical structures while keeping the failures and error identification systems unaware of the attack.

2.3.4.2 DOS threat

One of the most popular and straightforward tactics cyber-physical adversaries use is DoS assault [31]. To obstruct the transmission of lawful data entails flooding the network’s communication link with high traffic, congealing communication channels, or hacking equipment. These assaults can seriously impair the control network or only create minor disruptions [32].

2.3.4.3 Data integrity threat

A highly adept cyber-physical opponent may launch a more covert, and maybe more destructive, attack called a data integrity assault [33]. When a data integrity assault succeeds, an intruder tracks a legitimate data message, changes its contents without revealing any evidence of their work, and then sends it to the desired target. This technique is simple to implement on vintage CPS infrastructure, frequently using antiquated communication standards with few security safeguards. By manipulating the data delivered to the controller, a hacker might cause physical harm to a working CPS without the user's knowledge by taking advantage of weaknesses in specific standards. Wu and Sun [34] suggest a way to magnify the differences between how the framework behaves while it is under assault and when it is operating normally. In the same way, [35] hackers can record data collected by sensors, examine the system's reactions, and alter control inputs while tampering with readings from sensors to simulate regular functioning.

In the aforementioned situation, a hacker can read and transmit any CAN signal to the in-vehicle communication [36]. The injection assault is carried out at the CAN layer by infecting the system with fraudulent communications. It has two phases: First, the hacker gathers data about the intended CAN network, such as the frequency and the type of messages. After selecting the intended message, the hacker introduces counterfeit signals into the system, employing a quicker phase time and linking them with legal communications.

2.3.4.4 Fuzzing threat

An automated technique to evaluate networks using erroneous, unanticipated, or unpredictable inputs is called fuzzing. According to the proposed framework, a fuzzing attack entails using modified data input by an intruder to change the control system's output. This is a two-stage assault where the attacker gathers data on legitimate inputs before inserting an illegal input string into the system. Control systems [37] and CAN communications [38] have both been studied about this attack. Interestingly, the effect is the same if the fuzzing happens at the sensor's level or by changing the associated CAN message.

2.3.4.5 Replay threat

An adversary collecting and sending back control messages at a later period is known as a replay assault. The receiver considers the message authentic since its CRC is valid and tries to apply its control input modifications. The malicious message may stay under the background noise level of the system's flaw sensors, making it extremely difficult to identify, especially in devices with loud sensor inputs to operate. In the proposed threat model, the replay attack includes a process with two stages where the intruder collects an array of inputs and their matching outputs. After that, a hacker replays these results while feeding the network inaccurate input patterns. This kind of assault has been researched in CAN communication and control systems [39]. Table 2.2 highlights some security challenges in CPS.

2.3.5 CPS security strategies

In contrast to standard IT components, several properties of CPS could render its defense easier, yet substantial safety issues exist [40].

2.3.5.1 Intrinsic security benefits of CPS

CPS security specialists recommend a multi-layered strategy that can significantly reduce assault to reduce possible breaches and losses. Even while CPS presents a lot of difficult security concerns, some of its features truly render them less difficult to secure than conventional IT systems. In the study by Ashibani and Mahmoud [41], some advantages of privacy are presented. CPS networks are relatively stable; besides repair or malfunctions, devices often stay placed and never alter. Network arrangements, standards, and links hardly change until movement is required. Furthermore, a user base for CPS is often confined to operational people, leading to few changes among operators. Constant communication trends are produced by CPS activities, allowing users to track changes from regular operations over time by monitoring network activity, sensor readings, and control instructions.

2.3.5.2 Strategies for integrity attack prevention

A method of guaranteeing integrity considers the network configuration and the data inside. The work of Vegh and Miclea [42] suggested that the security system manages access through a hierarchy and provides integrity validation using a split secret key. Limiting access to data from compromised nodes to those within an identical hierarchy level. This technique lessens the data that adversaries may obtain and lowers the possibility of status elevation. However, the crucial facets of key allocation and management required for the network to function continuously are not covered.

Table 2.2 Security challenges in CPS.

Threats	Sources	Description	Effects on CPS
Types of attackers	• Malevolent insiders or unhappy workers • The hackers • Internet thieves • A state-sponsored attacker	• Attempting to take advantage of weaknesses maliciously • Keep identification systems unaware of the attack	• Sensitive information leak • Unauthorized command activities • Compromised system integrity and trust
DOS	• Compromised devices or networks of bots • Planned strikes by outsiders • Security flaws in networking protocols	• Interfere with CPS service availability, making it impossible for them to operate and impair vital activities	• Service unavailability • Disruption of critical operations • Financial losses • Potential safety hazards
Data integrity	• Threat target control systems • Deficient devices (detectors/ actuators) • Inadequate identification and accessibility controls	• Unauthorized data alteration inside the CPS is the source of this danger, which could result in harmful situations and improper system functioning	• Incorrect sensor reading • Safety risks • Doubt in system information
Fuzzing	• Automated fuzzing devices • Insider security testing • Flaws in the software development phase	• Fuzzing attacks deliver erroneous or invalid information to the CPS to exploit faults	• System crashes or erratic behavior • Discovery of vulnerabilities that can be exploited further • Degradation of system performance
Replay	• Incorrect series number or timestamping • Poor session administration • Protocol flaws in communication	• Rival capturing legal data packets and retransmitting them into carrying out successful orders, sometimes leading to illegal tasks	• Unauthorized command execution • Possibility of dangerous physical behavior • Safety in operation is compromised

2.3.5.3 CPS data protection strategies

Experts advise techniques that impede adversary access to strengthen the security of CPS systems. Installing encryption/decryption devices at the two ends of unprotected links, such as Modbus communications, is one practical solution [43]. A comprehensive method for encoding was presented in this research for Modbus that improves privacy but necessitates additional computing power, which could affect the reaction times needed to control real operations. Furthermore, implementing encryption techniques becomes more complicated due to safe key-sharing between central and sub-controllers.

2.3.6 Detection of hazard in CPS

The work of Kordy et al. [44] suggests attack trees make it possible to assess safety risks using real hardware testing and quantifiable goals. It assists in identifying the degree of complexity of different assaults and reveals objectives like data stealing or hacking of systems. Attack trees can also highlight threats to distant systems, such as field stations, communication networks, and outside vendors. An agent-based game theoretic (ABGT) strategy [45] can mimic attacker–defender exchanges and predict the likelihood of succeeding assaults, which can be used to measure hazards in CPS quantitatively. Researchers can examine these patterns with ABGT to find low-risk, high-reward assault pathways. By using this strategy, security groups can better focus assets to counteract the most significant and foreseeable risks from cyber-physical adversaries. Table 2.3 provides valuable information on CPS security techniques.

2.4 Case Studies

A general internal combustion engine is dynamically modeled, and dangerous situations are examined. Furthermore, a thorough analysis of an electric vehicle cyber-physical security framework and the outcomes of mock attacks are given.

2.4.1 A detailed analysis of generic internal combustion engine

The case study aims to increase public awareness of the potential hazards of integrating external connectivity into the automotive system. An experimental investigation using a speed controller connected via CAN and a general internal combustion engine model is presented in [46]. Four detection methods derived from computer safety and control theory across various

Table 2.3 CPS security techniques.

CPS security methods	Overview	Case studies of implementation	Implementation-related hazards
Intrinsic security benefits of CPS	Some features of CPS naturally enhance their safety and make them simpler to defend	• Static network settings minimize the need for regular adjustments • Fewer users with direct operational responsibilities mean fewer points of attack	• Due to the lack of updates, there is potential for outdated hardware or software • People get complacent about security procedures
Strategies for integrity attack prevention	Precautions are taken to prevent unauthorized changes from compromising the security of data and systems	• Attack trees are used to find flaws • Putting robust access controls and verification into place • Encrypting data both at idle and in motion	• Complexity may lead to failures • Stakeholders‘ opposition due to practical effect
CPS data protection strategies	Strategies aimed at guaranteeing the reliability and privacy of information within CPS	• Encoding/decoding units for secure transmission, i.e., Modbus • Safe key administration procedures • Frequent audits and observations of data access trends	• Introduce latency and affect real-time tasks • Incorrect handling of encryption keys may result in data loss
Detection of hazard in CPS	Techniques for safe communication routes that are employed in CPS to prevent illegal access and detection	• Secure communication technologies (like SSH and TLS) • Performing routine software updates and patches to address hazards	• Vulnerabilities may arise from integration issues with legacy systems • Insufficient staff training on fresh safety protocols

cyber assault situations are assessed to indicate risks facing contemporary automobiles.

2.4.1.1 Dynamic model of engine and controller

The average value model (AVM) of the spark ignition (SI) engine comprises five interrelated sub-modules: throttle assembly, intake chamber, gas exchange process, combustion process, and torque generation, along with engine inertia. The SI engine has the following dynamic model:

$$\frac{dp_c(t)}{dt} = \frac{K\Theta_c}{V_d}\left(\dot{m}_\alpha(t) - \dot{m}_\beta(t)\right) \tag{2.1}$$

$$\frac{d\omega_g(t)}{dt} = \frac{1}{\Theta_g}\left[\tau_g(t) - \tau_l(t)\right], \tag{2.2}$$

where p_c is intake chamber pressure, $\dot{m}_\alpha$ is the mass air-flow mass arriving through the throttle valve, $\dot{m}_\beta$ is the mass air flow leaving the intake chamber and entering the cylinders, ω_g is the engine speed, τ_g the torque generated by the engine, and τ_l is the load torque. Establishing the connection between eqn (2.1) and (2.2) will help derive an appropriate model expression for controller design. The engine speed ω_g is related to $\dot{m}_\alpha$ and $\dot{m}_\beta$ from eqn (2.1). With the assumption that the throttle is isenthalpic and the air is a perfect gas, $\dot{m}_\alpha$ can be written as:

$$\dot{m}_\alpha(t) = \begin{Bmatrix} A_\alpha(t)\dfrac{p_a}{\sqrt{2K\Theta_a}} & \dfrac{p_c(t)}{p_a} \leq 0.5 \\ A_\alpha(t)\dfrac{p_a}{\sqrt{K\Theta_a}}\sqrt{\dfrac{p_c(t)}{p_a}\left[1 - \dfrac{p_c(t)}{p_a}\right]} & \text{else} \end{Bmatrix}, \tag{2.3}$$

where region A_α of the throttle valve is open:

$$A_\alpha(\alpha_v) = \frac{\pi d_v^2}{4}\left(\frac{\cos(\alpha_v)}{\cos(\alpha_v,0)}\right) + A_{v,\text{leak}} \tag{2.4}$$

$$\alpha_v = \alpha_{v,0} + \left(\frac{\pi}{2} - \alpha_{v,0}\right)\mu_\alpha. \tag{2.5}$$

In this case, throttle actuation is disregarded, and $\mu_\alpha \in [0, 1]$ [0, 1] is the control input. α_v is the throttle angle. Before relating $\dot{m}_\beta$ to ω_g, the following relation is taken into account.

$$\xi(t) = \frac{1}{\sigma_s} \cdot \frac{\dot{m}_\beta(t)}{\dot{m}_f(t)} \tag{2.6}$$

In relation to the stoichiometric constant σ_s, this is the air-to-fuel ratio in the cylinders. $\dot{m}_f$ is the fuel mass that flows into the cylinder. Given the insignificant effects of injector dynamics and wall-wetting processes and an approximation constant ξ, the fuel flow mass entering the cylinder is:

$$\dot{m}_f = \frac{\dot{m}_{\dot{\beta}}(t)}{\sigma_s \xi}. \tag{2.7}$$

The gas-mixture mass flow desired in the cylinder is obtained from this expression:

$$\dot{m}(t) = \dot{m}_\beta + \dot{m}_f = \dot{m}_\beta \left(1 + \frac{1}{\sigma_s \xi(t)}\right). \tag{2.8}$$

The airflow mass $\dot{m}_\beta$ that is, leaving the intake chamber for the cylinders at this spot is associated with $\dot{m}$ in the following way:

$$\dot{m}_\beta(t) = \frac{\dot{m}(t)}{1 + \frac{1}{\sigma_s \xi}}. \tag{2.9}$$

When the engine is viewed as a volumetric pump, the mass flow of gas and mixture aspirated in the cylinders is determined by:

$$\dot{m}(t) = \frac{p_c(t)}{K\theta_c} . \xi_l\left(\omega_g(t), p_c(t)\right) V_d \frac{\omega_{g(t)}}{4\pi}. \tag{2.10}$$

The volumetric efficiency is represented by ξ_l, and can be approximated as follows:

$$\xi_{l\omega}\left(\omega_g, p_c\right) = \xi_{l\omega}\left(\omega_g\right) . \xi_{lp}\left(p_c\right), \tag{2.11}$$

where

$$\xi_{l\omega}\left(\omega_g\right) = \xi_s + \xi_1 \omega_g + \xi_2 \omega_g^2 \tag{2.12}$$

$$\xi_{lp}(p_c) = \frac{V_c + V_d}{V_d} - \frac{V_c}{V_d}\left(\frac{p_{\text{out}}}{p_c}\right)^{\frac{1}{R}}. \tag{2.13}$$

The V_c, and V_d is the compression and displaced volume, R is the specific heat ratio ($R \approx 1.4$), and pout is the engine's exhaust side pressure in eqn (2.13). The break mean effective pressure p_{cg} is necessary pressure that must remain on the piston for the span of the expanding stroke to complete an engine cycle.

$$p_{cg} = \frac{4\pi \,.\, \tau_g}{V_d}. \tag{2.14}$$

The break mean effective pressure that the engine produces for the amount of fuel mass m_ϕ burnt during each engine period, which converts all of the fuel's heat into mechanical energy, is known as the average effective pressure of fuel.

$$p_{cf} = \frac{m_f \,.\, H_l}{V_d}. \tag{2.15}$$

The fuel mass flow and the fuel mass mass m_f have the following relationship:

$$\dot{m}_f(t) = m_f(t)\frac{\omega_g(t)}{4\pi}. \tag{2.16}$$

The relationship between engine speed and intake manifold air pressure makes the above equation significant. According to this definition of effective efficiency:

$$\eta_g = \frac{p_{cg}}{p_{cf}} = \frac{\tau_g \,.\, 4\pi}{m_f \,.\, H_f}. \tag{2.17}$$

A function for τ_g can be found. Indeed, from eqn (2.17)

$$p_{cg} = \eta_g(-)\,.\,p_{cf}, \tag{2.18}$$

where there exist various methods to generate $\eta_g(-)$, and the following approximation could be used:

$$p_{cg} \approx p_{ci}(\omega_g) - \left(p_{c0s}(\omega_g) + p_{c0q}(\omega_g)\right). \tag{2.19}$$

The specified mean pressure p_{ci} is given by:

$$p_{ci} = \frac{\omega_i}{V_d} = \eta_i \frac{H_f \,.\, m_f}{V_d}. \tag{2.20}$$

Groza et al. [47] specified the ω_i. The Willian's approximation can be used to estimate the given thermodynamic efficiency η_i as follows: $\eta_i(\omega_g) \approx \eta_0 + \omega_g \eta_l$.

Table 2.4 Parameters values.

Parameters	Units	Values	Parameters	Units	Values
K	[*J/KgK*]	287	ξ_1	3.42e–3	[S]
θ_a	[K]	298	ξ_2	–7.7e–6	[S²]
θ_c	[K]	340	η_0	0.16	[*J/Kg*]
α_v	[degree]	7.9	η_1	2.21e–3	[*Js/Kg*]
d_v	[m]	58.7e–3	β_0	15.6	[Nm]
$A_{(v,\text{leak})}$	[m²]	5.6e–6	β_1	0.175e–3	[NmS²]
V_d	[m³]	2.77e–3	θ_g	0.2	[Kg/m²]
V_c	[m³]	0.277e–3	H_f	45.8e6	[-]
p_a	[Pa]	1e5	R	1.35	[-]
p_{out}	[Pa]	1e5	α	14.70	[-]
ξ_s	[-]	0.45			

The terms p_{c0s} is the loss due to friction and p_{c0q} due to gas exchange. According to eqn (2.14), (2.18), and (2.19)

$$\tau_g(t) = p_{cg}(t)\frac{V_d}{4\pi} = \left(\eta_i(\omega_g)p_{cf} - p_{c0s}(\omega_g) - p_{c0q}(\omega_g)\right)\frac{V_d}{4\pi}. \tag{2.21}$$

Substituting the p_{cf} from eqn (2.17), the engine's torque is:

$$\tau_g(t) = \left(\left(\eta_0 + \eta_l\omega_g\right)\frac{H_f m_f(t)}{V_d} - p_{c0s}(\omega_g) - p_{c0s}(\omega_g)\right)\frac{V_d}{4\pi}. \tag{2.22}$$

Lastly, from eqn (2.16), we may represent m_f as function of $\dot{m}_f$ which can be derived from eqn (2.8) as:

$$m_f(t) = \frac{4\pi \,.\, \dot{m}_\beta}{\alpha \,.\, \omega_g}, \tag{2.23}$$

where $\alpha = \xi.\sigma_s$. Table 2.4 provides the parameter values [48].

2.4.1.2 A non-linear SI engine model addressing the cruise control issue

The following non-linear SI engine model addresses the cruise control issue. Figure 2.5 gives the integrated IC engine model.

$$\frac{dp_c(t)}{dt} = \frac{K\theta_c}{V_d}\left(A_\alpha(t)\frac{p_a}{\sqrt{2K\theta_a}} - \left(\frac{p_c(t)}{K\theta_c}\left(\xi_s + \xi_1\omega_g(t) + \xi_2\omega_g^2(t)\right)\left(\frac{V_c + V_d}{V_d} - \frac{V_c}{V_d}\left(\frac{p_{\text{out}}}{p_c}\right)^{\frac{1}{R}}\right)V_d\frac{\omega_{g(t)}}{4\pi}\frac{\alpha}{\alpha+1}\right)\right) \tag{2.24}$$

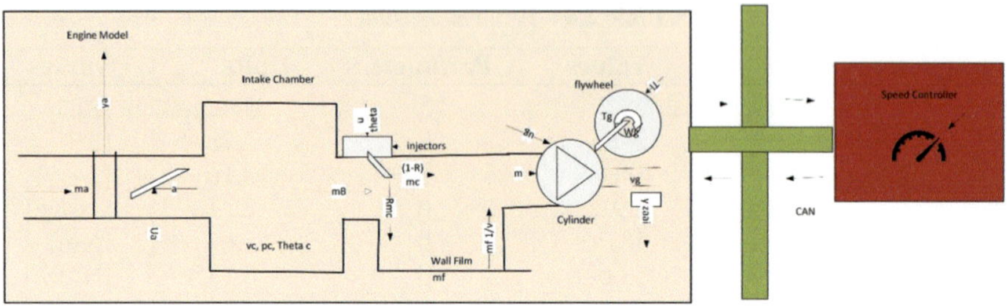

Figure 2.5 Integrated IC engine model.

$$\frac{d\omega_g(t)}{dt} = \frac{1}{\theta_g}\left[\begin{array}{l}\left(\xi_s + \xi_1\omega_g(t)\right)\frac{H_f p_c(t)}{K\theta_c}\left(\xi_s + \xi_1\omega_g(t) + \xi_2\omega_g^2(t)\right)\left(\frac{V_c + V_d}{V_d} - \frac{V_c}{V_d}\left(\frac{p_{\text{out}}}{p_c}\right)^{\frac{1}{R}}\right)\frac{V_d}{\alpha + 1} \\ -\left(\beta_0 + \beta_2\omega_g^2(t) + \left(p_{\text{out}} - p_c(t)\right)\frac{V_d}{4\pi}\right) - \tau_l(t)\end{array}\right]. \tag{2.25}$$

2.4.1.3 Flow chart

Ensuring safety and resilience, the multifunctional detection system for cyber-attacks on powertrain CPS adheres to a systematic procedure. The first step is acquiring physical and communication data from powertrain components, such as engine sensors and communication modules. After pre-processing and cleaning the raw data to eliminate noise, essential aspects of the system behavior are extracted for analysis. Then, anomaly detection algorithms, such as statistical techniques, rule-based systems, or machine learning models, are employed to find odd patterns that might point to a cyberattack. To prevent false alarms from the detection system, mechanical, electrical, and cybersecurity specialists work together to identify if a cyberattack or normal system behavior causes an anomaly. Anomalies that are verified to be assaults fall under many categories into attack types, such as fuzzing attacks, replay attacks, and injection attacks if it is determined that it is an attack. Then, appropriate response and mitigation techniques are implemented, like resetting system parameters, shutting down activities, or isolating impacted components.

The system is anticipated to develop, enhancing detection precision and adjusting to novel forms of attack. It can be strengthened by linking it with other car subsystems and encouraging cooperation between engineers and cybersecurity specialists. As time passes, it might start anticipating and stopping attacks before they happen, improving the security of contemporary machines and automobiles. Figure 2.6 gives the flow chart for the hybrid model.

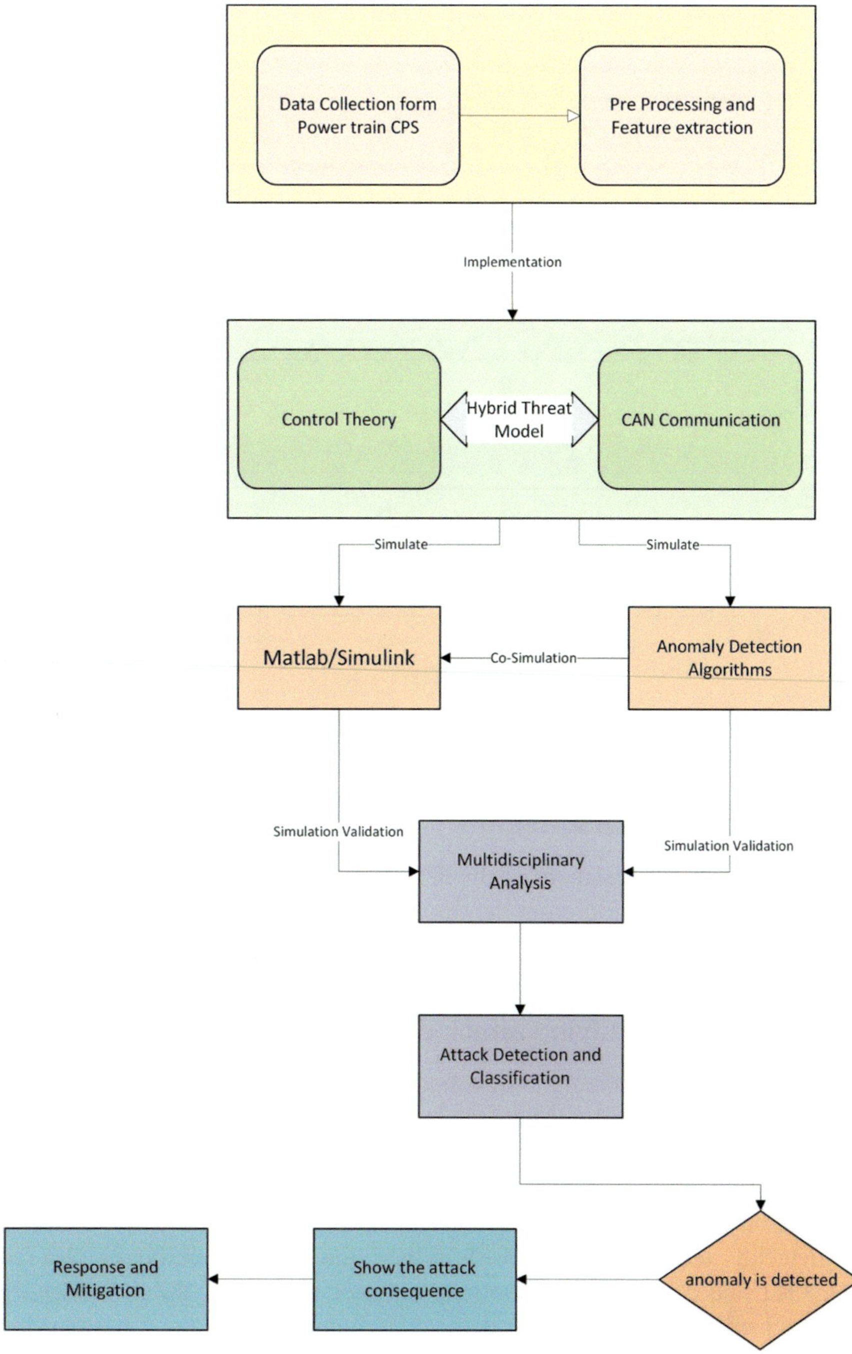

Figure 2.6 Flow chart for the hybrid model.

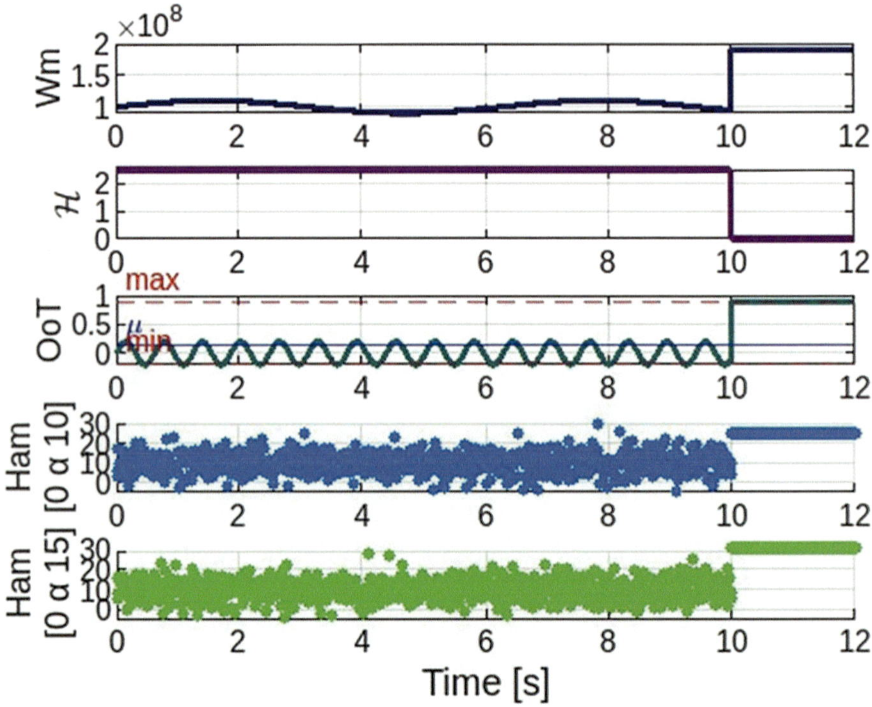

Figure 2.7 Fuzzing identifying attacks on the LQG controller μ_r^*.

2.5 Results and Discussion

The experimental assessment of the detection framework using a simulation of the assaults is considered in the threat framework of the proposed power-train structure.

2.5.1 Fuzzing identifying attack outcomes

This threat model's fuzzing attack modifies the ThrottleRequest CAN message or the LQG controller by injecting random input values into the system. Figures 2.7 and 2.8 display the detection results of the tests conducted on the two scenarios. Watermarking, bus entropy, out-of-time (OoT), and Hamming distance on CAN messages (ThrottleRequest and EngineSpeed) were among the detecting techniques employed. In the figures, the attack begins at a red line. OoT and conventional Hamming distance algorithms failed to identify the attack on the LQG controller depicted in Figure 2.7, but the watermarking approach and bus entropy did. When the red crosses overstep the threshold mark the detection system activated through the modified Hamming distance

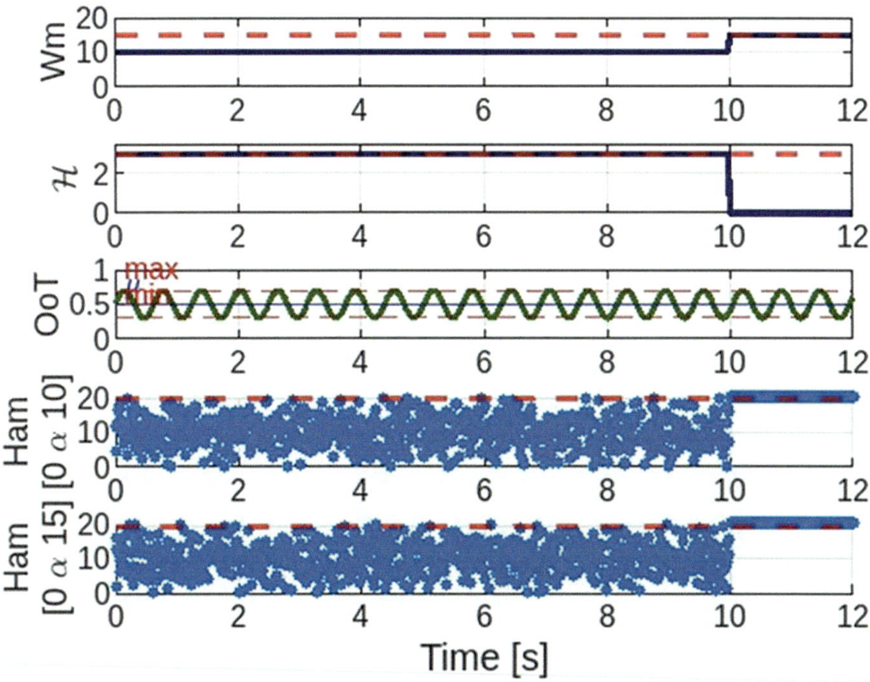

Figure 2.8 Fuzzing identifying attacks on CAN message ThrottleRequest.

method. Like a replay attack, the attack produced fixed input values, which resulted in zero Hamming distance, low entropy, and constant CAN data fields. To find it, the modified Hamming distance algorithm was necessary. The messages' useful content is below the typical entropy barrier because they don't change over time. Furthermore, the assault is not detected by the out-of-time detection approach since it does not change the frequency of messages.

The watermarking approach could not identify the CAN communication attack depicted in Figure 2.8 because it did not affect sensor data. EngineSpeed was unchanged; however, the modified Hamming distance was able to identify changes in the ThrottleRequest message. The attack's effect on CAN data fields also changed system entropy and facilitated anomaly detection.

2.5.2 Replay identifying attack outcomes

The replay attack targets the sensors or modifies CAN messages by replaying input values and matching outputs on the system. After testing both scenarios,

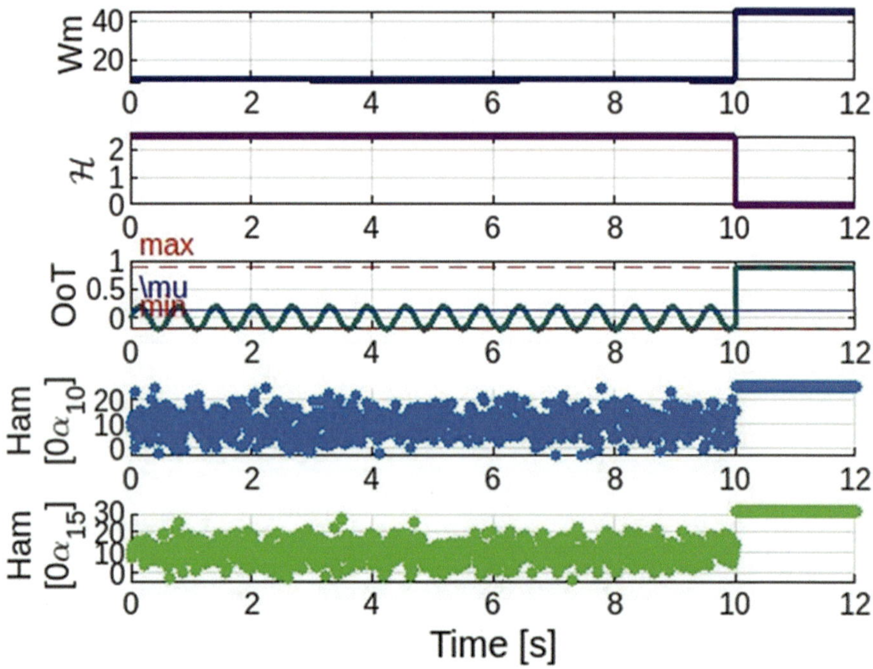

Figure 2.9 Replay identifying attacks on the LQG controller.

the results are displayed in Figure 2.7 (sensor replay) and Figure 2.8 (CAN replay), which are organized identically to the assault scenario that came before. The sensor replay assault, as shown in Figure 2.9, was detected using the same techniques as the previous fuzzing attack, except the out-of-time (OoT) algorithm. Given that the replay assault is a more sophisticated variant of the fuzzing technique, this resemblance makes sense.

As with the fuzzing attack, the detection performance of the CAN replay assault (Figure 2.10) was comparable to that of the technique for calculating the Hamming distance. Unlike in the previous instance, when only the target message could be utilized for detection, in this case, both CAN messages exhibited stable values due to the replayed data, enabling the updated Hamming distance technique to locate the attack on both messages.

2.5.3 Injection identifying attack outcome

The injection attack targets CAN communication solely by sending malicious values to the system input at a higher frequency than valid ones. Figure 2.11

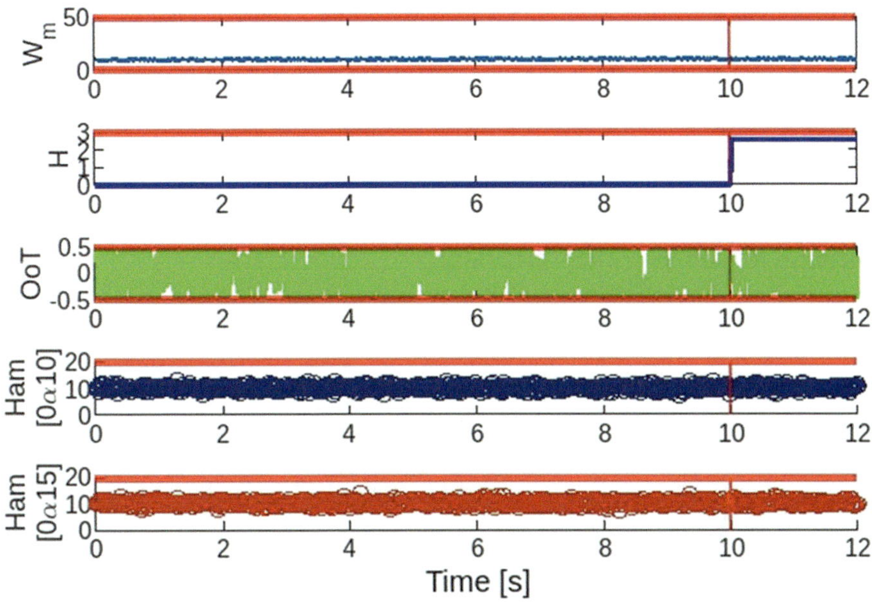

Figure 2.10 Replay identifying attacks on the CAN communication.

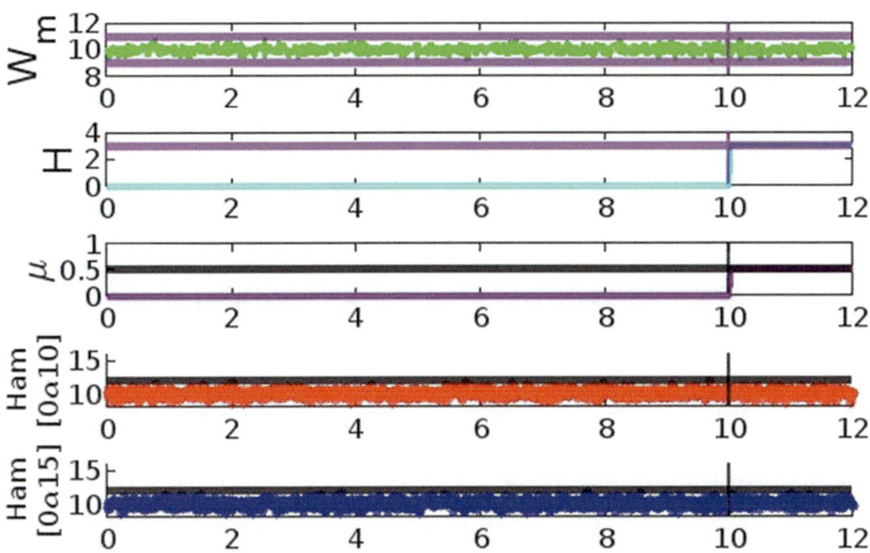

Figure 2.11 Injection identifying attacks on the CAN communication.

displays the detection results in a format similar to earlier attacks. This scenario's detection performance is different from previous ones. The attack happens at intervals of 0.1 milliseconds, evading detection, and the watermarking method's sampling interval of 1 millisecond prevents it from detecting it. However, because the assault modifies the CAN message frequency, the out-of-time (OoT) algorithm detects it correctly. Bus entropy and the modified Hamming distance algorithms also detect the attack for reasons identical to those of earlier scenarios.

2.5.4 An overview of cyber-physical security framework for automotive systems

The research [49] emphasizes the importance of addressing security issues early in the system design process, as it's more cost-effective. They propose modeling cybersecurity attacks and countermeasures before the system is built, using a security-aware functional model. This model allows for the analysis of cyber and physical attack vectors, such as those targeting the velocity controls of a car. Through system-level simulations, the impact of these attacks is assessed, and vulnerable functions are identified. The model is then refined iteratively by adding countermeasures, enabling the analysis of increasingly complex scenarios. This method is implemented in commercial design and simulation tools to validate system vulnerabilities.

2.5.4.1 Functional-level security modeling

An illustration of a security-conscious functioning model for an automobile is shown in Figure 2.12, which shows both physical and cyberattacks. Blue arrows represent the cyberattack vectors in this model, and red arrows represent the physical attack vectors. Determining if the velocity controls are vulnerable to cyber-physical assaults is the aim of the analysis, which evaluates the effect of such assaults on the Export TME functionality that regulates the car's speed. The model is simulated to examine the impact of the assault at the system level and assess the level of safety of the Export TME function. This stage aids in identifying weak points in the system that can be protected by improving the model and adding cybersecurity protections.

2.5.4.2 Simulation scenario

A framework was created using standard commercial software to validate the suggested methodology [50], as shown in Figure 2.13. Amesim was used to simulate system functions, cybersecurity features, and various scenarios, including environmental circumstances, using subsystem libraries.

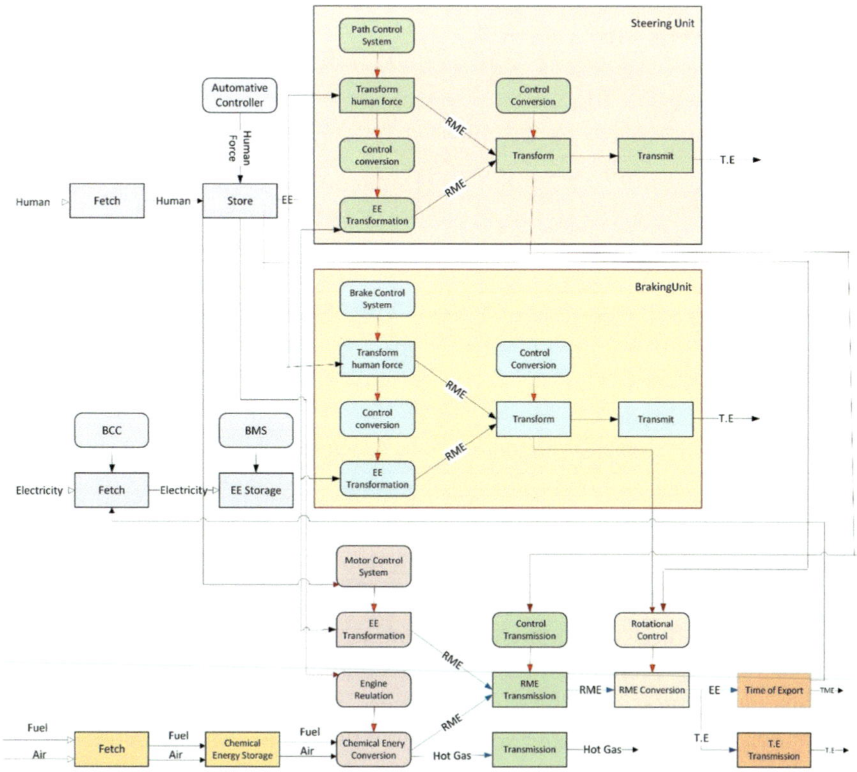

Figure 2.12 Cyber-physical security functional model for automotive systems.

Furthermore, Matlab/Simulink was used to model cybersecurity assaults because of its solid mathematical capabilities. There are six different kinds of assault models included in the current design automation tool. The application of the system to the design of an electric vehicle (EV) is an example that demonstrates the efficacy of the suggested framework and the threat scenarios during the initial design stages.

The flowchart, which describes a security-aware design space exploration approach for CPS, focuses on system design and security. It starts with continuous exploration to simulate various configurations, where context, multi-physics functions, and cyber defense functions are considered and modified. Threat models are used to evaluate vulnerabilities, and then co-simulation with Matlab/Simulink and Amesim is used to thoroughly test the physical and cyber aspects. The simulation results are examined, assessed, and improved upon iteratively to enhance system security and performance.

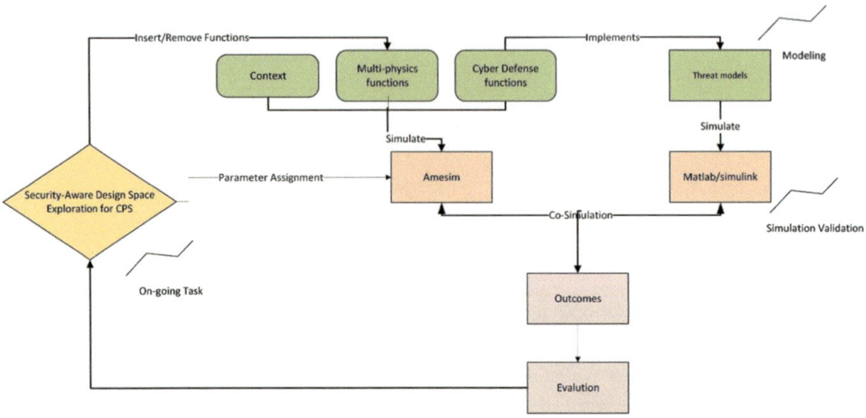

Figure 2.13 Schematic of the design automation tool.

Potential future developments for this approach include using AI and machine learning to automate threat modeling and design exploration, allowing for dynamic attack vector prediction and security measure optimization. Advanced real-time co-simulation technologies might be used to respond to threats in real time, and digital twin technology could enable testing and continuous monitoring using virtual copies. Furthermore, high-performance computing could enable more sophisticated multi-physics and cyber-defense models, increasing simulation accuracy and speed. Finally, industry-wide cooperation might create standardized practices and resources to advance security-conscious CPS design.

2.5.5 Attack consequences

An interface for the attack model was created by selecting one from the library and placing it between the motor and the motor-controlling ECU. As shown in Figure 2.14 and Figure 2.15, the fuzzy attack effectively disrupts the motor‘s behavior by introducing noise into the control signals. A functional model was developed to assess security challenges at the early design stage.

The effect of a fuzzy-based attack on the motor torque control system in an EV application is depicted in Figure 2.14. Two curves are displayed in the plot: the dashed line shows the torque command at port 3, which stays flat, indicating that the intended command signal is unaffected, and the red line shows the actual motor torque at port 2, which varies between 0 and 100 Nm over 1.2 seconds. This disparity demonstrates that the attack

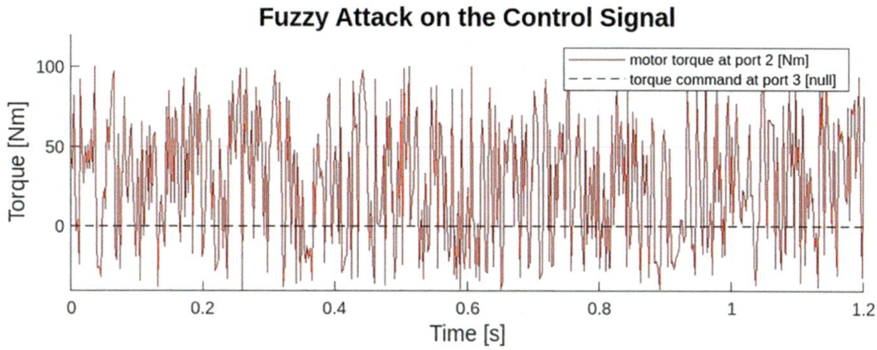

Figure 2.14 Fuzzy attack consequence on the control.

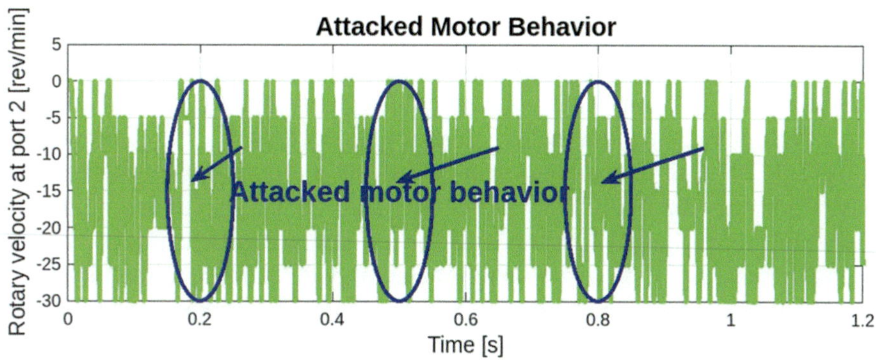

Figure 2.15 Attack consequence on the motor.

modifies the control signal supplied to the motor rather than changing the torque instruction, which results in notable torque differences. The torque of an automobile's motor is essential to its acceleration and general performance. Despite consistent command inputs, a fuzzy attack, as depicted in the image, might cause the motor to react erratically and produce irregular torque output. Unexpected changes in acceleration or deceleration could result in risky driving conditions. The findings highlight how susceptible automotive cyber-physical systems are to these kinds of attacks, showing how they might interfere with control signals without altering directives to interfere with regular car operation.

The time-series graph in Figure 2.15 records a motor's rotating velocity at port 2 for 1.2 seconds, expressed in revolutions per minute (rev/min). The green line indicates the motor's rotating velocity and blue ovals and remarks highlight instances of aberrant or irregular motor behavior that could result from a cyber-physical attack. The motor rotary velocity in electric vehicles (EVs) affects acceleration, deceleration, and overall control and is critical for a smooth power delivery system. The graph's irregular oscillations, highlighted by circled areas that display anomalous velocity spikes and decreases, reveal that the motor is being attacked. The functioning of the vehicle may be hampered by these interruptions, leading to erratic behavior, including abrupt slowdown, jerky acceleration, or even motor breakdown. This illustrates the susceptibility of EV motor control systems to cyber-physical attacks, underlining the necessity for strong security measures to prevent these concerns.

2.6 Conclusions and Future Scope

This chapter looks into the security risks that CPS in critical infrastructure face. It also offers solutions against adversarial assaults, both current and suggested. Strong security is required at many levels. It also examines how developments in computing and communication technologies have affected the development of industrial cyber-physical systems (ICPS). The chapter looks at ICPS design, communication protocols, and actual cyber incidents to assess current issues in ICPS cybersecurity and scholarly solutions. Anomaly detection techniques are implemented for self-defense in Industry 4.0, outlining major security risks and integrating anomaly detection into the MAPE-K control loop, further developing, assessing, and showing the viability of our approach in a working industrial setting for producing semiconductors. The chapter presents a threat model with three distinct attacks that modify system output by focusing on the engine model and CAN communication. The results of experiments show that output can be greatly impacted by even little adjustments to sensor readings or CAN signals. The detection framework uses four algorithms from network security and control theory: CAN message analysis, timing analysis, network analysis, and signal analysis. It shows how these techniques work together to efficiently identify and classify different kinds of attacks. There is also a discussion of the minimal setup needed to pinpoint attack targets. Future studies examine the proposed detection framework concerning potential additions to the current powertrain model by other vehicle subsystems. This chapter examines the design issues of protecting CPS, emphasizing essential instruments, strategies, and parts for efficient security. Three complimentary techniques are discussed: security concerns connected to the design and usage of computing hardware in CPS, control-aware design framework for strengthening attack resilience, and multi-domain modeling, simulation, and software synthesis tools. Future studies will look at how the functional model might be used to automatically generate or combine system-level simulation models in response to security analyses and assist such analyses. In the future, more assault models that can capture physical and cyber-domain attacks will also be developed. The development of security cost metrics will be integrated with the recommended security-aware functional models.

References

[1] S. Gujrati, H. Zhu, and G. Singh. "Composable algorithms for interdependent cyber physical systems," in *Proceedings of the Resilience Week (RWS) IEEE*, Philadelphia, PA, USA, 2015, pp. 1–6, doi: 10.1109/RWEEK.2015.7287431.

[2] H. Lasi, P. Fettke, H.-G. Kemper, T. Feld, and M. Hoffmann, "Industry 4.0," *Business & Information Systems Engineering*, vol. 6, no. 4, pp. 239–242, Aug. 2014, doi: 10.1007/s12599-014-0334-4.

[3] N. Jazdi, "Cyber physical systems in the context of Industry 4.0," in *Proceedings of the IEEE International Conference on Automation, Quality and Testing, Robotics*, Cluj-Napoca, Romania, 2014, doi: 10.1109/AQTR.2014.6857843.

[4] A. Cui and S. J. Stolfo, "A quantitative analysis of the insecurity of embedded network devices: Results of a wide-area scan," in *Proceedings of the 26th Annual Computer Security Applications Conference (ACSAC)*, Austin, TX, USA, 2010, pp. 97–106, doi: 10.1145/1920261.1920276.

[5] S. Bansal and D. Kumar, "IoT Ecosystem: A Survey on Devices, Gateways, Operating Systems, Middleware and Communication," *International Journal of Wireless Information Networks*, vol. 27, pp. 340–364, Feb,2020, doi: 10.1007/s10776-020-00484-y.

[6] J. Lee, B. Bagheri, and H.-A. Kao, "A Cyber-Physical Systems architecture for Industry 4.0-based manufacturing systems," *Manufacturing Letters*, vol. 3, pp. 18–23, Jan. 2015, doi:10.1016/j.mfglet.2014.12.001.

[7] K. Thramboulidis, "Model-integrated mechatronics - toward a new paradigm in the development of manufacturing systems," *IEEE Transactions on Industrial Informatics*, vol. 1, no. 1, pp. 54-61, April, 2005, doi: 10.1109/TII.2005.844427.

[8] Y. Liu, X. Liu, A. Liu, N. N. Xiong, and F. Liu, "A trust computing-based security routing scheme for cyber physical systems," *ACM Transactions on Intelligent Systems and Technolnology (TIST)* , vol. 10, no. 6, pp. 1–27, Dec. 2019, doi: 10.1145/3321694.

[9] H. Kayan, M. Nunes, O. Rana, P. Burnap, and C. Perera, "Cybersecurity of industrial cyber-physical systems: A review," *ACM Computing Surveys*, vol. 53, no. 2, pp. 1–36, Jan, 2021, doi: 10.1145/3510410.

[10] A. Sahu, K. Davis, H. Huang, A. Umunnakwe, S. Zonouz, and A. Goulart, "Design of Next-Generation Cyber-Physical Energy Management Systems: Monitoring to Mitigation," *IEEE Open Access Journal of Power and Energy*, vol. 10, pp. 151–163, Jan, 2023,doi: 10.1109/OAJPE.2023.3239186.

[11] A. Ashok, M. Govindarasu, and J. Wang, "Cyber–Physical Attack-Resilient Wide-Area Monitoring, Protection, and Control for the Power Grid," *IEEE Transactions on Smart Grid,* vol. 9, no. 5, pp. 5083–5093, Sep. 2018, doi: 10.1109/TSG.2017.2686394.

[12] R. Pinto, G. Gonçalves, J. Delsing, and E. Tovar, "Enabling data-driven anomaly detection by design in cyber-physical production systems," *Cyber security*, vol. 5, May, 2022, doi: 10.1186/s42400-022-00114-z.

[13] N. Jeffrey, Q. Tan, and J. R. Villar, "A Review of Anomaly Detection Strategies to Detect Threats to Cyber-Physical Systems," *Electronics*, vol. 12, no. 15, pp. 3283, July, 2023, doi: 10.3390/electronics.

[14] O. Morth, C. Emmanouilidis, N. Hafner, and M. Schadler, "Cyber-physical systems for performance monitoring in production intralogistics," *Computers & Industrial Engineering*, vol. 142, p. 106333, Apr. 2020, doi:10.1016/j.cie.2020.106333.

[15] A. Sahu and K. Davis, "Inter-domain fusion for enhanced intrusion detection in power systems: An evidence theoretic and meta-heuristic approach," *Sensors*, vol. 22, no. 6, p. 2100, Mar. 2022, doi: 10.3390/s22062100.

[16] A. Sahu, Z. Mao, P. Wlazlo, H. Huang, K. Davis, A. Goulart, and S. Zonouz, "Multi-source multi-domain data fusion for cyberattack detection in power systems," *IEEE Access*, vol. 9, pp. 119118–119138, June, 2021, doi: 10.1109/ACCESS.2021.3106873.

[17] C. Hewage, "Opportunities, challenges and strategies for integrating cyber security and safety in engineering practice," *Engineering Technology Open Access Journal*, vol. 3, no. 5, p. 555622, Feb, 2021, doi: 10.19080/ETOAJ.2021.03.555622.

[18] L. Zhang, Y. Chen, and M. Li, "Resilient Predictive Control for Cyber–Physical Systems Under Denial-of-Service Attacks," *IEEE Transactions on Circuits and Systems II: Express Briefs*, vol. 69, no. 1, pp. 67–71, Jan. 2022, doi: 10.1109/TCSII.2021.3076764.

[19] M. Gidlund, G. P. Hancke, M. H. Eldefrawy, and J. Akerberg, "Guest Editorial: Security, Privacy, and Trust for Industrial Internet of Things,"

IEEE Transactions on Industrial Informatics, vol. 16, no. 1, pp. 625–628, Jan. 2020, doi: 10.1109/TII.2019.2953241.

[20] D. Stabili, L. Ferretti, M. Andreolini, and M. Marchetti, "DAGA: Detecting attacks to in-vehicle networks via n-gram analysis," *IEEE Transactions on Vehicular Technology*, vol. 10, no. 15, Nov, 2022, doi: 10.1109/TVT.2022.3190721.

[21] D. Stabili, R. Romagnoli, M. Marchetti, B. Sinopoli, and M. Colajanni, "Exploring the consequences of cyber attacks on Powertrain Cyber Physical Systems," *arXiv:2202.00743,* Feb, 2022, doi:10.48550/arXiv.2202.00743.

[22] R. Falk and S. Fries, "Enhancing the resilience of cyber-physical systems by protecting the physical-world interface," *Internationa Journal of Advance and Secience*, vol. 13, no. 1 & 2, pp. 54–65, June, 2020.

[23] P. Arcaini, E. Riccobene, and P. Scandurra, "Modeling and analyzing MAPE-K feedback loops for self-adaptation," *in Proceedings of the 10th International Symposiumon Software Engineering for Adaptive and Self-Managing Systems*, Florence, Italy, IEEE Press, 2015, pp. 13–23, doi: 10.1109/SEAMS.2015.10.

[24] P. Garcia-Teodoro, J. Diaz-Verdejo, G. Maci-Fernandez, and E. Vazquez, "Anomaly-based network intrusion detection: Techniques, systems and challenges," *Computers & Security*, vol. 28, no. 1–2, pp. 18–28, March, 2009, doi:10.1016/j.cose.2008.08.003.

[25] G. Settanni, F. Skopik, A. Karaj, M. Wurzenberger, and R. Fiedler, "Protecting cyber physical production systems using anomaly detection to enable self-adaptation," in *Proceedings of the IEEE Industrial Cyber-Physical Systems (ICPS)*, St. Petersburg, Russia, 2018, pp. 173–180, doi: 10.1109/ICPHYS.2018.8387655.

[26] A. B. Sharma, F. Ivancic, A. Niculescu-Mizil, H. Chen, and G. Jiang, "Modeling and analytics for cyber-physical systems in the age of big data," *ACM Sigmetrics Performance Evaluation Review*, vol. 41, no. 4, pp. 74–77, April, 2014, doi: 10.1145/2627534.2627558.

[27] G. Hayes and K. El-Khatib, "Securing Modbus transactions using hash-based message authentication codes and stream transmission control protocol," in *Proceedings of the 3rd International Conference on Communications and Information Technology (ICCIT-2013): Networks and Internet Technologies*, Beirut, Lebanon, 2013, doi: 10.1109/ICCITechnology.2013.6579545.

[28] R. S. H. Piggin and H. A. Boyes, "Safety and security - a story of interdependence," in *Proceedings of the 10th IET System Safety and Cyber-Security Conference*, Bristol, UK, 2015, doi: 10.1049/cp.2015.0292.

[29] J. Rubio-Hernan, L. D. Cicco, and J. Garcia-Alfaro, "Revisiting a watermark-based detection scheme to handle cyber-physical attacks," in *Proceedings of the 11th International Conference on Availability, Reliability and Security*, Salzburg, Austria, 2016, pp. 21–28, doi:10.1109/ARES.2016.2.

[30] S. Amin, A. A. Cardenas, and S. S. Sastry, "Safe and secure networked control systems under denial-of-service attacks," in *Proceedings of the International Conference on Hybrid Systems: Computation and Control*, LNCS, Berlin Heidelberg: Springer, San Francisco, CA, 2009, pp. 31–45, doi: 10.1007/978-3-642-00602-9_3.

[31] H. He, C. Maple, T. Watson, A. Tiwari, J. Mehnen, Y. Jin, and B. Gabrys, "The security challenges in the IoT enabled cyber-physical systems and opportunities for evolutionary computing & other computational intelligence," in *Proceedings of the IEEE Congress on Evolutionary Computation (CEC)*, Vancouver, BC, Canada, 2016, pp. 1015–1021, doi: 10.1109/CEC.2016.7743900.

[32] H. Jeon and Y. Eun, "A stealthy sensor attack for uncertain cyber-physical systems," *IEEE Internet Things J*, vol. 6, no. 4, pp. 6345–6352, 2019, doi: 10.1109/JIOT.2019.2905878.

[33] Y. Mo and B. Sinopoli, "Integrity attacks on cyber-physical systems," in Proceedings of the 1st International Conference High Confidence Networked Systems, Beijing, China, 2012, pp. 47–54. doi: 10.1145/2185505.2185514.

[34] G. Wu and J. Sun, "Optimal data integrity attack on actuators in cyber-physical systems," in *Proceedings of the American Control Conference (ACC)*, Boston, MA, USA, 2016, pp. 1–6, doi: 10.1109/ACC.2016.7962252.

[35] Y. Mo and B. Sinopoli, "Secure control against replay attacks," in *Proceedings of the 47th Annual Allerton Conference on Communication, Control, and Computing (Allerton)*, Urbana-Champaign, IL, USA, 2009, pp. 1–6, doi: 10.1109/ALLERTON.2009.5393878.

[36] N. Nowdehi, W. Aoudi, M. Almgren, and T. Olovsson, "CASAD: CAN-aware stealthy-attack detection for in-vehicle networks," ArXiv abs/1909.08407, Sep, 2019, doi: 10.48550/arXiv.1909.08407.

[37] Y. Chen, C. M. Poskitt, J. Sun, S. Adepu, and F. Zhang, "Learning-guided network fuzzing for testing cyber-physical system defenses," in *Proceedings of the 34th IEEE/ACM International Conference on Automated Software Engineering (ASE)*, San Diego, California, 2019, pp. 962–973, doi: 10.1109/ASE.2019.00093.

[38] F. Martinelli, F. Mercaldo, V. Nardone, and A. Santone, "Car hacking identification through fuzzy logic algorithms," in *Proceedings of*

the IEEE International Conference on Fuzzy Systems (FUZZ-IEEE), Naples, Italy, 2017, pp. 1–7, doi: 10.1109/FUZZ-IEEE.2017.8015464.

[39] B. Groza and P.-S. Murvay, "Efficient intrusion detection with Bloom filtering in controller area networks," *IEEE Transactions on Information Forensics and Security*, vol. 14, no. 4, pp. 1037–1051, April, 2019, doi: 10.1109/TIFS.2018.2869351.

[40] J. M. Taylor Jr. and H. R. Sharif, "Security challenges and methods for protecting critical infrastructure cyber-physical systems," in *Proceedings of the International Conference on Selected Topics in Mobile and Wireless Networking (MoWNeT)*, Avignon, France, 2017, pp. 1–6, doi: 10.1109/MoWNet.2017.8045959.

[41] Y. Ashibani and Q. H. Mahmoud, "Cyber physical systems security: Analysis, challenges and solutions," *Computers & Security*, vol. 73, pp. 124-144, July, 2017, doi: 10.1016/j.cose.2017.04.005.

[42] L. Vegh and L. Miclea, "A framework for verifying the integrity of the components of a secure cyber-physical system," in *Proceedings of the International Conference on System Theory, Control, and Computing*, Sinaia, Romania, 2014, pp. 763–768, doi: 10.1109/ICSTCC.2014.6982510.

[43] A. Shahzad, M. Lee, Y. Lee, S. Kim, N. Xiong, J. Choi, and Y. Cho, "Real time modbus transmissions and cryptography security designs and enhancements of protocol sensitive information," *Symmetry*, vol. 7, no. 3, pp. 1176–1210, July, 2015, doi: 10.3390/sym7031176.

[44] B. Kordy, S. Mauw, and P. Schweitzer, "Quantitative Questions on Attack–Defense Trees," in *Proceedings of Information Security and Cryptology – ICISC*, Seoul, South Korea, 2013, pp. 49–64, doi: 10.1007/978-3-642-37682-5_5.

[45] R. K. Abercrombie and F. T. Sheldon, "Security analysis of smart grid cyber physical infrastructures using game theoretic simulation," in *Proceedings of IEEE Symposium Series on Computational Intelligence (SSCI)*, Hangzhou, China, 2015, pp. 1–8. doi: 10.1109/SSCI.2015.120.

[46] D. Stabili, R. Romagnoli, M. Marchetti, B. Sinopoli, M. Colajanni, "A multidisciplinary detection system for cyber attacks on Powertrain Cyber Physical Systems," *Future Generations Computer Systems*, vol. 144, pp. 151–164, March, 2023, doi: 10.1016/j.future.2023.02.019.

[47] B. Groza, S. Murvay, A. van Herrewege, and I. Verbauwhede, "LiBrA-CAN: A lightweight broadcast authentication protocol for controller area networks," in *Proceedings* of *Cryptology and Network Security*, Berlin, Heidelberg: Springer, 2012, pp. 185–200, doi: 10.1007/978-3-642-35404-5_15.

[48] L. Guzzella and C. Onder, *Introduction to Modeling and Control of Internal Combustion Engine Systems*. Springer Science & Business Media, 2009.

[49] M. Al Faruque, F. Regazzoni, and M. Pajic, "Design methodologies for securing cyber-physical systems," in *Proceedings of the International Conference on Hardware/Software Codesign and System Synthesis (CODES+ISSS)*, Amsterdam, Netherlands, 2015, pp. 30–36, doi: 10.1109/CODESISSS.2015.7331365.

[50] J. Wan, A. Canedo, and M. A. A. Faruque, "Security-Aware Functional Modeling of Cyber-Physical Systems," in *Proceedings of the 20th IEEE International Conference on Emerging Technology and Factory Automation (ETFA'15)*, Luxembourg, 2015, pp. 1–6. doi: 10.1109/ETFA.2015.7300954.

3

Explainable Artificial Intelligence for Intrusion Detection in Cyber-physical Systems

Yakubu Tsado[1], Shokooh Khandan[1] and Segun I. Popoola[2]

[1]Department of Computing and Mathematics, Manchester Metropolitan University, UK
[2]School of Computing and Information Science, Anglia Ruskin University, UK

Email: y.tsado@mmu.ac.uk; s.khandan@mmu.ac.uk; segun.popoola@aru.ac.uk

Abstract

Cyber-physical systems (CPSs) play a critical role in modern infrastructure and are regarded as a leading technology in advancing Industry 5.0 – a paradigm that integrates human interaction within CPS to enhance human capabilities, addressing concerns from Industry 4.0 where advanced technologies could substitute human roles. Due to the massive data generated by CPS, various predictive machine learning (ML) and deep learning (DL) models have been deployed for performance monitoring, optimization, preventive maintenance, and threat detection. However, a significant challenge in adopting these models in critical domains like CPS is their "black box" nature, which makes them difficult to interpret and trust. This chapter explores how explainable AI (XAI) can be utilized to enhance the interpretability of intrusion detection systems (IDS) within CPS. Firstly, we review recent studies on XAI methods applied to attack detection and provide a taxonomy of XAI techniques, encompassing model-specific and model-agnostic approaches that can be applied to ML and DL models. This taxonomy supports transparent insights into each model's learning and decision-making processes.

DOI: 10.1201/9788743801306-3

Furthermore, we discuss local and global explainability, where local explainability focuses on how individual features influence specific predictions, and global explainability reveals how features affect the overall model behavior. These insights aim to provide clearer, actionable explanations to strengthen IDS deployment within CPS.

3.1 Introduction

The distinguishing features of cyber-physical systems (CPS), to the Internet of Things (IoT), and industrial IoT (IIoT) systems are their ability to provide autonomous operation, real-time monitoring and decision, and a feedback loop. According to authors in [1] and [2], a precise definition of CPS is the integration of sensors, embedded computing and networking into physical objects, with feedback loops for monitoring and controlling close physical environments interconnected collaboratively and further connected to the Internet. These distinguishing functionalities of CPS have facilitated the transformation of processes across various critical industry sectors, including smart grid, healthcare, transportation, and manufacturing. For example, in healthcare, CPS is used in robotic surgery systems, such as the da Vinci surgical system [3], to enable precision and minimally invasive procedures. In transportation, Tesla and Waymo leverage CPS in autonomous vehicles, using real-time data from sensors to make decisions about speed, steering, and braking [4]. In a smart grid, sensors and control devices monitor real-time power consumption across the grid, and if demand increases in one area, the smart grid can automatically reroute power from areas with lower demand, it can autonomously manage the balance between energy supply from power plants or renewable sources like solar or wind and demand to avoid overloading the system [5].

In addition, CPS has strengthened manufacturing with digital, networked, and intelligent abilities by engendering systems to be intelligent, interconnected, and automated in line with the context of Industry 4.0 paradigm [6], [7]. CPS will also be integral to Industry 5.0, a paradigm that will further integrate humans into CPS to complement human capabilities rather than substitute humans with advanced technologies, which was a concern in Industry 4.0 paradigm [8].

3.1.1 Cybersecurity issues in CPS

Interconnection of the physical world (observable and measurable natural phenomena that are subject to monitoring or regulation) and the cyber world (embedded devices capable of processing information), along with the generation of vast amounts of data in CPS, introduces new vulnerabilities and security challenges. These challenges are particularly pronounced as communication networks grow increasingly complex. Due to the heterogeneous nature of CPS and the reliance on sensitive and private data, attacks on systems like the CPS can have substantial cascading effects, impacting digital assets (such as software and data), physical assets (such as machinery and critical infrastructure), and human activity that depend on CPS functionality [9]. For instance, in CPS, sensors used for real-time analysis, monitoring, and system forecasting play a critical role. Malfunctions in these systems, if caused by contamination or compromise through cyberattacks, can impact the entire manufacturing process by providing false predictions and insights, ultimately leading to catastrophic failures [10].

CPS operates through interconnected layers that manage physical processes, data applications, and network communications. Each layer plays a critical role in ensuring the seamless operation of CPS; however, these layers also introduce distinct vulnerabilities. The physical, application, and network layers of CPS are particularly susceptible to attacks such as false data injection, malware injection, and denial of service (DoS). Some CPS attacks are multifaceted, targeting all three layers simultaneously. Prominent examples include the Stuxnet attack on Iranian nuclear facilities in 2010, which altered operational speeds and caused physical damage to industrial equipment [11], and an attack on the Ukrainian power grid, which caused power outages for approximately 225,000 people in 2016 [12].

3.1.2 Intrusion detection system in CPS

Ensuring data protection against security threats and cyberattacks is one of the most challenging issues within the CPS environment. One major approach to defending and mitigating cyberattacks in CPS is through intrusion detection system (IDS), which enables the detection and prevention of malicious activities. IDS are essential tools for identifying threats in Internet-connected networks, supporting the core principles of information security: confidentiality, integrity, and availability. They play a vital role in securing CPS by continuously monitoring for irregularities and potential threats, thereby enhancing the resilience of critical infrastructure through prompt alerts and responses to cyberattacks [13].

IDS can operate in two primary modes in CPS: signature-based detection, which identifies known attack patterns, and anomaly-based detection, which monitors for deviations from normal behavior, flagging any irregular activity that may suggest an attack and it is well suited for an unknown (zero-day) attack. In addition, IDS can be implemented as host-based and network-based, where the host-based monitors activity on specific devices or hosts within the system, detecting suspicious behaviors locally, and network-based monitors traffic across the entire network, identifying malicious activities by analyzing network packets in real-time.

3.1.3 Application of artificial intelligence (AI) for IDS in CPS

Tradition algorithms such as pattern matching, rule-based systems, and statistical models were used for implementing IDPS. However, artificial intelligence (AI) is mostly used currently because of its robustness, scalability, and ability to detect complex, sophisticated, and zero-day attack. The growing dependence on AI is evident in its widespread use across various applications. Subsections of AI – machine learning (ML) and deep learning (DL) are currently used for the detection of cyberattacks, such as threat detection, malware clarification, and intrusion detection. Extensive research has been conducted on using ML and DL algorithms to enhance cyberattack issues in the CPS environment [10]. Though the majority of these algorithms have produced highly successful prediction models, there are inherent drawbacks regarding the explainability and trust of the models being developed. Most of the AI techniques used in IDS are not explainable. Understanding the logic behind decisions and recommendations from AI, ML, or DL models is of great importance; governments are even beginning to implement legislation to require explainability as a part of AI-based applications [14].

3.1.4 Explainable AI (XAI) for IDS in CPS

Over the past few years, different IDSs using different ML, DL, or hybrid approaches have been proposed, developed, and evaluated. Most of these methods exhibit excellent detection accuracy and low false-positive rates in the detection of attacks [15]. However, there are still some problems, especially with the transparency and trust of the systems, in the field of intrusion detection that have sparked significant concerns regarding the opacity of AI models. As a result, in addition to high detection accuracy, many cybersecurity experts now also consider interpretability, explainability, and trust of the models as essential characteristics of a robust IDS, especially for CPS environments, which are always deployed for critical infrastructures.

When a model makes a prediction, explainable AI (XAI) methods generate an explanation that gives insight into the model's behavior and how it arrived at that prediction [16]. A black-box model in XAI refers to an ML or DL algorithm whose internal operations are not easily interpretable or accessible. These models generate predictions based on input data, but the underlying decision-making processes remain opaque to users, thus limiting transparency. Such black-box characteristics are prevalent in many IDS models presented in current research, where interpretability is often compromised for model complexity and predictive accuracy. Thus, there is a pressing need for enhanced transparency in IDS, particularly for the professionals involved in their development. Such explainability not only aids in knowledge and data discovery but also enhances the processes of debugging, diagnosis, and identifying important features to foster greater trust in the underlying model [14]. The interpretability of AI techniques is not a new concept. Transparent ML models, such as decision trees (DTs), offer ante-hoc and intrinsic interpretability, which aligns with traditional AI practices that emphasize working directly with the data. Data evaluation provides essential insights and enhances understanding of the model, facilitating effective explanation [17]. Post-hoc interpretability refers to the class of techniques that involve the research and development of black-box models such as deep neural networks (DNNs) after their training. Post-hoc methods have diversified applications and can be extended to applications in intrinsically interpretable models. XAI techniques for post-hoc interpretability have led to a new wave of cybersecurity works that now include additional layers of explainability for a human-in-the-loop (HITL).

This chapter presents an XAI-based IDS for CPS. We employed post-hoc interpretability techniques using XAI to analyze and identify how features contribute to the predicted output value or class in both transparent and black-box ML and DL models, enhancing transparency, trustworthiness, and explainability for HITL systems.

3.1.5 Contributions of the chapter

The contributions are as follows:

- Developed and evaluated both transparent (DT) and black-box (deep neural network and random forest) intrusion detection models for cyber-physical systems (CPSs) using a recent dataset, X-IIoTID, which includes CPS-specific features.
- Demonstrated the use of post-hoc explainability techniques – both model-specific and model-agnostic – such as Shapley SHAP, LIME, and feature importance, to assess the contribution and impact of each feature on the model's decisions.

- Provided insights into both local and global explainability for each model, showing how features influence the prediction for specific input instance (local), as well as the overall contribution of the features of all input samples on the predicted output (global).

The remainder of the chapter is organized as follows: Section 3.2 presents the related work, Section 3.3 presents the methodology, Section 3.4 gives the experimental results and discussions, and finally, Section 3.5 concludes the chapter and highlights the future scope.

3.2 Literature Review

In recent literature, various researchers have extensively applied XAI for interpretability and explainability in IDS. This section examines transparent and black-box ML and DL models alongside post-hoc XAI techniques and provides a taxonomy of these techniques. In addition, recent XAI implementations are reviewed to highlight specific areas of XAI that have been considered in these studies and identify existing gaps in the literature.

3.2.1 Post-hoc XAI techniques

The process of explaining ML and DL predictions has generated a lot of discussions and several methods and techniques have advanced at such a rapid rate that it has resulted in the emergence of a new field that seeks to develop AI systems that not only provide accurate predictions but also provide explicit and interpretable explanations for their decisions and actions, thereby making them more trustworthy for human users. Vikas et al. [17] develop a framework that categorizes all the types of explanations which aim to interpret the logic of black-box algorithms. They proposed a based-on-stage categorization of interpretability that include ante-hoc interpretations, which comprise classical approaches for analyzing black-box models before their training, and post-hoc interpretation, which comprise approaches for analyzing black-box models after their training. Ante-hoc or intrinsic interpretability applies to transparent models, which are inherently interpretable by design, providing insights into their decision-making process without additional explanation tools. These models allow users to understand how input features contribute to the output due to their simple and interpretable structures. Post-hoc interpretability, on the other hand, applies to black-box models, which are complex and not inherently interpretable by design. These models' interpretability is achieved after training by applying external techniques that explain

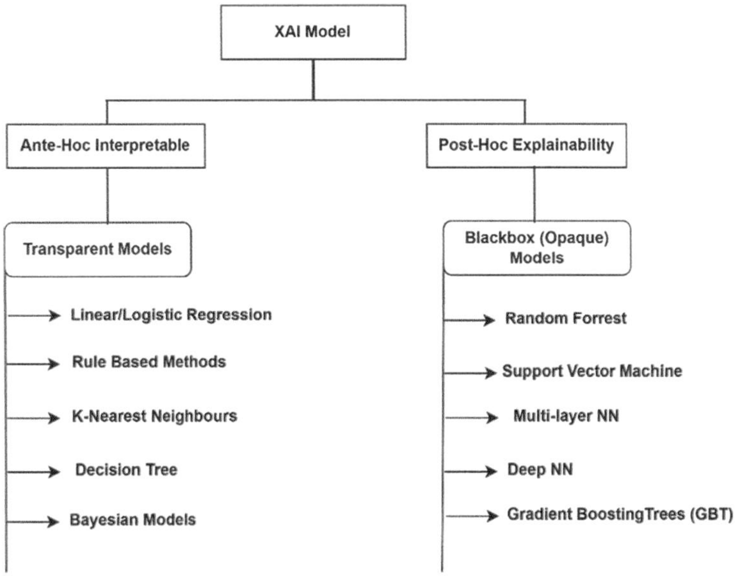

Figure 3.1 Transparent and explainable ML and DL models.

their predictions. Figure 3.1 illustrates the classification and examples of ante-hoc and post-hoc models.

Post-hoc XAI methods can be further classified into model-specific and model-agnostic techniques. Model-specific refers to any explainable method that has been designed and developed to work with a single model or specific groups of algorithms [17]. In model-specific approaches, the interpretation relies on the internal workings and architecture of the ML or DL models, such as the weights in a linear model, which are designed specifically to explain the model's decisions and are not generalizable to other types of models. Conversely, model-agnostic methods provide a more flexible and generalizable framework, offering explanations that can be applied to any model or algorithm, regardless of the model's underlying architecture or complexity.

Model agnostic XAI methods also provide either local or global explanations, the local explanations for a specific or random instance; for example, in IDS, it could be for a specific feature or attack category, whereas global explanations apply to all instances of the model. Many explainability methods are either built for a specific model, focus on specific data, or provide either local or global explanations; as such, there is no best-in-class method. The local interpretable model-agnostic explanations (LIME) and Shapley additive explanations (SHAP) are examples of model-agnostic XAI

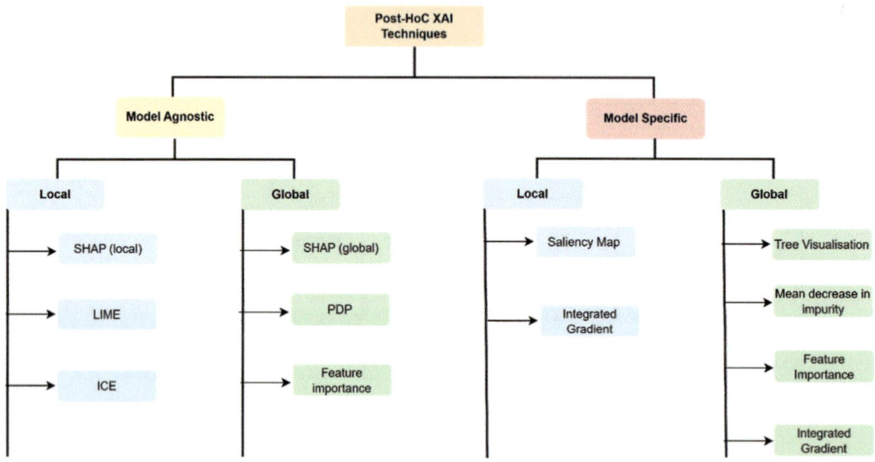

Figure 3.2 Post-hoc XAI techniques for IDS in CPS.

methods that can provide local and global explanations. SHAP is comprehensive because it is model agnostic and provides both local and global explanation.

As noted by authors in [18], most of the analyzed XAI intrusion detection systems rely on post-hoc explanation techniques, with SHAP being particularly prominent. Figure 3.2 illustrates post-hoc XAI techniques that can be applied to IDS models in CPS. These techniques encompass model-agnostic and model-specific methods, offering global and local explainability. Examples include SHAP, partial dependence plot (PDP), feature importance, tree visualization, saliency map, individual conditional expectation (ICE) plot, mean decrease in impurity, and integrated gradients. Figure 3.2 shows the post-hoc XAI techniques for IDS in CPS.

Questions are often raised regarding the need to explain complex AI algorithms when inherently interpretable models, such as DT, linear regression (LR), and rule-based techniques, are available for developing IDS models. The reason lies in the trade-off between interpretability and performance: while simpler models offer transparency, many IDS applications prioritize high accuracy and detection performance. To achieve these goals, increasingly complex models, such as deep neural networks (DNNs), recurrent neural networks (RNNs), and convolutional neural networks (CNNs), are being employed due to their capacity to capture intricate patterns within data. However, as model complexity increases, explainability often decreases, necessitating applying post-hoc interpretability methods to make these complex models understandable.

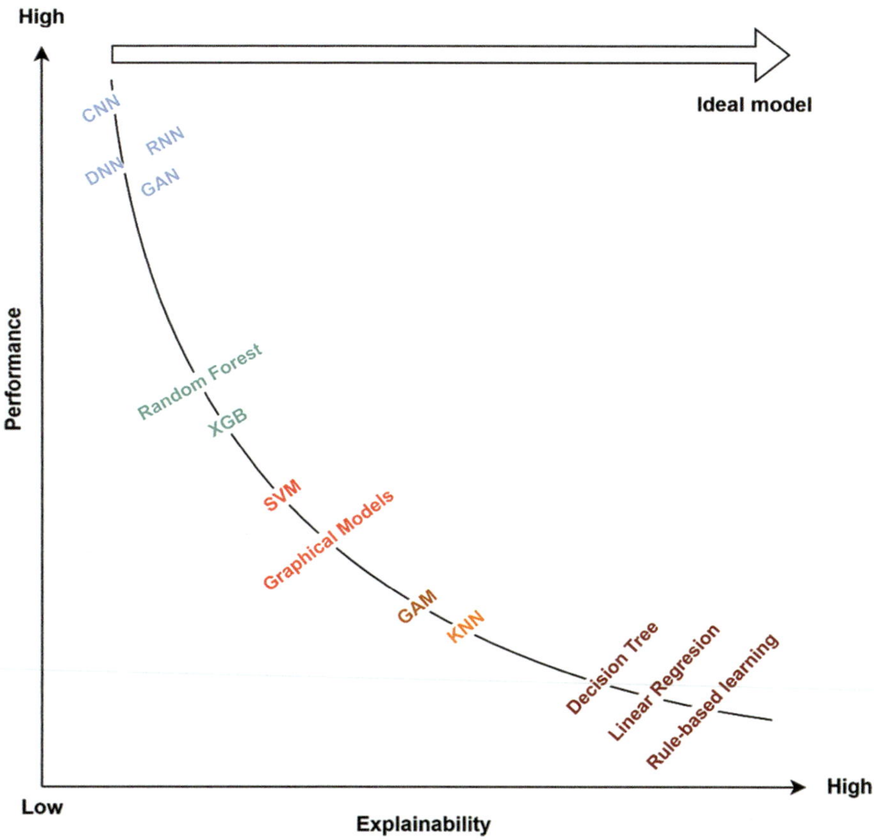

Figure 3.3 Trade-off between model complexity, explainability, and accuracy in machine learning Models for IDS.

Figure 3.3 illustrates the relationship between AI models, model explainability, and accuracy, highlighting the balance between using interpretable models and achieving high predictive performance.

3.2.2 Related work

Various researchers have extensively applied XAI in intrusion detection in recent literature. This section analyzes recent implementations of XAI in the current literature and highlights specific areas of XAI that have been considered in these studies. In [19], Oki et al. implemented XAI using SHAP to assess feature set similarity based on SHAP values in federated learning (FL)-based ML to distributed IDS for IoT devices. They introduced a "feature distance" metric, calculated as the Euclidean distance between SHAP values of two feature sets, where a shorter distance indicates greater similarity. This metric was used to compare feature sets for each attack class in distributed and non-distributed IDS environments. They concluded that feature distance increases in independent learning scenarios but decreases with FL in an IDS setup. In [20], the authors identified key features that influence attack detection by using SHAP values within XAI framework. They applied this XAI algorithm to the prediction results of both binary and multi-class classification models, where SHAP values quantify each feature's contribution to a specific detection outcome. The authors in [21] evaluated the differences in attack detection accuracy between random forest (RF) and multi-layer perceptron (MLP) techniques, and interpreted the detection results by calculating the SHAP values for each feature. In [22], SHAP values were utilized to train an autoencoder to distinguish between previously seen and unseen attacks. Their approach combines the detection capabilities of both supervised and unsupervised intrusion detection systems (IDSs) within a two-stage pipeline to enhance robustness in network intrusion detection. The proposed pipeline first employs an XGBoost model for supervised intrusion detection, followed by an autoencoder trained on SHAP explanations that capture the behavior of the initial model during training. Similarly, in [23], authors developed a DL model for botnet detection and classification, incorporating decision explanation using local and global SHAP interpretations. The authors in [24] utilized feature importance to select the top-ranked features and developed a model called "IntruDTree," a DT classifier built using these selected security features. They compared its performance against other machine learning models to assess its effectiveness. In a related study, the same authors [25] focused on detecting cyber anomalies and various cyberattacks. They employed feature importance techniques to design both a binary classification model for detecting anomalies and a multi-class classification model for distinguishing between multiple cyberattack types. In [26], explainability methods are explored for analyzing runtime trade-offs in both supervised and unsupervised IDS models, using SHAP for both local (feature-level for single instances) and global explainability. They also implemented LIME and feature importance. In [27], a hardware-assisted malware detection framework is proposed that utilizes explainable machine learning techniques, incorporating tree pruning for DT and outlier elimination for recurrent neural networks (RNNs). The framework employs high probability concepts (HPCs), example-based techniques (ETBs), and a combined HPC+ETB approach to explain model decisions. However, HPC and ETB are generally not classified as XAI techniques. An ensemble machine learning approach for explainable, multi-class bot detection, utilizing LIME to enhance model interpretability, was proposed by authors in [28]. In [29], the authors designed an explainable unsupervised machine learning model for CPS and proposed a novel model-specific explainable method for the self-organizing map (SOM) algorithm, generating local and global explanations. Using five CPS datasets, they developed a feedforward neural network (FFNN) and analyzed the model's explainability through LIME and feature importance techniques. In [30], an XAI-based IDS model, termed XAIIDS-FSDVAE, is proposed for securing CPS. This model integrates a Dirichlet variational autoencoder (DVAE) with a feature selection approach, utilizing the Coyote optimization algorithm (COA) to select an optimal subset of features. Although DVAE and COA can be applied in ML and XAI contexts to potentially enhance interpretability, they are not inherently XAI techniques.

While the XAI techniques implemented by authors in the current literature provided a level of explainability for the models used, the post-hoc XAI techniques applied did not comprehensively cover all aspects of post-hoc explainability. Additionally, these techniques were tested on older CPS datasets with limited feature sets. In contrast, this chapter utilizes a broader range of post-hoc XAI techniques, ensuring a more thorough exploration of model interpretability. We have also employed the X-IIoTID dataset, a recent and feature-rich CPS dataset, which offers a more robust representation of CPS characteristics, enhancing both the relevance and depth of the explainability analysis. Table 3.1 shows a summary of the review of related work.

3.3 Methodology and Experimental Setup

In this section, we provide a brief overview of the X-IIoTID dataset and describe our experimental setup, including the description of models and XAI techniques used.

3.3.1 Dataset

The X-IIoTID dataset was developed in 2021 by authors in [31] and is one of the most common datasets used for IDS IIoT systems. It was developed using a testbed of Brownfield IIoT devices to provide a platform that could be used for subsequent research on IIoT security in a similar way to other datasets. The testbed included various IP-based protocols, some general-purpose ones (e.g., HTTP, DNS, WebSocket), whereas others are designed for IoT/IIoT environments (Modbus, MQTT, CoAP). They leveraged the testbed to create the X-IIoTID publicly available dataset [32]. It contains benign and malicious network traffic recorded on the testbed, logs, and hardware metrics.

Table 3.1 Review of related work.

				XAI						
					Model agnostic					
				Model	SHAP					
Ref	**Year**	**Method**	**Dataset**	**specific**	**Local**	**Global**	**LIME**	**F-Importance**	**F-Distance**	**ICE/PDP**
[19]	2024	MLP	UNSW-NB15	×	×	ü	×	×	ü	×
[20]	2020	KNN, RF, ResNet50, SVM-rbf, DNN5 Layers	NSL-KDD	×	ü	ü	×	×	×	×
[21]	2022	MLP, RF	NF-CSE-CIC-IDS2018-v2, CSE-CIC-IDS2018, NF-ToN-IoT-v2, CIC-ToN-IoT, NF-BoT-IoT-v2, CIC-BoT-IoT	×	×	ü	×	×	×	×
[22]	2022	XGBoost	NSL-KDD	×	ü	ü	×	×	×	×
[24]	2020	NB, LR, KNN, SVM, IntruDTree	KDD'99 cup	ü	×	×	×	ü	×	×
[25]	2021	NB, LR, KNN, SVM, IntruDTree	UNSW-NB15, NSL-KDD	ü	×	×	×	ü	×	×

[26]	2021	LR, RF, DT, LR, IF, GB, Autoencoder, NN	Fraud data	ü	ü	ü	ü	×	×	×
[27]	2022	RNN, DT	Real-world malware dataset	ü	×	×	×	×	×	×
[23]	2022	CNN	Stratosphere IPS, Kitsune Dataset, Synthetic Dataset	×	ü	ü	×	×	×	×
[28]	2021	RF, Ensemble classifier	New dataset	×	×	×	ü	×	×	×
[29]	2021	ANN	KDD, German Credit, Bank marketing, Adult Income, DoHBrw-2020	×	×	×	ü	ü	×	×
[30]	2022	MLP	NSL-KDD-2015, CICIDS-2017	×	×	×	×	×	×	×
Ours	2024	DNN	XIIoTID	ü	ü	ü	ü	ü	ü	ü

Table 3.2 X-IIoTID data distribution.

Binary	10-Class	Samples
Normal	Normal	421417
Attack	RDoS	141261
	Reconnaissance	127590
	Weapon	67260
	Lateral _Movement	31596
	Exfiltration	22134
	Tampering	5122
	C&C	2863
	Exploit	1133
	Crypto_ransom	458

The data was collected over 114 days, though not continuously for 24 hours each day. A total of 18 distinct attacks, belonging to nine different attack families, were executed to generate the attack traffic. During the pre-processing of the X-IIoTID dataset, there were 68 columns on the dataset, 3 columns represent the attack-type labels, and 65 columns represent the features. We removed six features: date, timestamp, source IP, destination IP, source port, and destination port which decreased the number of features to 59. A detailed representation of the features presented in [31]. Table 3.2 presents the binary and 10-class label attack categories and the number of data samples per class. Figure 3.4 gives the model and experimental setups.

3.3.2 Model performance evaluation

In recent studies, the classification performance of ML and DL models for IDS has generally been evaluated using metrics such as accuracy, recall, precision, and F1 score, as given in eqn (3.1)-(3.4). Other performance metrics, such as the receiver operating characteristic (ROC) curve, exist. However, since the focus of this chapter is not on the detailed performance evaluation of the model, we have only presented a confusion matrix to illustrate the models' performance. The primary emphasis will be on the explainability of the ML and DL models.

$$\text{Accuracy} = \frac{TP + TN}{TP + TN + FP + FN} \tag{3.1}$$

$$\text{Recall} = \frac{TP}{TP + FN} \tag{3.2}$$

$$\text{Precision} = \frac{TP}{TP + FP} \tag{3.3}$$

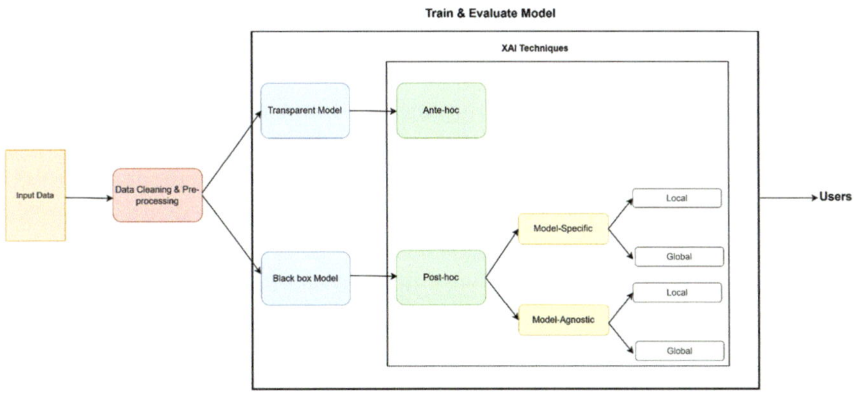

Figure 3.4 Model and experimental setup.

$$\text{F1 score} = \frac{2 \times \text{Precision} \times \text{Recall}}{\text{Precision} + \text{Recall}} \tag{3.4}$$

Here, true positive (TP) is the number of malicious samples in the testing set that were correctly classified. True negative (TN) is the number of benign samples that were correctly classified. False positive (FP) is the number of benign samples misclassified as malicious. False negative (FN) is the number of malicious samples misclassified as benign.

Figure 3.4 illustrates the experimental workflow. After uploading the dataset, data cleaning and preprocessing steps were applied prior to training and evaluating three models: one ML (DT) and two DL models (DNN and RF). Subsequently, intrinsic and extrinsic XAI techniques were applied to enhance model interpretability. First, DT was used as an example of a transparent model, with a DT plot demonstrating its inherently interpretable structure. We then applied model-specific (techniques limited to models) and model-agnostic (techniques applicable across any machine learning model) interpretability methods to the models, using both local (explains a specific feature or prediction) and global (explains the overall model behavior) configurations for a comprehensive explanation. The steps implemented are explained in the following section.

3.3.3 Implemented interpretable and transparent AI model

3.3.3.1 Decision tree (DT)

A DT is a non-parametric, interpretable model that operates based on rules and conditions, this makes it accessible to non-experts, and it is visualized easily. Its goal is to predict the value of a target variable (label) by learning simple decision rules from data features. When a decision tree splits on a feature, it aims to make the resulting groups purer (i.e., dominated by a single class). This purity is measured using metrics like Gini impurity or entropy. When the node is pure, the value of the Gini index is 0. Therefore, this node will not be split again. Thus, the optimum split is chosen by the features with less Gini index. Moreover, Gini gets the maximum value of one when the probability of the two classes is the same.

However, decision trees are very flexible and are subject to overfitting training data, where they become too complex and fail to generalize well to new data. Techniques such as pruning, setting a minimum number of samples needed at a leaf node, or restricting the maximum tree depth are used to avoid overfitting. Another limitation is that decision trees can be unstable; small variations in data can lead to hugely different tree structures. This instability is mitigated by using decision trees within ensemble methods, such as RF, which aggregate multiple trees to enhance stability and predictive performance.

3.3.4 Implemented explainable and black-box model

3.3.4.1 DNN

We utilize a DNN model, which contains three hidden layers with 32, 16, and 8 neurons, respectively. The neurons in three hidden layers allow the network to learn complex patterns and features in the data, as shown in Figure 3.5. The ReLU (rectified linear unit) activation function is employed for the hidden layers. ReLU is widely used due to its ability to introduce non-linearity into the model while maintaining efficient computation. It outputs the input directly if it is positive; otherwise, it outputs zero, which helps the model learn faster and mitigate the vanishing gradient problem. A sigmoid activation function is employed for the output layer. Sigmoid function curve is S shape and its range is between 0 and 1, therefore it is the most suitable activation function for binary classification tasks.

3.3.4.2 Random forest (RF)

A RF is an ensemble learning model that fits several decision tree classifiers on various subsamples of the dataset and uses averaging to improve predictive accuracy and control overfitting. It achieves high predictive accuracy by functioning like a team of decision-making wizards; each decision tree examines a segment of the problem, and together, they weave their insights into a powerful prediction tapestry. This collaborative effort typically yields

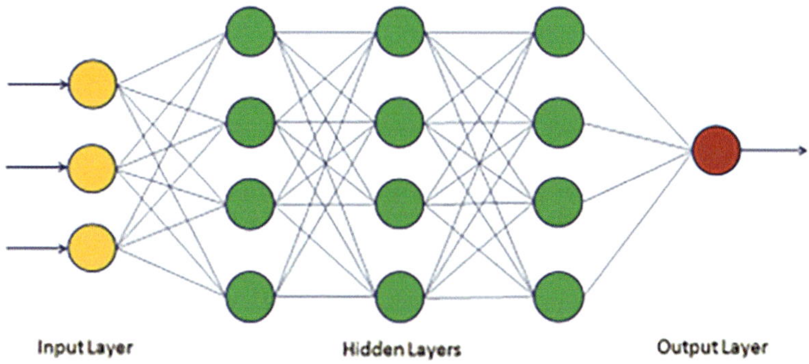

Figure 3.5 DNN layers.

a more accurate model than any single tree could produce. Furthermore, RF demonstrates resistance to overfitting. Rather than allowing them to memorize every detail of the training data, it fosters a well-rounded understanding, making the model less prone to overfitting. When confronted with large datasets, RF behaves like a seasoned explorer with a team of helpers, efficiently dividing the dataset among decision trees for thorough yet quick analysis. Additionally, it provides variable importance assessment, functioning as a detective that identifies which features are most influential in making predictions, allowing users to focus on critical elements. It effectively handles missing values, adapting to uncertainties by making predictions based on the available information without becoming flustered by incomplete data. Finally, RF enhances efficiency through parallelization for speed, with each decision tree acting as a worker tackling pieces of a puzzle simultaneously, leveraging modern technology to expedite the process, especially in large-scale projects.

3.3.5 Model interpretation and explainable technique

Different ML or DL models can be explained using various XAI techniques. Out of the models listed in Figure 3.1, we have applied XAI to DNN and RF, and provide both global and local explanations of the model performance.

3.3.5.1 SHAP

SHAP can be quite computationally expensive; in practice, it is often approximated. Kernel SHAP is used for a model-agnostic approach, while TreeSHAP is specific to tree-based ensembles, improving both quality and performance for these models. SHAP values quantify effects in the same units as the predictions (labels). Additionally, SHAP values are additive, meaning that for a single prediction:

Outcome = base value + sum of each feature's contribution.

To compute SHAP values, we start with a single observation and generate all subsets (the power set) of the feature of interest. For each subset, we obtain predictions with and without the feature to observe the change in prediction, measuring this difference as the feature's effect or attribution. By averaging these effects across all subsets, we calculate the SHAP value, quantifying the feature's contribution for that specific instance.

3.3.5.2 Feature importance

Feature importance is calculated by assessing each feature's contribution to the predictions, with one popular method being permutation feature importance (PFI) for RF. In PFI, the importance of a feature is determined by the extent to which prediction error increases when that feature's values are randomly shuffled. In tree-based models, feature importance is computed as the mean and standard deviation of the impurity decreases accumulated within each tree. This means that for each feature, the model tracks the total reduction in impurity achieved across all nodes where the feature is used to split the data. This accumulated reduction signifies how useful the feature is in accurately classifying or predicting outcomes.

In essence, feature importance in tree-based models reflects the feature's ability to decrease impurity (or uncertainty) in predictions averaged across the ensemble of trees.

3.3.5.3 PDP and ICE

A partial dependence plot (PDP) provides a global view of how a feature influences the model's predictions on average. It examines overall effects rather than focusing on individual cases, making it useful for understanding broad trends.

To generate a PDP, we vary the selected feature(s) values while keeping other features constant and then compute predictions for these modified instances. The resulting points, plotted against the varied feature values. PDPs can reveal linearity, monotonicity, or complexity patterns in feature–target relationships. However, by averaging across instances, PDPs may obscure interactions between features, potentially limiting interpretability in overly complex models.

In contrast, an individual conditional expectation (ICE) plot is a local method visualizing how a feature affects predictions for each instance individually, resulting in one line per instance compared to the single averaged line in a PDP. A PDP is the average of all ICE lines, allowing us to interpret the aggregate effect of a feature across the entire dataset. ICE plots address this limitation by preserving individual instance-specific effects, showing how each instance's prediction changes when only one feature value is altered over a range. This provides a more detailed view of the model's response to changes in the feature for specific cases. However, displaying multiple ICE lines together can lead to cluttered visualizations. A combined approach that leverages PDPs and ICE plots can help provide clarity and reveal feature effects at both global and local levels.

3.3.5.4 LIME

LIME (local interpretable model-agnostic explanations) provides explanations that highlight the most relevant features of a model's output. This is a local explanation technique, so it does not attempt to interpret all the decisions a model might make across every possible input. Instead, it focuses on the specific factors that influence the classification for an individual prediction.

LIME approximates any black-box machine learning model with a local, interpretable model to explain each prediction. It generates multiple samples like the input. By assigning a weight to each modified sample, LIME calculates the importance of different features, allowing the most significant ones to be identified.

3.4 Experimental Results and Analysis

We use 10 top features found from feature importance as *{'Avg_ideal_time', 'is_with_payload*', *'service',' Avg_nice_time', 'R_W_physical', 'Login_attmp', 'is_syn_only', 'Conn_state','FIN.or.RST', 'resp_ip_bytes'}*, to illustrate the structure of a DT model, as seen in Figure 3.6. We set the max_depth of tree to 4, this parameter controls the maximum depth of the tree. The deeper the tree, the more complex the model. A deeper tree can fit the training data better, but it can also lead to overfitting. To prevent overfitting, we can limit the depth of the tree by setting a maximum value for max_depth. Figure 3.6 displays the split on each feature value from root node to leaf node.

3.4.1 DNN performance evaluation and post-hoc XAI techniques

Figure 3.7 displays the DNN classification report, where for class 0, Accuracy: 99.19%, Recall: 99.54%, Precision: 98.90%, F1 score: 99.22%

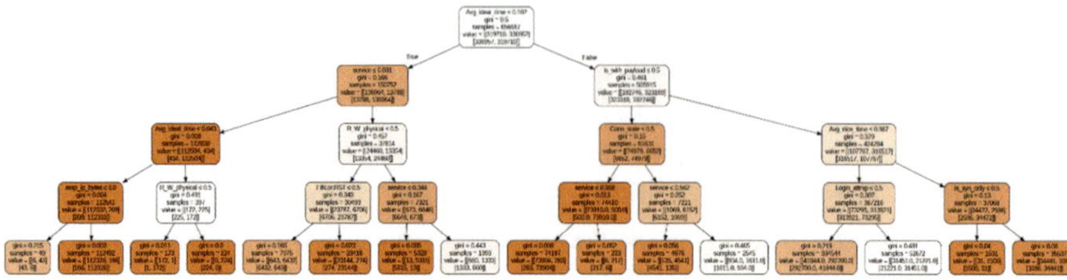

Figure 3.6 The DT plot.

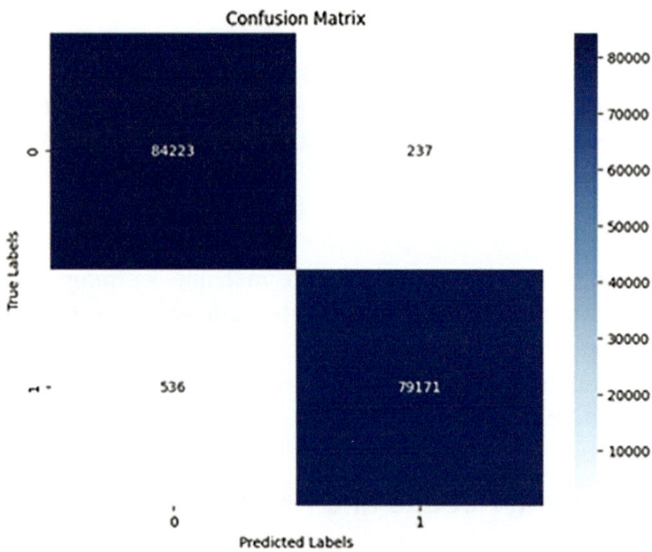

Figure 3.7 DNN confusion matrix.

and for class 1, Accuracy: 99.19%, Recall: 98.83%, Precision: 99.51%, F1 score: 99.17%.

LIME is a model agnostic local explainer that focuses on explaining the model's prediction for individual instances. Figure 3.8 displays a LIME explanation for an instance in the test data using the DNN classifier and presenting the final feature contribution in a tabular format. The result contains three main pieces of information from left to right: (1) the model's predictions, (2) feature contributions, and (3) the actual value for each feature.

The ICE plot is a local, model-agnostic explainer that visualizes the dependence of the prediction on one feature for *each* instance separately.

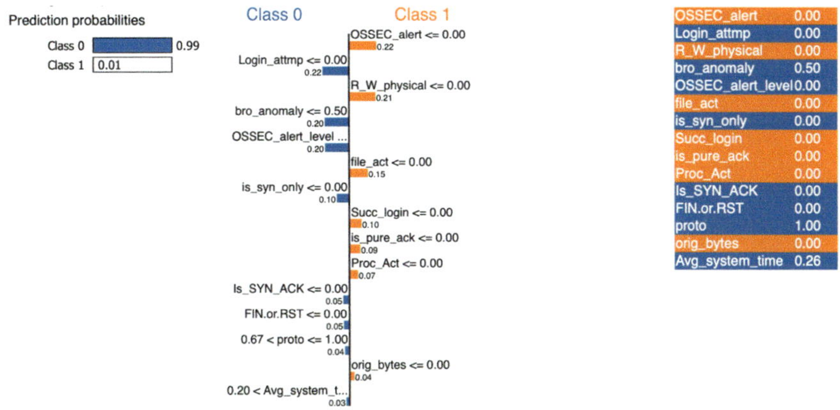

Figure 3.8 LIME plots for DNN model.

Figure 3.10 illustrates ICE plots for *{'Avg_ideal_time,' 'service,' 'R_W_physical,' 'Conn_state'}* features for the DNN. ICE plot is in one line per instance, compared to one line overall in partial dependence plots. A PDP is the average of the lines of an ICE plot that it is a global and model-agnostic technique.

The waterfall plot demonstrates that SHAP values of all the input features, as in Figures 3.12 and 3.13, will always sum up to the difference between baseline (which is 0.515 in this example) model output and the current model output for the prediction being explained. Figures 3.12 and 3.13 demonstrate the local explainability of the SHAP technique.

3.4.2 Random forest post-hoc XAI techniques

Figure 3.9 shows the LIME plot for the RF model. The result contains three main pieces of information from left to right: (1) the model's predictions, (2) feature contributions, and (3) the actual value for each feature. Figure 3.11 shows PDP and ICE plots for RF model. ICE plot is in one line per instance, compared to one line overall in partial dependence plots. A PDP is the average of the lines of an ICE plot that it is a global and model-agnostic technique. Figure 3.14 shows the feature important ranking on RF model and Figure 3.15 shows the 10 top important features which are *{'Avg_ideal_time', 'is_with_payload', 'service',' Avg_nice_time', 'R_W_physical', 'Login_attmp', 'is_syn_only', 'Conn_state','FIN.or.RST', 'resp_ip_bytes'}*. Feature importance technique is a global model specific technique. Feature importance values are in percentage.

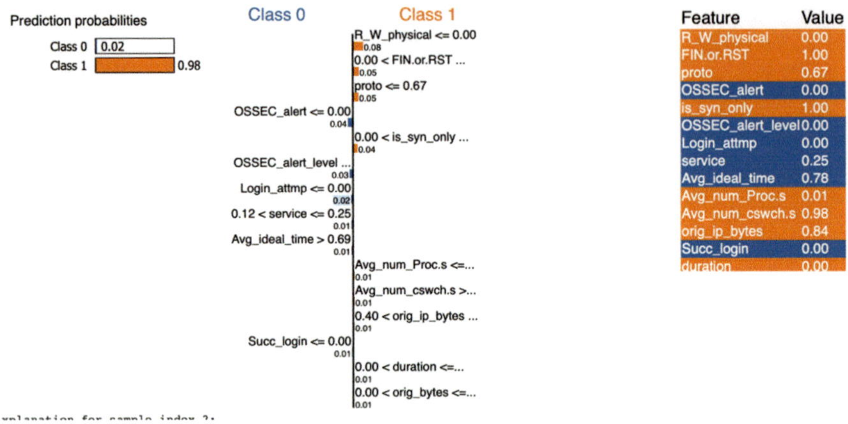

Figure 3.9 LIME plots for RF model.

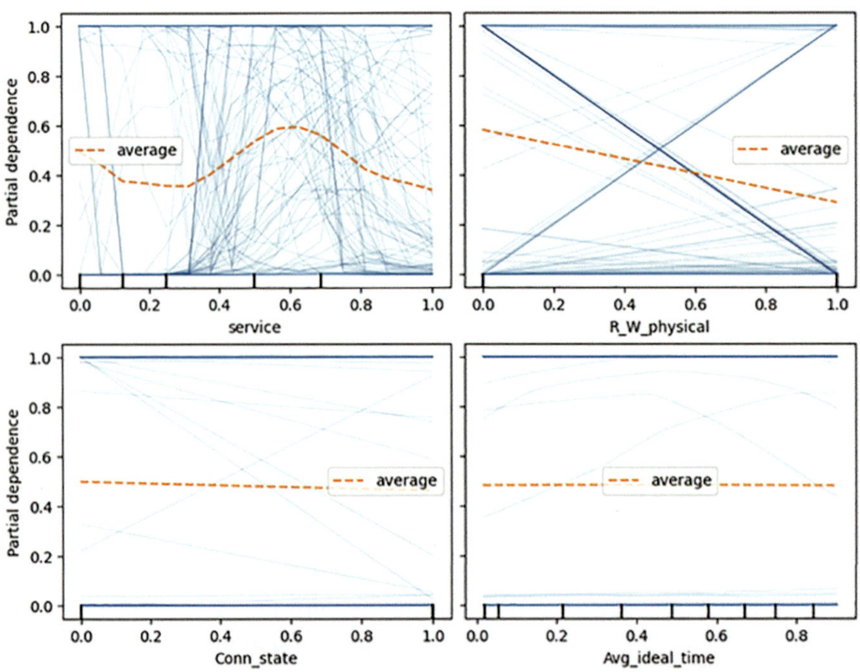

Figure 3.10 PDP and ICE plots for DNN.

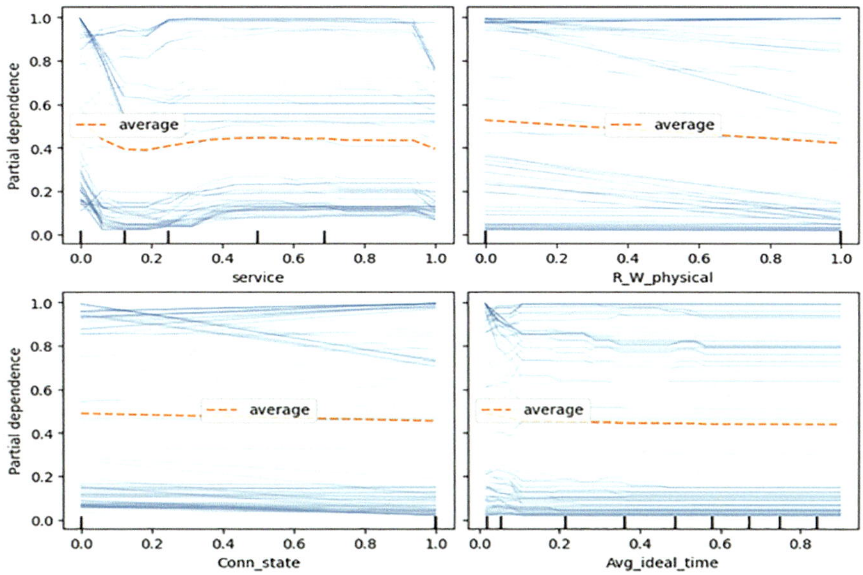

Figure 3.11 PDP and ICE plots for RF model.

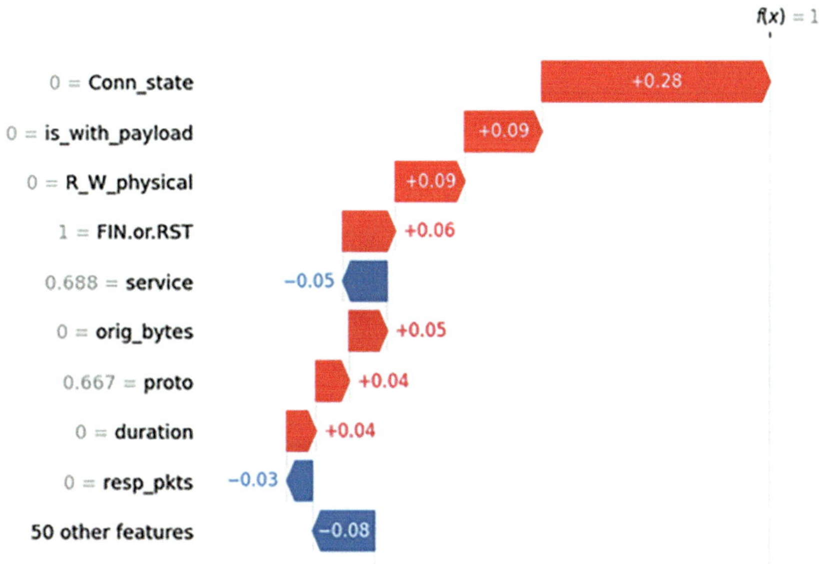

Figure 3.12 DNN SHAP.

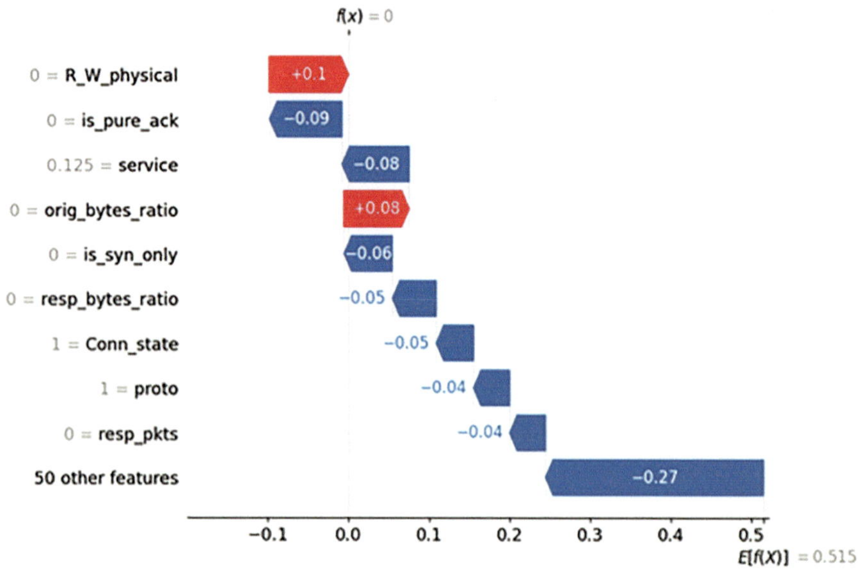

Figure 3.13 DNN SHAP.

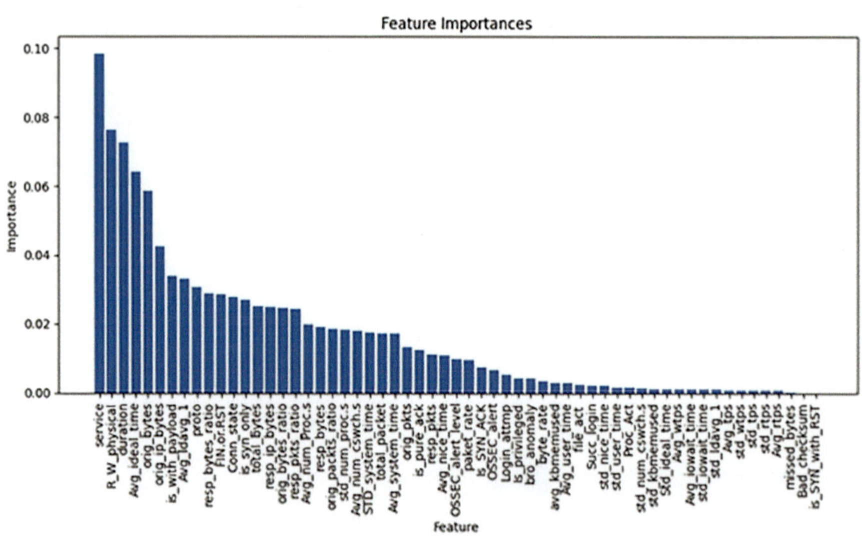

Figure 3.14 Feature importance for all features.

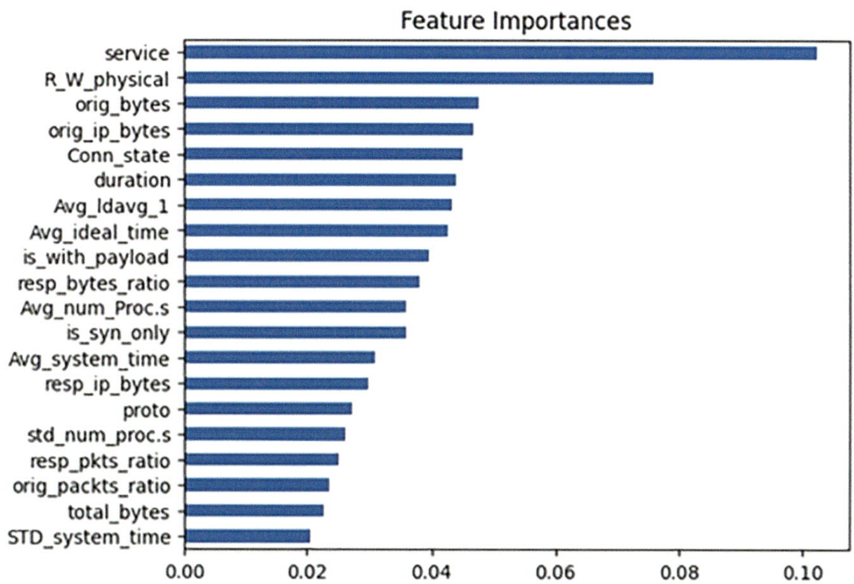

Figure 3.15 Best performing feature for RF.

Figure 3.16 is the SHAP-value summary plot. The figure illustrates the mean SHAP value for each feature impact on each class predicted value from the RF model. The length of each bar in the SHAP bar plot corresponds to the magnitude of a feature's contribution to the prediction. Longer bars indicate greater importance, signifying that the corresponding feature substantially impacts the model's output.

Figures 3.17 and 3.18 display the SHAP force plot for two instances of the RF model. The SHAP force plot and waterfall plot are similar in that they both show how the features of a data point contribute to the model's prediction, as they both show the magnitude and direction of the contribution as arrows or bars. The main difference between the two plots is the orientation. SHAP force plots show the features from left to right, with positive contributions on the left and negative ones on the right. Waterfall plots show the features from top to bottom, with the positive contributions at the top and the negative contributions at the bottom.

Figures 3.19 and 3.20 show the SHAP beeswarm plot for the RF model. It is designed to display an information-dense summary of how the top features in a dataset impact the model's output globally. Each instance a single dot on each feature represents the given explanation. By default, the features are ordered using the mean absolute value of the SHAP values for each

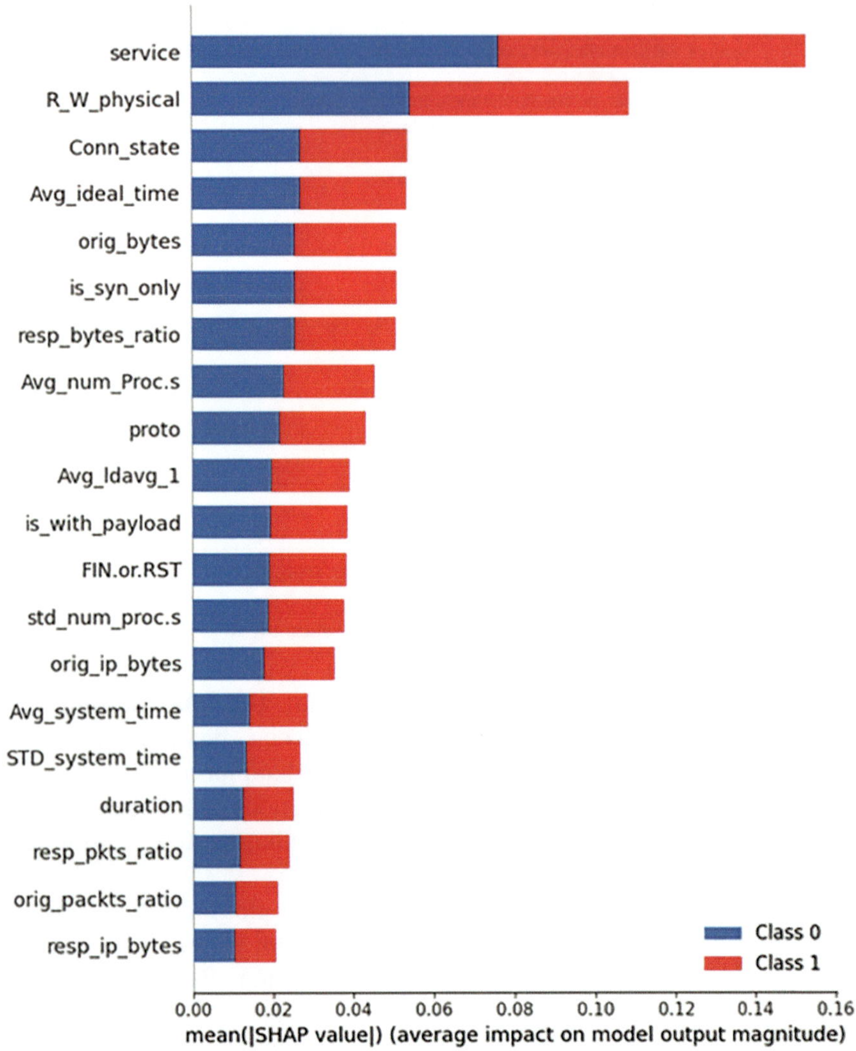

Figure 3.16 SHAP values for each class.

feature. This order, however, places more emphasis on broad average impact and less on rare but high-magnitude impacts.

3.5 Conclusion and Future Scope

In this chapter, we explored the current literature on the application of XAI techniques to IDS models for CPS, utilizing the XIIoTID dataset – a recent

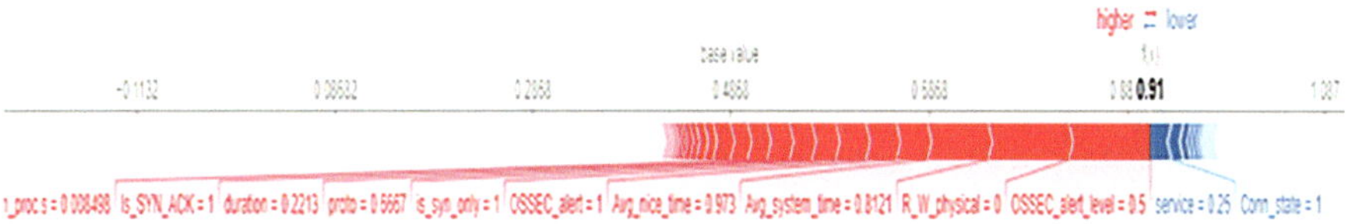

Figure 3.17 SHAP (local).

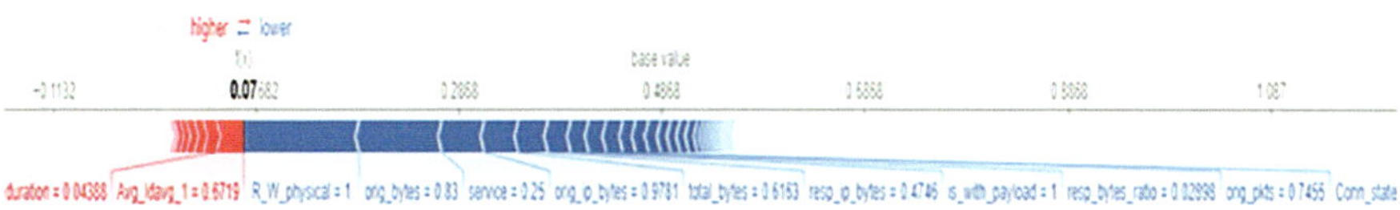

Figure 3.18 SHAP (local).

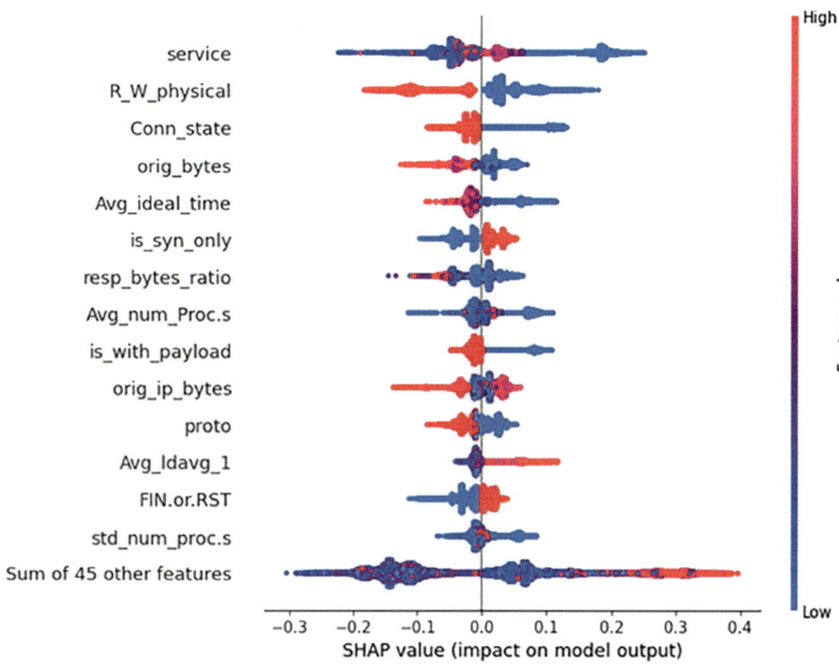

Figure 3.19 SHAP.

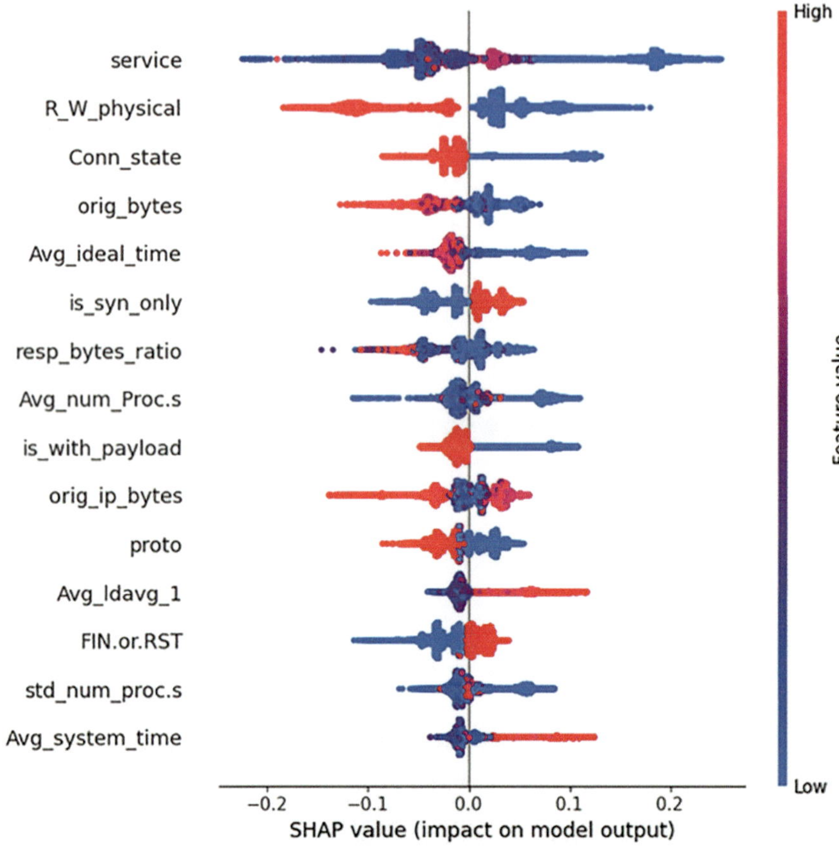

Figure 3.20 SHAP values.

dataset designed to represent features specific to CPS networks. We presented a taxonomy of XAI techniques applied to IDS and implemented these techniques on three IDS models: DT, RF, and DNN. The XAI techniques employed include both model-specific and model-agnostic approaches, such as DT structure analysis, SHAP (for local and global interpretability), LIME, feature importance metrics, partial dependence plot (PDP), and individual conditional expectation (ICE). Our findings indicate that these XAI techniques significantly enhance the interpretability of IDS models, providing a deeper understanding of and confidence in their predictions. Notably, SHAP and LIME offered crucial insights into feature contributions at both local and global scales, while feature importance metrics enabled identifying the most influential features. Furthermore, PDP and ICE visualizations provided valuable perspectives on model behavior, facilitating a clearer interpretation of complex model decisions. This integration of XAI techniques demonstrates the feasibility of achieving a balance between performance and interpretability in IDS models, which is essential for deploying advanced ML and DL IDS solutions in practical, real-world environments.

This work highlights the critical role of explainability in developing and implementing robust IDS models, setting a foundation for more transparent and accountable AI systems in cybersecurity. We believe that the XAI techniques explored here contribute to model transparency and interpretability and foster trust in AI-driven intrusion detection systems. This, in turn, enables effective human-in-the-loop (HITL) interactions, facilitating collaboration between human analysts and automated systems, which is a key component of Industry 5.0. Future work will focus on expanding the application of XAI techniques toward refining feature selection processes, model efficiency, and enhancing HITL capabilities to support ongoing advancements in this field.

References

[1] E. A. Lee, "The past, present and future of cyber-physical systems: A focus on models," *Sensors,* vol. 15, no. 3, pp. 4837–4869, 2015.

[2] M. Sverko, T. G. Grbac, and M. Mikuc, "Scada systems with focus on continuous manufacturing and steel industry: A survey on architectures, standards, challenges and industry 5.0," *IEEE access,* vol. 10, pp. 109395–109430, 2022.

[3] B. S. Peters, P. R. Armijo, C. Krause, S. A. Choudhury, and D. Oleynikov, "Review of emerging surgical robotic technology," *Surgical endoscopy,* vol. 32, pp. 1636–1655, 2018.

[4] R. Song, M. O. Ozmen, H. Kim, R. Muller, Z. B. Celik, and A. Bianchi, "Discovering adversarial driving maneuvers against autonomous vehicles." pp. 2957–2974.

[5] Y. Tsado, D. Lund, and K. A. Gamage, "Resilient communication for smart grid ubiquitous sensor network: State of the art and prospects for next generation," *Computer Communications,* vol. 71, pp. 34–49, 2015.

[6] C. Hildebrandt, A. Köcher, C. Küstner, C.-M. López-Enríquez, A. W. Müller, B. Caesar, C. S. Gundlach, and A. Fay, "Ontology building for cyber–physical systems: Application in the manufacturing domain," *IEEE Transactions on Automation Science and Engineering,* vol. 17, no. 3, pp. 1266–1282, 2020.

[7] W. Hao, T. Yang, and Q. Yang, "Hybrid statistical-machine learning for real-time anomaly detection in industrial cyber–physical systems,"

IEEE Transactions on Automation Science and Engineering, vol. 20, no. 1, pp. 32–46, 2021.

[8] K. B. Virupakshar, M. Asundi, K. Channal, P. Shettar, S. Patil, and D. Narayan, "Distributed denial of service (DDoS) attacks detection system for OpenStack-based private cloud," *Procedia Computer Science,* vol. 167, pp. 2297–2307, 2020.

[9] S. Gaba, I. Budhiraja, V. Kumar, S. Martha, J. Khurmi, A. Singh, K. K. Singh, S. S. Askar, and M. Abouhawwash, "A systematic analysis of enhancing cyber security using deep learning for cyber physical systems," *IEEE Access*, 2024.

[10] M. Abdullahi, H. Alhussian, N. Aziz, S. J. Abdulkadir, A. Alwadain, A. A. Muazu, and A. Bala, "Comparison and investigation of AI-based approaches for cyberattack detection in cyber-physical systems," *IEEE Access*, 2024.

[11] Ş. Çetinkaya, and S. Terzi, "Analysing the Effects of Cyber Security on National Security from a Realist Perspective:" Stuxnet" Example," *Güvenlik Çalışmaları Dergisi,* vol. 26, no. 1, pp. 38–51, 2024.

[12] V. Makkada, and I. Rai, "Case Study: Cyber-attack on Ukrainian Power Grid," *Information Technology Security and Risk Management*, pp. 18–24: CRC Press.

[13] Z. U. I. Nasir, A. Iqbal, and H. K. Qureshi, "Securing Cyber-Physical Systems: A Decentralized Framework for Collaborative Intrusion Detection with Privacy Preservation," *IEEE Transactions on Industrial Cyber-Physical Systems*, 2024.

[14] A. Hoenig, K. Roy, Y. Acquaah, S. Yi, and S. Desai, "Explainable AI for Cyber-Physical Systems: Issues and Challenges," *IEEE Access*, 2024.

[15] M. A. Ferrag, O. Friha, D. Hamouda, L. Maglaras, and H. Janicke, "Edge-IIoTset: A new comprehensive realistic cyber security dataset of IoT and IIoT applications for centralized and federated learning," *IEEE Access,* vol. 10, pp. 40281–40306, 2022.

[16] M. Munn, and D. Pitman, *Explainable AI for practitioners*: " O'Reilly Media, Inc.", 2022.

[17] V. Hassija, V. Chamola, A. Mahapatra, A. Singal, D. Goel, K. Huang, S. Scardapane, I. Spinelli, M. Mahmud, and A. Hussain, "Interpreting black-box models: a review on explainable artificial intelligence," *Cognitive Computation,* vol. 16, no. 1, pp. 45–74, 2024.

[18] N. Capuano, G. Fenza, V. Loia, and C. Stanzione, "Explainable artificial intelligence in cybersecurity: A survey," *Ieee Access,* vol. 10, pp. 93575–93600, 2022.

[19] A. Oki, Y. Ogawa, K. Ota, and M. Dong, "Evaluation of Applying Federated Learning to Distributed Intrusion Detection Systems Through Explainable AI," *IEEE Networking Letters*, 2024.
[20] M. Wang, K. Zheng, Y. Yang, and X. Wang, "An explainable machine learning framework for intrusion detection systems," *IEEE Access,* vol. 8, pp. 73127–73141, 2020.
[21] M. Sarhan, S. Layeghy, and M. Portmann, "Evaluating standard feature sets towards increased generalisability and explainability of ML-based network intrusion detection," *Big Data Research,* vol. 30, pp. 100359, 2022.
[22] P. Barnard, N. Marchetti, and L. A. DaSilva, "Robust network intrusion detection through explainable artificial intelligence (XAI)," *IEEE Networking Letters,* vol. 4, no. 3, pp. 167–171, 2022.
[23] P. P. Kundu, T. Truong-Huu, L. Chen, L. Zhou, and S. G. Teo, "Detection and classification of botnet traffic using deep learning with model explanation," *IEEE Transactions on Dependable and Secure Computing*, 2022.
[24] I. H. Sarker, Y. B. Abushark, F. Alsolami, and A. I. Khan, "Intrudtree: a machine learning based cyber security intrusion detection model," *Symmetry,* vol. 12, no. 5, pp. 754, 2020.
[25] I. H. Sarker, "CyberLearning: Effectiveness analysis of machine learning security modeling to detect cyber-anomalies and multi-attacks," *Internet of Things,* vol. 14, pp. 100393, 2021.
[26] I. Psychoula, A. Gutmann, P. Mainali, S. H. Lee, P. Dunphy, and F. Petitcolas, "Explainable machine learning for fraud detection," *Computer,* vol. 54, no. 10, pp. 49–59, 2021.
[27] Z. Pan, J. Sheldon, and P. Mishra, "Hardware-assisted malware detection and localization using explainable machine learning," *IEEE Transactions on Computers,* vol. 71, no. 12, pp. 3308–3321, 2022.
[28] I. Dimitriadis, K. Georgiou, and A. Vakali, "Social botomics: A systematic ensemble ml approach for explainable and multi-class bot detection," *Applied Sciences,* vol. 11, no. 21, pp. 9857, 2021.
[29] C. S. Wickramasinghe, K. Amarasinghe, D. L. Marino, C. Rieger, and M. Manic, "Explainable unsupervised machine learning for cyber-physical systems," *IEEE Access,* vol. 9, pp. 131824–131843, 2021.
[30] B. A. Alqaralleh, F. Aldhaban, E. A. AlQarallehs, and A. H. Al-Omari, "Optimal machine learning enabled intrusion detection in cyber-physical system environment," *Computers, Materials & Continua,* vol. 72, no. 3, pp. 4691–4707, 2022.

[31] M. Al-Hawawreh, E. Sitnikova, and N. Aboutorab, "X-IIoTID: A connectivity-agnostic and device-agnostic intrusion data set for industrial Internet of Things," *IEEE Internet of Things Journal,* vol. 9, no. 5, pp. 3962–3977, 2021.

[32] F. De Keersmaeker, Y. Cao, G. K. Ndonda, and R. Sadre, "A survey of public IoT datasets for network security research," *IEEE Communications Surveys & Tutorials,* vol. 25, no. 3, pp. 1808–1840, 2023.

4

Addressing Security and Privacy Issues in Cyber-physical Systems

Yunus Olusola Kareem[1], Adetola Abdulfattah Sogbesan[2] and Habeeb Quadri[3]

[1]Department of Cybersecurity, College of Engineering, University of West England, United Kingdom
[2]Centre for Cyberspace, Nasarawa State University, Nigeria
[3]University of Kent, United Kingdom

Email: yunus.kareem@uwe.ac.uk; tolasogbesan@ieee.org; h.quadri@kent.ac.uk

Abstract

Security and privacy are paramount concerns in cyber-physical systems (CPS), where the convergence of physical and digital components exposes them to various threats. While traditional security measures like encryption and firewalls have been employed, and more recent technologies like machine learning have been explored to address these challenges, they need to address CPS's distributed nature and real-time requirements. The physical threats are also inherent, and automation cannot completely solve them. This chapter explains security and privacy issues in CPS and how emerging technology, such as blockchain, can help solve its cyber threats. With its decentralized architecture and immutable ledger, blockchain technology offers a promising solution to these challenges. Compared to machine learning-based approaches, blockchain provides enhanced data integrity, resistance to tampering, and improved privacy protections.

4.1 Introduction

Cyber-physical systems (CPS) are a subset of the Internet of Things (IoT). It represents a transformative integration of embedded technologies with

DOI: 10.1201/9788743801306-4

physical processes, enabling seamless interaction between the cyber and physical domains [1]. These systems are increasingly pivotal across various sectors, including healthcare, agriculture, autonomous systems, and industrial automation, due to their ability to enhance efficiency and automation through advanced technologies like artificial intelligence (AI) and machine learning (ML)[2]. The growing importance of CPS is underscored by its application in critical areas such as smart grids, autonomous vehicles, and industrial control systems. These applications demonstrate CPS's potential to revolutionize industries by providing real-time monitoring and control, which is crucial for tasks that protect human lives and strategic assets [1], [2].

CPS systems have been used in many industries. For instance, CPS has been employed in the sports industry to enhance athlete training environments through real-time monitoring and precise physical fitness assessment, thereby improving performance and reducing injury risks [3]. However, integrating cyber and physical components introduces significant challenges, particularly regarding security, privacy, and safety [4], [5].

The cyber-physical system comprises interconnected hardware and software that interact with people (physical environment), as shown in Figure 4.1, enabling real-time data exchange and decision-making. These components include sensors, actuators, communication networks, and data processing units, all working together to create a seamless interface between the digital and physical realms [6]. This integration allows for enhanced monitoring and control, but it also necessitates a comprehensive understanding of the potential risks associated with each component [1]. As these systems become more complex, robust security measures become increasingly critical to protect against vulnerabilities that could lead to catastrophic failures or data breaches [7].

CPSs are vulnerable to cybersecurity threats due to their complexity and interdependencies, which can lead to severe consequences such as production performance deterioration and regulatory violations [8]. Traditional IT threat models are insufficient for CPS. AI and machine learning methods were also inadequate to cover the ever-growing threat in their ecosystem, necessitating the development of inclusive technology with optimum security measures and proactive risk assessments to address these vulnerabilities effectively.

Privacy is another primary concern in CPS, as sensitive data is often collected and processed, necessitating robust data protection measures to safeguard against unauthorized access and misuse [2]. Existing solutions usually need to be revised, highlighting the need for innovative approaches that integrate privacy by design principles and advanced encryption techniques to

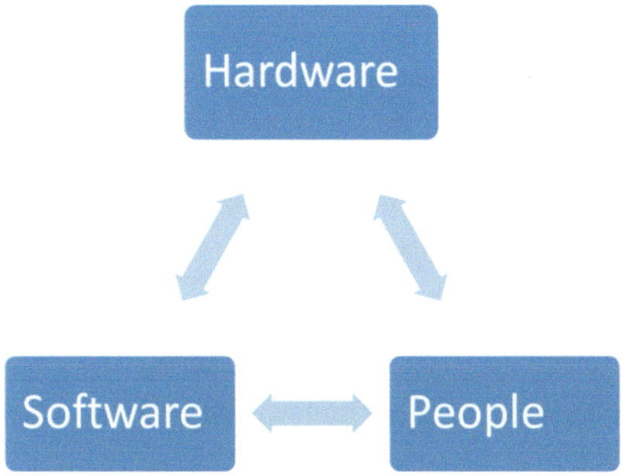

Figure 4.1 Cyber-physical system.

ensure data integrity and confidentiality. Also, the complexity of CPS raises issues related to transparency, bias, and trust in AI-driven decision-making processes. Ensuring the reliability and trustworthiness of AI systems within CPS is critical, with explainable AI (XAI) playing a pivotal role in enhancing transparency and accountability.

In summary, cyber-physical systems are crucial for advancing technological integration across various domains, offering significant benefits in efficiency and automation. However, their complexity necessitates robust security measures to fight the growing threat and vulnerability. Privacy concerns also emerge as the data collected by these systems can be sensitive, requiring stringent protocols to safeguard personal information while maintaining functionality and user trust. Several technologies as emerged with the possibility to address these issues. These technologies include advanced encryption methods, decentralized data storage solutions, and machine learning algorithms to detect real-time anomalies.

This work will focus on evaluating the effectiveness of these technologies in enhancing the security and privacy of cyber-physical systems, ultimately aiming to propose a comprehensive framework that balances innovation with protection using blockchain. We will review how blockchain can provide a transparent and immutable ledger for transactions, ensuring that data integrity is maintained while allowing for secure access controls that empower users to manage their information. Additionally, we will explore the potential of smart contracts to automate processes and enforce compliance, reducing the risk of human error and increasing operational efficiency.

4.1.1 Chapter contribution

The following are the significant contributions of the chapter.

1. The chapter examines some security and privacy issues in CPS.
2. The technology used in previous work to address security and privacy issues in CPS.
3. Explore using blockchain technology to address security and privacy issues in CPS.
4. Propose a blockchain-based framework to address security and privacy issues in CPS.

4.1.2 Chapter organization

The chapter is structured as follows: Section 4.1 introduces the chapter, focusing on the summary of CPS's security and privacy issues and current solution trends. Section 4.2 covers the background and related works. Section 4.3 delves into the CPS architecture and components. The security issues and vulnerabilities are broached in Section 4.4. The proposed technology and framework, exploring CPS integrations with blockchain technology are highlighted in Section 4.5. Finally, Section 4.6 concludes with future works.

4.2 Background and Related Work

Concerns regarding security and privacy are critical factors in all systems, including cyber-physical systems, which various researchers have explored. This section examines a multitude of scholarly works associated with the topic. One of the pioneering researchers in this field is George Loukas [9], whose research examined the attacks and their effects on CPS. Wardell et al. [10] also pointed out the weaknesses in industrial control systems, stressing the necessity for solid security protocols. They suggested modeling systems alongside their malicious agents to uncover security flaws.

In 2017, further advancement in active scholarship of the investigation of security and privacy within cyber-physical systems (CPS) was witnessed, highlighted by the contributions of Fink et al. [11], Ashibani and Mahmoud [12], Orojloo and Azgomi [13], Nguyen et al. [14], Dai et al. [15], and Martin [16]. These studies collectively underscored the critical importance of integrating security protocols early in the design phase of CPS to mitigate

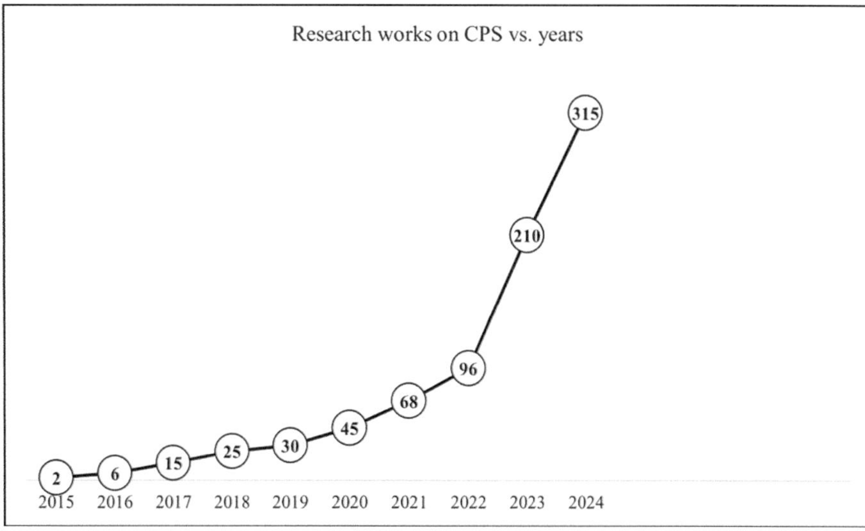

Figure 4.2 Advancement in CPS security research from 2015 to 2024.

potential threats effectively. Figure 4.2 shows the progressive nature of active research in the field from 2015 to 2024.

As the technology landscape evolves, ongoing research continues to explore innovative methodologies for enhancing the resilience of CPS against emerging vulnerabilities. Jain and his esteemed colleagues, as referenced in their notable work [17], significantly enhance data privacy security by implementing a more advanced and sophisticated version of the well-known ChaCha20 algorithm, improving its effectiveness in safeguarding sensitive information. Another similar work is by authors in [18].

Alternative methodologies documented in the preceding literature encompass a variety of innovative approaches designed to enhance security and efficiency in various systems. Access controls have been extensively researched among these methodologies, with notable contributions from authors such as Mikel et al. and Liang et al. These studies explore strategies for implementing robust access control mechanisms that ensure only authorized users can access sensitive information, thereby mitigating potential security risks [19], [20]. Secure communication protocols have also been a focal point of research, as highlighted by the work of Sun et al. and Zhang et al. in [21] and [22], respectively. These protocols are essential for protecting data in transit, ensuring that information exchanged over networks remains confidential and tamper-proof. Their research delves into the design and implementation of these protocols, addressing various vulnerabilities

Table 4.1 Summary of related work.

Author work	CPS components	Security issues	Privacy issues	Technologies	Case study
[11]	Yes	Yes	Yes	None	No
[4]	Yes	Yes	Yes	Blockchain	No
[2]	No	Yes	Yes	Artificial intelligence	No
[32]	No	Yes	Yes	LightGBM model	No
[33]	Yes	Yes	Yes	Blockchain	No
[34]	No	Yes	Yes	Review	No
[26]	No	Yes	Yes	Review	No
[21]	Yes	Yes	Yes	Deep learning	No
[22]	No	Yes	Yes	-	No
[35]	Yes	Yes	Yes	IDS	No
This	Yes	Yes	Yes	Review, Blockchain	Yes

that can arise during data transmission. Incorporating machine learning techniques has gained traction in recent years, with significant contributions from Srinath et al. [23], Djamel et al. [24], Kumar et al. [25], and Ramkumar et al. [26]. Their studies investigate how machine learning algorithms can detect anomalies, predict potential threats, and enhance decision-making processes in security systems. This innovative approach leverages data-driven insights to improve the overall resilience of the security framework.

Lastly, blockchain technology has emerged as a transformative methodology, with research conducted by Shukla et al., Xu et al., and Kuljeet et al. These authors examine the potential of blockchain to provide decentralized, transparent, and immutable records of transactions, which can significantly bolster security in various applications [27], [28]. A quick summary of existing work is captured in Table 4.1. By exploring the intricacies of blockchain implementation, their work sheds light on how this technology can be harnessed to create more secure and trustworthy systems. Overall, these alternative methodologies collectively contribute to the evolving landscape of security and privacy practices, each offering unique advantages and addressing different security and privacy challenges modern systems face. However, the current trend tends to focus on blockchain as it's becoming increasingly recognized for its potential to revolutionize data integrity and enhance user trust in digital transactions. This chapter focuses on integrating blockchain with CPS and how security and privacy are achieved due to the integration.

4.3 Components of Cyber-physical Systems

Cyber-physical system components can be categorized into three categories: Control systems, sensors and actuators, the network or communication

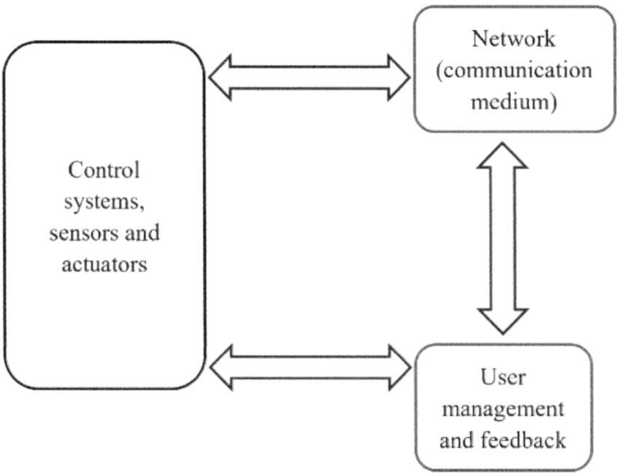

Figure 4.3 Block diagram of a CPS.

medium, and user management/ feedback systems [11]. Figure 4.3 gives the block diagram of a CPS.

4.3.1 Control systems, sensors, and actuators

This block manages, monitors, and interacts with the physical world. Control systems are the "brains' of a CPS, responsible for making decisions and coordinating the interactions between the physical and digital components [32]. Control systems in CPS are often implemented as embedded software. They analyze data from sensors, process it using algorithms, and send commands to actuators.

4.3.2 Network or communication medium

The network or communication medium is the backbone of a cyber-physical system (CPS), connecting its various components and enabling data exchange. It is crucial in ensuring the system's functionality, reliability, and security.

1. **Key characteristics of communication networks in CPS**:

   - Real-time capability: Networks must be able to transmit data with minimal latency to support timely decision-making and control actions.
   - Reliability: The network should be resilient to failures and disruptions to maintain system operation.
   - Security: Robust security measures are essential to protect sensitive data and prevent unauthorized access.

- Scalability: The network should be capable of accommodating the growth of the system and increasing data volumes.

2. **Common network technologies used in CPS:**

   - Ethernet: A widely used wired network technology offering high bandwidth and flexibility.
   - Wireless networks: Wi-Fi, Bluetooth, cellular networks, and other wireless technologies provide connectivity in various environments.
   - Fieldbus networks: Specialized networks designed for industrial automation and control applications, such as CAN bus, Profibus, and Modbus.
   - Industrial Ethernet: Ethernet-based networks optimized for industrial environments, including Profinet, EtherCAT, and EtherNet/IP.

3. **Network architectures**:

   - Centralized: A single central node (e.g., a server) coordinates communication between other devices.
   - Distributed: Communication is decentralized, with multiple nodes sharing the workload and reducing the impact of failures.
   - Hybrid: A combination of centralized and distributed architectures, offering flexibility and scalability.

4.3.3 User management and feedback systems

These elements facilitate human interaction and provide feedback to the system.

4.4 Security Threats and Vulnerabilities

The convergence of cyber and physical elements creates unique vulnerabilities that can be exploited by malicious actors, leading to severe consequences ranging from data breaches to physical harm [33], [34]. Understanding the security threats and vulnerabilities inherent in CPS is essential for developing robust protective measures and ensuring the safety and reliability of these systems in our daily lives [15], [36]. These threats and vulnerabilities are categorized into two categories.

4.4.1 Physical threat

Physical threats pose a significant risk to the security and integrity of cyber-physical systems. These threats range from simple tampering to more sophisticated attacks that exploit physical vulnerabilities [11]. Some common physical threats include unauthorized access and tempering, environmental factors, physical damage, espionage, and supply chain [37].

Unauthorized access and tampering: The act of gaining entry to a tangible infrastructure, be it a physical facility or a range of devices, without the requisite permissions or formal authorization is undeniably a grave and significant threat that has the potential to result in tampering or modification of various devices or components, an occurrence which could ultimately undermine their operational functionality or compromise the integrity of their security mechanisms.

1. **Environmental factors**: This phenomenon may occur because of intense thermal conditions or environmental catastrophes (for instance, hurricanes, seismic activities, inundations, and other ecological disturbances can considerably impact operational systems and infrastructural frameworks). Such disasters can impair technological apparatus or constituent parts, resulting in operational anomalies or complete breakdowns. Additional instances include interruptions in electrical supply.
2. **Physical damage and destruction**: Vandalism is intentional damage to devices or infrastructure. Theft is the theft of devices or components, potentially leading to data loss or unauthorized access. Acts of war or terrorism are physical attacks on critical infrastructure.
3. **Supply chain attacks**: Supply chain disruptions: Disruptions in the supply chain can lead to shortages of critical components or delays in maintenance and repairs.
4. **Espionage and sabotage**: Obtaining sensitive information or technology through physical means. Sabotage: Intentionally damaging or disrupting systems to cause harm or gain a strategic advantage.

4.4.2 Cyber threat

Cyber-physical systems (CPSs) are increasingly integral to critical infrastructure, yet they face numerous cyber threats due to their complex integration of physical and digital components [9]. These threats can severely impact the functionality and safety of CPS, necessitating robust security measures. CPS's most common cyber threats include denial-of-service attacks, data modification, information leakage, and malware dissemination [6]. These threats exploit the vulnerabilities inherent in the interconnected nature of

CPS, affecting sectors such as healthcare, transportation, and energy. Some of the common cyber threats include:

Denial-of-service attack: A denial-of-service attack is a malicious attempt to disrupt a service's normal functioning by overwhelming it with traffic, rendering it unavailable to legitimate users. This attack can lead to significant downtime and loss of trust among users, particularly in critical systems where reliability is paramount. Developing advanced intrusion detection systems and real-time monitoring tools is essential to mitigate these risks [35], [38].

1. **Data breach**: A security incident where unauthorized access to sensitive data occurs, potentially exposing personal information and compromising user privacy. Organizations must implement robust encryption methods and access controls to safeguard against such breaches and conduct regular security audits to identify vulnerabilities before they can be exploited. Current scholarly investigations concerning access control, exemplified by sources [19] and [40], in conjunction with studies on blockchain technology, as referenced in [18] and [32], have elucidated a commendable resolution.

2. **Malicious code injection** remains a significant threat, as attackers exploit vulnerabilities in software to insert harmful scripts that can manipulate or steal data. To mitigate this risk, organizations must implement robust input validation techniques and employ web application firewalls to detect and block such attacks before they can cause harm [41]. Li et al. and other researchers have emphasized the importance of continuous monitoring and updating security protocols to adapt to evolving threats [39], [40].

3. **Man-in-the-middle (MitM) attacks** attacks pose a severe risk as they allow attackers to intercept and alter communications between two parties [36]. To counteract this, encryption protocols such as TLS should be utilized to secure data in transit, ensuring that even if data is intercepted, it remains unreadable to unauthorized users [41]. Additionally, technologies such as blockchain can offer enhanced security by providing a decentralized ledger that verifies transactions, making it more difficult for attackers to manipulate data [20], [31], [36].

4. **Supply chain attacks** attacks exploit vulnerabilities in third-party vendors, highlighting the need for rigorous vetting and monitoring of all partners involved in the supply chain. Implementing strong security

measures, such as regular audits and compliance checks, can help mitigate these risks and ensure that all supply chain components adhere to the highest standards of security [42]. Also, access control measures should be enforced to limit who can access sensitive information, ensuring that only authorized personnel can view or modify critical data [19], [43].

4.4.3 Privacy concerns and risks

As organizations increasingly rely on digital platforms, the potential for data breaches and unauthorized access grows, necessitating a comprehensive approach to privacy that includes employee training and awareness programs. Specific activities that may pose privacy risks include:

1. **Data collection and sharing**: The methodologies employed for collecting information, the regulatory frameworks that dictate the parameters for data dissemination among stakeholders, and the repercussions of these practices on user privacy. Each dimension necessitates meticulous scrutiny to reconcile operational efficacy with ethical benchmarks such as the Information Commissioner's office (ICO), International Organization for Standardization (ISO), and General Data Protection Regulation (GDPR), thereby ensuring that users are adequately informed and that their consent is duly emphasized.

2. **User consent and control**: The capacity for individuals to oversee their data, which encompasses the alternatives to either consent to or withdraw from data collection, is of utmost importance. This capability enables individuals to make well-informed decisions regarding their personal information and cultivates a sense of ownership concerning their digital presence. Moreover, transparency in data management practices is critical; organizations must explicitly convey their data utilization policies and the objectives for which data is gathered, as delineated in ISO 27001. This practice enhances trust and ensures compliance with international regulations that champion user rights and data protection, such as the General Data Protection Regulation (GDPR).

4.4.4 Security and privacy-preserving technologies

Technologies and frameworks are crucial in addressing insecurity and privacy issues in CPS [44]. Techniques such as blockchain, artificial intelligence, differential privacy, homomorphic encryption, zero knowledge of proof, and federated learning enable organizations to ensure security and privacy without compromising data. By implementing these methods, companies can enhance their data analytics capabilities while ensuring compliance with stringent privacy standards, ultimately leading to a more secure digital environment for all users.

1. **Blockchain technology**: This decentralized ledger technology enhances security and transparency in data transactions. By providing a tamper-proof record of data exchanges, blockchain can help ensure the integrity of sensitive information and facilitate trust among stakeholders.
2. **Federated learning**: This approach allows machine learning models to be trained across multiple decentralized devices without sharing raw data. By keeping data localized, federated learning enhances privacy while enabling valuable insights from aggregated data.
3. **Homomorphic encryption**: This encryption method allows computations on encrypted data without decrypting it first. This means sensitive information can be processed securely, ensuring privacy even during data analysis.
4. **Differential privacy**: This technique adds noise to datasets to protect individual privacy while allowing for valuable data analysis. By ensuring that the output of data queries does not reveal too much about any individual, differential privacy helps organizations comply with privacy regulations.
5. **Zero-knowledge proofs**: This cryptographic method allows one party to prove to another that they know a value without revealing it. It can enhance authentication processes and secure transactions in CPS.
6. **Privacy-preserving data sharing platforms**: These platforms enable organizations to share data securely while maintaining user privacy. They often incorporate advanced encryption and access control mechanisms to ensure sensitive information is only accessible to authorized users.
7. **Secure multi-party computation (SMPC)**: This technology allows multiple parties to jointly compute a function over their inputs while keeping those inputs private. SMPC is particularly useful in collaborative environments where data sharing is necessary, but privacy must be preserved.
8. **Artificial intelligence and machine learning**: AI and ML can be employed to identify unusual patterns or behaviors in CPS that may

indicate security threats. These technologies can enhance detection and response to potential breaches in real-time.

9. **Privacy-enhancing technologies (PETs)**: These include tools and methodologies to protect user privacy, such as anonymization techniques and secure data storage solutions.

10. **Regulatory compliance tools**: Technologies that help organizations comply with privacy regulations (like GDPR and CCPA) are becoming essential. These tools assist in data governance, consent management, and audit trails to ensure user rights are respected.

4.5 Proposed Technology and Framework

Among the listed technologies and frameworks, blockchain excels in both addressing security and privacy due to its decentralized nature and supporting framework sucks as zero-knowledge of proof. This unique combination allows for secure transactions while maintaining user anonymity, making it a powerful tool in cyber-physical systems. Blockchain components are designed to facilitate transparency and traceability, ensuring that all interactions within the system are recorded immutably. This helps verify data integrity and enables organizations to conduct audits more efficiently and accurately. Several blockchain technologies have emerged, each offering unique features and capabilities that cater to different use cases, from supply chain management to healthcare data sharing. Among these, the most notable are Ethereum, Hyperledger, and Corda, each providing distinct advantages depending on the application's specific requirements.

Kareem et al. highlight the importance of selecting the appropriate blockchain framework, as it can significantly impact scalability, security, and overall performance [45]. As organizations explore these options, they must also consider factors such as community support, development resources, and regulatory compliance to ensure a successful implementation. Figure 4.4 gives the convention centralized CPS and Figure 4.5 depicts a blockchain-based CPS.

Blockchain is built around several components that create a secure and transparent environment. These components include consensus mechanisms, smart contracts, and cryptographic techniques, all of which play crucial roles in maintaining the network's integrity and functionality. Integrating blockchain technology into cyber-physical systems (CPSs) enhances security, transparency, and resilience but requires a structured approach to address CPS's unique challenges.

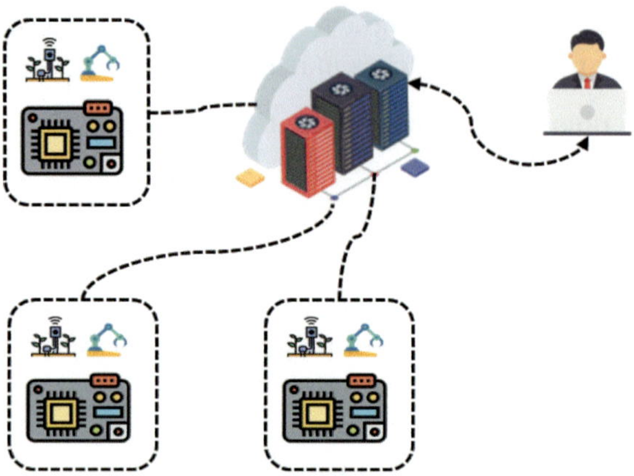

Figure 4.4 Convention centralized CPS.

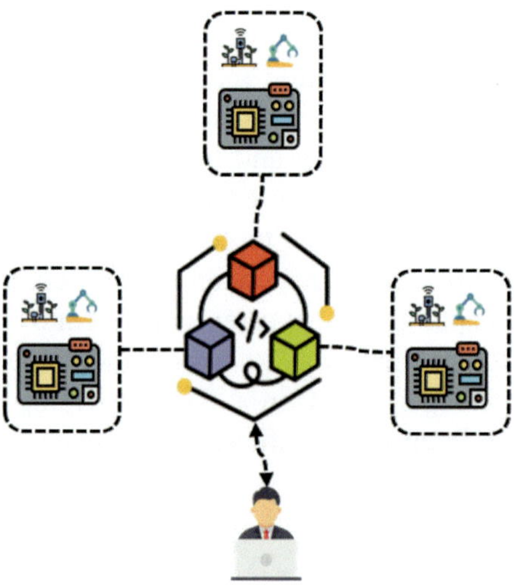

Figure 4.5 Blockchain-based CPS.

First, clear objectives and use cases must be defined to determine the specific benefits of blockchain, such as improving data integrity, decentralized control, or traceability. Following this, the existing CPS architecture and data flow are analyzed to identify optimal points for integration, carefully selecting blockchain platforms and consensus mechanisms that balance security with performance, especially for resource-constrained devices. Smart contracts are then designed to automate critical processes and enforce security policies. At the same time, data management strategies determine which information is stored on-chain versus off-chain, considering CPS's high data volume and real-time requirements. Device identity management and authentication are essential, employing decentralized identifiers and cryptographic protocols to secure communication channels and prevent unauthorized access. Privacy and access control mechanisms, such as attribute-based permissions and zero-knowledge proofs, further ensure data confidentiality.

Comprehensive testing, including simulation, stress, and security testing, is vital before deployment. This is followed by continuous monitoring and regular updates to maintain security and scalability. This stepwise approach enables blockchain integration that enhances CPS functionality while addressing latency, data sensitivity, and scalability concerns critical to CPS environments.

4.5.1 Case study

Considering the privacy and security-enhanced CPS system requirement, Hyperledger Fabric and Ethereum stand as strong candidates. Hyperledger Fabric offers modular architecture and fine-grained access control, while Ethereum provides a robust smart contract framework that can be adapted for private use cases. For the sake of this work, Hyperledger Fabric is proposed for a blockchain platform, leveraging its capabilities to create a secure and efficient environment for managing transactions and data sharing among trusted parties. This choice allows us to implement a permissioned network where participants can be authenticated and authorized, ensuring that only designated entities can access sensitive data and functionalities. Hyperledger zero-knowledge proofs can further enhance privacy by allowing parties to validate transactions without revealing the underlying data, thus maintaining confidentiality while ensuring trust in the system.

In order to develop a private blockchain using Hyperledger Fabric, the following steps are required:

1. Define the network architecture and identify the key stakeholders involved in the project.
2. Set up the necessary infrastructure, including nodes and servers, to support the network's operations.
3. Configure the Hyperledger Fabric components, such as the orders, peers, and channels, to facilitate secure communication and data sharing among participants.
4. Implement access control policies to safeguard sensitive information by ensuring only authorized users can interact with the blockchain.

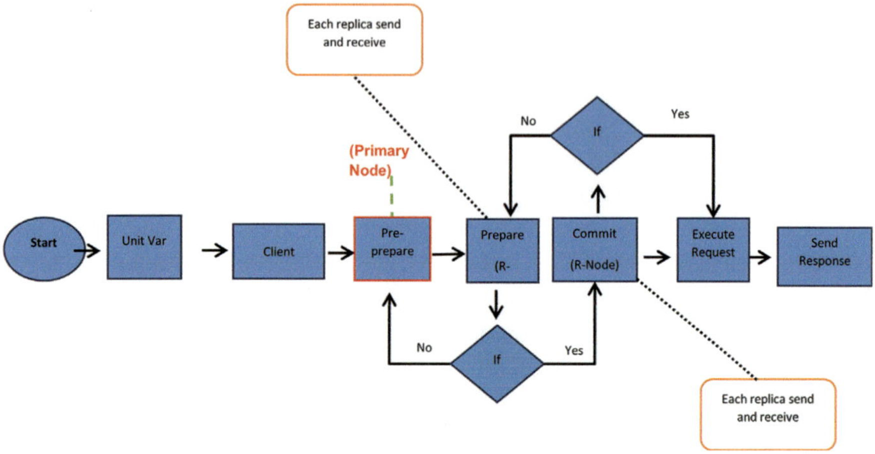

Figure 4.6 Hyperledger PBFT consensus flowchart

5. Develop chain contracts tailored to the specific use case, ensuring they adhere to the privacy requirements established in the initial planning phase.

6. Conduct thorough testing of the network and its components to identify and resolve potential vulnerabilities before going live.

Integrating CPS with Hyperledger following the steps above will ensure all nodes are prepared for the operation; one of the most important aspects of blockchain is the agreement. Hyperledger uses Practical Byzantine Fault Tolerant (PBFT) to achieve consensus and this required series of steps which is represented with flowchart in Figure 4.6. Once the consensus is achieved the block will then be added to blockchain.

4.6 Conclusion and Future Scope

Security and privacy are essential in ensuring the integrity and confidentiality of data within cyber-physical systems, necessitating ongoing research and development to address emerging threats and enhance resilience. This work has introduced the importance of integrating robust security technology and frameworks such as blockchain that safeguard data and promote trust among users and stakeholders, paving the way for more secure and efficient cyber-physical interactions. Moreover, embracing decentralized solutions can significantly minimize the likelihood of encountering single points of failure, thus improving the overall reliability and effectiveness of the system.

Hyperledger Fabric is an example of a blockchain framework that provides a modular design, facilitating seamless integration with CPS and enabling organizations to customize their solutions to meet specific requirements while adhering to regulatory guidelines. While this integration presents new hurdles, including challenges related to scalability and interoperability, it also paves the way for creative security strategies that can evolve in response to the changing landscape of cyber threats. This can serve as a foundation for research in future endeavors.

References

[1] S. Rani, A. Kataria, S. Kumar, and V. Karar, “A new generation cyber-physical system: A comprehensive review from security perspective,” Jan. 01, 2025, *Elsevier Ltd.* doi: 10.1016/j.cose.2024.104095.

[2] A. Bandi, “A Taxonomy of AI Techniques for Security and Privacy in Cyber–Physical Systems,” May 21, 2024, *Bon View Publishing Pte Ltd.* doi: 10.47852/bonviewJCCE42021539.

[3] P. H. J. Nardelli, *Cyber-physical Systems: Theory, Methodology, and Applications*, 1st edition. in IEEE Press. Newark: John Wiley & Sons, Inc, 2022.

[4] D. Das, S. Banerjee, P. Chatterjee, U. Ghosh, U. Biswas, and W. Mansoor, “Security, Trust, and Privacy Management Framework in Cyber-Physical Systems using Blockchain,” in *Proceedings - IEEE Consumer Communications and Networking Conference, CCNC*, Institute of Electrical and Electronics Engineers Inc., 2023. doi: 10.1109/CCNC51644.2023.10060483.

[5] A. R. Mahlous, “Security Analysis in Smart Agriculture: Insights from a Cyber-Physical System Application,” *Computers, Materials and Continua*, vol. 79, no. 3, pp. 4781–4803, 2024, doi: 10.32604/cmc.2024.050821.

[6] C. Koulamas and A. Kalogeras, “Cyber-physical systems and digital twins in the industrial internet of things,” Nov. 01, 2018, *IEEE Computer Society*. doi: 10.1109/MC.2018.2876181.

[7] Callum Cyrus, “IoT Cyberattacks Escalate in 2021, According to Kaspersky,” IoT World Today.

[8] S. Rani, A. Kataria, M. Chauhan, P. Rattan, R. Kumar, and A. Kumar Sivaraman, “Security and Privacy Challenges in the Deployment of Cyber-Physical Systems in Smart City Applications: State-of-Art Work,” in *Materials Today: Proceedings*, Elsevier Ltd, Jan. 2022, pp. 4671–4676. doi: 10.1016/j.matpr.2022.03.123.

[9] G. Loukas, "2 - A History of Cyber-Physical Security Incidents," in *Cyber-Physical Attacks*, G. Loukas, Ed., Boston: Butterworth-Heinemann, 2015, pp. 21–57. doi: https://doi.org/10.1016/B978-0-12-801290-1.00002-3.
[10] D. C. Wardell, R. F. Mills, G. L. Peterson, and M. E. Oxley, "A Method for Revealing and Addressing Security Vulnerabilities in Cyber-physical Systems by Modeling Malicious Agent Interactions with Formal Verification," *Procedia Comput Sci*, vol. 95, pp. 24–31, Jan. 2016, doi: 10.1016/J.PROCS.2016.09.289.
[11] G. A. Fink, T. W. Edgar, T. R. Rice, D. G. MacDonald, and C. E. Crawford, "Security and Privacy in Cyber-Physical Systems," *Cyber-Physical Systems: Foundations, Principles and Applications*, pp. 129–141, Jan. 2017, doi: 10.1016/B978-0-12-803801-7.00009-2.
[12] Y. Ashibani and Q. H. Mahmoud, "Cyber physical systems security: Analysis, challenges and solutions," *Comput Secur*, vol. 68, pp. 81–97, Jul. 2017, doi: 10.1016/J.COSE.2017.04.005.
[13] H. Orojloo and M. A. Azgomi, "A method for evaluating the consequence propagation of security attacks in cyber–physical systems," *Future Generation Computer Systems*, vol. 67, pp. 57–71, Feb. 2017, doi: 10.1016/J.FUTURE.2016.07.016.
[14] P. H. Nguyen, S. Ali, and T. Yue, "Model-based security engineering for cyber-physical systems: A systematic mapping study," *Inf Softw Technol*, vol. 83, pp. 116–135, Mar. 2017, doi: 10.1016/J.INFSOF.2016.11.004.
[15] H. Dai, S. Zhao, and K. Chen, "A chaos-oriented prediction and suppression model to enhance the security for cyber physical power systems," *J Parallel Distrib Comput*, vol. 103, pp. 87–95, May 2017, doi: 10.1016/J.JPDC.2016.11.015.
[16] M. Novotný, "Cryptanalytic attacks on cyber-physical systems," *Microprocess Microsyst*, vol. 52, pp. 534–539, Jul. 2017, doi: 10.1016/J.MICPRO.2017.04.017.
[17] D. K. Jain, P. Mohan, K. Lakshmanna, and A. K. Nanda, "Enhanced Data Privacy in Cyber-physical System Using Improved Chacha20 Algorithm," May 13, 2022. doi: 10.21203/rs.3.rs-1558846/v1.
[18] K. R. Saraf and P. Malathi, "Security enhancement of cyber-physical system using modified encryption AESGNRSA technique," *Indonesian Journal of Electrical Engineering and Computer Science*, vol. 33, no. 2, pp. 1177–1185, Feb. 2024, doi: 10.11591/ijeecs.v33.i2.pp1177-1185.
[19] J. and J. E. and H. M. and L. O. Uriarte Mikel and Astorga, "Survey on Access Control Models Feasible in Cyber-Physical Systems," in *Cyber-Physical Systems: Architecture, Security and Application*, D. Guo Song

and Zeng, Ed., Cham: Springer International Publishing, 2019, pp. 103–152. doi: 10.1007/978-3-319-92564-6_6.

[20] L. Tan, N. Shi, C. Yang, and K. Yu, "A Blockchain-Based Access Control Framework for Cyber-Physical-Social System Big Data," *IEEE Access*, vol. 8, pp. 77215–77226, 2020, doi: 10.1109/ACCESS.2020.2988951.

[21] G. and C. Z. and Z. X. and L. Z. and L. L. and J. Y. and Z. T.-X. Sun Qiangqiang and Lian, "Deep Reinforcement Learning Based Secure Communication and Computing Resource Allocation for Grid Cyber-Physical System," in *Proceedings of the 2nd International Conference on Internet of Things, Communication and Intelligent Technology*, L. and C. D. Dong Jian and Zhang, Ed., Singapore: Springer Nature Singapore, 2024, pp. 274–283.

[22] J. Zhang, R. Ying, J. Cui, H. Zhong, I. Bolodurina, and D. He, "Secure and Efficient User-Centric V2C Communication for Intelligent Cyber-Physical Transportation System," *IEEE Transactions on Information Forensics and Security*, vol. 19, pp. 7674–7689, 2024, doi: 10.1109/TIFS.2024.3442609.

[23] S. Srinath and S. Dey, "A Machine Learning Approach toward Cyber-Physical Security of Battery Systems," *J Dyn Syst Meas Control*, vol. 146, no. 6, Jun. 2024, doi: 10.1115/1.4065703.

[24] D. Djenouri, R. Laidi, Y. Djenouri, and I. Balasingham, "Machine Learning for Smart Building Applications: Review and Taxonomy," *ACM Comput. Surv.*, vol. 52, no. 2, Mar. 2019, doi: 10.1145/3311950.

[25] P. J. Kumar, L. H. J. Alzubaidi, N. Nagarjuna, R. Deshmukh, and G. K. Madhura, "Classifying Network Abnormalities Into Faults and Attacks in Iot-Based Cyber-Physical Systems using Machine Learning," in *2nd International Conference on Integrated Circuits and Communication Systems, ICICACS 2024*, Institute of Electrical and Electronics Engineers Inc., 2024. doi: 10.1109/ICICACS60521.2024.10498664.

[26] P. Ramkumar *et al.*, "A Smart Anomaly Detection Method in Cyber Physical Systems Using Machine Learning," in *https://services.igi-global.com/resolvedoi/resolve.aspx?doi=10.4018/979-8-3693-4159-9.ch021*, IGI Global, 2024, pp. 354–363. doi: 10.4018/979-8-3693-4159-9.ch021.

[27] D. Shukla, S. Chakrabarti, and A. Sharma, "Blockchain-based cyber-security enhancement of cyber–physical power system through symmetric encryption mechanism," *International Journal of Electrical Power & Energy Systems*, vol. 155, p. 109631, Jan. 2024, doi: 10.1016/J.IJEPES.2023.109631.

[28] Y. Xu *et al.*, "Enhancing privacy in cyber–physical systems: An efficient blockchain-assisted data-sharing scheme with deniability," *Journal of*

Systems Architecture, vol. 150, p. 103132, May 2024, doi: 10.1016/J.SYSARC.2024.103132.

[29] Y. Xu *et al.*, "Enhancing privacy in cyber–physical systems: An efficient blockchain-assisted data-sharing scheme with deniability," *Journal of Systems Architecture*, vol. 150, May 2024, doi: 10.1016/j.sysarc.2024.103132.

[30] A. Alkhodair, S. Mohanty, E. Kougianos, and D. Puthal, "McPoRA: A multi-chain proof of rapid authentication for post-blockchain based security in large scale complex cyber-physical systems," in *Proceedings of IEEE Computer Society Annual Symposium on VLSI, ISVLSI*, IEEE Computer Society, Jul. 2020, pp. 446–451. doi: 10.1109/ISVLSI49217.2020.00-16.

[31] K. Kaur, G. Kaddoum, and S. Zeadally, "Blockchain-Based Cyber-Physical Security for Electrical Vehicle Aided Smart Grid Ecosystem," *IEEE transactions on intelligent transportation systems*, vol. 22, no. 8, pp. 5178–5189, 2021.

[32] S. Dalal *et al.*, "Optimized LightGBM model for security and privacy issues in cyber-physical systems," *Transactions on Emerging Telecommunications Technologies*, vol. 34, no. 6, Jun. 2023, doi: 10.1002/ett.4771.

[33] L. Wu, H. Wang, K. Liu, L. Zhao, and Y. Xia, "Privacy and security trade-off in cyber-physical systems: An information theory-based framework," *International Journal of Robust and Nonlinear Control*, vol. 34, no. 8, pp. 5110–5125, May 2024, doi: 10.1002/rnc.7252.

[34] A. Alabdulatif, N. N. Thilakarathne, and Z. K. Lawal, "A Review on Security and Privacy Issues Pertaining to Cyber-Physical Systems in the Industry 5.0 Era," 2024, *Tech Science Press*. doi: 10.32604/cmc.2024.054150.

[35] F. A. Dotty and Y. Asnar, "Intrusion Detection System Architecture for Cyber-Physical System," in *2023 International Conference on Electrical Engineering and Informatics (ICEEI)*, 2023, pp. 1–6. doi: 10.1109/ICEEI59426.2023.10346839.

[36] X. Xiang, J. Cao, and W. Fan, "Lightweight privacy-preserving authentication mechanism in 5G-enabled industrial cyber physical systems," *Inf Sci (N Y)*, vol. 666, May 2024, doi: 10.1016/j.ins.2024.120391.

[37] Z. Liu, Q. Wang, and Y. Tang, "Design of a Cosimulation Platform with Hardware-in-the-Loop for Cyber-Attacks on Cyber-Physical Power Systems," *IEEE Access*, vol. 8, pp. 95997–96005, 2020, doi: 10.1109/ACCESS.2020.2995743.

[38] S. A. Mahboub, E. Sayed Ali Ahmed, R. A. Saeed, S. A. Mahboub, E. Sayed Ali Ahmed, and R. A. Saeed, "Smart IDS and IPS for

Cyber-Physical Systems," in *https://services.igi-global.com/resolvedoi/resolve.aspx?doi=10.4018/978-1-7998-5101-1.ch006*, IGI Global, 2021, pp. 109–136. doi: 10.4018/978-1-7998-5101-1.ch006.

[39] S. Li, S. Zhao, P. Yang, P. Andriotis, L. Xu, and Q. Sun, "Distributed Consensus Algorithm for Events Detection in Cyber Physical Systems."

[40] S. Li, S. Zhao, P. Yang, P. Andriotis, L. Xu, and Q. Sun, "Distributed Consensus Algorithm for Events Detection in Cyber Physical Systems."

[41] P. Urien, "Demonstrating Trusted Blockchain IoT Device Based on TLS-PSK Secure Element," in *5th Conference on Blockchain Research and Applications for Innovative Networks and Services, BRAINS 2023*, Institute of Electrical and Electronics Engineers Inc., 2023. doi: 10.1109/BRAINS59668.2023.10316975.

[42] A. Association for Computing Machinery. Special Interest Group on Security, *WiSec '08 : proceedings of the First ACM Conference on Wireless Network Security : Alexandria, Virginia, USA, March 31-April 2, 2008*. Association for Computing Machinery, 2008.

[43] M. and L. W. S. Greaves Brian and Coetzee, "Access Control in Cyber-Physical Spaces Using Virtual Perimeters," in *Proceedings of Sixth International Congress on Information and Communication Technology*, S. and D. N. and J. A. Yang Xin-She and Sherratt, Ed., Singapore: Springer Singapore, 2022, pp. 369–378.

[44] Clark Nathan, Maglaras A Leandros, Kantzavelou Ioanna, Chouliaras Nestoras, and Ferrag Mohamed Amine, "Blockchain Technology: Security and Privacy Issues," in *Blockchain Technology and Innovations in Business Processes*, T.-S. and S. T. and P. S. K. Patnaik Srikanta and Wang, Ed., Singapore: Springer Singapore, 2021, pp. 95–107. doi: 10.1007/978-981-33-6470-7_6.

[45] Y. Kareem, D. Djenouri, and E. Ghadafi, "A Survey on Emerging Blockchain Technology Platforms for Securing the Internet of Things," Aug. 01, 2024, *Multidisciplinary Digital Publishing Institute (MDPI)*. doi: 10.3390/fi16080285.

5

Physical Layer Security of 6G Vehicle Visible Light Communications for Cyber-physical Systems

Jupeng Ding[1,2], Chih-Lin I[3], Jintao Wang[4] and Hui Yang[5]

[1]College of Technology and Data, Yantai Nanshan University, China
[2]Key Laboratory of Signal Detection and Processing in Xinjiang Uygur Autonomous Region, School of Computer Science and Technology (School of Cyberspace Security), Xinjiang University, China
[3]China Mobile Research Institute, China
[4]Department of Electronic Engineering, Beijing National Research Center for Information Science and Technology, Tsinghua University, China
[5]Department of Electronic Engineering, Beijing National Research Center for Information Science and Technology, Tsinghua University, China

Email: jupeng7778@163.com; icl@chinamobile.com; wangjintao@tsinghua.edu.cn; huiyang@tsinghua.edu.cn

Abstract

As one complementary approach to the well-discussed radio frequency (RF) technology in 6G vehicular-to-vehicular communications (V2V) and 6G Internet of vehicles (IoV), light emitting diodes (LED)-based emerging vehicular visible light communication (VLC) is gaining the unprecedented focus and investigation, main thanks to the abundant optical spectrum resource, the high directivity, and the immunity to conventional electromagnetic interference of the utilized lightwave signal. Due to the broadcasting propagation nature of vehicle VLC signals, it is essential to improve the security performance metrics of the edge-cutting vehicle VLC, especially from the view of the physical layer. Numerous physical layer security (PLS) designs and schemes have been proposed to enhance security performance of vehicular

DOI: 10.1201/9788743801306-5

VLC. However, these works are limited to the studies of the emerging secure vehicular VLC with traditional Lambertian light beam configurations, which objectively cannot characterize the PLS performance of emerging vehicular VLC scenarios with emerging and distinctive non-Lambertian light beam patterns. To address this challenge, in this chapter, one typical secure vehicular VLC deploying representative non-Lambertian light beams is envisioned and comparatively studied from the view of PLS. Numerical results demonstrate that, for this typical V2V VLC scenario of stop mode, compared with 5.27 bps/Hz secrecy capacity of the vehicular VLC with benchmark Lambertian configuration, the effect of the non-Lambertian light beams could be up to about 2.66 bps/Hz for the PLS performance gain of the 6G IoV-oriented typical inter-vehicle VLC application.

5.1 Introduction

As one complementary solution to the well-discussed radio frequency (RF) technology in the upcoming 6G Internet of vehicles (IoV), the vehicular visible light communication (VLC) based on light-emitting diodes (LED) is gaining continuous attention and discussion since its inherent advantages in the lower cost, the lower complexity, the abundant light spectrum resource, the high directivity, the immunity to conventional electromagnetic interference, and the ubiquity of LED installed in vehicles [1-4]. At the same time, it must be noted that, like conventional RF vehicular communications, vehicle VLC could also be intercepted by potential malicious users due to the broadcasting propagation nature of vehicle VLC signals [5-8]. Particularly in conventional RF-based vehicular communications, physical layer security (PLS) has been widely explored by mainly utilizing physical layer characteristics to protect vehicular wireless links from eavesdroppers [9-11]. Similarly, following this research path, in the research community of vehicular VLC, numerous PLS designs and schemes have been actively proposed and anticipated to enhance security performance of vehicular VLC systems [12-16].

Specifically, the authors in [17] investigated VLC-IEEE 802.11p-based protocol to improve reliability and delay of safety message dissemination in hybrid multiphoton architecture for vehicular VLC. Moreover, the study in [18] presented a VLC-based information debugging system for IoV, with one new security enhancement optimization scheme based on artificial noise proposed. Furthermore, based on the successive usage of multiple deep neural network (DNN) blocks, the authors in [19] proposed one hybrid learning framework for jamming detection and pathloss predictions in hybrid RF-VLC vehicular networks. In addition, by leveraging the biometric fingerprints as authentication keys, the work in [20] enhanced the security of the vehicular platooning VLC network, which facilitates the secure vehicular VLC establishment within one platoon,

Objectively, these works are usually limited to the studies of the secure vehicular VLC with traditional Lambertian light beam configurations, which could not characterize the PLS performance of vehicular VLC scenarios adopting emerging and distinctive non-Lambertian light beam configurations. As for the diverse LED-based 6G outdoor applications, numerous fundamental works have illustrated that international LED luminaries manufacturers could design and implement the emerging and distinct non-Lambertian light beams well [21-23]. Additionally, that non-Lambertian spatial light beams have been successfully investigated in numerous technical branches of promising 6G VLC community [24-27], including but not limited to channel modeling and characterization [24], optical beam switching [25], non-orthogonal multiple access [26], and simultaneous lightwave information and power transfer [27]. The effects of distinct spatial light beams and the relevant performance features have been explored and demonstrated for the 6G VLC typical application scenarios and the research branch directions.

5.1.1 Key contributions of the chapter

Nevertheless, to the best of our knowledge, up to now, the potential PLS effects of the distinctive non-Lambertian light beams and the related spatial beam configurations are still waiting for a comparative study and numerical analysis in this branch domain of secure 6G vehicular VLC. Motivated by the above discussions, the PLS performance metrics of secure 6G emerging vehicular VLC transmission with the distinctive light beam configurations is comparatively studied in this chapter. Moreover, it is anticipated that this original work will pave the fundamental way for the following PLS study of the non-Lambertian secure 6G vehicular VLC.

5.1.2 Chapter organization

In this chapter, the PLS for Lambertian spatial light beam-based emerging vehicular VLC is presented in Section 5.2. The PLS for that typical non-Lambertian light beam-based emerging vehicular VLC is investigated

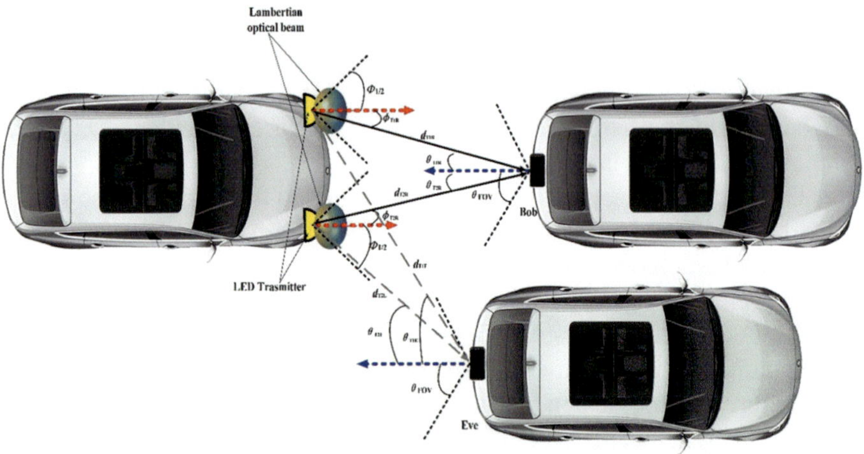

Figure 5.1 Schematic of PLS for Lambertian spatial light beam-based vehicular VLC for 6G IoV.

in Section 5.3. Numerical results and discussion evaluation are presented in Section 5.4. Finally, the Section 5.5 concludes this chapter.

5.2 PLS for Lambertian Spatial Beam Configurations based on 6G Emerging Vehicular VLC

5.2.1 Lambertian spatial light beam configurations

In performance analysis of current secure vehicular VLC, the LEDs generally follow the Lambertian light spatial beam. This beam characteristic means the light intensity is one cosine function of the viewing angle and can be given as [22]

$$I_{Lam}(\phi) = \frac{m_{Lam}+1}{2\pi}\cos^{m_{Lam}}(\phi), \tag{5.1}$$

where ϕ denotes the irradiance angle relative to the light axis of LED light source, and m_{Lam} denotes the Lambertian order. The order m_{Lam} can be given by

$$m_{Lam} = -\frac{\mathrm{In}2}{\mathrm{In}\left(\cos\phi_{1/2}\right)}, \tag{5.2}$$

where $\phi_{1/2}$ is half-power angle of the Lambertian light beam [22]. For clarity, in Figure 5.1, the application scenario of PLS for Lambertian light beam-based vehicular VLC for 6G IoV is illustrated.

5.2.2 Lambertian 6G secure vehicular VLC link gain

For the well-known Lambertian spatial light beam configuration, the secure vehicular VLC link gain includes a line of sight (LOS) and non-line of sight (NLOS) components. And for the convenience of analysis, the NLOS components are usually ignored. Such that, between the jth Lambertian headlight source S_j^{Lam} of host vehicle and tail light receiver R of the target vehicle, the related secure vehicular VLC link gain is given as [22]

$$H(S_j^{\text{Lam}}, R) = \begin{cases} \dfrac{A_R}{d_j^2} I_{\text{Lam}}(\phi)\cos(\theta) g(\theta), & 0 \le \theta \le \theta_{\text{FOV}} \\ 0, & \theta > \theta_{\text{FOV}} \end{cases} = \begin{cases} \dfrac{A_R}{d_j^2}\left(\dfrac{m_{\text{Lam}}+1}{2\pi}\cos^{m_{\text{Lam}}}(\phi)\right)\cos(\theta) g(\theta), & 0 \le \theta \le \theta_{\text{FOV}} \\ 0, & \theta > \theta_{\text{FOV}} \end{cases}, \tag{5.3}$$

where d_j is the LOS distance between the jth Lambertian light source S_j^{Lam} of the host vehicle and the PD of light receiver R of the target vehicle, A_R denotes the physical area of photodetector (PD) for the tail light receiver, $g(\theta)$ is the light concentrator gain, θ denotes the incidence angle from the Lambertian light source S^{Lam} of host vehicle and light receiver R, and θ_{FOV} denotes the vehicle receiver field of view (FOV). Specifically, the gain of light concentrator $g(\theta)$ could be given by

$$g(\theta) = \begin{cases} \dfrac{n^2}{\sin^2(\theta_{\text{FOV}})}, & 0 \le \theta \le \theta_{\text{FOV}} \\ 0, & \theta > \theta_{\text{FOV}} \end{cases}, \tag{5.4}$$

where n denotes internal refractive index for receiver.

5.2.3 PLS performance metrics for Lambertian 6G secure vehicular VLC

Following the study of Ding J et al., as shown in Figure 5.1, for the legitimate receiver, i.e., target vehicle Bob, the signal-to-noise ratio (SNR) of secure vehicular VLC is given by [25-27]

$$\mathrm{SNR}_{\mathrm{Bob}}^{\mathrm{Lam}} = \frac{(rI_{\mathrm{TX}})^2}{N_0 N_t^2}\left(\sum_{j=1}^{N_t} H(S_j^{\mathrm{Lam}}, R_{\mathrm{Bob}})\right)^2$$
$$= \begin{cases} \dfrac{(rI_{\mathrm{TX}})^2}{N_0 N_t^2}\left(\sum_{j=1}^{N_t}\left(\dfrac{A_R}{d_{\mathrm{T}_j\mathrm{R}}^2}\left(\dfrac{m_{\mathrm{Lam}}+1}{2\pi}\cos^{m_{\mathrm{Lam}}}\left(\phi_{\mathrm{T}_j\mathrm{R}}\right)\right)\cos\left(\theta_{\mathrm{T}_j\mathrm{R}}\right)g\left(\theta_{\mathrm{T}_j\mathrm{R}}\right)\right)\right)^2, & 0 \le \theta_{\mathrm{T}_j\mathrm{R}} \le \theta_{\mathrm{FOV}} \\ 0, & \theta_{\mathrm{T}_j\mathrm{R}} > \theta_{\mathrm{FOV}} \end{cases} \tag{5.5}$$

where r denotes the PDs responsivity, I_{TX} is the emitted signal power of all headlight transmitters, N_0 is the noise power, $N_t = 2$ is the amount of the headlight transmitters, while $d_{\mathrm{T}_j\mathrm{R}}$ is the LOS distance between the jth Lambertian source S_j^{Lam} of host vehicle and the legitimate receiver PD, $\phi_{\mathrm{T}_j\mathrm{R}}$ denotes that irradiance angle relative to the jth Lambertian source S_j^{Lam} of the host vehicle to the PD of the legitimate receiver, $\theta_{\mathrm{T}_j\mathrm{R}}$ denotes the incidence angle from the jth Lambertian source S_j^{Lam} of host vehicle to the legitimate light receiver R. In a typical secure vehicular VLC scenario, at the light receiver the shot noise denotes one dominant contributor. Thus, the noise power is given as [22]

$$N_0 = 2qI_{\mathrm{bg}}B + \frac{4K_{\mathrm{b}}TB}{R_{\mathrm{f}}}, \tag{5.6}$$

where K_{b} denotes the Boltzmann constant, T denotes the absolute temperature, B is the system modulation bandwidth, q denotes the electron charge in coulombs, I_{bg} denotes the current due to background light, and R_{f} denotes the feedback resistance of the trans-impedance amplifier (TIA) [22].

Similarly, for that malicious receiver, i.e., eavesdropper vehicle Eve, as shown in Figure 5.1, the SNR of emerging secure vehicular VLC can be given by

$$\mathrm{SNR}_{Eve}^{Lam} = \frac{(rI_{TX})^2}{N_0 N_t^2}\left(\sum_{j=1}^{N_t} H(S_j^{Lam}, R_{Eve})\right)^2$$

$$= \begin{cases} \dfrac{(rI_{TX})^2}{N_0 N_t^2}\left(\sum_{j=1}^{N_t}\left(\dfrac{A_R}{d_{T_jE}^2}\left(\dfrac{m_{Lam}+1}{2\pi}\cos^{m_{Lam}}\left(\phi_{T_jE}\right)\right)\cos\left(\theta_{T_jE}\right)g\left(\theta_{T_jE}\right)\right)\right)^2, & 0 \le \theta_{T_jE} \le \theta_{FOV} \\ 0, & \theta_{T_jE} > \theta_{FOV} \end{cases} \quad (5.7)$$

where $d_{\mathrm{T}_j\mathrm{E}}$ is the LOS distance between the jth Lambertian source S_j^{Lam} of host vehicle and the malicious receiver PD, $\phi_{\mathrm{T}_j\mathrm{E}}$ is the irradiance angle relative to the jth Lambertian light source S_j^{Lam} of the host vehicle to the PD of the malicious receiver, $\theta_{\mathrm{T}_j\mathrm{E}}$ denotes the incidence angle from the jth Lambertian source S_j^{Lam} of host vehicle to the malicious light receiver R. The secrecy capacity (SC) of the legitimate optical receiver, also known as Bob, is given by [12]

$$C_{\mathrm{Lam}} = \left[\log_2(1+\mathrm{SNR}_{\mathrm{Bob}}^{\mathrm{Lam}}) - \log_2(1+\mathrm{SNR}_{\mathrm{Eve}}^{\mathrm{Lam}})\right]^+, \quad (5.8)$$

where [b]+ denotes the max{0, b}.

5.3 PLS for Non-Lambertian Spatial Beam Configurations based 6G Secure Vehicular VLC

5.3.1 Non-Lambertian spatial light beam configurations

Without loss of generality, in this chapter, two representative non-Lambertian light beams are considered for the discussed secure vehicular visible light communications. Specifically, these beams are derived from the LUXEON Rebel LED and NSPW345CS LED.

For the secure vehicular VLC case of the LUXEON Rebel non-Lambertian light beam, the radiation intensity can be given by one sum of two Gaussian functions [23]

$$I_{\mathrm{Rebel}}(\phi) = \sum_{i=1}^{N_1} g_{1i}^{\mathrm{Rebel}} \exp\left[-\ln 2\left(\frac{|\phi| - g_{2i}^{\mathrm{Rebel}}}{g_{3i}^{\mathrm{Rebel}}}\right)^2\right], \quad (5.9)$$

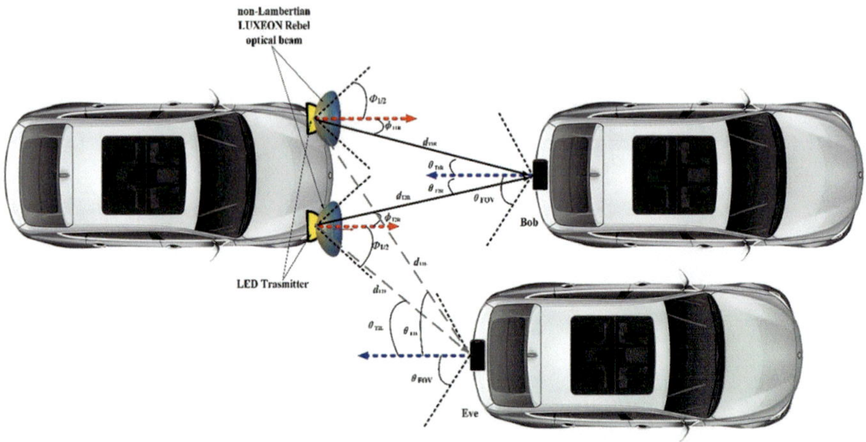

Figure 5.2 Schematic of PLS for LUXEON Rebel spatial light beam-based vehicular VLC.

where the coefficient values are identified as $N_1 = 2$, $g_{11}^{\text{Rebel}} = 0.76$, $g_{21}^{\text{Rebel}} = 0°$, $g_{31}^{\text{Rebel}} = 29°$, $g_{12}^{\text{Rebel}} = 1.10$, $g_{22}^{\text{Rebel}} = 45°$, and $g_{32}^{\text{Rebel}} = 21°$. Correspondingly, the application scenario of PLS for LUXEON Rebel beam-based emerging vehicular VLC for 6G IoV are illustrated in Figure 5.2.

As for the emerging secure vehicular VLC case of the NSPW345CS light beam pattern, the radiation intensity could be given by one sum of two Gaussian functions [23]

$$I_{\text{NSPW}}(\phi,\alpha) = \sum_{i=1}^{N_2} g_{1i}^{\text{NSPW}} \exp\left[-(\text{In}2)(|\phi| - g_{2i}^{\text{NSPW}})^2\left(\frac{\cos^2\alpha}{(g_{3i}^{\text{NSPW}})^2} + \frac{\sin^2\alpha}{(g_{4i}^{\text{NSPW}})^2}\right)\right], \quad (5.10)$$

where α is the azimuth angle, the coefficient values of Gaussian functions are given as $N_2 = 2$, $g_{11}^{\text{NSPW}} = 0.13$, $g_{21}^{\text{NSPW}} = 45°$, $g_{31}^{\text{NSPW}} = g_{41}^{\text{NSPW}} = 18°$, $g_{12}^{\text{NSPW}} = 1$, $g_{22}^{\text{NSPW}} = 0$, $g_{32}^{\text{NSPW}} = 38°$, and $g_{42}^{\text{NSPW}} = 22°$. Similarly, in Figure 5.3, the 3D display of NSPW345CS beam pattern is described.

5.3.2 Non-Lambertian 6G secure vehicular VLC link gain

The DC link gain of secure vehicular VLC based on non-Lambertian beam is tightly related to the light radiation pattern. Accordingly, for the LUXEON Rebel beam case, the VLC link gain between the jth non-Lambertian headlight source S_j^{Rebel} of the host vehicle and the tail light receiver R of that target vehicle is given by

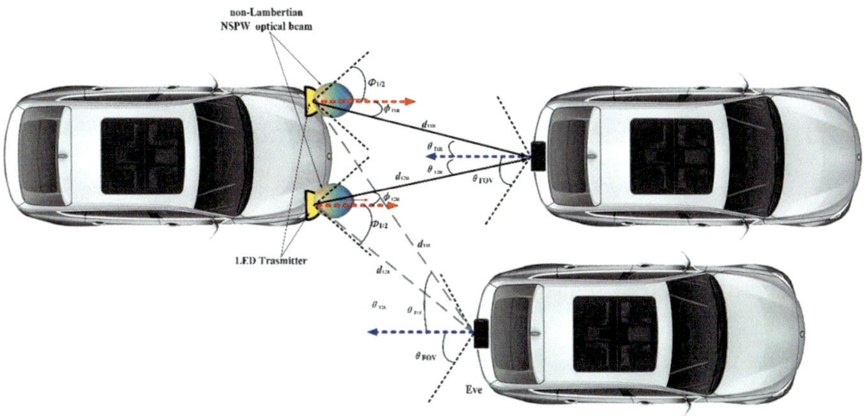

Figure 5.3 Schematic of PLS for asymmetric NSPW light beam-based vehicular VLC.

$$H(S_j^{\text{Rebel}}, R) = \begin{cases} \dfrac{A_R I_{\text{Rebel}}(\phi)}{P_{\text{normRebel}} d_j^2} \cos(\theta) g(\theta), & 0 \le \theta \le \theta_{\text{FOV}} \\ 0, & \theta > \theta_{\text{FOV}} \end{cases}$$

$$= \begin{cases} \dfrac{A_R}{P_{\text{normRebel}} d_j^2} \left(\sum_{i=1}^{N_1} g_{1i}^{\text{Re bel}} \exp\left[-\ln 2 \left(\dfrac{|\phi| - g_{2i}^{\text{Re bel}}}{g_{3i}^{\text{Re bel}}} \right)^2 \right] \right) \cos(\theta) g(\theta), \\ \qquad 0 \le \theta \le \theta_{\text{FOV}} \\ 0, \qquad \theta > \theta_{\text{FOV}} \end{cases} \tag{5.11}$$

where $P_{\text{normRebel}}$ is the LUXEON Rebel beam's emitted power normalization factor, to ensure that the total emitted power equals 1 W.

Similarly, for the NSPW345CS beam case, the DC link gain could be replaced by

$$H(S_j^{\text{NSPW}}, R) = \begin{cases} \dfrac{A_R I_{\text{NSPW}}(\phi, \alpha)}{P_{\text{normNSPW}} d_j^2} \cos\theta g(\theta) r, & 0 \le \theta \le \theta_{FOV} \\ 0, & \theta > \theta_{FOV} \end{cases}$$

$$= \begin{cases} \dfrac{A_R}{P_{\text{normNSPW}} d_j^2} \left(\sum_{i=1}^{N_2} g_{1i}^{\text{NSPW}} \exp\left[-(\text{In}2)(|\phi| - g_{2i}^{\text{NSPW}})^2 \left(\dfrac{\cos^2\alpha}{(g_{3i}^{\text{NSPW}})^2} + \dfrac{\sin^2\alpha}{(g_{4i}^{\text{NSPW}})^2} \right) \right] \right) \\ \times \cos(\theta) g(\theta), \qquad 0 \le \theta \le \theta_{\text{FOV}} \\ 0, \qquad \theta > \theta_{\text{FOV}} \end{cases} \tag{5.12}$$

where P_{normNSPW} denotes the NSPW345CS beam's power normalization factor, for ensuring the whole emitted power equals 1 W as well.

5.3.3 PLS performance metrics for non-Lambertian 6G secure vehicular VLC

In the studied configuration of LUXEON Rebel beam, the secure links are implemented between the two LUXEON Rebel non-Lambertian sources and the receiver located at rear center of vehicle ahead. In this scenario, for the legitimate receiver, i.e., target vehicle Bob, as shown in Figure 5.2, the SNR at the light receiver $\text{SNR}_{\text{Bob}}^{\text{Rebel}}$ is given by

$$\text{SNR}_{\text{Bob}}^{\text{Rebel}} = \frac{(rI_{\text{TX}})^2}{N_0 N_t^2}\left(\sum_{j=1}^{N_t} H(S_j^{\text{Rebel}}, R_{\text{Bob}})\right)^2$$
$$= \begin{cases} \frac{(rI_{\text{TX}})^2}{N_0 N_t^2}\left(\sum_{j=1}^{N_t}\left(\frac{A_R}{P_{\text{normRebel}} d_{\text{T}_j\text{R}}^2}\left(\sum_{i=1}^{N_1} g_{1i}^{\text{Rebel}} \exp\left[-\ln 2\left(\frac{\left|\phi_{\text{T}_j\text{R}}\right| - g_{2i}^{\text{Rebel}}}{g_{3i}^{\text{Rebel}}}\right)^2\right]\right) \times\cos(\theta_{\text{T}_j\text{R}})g(\theta_{\text{T}_j\text{R}})\right)\right)^2, & 0 \le \theta_{\text{T}_j\text{R}} \le \theta_{\text{FOV}} \\ 0, & \theta_{\text{T}_j\text{R}} > \theta_{\text{FOV}} \end{cases} \tag{5.13}$$

Accordingly, the legitimate receiver, i.e., Bob's secrecy capacity (SC) under LUXEON Rebel beam configuration, is given by

$$C_{\text{Rebel}} = \left[\log_2(1 + \text{SNR}_{\text{Bob}}^{\text{Rebel}}) - \log_2(1 + \text{SNR}_{\text{Eve}}^{\text{Rebel}})\right]^+, \tag{5.14}$$

where $\text{SNR}_{\text{EVE}}^{\text{Rebel}}$ denotes the SNR of secure vehicular VLC for the malicious receiver, i.e., eavesdropper vehicle Eve, as shown in Figure 5.2 under LUXEON Rebel beam configuration, which could be easily derived according to eqn (5.7) and (5.13).

In the left NSPW345CS non-Lambertian configuration, the secure vehicular links are connected between the two non-Lambertian NSPW345CS sources and the light receiver located at rear center of vehicle ahead as well. For legitimate receiver, i.e., target vehicle Bob, as shown in Figure 5.3, the resultant SNR at the light receiver $\text{SNR}_{\text{Bob}}^{\text{NSPW}}$ is given by

$$\mathrm{SNR}_{\mathrm{Bob}}^{\mathrm{NSPW}} = \frac{(rI_{\mathrm{TX}})^2}{N_0 N_t^2}\left(\sum_{j=1}^{N_t} H(S_j^{\mathrm{NSPW}}, R_{\mathrm{Bob}})\right)^2$$

$$= \begin{cases} \dfrac{(rI_{\mathrm{TX}})^2}{N_0 N_t^2}\left(\sum_{j=1}^{N_t}\left(\dfrac{A_R\left(\sum_{i=1}^{N_2} g_{1i}^{\mathrm{NSPW}} \exp\left[-(\mathrm{In}2)(\left|\phi_{\mathrm{T}_j\mathrm{R}}\right| - g_{2i}^{\mathrm{NSPW}})^2\left(\dfrac{\cos^2\alpha_{\mathrm{T}_j\mathrm{R}}}{(g_{3i}^{\mathrm{NSPW}})^2} + \dfrac{\sin^2\alpha_{\mathrm{T}_j\mathrm{R}}}{(g_{4i}^{\mathrm{NSPW}})^2}\right)\right]\right)}{P_{\mathrm{normNSPW}} d_{\mathrm{T}_j\mathrm{R}}^{\ 2}} \times \cos\left(\theta_{\mathrm{T}_j\mathrm{R}}\right) g\left(\theta_{\mathrm{T}_j\mathrm{R}}\right)\right)\right)^2, & 0 \le \theta_{\mathrm{T}_j\mathrm{R}} \le \theta_{\mathrm{FOV}} \\ 0, & \theta_{\mathrm{T}_j\mathrm{R}} > \theta_{\mathrm{FOV}} \end{cases} \tag{5.15}$$

Accordingly, the legitimate receiver, i.e., Bob's SC of under NSPW345CS beam configuration, could be given by

$$C_{\mathrm{NSPW}} = \left[\log_2(1 + SNR_{\mathrm{Bob}}^{\mathrm{NSPW}}) - \log_2(1 + SNR_{\mathrm{Eve}}^{\mathrm{NSPW}})\right]^+, \tag{5.16}$$

where $\mathrm{SNR}_{\mathrm{Eve}}^{\mathrm{NSPW}}$ denotes the SNR of secure vehicular VLC for the malicious receiver, i.e., eavesdropper Eve, under NSPW345CS beam configuration, as shown in Figure 5.3. This could be easily derived according to eqn (5.7) and (5.15).

5.4 Numerical Results and Discussions

In the following portion, for emerging secure vehicular application scenario for 6G IoV, the secrecy capacity performance for this concerned baseline Lambertian and the novel two non-Lambertian light configurations based on vehicular VLC secure transmission are evaluated and analyzed. In addition, Table 5.1 summarizes the main system parameters of this chapter [22, 23]. Particularly, following the study of [12], for all concerned vehicles, the vehicle width is set as 1.6 m, while for the stop mode and traffic mode, inter-vehicle spacing is set as 2 m and 8 m accordingly. Moreover, the concerned lane width is typically set as 4 m.

As shown in Figure 5.4(a), once the eavesdropper vehicle Eve is fixed at the location with 8 m longitudinal displacement along the lane, the secrecy capacity of emerging vehicular VLC for emerging 6G is deeply affected by the target vehicle Bob's longitudinal displacement along the vehicle lane, regardless of applied light beam configuration. When the target vehicle

Table 5.1 Main parameters configuration.

Parameter	**Value**
LED optical source spacing	1.20 m
Emitted power of transmitter	1 W
Absolute temperature	298 K
Background light current	5100 μA
Receiver field of view	90°
LED Lambertian index	1
Responsively of PD	0.28 A/W
Physical area of PD	1 cm^2
LED modulation bandwidth	20 MHz
Concentrator refractive index	1.54
Modulation	OOK-NRZ
Channel	LOS

Bob's longitudinal displacement is increased to 8 m from the original 2 m, the secrecy capacity is reduced to 0.47 bps/Hz from the original 7.46 bps/Hz. Once LUXEON Rebel light beam is applied, the secrecy capacity is reduced to 0.06 bps/Hz from the original 6.90 bps/Hz, with the above longitudinal displacement varied to 8 m from the 2 m. As for the last NSPW345CS non-Lambertian beam configuration, one similar phenomenon and change trend is observed. At the same time, the respective secrecy capacity is reduced to 1.20 bps/Hz from the original 7.99 bps/Hz with the same longitudinal displacement increase for target vehicle Bob. The above numerical results indicate that compared with the Lambertian configuration, the secrecy capacity gain is varied to 0.73 bps/Hz from the original 0.53 bps/Hz via adopting novel NSPW345CS beam with rotated asymmetrically spatial radiation characteristics, compared to the counterpart of the Lambertian configuration.

As shown in Figure 5.4(b), a similar change trend of secrecy capacity reduction could be identified when the longitudinal displacement for target vehicle Bob and eavesdropper vehicle Eve is simultaneously increased to 8 m from the original 2 m along the lane. Although the superiority of the target vehicle Bob is mitigated by the simultaneous displacement of the eavesdropper Eve, the secrecy capacity gain can be observed by applying NSPW345CS non-Lambertian configuration. Specifically, for that most challenging situation with the longitudinal displacement of 8 m, the secrecy capacity is enhanced to about 1.20 bps/Hz by adopting the NSPW345CS non-Lambertian beam from the original about 0.47 bps/Hz of the baseline Lambertian configuration, which means that about 155% improvement ratio for secrecy capacity could be still achieved in this harsh longitudinal displacement condition.

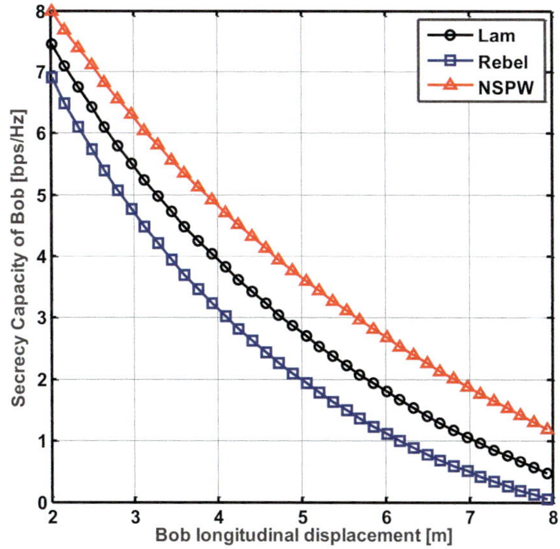

(a)

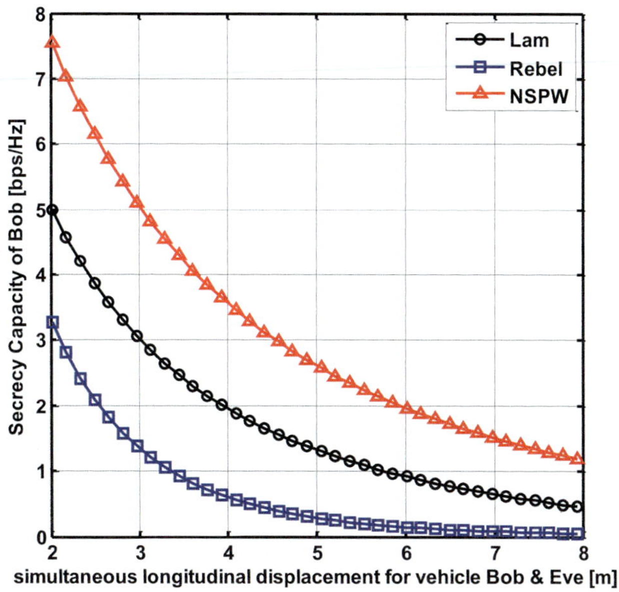

(b)

Figure 5.4 Secrecy capacity of emerging vehicular VLC for the case of (a) target vehicle's different longitudinal displacement along the vehicle lane, (b) simultaneous longitudinal displacement for target vehicle Bob and eavesdropper vehicle Eve along the lane.

As shown in Figure 5.5(a), once the target vehicle Bob is fixed at the location with 8 m longitudinal displacement along the lane, the secrecy capacity of vehicular communications is deeply degraded by the reduction of eavesdropper vehicle's longitudinal displacement along the lane, regardless of the applied light beam configuration. For case of baseline Lambertian beam, the total secrecy outage could be observed and kept once the eavesdropper's longitudinal displacement is reduced to less than about 7 m since the sufficient superior channel condition could be obtained and maintained for the eavesdropper vehicle Eve. Thanks to the unique rotated asymmetrically emission characteristic of NSPW345CS beam, the respective channel condition improvement is more limited, which makes the total secrecy capacity outage not appear until the longitudinal displacement for Eve is reduced to less than about 4.5 m. Moreover, the special secrecy capacity recovery could be observed when the longitudinal displacement for Eve is reduced to less than about 3 m since the quite sharp radiation intensity reduction for this novel non-Lambertian beam in these emission directions, which fundamentally counteracts the transmission channel improvement provided by the so little longitudinal displacement to these Eve locations.

Figure 5.5(b) shows that the secrecy capacity could be apparently improved for all concerned light beam configurations by increasing the lateral displacement for eavesdropper vehicle Eve within the neighboring lane. In particular, when the lateral displacement is changed to 0.8 m from the initial 0 m, the secrecy capacity is almost linearly increased to 7.06 bps/Hz from the original 5.18 bps/Hz for baseline Lambertian beam configuration. The reason for this result is that further introducing more lateral displacement along the direction perpendicular to the traffic lane gradually degrades the achievable transmission capacity of eavesdropper vehicle Eve. In contrast, the achievable transmission capacity difference between the target vehicle, Bob, and the eavesdropper vehicle, Eve, is enlarged accordingly, to a large extent.

As shown in Figure 5.6, the secrecy capacity of vehicular communications reaches the saturation status once the emitted power is increased to about 4 W, regardless of the applied light beam, which indicates that the more emitted power will not enlarge the achievable VLC transmission capacity between the target vehicle Bob and the eavesdropper vehicle Eve. For the stop mode, the saturation status of secrecy capacity is about 7.93 bps/Hz for impressive NSPW345CS non-Lambertian beam, which means that steady about 2.66 bps/Hz capacity gain can be obtained compared to Lambertian beam configuration with about 5.27 bps/Hz secrecy capacity performance. On the other hand, in Figure 5.6(b), similar results can be found for the traffic

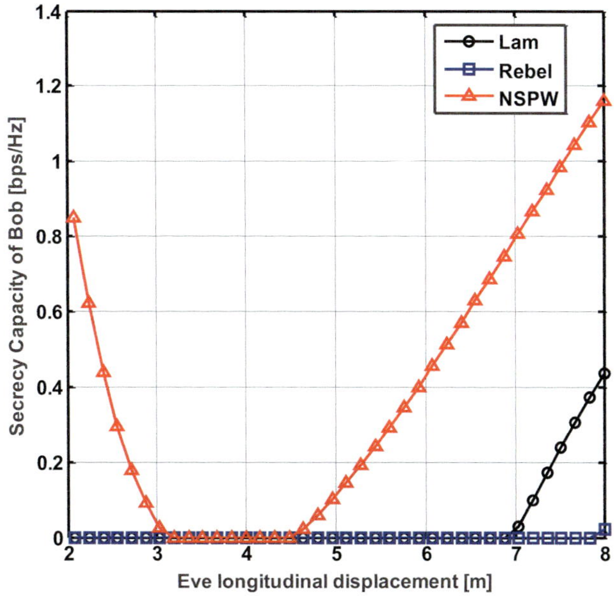

(a)

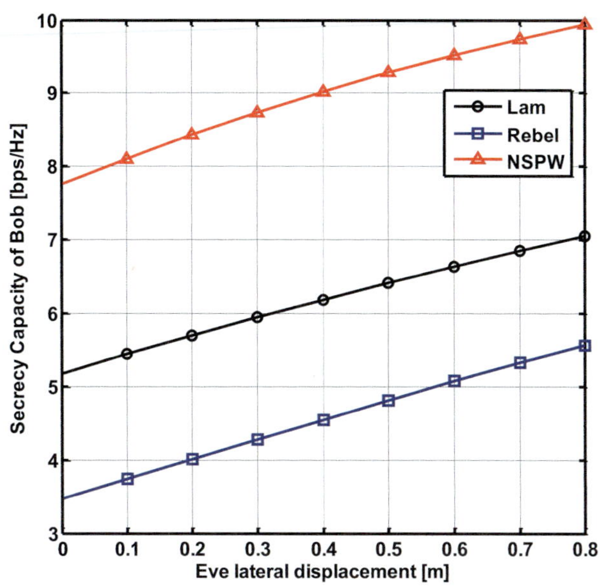

(b)

Figure 5.5 Secrecy capacity of emerging vehicular VLC for the case of (a) eavesdropper vehicle's longitudinal displacement along the lane, (b) eavesdropper vehicle's lateral displacement.

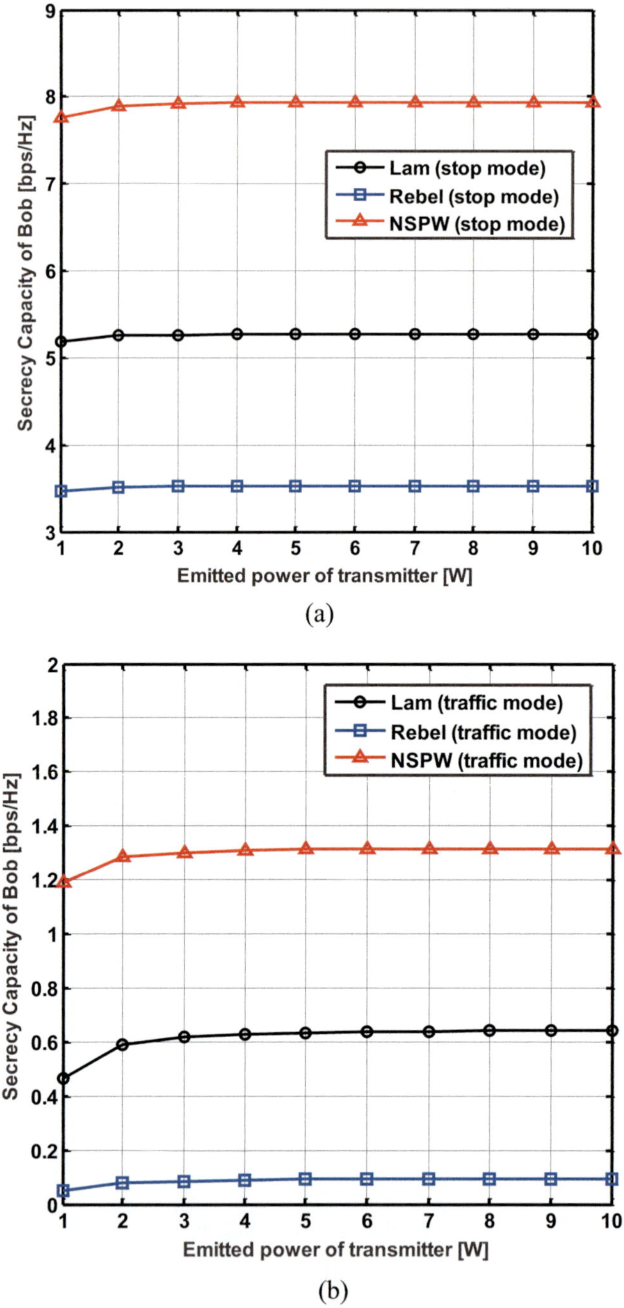

Figure 5.6 Secrecy capacity of emerging vehicular VLC versus the emitted power for the case of (a) stop mode, (b) traffic mode.

mode with more challenging longitudinal displacement 8 m. Numerically, the saturation status of the secrecy capacity is varied to about 1.31 bps/Hz for the impressive NSPW345CS non-Lambertian beam, which means that robust about 0.68 bps/Hz secrecy capacity gain could be achieved compared to Lambertian beam configuration with about 0.63 bps/Hz capacity performance.

5.5 Conclusions and Future Directions

It is expected that this work could fill the gap of the PLS for secure vehicular communication based on conventional Lambertian light beam configurations, which definitely cannot describe the PLS performance of the secure vehicular communication adopting emerging non-Lambertian light beam setting. This chapter uses the representative non-Lambertian LED light pattern to construct the secure inter-vehicle transmission links. Accordingly, for the case of traffic mode, this average secrecy capacity could be increased to about 1.31 bps/Hz from about 0.63 bps/Hz for the benchmark secure inter-vehicle VLC transmission link. In the near future, based on diverse non-Lambertian light beams, the PLS study of vehicular vehicular communication using visible light can be further extended to the secure platoon management and control, secure hybrid communications, artificial noise, resource management, multiple-input multiple-output precoding, transmit beam selection, and other key techniques design.

Acknowledgment

This work was supported in part by the National Natural Science Foundation of China (Grants No. 62061043), Yantai Nanshan University Research and Development Fund Project (Grants No. 2025KJ01001), Tianshan Cedar Project of Xinjiang Uygur Autonomous Region (Grants No. 2020XS27), and High-level Talents Introduction Project in Autonomous Region (Grants No. 042419004).

References

[1] Zadobrischi, Eduard. "The Concept regarding Vehicular Communications Based on Visible Light Communication and the IoT" *Electronics* 12, no. 6: 1359. 2023. https://doi.org/10.3390/electronics12061359

[2] H. Mei, J. Ding, J. Zheng, X. Chen and W. Liu, "Overview of Vehicle Optical Wireless Communications," *IEEE Access*, vol. 8, pp. 173461–173480, 2020, doi: 10.1109/ACCESS.2020.3024854.

[3] M. Z. Chowdhury, M. K. Hasan, M. Shahjalal, M. T. Hossan and Y. M. Jang, "Optical wireless hybrid networks: trends, opportunities, challenges, and research directions," *IEEE Communications Surveys & Tutorials*, vol. 22, no. 2, pp. 930–966, Secondquarter 2020.

[4] S. Refas, D. Acheli, S. Yahia and Y. Meraihi, "Energy Harvesting Based on SLIPT in I2V-VLC System," 2023 International Conference on Advances in Electronics, Control and Communication Systems (ICAECCS), BLIDA, Algeria, 2023, pp. 1–5, doi: 10.1109/ICAECCS56710.2023.10105093.

[5] T. Pal, G. Singh, V. A. Bohara and A. Srivastava, "Optical IRS Aided B5G V2V Solution for Road Safety Applications," 2022 IEEE International Conference on Advanced Networks and Telecommunications Systems (ANTS), Gandhinagar, Gujarat, India, 2022, pp. 169–174, doi: 10.1109/ANTS56424.2022.10227754.

[6] S. Refas, D. Acheli, S. Yahia and Y. Meraihi, "Energy Harvesting Based on SLIPT in I2V-VLC System," 2023 International Conference on Advances in Electronics, Control and Communication Systems (ICAECCS), BLIDA, Algeria, 2023, pp. 1–5, doi: 10.1109/ICAECCS56710.2023.10105093.

[7] S. Yahia, Y. Meraihi, A. Ramdane-Cherif, T. D. Ho and H. B. Eldeeb, "Enhancement of Vehicular Visible Light Communication Using Spherical Detector and Custom Lens Combinations," *IEEE Access*, vol. 11, pp. 21600–21611, 2023, doi: 10.1109/ACCESS.2023.3250397.

[8] S. Refas et al., "Performance Analysis of Bidirectional Multi-Hop Vehicle-to-Vehicle Visible Light Communication," *IEEE Access*, vol. 11, pp. 129436–129448, 2023, doi: 10.1109/ACCESS.2023.3333046.

[9] L. Mucchi et al., "Physical-Layer Security in 6G Networks," *IEEE Open Journal of the Communications Society*, vol. 2, pp. 1901-1914, 2021.

[10] M. Rice et al., "Physical-Layer Security for Vehicle-to-Everything Networks: Increasing Security While Maintaining Reliable Communications," *IEEE Vehicular Technology Magazine*, vol. 15, no. 3, pp. 68–76, Sept. 2020.

[11] X. Luo, Y. Liu, H. -H. Chen and Q. Guo, "Physical Layer Security in Intelligently Connected Vehicle Networks," *IEEE Network*, vol. 34, no. 5, pp. 232–239, September/October 2020.

[12] Rana Shaaban, Saleh Faruque, " Cyber security vulnerabilities for outdoor vehicular visible light communication in secure platoon network: Review, power distribution, and signal to noise ratio analysis," *Physical Communication*, vol. 40, no. 5, pp. 101094, September/October 2020.

[13] S. Yahia, V. Loscri and P. Saxena, "Enhancing Security in 6G Vehicular Networks: Leveraging VLC and MMW Integration and Cooperative

Relaying Technique," 2023 IEEE Intl Conf on Dependable, Autonomic and Secure Computing, Intl Conf on Pervasive Intelligence and Computing, Intl Conf on Cloud and Big Data Computing, Intl Conf on Cyber Science and Technology Congress, Abu Dhabi, United Arab Emirates, 2023, pp. 0711–0716.

[14] B. Elghorab, S. M. Abd El-atty, I. M. El-Dokkany, F. E. Abd El-Samie and M. S. Arafa, "Securing Vehicular Platoons with Visible Light Communication and Fingerprint-based Authentication," 2023 3rd International Conference on Electronic Engineering (ICEEM), Menouf, Egypt, 2023, pp. 1–5, doi: 10.1109/ICEEM58740.2023.10319599.

[15] S. Ucar, S. C. Ergen and O. Ozkasap, "Security vulnerabilities of IEEE 802.11p and visible light communication based platoon," 2016 IEEE Vehicular Networking Conference (VNC), Columbus, OH, USA, 2016, pp. 1–4, doi: 10.1109/VNC.2016.7835972.

[16] S. Ucar, S. C. Ergen and O. Ozkasap, "IEEE 802.11p and Visible Light Hybrid Communication Based Secure Autonomous Platoon," *IEEE Transactions on Vehicular Technology*, vol. 67, no. 9, pp. 8667–8681, Sept. 2018, doi: 10.1109/TVT.2018.2840846.

[17] S. Ucar, S. C. Ergen and O. Ozkasap, "Visible light communication assisted safety message dissemination in multiplatoon," 2017 IEEE International Black Sea Conference on Communications and Networking (BlackSeaCom), Istanbul, Turkey, 2017, pp. 1–5, doi: 10.1109/BlackSeaCom.2017.8277704.

[18] C. Gu et al., "Visible Light Secure Communication Method for Internet of Vehicles," 2024 27th International Conference on Computer Supported Cooperative Work in Design (CSCWD), Tianjin, China, 2024, pp. 139–144, doi: 10.1109/CSCWD61410.2024.10580847.

[19] A. Ullah, W. Choi and S. Coleri, "Path Loss Estimation and Jamming Detection in Hybrid RF-VLC Vehicular Networks: A Machine-Learning Framework," *IEEE Sensors Journal*, vol. 23, no. 24, pp. 31325–31336, 15 Dec.15, 2023, doi: 10.1109/JSEN.2023.3329490.

[20] B. Elghorab, S. M. Abd El-atty, I. M. El-Dokkany, F. E. Abd El-Samie and M. S. Arafa, "Securing Vehicular Platoons with Visible Light Communication and Fingerprint-based Authentication," 2023 3rd International Conference on Electronic Engineering (ICEEM), Menouf, Egypt, 2023, pp. 1–5, doi: 10.1109/ICEEM58740.2023.10319599.

[21] S. Wang, K. Wang, F. Chen, S. Liu, "Design of primary optics for LED chip array in road lighting application," *Optics Express*, vol. 19, no. S4, pp. A716–A724, 2011.

[22] T. Komine, M. Nakagawa, "Fundamental analysis for visible-light communication system using LED lights," *IEEE Transactions on Consumer Electronics*, vol. 50, no. 1, pp. 100–107, 2004.
[23] I. Moreno, C. Sun, "Modeling the radiation pattern of LEDs," *Optics Express*, vol. 16, no. 3, pp. 1808–1819, 2008.
[24] J. Ding, C. I, Z. Xu, "Indoor optical wireless channel characteristics with distinct source radiation patterns," *IEEE Photonics Journal*, vol. 8, no. 1, pp. 1–15, 2015.
[25] J. Ding, C. -L. I, J. Wang and H. Yang, "Optical Beams Switching-Based Coverage Enhancement Scheme for Compact Visible Light Communications," *Journal of Lightwave Technology*, vol. 40, no. 18, pp. 6139–6150, 15 Sept.15, 2022.
[26] J. Ding, C. -L. I, J. Wang and H. Yang, "NOMA Visible Light Communications with Distinct Optical Beam Configurations," *Photonics*, vol. 11, no. 10, pp. 944(1–16), Oct. 2024.
[27] Jupeng Ding, Chih-Lin I, Jintao Wang and Jian Song, "Performance Evaluation of Non-Lambertian SLIPT for 6G Visible Light Communication Systems," *Photonics*, vol. 11, no. 9, pp. 856(1–17), Sep. 2024.

6

Hardware Security and Privacy for Cyber-physical Systems

Kinzah Noor[1], Hasnain Ahmad[2], Mercy Oka Ebute[3] and Agbotiname Lucky Imoize[4]

[1]Office of Research Innovation and Commercialization, University of Management and Technology, Pakistan
[2]Department of Computer Science, COMSATS University Islamabad-Lahore Campus, Pakistan
[3]Department of Accounting, Anderson School of Management, University of New Mexico, USA
[4]Department of Electrical and Electronics Engineering, Faculty of Engineering, University of Lagos, Nigeria

Email: kinzah.noor@umt.edu.pk; sp22-bcs-140@cuilahore.edu.pk; mercyebute02@gmail.com; aimoize@unilag.edu.ng

Abstract

The current cyber-physical systems (CPSs) face several significant challenges, such as insufficient security consideration in the physical domain, insecure CPS design from the start, attack identification, and survivability limitations. This study analyzes practical applications of industrial robots and wireless medical systems to address these issues. This study provides a generalized CPS that uses an adaptable communications system to control an autonomous multi-robot community. During robotic tasks, the main goal is to provide accurate and almost instantaneous observation of the distant surroundings by digital layer. Our method uses data contraction, downsizing, and dynamic bandwidth control to facilitate successful interaction and joint surveillance operations. The system's functionality is much improved by this foundation, which makes simultaneous data interchange between digital and real-world counterparts trivial. An enhanced, updated wireless

DOI: 10.1201/9788743801306-6

cyber-physical medical system (UWCPMS) is presented that uses machine learning for intrusion recognition and classification to address the abovementioned issues. Deep neural networks are integrated into the proposed system to counteract attacks such as data injection, alteration, and denial of service. Three primary elements comprise the UWCPMS framework: actual time management of resources, computational and security, and connectivity and supervision. It is patient-oriented and enables smartphone-based data control, guaranteeing secure sharing of health information. Our approach proved effective against cyber-physical threats with a reduced computing time of 13 seconds and a 92% detection accuracy.

6.1 Introduction

Cyber-physical systems (CPSs) integrate the digital and physical domains. Embedded digital controllers communicate with the physical world via actuators and environmental sensors. The modern world depends on integrated embedded systems to operate and manufacture smart grids, automobiles, home appliances, medical equipment, and other items. They are characterized by highly stringent battery and processing power limitations, necessitating dependability and fault tolerance [1]. CPS designers must prioritize security due to the increasing complexity of CPSs and the nature of threats by unforgiving surroundings, which calls for concurrently executing several security standards [2]. Most studies in CPS security focus on its cyber component and aim to secure information flow security from sources to sinks, like a sensor to a PLC. Cyber and physical threats must be considered while designing a security system for a CPS. Comprehending the physical subsystem and its weaknesses is crucial to guarantee CPS security [3].

Security and privacy protection are made more difficult by embedded systems, sensors, actuators, control and monitoring software, and other CPS components that are heterogeneous and sophisticated. Attacks can originate from, move between, and target many CPS components – cyber, physical, and cyber-physical – making identifying, tracing, and examining them challenging. Along with suggestions for improving security at every stage of CPS development, the efficacy of risk analysis, threat detection, and defense responses in smart grids is investigated in this study [4]. The main study focus of Konstantinou et al. [5] is to accomplish the objectives of performance, robustness, efficiency, and reliability for physical systems. For instance, miscommunication of location could result in mishaps if a vehicle-to-vehicle communication network is disrupted. Studies on cybersecurity issues related to smart grids can be divided into two primary categories: techniques that compromise devices and systems and methods that impact connectivity. A partially observable Markov decision process (POMDP) and support vector regression (SVR) are used by Gislason [6] to create a long-run identification approach that forecasts guideline power prices based on past data.

Protected control, network administration, and data-driven tactics are all included in resilient CPS systems. These designs include network-based attack segmentation and data route restoration to maintain stability, mitigate the physical effects of cyber-physical attacks, and ensure safe operation. Network and control must be co-designed to make CPS resilient to cyber-physical threats. Cyber-physical assaults are classified into intervention area, stealthiness, and position. These perspectives specify the necessary conditions for an attack, such as altering target data, gaining access to intrusion channels, and understanding the behavior of physical systems [7]. The Secure by Design strategy is not applied to manufacturing a significant amount of elements and communication methods, which lessens their resilience to cyberattacks. In this chapter, CyberSeg – a new method for identifying which parts of cyber-physical production networks should be segregated in case of a cyberattack – is presented by Otto et al. [8].

Survivability includes avoiding ongoing service deterioration, failures, or fidelity breaches. Sophisticated model-checking methods are employed for validation to demonstrate predicted survivability characteristics on the protection requirement [9]. This study area seeks to attain high degrees of resilience and self-healing qualities through reconfigurable hardware computing. In closing, researchers would like to point out that creating and utilizing a self-healing hardware structure has produced more insights than only measuring the system's resilience and self-healing features. For various stakeholders, ranging from automating to the Internet of Things, these insights provide fresh perspectives on developing bio-inspired autonomous systems [10]. The hardware architecture often includes combinational circuits and sequential logic systems with flip-flops, latches, and logic gates to perform hazardous operations. These components are vulnerable to software errors and hardware failures, which can have severe repercussions and impair vital state functions [11].

Currently employed CPSs suffer from problems such as not considering security issues in physical aspects and secure CPS system design from the beginning, identification, type of attacks, surveillance, and system survivability. This study proposed a comprehensive approach for blocking unnecessary network access and analyzing physical components exposed to attacks. Additionally, the proposed architecture is survivable in the presence of an attack and considers security aspects from the start. The chapter will provide a detailed methodology for improving CPS security and privacy and an exhaustive approach for assessing these solutions' efficacy through simulation and real-world case studies in industrial robots and medical devices.

Robust security and privacy safeguards are needed due to CPS's rapid improvement and broad integration in different fields, including smart grids, healthcare, and industrial automation. Cyber-physical systems are becoming increasingly vulnerable to advanced cyberattacks, which can have disastrous effects such as disruptions to operations, monetary losses, and even dangers to human safety. The rationale of this study comes from the urgent necessity to improve these systems' security and privacy to guarantee their dependable and secure operation. By conducting a thorough study of hardware security and privacy concerns unique to CPS and proposing fresh perspectives and risk-reduction strategies, this chapter seeks to close the gaps in the present study.

6.1.1 Key contributions of the chapter

The noteworthy additions made by this chapter are outlined below:

i. The chapter analyzes how physical vulnerabilities in CPS affect hardware security and privacy. Because physical and cyberattacks have potential in a CPS, security measures should be considered. To ensure CPS security, it is crucial to comprehend how a CPS's physical subsystem might be exploited. Advertisers can alter or substitute some physical elements, potentially leading to unfavorable outcomes. Sensor measurements detect physical attacks.

ii. Focus on incorporating security and privacy concerns into CPS to provide strong protection from the beginning. This chapter discusses the development of secure CPS as a component of the overall CPS design process. It offers insights into the new platform-aware control component, design methodology, and architecture requirements CPS development brings. Investigate how physical systems react in real time to cyber-physical threats.

iii. Examine different attack routes and their identification and prevention methods. This study aims to give a thorough overview of how physical systems are harmed by cyber-physical attacks via networks and the strategies that can be used to build strong CPS defenses against such attacks.

iv. Thorough examination of hardware security and privacy in industrial robots and medical devices, emphasizing particular issues and potential solutions for each industry. Proposed changes in the practical applications of industrial robots and medical equipment.

6.1.2 Chapter organization

Section 6.2 presents the related work on hardware security and privacy affected by physical flaws. Section 6.3 investigates the structure and components of CPS hardware and control theory system model description. Section 6.4 explores several attacks particular to CPS and techniques for identifying and avoiding them. Section 6.5 is a detailed analysis of CPS architecture in robots and medical care, focusing on industry-specific problems and possible solutions. Section 6.6 concludes the chapter with future directions.

6.2 Related Work

Cyber Physical System (CPS) due to their decreased cost and increased computational ability. They have recently become widely used in various industries, including aviation, the automotive sector, infrastructure construction, power, medical care, and the production of resources. This is due to their decreased cost and increased computational ability. According to Yu et al. [12], the framework's objectives are to recognize attack patterns, comprehend possible new threats, and encourage the creation of defenses against developing physical and cyber threats by deriving a general assault paradigm from prior studies. Countermeasures need to take into consideration growing threats from a variety of attack channels. There is a lack of studies on the best way to coordinate and communicate between defenses. Current physical, cyber, and hybrid assaults, as well as both cryptographic and non-cryptographic defenses, are discussed by Yaacoub et al. [13], and examining the reasons behind CPS-related robberies and assaults. Security aspects like availability, integrity, and secrecy can all be targeted and examined by the computing level's security. The perception, transmission, and application layers are the three primary levels of the CPS system. The study does not consider multi-factor authentication and cyber environment with secure communications and computing. Risks are continually seen, recorded, examined, and reduced before a suspicious action. CPS must regularly update its firmware, software, and hardware through certified repairs and upgrades.

The purpose of the study by Keshk et al. [14] is to examine safe strategies for defending CPSs against cyberattacks and assess how well they work for intrusion detection and privacy preservation. One important outcome is the requirement for efficient methods to find breaches while protecting data and system components from unwanted access and identifying cyberattacks. Studies are lacking to ensure critical infrastructure security, including creating information sets, managing information confidentiality and utility, and accurately detecting sophisticated and ongoing threats in complex environments. The primary objective of Lanotte et al. [15] is to formally study the timing elements associated with security and denial of service (DoS) attacks against the actual components of CPSs. It employs formal calculus approaches to establish theoretical foundations for formal attack detection. The study is deficient in its coverage of threat scenarios, practical assessment, protective methods that are reactive and responsive, and interoperability with existing protection structures. The development challenge raised by Jiang et al. [16] is multifaceted, with the main goals being to reduce the uneven level of safety power to withstand fault injection across the entire risk-critical application in real time and to optimize mean failure protection. Additionally, it reduces the program's schedule duration and the computer nodes' heterogeneous tasks. A practical method for obtaining pareto-optimal outcomes using multiple optimization objectives has been suggested.

Avula et al. suggested [17] a Bayesian approach to manage hostile inference and lower the risks to CPS secrecy. A control plan is also created for the worst-case situation in which the adversary is fully aware of the user's control plan. The publicly available "Co-LivEn" dataset, including detailed electrical inspections of devices in a shared home, is presented to promote studies on smart meter protection. The proposed reinforcement learning method is benchmarked against this dataset. Scalability, real-time application, integration, and thorough security measures are ways to enhance the study. Most CPSs lack authentication for messages and other cybersecurity characteristics, making it difficult to identify information injection assaults. Large datasets are specifically designed [18] to be handled by deep learning algorithms instead of tiny ones with many characteristics. The effectiveness of the information demands, current performance optimization, and adaptation over various CPSs are areas where the investigation falls short. The development of Self-CPS, which necessitates self-defense, observability, and runtime adaptation, is the aim of this study by de O et al. [19] This design has no industrial applications and does not assess how Self-CPS behaves if deployed to operate in a nearby system region.

Deebak and Al-Turjman designed Lightweight Privacy-Aware Secure Authentication (LPASA) [20] which incorporates lightweight cryptographic operations for health information protection because of its vulnerability. By raising the proportion of low-latency packets, decreasing energy usage per data bit, and boosting packet delivery ratios, the suggested LPASA system improves service levels in contexts with limited resources. Scalability problems and resilience against advanced persistent threats are two areas where the study lacks. Using a patient-focused approach to counteract CPS threats, the architecture of the improved wireless medical cyber-physical system (IWMCPS) [21] applies mobile devices to govern information access. IWMCPS concentrates on a few design components, like safety and connectivity. The accidental contact of ICS parts requires further investigation due to insufficient physical safeguards, and the actual manipulation of information may corrupted.

ATT&CK's threat model [22] spans various technology areas, including ICS, mobile devices, and business, all relevant to the autonomous passenger ships (APSs) application scenario. Subsequent activities are imperative to tackle the dissemination of hazards, enhance safety and economic consequences assessment, and compute the efficacy of countermeasures. Future uses include enabling opponent simulation, risk residual estimation, and the creation of threat-informed safety designs. Furthermore, they develop mitigation techniques against threats, including DOS, resource hijacking, account access revocation, and jamming.

Khalaf et al. [23] provide an initial contemporary assessment of the study on the CPS of active distribution networks (ADNs), emphasizing the vital procedures and elements that make up ADNs. There is a thorough discussion of the trustworthiness of ADN sensors and devices, such as protection relays, smart meters, sophisticated metering structures, and phasor measurement devices. A comprehensive analysis of the practical drivers and facilitators of ADNs, such as intelligent homes, electrical vehicles (EVs), microgrids, and the Internet of Things (IoT), is carried out. The prospect is to develop efficient monitoring systems with continuous operation in the presence of attacks. Additionally, safety experts must balance efficiently handling enormous information, fast speeds, and an intelligent grid that is frequently overpowering. A summary of the related work on CPS is given in Table 6.1.

6.3 Structure and Components of CPS

The structure and components of CPS are shown in Figure 6.1. Secure CPSs are complicated structures typically comprising various software and hardware processing components, as shown in Figure 6.1. The electronic module performs environmental data acquisition before sending it to the computing unit which activates the communication channel. The final module of an electronic device enables the device to perform specific targeted actions in the environment with high precision.

Table 6.1 Related work in the CPS.

Reference number	Key contributions	Approach	Study gap	Future recommendations
[7]	Robust CPS design techniques and classification of cyber-physical threats	Numerical examples for cyber-physical threats and examine CPS in the control theory	Network-based privacy and the physical system's irreversible state	Durability for control and organization of resources
[8]	Identifying the gadgets to isolate in the event of an assault	Integer linear programming approach modified by the critical node problem	Direct communication between devices and turning off pricy electronics	A version of the issue with weighted gadgets and practical applications
[9]	Demonstrating safety by misuse cases and automatic confirmation of survivability possessions	Surreal framework. Misuse of UML profile annotations yielding an assessment model (SAM)	Services, misuses, and recovery actions are the probability of their occurrence	Evaluate the tool framework using new attributes and in various case scenarios
[10]	Fresh approaches to error tolerance and self-healing architecture based on biological concepts	Architecture is arranged in two levels: essential operations and the layer of healing. Two practical applications have been mapped	Essential components were verified to confirm the data and control flow	Develop independent control and information about problem handling
[11]	Proper certifiable and fault-tolerant hardware design uses the concepts of the state machine	Analysis, design, validation, and verification model of railway interlocking system (RIS)	Verify run time and tolerance for errors	Self-checking for errors and other crucial attributes; other applications of the real world
[12]	Identify attack patterns, comprehend new threats, and protect against future assaults	Derive a generic assault paradigm, inattentive CPS design, and the interaction between components	The optimum method for safely correlating and communicating among defenses	Makeup of countermeasures, more risks use a combination of vectors of attack
[13]	Reviews the key features of CPS and the matching applications, technologies, and values	Attack assessments, security measures, and forensics are thoroughly analyzed	Multi-factor authentication, cyber environment with secure communications and computing	Continuous monitoring, risks, and up-to-date system. Certified repairs and upgrades
[14]	Analyze the state of secure methods for CPSs and their connections from cyber-attacks	Machine learning (ML), cryptography, and blockchain are learning (ML); cryptography, and blockchain have been enlightened and employed for data privacy preservation	The protection of CPSs depends on the effective creation of information sets together with the correct handling of information confidentiality and usefulness and the optimized data processing and transmission.	Highly accurate detection of sophisticated and ongoing risks in these problematic environments
[15]	The formal study of the timing elements with attacks against the actual components of CPSs	Studied using calculus techniques to establish theoretical foundations for formal attack detection	Limited coverage of threat situations, compatibility with current protection structures	Reactive and responsive protection measures, and practical evaluation

[16]	The fault dispersion model to quantify the security strength	Optimization challenge and implementation reliance restrictions for encryption/decryption of communications	Program's schedule duration and the compute nodes' heterogeneous task	Method for obtaining pareto-optimal outcomes using multiple optimization objectives
[17]	Electrical inspections of all the devices in a shared housing home and study smart meter protection	A Bayesian strategy for controlling hostile inference and a control plan for the worst-case situation	Inference control data protection and improve efficiency	Scalability, real-time application, and integration, along with thorough security measures
[18]	The public can readily access high-quality datasets, contributing to the impressive performance	Deep learning approximates any function and is suitable for use in CPS. It analyzes different ways of attack detection	The credibility of information depends on its validity along with its protection from unauthorized alterations combined with its defense against additional route attacks.	Current performance optimizing and adaptation over various CPS and new data for the model
[19]	Development of self-CPS, self-defense, observability, and runtime adaptation	RA4Self-CPS is a reference architecture that supports the development of self-CPS	Assess how self-CPS behaves if it is deployed to operate in a nearby system region	Evaluate its structure in other programming languages and apply it in other practical applications
[20]	Obtain higher efficiency and resilience to potential active and passive threats	Employ lightweight cryptographic procedures, bitwise exclusive-OR, and one-way hashing functions	It improves the level of services to achieve better delivery ratios and consumes less energy per data delivery ratios	Scalability problems and resilience against advanced persistent threats are two areas
[21]	Maintains end-user's mobile devices to control information access and guarantee confidentiality	The improved wireless medical cyber-physical system (IWMCPS) architecture is based on a patient-focused strategy	Actual manipulation of information may get corrupted, and the accidental contact of ICS parts is considered an issue	Concentrate on a few IWMCPS design components, like safety and connectivity
[22]	The technique revises risk values by modifying input values according to current threats and computes the efficacy of countermeasures	ATT&CK's threat model applies to the autonomous passenger ships (APS) scenario	Incorporation of outside-the-band communication channels, networking, duplication of assistance, and information backup	Develop mitigation techniques against hijacking, account access revocation, and jamming
[23]	Study on CPS active distribution networks and vital procedures and elements	Comprehensive analysis of the practical drivers and facilitators of ADNs	Balance to efficiently handle information in a fast-speed intelligent grid	Carry out monitoring systems that offer immediate detection of intrusions without interception

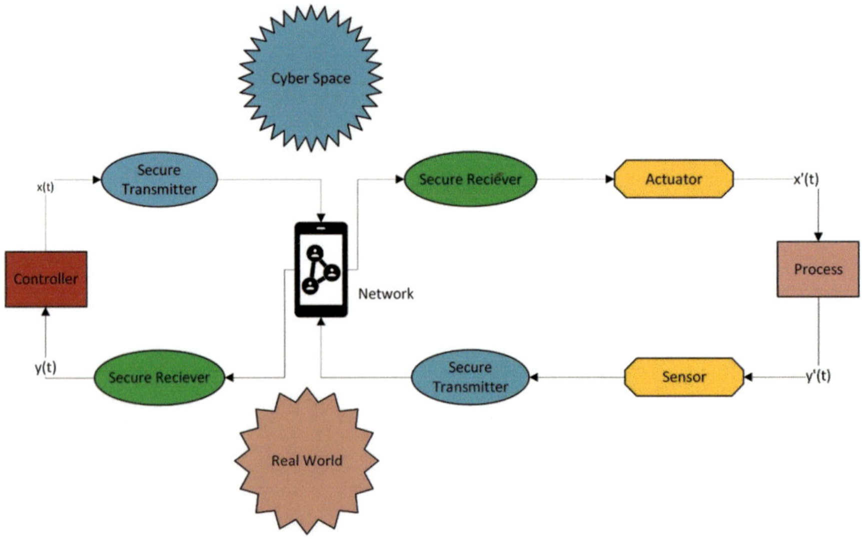

Figure 6.1 Cyber-physical system.

Moreover, the safety-critical CPS usually consists of several electronic processing elements that need to be constantly tracked for optimal performance and managed by robust and fault-tolerant real-time validation approaches [24].

6.3.1 CPS structural hierarchy

Figure 6.2 shows the CPS structural hierarchy. The physical, network, and application layers are the three tiers of a layered CPS architecture that are considered. Structured CPS offers significant advantages in maintaining systems and innovative technical problem resolution over non-hierarchical CPS. This multilevel CPS design can be used for practical CPS, including smart grids, intelligent transportation systems, and many other practical applications [25].

1. **Physical layer**
   It is the reality of the world's physical structures. The physical layer consists of networking the physical systems and detectors, which are affixed to the components and regularly provide readings to a central server. Furthermore, the application layer inside the computer system sends an input control signal across the network to the physical devices,

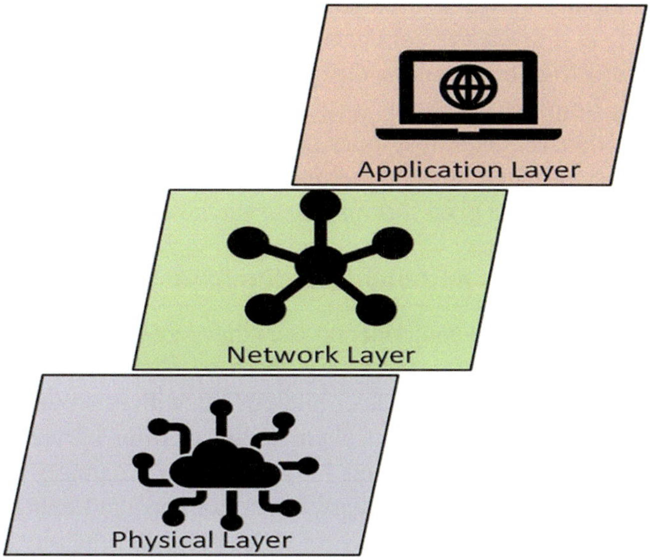

Figure 6.2 CPS structural hierarchy.

which causes them to actuate. Performance of tasks involving complicated calculations across the application layer typically relies on the physical layer due to power constraints on the physical structures. The physical layer of an intelligent grid consists of power plants, distribution centers, and electric equipment that transfers electricity.

2. **Network layer**
The network layer facilitates interaction among the application and physical layers and represents the CPS feedback loop. It handles data flow between the physical and application layers and links them via wireless or wired networks [26]. The network in CPS needs to ensure real-time communication as it has to supply functions to the physical components running in a continuous-time domain – an intelligent grid and power equipment exchange data via the IEC 61850 networks [27].

3. **Application layer**
The application layer is used for the computer infrastructure in the virtual world. Physical structures are supervised by the application layer, which offers features to CPS clients. The computer algorithms calculate the complete CPS's general condition depending on the sensors' obtained readings via several different physical structures [28]. Next,

the computer networks ascertain the actual system's subsequent state. After this, it sends the command signal required to operate the actual system instructions found within the programs. Using data collected by sensors from the structures, a smart energy system's supervisory control and data acquisition systems may estimate energy demands, govern electricity production, and offer tolerance of faults in electricity transmission. Table 6.2 gives a summary of the layers in the CPS.

6.3.2 Bridging cyber and physical domains

Sensing and actuation components are the key elements for cyber-physical domain interaction. Generally speaking, sensors in CPS function as physical-interfacing hubs that communicate with surroundings, parts, or other random objects. Through their ability to offer useable outputs in response to particular measurements [29], CPSs can accurately perceive the outside world and develop into smarter, autonomous, and dependable systems. Conversely, actuators allow cyber systems to alter the physical conditions in which they operate. In addition to conventional actuators found in larger-scale CPSs, actuator elements are also found in emerging IoT devices, which allow them to interact with their surroundings and communicate with other IoT devices.

However, since an actuator does not get data from the outside world, most harmful assaults are typically started by the user; hence, most current cyberattacks remain.

For this reason, most current assaults concentrate on delivering erroneous orders to enable them to carry cyber-to-physical manipulation. Fake cyber-domain communications, like leaked network transmissions or program flow control hijackings, can be used to achieve this fake signal input. Alternatively, harmful impulses may be transmitted by using an unintentional receptor in the electronic device. In addition, because the nodes that collect data are located where the CPS and non-CPS boundaries meet, they are exposed to both the physical and cyber worlds, making them more vulnerable to intrusions. Thus, the sensor system is the main topic of discussion here.

Two kinds of sensors, passive and active sensors, can be distinguished based on how they investigate their environment.

1. Passive sensors, like MEMS movement and microphone detectors, take in existing physical signals and do not release outside stimuli. In essence, they are physical phenomenon detectors and only send the acquired signals to the program at the top layer.

Table 6.2 Layers in the CPS.

Layers	Components	Function	Possible threats	Target of attacks	Risk mitigations
Physical layer	Chips, electronics tags, sensors, actuators, integrators, navigation system	Data gathering from physical objects	Zero-day exploits interception attacks, injection attacks, port scans, and passive replay	Privacy, authentication, and privacy	Data protection, trust management, source verification, and secure information
Network layer	Global network, cloud platform, network access point, Wifi hotspot, routing devices, Zigbee, Bluetooth	Data communication via channel	Replay attack, DOS, preventing repudiation, routing attacks, malware attacks	Change the communication path, interrupt the flow of data, and disrupt connectivity	Monitor unauthorized access, protect system using strong passwords and protection, anti-virus
Application layer	Electrical vehichle, smart grids, smart infrastructures, smart waste solutions, advanced traffic control	Data analysis and strategic decision-making in real world	Hijacking, misconfiguration, injection of SQL	Web applications, online services, and DNS and management services	Firewall protection, authenticity, confidentiality, and regular security checks

2. Active sensors, like radar and LiDAR, proactively explore the environment by sending out signals that cause measurable entities, including nearby objects, to respond physically. The receiver subsequently detects the signal. It has an internal control system that deduces characteristics of the environment around it, including the form, closeness, and comparative angle of objects in the vicinity, by analyzing the correspondence among the emitted and received signals.

Despite their wide range and complexity, sensors frequently share similar fundamental parts, including amplification techniques and filtering methods, sensing and detection systems, and analog-to-digital conversion (ADC).

1. **Sensing and detection system**
   Active detectors possess similar sensor-receiving subsystems to passive systems although their operations for active sensing prove more intricate. The part that responds to changes in a specific physical parameter, $x(t)$, and produces an output, $y(t)$, that is precisely proportionate to the physical signal is known as the sensing mechanism. The formula for this is $y(t) = \alpha \cdot x(t)$, where α is the proportional constant or the device's sensitivity. A desired feature in a sensor is this relationship, known as linearity. In actuality, sensors behave non-linearly, meaning that the outcome of the sensor is not exactly proportional to the input within the boundaries of the actual signal. Although non-linearity is a less-than-ideal characteristic of sensors, attackers may benefit from it by trying to introduce out-of-band signals.

2. **Amplification techniques and filtering methods**
   In specific sensors, the output signal, $y(t)$, is filtered to eliminate undesired frequency components and amplified to meet the microcontroller's voltage specification. Attackers may encounter difficulties when inserting out-of-band data during filtration, as the filter may significantly reduce the input signals.

3. **Analog-to-digital conversion (ADC)**
   The ADC transforms an analog signal into a distinct digital stream. It samples the signal at a specific frequency, called the ADC's sample rate, and transforms each sample into certain-bit integers, known as its resolution.

6.3.3 Formal verification of CPS

Verification and validation are generally crucial techniques for guaranteeing the reliability and correctness of digital CPS, as seen in Figure 6.3. Furthermore, the layout of a digital system satisfies a set of user-specified

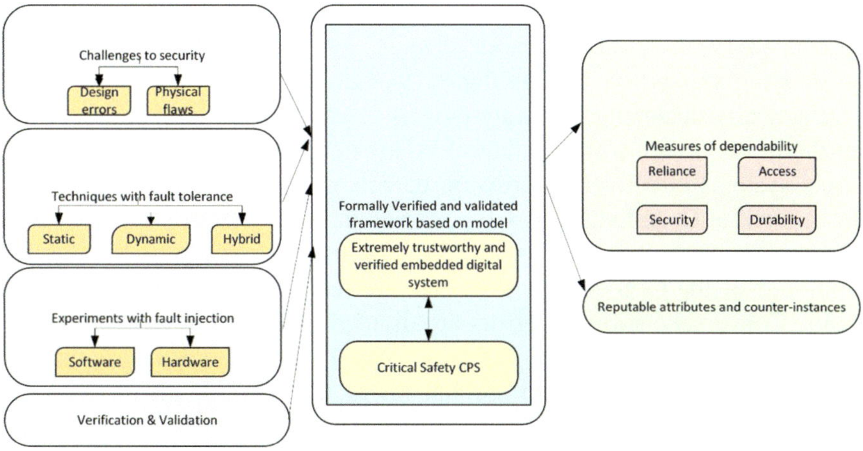

Figure 6.3 Formal verification and validation of CPS.

criteria. On the other hand, validation is a technique to assess whether the digital embedded system meets the customer's requirements. The study [30] has employed a variety of formal verification and validation approaches to demonstrate a wide range of time-associated features, such as life or security, as well as specifications for both the software and hardware layers that comprise safety-critical CPS.

When a system is executed, for instance, an authenticity property implies that a certain benefit will happen, while a security property indicates nothing undesirable will occur during the process of execution, which is both finite and unlimited. NuSMV is a formal verification tool checker that can define system constants for safety and liveness standards. This tool evaluates the result of the digital system against its particular qualities, characterized by a mathematical model embodied in temporal logic [31]. Symbolic Model Verification (SMV), an officially recognized language that supports finite state machine requirements and establishes the fundamental concepts of digital systems, is a case study of a symbolic modeling verification language. A textual description characterized by attributes based on either computation tree logic (CTL) or linear temporal logic (LTL) is the input for the SMV model. The variable, assign, and specification subsections comprise the three submodules that comprise the basic SMV module [32].

6.3.4 Tolerance for faults in CPS

The fundamental schematic of a highly verifiable and safety-critical CPS is depicted by Singh and Rajput [33]. The system can be formally verified using a hybrid approach that combines classic verified tolerance for faults approaches with modeling-based design. Adequate safety requirements, outstanding reliability, and immunity to various breakdown modes, such as practically occurring hardware defects resulting from ionizing radiation. Furthermore, design software flaws [34] are necessary to function CPS electronic systems effectively. Hardware defects of the single and multiple-bit upset stuck-at-0, and stuck-at-1 types brought on by electromagnetic radiation or alpha particles can all occur [35]. For instance, bit flips in the flip-flop memories of the CPS electronic system are the primary result of single-bit faults. Conversely, software errors are divided by zero, useless logic, overflowing facts, and violations of array access. Hazardous CPS systems have to be designed and verified to account for each of these kinds of flaws and failures [36].

6.3.5 CPS in the context of control

CPS's primary purpose is to enable numerous physical systems to perform as the user plans. Consequently, disrupting the immediate nature of the physical systems is the primary goal of a cyber-physical attack. In CPS, control theory examines the physical system's time reaction to cyber-physical threats. As seen in Figure 6.4, the constituent parts are a four-component control system: physical system, controller, sensor, and state estimator. The sensor measures the specific physical parameters of the system's structure. The state estimator uses a mathematical model of a physical structure to determine all physical characteristics are based on the sensor measurements. The controller creates an input control signal to function in the physical infrastructure as the user requests. These four parts create a feedback control loop to produce the right control signal to run the physical system.

1. **Physical system status and parameters**
   There are several time-varying physical quantities in a physical system. A car, for instance, has several parameters, such as engine temperature, driving angle, direction, angular speed, acceleration, and velocity. According to control theory, x is the vector $x(\mathrm{t}) \in \mathbb{R}^w$, where w is the total number of physical values, representing the physical procedure corresponding to the state. The state parameter is any component of the current state vector $x(\mathrm{t})$ that describes something physical. With the right inputs for control signals, control aims to maintain the state $x(\mathrm{t})$ as the user desires.

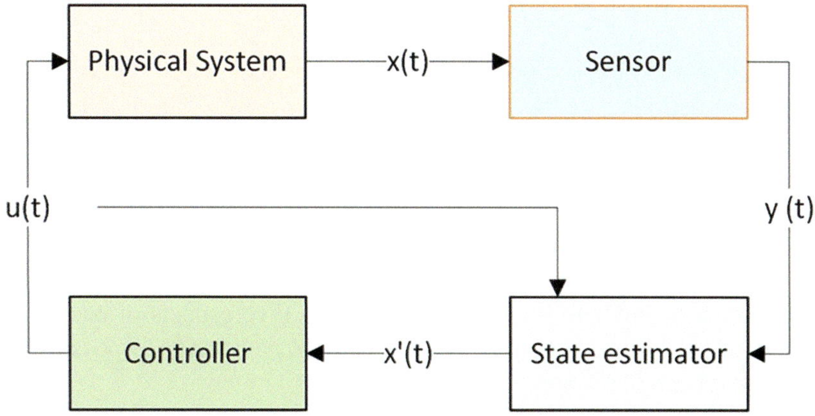

Figure 6.4 Control system.

2. **System model description**
Multiple sensor measurements, $y(t)$, from sensors linked to the physical structure, along with control input signals, $u(t)$, handling the current state $x(t)$, might be found in a physical system. An equation in differential form is used to depict the physical framework quantitatively based on the input–output connection. Furthermore, the condition estimator, which calculates internal physical values not immediately detected by detectors, is designed using a numerical representation of the physical system, which also offers features of the real system about pole and zero changes.

3. **Dynamic behavior of the CPS physical plant**
The dynamic behavior of a CPS's physical plant [37], [38] is often represented by a discrete-time state-space model, typically expressed as two equations, eqn (6.1) and (6.2).

$$x_{m+1} = Dx_m + Eu_m + v_m \tag{6.1}$$

$$y_m = Fx_m + e_m, \tag{6.2}$$

where $x_m \in P^w$ is the current (physical) state, $u_m \in P^z$ is the input (i.e., the control actions implemented through actuators), and $y_m \in P^q$ is the output (i.e., the measurements from the sensors). The uncertainty $v_m \in P^w$ and the measurement error $e_m \in P^q$ represent perturbation and sensor noise, respectively, and D, E, and F are matrices modeling the dynamics of the physical system. Here, the next state depends on the current state and the corresponding control actions , at the sampling instant $m \in N$. The state cannot be directly observed; only its measurements can be observed.

6.4 Attacks Identification in CPS

Generally, a system must meet the confidentiality, integrity, and availability requirements in order to be considered secure. Five aspects of each threat: (1) source, (2) target, (3) motivation, (4) attack path, and (5) possible outcomes have been identified.

1. Source: The origin of a threat is the instigator of an attack. There are three categories of risk sources.
   a. Adversarial threats are acts of malice from individuals, corporations, teams, states, or countries.
   b. Incidental threats have arisen unintentionally or due to valid CPS elements.
   c. Natural risks include flooding, quakes, and explosions; human-caused disasters, such as wildfires and explosions; and infrastructure failures, such as power outages or lost telecommunications [39].
2. Target: CPS applications, as well as any users or parts, are targets.
3. Motive: Criminal, espionage, terrorist, political, or cyberwar motivations are the usual motives of CPS attackers.
4. Assault vector: To successfully launch an assault, a threat may employ one or more of the following four processes: (1) creation, (2) disruption, (3) alteration, or (4) interception.
5. Consequence: Jeopardizing the safety, confidentiality, accessibility, accuracy, or confidence of the CPS. There are five different kinds of threats: (1) financial, (2) political, (3) criminal, (4) privacy, and (5) physical.

6.4.1 Concerns from crime

1. Industrial control system (ICS): By using the capabilities of an ICS application's wireless links, a malicious party with system knowledge might wirelessly alter it and perhaps disrupt its functionality.

2. Intelligent grids: Hackers targeting sources that want to steal confidential data, such as the existence of a house occupant, may be deduced by the target via the connections to carry out a practical theft between the energy provider and the smart meter.

3. Medical devices: Unauthorized thieves can add or send back trusted commands that small devices have already captured in an attempt to harm patients and their health, altering the device's expected functions and indications and leading to an unfavorable situation. Moreover, an attacker could also trigger damage by rendering the equipment unusable and averting it from providing the expected treatments by tampering with the wireless signaling that medical apparatus exchanges with each other to maintain unharmed health [40].

4. Smart cars: An unwanted user may be able to take advantage of a weakness in communication through wireless systems to gain access to an automobile, leading to an accident or a loss of command.

6.4.2 Risk to finance from crime

1. ICS: An informed customer looking to cut their electricity costs could likely trick their energy provider by altering physical equipment or introducing deceptive data, causing it to face a financial loss.

2. Smart grid: Intelligent meters may be tampered with by a customer wishing to pretend to be a utility company to lower their electricity cost. Utility companies put customers' confidentiality at risk by tracking consumers' electrical consumption to determine their habits and the types of devices they own. As a result, these companies violate customers' privacy when they give this data to advertisers. Moreover, criminals attempting to tear down many smart meters and perhaps cause an interruption is a case of bribery [41].

6.4.3 Political challenges

1. ICS: An adversarial nation may initiate a cyberattack against a target nation by breaching critical networks, like air pipes and radioactive plants, dispersing malware remotely, or fragmenting into field gadgets. These actions could force a plant to shut down, jeopardize vital sections, or contaminate the surrounding environment [42]. A nation's essential structures may be the subject of monitoring operations by espionage

agencies, maybe through the spread of viruses that jeopardize the confidentiality of essential data.

2. Smart grids: An opponent country may initiate a digital conflict against the national power grid of an opponent nation (target) by gaining worldwide authority over the tangible parts of electrical networks, leading to extensive power cuts, delays, or financial harm.

3. Medical devices: An enemy nation could attack legislators by suppressing their medical supplies and using the devices' wireless communication as a path, possibly resulting in a fatal medical condition.

4. Smart automobiles: An enemy may initiate a digital fight targeting national transport highway conflict and travelers by infiltrating smart cars, which are vulnerable to fully autonomous attacks, perhaps leading to several crashes and severe harm.

6.4.4 Dangers to privacy

1. Medical equipment: The hacker's objective is to use patient conversations to reveal the existence of any medical equipment, illnesses, or any related information that a patient considers private. Medical equipment compromised by vector-based wireless malware suffers from a safety and privacy violation. In addition, a lot of sensitive data is stored in multiple locations, and medical gadgets exchange data with different organizations, such as medical facilities. The need to monitor individuals may encourage an intruder to breach privacy by breaking into the networks connecting the relevant lawful parties to gain unauthorized access to such data.

2. Smart cars: An attacker may be able to listen in on talks inside a car by exploiting security holes, which would violate the privacy of the car's occupants. Confidentiality violations may result from using the global GPS and directions by an attacker or a police officer, primarily intended to steer and train drivers. Automakers can covertly gather vehicle information without the knowledge or consent of drivers, which exposes particular driving behaviors and infractions and is against confidentiality consequences [43]. Another option is for corporations to gather information about motorists that insurers might exploit. This information could include valuable private information for accident investigations or policy customization.

6.4.5 Physical dangers

1. ICS: The control center could receive inaccurate and deceptive readings if an attacker uses heat or cold to spoof a sensor that detects the ambient temperature of a particular environment.

2. Smart grids: To disrupt services and perhaps result in blackouts, an attacker may damage parts of smart electricity systems that are visibly accessible throughout the electrical grid.

3. Medical devices: An attacker could physically interfere with a piece of medical equipment to alter its settings and interrupt the delivered medical service, perhaps leading to unfavorable health outcomes.

4. Smart cars: Since automobiles are typically physically revealed, it is easy for an intruder to access a car and install a malicious device or alter its external components to accomplish various objectives, from tracking to inducing mishaps. Table 6.3 highlights the types of attacks in CPS.

6.4.6 Types of CPS attacks

Common cyber-physical attacks are the DoS attack, the replay attack, the zero dynamics attack (ZDA), the pole dynamics attack (PDA), and the covert attack.

1. **DOS attacks**: One common type of network assault that disrupts packet transmissions by taking advantage of network vulnerabilities is a denial-of-service attack. Two major communication errors brought on by a denial-of-service assault are packet losses and communication network delays. Among the most popular methods of DoS attacks is packet dropping. Furthermore, a DoS attack might cause severe delays by depleting the system‘s resources. DoS attacks cause latency and timeouts by intentionally filling the memory in network equipment or requesting excessive replies from the computer system. These attacks include ICMP flooding [44], UDP flooding, and TCP connection flooding.

2. **Enhanced attacks**: One of the best techniques is reactive jamming [45], during which an intruder monitors the message channel and responds by clashing with the transmitted signal. Reactive jamming offers benefits for cost-effective transmission disruptions and difficult detection.

Table 6.3 Types of attacks in CPS.

Attack type	Description	Target	Impact	Mitigation technique
DOS	Slow down the operation	System and network services	Reduced availability and diminished performance	Traffic filtering, rate limitation, redundant systems
Replay attacks	To impede operations, provide genuine data packets that have already been captured	Control systems, sensors	Interrupting regular activities and falsifying data	Timestamping, sequence numbers, random data in communication
Zero dynamics attacks	Exploits the zero dynamics of the system, hidden modes of the system that remain undetectable from the system's output	Feedback loops, system controllers	Gradual system degradation, undetectable deviation from expected behavior	Disturbance rejection, robust control design, system observability analysis
Pole dynamics attacks	Manipulate the poles of the system dynamics to destabilize the system, often by injecting signals that alter the system's characteristic equation	Feedback loops, system controllers	Eventual system failure, system instability, oscillations	Secure feedback mechanisms, pole-placement control, stabilization algorithms
Covert attacks	Attackers inject malicious inputs while compensating with false outputs to keep the attack hidden from monitoring systems	Communication channels, sensors, actuators	Stealthy manipulation of system state without triggering alarms	Redundancy, anomaly detection algorithms, dynamic watermarking, multi-layered security checks
Physical attacks	Direct tampering or damage to components of the CPS	Hardware Components	Operational failure, system destruction, unauthorized access	Physical security measures, tamper detection, surveillance

3. **Replay attacks**: The replay attack [46] is a covert cyber-physical exploit in which a hacker inserts prior sensor readings into a computer system. The hacker must be enabled to breach both the controller input signaling channel and the sensor measurement channel to carry out the assault. Unlike other attacks, the replay attack doesn't need physical system modeling. Rather, the replay attack is divided into two stages: the recording and injection phases.

4. **Zero dynamics attack (ZDA)**: The control input attacks via injection, known as the ZDA [47], take advantage of a framework's zero dynamics when it has a non-minimum phase zero. A criminal must know the intended system's zero dynamics and the precise control signal that causes the output $y(\mathrm{t}) = 0$ to perform a zero-dynamics attempt. Combining the particular incoming to the standard input communication and an intruder can cause a specific internal configuration of the system to diverge. It should be mentioned that since the ZDA does not affect the output, it cannot be found simply by looking at the output $y(\mathrm{t})$.

   It could be assumed that the ZDA may only apply to systems with an inherent non-minimum phase zero. So, discretizing a continuous framework for digital control can add a second non-minimum phase zero to the framework that an adversary can exploit [48].

5. **Pole dynamics attack (PDA)**: PDA [49] can be viewed as a pair of the ZDAs. The PDA utilizes unreliable pole patterns by misleading the sensors, while the ZDA leverages the unsteady zero behavior by tricking the actuators. PDA is a detector evaluation alteration assault that aims to delude the control system by removing the variations of the erratic poles in the output detector evaluation.

6. **Covert attack**: The covert strike is a cunning combination of sensor and control assault that misleads the computer system while seizing control of the physical system. The covert attack necessitates simultaneously sensing the control signal that is input $u(\mathrm{t})$ and the corresponding sensor measurement $y(\mathrm{t})$, compared to the replay attack, which merely detects the sensor measurement $y(\mathrm{t})$. The two procedures that make up the covert attack are insertion and illusion. These two operations – manipulating data from sensors and infiltrating the actual system with illegal control inputs – are carried out simultaneously under the covert assault.

6.5 Practical Applications of CPS

This section analyzes industrial robots and wireless medical systems in a real-world scenario.

6.5.1 Autonomous robot to monitor industrial assets

The experiment is conducted and designed to confirm and demonstrate the viability of the suggested CPS architecture [50] that satisfies the needs of heterogeneous multi-robot inspection. A fleet of robots will investigate or scan an unidentified area in a simulation-based experiment to collect data for 3D environmental construction, which will be utilized to plan the next inspection missions.

1. **Case study of robots**
   A diverse multi-robot evaluation is conducted in a real-world industrial environment as part of the experiment. Because of resource limitations, ROS software is used to simulate the environment and robots, as seen in the figure. These technologies are developed for scaled multi-robot evaluation, efficient information handling to maximize bandwidth and adjust to the fleet's requirements, and communication with low latency for actual time collaboration [51]. Three instruments comprise the suggested system: a digital replica, a real-world counterpart, and a digital layer. Every robot uses its reference frame to modify its attitude and data from sensors. Each robot sends data to the digital cells, compressing, downsampling, and managing points clouds for the best possible bandwidth usage. Once transmitted, the receiver can view the collapsed point cloud on an interface sent to the digital layer.

   A live map is created by the centralized digital replica node using all of the robots' data collected from sensors. Although not having immediate access to the map could restrict the ability to decide on individual robots, this centralized solution guarantees effective data management and minimizes network congestion. Because of the flexibility of the proposed approach, robots have access to the live map whenever required, striking a balance between autonomy and connection overhead. The digital layer user experience, which links robots and drivers in continuous teleoperation, displays a three-dimensional map of coverage and the present status of the robots. Preserving low latency and accurate data is essential. The user interface relays navigational and perceptual instructions from the user to the robots, ensuring communication in both directions. The CPS diagram and flow chart are shown in Figure 6.5.

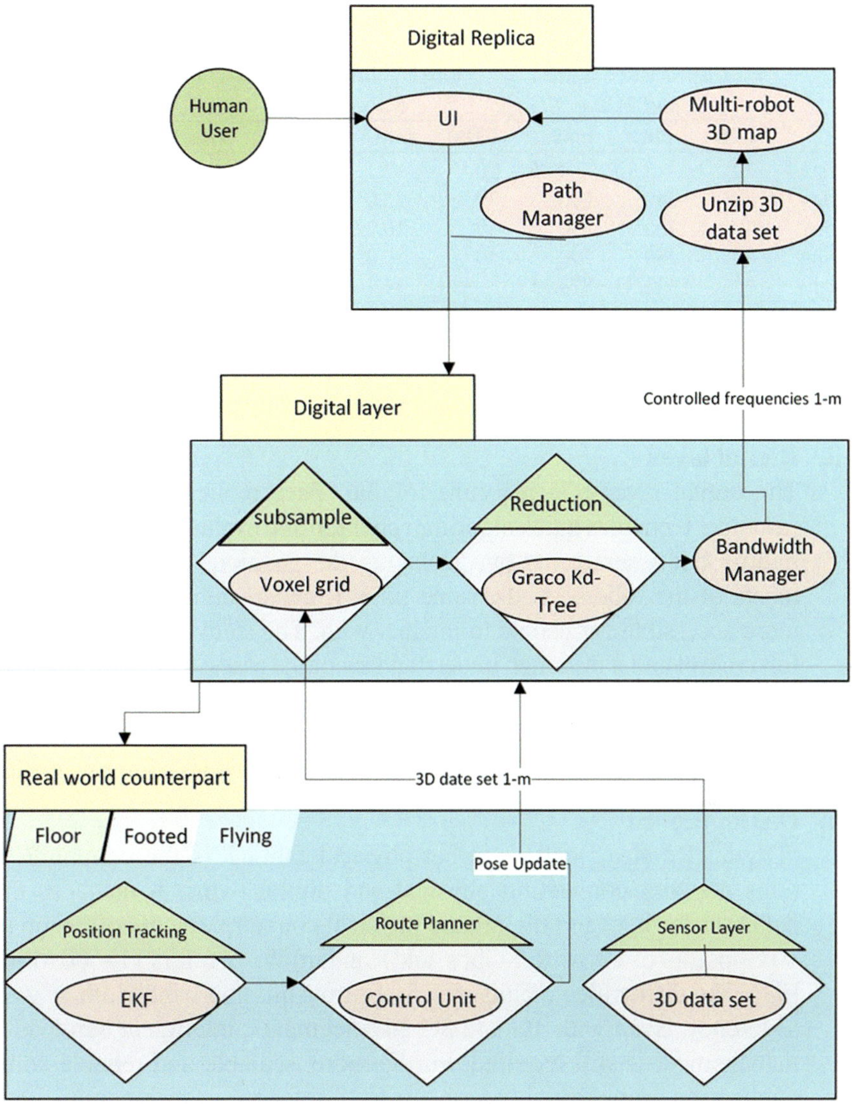

Figure 6.5 CPS diagram and flow chart.

i. **Real world counterpart**
The construction framework, robotics, indicators, and other equipment are represented by the real-world counterpart and the real-life project context. The fleet includes many aerial, wheeled, and legged robots and is outfitted with IMUs, depth cameras, wheel encoding devices, and

Table 6.4 Statistics from analyzing data from point clouds at voxel size 10 cm in terms of bandwidth use.

	Unprocessed point cloud MBps			Filter point cloud MBps			Compress point cloud MBps		
	f(Hz)	min	max	f(Hz)	min	max	f(Hz)	min	max
Series 4	20	2.90	4.55	20	2.1	2.67	20	0.39	0.48
Series 3	40	280	290	40	22.01	22.49	40	4.15	4.47
Footed	40	280	290	40	10.22	12.45	40	1.69	2.46
Flying	40	280	290	40	10.43	12.69	40	1.9	2.8
Total		842.93	874.55		44.76	50.3		8.13	10.21

three-dimensional lidars. These sensors support vital functions for driverless evaluations, like directions, mapping, and localization.

ii. Digital layer

The digital layer is a real-time, digital space replicating the physical resource. It enables quick algorithm creation and evaluation and improves multi-robot assessments by displaying the positions as well as movements of the robots. At the same time, it makes digital user interfaces more accessible for people to interact with. The study [52] gives drivers full control and a thorough understanding of the assessment surroundings by using the digital layer to produce a unified three-dimensional map from three-dimensional lidar and depth perception cameras. It also offers distant remote operation with continuous footage and map improvements.

iii. Digital replica

"Digital Replica," called "cyber-physical fabric," is the communications network connecting physical and digital twins. It manages the data transfer between digital and physical counterparts. 5G offers up to 10 Gbps, 4G offers up to 1 Gbps, and standard Wi-Fi offers 11–600 Mbps [53]. The difficulties include restricted transmission bandwidth as well as latency. Even with 4G and 5G advancements, intelligent bandwidth management is still required. Furthermore, scalable and reliable communication availability is necessary. ROS software supports multi-robot collaborative investigations with a digital twin in this work.

iv. Results and discussion

Actual transmission of data and system scalability are assessed using network efficiency measurements. Metrics like latency measures, publishing rate, and bandwidth are important indicators of how well the CPS system performs. Table 6.4 provides the statistics from analyzing data from point clouds at a voxel size of 10 cm in terms of bandwidth use [50].

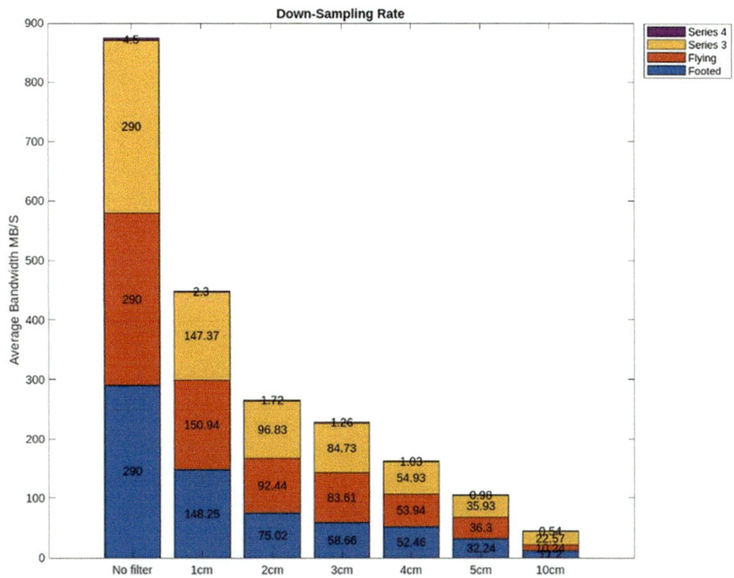

Figure 6.6 The downsampling rate of grid filters for voxels with different sizes in proportion to the bandwidth used.

v. Analysis of scalability

Simulations were used to assess the CPS design, incorporating scalability experiments using fleets of several robots. Figure 6.6 displays the average bandwidth used for various voxel sizes. Except for Series 4.0, where 1 cm voxels were preferable for maintaining point cloud information, a 10 cm voxel size was usually ideal. Figure 6.6 also illustrates how bandwidth was lowered from 873.5 MB/s to 44.55 MB/s, a 94.85% reduction, by downsampling point cloud information in a 10 cm voxel size. Downsampling and compressing lowered the data to 8.71 MB/s, a 99.4% reduction.

vi. Analysis of bandwidth

Figure 6.7 shows how well Draco's compression works when downsampling point cloud signals at different voxel sizes and reducing the average bandwidth needed. The results in Figure 6.7 enable one to modify the downsampling rate or apply compression algorithms as necessary. Bandwidth management will play a vital role as robot numbers expand because it ensures smooth communication between groups A and B. Figure 6.8 illustrates a rise in bandwidth employed. The highest data rate for category A robots with 3D lidar is around 3.78 Mbps

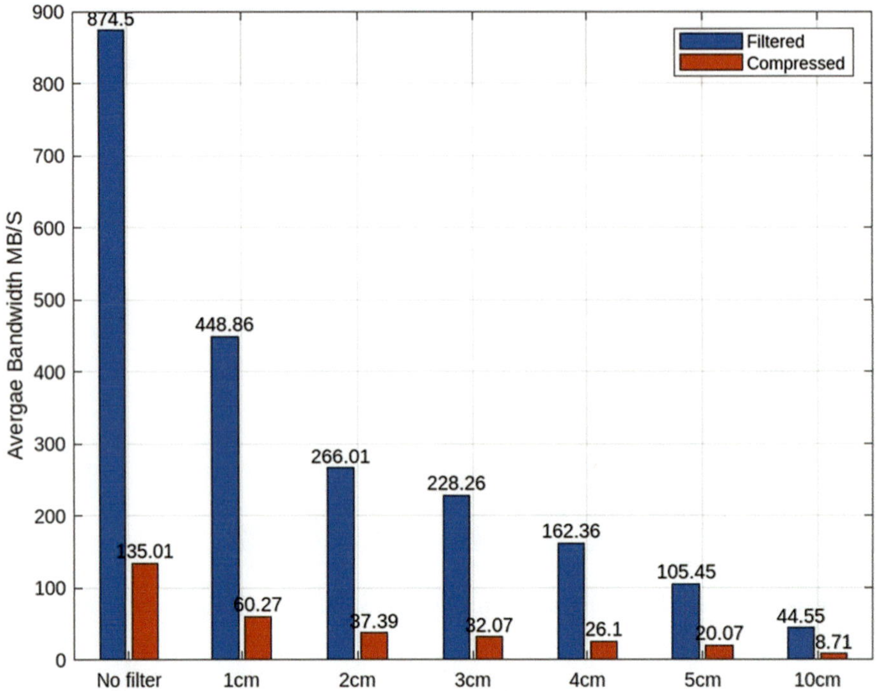

Figure 6.7 Comparing multi-robot point cloud streams that have been filtered and compressed.

(0.47 MB/s), whereas category B robots with depth imaging can function at the highest rate of approximately 35.04 Mbps (4.13 MB/s).

The fleet size is impacted by the kind of robot selected. A bigger fleet can be operated using reduced speeds for robots, such as category Robot A, if bandwidth is limited, like 16 category A robots vs. 2 group B robots on 70 MB/s. On the other hand, few high-data-rate robots like B were used if visual abilities were given priority. Fleet size and abilities can be balanced by combining the two types. While preventing bandwidth overabundance, fleet size can be significantly optimized, and actual time agility can be improved with bandwidth management techniques like frequency control.

Vast regions may present stability difficulties for the consolidated strategy of the system because of interruptions from wireless technology and obstructions. Decentralized connectivity and interconnected wireless mesh networks may offer flexible links to increase resiliency and accessibility. In real-life circumstances, variables like signal intensity might alter communication, necessitating

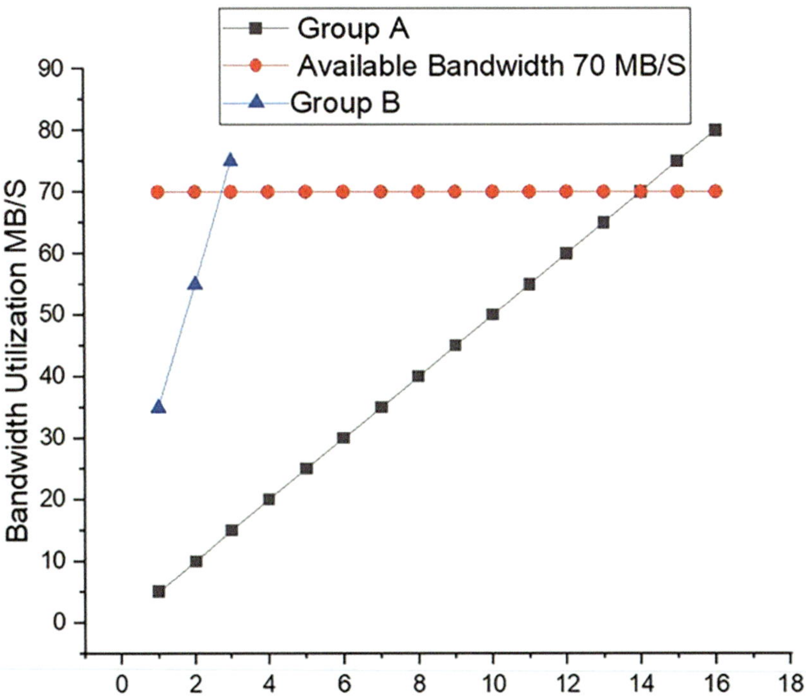

Figure 6.8 Maximum number of deployable robots for groups A and B, considering uniform bandwidth allocation and a 70 Mbps bandwidth.

bandwidth estimations. This is why the bandwidth management method requires previous bandwidth information. The findings indicate that resolving bandwidth constraints in multi-robot fleets requires intelligent data management, not merely 5G/6G. To ensure smooth communication, flexible data utilization approaches must be used to obtain minimal latency and sufficient bilateral bandwidth. Because evaluation duties identify the autonomy stages, minimal latency is essential for actual time visualization, control, and interconnection. Level 3 autonomy with conditions is best for exploring dangerous environments.

6.5.2 Upgraded wireless cyber-physical medical system (UWCPMS)

CPMS designs [54] consist of four basic components: (i) the information acquisition level, (ii) the preliminary information level, (iii) the cloud analyzing level, and (iv) the execution level.

6.5.2.1 Case study of UWCPMS

The computer foundation, sensors, and connectivity are separated into tiny parts by the UWCPMS. Various data are gathered, such as medical service user behavior and information about public health. Structures are equipped with sensors, and cameras adopt a video-centered technique to record motions such as strolling, lying down, and racing. Secure and flexible accessibility is improved by image-based authentication and movement tracking. Connectivity and computation are integrated with the safety core, and data processing in the cloud is utilized for cost-effectiveness. Huge-scale wireless transmission varies from ad hoc links using fewer devices and being more associated with the physical situation. Wireless networks must carry out activities within time limits and with minimal energy to prevent unfavorable consequences. One of the main research challenges is supporting wireless sensor nodes on a big scale.

Time constraints for computations and messages in CPS platforms must be adhered to avoid major repercussions. One of the primary investigation challenges is providing support for wireless sensor nodes. Movement tracking and image-based authorization may increase individuals' access reliability and flexibility. The safeguarding core combines processing and connectivity units, using cloud computing to save costs. The process flow of the UWCPMS model, comprising limit control devices, cloud computing, protection designs, WBANs, and sensor nodes, is shown in Figure 6.9. Sensors transmit data to pathways, where it is saved for assessment. Scheduling, path, and medium accessibility are important research subjects. Activities were divided via layered interactions, allowing CPMS devices to keep track in actual time and with flexibility. The objective is to construct an abstract actual time level for efficient wireless transmission in changing surroundings.

This study demonstrates the medical use in three settings: job sites, residences, and healthcare. This application allows everyday information about health from cameras, biomarkers, and other equipment to be saved in an external cloud, strengthening care for seniors while decreasing medical expenditures. Wireless or wired, medical professionals or caretakers can examine this information and offer guidance or treatment virtually. Doctors and family members receive information rapidly in situations such as a fall.

The UWCPMS data handling unit employs a communication system to gather and evaluate data collected by sensors and actuators. Information is processed by processing and control modules using wireless or wired connections. Indoors, actual time scheduling and tracking are done using a variety of security measures. Healthcare facilities employ ZigBee devices or RFID tags

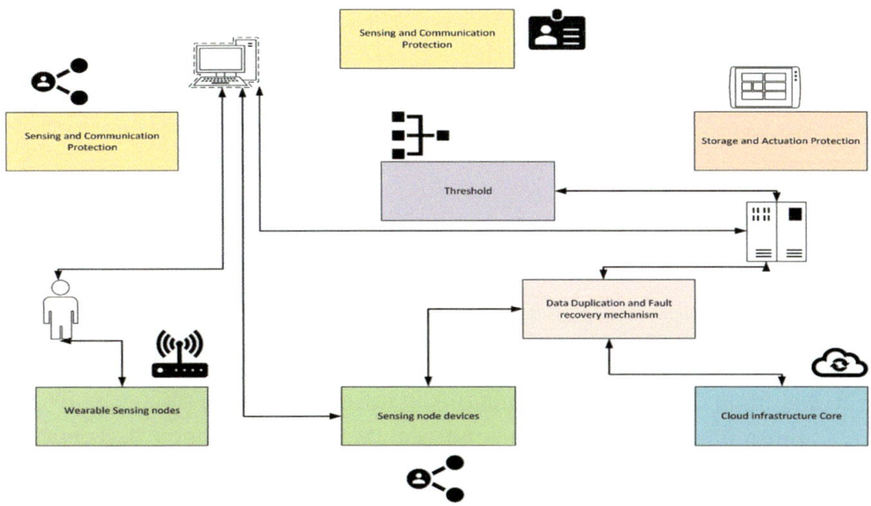

Figure 6.9 Proposed UWCPMS workflow.

in locations where recording devices are inappropriate. The concerns that need to be handled in the CPMS study are transparency, security, confidence, and reliability. To tackle these problems, machine learning utilization [55] is suggested to create a better wireless medical cyber-physical system. Deep neural networks are needed to identify and categorize cyberattacks because the variety of components in medical facilities offers broad areas for attack. Endpoint devices, from mobile phones to hard drives, contribute to this attack surface. Solutions are evaluated against threats such as data injection, DoS, and data alteration using patient data. DoS attacks are frequent and destructive; they obstruct network connections by depleting system assets. Deep neural networks were used to improve privacy by identifying and categorizing these assaults.

6.5.2.2 Results and discussion

Three unique statistics were computed to evaluate the proposed models. The lambda design, which relies upon the Apache Spark and Apache Kafka methods adopted for a simulation, was introduced in the framework. The model's parameters were analyzed depending on the inner framework and verified by relying on the information provided automatically, while the model's hyperparameters were defined independently. Prioritizing communication latency is the first step in assessing an infrastructure's effectiveness. The performance, half-total rate of error, and computational efficiency of the suggested forecasting approaches were evaluated. Finally, the precision,

Table 6.5 Analysis of simulation results.

Technique	Precision %	Effectiveness %
FL	51	43
RF	48	49
CNN	67	56
DNN	73	69
DT	79	71
UWCPMS	92	89

efficacy, hold-up, and usage period of the proposed model were evaluated. The lag graph displays the fluctuations in information size.

Table 6.5 presents the specific accuracy and efficiency percentages, highlighting UWCPMS's higher performance. The simulation analysis of the proposed UWCPMS shows superior accuracy and efficiency compared to existing models like convolutional neural network (CNN), deep neural network (DNN), random forest (RF), decision tree (DT), and fuzzy logic (FL). UWCPMS consistently outperformed these models, especially with larger data sizes. The UWCPMS also demonstrated improved classification accuracy and efficiency, supported by its theoretical error calculation and avoidance model.

6.5.2.3 Analysis of delay

Figures 6.10(a) and (b) display the findings of the delay investigation between the suggested UWCPMS model and the current CPS model. Simulation data sizes ranged from 500 kB to 5000 kB in steps of 500 kB. Compared to the current model, the UWCPMS model continuously offered reduced delays because it made better decisions and had more reliable errors.

6.5.2.4 Analysis of time

The computation time analysis between the suggested UWCPMS framework and the current CPS model is displayed in Figures 6.11(a) and (b). Data sizes for the simulation changed, and a graph of the last output's time to compute was generated. The UWCPMS model required less time due to fewer components and processing blocks, while the existing model needed multiple layers and feedback loops to achieve optimized results. The computation time analysis for the proposed UWCPMS model is compared to the existing CPS model. As data size increased, so did computation time, but the UWCPMS model had shorter times due to its simpler processing layers. Its theoretical error calculation and avoidance model also resulted in faster accuracy.

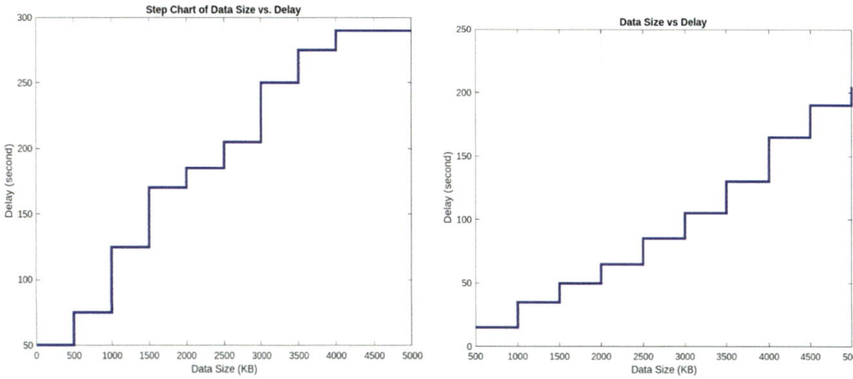

(a) (b)

Figure 6.10 Delay analysis of (a) proposed UWCPMS (b) current CPS.

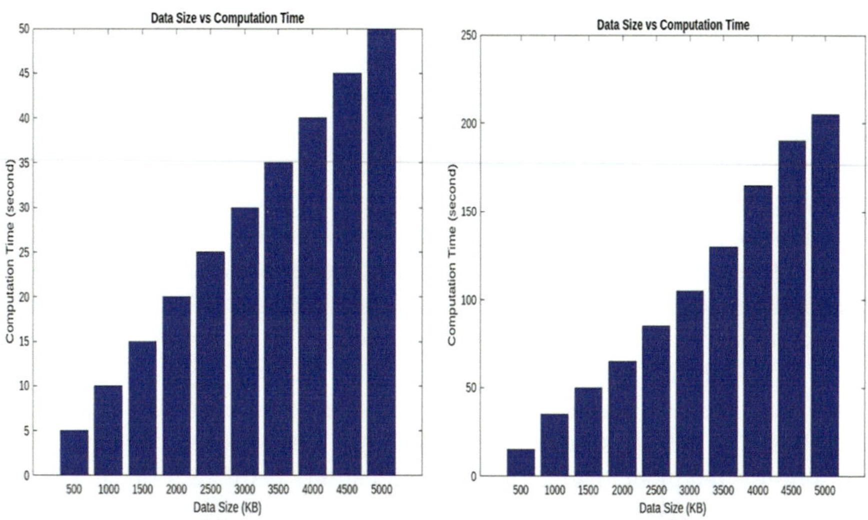

(a) (b)

Figure 6.11 Computation time analysis of (a) proposed UWCPMS (b) current CPS.

6.5.2.5 Analysis of efficiency and accuracy

Figures 6.12(a) and (b) display the suggested UWCPMS model's precision and effectiveness assessments alongside those of other models, such as CNN, DNN, RF, DT, and FL. Because of its reduced complexity and enhanced error prediction – achieved by lowering the number of computation layers – the UWCPMS model fared better than the others.

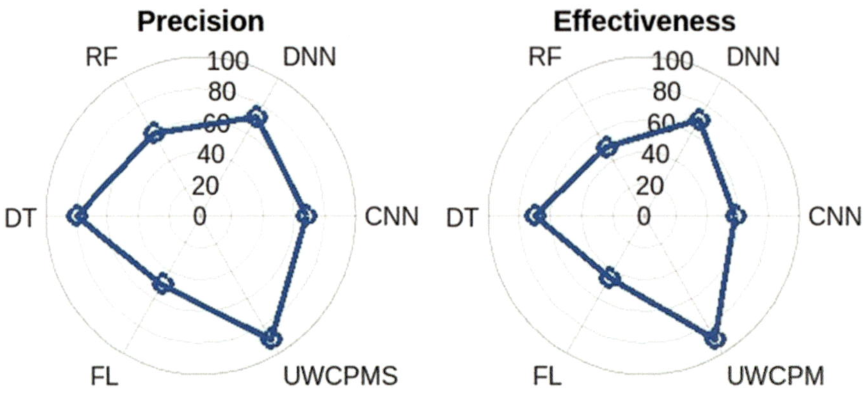

(a) (b)

Figure 6.12 (a) Precision analysis (b) effectiveness.

6.5.2.6 Analysis of attack rate

Figure 6.13 illustrates how the UWCPMS framework, which used deep neural networks to identify attacks, provided a successful security measure due to its significant detection rate. The DNN and CNN approaches were used to determine this rate. The UWCPMS framework was evaluated against risks, including data manipulation, DoS, and data injection using actual patient information because medical information is sensitive. The test outcomes showed that the UWMCPS model performed better because of its enhanced selection sections and reduced complication. Additionally, the framework decreased delay choices without using the cloud.

The results illustrate how the suggested UWCPMS approach functions better than the rest because of its sophisticated choice units and reduced complication. It lowers delay without using cloud services. According to the scrutiny, the model had a threat identification rate of 98.92%, an execution time of 13 seconds, a precision of 92%, and an effectiveness of 89%. Subsequent research endeavors will use compact deep neural networks to expedite bio-modality categorization and enhance communication and security protocols inside the UWCPMS framework.

6.6 Conclusions and Future Scope

This study presents CPS security and privacy, focusing on two major application areas: industrial robots and wireless medical systems. The classification of dangers, weaknesses, known attacks, and available countermeasures are also introduced. Furthermore, an approach for cyber-physical security

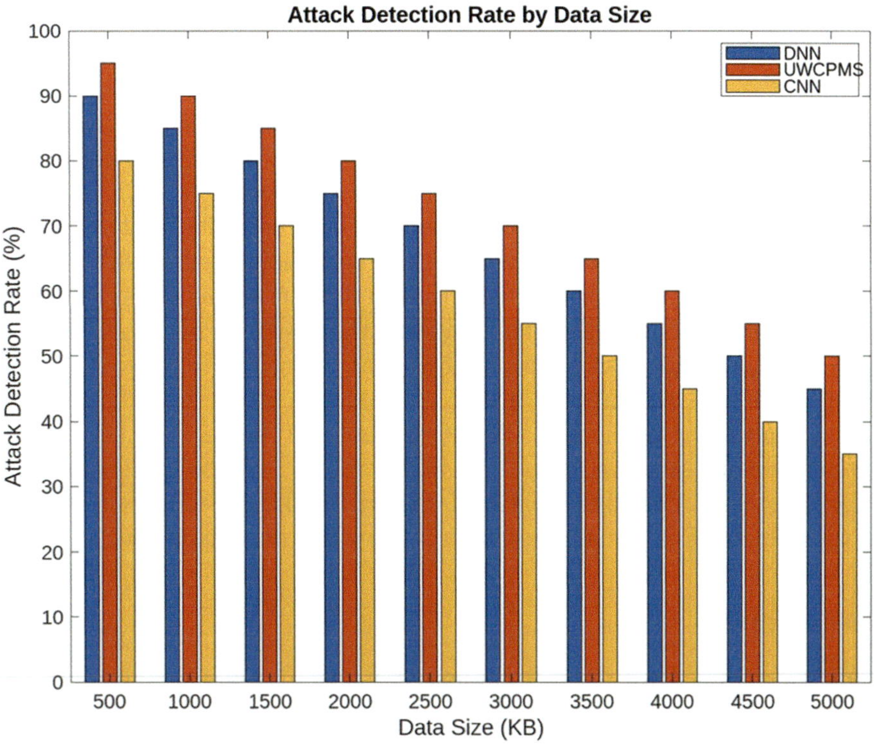

Figure 6.13 UWCPMS attack detection rate.

incorporates the special features of CPS into the wider scenario of security procedures. A CPS architecture intended for multi-robot operation that is both robust and easy to set up is presented. By uniting disparate robots into a single unit, the structure facilitates smooth communication and increases the utility of monitoring tasks. Joint tasks and actual time simultaneous exchange of information are supported by the framework, which has a minimal delay, flexible communication systems, and digital twin technologies. Using a digital layer layout, this technology enables administrators to oversee and manage networks of autonomous robots, greatly enhancing industrial assessments, task scheduling, and efficiency while lowering hazards and related expenses. In the future, unmanned robot fleets with robots specifically designed for data collection and repair will be deployed in settings such as power plants and nuclear facilities. This research will examine AI-driven adaptive data processing and optimization strategies to minimize bandwidth consumption while improving system reliability. It will also involve distant communication tests, practical application testing, and commercial implementation. Two critical topics for improvement are putting data distribution on ROS2 and comprehending the semantic handling of assets in examination and management. A unique architecture that combines privacy and cloud platforms with detecting, exchanges, computing, cloud-based services, and safeguarding cores is presented. The real-world situation was also described for the upgraded wireless medical cyber-physical medical system (UWCPMS). The suggested methodology improves precision and computational effectiveness across three bio-modalities while lowering choice-making delay without depending on cloud computing. Though the data collection is restricted, future studies will examine extending this framework to bio-modality task classification utilizing compressed deep neural networks to improve execution speed. Subsequent investigations should concentrate on cybersecurity and connectivity within the UWCPMS structure, broadening the testing ground from federal initiatives. Physical defenses must be strengthened to stop communication distortion from compromised cyber-physical systems. Exposure of ICS elements is a significant flaw that needs to be fixed.

References

[1] M. Al Faruque, F. Regazzoni, and M. Pajic, "Design methodologies for securing cyber-physical systems," in *Proceedings of the International Conference on Hardware/Software Codesign and System Synthesis (CODES+ISSS)*, Amsterdam, Netherlands, 2015, pp. 30–36, doi: 10.1109/CODESISSS.2015.7331365.

[2] A. Baird, A. Panda, H. Pearce, S. Pinisetty, and P. Roop, "Scalable security enforcement for cyber physical systems," *IEEE Access*, vol. 12, pp. 14385–14410, November, 2024, doi: 10.1109/ACCESS.2024.3357714.

[3] C. M. Ahmed and A. P. Mathur, "Hardware identification via sensor fingerprinting in a cyber-physical system," in Proceedings of the *IEEE International Conference on Software Quality, Reliability and Security Companion (QRS-C)*, Prague, Czech Republic, 2017, doi: 10.1109/QRS-C.2017.89

[4] A. Humayed, J. Lin, F. Li, and B. Luo, "Cyber-physical systems security—A survey," *IEEE Internet of Things Journal*, vol. 4, no. 6, pp. 1802–1831, December 2017, doi: 10.1109/JIOT.2017.2703172.

[5] C. Konstantinou, M. Maniatakos, F. Saqib, S. Hu, J. Plusquellic, and Y. Jin "Cyber-Physical Systems: A Security Perspective," in *Proceedings of the 20th IEEE European Test Symposium (ETS)*, Cluj-Napoca, Romania, 2015, doi:10.1109/ETS.2015.7138763.

[6] D. Gislason, *ZigBee Wireless Networking,* Burlington, MA, USA: Newnes, 2008.

[7] S. Kim, K.-J. Park, and C. Lu, "A survey on network security for cyber–physical systems: From threats to resilient design," *IEEE Communications Surveys & Tutorials,* vol.24, no. 3, pp. 1534–1573, June, 2022, doi: 10.1109/COMST.2022.3187531.

[8] J. Otto, N. Gruttemeier, and F. Specht, "Security Decisions for Cyber-Physical Systems based on Solving Critical Node Problems with Vulnerable Nodes," *Cryptography and Security,* June, 2024, doi: 10.48550/arXiv.2406.10287.

[9] S. Bernardi, U. Gentile, S. Marrone, J. Merseguer, and R. Nardone, "Security modelling and formal verification of survivability properties: Application to cyber–physical systems," *Journal of Systems and Software,* vol. 117, p. 110746, January, 2021, doi:10.1016/j.jss.2020.110746.

[10] S. S. Khairullah and C. R. Elks, "Self-repairing hardware architecture for safety-critical cyber-physical-systems," *IET Cyber-Physical Systems: Theory & Applications*, vol. 5, no. 1, pp. 92–99, October, 2020, doi: 10.1049/iet-cps.2019.0022.

[11] S. S. Khairullah, "Formal verification of a dependable state machine-based hardware architecture for safety-critical cyber-physical systems: Analysis, Design, and Implementation,"*Journal of Electronic Testing springer*, July, 2024, doi: 10.1007/s10836-024-06126-6.

[12] Z. Yu, Z. Kaplan, Q. Yan, and N. Zhang, "Security and privacy in the emerging cyber-physical world: A survey," *IEEE Communications Surveys & Tutorials*, vol. 23, no. 3, pp. 1879–1919, May, 2021, doi: 10.1109/COMST.2021.3081450.

[13] J.-P. A. Yaacoub, O. Salman, H. N. Noura, N. Kaaniche, A. Chehab, and M. Malli, "Cyber-physical systems security: Limitations, issues and future trends," *Microprocessors and Microsystems: Embedded Hardware Design*, vol. 77, pp. 103201, July, 2020, doi:10.1016/j.micpro.2020.103201.

[14] M. Keshk, B. Turnbull, E. Sitnikova, D. Vatsalan, and N. Moustafa, "Privacy-preserving schemes for safeguarding heterogeneous data sources in cyber-physical systems," *IEEE Access*, vol. 9, pp. 55077–55097, March, 2021, doi: 10.1109/ACCESS.2021.3069737.

[15] R. Lanotte, M. Merro, A. Munteanu, and L. Vigano, "A formal approach to physics-based attacks in cyber-physical systems," *ACM Transactions on Privacy and Security (TOPS)*, vol. 23, no. 1, pp. 1–41, February, 2020, doi: 10.1145/337327.

[16] W. Jiang, L. Wen, J. Zhan, and K. Jiang, "Design optimization of confidentiality-critical cyber-physical systems with fault detection,"

Journal of Systems Architecture, vol. 107, pp. 101739, August, 2020, doi:10.1016/j.sysarc.2020.101739.

[17] R. R. Avula, T. J. Oechtering, and D. Mansson, "Adversarial inference control in cyber-physical systems: A Bayesian approach with application to smart meters," *IEEE Access*, vol. 12, pp. 24933–24948, February, 2024, doi:10.1109/ACCESS.2024.3365270.

[18] S. Gaba, I. Budhiraja, V. Kumar, S. Martha, J. Khurmi, A. Singh, K. K. Singh, S. S. Askar, and M. Abouhawwash, "A systematic analysis of enhancing cyber security using deep learning for cyber physical systems," *IEEE Access*, vol. 12, pp. 6017–6035, January, 2024, doi: 10.1109/ACCESS.2023.3349022.

[19] M. P. de O. Camargo, G. dos S. Pereira, D. de Almeida, L. A. Bento, W. F. Dorante, and F. J. Affonso, "RA4Self-CPS: A reference architecture for self-adaptive cyber-physical systems," *IEEE Latin America Transactions*, vol. 22, no. 2, pp. 113–125, February, 2024, doi: 10.1109/TLA.2024.10412036.

[20] D. B. Deebak and F. Al-Turjman, "Lightweight privacy-aware secure authentication scheme for cyber-physical systems in the edge intelligence era," *Concurrency and computation practise and experience*, vol. 35, July, 2021, doi: 10.1002/cpe.6510.

[21] M. Bagheri, J. Lamp, X. Zhou, L. Feng, and H. Alemzadeh, "Towards developing safety assurance cases for learning-enabled medical cyber-physical systems," *arXiv*, December, 2022, doi: arXiv:2211.15413.

[22] A. Amro, V. Gkioulos, and S. Katsikas, "Assessing cyber risk in cyber-physical systems using the ATT&CK framework," *ACM Transactions on Privacy and Security*, vol. 26, no. 2, pp. 1–33, March, 2023, doi: 10.1145/357173.

[23] M. Khalaf, A. Ayad, M. H. K. Tushar, M. Kassouf, and D. Kundur, "A survey on cyber-physical security of active distribution networks in smart grids," *IEEE Access*, vol. 12, pp. 29414–29444, February, 2024, doi: 10.1109/ACCESS.2024.3364362.

[24] H. Ibrahim, H. Azmi, M. W. El-Kharashi, and M. Safar, "Noninvasive hardware trojans modeling and insertion: A formal verification approach," *Journal of Electron Testing*, vol. 40, pp. 117–135, March, 2024, doi: 10.1007/s10836-024-06100-2.

[25] J. Farooq and J. Soler, "Radio communication for communications-based train control (CBTC): A tutorial and survey," *IEEE Communications, Surveys and* Tutorials, vol. 19, no. 3, pp. 1377–1402, 3rd Quart, 2017, doi: 10.1109/COMST.2017.2661384.

[26] P. Park, S. C. Ergen, C. Fischione, C. Lu, and K. H. Johansson, "Wireless network design for control systems: A survey," *IEEE Commuications, Surveys and Tutorials*, vol. 20, no. 2, pp. 978–1013, 2nd Quart, 2018, doi: 10.1109/COMST.2017.2780114.

[27] N. Etherden, V. Vyatkin and M. H. J. Bollen, "Virtual Power Plant for Grid Services Using IEC 61850," in *IEEE Transactions on Industrial Informatics*, vol. 12, no. 1, pp. 437–447, Feb. 2016, doi: 10.1109/TII.2015.2414354.

[28] N. Higgins, V. Vyatkin, N. C. Nair, and K. Schwarz, "Distributed power system automation with IEC 61850," *IEEE Transactions on Systems, Man, and Cybernetics, Part C (Applications and Reviews)*, vol. 41, no. 1, pp. 81–92, January, 2011, doi: 10.1109/TSMCC.2010.2046322.

[29] M. J. McGrath and C. N. Scanaill,"Sensing and Sensor Fundamentals" in *Sensor Technologies, Berkeley*, CA: Apress, 2013, pp. 15–50, doi:10.1007/978-1-4302-6014-1 2.

[30] C. Seceleanu, M. Johansson, J. Suryadevara, G. Sapienza, T. Seceleanu, S.-E. Ellevseth, and P. Pettersson,"Analyzing a wind turbine system: From simulation to formal verification," *Science of Computer Programming*, vol. 133, pp. 216–242, January, 2017, doi: 10.1016/j.scico.2016.09.007.

[31] O. Ljungkrantz, K. Akesson, M. Fabian, and Y. Chengyin, "Formal specification and verification of industrial control logic components," *IEEE Transactions on Automation Science and Engineering*, vol. 7, no. 3, pp. 538–548, July, 2010, doi:10.1109/TASE.2009.2031095.

[32] E.-Y. Kang, D. Mu, L. Huang, and Q. Lan, "Verification and validation of a cyber-physical system in the automotive domain," in *Proceedings of the IEEE International Conference on Software Quality, Reliability and Security Companion (QRS-C),* Prague, Czech Republic, 2017, pp. 326–333, doi: :10.1109/QRS-C.2017.62.

[33] L. K. Singh and H. Rajput, "Dependability analysis of safety critical real-time systems by using Petri nets," *IEEE Transactions on Control Systems Technology*, vol. 26, no.3, pp. 415–426, March 2018, doi: 10.1109/TCST.2017.2669147.

[34] Z. Li, Y. Wang, Z. Huang, "Ada-FA: A comprehensive framework for adaptive fault tolerance and ageing mitigation in FPGAs," *IEEE Internet Things Journal*, vol. 11, no.10, pp. 17688–17699, February, 2024, doi: 10.1109/JIOT.2024.3361036.

[35] A. Pakonen and I. Buzhinsky, "Verification of fault-tolerant safety I&C systems using model checking," in *proceedings of the IEEE*

International Conference on Industrial Technology (ICIT), Melbourne, Australia, 2019, pp. 969–974, doi: 10.1109/ICIT.2019.8755014.

[36] Y. Z. Lun, A. D'Innocenzo, I. Malavolta, and M. D. Di Benedetto, "Cyber-physical systems security: A systematic mapping research," *arXiv preprint arXiv:1605.09641*, May, 2016, doi: 10.1016/j.jss.2018.12.006.

[37] Y. Z. Lun, A. D'Innocenzo, F. Smarra, I. Malavolta, and M. D. Di Benedetto, "State of the art of cyber-physical systems security: An automatic control perspective," *Journal of Systems and. Software,* vol. 149, pp. 174–216, March, 2019, doi: 10.1016/j.jss.2018.12.006.

[38] A. Nicholson, S. Webber, S. Dyer, T. Patel, and H. Janicke, "SCADA security in the light of cyber-warfare," *Computer & Security*, vol. 31, no. 4, pp. 418–436, June, 2012, doi: 10.1016/j.cose.2012.02.009

[39] S. Sridhar, A. Hahn, and M. Govindarasu, "Cyber–physical system security for the electric power grid," *Proceedings of IEEE*, vol. 100, no. 1, pp. 210–224, January, 2012, doi: 10.1109/JPROC.2011.2165269.

[40] D. Halperin, T. S. Heydt-Benjamin, K. Fu, T. Kohno, and W. H. Maisel, "Security and privacy for implantable medical devices," *IEEE Pervasive Computing* , vol. 7, no. 1, pp. 30–39, January, 2008, doi: 10.1109/MPRV.2008.16.

[41] M. Rushanan, A. D. Rubin, D. F. Kune, and C. M. Swanson, "Sok: Security and privacy in implantable medical devices and body area networks,"in *proceedings of the IEEE Symposium on Security and Privacy*, Berkeley, CA, USA, 2014, pp. 524–539 ,doi:10.1109/SP.2014.40.

[42] R. Anderson and S. Fuloria, "Who controls the off switch?", in *proceedings of the IEEE International Conference on Smart Grid Communications,* Gaithersburg, MD, USA, 2010, pp. 96–101, doi: 10.1109/SMARTGRID.2010.5622026.

[43] D. H. Ryu, H. Kim, and K. Um, "Reducing security vulnerabilities for critical infrastructure," *Journal of Loss Preventention in the Process Industries*, vol. 22, no. 6, pp. 1020–1024, November, 2009, doi: 10.1016/J.JLP.2009.07.015.

[44] K. Munro, "Deconstructing flame: The limitations of traditional defences," *Computer Fraud & Security*, vol. 2012, no. 10, pp. 8–11, October, 2012, doi:10.1016/S1361 3723(12)70102-1.

[45] T. Hoppe, S. Kiltz, and J. Dittmann, "Security threats to automotive CAN networks—Practical examples and selected short-term countermeasures," *Reliability Engineering & System Safety*, vol. 96, no.1, pp. 11–25, January, 2011, doi:10.1016/j.ress.2010.06.026.

[46] Y.-M. Kwon, J. Yu, B.-M. Cho, Y. Eun, and K.-J. Park, "Empirical analysis of MAVLink protocol vulnerability for attacking unmanned aerial

vehicles," *IEEE Access*, vol. 6, pp. 43203–43212, August, 2018, doi: 10.1109/ACCESS.2018.2863237.

[47] Y. Mo and B. Sinopoli, "Secure control against replay attacks," *47th Annual Allerton Conference on Communication, Control, and Computing (Allerton)*, Monticello, IL, USA, 2009, pp. 911–918, doi: 10.1109/ALLERTON.2009.5394956.

[48] A. Teixeira, D. Perez, H. Sandberg, and K. H. Johansson, "Attack models and scenarios for networked control systems," in *Proceedings of the. International Conference High Confidence Network Systems*, 2012, pp. 55–64, doi: 10.1145/2185505.218551.

[49] H. Jeon and Y. Eun, "A stealthy sensor attack for uncertain cyber-physical systems," *IEEE Internet Things Journal*, vol. 6, no. 4, pp. 6345–6352, March, 2019, doi: 10.1109/JIOT.2019.2905878.

[50] H. Kivrak, M. Z. Karakusak, S. Watson, and B. Lennox, "Cyber–physical system architecture of autonomous robot ecosystem for industrial asset monitoring," *Computer Communications*, vol. 218, pp. 72–84, March, 2024, doi:10.1016/j.comcom.2024.02.013.

[51] G.S. Martins, D. Portugal, R.P. Rocha, "mrgs:A multi-robot SLAM framework for ROS with efficient information sharing," in *Robot Operating System, ROS,* Cham, Switzerland: Springer, 2021, pp. 45–75, doi:10.1007/978-3-030-45956-7_3.

[52] Y. Yue, C. Yang, Y. Wang, J. Zhang, M. Wen, X. Tang, H. Zhang, D. Wang, "Multi-robot map fusion framework using heterogeneous sensors", in *Proceedings of the IEEE International Conference on Cybernetics and Intelligent Systems (CIS) and Robotics, Automation and Mechatronics (RAM)*, Bangkok, Thailand, 2019, pp. 536– 541, doi: 10.1109/CIS-RAM47153.2019.9095798.

[53] M. Giordani, M. Polese, M. Mezzavilla, S. Rangan, M. Zorzi, "Toward 6G networks: Use cases and technologies", *IEEE Communication Magazine*, vol. 58, no. 3, 55–61, March, 2020, doi: 10.1109/MCOM.001.1900411.

[54] A. Alzahrani, M. Alshehri, R. AlGhamdi, and S. K. Sharma, "Improved wireless medical cyber-physical system (IWMCPS) based on machine learning," *Healthcare (Basel)*, vol. 11, no. 3, pp. 384, January, 2023, doi: 10.3390/healthcare11030384.

[55] S. Kim, and K.-J. Park, "A survey on machine-learning based security design for cyber-physical systems," *Applied Science*, vol. 11, no. 5458, June, 2021, doi: 10.3390/app11125458.

7

A Secure Biometric Authentication Architecture for Blockchain-driven Cyber-physical Systems

Oleksandr Kuznetsov[1], Emanuele Frontoni[2], Kateryna Kuznetsova[2,3], Marco Arnesano[1] and Oleksii Smirnov[4]

[1]Department of Theoretical and Applied Sciences, eCampus University, Italy
[2]Department of Political Sciences, Communication and International Relations, University of Macerata, Italy
[3]Vision, Robotics and Artificial Intelligence Lab, Italy
[4]Department of cyber security and software, Central Ukrainian National Technical University, Ukraine

Email: oleksandr.kuznetsov@uniecampus.it; emanuele.frontoni@unimc.it; kate7smith12@gmail.com; marco.arnesano@uniecampus.it; dr.SmirnovOA@gmail.com

Abstract

With the increased usage of cyber-physical systems (CPSs) in different critical domains, there is an emerging need for sound mechanisms for security and privacy. A deep learning-based biometric authentication system using feature extraction integrated with zero-knowledge proof and blockchain-based storage techniques is proposed for a secure authentication system providing better assurance in data privacy. The proposed architecture consists of three modular layers: a biometric processing layer responsible for extracting discriminative features using the FaceNet model, a cryptographic layer transforming these features into keys and generating ZKP-based proofs, and a blockchain layer for immutable authentication results storage. The system was tested on the Database of Faces, which resulted in 100% classification accuracy, reliably

DOI: 10.1201/9788743801306-7

integrated cryptographic functions through proof generation and verification times averaging 1.884 ms and 4.062 ms, respectively. Its compact proof size of 340 bytes speaks to the efficiency of the system. While these results clearly confirm the potential of such a system to be actually deployed in CPS applications, future work will address those challenges related to real-world conditions, such as diverse environments and additional biometric modalities. The proposed system enables a scalable and secure framework for CPS applications where privacy, transparency, and reliability are paramount.

7.1 Introduction

The rapid proliferation of cyber-physical systems (CPSs) into critical domains such as healthcare [1], [2], smart cities [3], [4], and industrial automation [5], [6] has caused unprecedented security and privacy challenges. The integration of physical processes with computational elements in CPS creates complex attack surfaces that traditional security mechanisms struggle to protect [7], [8]. Because these systems are increasingly managing sensitive data and controlling critical operations, robust authentication mechanisms are required for preventing unauthorized access while preserving user privacy. This requirement becomes particularly crucial as CPS deployments expand in scale and complexity, handling everything from patient health records to critical infrastructure control [9], [10].

Conventional authentication methods based on passwords or PINs prove inadequate in the case of CPS with regard to their vulnerability against various attacks and poor user experience [11]. These traditional approaches suffer from multiple weaknesses: they can be forgotten, stolen, or shared; they are susceptible to brute force and dictionary attacks; and they provide no inherent binding between the authenticator and the legitimate user [12], [13]. Furthermore, the distributed nature of CPS environments makes password management and access control particularly challenging.

Biometric authentication, on the other hand, offers a promising alternative through the use of hard-to-forge physiological or behavioral traits, combining high security with user convenience [10], [14]. Biometric traits such as fingerprints, facial features, and iris patterns are unique to individuals, cannot be easily forgotten or transferred, and provide a natural link between the authentication credential and its rightful owner. Recent advances in machine learning and computer vision have significantly improved the accuracy and reliability of biometric recognition systems [18], [19].

However, this adoption of biometric systems in CPS introduces challenges with respect to three critical aspects. First, the protection of sensitive biometric data during storage and transmission remains a significant concern, as compromise of biometric information is irreversible – unlike passwords, biometric traits cannot be changed if compromised [20]. Second, ensuring reliable authentication while accounting for natural variations in biometric traits presents technical challenges, as environmental factors, aging, and sensor variations can affect biometric measurements [10]. Third, maintaining transparent and auditable authentication processes without compromising privacy requires careful system design, especially in regulated industries where accountability is mandatory.

Accordingly, in this regard, we propose a novel biometric authentication system based on integrating three important technologies: deep learning-based feature extraction, zero-knowledge proofs (ZKPs), and blockchain. This approach leverages recent advances in deep learning through the FaceNet model to extract highly discriminative biometric features with state-of-the-art accuracy. The system employs a carefully designed feature extraction pipeline that maintains consistency across varying environmental conditions while capturing the essential distinguishing characteristics of individual users.

These extracted features are then securely transformed into cryptographic keys using a novel methodology that preserves the discriminative power of the biometric features while ensuring the generated keys meet the cryptographic requirements of the ZKP protocol. The Schnorr ZKP protocol enables authentication without exposing the original biometric information or the derived cryptographic secrets, providing a robust security guarantee through well-established cryptographic principles.

The final component of our system, the blockchain layer, provides immutable storage for authentication records while maintaining user privacy through pseudonymization. This approach ensures that authentication events are permanently recorded and tamper-evident, while the use of cryptographic techniques prevents the linking of blockchain records to individual biometric data or user identities. The blockchain's distributed nature also enhances system availability and eliminates single points of failure in the authentication infrastructure.

7.1.1 Chapter contributions

This chapter adds the following original contributions:

1. A secure and privacy-preserving framework for biometric authentication using deep learning, ZKP, and blockchain technologies.

2. Implementation of an efficient version of the Schnorr ZKP protocol, optimized for authentication using biometric data.
3. The methodology of comprehensive evaluation based on the ORL Database of Faces.
4. Thorough performance analysis including discussions about accuracy, computational efficiency, and security aspects.
5. Critical analysis of system limitations and suggesting future research directions.

7.1.2 Chapter organization

The rest of this chapter is organized into seven main sections: Section 7.2 provides a comprehensive literature review focusing on recent advances in biometric authentication, cryptographic protocols, and blockchain integration in CPS. Section 7.3 details the proposed system architecture and its three main components. It also involves, in Section 7.4, the technical implementation that includes the FaceNet model, Schnorr ZKP protocol, and blockchain integration. Section 7.5 presents the experimental methodology and evaluation metrics. Sections 7.6 and 7.7 present the analysis and discussion of results. Section 7.8 concludes the chapter, mentioning some future research directions.

7.2 Literature Review

Recent developments in biometric authentication [10], [15] and zero-knowledge proofs [16], [17] have received considerable attention in the context of secure CPS and IoMT. This section provides a comprehensive analysis of recent developments in this domain.

7.2.1 Authentication in modern systems

The ever-increasing complexity of the cyber-physical system and IoT networks influence the development of different mechanisms for authentication. Al-Mhiqani et al. (2024) [7] discussed a systematic review in insider threat detection in CPS, showing that 39.1% of the works focused on specification-based methods and 27.5% dealt with cryptographic approaches, showing the increased interest in cryptographic solutions for modern authentication systems.

Alrawili et al. (2024) [10] introduce a detailed analysis concerning biometric user authentication, considering physiological and behavioral characteristics. The authors underline that security enhancement should be balanced with system usability and performance. Indeed, striking a balance between security and usability is one of the main challenges in the design of authentication systems.

7.2.2 Blockchain-based authentication

Recent research is pointing out a strong trend in integrating blockchain with the authentication system. Alsaeed et al. (2024) [18] presented an integrated blockchain and fog computing for IoMT to provide scalable authentication. Their approach has been proven with an improvement in latency, which is 0.5 s, and increased throughput, which is about 400 transactions per second, compared to traditional approaches.

Kumar and Ali (2024) [19] present blockchain-enabled authentication to 6G-IoT-empowered maritime transportation systems; they focus on the necessity of decentralized authentication in a complex networked environment. On the other hand, Iftikhar et al. (2025) [20] introduce BCAuthEN-a blockchain-based authentication technique that reduces computation cost and communication overhead by 10% and 7%, respectively.

7.2.3 Zero-knowledge proofs in authentication

Wang et al. (2023) [21] introduce LZIA, a lightweight zero-knowledge authentication scheme for IoT-embedded devices. Their method solves the computational constraints of the resource-constrained devices while ensuring security guarantees. Kumar et al. (2025) [22] propose iZKP-AKA an improved ZKP-based authenticated key agreement protocol for healthcare applications that addresses issues such as perfect forward secrecy and ephemeral secret leakage.

7.2.4 Integration of modern technologies

Recent works have demonstrated the convergence of multiple technologies in authentication systems. Krishnan (2024) [23] introduces AI-HybridChain, a system that integrates picturized authentication with deep reinforcement learning to improve the security of cloud computing. Lin et al. (2024) [24] introduced blockchain integrated with IoMT using the ECMQV-MAC authentication protocol and achieved better throughput and lower privacy leakages.

7.2.5 Research gap

Although there are many active researches in the area of both biometric authentication and zero-knowledge proof, there lacks a good integration of the two. Current solutions either use very light-weight implementations, thereby losing some key security features, or comprehensive solutions which come out to be highly computation-intensive. We fill this gap by proposing a novel integration of biometric authentication with zero-knowledge proofs, which maintains both aspects.

Particularly, most of the existing solutions:

- Do not provide formal security proofs for biometric-based ZKP systems;
- Lacking efficient implementations for resource-constrained environments;
- Do not address the peculiar challenges in the protection of biometric templates in ZKP contexts.

Our work contributes to filling these gaps by proposing a mathematically rigorous yet practically implementable solution that bridges the theoretical foundations of ZKPs with the practical requirements of biometric authentication systems.

7.3 System Architecture

This section highlights the architecture of the proposed biometric authentication, which embeds advanced feature extraction techniques together with cryptographic zero-knowledge proofs. The architecture is devised to solve critical security and privacy issues related to blockchain CPS in a scalable and robust manner. The overall system is divided into three main layers: a biometric processing layer, a cryptographic layer, and a blockchain layer. Each layer is designed for specific functions, hence working together in view to enable safe and private authentication.

The biometric processing layer is responsible for capturing and filtering the biometric data from which high-dimensional feature vectors are extracted as unique to the users. Then, the cryptographic layer transforms such features into secure cryptographic keys and invokes a Schnorr-based ZKP, which performs the non-revealing authentications. Finally, the immutability of authentication outcomes is enabled at the blockchain layer while maintaining privacy for users in a pseudonymous manner. The separation of this architecture, therefore, guarantees adaptability against different contexts of CPS, ranging from IIoT to smart cities' scenarios. A high-level representation of the system is illustrated in Figure 7.1.

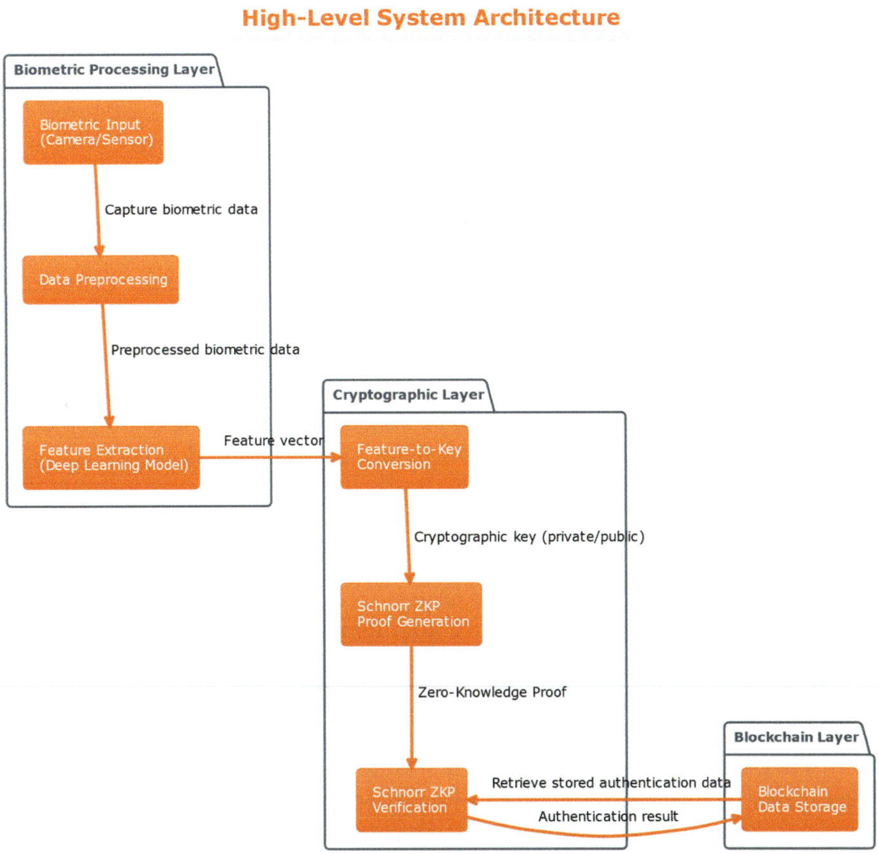

Figure 7.1 Architecture of high-level system.

The high-level architecture illustrates the seamless integration of three critical layers through well-defined interfaces. Each component shall be designed based on separation of concerns while the flow of data between layers is allowed securely. In the biometric processing layer, the pipeline architecture is employed to perform efficient feature extraction, and stateless processing is utilized in the cryptographic layer to enhance security. The blockchain layer will be processed asynchronously to avoid any delay in authentication while allowing immutability of data.

7.3.1 Biometric processing layer

In principle, a system usually has the biometric processing layer, which forms its entry and is tasked with various activities related to the collection, quality testing, enhancement, and matching of the biometric samples input. It is in charge of delivering standardized and suitable data at its output to subsequent cryptographic operation. It comprises mainly of layers of data acquisition and preprocessing. Biometric data – facial images – are first captured by cameras or sensors. These captured raw input data will need to be preprocessed. These include very essential steps for at least reducing variability due to illumination or pose, in addition to other environmental factors – all to maintain coherence in the data that has reached the feature extractor stage.

The processed biometric data then passes through the feature extraction module, which uses a pretrained deep learning model such as FaceNet or InceptionResNetV1. These models showed state-of-the-art results regarding the generation of compact and highly discriminative feature embeddings. Every feature vector is a numerical representation of the user's biometric identity. It usually consists of a 128-dimensional vector and is passed to the cryptographic layer for further processing.

7.3.2 Crypto layer

At the core of the system lies a cryptographic layer providing secure and privacy-preserving authentication, converting extracted biometric features into cryptographic keys, using Schnorr-based zero-knowledge proofs for its integrity and confidentiality.

First, this layer converts biometric feature vectors into cryptographic keys. It normalizes the feature vector to lie within a specified numerical range, followed by quantizing it into discrete integers. Selected components of the quantized feature vector are used for generating a private key that is unique and reproducible for the same biometric input of the derived key. Using this private key, a corresponding public key will be derived using elliptic curve cryptography.

The Schnorr ZKP module uses the generated keys to provide a secure authentication mechanism. In all, there are three major steps involved in generating the proof: it computes a commitment value by hashing the random nonce; then, it generates a challenge from hashing the commitment with the public key to make it secure against any tampering attacks. A response is computed based on the private key, random nonce, and challenge. The response and commitment are both included in the zero-knowledge proof.

The proof is then sent to the verifier, which verifies the validity of the proof without showing the private key. The verification process depends on the properties of elliptic curve cryptography and checks that the given proof meets the Schnorr equation. This ensures that the prover actually has the private key corresponding to the public key, but the private key itself is not revealed. Figure 7.2 shows the step-by-step interaction between the prover and verifier.

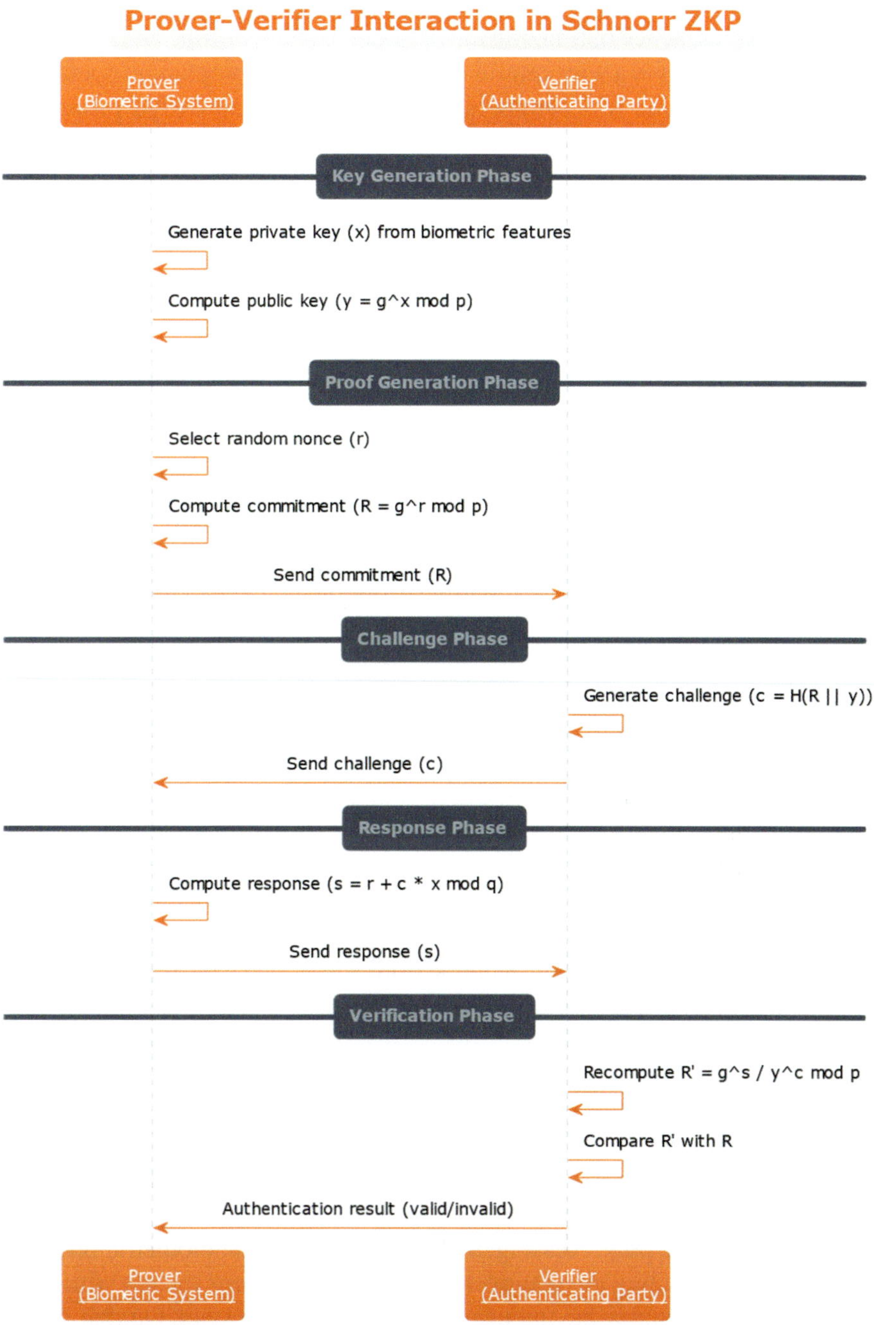

Figure 7.2 UML sequence diagram for prover-verifier interaction.

The sequence diagram depicts that the implemented Schnorr ZKP is non-interactive, hence optimizing the protocol to suit real-time authentication requirements. This is a very careful orchestration of cryptographic operations with minimal round-trip communications and zero-knowledge properties. The diagram highlights that the entire proof cycle can be completed within one authentication session, which is very important for practical deployment in CPS environments.

7.3.3 Blockchain layer

The blockchain layer completes the system, ensuring immutability of the records of authentication events. It ensures transparency with privacy in users' biometric and cryptographic data.

Once the cryptographic layer confirms an authentication attempt, a result is hashed and kept on the blockchain. The data recorded is non-sensitive in nature, such as a hash of the verification result and a timestamp, which does not disclose any identifiable biometric data. Besides, pseudonymous identifiers are used to decouple user identities from blockchain records for further enhancement of privacy.

This layer not only makes the authentication records immutable but also allows auditability by third parties without compromising user confidentiality. Figure 7.3 illustrates the data structures and interactions in the blockchain layer.

The class structure indicates that the blockchain layer is of extensible design, thereby making different consensus mechanisms with varied storage strategies easy in the near future. Its relationships, such as compositions between classes, enable modular updating of the cryptographic primitives, not disturbing the overall system architecture. It also makes a thoughtful segregation of the authentication records from block management, enabling a query facility efficiently while guarantees privacy.

7.3.4 Workflow

It means the proposed system goes through a sequential workflow in which the aforementioned three-layer system integrates the user. It starts with the input provided by the user in some biometric form, such as in facial images, that undergo some preprocessing and then are sent to the biometric processing layer for extracting the feature vector. Later, it converts the resulting vector into a cryptographic key by using the cryptographic layer. On that proof, generated by the Schnorr ZKP module, its correctness is verified by the system and recorded via the blockchain layer.

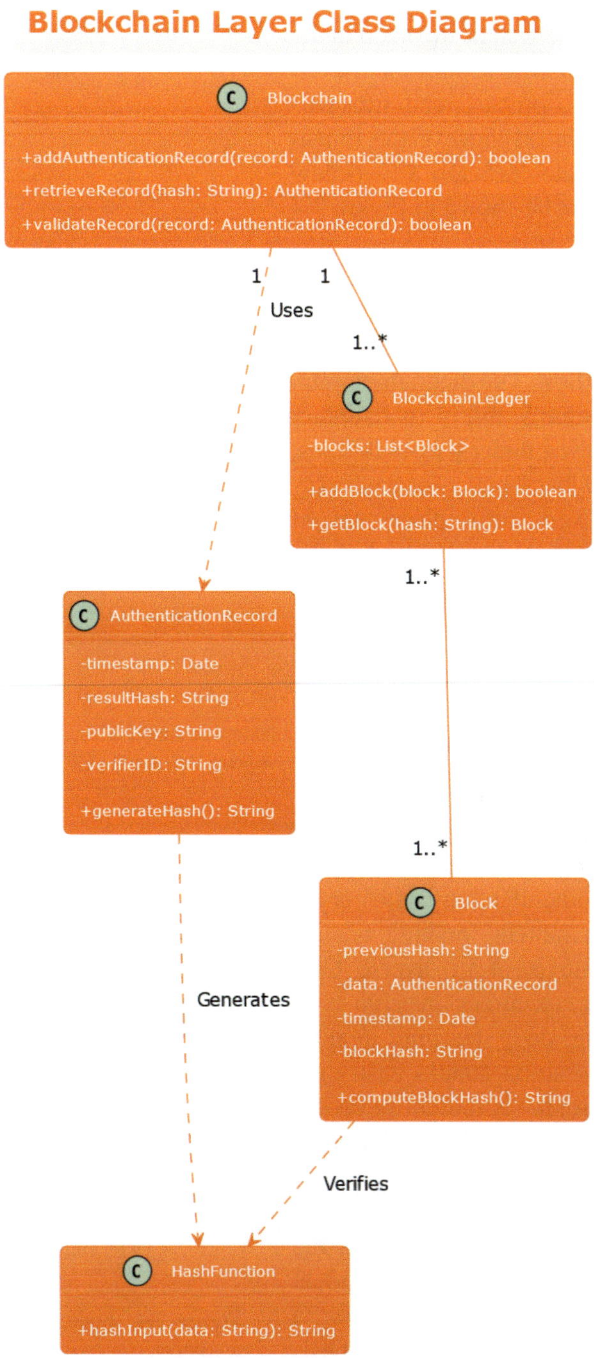

Figure 7.3 UML class diagram of the blockchain layer.

In other words, this workflow ensures that all the steps involved in the processes contribute toward the overall aims: security, privacy, and transparency. An enhanced view of the transitions about states through a workflow in a system can be shown in Figure 7.4 below.

The state transitions reveal sophisticated error handling and recovery mechanisms integrated into the authentication workflow. The diagram emphasizes the system's ability to maintain consistency even under partial failures, with clear rollback paths for each critical state. The careful placement of validation checkpoints ensures that the system can't enter an invalid state, crucial for maintaining security properties in a distributed CPS environment.

7.3.5 Discussion of system architecture

The modular architecture of the proposed system effectively combines biometric authentication with cryptographic guarantees, making it suitable for deployment in diverse CPS environments. Accuracy may go high due to using deep learning feature extraction, common attacks easily get defeated by replay and identity spoofing applying Schnorr ZKP, but also provides higher layer transparency while enhancing user privateness via its blockchain layer. It showcases the efficiency of the system in an ideal environment since it depends on a controlled dataset, for example, ORL

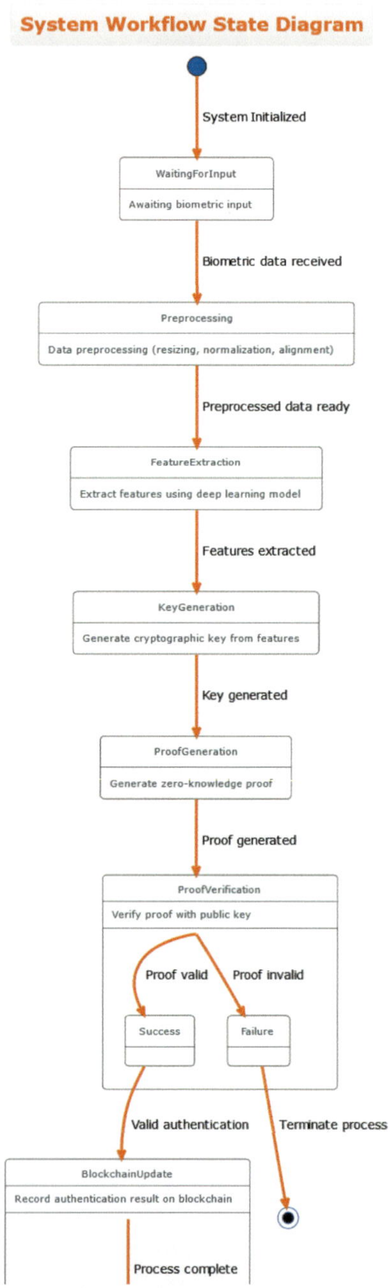

Figure 7.4 State diagram for system workflow.

[25], [26]. Future work will be required to extend this performance on more diverse datasets and realistic conditions to validate its generalization.

7.4 Technical Implementation

In particular, the technical description of our solution encompasses these core sections regarding features taken from the FaceNet model of critical components: the generation of cryptographic keys from features that refer to a biometric trait; finally, using zero-knowledge proof and verification through the Schnorr protocol. These enable us to ensure high accuracy regarding correct recognition of the person possessing any kind of biometric while preserving cryptographic security with necessary guarantees related to user privacy.

Each subsection presents a detailed explanation of the methodologies and algorithms applied, with pseudocode and explanations to facilitate implementation.

7.4.1 FaceNet feature extraction

Feature extraction in biometric processing is the process by which raw biometric input gets represented into a compact yet discriminative format. A very recent state-of-the-art deep convolutional neural network, FaceNet, is adopted, given its excellent previous record in various facial recognition applications.

7.4.1.1 Preprocessing

The preprocessing of input biometric data normalizes the data for consistency before features can be extracted:

1. The original image is resized to a fixed resolution of 160 × 160 pixels.
2. The pixel intensity values are normalized to the range [0, 1].
3. The key facial landmarks aligned in such a way so as to standardize the orientation of the facial features.

7.4.1.2 Feature extraction workflow

The FaceNet model projects the preprocessed image into a 128-dimensional feature vector keeping the identity of the image. The pseudo code for the following is as follows:

Pseudocode for Feature Extraction:

```
function extract_features(image_path):
```

```
# Load image
image = load_image(image_path)
# Preprocess image
preprocessed_image = preprocess_image(image, resolution = (160,
160), normalize=True, align=True)
# Extract features using FaceNet
feature_vector = FaceNet(pretrained_model).
forward(preprocessed_image)
return feature_vector
```

The feature vector extracted from the above process is fed as input to the cryptographic module for secure and accurate representation of the user.

7.4.2 Feature conversion to cryptographic keys

This transformation is an additional pipeline step in order to take the biometric feature vector and turn it into a cryptographic key, meaning securely coupling the biometric with some sort of cryptography, given reproducibility.

7.4.2.1 Feature normalization and quantization

Normalizing it within the known range of feature vectors allows various inputs consistently, which can be taken between [0, 1]. A selection of dimensions of this normalized vector is quantized into integers and forms the foundation of the cryptographic key.

7.4.2.2 Key generation workflow

The private key is derived from the quantized feature vector, and a corresponding public key is generated using elliptic curve cryptography. The pseudocode for this procedure is as follows:

```
Pseudocode for Key Generation:
function generate_keys(feature_vector):
    # Normalize feature vector to range [0, 1]
    normalized_features = (feature_vector - min(feature_vector)) / (max(-
    feature_vector) - min(feature_vector))
    # Quantize normalized features
    quantized_features = quantize(normalized_features, num_bits=10)
    # Derive private key from quantized features
    private_key = hash_function(quantized_features)
    # Generate public key using elliptic curve cryptography
```

```
public_key = elliptic_curve_multiply(generator_point, private_key)
return private_key, public_key
```

The generated keys are then fed to the Schnorr ZKP module that handles authentication.

7.4.3 Generation and verification of Schnorr ZKP

The Schnorr protocol operates in a cyclic group of prime order where the discrete logarithm problem is assumed to be hard. Let G be a cyclic group of prime order q with generator g. The protocol's security is based on the following mathematical principles.

The private key x is chosen randomly from $\mathbb{Z}_q$ (integers modulo q), and the corresponding public key y is computed as:

$$y = g^x \bmod p,$$

where p is a large prime modulus defining the finite field.

During proof generation, the prover first selects a random nonce $r \in \mathbb{Z}_q$ and computes the commitment R:

$$R = g^r \bmod p.$$

The challenge c is then computed as a hash of the commitment and public key:

$$c = \mathcal{H}(R \mid y),,$$

where $\mathcal{H}$ denotes a cryptographic hash function and $|$ represents concatenation.

The response s is calculated using the private key, nonce, and challenge:

$$s = (r + cx) \bmod q.$$

The verification equation checks if:

$$g^s \stackrel{?}{=} R \cdot y^c \bmod p.$$

This equation holds because:

$$g^s = g^r + cx = g^r \cdot (g^x)^c = R \cdot y^c \bmod p.$$

The zero-knowledge property is maintained because:

1. the commitment R is random due to the random nonce r;
2. the challenge c is deterministically derived from public information;
3. the response s masks the private key x with random value r.

The soundness of the protocol relies on the discrete logarithm assumption: without knowing x, it is computationally infeasible to generate a valid response s that satisfies the verification equation. The commitment scheme ensures that the prover cannot change their response after seeing the challenge, as R is bound to both r and the eventual response s.

In the biometric context, x is derived from the biometric features through a deterministic yet irreversible transformation. The protocol proves knowledge of this derived key without revealing either the original biometric data or the key itself, providing a secure bridge between biometric authentication and cryptographic verification.

7.4.3.1 Proof generation

The prover creates a random nonce and calculates a commitment using elliptic curve arithmetic. The commitment is the first part of the proof sent to the verifier.

Pseudocode for Proof Generation:

```
function generate_proof(private_key):
    # Generate random nonce
    nonce = random_integer(1, group_order - 1)
    # Compute commitment
    commitment = elliptic_curve_multiply(generator_point, nonce)
    return commitment, nonce
```

7.4.3.2 Challenge computation

The verifier then creates a challenge by hashing together the commitment and the public key of the prover; this binds the proof securely to the particular authentication session.

Pseudocode for Challenge Computation:

```
function generate_challenge(commitment, public_key):
    challenge = hash_function(commitment || public_key)
    return challenge
```

7.4.3.3 Proof completion and verification

Using the response to compute with the nonce, private key, and challenge completes the proof. Then, the verifier will recompute the commitment with the response and compare it with the commitment from before.

Pseudocode for Proof Verification:

```
function verify_proof(commitment, response, public_key, challenge):
    # Recompute commitment
    recomputed_commitment = elliptic_curve_multiply(generator_point,
response) -
    elliptic_curve_multiply(public_key, challenge)
    # Check if recomputed commitment matches original
    return recomputed_commitment == commitment
```

7.4.4 Integration of components

The above components are integrated into a single pipeline that actually realizes the concept of end-to-end biometric authentication. In summary, the steps involved will be as follows:

- Biometric input is preprocessed, and features are extracted using FaceNet.
- Normalization and quantization are applied to the features in order to transform them into cryptographic keys.
- A zero-knowledge proof is generated, sent to the verifier, and validated.
- Successful authentication results are stored on the blockchain.

The result of each step is a system that is both highly accurate and robustly secure.

The above section has presented a technical explanation of the implementation of the proposed system in pseudocode, representing major processes. Such an implementation is modular; hence, it is assuredly adaptable and scalable to deploy into a wide range of cyber-physical systems.

7.5 Experimental Methodology

The methodology of the proposed biometric authentication system is presented in this section. The experimental evaluation was performed on a publicly available dataset called the Database of Faces for assessing three very important properties of the system: classification accuracy, robustness against data variations, and reliability of its cryptographic integration. It includes dataset description, experimental setup, evaluation metrics, and visualization techniques.

7.5.1 Dataset description

These experiments made use of the Database of Faces, previously known as the ORL Database of Faces [25], [26], a database of facial images taken between April 1992 and April 1994 at AT&T Laboratories Cambridge. Coauthored in association with Speech, Vision, and Robotics Group, Cambridge University Engineering Department, this collection has, for the most part, stayed a benchmark for several related analyses concerning face recognition [25], [26].

Dataset structure [25], [26]:

- Subjects: 40 individual.
- Images per subject: 10 grayscale images in grayscale
- Variations: The images are in variations of lighting, facial expressions that include smiling and neutral, and whether or not the subjects wore glasses.
- Resolution: 92 × 112 pixels, 256 gray levels
- File structure: sX, where X ranges from 1 to 40, which corresponds to the subject number and each directory contains a total of 10 files named Y.pgm, where Y ranges from 1 to 10, corresponding to image number.

This consistency of the dataset is quintessential in testing the system because these conditions provide a controlled environment to ensure that the variation in accuracy is indeed from the algorithmic side and not some other noisy, extraneous issues. The only drawbacks with this dataset are its low variability in pose, lighting, and demographic variation. These reduce its application potential for real-world scenarios. In this chapter, the same has been noted, and further work would target such datasets incorporating complexities.

7.5.2 Experimental setup

The primary aim of the experiments was an evaluation of the system:

- Classification accuracy (Accuracy): The accuracy may be defined by the capability of the system to correctly separate the pairs into "same_person" and "different_person."
- Robustness: Invariant performance across changes in illumination, facial expressions, and other details.
- Cryptographic reliability (P_{verify}): the number of generated and verified zero-knowledge proofs.

Key metrics:

1. Accuracy:

$$\text{Accuracy} = \frac{\text{TP} + \text{TN}}{\text{TP} + \text{TN} + \text{FP} + \text{FN}},$$

where TP, TN, FP, and FN represent true positives, true negatives, false positives, and false negatives, respectively.

2. Similarity score (S_{ij}). The cosine similarity of two features vectors f_i and f_j is computed as:

$$S_{ij} = \frac{f_i \cdot f_j}{\|f_i\| \cdot \|f_j\|}.$$

3. Proof verification rate (P_{verify}). Proportion of proofs successfully verified:

$$P_{verify} = \frac{\text{Valid Proofs}}{\text{Total Proofs}}.$$

7.5.3 Experimental stages

7.5.3.1 Pair generation

Using this dataset, the following are image pairs of size 500 generated:

- Same person pairs: The 250 pairs were obtained by randomly selecting two different images of the same subject.
- Different person pairs: 250 pairs were generated by randomly picking images of two different subjects.
- Balanced pairing made sure that the numbers in both categories were equal, thus not leading to biased classification.

7.5.3.2 Feature extraction

Each image was processed using the FaceNet model. Preprocessing included

- It resizes each photo to 160 × 160 pixels.

- Normalization of the pixel intensity values into the range [0 1].
- Alignment of the key facial landmarks across inputs.

This model returned a 128D feature vector from each image describing the peculiarities of the image. Feature vectors were checked for their discriminative power, and indeed there was a clear separation of "same_person" and "different_person" categories.

7.5.3.3 Computation of similarity metric

For each pair, the cosine similarity score (S_{ij}) was calculated between the feature vectors. Finally, all the classification results were noted down for reference and also for calculating the accuracy metric in order to determine the performance of the system.

7.5.3.4 Crypto integration

Feature vectors from the first image in each pair were then projected into cryptographic keys. Corresponding private keys generated Schnorr zero-knowledge proofs, which were verified with the public keys. It also recorded the success rate of each proof generation and verification, reflecting the reliability of the cryptographic module.

7.5.4 Summary of the methodology

The experimental methodology was designed to rigorously test both the biometric and cryptographic components of the system. The use of the Database of Faces provided a consistent baseline for performance assessment, while the inclusion of metrics such as accuracy and proof verification rates offered a comprehensive evaluation framework. Results, underpinned by visualizations, highlighted strengths and limitations of the system, therefore providing valuable insights for further development and deployment in real-world scenarios.

7.6 Results

This section represents a deep analysis of the experimental results to underline the performance of the system with a focus on biometric classification, cryptography integration, and overall reliability. The results are presented under three separate sections:

1. Statistical analysis of similarity scores and classification accuracies.

Table 7.1 Similarity score statistics.

Category	Mean	Standard deviation	Minimum	Maximum
Same_Person	0.7022	0.0581	0.6782	0.7586
Different_Person	0.4555	0.0120	0.4361	0.4750

Table 7.2 Classification performance.

Metric	Value
Classification accuracy	100%
True positive rate (TPR)	1.0
False positive rate (FPR)	0.0

2. Evaluation of cryptographic performance: metrics related to the creation and verification of zero-knowledge proof.
3. Visual examples of "same_person" and "different_person" that demonstrate the efficacy of the system.

These results together point to the strengths of the system while showing the areas that need further investigation.

7.6.1 Biometric classification: Statistical analysis

Biometric classification results are summarized in the following Tables 7.1 and 7.2, representing similarity scores and the classification accuracy over 500 test cases: 250 "same_person" pairs and 250 "different_person" pairs.

Analysis:

- The results from Table 7.1 indicate clear separation for the score of mutual similarity in two categories with no overlap.
- Table 7.2 confirms the perfect performance of classification. The couple will all be correctly identified. Once again, the true positive rate and false positive rate, associated with this threshold-based classification system, will again be verified.

7.6.2 Cryptographic performance

Afterwards, an analysis of the cryptographic layer was done: key generation, proof generation, and verification of the ZKP supported by several metrics such as computation time, proof size, and verification success rate (Table 7.3).

Table 7.3 ZKP performance metrics.

Metric	Value
Key generation time	1.20 ms (avg)
Proof generation time	1.884 ms (avg)
Proof verification time	4.062 ms (avg)
Proof size	340 bytes
Proof generation success	100%
Proof verification success	100%

Analysis:

- Proof generation and verification: The average times for proof generation (1.884 ms) and verification (4.062 ms) demonstrate the computational efficiency of the cryptographic layer, making it suitable for real-time applications.
- Compact proofs: The average proof size of 340 bytes ensures minimal memory and bandwidth usage, critical for scalability in resource-constrained environments such as IoT devices.
- Reliability: The cryptographic module achieved a 100% success rate in both proof generation and verification, underscoring its robustness.

These results confirm the feasibility of integrating Schnorr ZKP into the biometric authentication system. The low computational overhead ensures that the cryptographic operations do not hinder the system's performance, while the compact proofs facilitate deployment in bandwidth-sensitive environments.

7.6.3 Visual examples

To further illustrate these capabilities of the system, Figures 7.5 and 7.6 give some examples of "same_person" and "different_person" pairs, respectively. Thus, the system is able to generate discriminative feature vectors in order to ensure high accuracy in classification.

These are pairs of two images of the same person, with similarity scores consistently above the threshold of 0.5. Challenges in pose, lighting, and facial expression are dealt with accordingly.

High measures of similarity will prove the robustness in feature extraction.

Figure 7.6 shows the pictures of different individuals, but the similarity scores are low, always below the threshold.

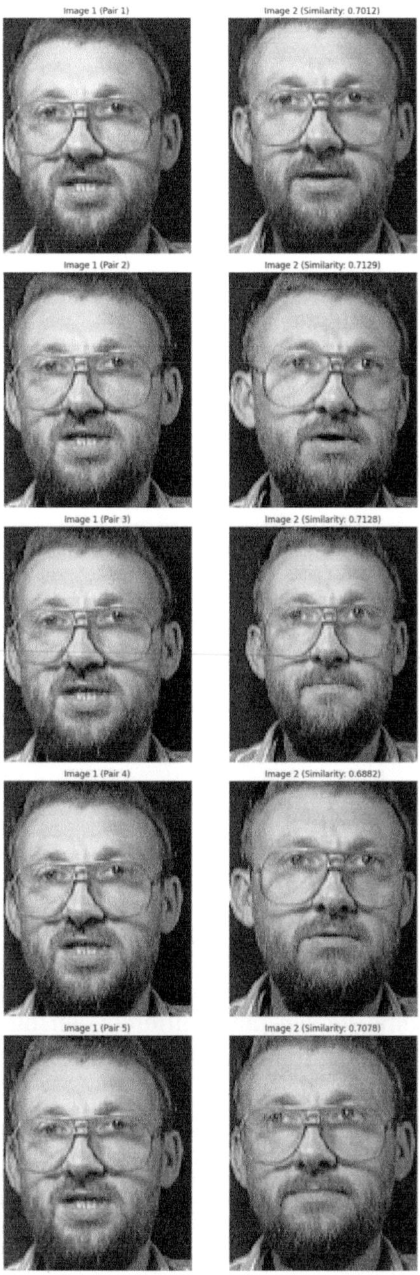

Figure 7.5 Examples of "Same_Person" pairs.

Figure 7.6 Examples of "Different_Person" pairs.

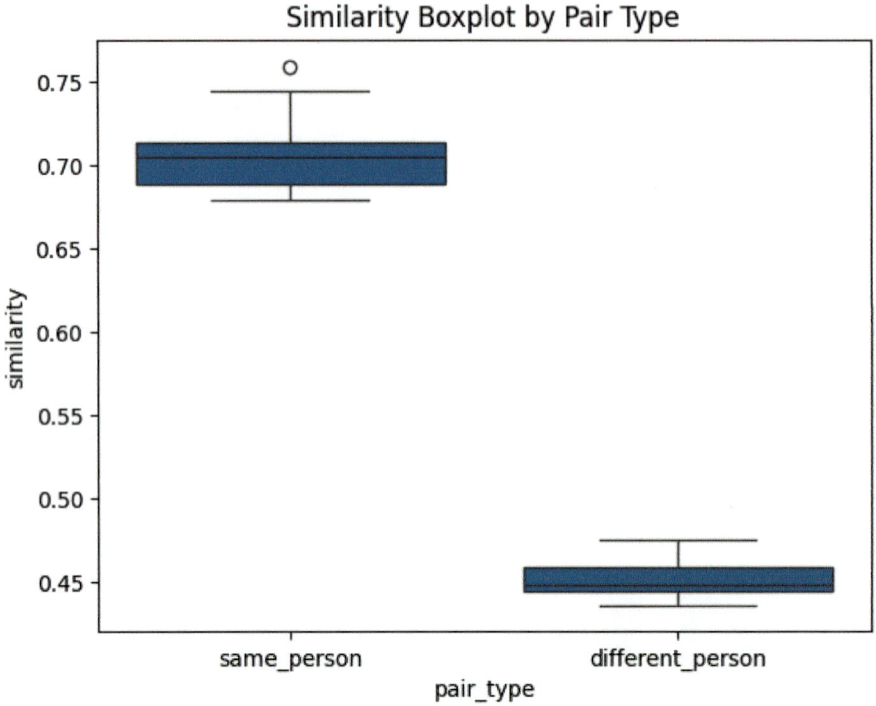

Figure 7.7 Similarity boxplot by pair type.

The classification can be consistent because the system would be able to generate unique and non-overlapping feature vectors.

7.6.4 Visualization of biometric classification results

Apart from the statistical tables, boxplots, and histograms of similarity scores allow one to separate between "same_person" and "different_person" pairs intuitively, which visualizes the system's classification performance (Figures 7.7 and 7.8).

This figure shows the distribution of similarity scores for both "same_person" and "different_person" pairs as a boxplot. The "same_person" similarities are bunched together very near the higher mean value (~0.70) while the "different_person" similarities are decidedly lower at approximately ~0.45 with low-overlap.

The clarity of separation between categories speaks to how robust the feature extraction and similarity scoring that has taken place is. The limited

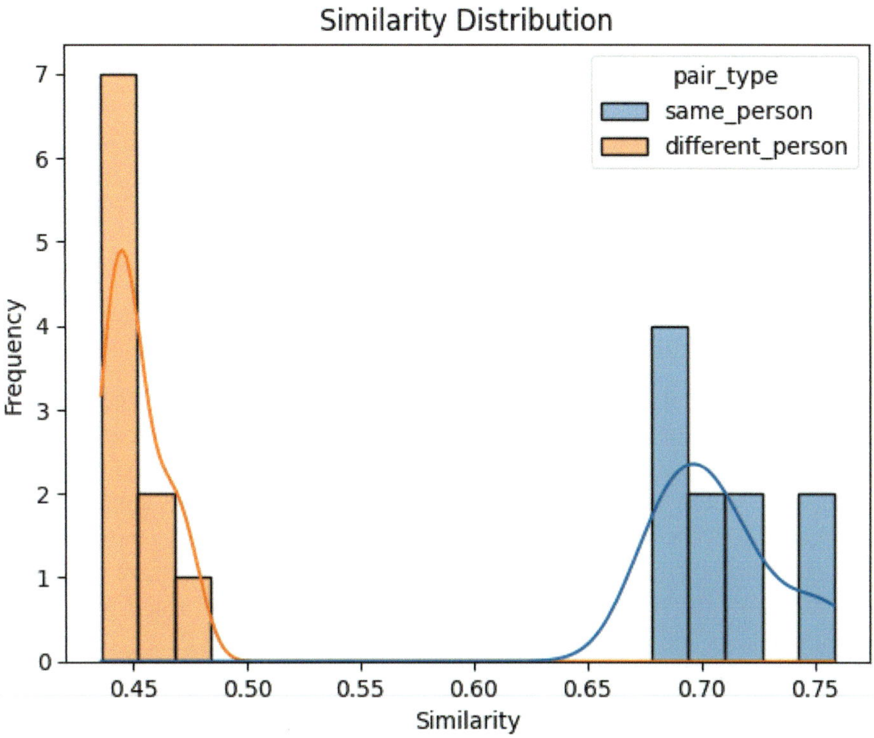

Figure 7.8 Distribution of similarity.

variance for "different_person" pairs speaks to how precisely the system is identifying different subjects.

The following histogram represents the frequency distribution of similarity scores for "same_person" and "different_person" pairs. The two categories show non-overlapping peaks, with "same_person" scores coming in above the threshold at 0.5 and "different_person" scores below the same threshold.

The complete separation of the two distributions underlines the efficiency of the system in keeping the feature embeddings discriminative even for variations in pose, lighting, and facial details.

Figures 7.7 and 7.8 give a very clear visual evidence of the system's performance in terms of biometric classification. The clear separation of the similarity scores proves the validity of the cosine similarity metric and the thresholding approach. Such results are a backup of the statistical data depicted in Tables 7.1 and 7.2, which leads to a more general conclusion: under controlled conditions, the system ensures good accuracy and robustness.

7.7 Discussion

The proposed biometric authentication system combines advanced feature extraction techniques with cryptographic zero-knowledge proofs for addressing the dual challenges of security and privacy in blockchain-based cyber-physical systems. This section provides an in-depth discussion of architectural innovations, implementation choices, testing methodology, and experimental results, together with implications for future work.

7.7.1 Architectural innovation

The system architecture is designed to achieve a balance between modularity and robustness. It consists of three layers, namely, biometric processing, cryptographic operations, and blockchain integration, and hence, the proposed system is scalable and adaptable for various CPS applications. Biometric processing relies on the latest deep learning model techniques for the extraction of distinctive features from facial images that have the highest degree of difference. These will seamlessly get transformed into cryptographic keys and thereafter verified by Schnorr-based ZKP.

The architecture's key strength will be the tight coupling of biometric data with cryptographic operations without compromising confidentiality. Its use of ZKP keeps it non-vulnerable for the authentication process while keeping the confidentiality of both the biometric key and the cryptographic key. Furthermore, integrating a blockchain layer further allows immutability and auditability, hence being able to work in an ecosystem where transparency will be an important role.

The modular nature of the architecture also enables extensibility. For example, other biometric modalities such as voice or fingerprints may be added, or cryptographic protocols like more efficient variants of ZKP with minimal changes in the core framework. This flexibility underlines the possible broader applicability of the system.

7.7.2 Technical implementation

Care had to be taken with the system implementation regarding computational efficiency, accuracy, and scalability. Feature extraction is based on the FaceNet model, which has already proven its capability of generating compact and highly discriminative embeddings. This preprocessing pipeline makes for a very standardized input, thus minimizing variability.

The implementation in the cryptographic layer was a performance-optimized implementation of the Schnorr ZKP. Results indicated that both prover and verifier are computational light and, on average, would take about 1.884 ms and 4.062 ms, respectively. The proof size taken equated to 340 bytes and underlined once more its suitability for bandwidth-limited applications.

The blockchain layer was easy to implement but provided critical functionality for the secure and immutable storage of authentication results. Hashing verification outcomes and storing them on-chain ensures data integrity and auditability without exposing sensitive biometric or cryptographic information.

7.7.3 Experimental methodology

The methodology of the scheme was designed to test both a biometric and cryptographic setup of the system in a rigorous sense. The use of the Database of Faces, with prepared conditions and structured organization, allowed tests on the performance of the system with no additional interference. Given that 500 pairs generated in each class "same_person" and "different_person," equal representation of both classes reduces the bias.

These experiments followed a multi-step pipeline, starting with feature extraction and ending with the verification of cryptographic proofs. Cosine similarity was used as a metric for the closeness of feature vectors, with a classification threshold of 0.5. This method yielded an easy and interpretable mechanism to separate the two classes.

In particular, ZKP performance testing was embedded within an experimental design. Regarding measurement of the generation and verification time along with the size of proof, the experiments had already confirmed the feasibility of real-time cryptographic integration.

7.7.4 Experimental results

The results obtained from the experiment support the capabilities of the system quite well. The statistical analysis of the similarity scores demonstrated that the "same_person" and "different_person" pairs are well separated, with no overlap observed. The average of similarity scores for "same_person" pairs was 0.7022, while in the case of "different_person" pairs, the average was 0.4555. These results thus obtained prove the fact that the FaceNet model is very effective in generating discriminative feature embeddings.

The classification performance was perfect, yielding 100% accuracy without any false positives or false negatives. This result illustrates the robustness of the threshold-based approach to classification. However, it has to be considered that this accuracy could be subject to the controlled conditions of the dataset, and further testing on more diverse datasets should be carried out in order to confirm generalizability.

These very good results are also confirmed by cryptographic evaluation. That the success rates in both proof generation and verification are 100% shows the strength of the implementation of the Schnorr ZKP. From the computational perspective, an average of 1.884 ms in generating a proof and 4.062 ms in its verification means the cryptographic layer can fit easily into real-time applications. Furthermore, since the size of one proof is equal to 340 bytes, the system has the ability to scale up even in bandwidth-sensitive environments.

More detailed visualizations of boxplots and histograms give more details about the system's performance. As illustrated in Figures 7.7 and 7.8, there is a good separation of similarity scores for both classes; thus, proving the extracted features' power for discrimination. Examples of "same_person" and "different_person" pairs are presented in Figures 7.5 and 7.6, respectively. They illustrate the capabilities of this system to work with pictures where different lighting conditions, facial expressions, and other factors have changed.

7.7.5 Limitations and future directions

Although these results are very promising, some limitations do need to be identified: the conditions of the Database of Faces are contrived; hence, it is expected that real-world conditions might pose different challenges. Such extreme light variations, large pose changes, and varied demographic traits have been kept out of this data collection. Future experiments must extend this work with harder datasets such as Labeled Faces in the Wild (LFW) or CASIA-WebFace that may stress the system to handle a scenario close to natural surroundings.

Besides this, the cryptographic layer did a great job and may be further optimized for proof generation and verification times for enhanced scalability. Further improvements could therefore come from looking into more advanced zero-knowledge proof protocols, such as Bulletproofs or zk-SNARKs. Other future work directions may be related to the integration of more biometric modalities. A combination of modalities, such as face with fingerprints or voice, may increase the accuracy and robustness of the system against spoofing attacks even further.

7.7.6 Implications and wider impact

This system represents a significant step forward toward secure and private biometric authentication. The modular design and computational efficiency, along with the strong performance in both the biometric and cryptographic dimensions, make the proposed system a promising candidate for deployment in various CPS applications such as smart cities, healthcare, and industrial IoT. The guarantee of data integrity and privacy ensures critical concerns in modern cybersecurity. Additionally, the addition of a blockchain layer brings an extra layer of transparency and trust to the system, which is suitable for applications that require auditability. This feature is highly applicable in cases involving sensitive data, such as financial transactions or medical records.

7.8 Conclusion

In this chapter, we have proposed a novel biometric authentication system that combines deep learning-based feature extraction with cryptographic ZKP to enable robust security and privacy. Overall, architecture design is done in three modular layers: biometric processing layer, cryptographic integration layer, and blockchain storage layer. This ensures scalability and adaptability for different CPS applications.

These experiments conducted on the Database of Faces proved that this system could work effectively in controlled conditions. Feature extraction, with the help of the FaceNet model, continuously showed highly discriminative embeddings where "same_person" and "different_person" pairs were clearly separated, which was reflected in perfect 100% classification accuracy supported by robust statistical metrics and visualizations.

The cryptographic integration, based on the Schnorr zero-knowledge proof, was reliable and effective, presenting respective average proof generation and verification time of 1.884 ms, 4.062 ms. Besides, the proof size is compact; it reaches as low as 340 bytes, again showing the best fit in case of real-time transmission with restricted available bandwidth.

While these results are encouraging, generalizing from them is limited because the nature of the dataset is quite controlled. Consequently, it should be considered that this work is going to continue to take more challenges that will put the system under conditions not provided earlier, such as real-world datasets and biometric modalities. This will explore better cryptography techniques to optimize scalability by the blockchain.

In all, the proposed system marks a significant step ahead in secure and private biometric authentication, thus providing a robust framework for deployment in CPS applications where trust and transparency are of utmost importance.

References

[1] G. Aceto, V. Persico, and A. Pescapé, "Industry 4.0 and Health: Internet of Things, Big Data, and Cloud Computing for Healthcare 4.0," *Journal of Industrial Information Integration*, vol. 18, p. 100129, Jun. 2020, doi: 10.1016/j.jii.2020.100129.

[2] A. Agarwal, R. Joshi, H. Arora, and R. Kaushik, "Privacy and Security of Healthcare Data in Cloud based on the Blockchain Technology," in *2023 7th International Conference on Computing Methodologies and Communication (ICCMC)*, Feb. 2023, pp. 87–92. doi: 10.1109/ICCMC56507.2023.10083822.

[3] X. Meng and L. Zhu, "Augmenting cybersecurity in smart urban energy systems through IoT and blockchain technology within the Digital Twin framework," *Sustainable Cities and Society*, vol. 106, p. 105336, Jul. 2024, doi: 10.1016/j.scs.2024.105336.

[4] I. Yaqoob, K. Salah, R. Jayaraman, and M. Omar, "Metaverse applications in smart cities: Enabling technologies, opportunities, challenges, and future directions," *Internet of Things*, vol. 23, p. 100884, Oct. 2023, doi: 10.1016/j.iot.2023.100884.

[5] C. Rao and L. Yu, "A particular method for the shortest path finding of mobile robots," in *2010 The 2nd International Conference on Industrial Mechatronics and Automation*, May 2010, pp. 221–224. doi: 10.1109/ICINDMA.2010.5538330.

[6] S. F. Ahmed *et al.*, "Industrial Internet of Things enabled technologies, challenges, and future directions," *Computers and Electrical Engineering*, vol. 110, p. 108847, Sep. 2023, doi: 10.1016/j.compeleceng.2023.108847.

[7] M. N. Al-Mhiqani, T. Alsboui, T. Al-Shehari, K. hameed Abdulkareem, R. Ahmad, and M. A. Mohammed, "Insider threat detection in cyber-physical systems: a systematic literature review," *Computers and Electrical Engineering*, vol. 119, p. 109489, Oct. 2024, doi: 10.1016/j.compeleceng.2024.109489.

[8] H. Harkat, L. M. Camarinha-Matos, J. Goes, and H. F. T. Ahmed, "Cyber-physical systems security: A systematic review," *Computers & Industrial Engineering*, vol. 188, p. 109891, Feb. 2024, doi: 10.1016/j.cie.2024.109891.

[9] A. Kuznetsov, I. Oleshko, K. Chernov, M. Bagmut, and T. Smirnova, *Biometric authentication using convolutional neural networks*, vol. 152.

in Lecture Notes in Networks and Systems, vol. 152. Springer, 2021, p. 98. doi: 10.1007/978-3-030-58359-0_6.

[10] R. Alrawili, A. A. S. AlQahtani, and M. K. Khan, "Comprehensive survey: Biometric user authentication application, evaluation, and discussion," *Computers and Electrical Engineering*, vol. 119, p. 109485, Oct. 2024, doi: 10.1016/j.compeleceng.2024.109485.

[11] M. Jakobsson, "Can Biometrics Replace Passwords?," in *Mobile Authentication: Problems and Solutions*, M. Jakobsson, Ed., in SpringerBriefs in Computer Science. , New York, NY: Springer, 2013, pp. 91–100. doi: 10.1007/978-1-4614-4878-5_7.

[12] M. Lutsenko, A. Kuznetsov, A. Kiian, O. Smirnov, and T. Kuznetsova, "Biometric cryptosystems: Overview, state-of-the-art and perspective directions," *Lecture Notes in Networks and Systems*, vol. 152, pp. 66–84, 2021, doi: 10.1007/978-3-030-58359-0_5.

[13] A. Kuznetsov, A. Kiyan, A. Uvarova, R. Serhiienko, and V. Smirnov, "New Code Based Fuzzy Extractor for Biometric Cryptography," in *2018 International Scientific-Practical Conference on Problems of InfocommunicationsScienceandTechnology,PICSandT2018-Proceedings*, 2019, pp. 119–124. doi: 10.1109/INFOCOMMST.2018.8632040.

[14] R. Amin, T. Gaber, G. ElTaweel, and A. E. Hassanien, "Biometric and Traditional Mobile Authentication Techniques: Overviews and Open Issues," in *Bio-inspiring Cyber Security and Cloud Services: Trends and Innovations*, A. E. Hassanien, T.-H. Kim, J. Kacprzyk, and A. I. Awad, Eds., in Intelligent Systems Reference Library. , Berlin, Heidelberg: Springer, 2014, pp. 423–446. doi: 10.1007/978-3-662-43616-5_16.

[15] H. El-Sofany, B. Bouallegue, and Y. M. Abd El-Latif, "A proposed biometric authentication hybrid approach using iris recognition for improving cloud security," *Heliyon*, vol. 10, no. 16, p. e36390, Aug. 2024, doi: 10.1016/j.heliyon.2024.e36390.

[16] D. Benarroch, M. Campanelli, D. Fiore, K. Gurkan, and D. Kolonelos, "Zero-knowledge proofs for set membership: efficient, succinct, modular," *Des. Codes Cryptogr.*, vol. 91, no. 11, pp. 3457–3525, Nov. 2023, doi: 10.1007/s10623-023-01245-1.

[17] S. Dutto, D. Margaria, C. Sanna, and A. Vesco, "Toward a Post-Quantum Zero-Knowledge Verifiable Credential System for Self-Sovereign Identity," 2022, 2022/1297. Accessed: Nov. 02, 2023. [Online]. Available: https://eprint.iacr.org/2022/1297

[18] N. Alsaeed, F. Nadeem, and F. Albalwy, "A scalable and lightweight group authentication framework for Internet of Medical Things using integrated blockchain and fog computing," *Future Generation*

Computer Systems, vol. 151, pp. 162–181, Feb. 2024, doi: 10.1016/j.future.2023.09.032.

[19] N. Kumar and R. Ali, “Blockchain-enabled authentication framework for Maritime Transportation System empowered by 6G-IoT,” *Computer Networks*, vol. 244, p. 110353, May 2024, doi: 10.1016/j.comnet.2024.110353.

[20] A. Iftikhar, K. N. Qureshi, F. B. Hussain, M. Shiraz, and M. Sookhak, “A blockchain based secure authentication technique for ensuring user privacy in edge based smart city networks,” *Journal of Network and Computer Applications*, vol. 233, p. 104052, Jan. 2025, doi: 10.1016/j.jnca.2024.104052.

[21] Z. Wang *et al.*, “Lightweight zero-knowledge authentication scheme for IoT embedded devices,” *Computer Networks*, vol. 236, p. 110021, Nov. 2023, doi: 10.1016/j.comnet.2023.110021.

[22] S. Kumar, K. Kumar, A. Anand, A. K. Yadav, M. Misra, and A. Braeken, “iZKP-AKA: A secure and improved ZKP-AKA protocol for sustainable healthcare,” *Computers and Electrical Engineering*, vol. 122, p. 109886, Mar. 2025, doi: 10.1016/j.compeleceng.2024.109886.

[23] S. C. Krishnan, “AI-HybridChain: Picturized authentication and DRL based access control method with secure two fold revocation for ensuring cloud computing security,” *Future Generation Computer Systems*, vol. 160, pp. 389–405, Nov. 2024, doi: 10.1016/j.future.2024.04.054.

[24] Q. Lin, X. Li, K. Cai, M. Prakash, and D. Paulraj, “Secure Internet of medical Things (IoMT) based on ECMQV-MAC authentication protocol and EKMC-SCP blockchain networking,” *Information Sciences*, vol. 654, p. 119783, Jan. 2024, doi: 10.1016/j.ins.2023.119783.

[25] F. S. Samaria and A. C. Harter, “Parameterisation of a stochastic model for human face identification,” in *Proceedings of 1994 IEEE Workshop on Applications of Computer Vision*, Dec. 1994, pp. 138–142. doi: 10.1109/ACV.1994.341300.

[26] “The Database of Faces.” Accessed: Dec. 08, 2024. [Online]. Available: https://www.cl.cam.ac.uk/research/dtg/attarchive/facedatabase.html

8

Secure IoT-based Smart Wheelchair System: From Implementation to Security Enhancement Strategy

Oleksandr Kuznetsov[1], Gianluca Atzeni[1], Marco Arnesano[1], Cristian Randieri[1] and Oleksii Smirnov[2]

[1]Department of Theoretical and Applied Sciences, eCampus University, Italy
[2]Department of cyber security and software, Central Ukrainian National Technical University, Ukraine

Email: oleksandr.kuznetsov@uniecampus.it; gianluca.atzeni@studenti.uniecampus.it; gianlucaatzeni@outlook.com; marco.arnesano@uniecampus.it; Cristian.randieri@uniecampus.it; dr.SmirnovOA@gmail.com

Abstract

This chapter develops and performs security analysis of an IoT-enabled smart wheelchair system with voice control, considering critical security considerations in healthcare mobility devices. Further, we also demonstrate how cost-effective solutions could be developed using Arduino microcontroller architecture with Bluetooth communication and dual controls through voice commands and override options manually. The designed system architecture is with prime emphasis on reliability and accessibility, ensuring basic security requirements. We identify potential vulnerabilities in wireless communication, access control, and user privacy aspects by comprehensive security analysis. In this respect, the chapter reviews existing commercial solutions by comparing their technical approaches and respective security features. The result shows significant trade-offs between system complexity and practical implementation considerations in healthcare environments. We now give a structured methodology for increasing the security in our proposed architecture,

DOI: 10.1201/9788743801306-8

based on several identified vulnerabilities but keeping in mind that usability should also be considered for the system. We make suggestions on encryption protocols to be adopted, mechanisms of authentication, and measurements on compliance with regulations. The contribution presented will serve to understand better the safety requirements about IoT devices being used within healthcare while facilitating practical guidelines to implement safety solutions using mobility assistance. The research carried out shows that while the basic functionality of IoT can be achieved with minimum hardware requirements, comprehensive security measures need considerable architectural consideration. This roadmap for enhancing security proposes a balanced approach toward implementing advanced features with system reliability and user accessibility and provides valuable insight into the future development of secure cyber-physical systems in healthcare applications.

8.1 Introduction

The rapid evolution of IoT technologies [1] has transformed healthcare delivery systems in general and the area of mobility assistance in particular [2], [3]. While this transformation opens up new and unparalleled opportunities to improve patient care and independence, it also introduces complex challenges related to system security, user privacy, and operational reliability [2], [4]. While embedding smart functionalities in conventional medical devices is one of the most critical developments for healthcare, most of the current studies fall short of considering security implications [5].

Recent analyses on markets show that IoT for healthcare is in explosive growth, with 30 billion connected devices predicted for 2025 [6]. A very important category of the ecosystem is mobility assistance, as it affects user independence and safety [2]. These systems are paradigm examples of how medical devices are transformed into cyber-physical systems – in this case, the interaction of physical mobility with capabilities for digital control and monitoring creates unique security challenges sometimes extending beyond those with traditional medical devices [7], [8].

The development of IoT-enabled mobility assistance devices faces several critical challenges [7], [9]. First, these systems must maintain robust functionality while ensuring user safety, particularly given their role in physical movement assistance. Second, they must implement comprehensive security measures to protect against unauthorized access and potential malicious control. Third, they have to balance advanced functionality with ease of use, ensuring that security features do not hinder usability for end-users with a wide range of technical competencies. Fourth, they must be designed to meet rigorous healthcare regulations while allowing flexibility and upgradability of the system.

Most of the current research in smart wheelchair systems has focused on functionality and autonomy, giving less attention to security implications [10]–[12]. While commercial solutions show advanced capabilities in navigation and obstacle avoidance, most of them lack comprehensive security frameworks necessary for healthcare applications. Besides, most of the implementations so far require complex infrastructure support, which restricts their practical deployment in diverse healthcare environments.

In this context, our research proposes a new direction in the development of secure IoT-enabled mobility assistance systems. We illustrate an example implementation of a low-cost smart wheelchair system that integrates voice control capabilities while allowing for manual override options – a starting point for developing investigation into security considerations in medical IoT devices. Our approach is practical in implementation while being cognizant of fundamental security requirements and regulatory requirements.

8.1.1 Contribution of the chapter

This chapter makes several significant contributions to the field of secure healthcare cyber-physical systems:

- The design of a holistic security framework for IoT-enabled mobility assistance devices and the realization of the concept through the implementation of an IoT-enabled smart wheelchair controlled by speech, with a manual override.
- Systematic analysis of security vulnerabilities in medical IoT devices: A structured approach toward the identification and addressing of potential threats in healthcare mobility systems.
- Novel approach in balancing security requirements against the aspect of system usability, therefore providing practical guidelines on implementing security measures while maintaining access by users of varied abilities.
- The chapter presents a detailed, comparative analysis of existing commercial solutions that reviews the security features of these solutions and outlines the key lessons to be learned from them for the future development of secure healthcare mobility systems.
- Framework for ensuring regulatory compliance in IoT-enabled healthcare devices, both with respect to present requirements and future scalability aspects.

8.1.2 Chapter organization

The rest of this chapter is organized as:

- Section 8.2 follows with a critical review of related literature that covers the existing state of research in healthcare IoT security, mobility assistance systems, and regulatory frameworks.
- Section 8.3 describes the implementation of our system, hardware architecture, software development, communication protocols, and integration methodologies.
- Section 8.4 elaborates on implementation security analysis, including some issues that could be attacked against the present design and other miscellaneous privacy issues.
- By performing a comparison with state-of-the-art commercial products, Section 8.5 discusses, for various market-available solutions, those features related to security-performance trade-offs.
- The recommended development that follows in Section 8.6 of the present document covers certain priority security enhancements and related implementation guidelines.
- Section 8.7 discusses the implications of our findings for the broader field of healthcare IoT security. Finally, Section 8.8 synthesizes the key findings along with considerations about future research directions in ending.

This research is among the several building blocks in the literature on secure IoT implementations in healthcare, with practical insights for researchers and developers working on similar systems. The findings and recommendations made here aim to advance the field of secure cyber-physical systems while maintaining focus on practical applicability and user needs.

This research builds upon and significantly expands the work originally presented in Atzeni's thesis "Development, Study and Implementation of an IoT System for Remote Monitoring of Medical Aid for People with Reduced Mobility" [13]. While the thesis focused on the practical implementation of an IoT-enabled wheelchair system, this chapter provides a comprehensive security analysis and enhancement strategy for healthcare mobility devices.

8.2 Literature Review

Recent development in IoT and smart healthcare systems has presented tremendous development in the area of mobility assistance devices. The current section is dedicated to the review of the existing trend in research being carried out on smart wheelchair systems from security consideration, control mechanisms, and integration into healthcare systems.

IoT technologies turned what used to be simple dumb medical devices into intelligent and further connected systems. Corsi et al. (2022) [14] noted that smart healthcare is a very important application within modern urban environments, pointing at the need for solid technological infrastructures while keeping citizen-centric approaches as the main focus of this area. Now this has been further exacerbated by the proliferation of IoT in healthcare or what some scholars (Shreya et al., 2022 [15]) have also referred to as IoMT – a facilitation of new possibilities in regard to patient monitoring and delivery of care, on one hand, and raising huge concerns pertaining to security, on the other hand.

Recent research has approached the smart wheelchair development in the following directions:

- Control mechanisms. Nowadays, modern smart wheelchairs have a long list of different control interfaces. Jiang et al. (2023) [16] have presented SmartRolling that was able to use EEG signals in addition to motion sensing to provide natural control. Another work from Hutamaputra et al. (2023) [17] has been able to achieve menu selections by using eye-gaze detection, for users without glass and for users with glasses with more than 90% and 86.99%, respectively.
- Navigation and safety. Safety is still one of the most important issues in smart wheelchair development. Chu and Chen (2022) [18] proposed Smart Wheelchair for Fall Risk Assessment (SWAF), which focuses on evaluating the risk of falling by implementing pressure sensors and filtering data with SVM. Jiao et al. (2018) [19] have proposed an adaptive polymorphic ant colony algorithm for efficient path planning; it showed a superior performance in obstacle avoidance and route optimization.
- Brain–computer interface integration. Badajena et al. (2023) [20] discussed a data-driven method including the use of a BCI with machine learning in order to enhance the accuracy of the control. An Attention Meditation Cost-Benefit Analysis (AMCBA) has been performed regarding meditating on attention and showed improved performance in the complicated operational situation.
- Security and privacy. Various aspects relating to security issues in IoT-enabled healthcare devices have received the attention of several researchers lately. Security implications related to remote patient monitoring using RFID-based authentication and end-to-end communications

were stressed by Imtyaz Ahmed and Kannan (2022) [21] for the need to ensure adequate levels of security. Alfayez and Khan (2024) [22] propose a design framework incorporating blockchain technology combined with federated learning toward providing increased security on virtual assistants targeted at disabled users.

  - Protection of data. Singh et al. (2022) [23] discussed large volumes of health data challenges and recommended some optimization algorithms which will work in line with efficient and secure handling. The research emphasized the need to reduce the time of services and loss of energy without forgetting data security.
  - Privacy preservation. The issue of healthcare data privacy is of vital concern. Rahman et al. (2022) [24], in their iRestroom project, demonstrated the importance of secure monitoring systems through a multisensory environment that ensures data collection mechanisms preserve the user's privacy.

- Challenges in implementation. Different challenges in the implementation of smart wheelchair systems include the following, annually:
  - System integration. Utaminingrum et al. (2024) [25] discuss the complexity of integrating safety features for staircase detection with limited computational delay, achieving 94% accuracy.
  - Environmental adaptation. Tomari et al. (2014) [26] address socially acceptable navigation by incorporating head cue information in human-aware motion planning.
  - Infrastructure requirements. Perez et al. (2023) [27] talk about the demanding infrastructure of IoT to support autonomy in elderly and disabled people, developing the necessity of reliable approaches to their implementation in practice.

The literature review reveals a number of issues that require further investigation:

- improved security mechanisms to be deployed especially on mobility assistance devices;
- improved integration of several control interfaces without loss of system security;
- the development of standardized security protocols regarding IoT devices in healthcare;
- implementation of privacy-preserving data collecting and processing methodologies.

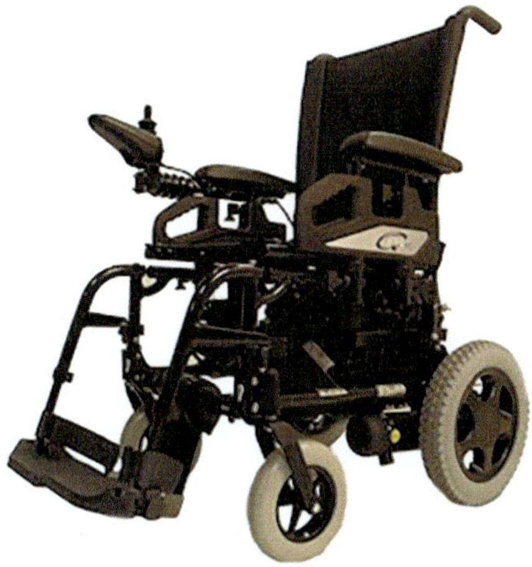

Figure 8.1 Sunrise Medical F40VR powered wheelchair platform, with a look at the base mechanical structure prior to IoT integration.

This review of the current research provides a basis for our implementation approach, especially in addressing security considerations while maintaining system usability and effectiveness.

8.3 System Implementation and Architecture

Any development regarding an IoT-enabled smart wheelchair is heavily based on the proper understanding of hardware integration, the role of control systems, and, finally, user interface design. This section provides the description of our implementation that would essentially change any ordinary powered wheelchair into an intelligent mobility assistance device. As noted, the implementation concentrates on reliable operation with minimal complication of the system and inaccessibility to the users. We describe the architecture of the system, its operation mechanism, and validation methods that ensure safety and efficacy of operation.

8.3.1 Hardware architecture

The implementation platform used in this investigation is the powered wheelchair from Sunrise Medical, F40VR featuring a robust mechanical design easy to adopt with control system. This base wheelchair provided the essential mobility, with capacity for up to 115 kg and programmable top of 6 km/h limit for various users' differing needs. Robust construction provides an excellent platform for smart system implementation (Figure 8.1).

Figure 8.2 Fracmo drive motor with electromagnetic brake assembly, showing compact integration of drive and safety systems.

The propulsion system is based on dual Fracmo motors, each with integrated electromagnetic brakes (Figure 8.2). These provide great precision in the control of wheelchair movement, maintaining safety due to their braking. Table 8.1 gives the detailed technical specifications of the drive system.

It utilizes an Arduino Uno microcontroller as its basis for an electronic control system, which interfaces other components in view of intelligent operation. Such integration allows the wide-range control architecture to process voice commands and manual inputs with consideration for system safety.

The key electronic components integrated into the control system are shown in the Table 8.2.

The integration of these components creates a comprehensive control system capable of:

1. processing voice commands received via Bluetooth;
2. managing motor control for precise movement;
3. providing manual control through the joystick;

Table 8.1 Motor technical specifications.

Parameter	Specification
Model	451-50-115-G31-29A
Current rating	10.5 A
Frequency	DC
RPM	115
Voltage	24 MTR 12 BRK
Rating	CONT
Output torque	11.0 Nm

Table 8.2 Electronic components specification.

Component	Quantity	Model/Type	Function
Microcontroller	1	Arduino UNO (A000066)	Central processing and control
Relay module	1	IT-EL-SM-005 8-Channel	Motor control switching
Motor drivers	2	BTS7960	Motor speed and direction control
Audio indicators	2	KPX-1212A Buzzer	User feedback and warnings
Bluetooth module	1	HC-05	Wireless communication
Manual control	1	HW-504 Joystick	Backup control system
Power supply	1	MKC1270P 12V Battery	System power

4. delivering audio feedback for system status and warnings;
5. maintaining stable power distribution across all components.

Figure 8.3 shows how the microcontroller, motor drivers, and communication modules are interconnected.

It has been built considering the careful prevision of components mounting and wiring management. Figure 8.4 shows how the Arduino-based control system is integrated with the already available electronics on the wheelchair.

A dual-control approach was followed for providing for the system operating reliably in un-apt conditions. Mainly, this control is done through voice commands using a smartphone interface, and for backup, a manual joystick control is incorporated (Figure 8.5). This adds to the redundancy of operation and makes the system very reliable and safe for the user.

The integration includes visual feedback mechanisms through LED indicators for notification of the status to be communicated to the user (Figure 8.6). In effect, these provide real-time feedback on the wheelchair's functioning state and any anomalies which may need attention.

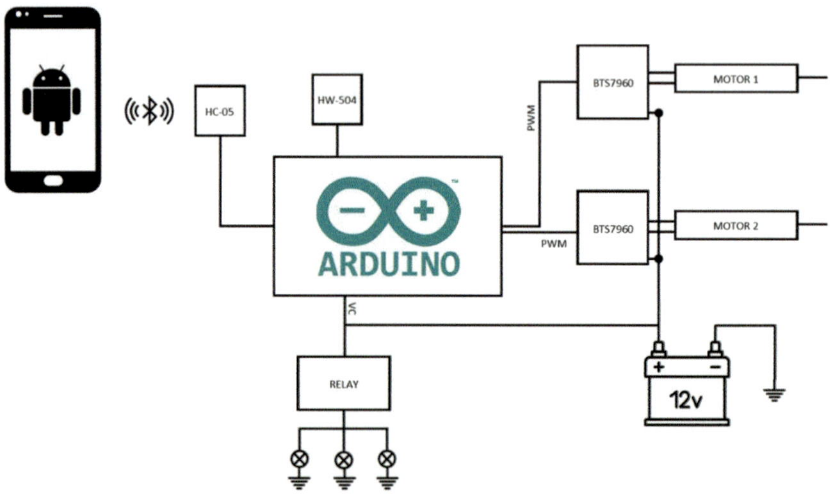

Figure 8.3 Complete electronics architecture with the integration of control components.

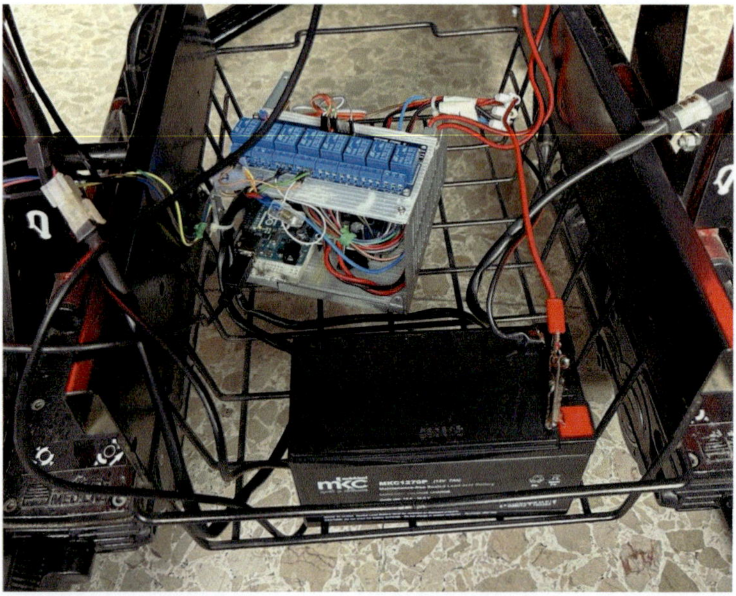

Figure 8.4 Physical implementation of the Arduino-wheelchair interface showing careful integration with the existing system.

Figure 8.5 Manual control joystick implementation providing direct mechanical control as a backup system.

Figure 8.6 Operational status indication system, with LEDs in an active state. The lightened "stop" LED indicates that the system is ready.

The hardware architecture here represents the embodiment of a successful integration effort of IoT capabilities onto traditional mobility assistive equipment. This shall retain much of the reliabilities of the original system through careful selection and implementation of componentry, adding intelligent functions of control.

8.3.2 Software architecture

The software implementation forms the critical component of the IoT-enabled wheelchair system, managing complex interactions between user inputs, control systems, and mobility functions. This implementation has followed a structured approach with a high regard for reliability and real-time performance, all while still maintaining the safety of the system.

The firmware architecture realizes a state-based control system responsible for the operational modes of the wheelchair and the processing of voice and manual control inputs. Figure 8.7 shows the main program flow diagram describing the operational logics and control pathways of the system. This is a flow diagram showing in detail the integration of speech commands, manual controls into the overall firmware architecture showing the integration with safety systems.

The source code of the system is modular, meaning different components handle different parts of the system operation. This, in turn makes the

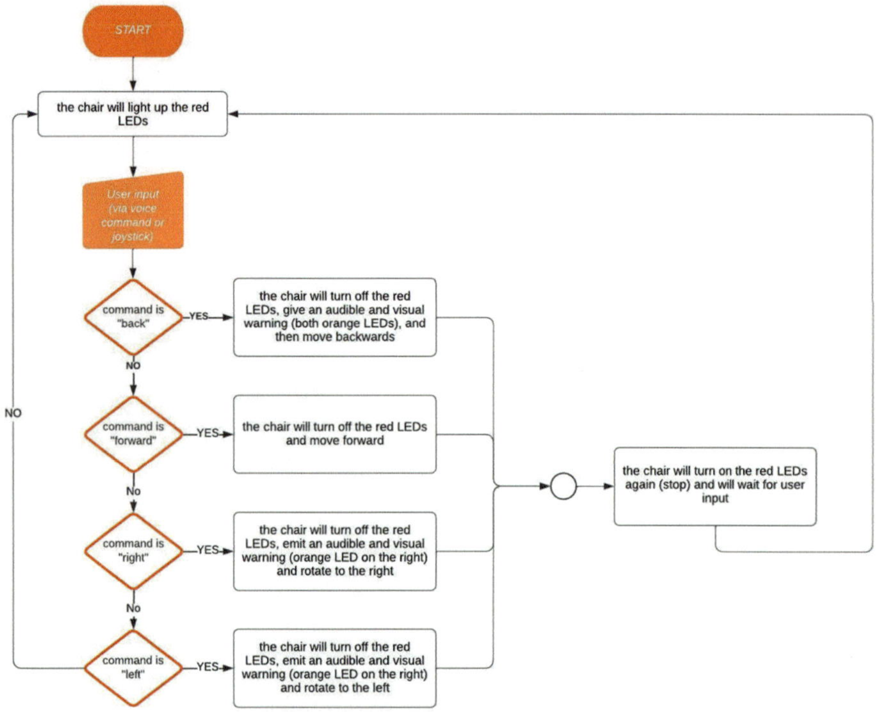

Figure 8.7 Overall software flow diagram showing primary control loops and decision pathways.

Figure 8.8 Arduino source repository structure showing an organized set of control algorithms with supporting functions.

maintenance easier, as well as future enhancements. Figure 8.8 shows the source code repository where one can find the complete implementation details.

The mobile application interface, which is the "Voice to Arduino" named, is the main interaction mechanism for users. This Android application provides both the functionalities of voice command processing and Bluetooth communication with the wheelchair control system. In the implementation of the application, three stages of the interaction process were followed and presented in Figures 8.9 through 8.11.

Figure 8.9 Initial interface of the mobile application, which guides the user through the interaction with the system and the initialization of the connection.

Figure 8.10 Interface showing Bluetooth device discovery for finding and connecting to the wheelchair system.

The interface of voice command processing is with the Google Voice Assistant API for robust speech recognition and command interpretation. Figures 8.12 and 8.13 show in detail a sequence of a voice command, from the very activation to the execution of the command.

Software architecture: The architecture implements all multiple technologies related to microcontroller firmwares, mobile application development to voice recognition systems. These interfaces are integrated harmoniously to provide users with an operational system that is easy to use, while maintaining important characteristics related to system reliability with embedded safety features. An accessible version, of how the system demonstratively works, is directly shown within operation videos through the availability provided by the QR within Figure 8.14.

In general, the software implementation emphasizes the safety of the user throughout various validation layers, always verifying the command

Figure 8.11 Active connection status screen, showing current state in the system and input options of command.

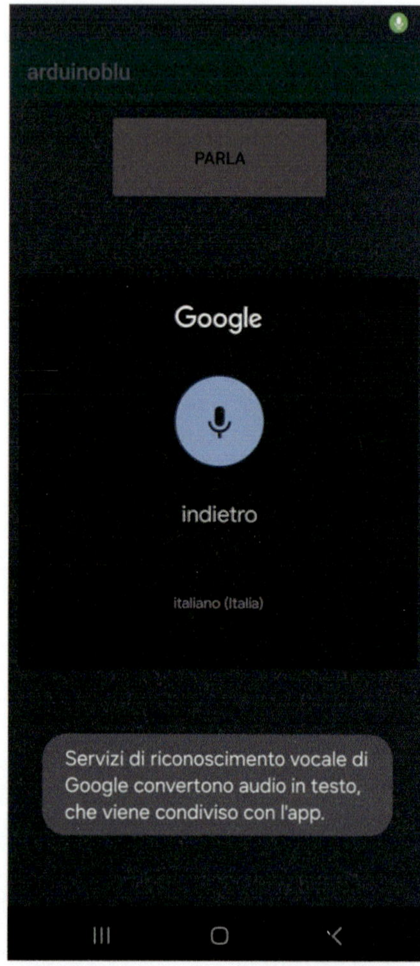

Figure 8.12 The voice command activation interface integrates the use of Google Voice Assistant in recognizing the commands.

properly before any execution. Such a mechanism maintains a trade-off between the responsiveness of the system and safety during operation, crucial for such a medical mobility assistant.

8.3.3 Communication protocol implementation

The communication infrastructure of the system is based on Bluetooth technology, selected due to its easy availability and relatively easy implementation in healthcare environments. Implementation of the protocol focuses

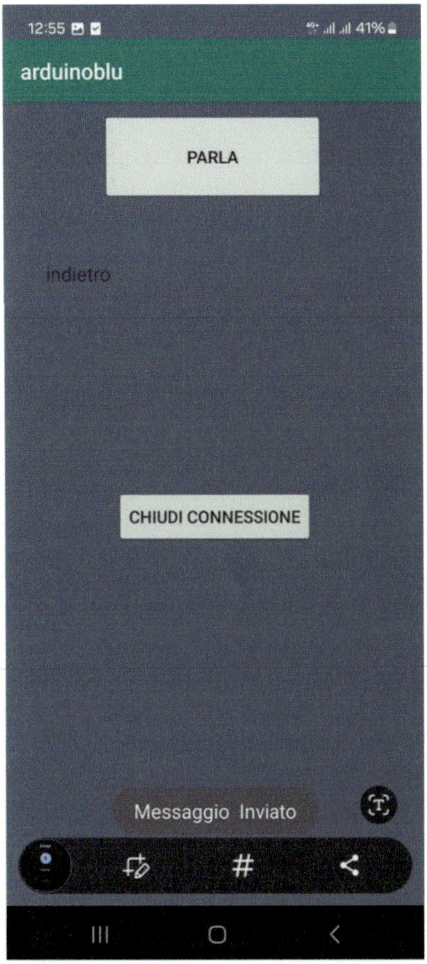

Figure 8.13 Command processing and confirmation screen. The successful interpretation of the command and transmission to the wheelchair system are shown.

Figure 8.14 QR code of the video of the system demonstration. This video provides the step-by-step operational sequence and examples of functionality.

on the creation of reliable connections with the integrity of the commands maintained during transmission.

The communication system uses the HC-05 Bluetooth module, configured as a slave to accept the mobile application's connections. This configuration is fairly stable in wireless communication and works within the usual operating range of 10 meters, enough for direct user control of the wheelchair system.

8.3.3.1 Protocol structure

This is accomplished using a specific, implemented protocol in a structured command format to effectively make sure the mobile application reliably communicates with the wheelchair's control system. Each time a command is transmitted, the following is included:

- Command identifier
- Parameter values
- Checksum verification
- Acknowledgement requirement

It provides integrity to commands and responsiveness of the system, using a protocol implementation that allows error detection and automatic retransmission in case of communication breaks.

8.3.4 Systems validating and testing

In a review where both testing and validation processes were fully outlined in a comprehensive program to aim at the system functionality, its reliability, and safety features, the testing procedure included a full range of tests on each of its components and in integrated operations and under various conditions.

8.3.4.1 Hardware integration testing

Initial testing was directed toward confirming that all hardware components were integrated properly. The electronic control system was tested extensively to ensure that all interconnections operated properly. Figure 8.15 illustrates the test setup of the integrated control system. The picture is showing that the correct function of LED indicators is implemented and appropriate reaction from a control system is obtained.

8.3.4.2 Control system validation

The verification of the control system reviewed both voice-activated and manual mechanisms of control. Testing procedures verified:

1. Voice command processing:
    - Command recognition accuracy

Figure 8.15 Hardware integration test set up, connected system components during the validation tests are shown.

- System response time
- Error-handling capabilities

2. Manual control operation:
   - Joystick calibration accuracy
   - Response characteristics
   - Emergency override functionality

8.3.4.3 Performance metrics

System performance evaluation incorporated the quantitative measurement of the following key operational parameters (Table 8.3).

8.3.4.4 Safety system validation

The approach toward the safety testing was to verify system behavior under a variety of operational scenarios and potential fault conditions. Among other things, testing was conducted to examine:

1. Emergency stop function:
   - Measuring response time
   - Reliability under varying conditions
   - System recovery procedures

Table 8.3 System performance metrics.

Parameter	Target value	Achieved result
Voice command recognition	>95%	97.2%
Command response time	<500 ms	425 ms
Manual control latency	<100 ms	85 ms
Connection stability	>99%	99.4%
Operating duration	8 h	8.5 h

2. Power management:
   - Battery level monitoring accuracy
   - Low-power operation behavior
   - System shutdown procedures
3. Control safety of movement:
   - Acceleration/deceleration characteristics
   - Enforcement of speed limit
   - Directional control accuracy

8.3.5 Implementation challenges

In the process of development, a number of technical issues came up which needed solutions.

8.3.5.1 Motor precision

Initial implementation showed the smoothness of control to be somewhat problematic, mainly at start and stop modes of operation. Gradual addition of PWM control incorporating ramp functions greatly improved comfort in operation and smoothness for users of the system.

8.3.5.2 Wireless communication

Early testing highlighted occasional communication instabilities between the mobile application and wheelchair control system. To address this issue, we implemented a robust error detection and recovery system with automatic reconnect capabilities, which proved effective in resolving these issues.

8.3.5.3 Power management

This proved challenging in power distribution and management in order to keep all the components of the system in stable operation. The solution implemented utilizes separate power systems for control electronics and drive systems, ensuring reliable operation with proper isolation between systems. These are just some of the problems addressed in a systematic way so as to develop a robust and reliable IoT-enabled mobility assistance system. Solutions performed to date demonstrate that it is feasible to design practical, user-friendly smart wheelchair systems which do not give in to certain necessary safety and reliability requirements.

8.4 Security Analysis of Current Implementation

The integration of IoT capabilities in medical mobility devices has considerable security considerations that are very sensitive and should be carefully analyzed. This section provides an extensive security analysis of the implemented system in terms of finding potential vulnerabilities and judging their impact on system safety and user privacy.

8.4.1 Architecture security assessment

Our security assessment starts from the communication layer, where, considering that the system will use Bluetooth technology, special security challenges arise. The implementation of the HC-05 Bluetooth module employs very simple pairing schemes that work but do not include more sophisticated authentication schemes. This simple architectural decision opens up possible vulnerabilities to man-in-the-middle attacks during pairing and raises other concerns about unauthorized attempts to pair devices.

Another area that raises security concerns is its data transmission mechanism, realized on the standard Bluetooth serial port profile. In its current implementation, end-to-end encryption of command data is missing, and that may expose the system against interception of commands and unauthorized injections of control signals.

The realization of the Arduino-based control system brings forth some other architectural security considerations: The existing firmware is functionally sound, but basic security features, such as secure boot mechanisms and verification of authenticity in the commands, are missing. On top of that, access control is quite primitive, using Bluetooth pairing but not implementing various levels of user authentication and session management features that a medical device should have.

8.4.2 Vulnerability assessment

Security analysis of the communication channel reveals crucial vulnerabilities in the implementation so far. For any of the operation ranges, a highly vulnerable Bluetooth signal opens several avenues for interception; indeed, it allows attackers to capture command sequences or simply perform device scanning. Indeed, it exposes vulnerability from command injection attacks – when some unauthorized device wants to transmit control commands or simply replays captured command sequences.

Within this system itself, at hardware as well as software levels, several vulnerabilities exist. Free physical access to the diagnostics' ports and the unattended ability for firmware updating stand as two of the paramount potential security hazards at a hardware level. In this, especially in the software layer, narrow input validation and crude basic error-handling mechanisms have eliminated all possibility of providing safety features in the said application area.

8.4.3 Privacy considerations

The operation of the system will inherently involve the collection and treatment of sensitive user data, such as movement patterns or regular routes and usage timing that can be derived from the operation of the system. This information, put in conjunction with the presence of the Bluetooth signal, creates potential privacy risks through unauthorized tracking or the analysis of movement patterns.

Adding voice command functionality via Google Voice Assistant will raise other privacy concerns. The fact that, in order to facilitate the current functionality, voice data has to be transferred to cloud services for processing raises a host of questions on how that data is handled and stored, not to mention possible voice command logging that may compromise users' privacy.

8.4.4 Risk analysis

Based on this comprehensive risk assessment, key security vulnerabilities are highlighted and categorized, which may be reflected in Table 8.4. Regarding the two parameters taken for valuation, these threats include likelihood of exploitation along with potential impact to system operation and user safety.

The risk assessment matrix underlines that Bluetooth interception and command injection are the most critical security risks because they combine medium likelihood with high potential impact. Although firmware tampering has a lower likelihood, its critical potential impact deserves significant attention in security planning. Privacy breaches are of moderate

Table 8.4 Security risk assessment

Vulnerability	Likelihood	Impact	Risk level
Bluetooth interception	Medium	High	Critical
Unauthorized access	Low	High	Significant
Command injection	Medium	High	Critical
Firmware tampering	Low	Critical	Significant
Privacy breach	Medium	Medium	Moderate

concern but present a balanced risk profile that needs appropriate mitigation strategies.

8.4.5 Security analysis implications

This security analysis points to some very critical areas that need to be addressed in the near future. First and foremost, enhanced communication security is achieved through the provision of robust encryption protocols together with strong authentication mechanisms. Security of the control system has to be done from the ground up: first, secure boot, and second, full-scale authentication protocols for every command.

Accordingly, the protection of privacy shows up as an important matter, especially when the setting is healthcare and the situation at hand involves confidential user information. Future development will need to take these challenges into account without sacrificing usability and the performance of the system in this endeavor. As is performed herein – an application development analysis – the foundation of proposed comprehensive security enhancement strategies described and contextualized in subsequent sections herein is formed based on identified findings.

8.5 Comparative Analysis

The rapid evolution of smart wheelchair technology has spawned a number of innovative solutions in the commercial and research domains. In this section, a wide-ranging comparison of the existing solutions is presented that analyzes their technical approaches, capabilities, and security features in relation to our implementation.

8.5.1 Commercial solutions overview

Recent breakthroughs in smart wheelchair mobility assistance have pointed out various sets of pathways through which wheelchair capacities are

Figure 8.16 A Whill autonomous wheelchair system is able to demonstrate integration of a navigation and obstacle avoidance system to provide better mobility in public spaces.

Figure 8.17 Practical deployment of the Whill system at Haneda Airport.

empowered using the IoT approach. The implementations in the commercial arena exhibit different solutions for tackling challenging mobility situations.

The Whill autonomous wheelchair system represents an advance in the state of the art in mobility assistance technology, especially for transportation hub applications. Figures 8.16 and 8.17 illustrate how such a system might be deployed in an airport environment.

Otis Corporation's Advanced Light Body Assistance (A.L.B.A.) system takes a different approach, focusing on healthcare facility integration. The system, shown in Figure 8.18, demonstrates sophisticated infrastructure interaction capabilities.

Honda Robotics have developed a system known as UNI-ONE that employs an approach wholly new to control mobility through sensing of the movement of the body. Figures 8.19 and 8.20 illustrate a special way of control the system is employing.

This has made the WHILL NEXT – a smart, next-generation, self-navigating device – a result of a partnership between Panasonic and Whill. Its airport application is shown in Figures 8.21 and 8.22.

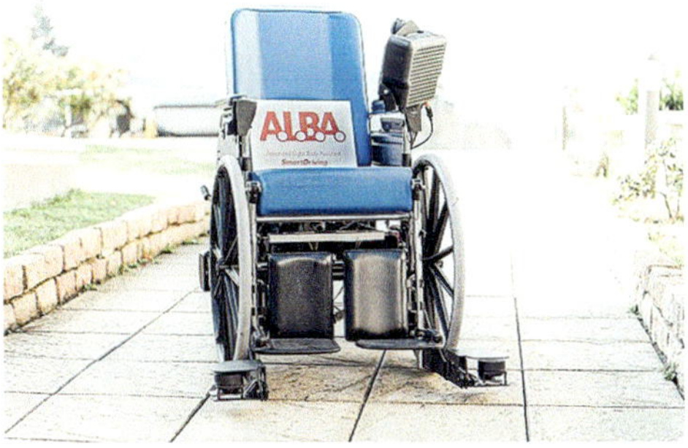

Figure 8.18 A.L.B.A. wheelchair system integration with facility infrastructure and elevator systems.

Figure 8.19 UNI-ONE operational demonstration, showing the body-movement control interface.

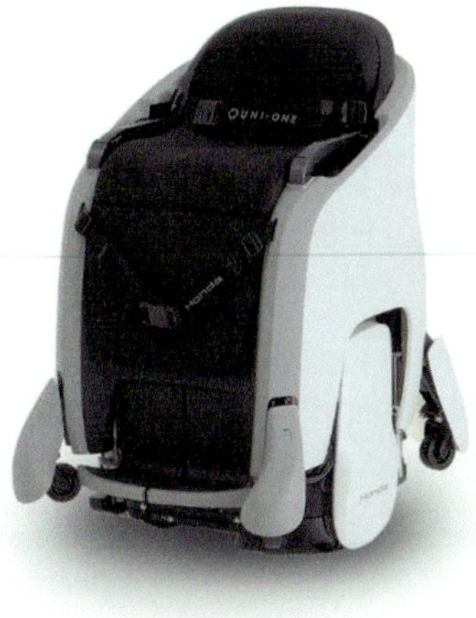

Figure 8.20 UNI-ONE system architecture, for the integration of movement and control systems.

Figure 8.21 WHILL NEXT demonstration – demonstration of the autonomous navigation capabilities.

8.5.2 Analyze technical capability

A comparison of the technical specifications indicates large differences in the capabilities of systems among a variety of implementations. Table 8.5 shows some key performance metrics comparison.

8.5.3 Implementation approaches

The analysis shows different strategies for the implementation of mobility assistance. Our prototype presents advantages in cost-effectiveness and ease

Figure 8.22 Panasonic autonomous wheelchair system, showing environment aware and navigation competencies.

Table 8.5 Technical comparison of wheelchair solutions.

System	Maximum speed	Operating range	Load capacity	Security features
Our implementation	6 km/h	1 h	115 kg	Acoustic signaling
WHILL [28]	8 km/h	19 km	112 kg	Obstacle detection
A.L.B.A. [11]	6 km/h	Not specified	Not specified	Infrastructure integration
IDSIA [29]	Not specified	Not specified	Not specified	Sensor and camera-based safety
UNI-ONE [30]	6.4 km/h	8 km or 2 h	Not specified	Auto-balancing sensors
WHILL NEXT [31]	Not specified	Not specified	Not specified	Collision avoidance

of operation by reusing existing components, while keeping the necessary functionality. This is opposed to commercial solutions, which in most cases use more complex and specialized systems.

The Whill system is focused on autonomous navigation, with a particular emphasis on large public spaces. Implementation practice at Whill is based on environmental awareness and obstacles to be avoided, using improved sensor arrays and processing. The integration of building infrastructure in the A.L.B.A. system shows a different approach: facility-specific optimization in focus, with system interoperability at the core.

8.5.4 Security and safety features

The security implementations vary radically among them. Commercial systems tend to implement highly advanced securities also, including improved obstacle detection and collision avoidance systems. These applications generally require complex infrastructure which creates challenges for system maintenance and limits flexibility for future upgrades.

Our implementation has a less complex but rather straightforward approach to security, where acoustic signaling and manual override capabilities are the most basic safety features. In this design, the trade-off in system reliability and maintainability may be advantageous, although additional security enhancements would be useful in future iterations.

8.5.5 Implications for future development

The comparison shows several directions of further development: the commercial solutions show how much more autonomous operation and infrastructure integration are possible, while our implementation shows that simplicity and reliability will be decisive in practical applications.

Key findings from this analysis will lead into further development iterations, specifically within:

- enhanced autonomous capabilities while maintaining system simplicity;
- improved security features, based on examples of commercial implementation;
- advanced user interface options that include successful elements of already existing solutions;
- full capabilities for infrastructure integration to provide higher operational efficiency.

The results from this analysis provide valuable insights into further developing accessible, secure, and effective mobility assistance solutions, contributing to the greater advancement of IoT-enabled healthcare devices.

8.6 Recommendations on Future Development

The analysis of our implementation, along with the security assessment and the comparative study of commercial solutions, establishes the foundation for key development priorities. The following section aims to recommend ways to improve the security, functionality, and compliance of the system with regulations while not affecting usability.

8.6.1 Priority security enhancements

The current implementation needs several specific security improvements needed in healthcare devices. Improvements to communication security can thus be considered the area currently receiving most attention. Recommendations can be made for a layered approach to security, first necessitating the replacement of standard HC-05 Bluetooth with a Bluetooth 5.0 module equipped with BLE mode that supports BLE security modes. This upgrade would implement Advanced Encryption Standard (AES) encryption for all data transmissions while also providing enhanced authentication protocols.

The cardinal improvement of the security architecture in the control system should be based on the introduction of the technology of secure boot mechanisms and also cryptographic verification in firmwares. We would also propose that the design include a discrete hardware security microcontroller such as Microchip ATECC608A, which could ensure both hardware-based key storage and cryptographic operations. With its addition, the solution could give way to secure authentication of different control commands and also assure protection against unauthorized modification of firmwares.

8.6.2 Implementation guidelines

All further implementation should be based on structured development of functionality and security-related aspects together. The architecture of a control system shall be guided through modular design patterns in a manner that will effectively decouple core functions that govern mobility from those having roles in security operations, hence making their improvement and updating possible without compromising any part of the basic functionalities.

The voice control system needs to be re-implemented using only local voice processing to minimize privacy risks due to cloud-based voice processing. We suggest to integrate an edge computing module that can perform the tasks of voice recognition locally and is able to use or implement solutions like CMU Sphinx, or other similar open-source voice recognition engines that are optimized for embedded systems.

8.6.3 Regulatory compliance considerations

IoT-enabled healthcare equipment includes some very demanding medical device regulations. Future development should focus on compliance with major regulatory frameworks, including:

FDA guidance for cybersecurity of medical devices enforces unique device identification, as well as extensive security logging capabilities. The system should support secure logging mechanisms for all critical operations. Keep a record of access and changes to the system configuration in a manner that is auditable.

Compliance with the European Medical Device Regulation requires enhanced risk management processes and detailed documentation of security measures taken. We recommend the implementation of a complete Security Information and Event Management (SIEM) system, adapted for healthcare mobility devices.

8.6.4 Balancing security with usability

Enhanced security features cannot come at the expense of usability of the system, especially in situations where the users may have limited technical expertise. We propose a multi-layered authentication system that is going to keep the security of the system intact but offer ease of access to the regular user. In the process, it includes:

Session-based authentication with temporary tokens: this would decrease the number of full authentications that are needed, without losing any advantage in terms of security. Such an implementation should use hardware security modules to manage the tokens, ensuring secure storage and processing of authentication data.

Adaptive security, whereby authentication requirements would change based on the usage pattern and risk assessment. This would keep the security level high but minimize user interaction requirements for routine operations.

Safety override capabilities should be supported but without the threat of being manipulated for unauthorized access. We hereby recommend that a dual-factor emergency access system is coupled with physical key access and electronic verification.

8.6.5 Roadmap for implementation

Based on this, we propose a phase-by-phase implementation approach:

- Phase 1 (Immediate priority): Implementation of enhanced Bluetooth security features, including local voice processing capabilities. This step provides a minimum set of modifications required to address the most critical security vulnerabilities while preserving current functionality.

- Phase 2 (Medium term): Hardware security module integration and secure boot functionality. This step sets the basic security architecture enhancement critical for healthcare deployment.
- Phase 3 (Long-term): Full deployment of extensive logging and monitoring systems concludes the security infrastructure necessary for complete regulatory compliance.

These recommendations give a structured approach toward the improvement of system security, keeping in mind practical usability. The improvements proposed will address current vulnerabilities and create a foundation for future development that is aligned with healthcare security requirements.

8.7 Discussion

The development and implementation of the IoT-enabled smart wheelchair system represent great opportunities and challenges in the context of healthcare mobility assistance. Our research shows the feasibility of creating cost-effective, intelligent mobility solutions while highlighting critical considerations for security and usability in medical IoT devices.

The implemented prototype, which combines voice control with manual override, can satisfy the basic functional requirements. This kind of dual-control strategy has already been particularly useful in some healthcare applications where system reliability is important. However, our security analysis identifies several vulnerabilities that must be fixed for healthcare deployment, particularly in wireless communication and access control systems.

A comparative analysis against the commercial solutions therefore gives an interesting trade-off between system complexity and practical implementation: although many commercial systems boast of autonomous navigation and infrastructure integration, their simplification can bring many advantages concerning maintenance accessibility and system reliability. The observation made therefore justifies a development line on implementing the advanced features but not losing the simplicity of the system and its maintainability.

Security in IoT-enabled healthcare devices creates unique challenges, extending well beyond traditional mobility assistance. Our study shows that while simple security can be supported using only very minor hardware modifications, more robust security actually involves fundamental architectural changes. The proposed security enhancements in this work will demonstrate how robust protection needs to balance system usability, especially in healthcare applications where user accessibility is considered paramount.

The regulatory landscape for medical IoT devices adds another layer of complexity to the development of a system. From our experience, it follows that early consideration of regulatory requirements in the design phase can reduce implementation challenges later on. This proposed roadmap is in line with current regulatory frameworks but maintains focus on practical implementation considerations.

8.8 Conclusion

This chapter considers security and some implementation aspects of IoT-enabled mobility assistance devices. The section shows the potential and, at the same time the challenges of integrating IoT in healthcare mobility devices by developing a prototype smart wheelchair system.

Key contributions of this study are:

- It describes the design and development connected with a low-cost voice-controlled smart wheelchair system, introducing manual override; it makes a presentation on the development viability of accessible IoT-related mobility solutions.
- A holistic security analysis framework for finding out critical vulnerabilities in medical IoT devices will provide valuable insight into the future development of secure healthcare mobility systems.
- How, taking a structured approach to such a system to strengthen the security while keeping the usability of the system intact, sets practical guidance on how all the safety measures could, in general, be implanted by healthcare IoT devices.
- Conclusive recommendations will be given for future development, both in technical and regulatory considerations, thus providing a road map for the creation of secure, compliant medical IoT devices.

The results of this research provide important lessons for the development of secure IoT-enabled healthcare devices. Our implementation represents an accessible approach to smart mobility solutions but also shows the crucial need for security considerations in medical IoT devices. The proposed security enhancements and implementation guidelines form a good basis for future development of secure, reliable healthcare mobility systems.

Future research directions should be focused on:

- development of sophisticated security architectures for healthcare mobility gadgets;

- integration of autonomous capabilities while ensuring system security and reliability;
- implementing improved user authentication that balances security with accessibility;
- standardization of security frameworks for IoT medical devices.

The contribution of this research would serve to extend the existing knowledge regarding the security of IoT devices within the healthcare arena and provide insights for creating functional and accessible methods of ensuring mobility assistance that is both secure and accessible. The results and recommendations obtained from this chapter would provide ground for developing a secure CPS in the application field of health care in future works.

References

[1] K. I. Roumeliotis and N. D. Tselikas, "An Effective SEO Techniques and Technologies Guide-Map," *Journal of Web Engineering*, vol. 21, no. 5, pp. 1603–1649, Jul. 2022, doi: 10.13052/jwe1540-9589.21510.

[2] G. Aceto, V. Persico, and A. Pescapé, "Industry 4.0 and Health: Internet of Things, Big Data, and Cloud Computing for Healthcare 4.0," *Journal of Industrial Information Integration*, vol. 18, p. 100129, Jun. 2020, doi: 10.1016/j.jii.2020.100129.

[3] C. Gong and V. Ribiere, "Chapter 1 - A historical outline of digital transformation," in *Digital Transformation in Healthcare in Post-Covid-19 Times*, M. D. Lytras, A. A. Housawi, and B. S. Alsaywid, Eds., in Next Generation Technology Driven Personalized Medicine and Smart Healthcare. , Academic Press, 2023, pp. 3–25. doi: 10.1016/B978-0-323-98353-2.00016-2.

[4] A. Agarwal, R. Joshi, H. Arora, and R. Kaushik, "Privacy and Security of Healthcare Data in Cloud based on the Blockchain Technology," in *2023 7th International Conference on Computing Methodologies and Communication (ICCMC)*, Feb. 2023, pp. 87–92. doi: 10.1109/ICCMC56507.2023.10083822.

[5] B. Coutinho, J. Ferreira, I. Yevseyeva, and V. Basto-Fernandes, "Integrated cybersecurity methodology and supporting tools for healthcare operational information systems," *Computers & Security*, vol. 129, p. 103189, Jun. 2023, doi: 10.1016/j.cose.2023.103189.

[6] Unit 42, "2020 Unit 42 IoT Threat Report," Unit 42. Accessed: Dec. 08, 2024. [Online]. Available: https://unit42.paloaltonetworks.com/iot-threat-report-2020/

[7] H. Harkat, L. M. Camarinha-Matos, J. Goes, and H. F. T. Ahmed, "Cyber-physical systems security: A systematic review," *Computers & Industrial Engineering*, vol. 188, p. 109891, Feb. 2024, doi: 10.1016/j.cie.2024.109891.

[8] P. P. Ray, "Web3: A comprehensive review on background, technologies, applications, zero-trust architectures, challenges and future directions," *Internet of Things and Cyber-Physical Systems*, vol. 3, pp. 213–248, Jan. 2023, doi: 10.1016/j.iotcps.2023.05.003.

[9] "J-BHI Special Issue on 'Cognitive Cyber-Physical Systems with AI Based Solutions in Medical Informatics' – EMBS." Accessed: Jul. 03, 2021. [Online]. Available: https://www.embs.org/j-bhi-special-issue-on-cognitive-cyber-physical-systems-with-ai-based-solutions-in-medical-informatics/

[10] S. Ibrahim, "Sedia a rotelle svizzera assistita da droni mette in luce promesse e problemi dell'IA," SWI swissinfo.ch. Accessed: Dec. 08, 2024. [Online]. Available: https://www.swissinfo.ch/ita/scienza/sedia-a-rotelle-svizzera-assistita-da-droni-mette-in-luce-promesse-e-problemi-dellia/87651808

[11] "Info dalle aziende - Otis presenta A.L.B.A., la sedia a rotelle a guida autonoma - INFOBUILD." Accessed: Dec. 08, 2024. [Online]. Available: https://www.infobuild.it/info_dalle_aziende/otis-presenta-alba-prima-carrozzina-autonoma-spostamento-pazienti/

[12] b.marcotulli, "Accessibilità: la sedia a rotelle a guida autonoma è rivoluzionaria," Maker Faire Rome. Accessed: Dec. 08, 2024. [Online]. Available: https://makerfairerome.eu/it/accessibilita-la-sedia-a-rotelle-a-guida-autonoma-e-rivoluzionaria/

[13] G. Atzeni, "Sviluppo, studio ed implementazione di un sistema IoT per il monitoraggio remoto di un ausilio medico per persone a mobilità ridotta," eCampus University, Novedrate, Italy, 2024.

[14] A. Corsi, F. Florencio de Souza, R. N. Pagani, and J. L. Kovaleski, "Ultimate approach and technologies in smart healthcare: A broad systematic review focused on citizens," *Smart Health*, vol. 26, p. 100310, Dec. 2022, doi: 10.1016/j.smhl.2022.100310.

[15] S. Shreya, K. Chatterjee, and A. Singh, "A smart secure healthcare monitoring system with Internet of Medical Things," *Computers and Electrical Engineering*, vol. 101, p. 107969, Jul. 2022, doi: 10.1016/j.compeleceng.2022.107969.

[16] L. Jiang *et al.*, "SmartRolling: A human–machine interface for wheelchair control using EEG and smart sensing techniques," *Information Processing & Management*, vol. 60, no. 3, p. 103262, May 2023, doi: 10.1016/j.ipm.2022.103262.

[17] W. Hutamaputra, F. Utaminingrum, A. S. Budi, and K. Ogata, "Eyes gaze detection based on multiprocess of ratio parameters for smart wheelchair menu selection in different screen size," *Journal of Visual Communication and Image Representation*, vol. 91, p. 103756, Mar. 2023, doi: 10.1016/j.jvcir.2023.103756.
[18] E. T.-H. Chu and K.-J. Chen, "SWAF: Smart Wheelchair for Fall Risk Assessment," *Journal of Systems Architecture*, vol. 131, p. 102694, Oct. 2022, doi: 10.1016/j.sysarc.2022.102694.
[19] Z. Jiao, K. Ma, Y. Rong, P. Wang, H. Zhang, and S. Wang, "A path planning method using adaptive polymorphic ant colony algorithm for smart wheelchairs," *Journal of Computational Science*, vol. 25, pp. 50–57, Mar. 2018, doi: 10.1016/j.jocs.2018.02.004.
[20] J. C. Badajena, S. Sethi, and R. K. Sahoo, "Data-driven approach to designing a BCI-integrated smart wheelchair through cost–benefit analysis," *High-Confidence Computing*, vol. 3, no. 2, p. 100118, Jun. 2023, doi: 10.1016/j.hcc.2023.100118.
[21] M. Imtyaz Ahmed and G. Kannan, "Secure and lightweight privacy preserving Internet of things integration for remote patient monitoring," *Journal of King Saud University - Computer and Information Sciences*, vol. 34, no. 9, pp. 6895–6908, Oct. 2022, doi: 10.1016/j.jksuci.2021.07.016.
[22] F. Alfayez and S. B. Khan, "User-centric secured smart virtual assistants framework for disables," *Alexandria Engineering Journal*, vol. 95, pp. 59–71, May 2024, doi: 10.1016/j.aej.2024.03.033.
[23] S. P. Singh *et al.*, "Dual adaption based evolutionary algorithm for optimized the smart healthcare communication service of the Internet of Things in smart city," *Physical Communication*, vol. 55, p. 101893, Dec. 2022, doi: 10.1016/j.phycom.2022.101893.
[24] M. M. Rahman, G. Hossain, R. Challoo, and M. Rizkalla, "iRestroom : A smart restroom cyberinfrastructure for elderly people," *Internet of Things*, vol. 19, p. 100573, Aug. 2022, doi: 10.1016/j.iot.2022.100573.
[25] F. Utaminingrum, A. W. S. B. Johan, I. K. Somawirata, T. K. Shih, and C.-Y. Lin, "Indoor staircase detection for supporting security systems in autonomous smart wheelchairs based on deep analysis of the Co-occurrence Matrix and Binary Classification," *Intelligent Systems with Applications*, vol. 23, p. 200405, Sep. 2024, doi: 10.1016/j.iswa.2024.200405.
[26] R. Tomari, Y. Kobayashi, and Y. Kuno, "Analysis of Socially Acceptable Smart Wheelchair Navigation Based on Head Cue Information,"

Procedia Computer Science, vol. 42, pp. 198–205, Jan. 2014, doi: 10.1016/j.procs.2014.11.052.

[27] A. J. Perez, F. Siddiqui, S. Zeadally, and D. Lane, "A review of IoT systems to enable independence for the elderly and disabled individuals," *Internet of Things*, vol. 21, p. 100653, Apr. 2023, doi: 10.1016/j.iot.2022.100653.

[28] "WHILL: Mobilità personale innovativa." Accessed: Dec. 08, 2024. [Online]. Available: https://whill.inc/it/

[29] "Safe Road-Crossing by Autonomous Wheelchairs – Trustworthy Autonomous Systems (TAS) @IDSIA USI-SUPSI." Accessed: Dec. 08, 2024. [Online]. Available: https://tas.idsia.ch/2024/03/15/safe-road-crossing-by-autonomous-wheelchairs/

[30] Venkat, "Introducing UNI-ONE: A Revolutionary Hands-Free Mobility Device Redefining Independence and Joy for Diverse Users," Assistive Technology Blog. Accessed: Dec. 08, 2024. [Online]. Available: https://assistivetechnologyblog.com/2023/11/honda-unione.html

[31] Redazione, "Whill Next: la carrozzina con il pilota automatico | CUENEWS," CUENEWS | Biomed. Accessed: Dec. 08, 2024. [Online]. Available: https://www.biomedicalcue.it/whill-next-carrozzina-pilota-automatico/10652/

9

Statistical Estimation of User Location Distribution via Anonymized Dummy Data Transmission

Yuichi Sei[1], Akihiko Ohsuga[1] and Agbotiname Lucky Imoize[2,3]

[1]Department of Informatics, Graduate School of Informatics and Engineering, The University of Electro-Communications, Japan
[2]Department of Electrical and Electronics Engineering, Faculty of Engineering, University of Lagos, Nigeria
[3]Department of Electrical Engineering and Information Technology, Institute of Digital Communication, Ruhr University, Germany

Email: seiuny@uec.ac.jp; ohsuga@uec.ac.jp; aimoize@unilag.edu.ng

Abstract

In this chapter, we explore a novel approach to collecting and utilizing users' location information from mobile devices while preserving their privacy within the context of cyber-physical systems (CPSs). CPS integrates computational algorithms with physical processes, enabling enhanced automation, precision, and efficiency in various applications. However, the continuous data collection inherent in CPS raises significant privacy concerns, particularly regarding location-based services. Our proposed method allows users to provide a candidate set containing their true location and randomly generated dummy locations, ensuring that the server cannot pinpoint their exact position. By gathering these candidate sets from many users, we can estimate the number of users in each grid cell with minimal error. This method introduces a flexible framework where the privacy protection level can be adjusted individually for each user, accommodating varying privacy preferences. We derive an equation to calculate the expected mean squared error of these estimations and demonstrate through simulations that our method

DOI: 10.1201/9788743801306-9

outperforms existing techniques in balancing privacy and estimation accuracy. Future work will address optimizing the computational efficiency of the server protocol. This chapter provides a comprehensive analysis and validation of our approach, showcasing its potential for enhancing location-based services with robust privacy guarantees, thus contributing to the broader field of CPS by ensuring user trust and data security.

9.1 Introduction

Cyber-physical systems (CPSs) represent the integration of computational algorithms and physical processes. This integration is achieved through the use of sensors, actuators, and network communication technologies that bridge the gap between the digital and physical worlds. CPS has become a cornerstone of modern technology, driving innovation in various fields such as healthcare [1], transportation [2], manufacturing [3], and smart cities [4],[5].

In a CPS, physical processes are monitored and controlled by embedded systems that are tightly coupled with computational algorithms. These systems continuously interact with the physical environment, enabling real-time data collection and analysis. This dynamic interaction allows for enhanced automation, precision, and efficiency in various applications.

While CPS offers numerous benefits, it also raises significant privacy concerns [6]. The continuous monitoring and data collection inherent in CPS can lead to the potential misuse of personal information. For instance, location-based services, which are a common application of CPS, collect vast amounts of data about users' movements. If this data is not properly anonymized and protected, it could be exploited for malicious purposes, such as tracking individuals without their consent.

In this chapter, we explore a novel approach to collecting and utilizing users' location information from mobile devices while preserving their privacy. Users' location information can be collected from mobile devices such as smartphones, enabling marketing analyses that link users' consumption behavior with their movement patterns. However, many users are hesitant to provide accurate location information, making privacy considerations essential.

To address this issue, research has been actively conducted on anonymizing location data for use in data mining. However, much of this research assumes that the server collecting user data is trustworthy, which is not always the case. There are growing concerns that collected location data could be sold to other companies without user consent or leaked due to attacks on the data collection server. Therefore, it is increasingly necessary to consider situations where users do not trust the data collection server.

Recently, methods for anonymizing location information on the user's own mobile device have been proposed [7]–[9]. These methods utilize a technique called negative survey [10], allowing them to be used even when the data collection server is not trusted.

The negative survey-based methods do not collect each user's precise location information. Instead, they can estimate the distribution of users in various locations with reasonable accuracy by gathering information from many users. However, to accurately estimate the distribution of users' location information on the data collection server, it is necessary to collect data from a large number of users.

This chapter proposes a method where each user generates dummy location information probabilistically and reports it to the server along with their true location information. Using this method, it is possible to achieve high-accuracy estimations from fewer users while maintaining the same level of privacy protection as existing methods. Under the privacy and utility metrics adopted in this chapter, mathematical analysis and simulation results show that our proposed method can improve estimation accuracy by approximately 85% to 99% compared to existing methods.

9.1.1 Key contributions of the chapter

The contributions of this book chapter are as follows:

i. The chapter introduces a novel method that allows users to set their own privacy protection levels by randomly generating dummy locations along with their true location. This flexibility accommodates varying privacy preferences among users, which is a significant advancement over existing methods that enforce a fixed privacy level.

ii. By collecting and analyzing candidate sets from numerous users, the proposed method enables the estimation of the number of users in each grid cell with minimal error. The chapter provides a detailed mathematical framework for calculating the expected mean squared error, demonstrating through simulations that the proposed method achieves a better trade-off between privacy and estimation accuracy compared to traditional techniques.

iii. The chapter not only introduces the theoretical underpinnings of the proposed method but also validates its effectiveness through extensive simulations. The derived equations for expected estimation errors closely match the simulation results, providing robust evidence of the method's reliability and practical applicability in real-world scenarios.

9.1.2 Chapter organization

The structure of this chapter is as follows. Section 9.2 defines the scenario, attack model, and privacy model assumed in this chapter. Section 9.3 describes the privacy and utility metrics adopted in this chapter. Section 9.4 reviews existing research. Section 9.5 details the proposed method, and Section 9.6 compares the proposed method with existing methods through mathematical analysis and simulations. Section 9.7 presents discussions, and Section 9.8 concludes the chapter.

The original version of this chapter is provided by Sei and Oshuga [11].

9.2 Assumed Environment

This section presents the assumed scenarios, the attack model, the representation of location information, and the privacy model used in this chapter.

9.2.1 Assumed scenario

Users send anonymized location information along with attribute information they do not want to be linked to their identity to a data collection server. The server attempts to estimate how many people with certain attributes are present at specific locations (Figure 9.1).

Some existing studies assume scenarios where users' location histories are used for data mining. However, this chapter does not consider users' movement histories as a data mining target. Therefore, even if a user sends multiple location data points to the server over time, the server does not need to recognize that the data comes from the same user. Participatory environmental sensing [12], [13] is one such scenario. In participatory environmental sensing, users sense environmental information, including location data, at various places and notify the server. The server performs statistical analysis on the location data received without considering whether the data is from the same person.

Additionally, it is assumed that surveillance cameras at stores, parks, etc., may identify the faces of individuals at a specific location and time. Typically, it is not possible to infer what applications those individuals use or what keywords they search for. However, providing location information

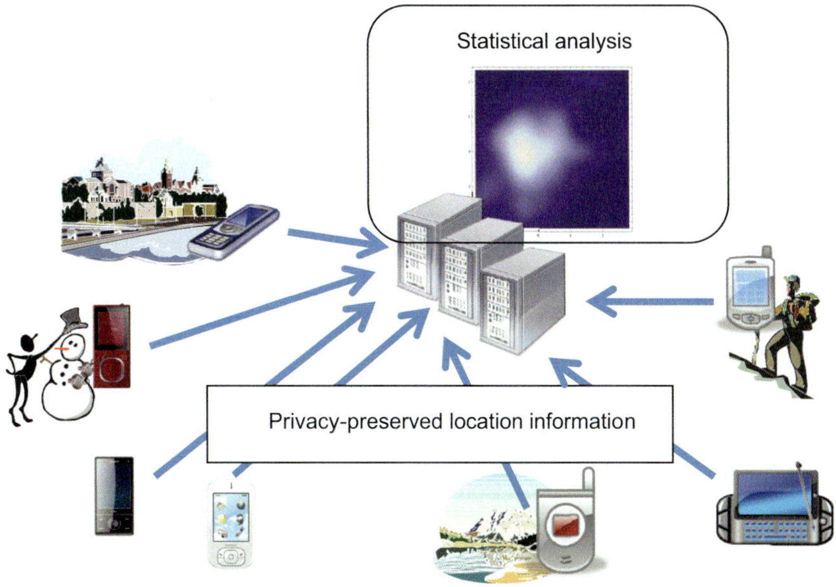

Figure 9.1 Scenario example.

could lead to attribute information being linked to an individual, which they may not want.

Furthermore, we assume that the location information obtained by a user's device is correct. Some works, such as [14], [15], assume that any location information may have a large measurement error. The treatment of large noisy location information is left for our future work.

Here are some examples of assumed scenarios:

Scenario 1:
Consider a situation where a municipality wants to know what types of people are present in various locations for urban development and public health purposes. Users might be willing to provide their age, gender, location, and other sensed information to the server for social contribution if the data is anonymized. This is an example of the aforementioned participatory environmental sensing.

Scenario 2:
Consider a situation where a mobile application development company wants to know where its applications are most frequently used. Users recognize that providing location information is not essential for using the application. However, if the data is anonymized, they might be willing to provide

information to the server in exchange for free or low-cost use of the application. In this case, "attribute information they do not want to be linked to their identity" is the fact that they are using the mobile application.

Scenario 3:
Consider a situation where a search engine service provider wants to know what keywords are searched for in specific locations. Users who want location-related search results may provide their exact location to the search engine service, while others do not need to provide location information. However, if the data is anonymized, users might be willing to provide location information when conducting keyword searches.

9.2.2 Attack model

We assume that the data collection server is semi-honest. In this chapter, the data collection server follows the protocol but attempts to infer users' location and attribute information from the received data. Additionally, users are anonymized, and the server cannot identify individual users. Therefore, even if the same user sends information to the server multiple times, the attacker cannot determine whether the information is from the same user.

Naturally, if the goal is to mine users' movement histories, each user must be assigned an ID for data collection, allowing the attacker to determine whether the information is from the same user. However, it is important to note that the scenarios targeted in this chapter do not involve mining movement histories.

Attacks on the sensing devices themselves, such as smartphones, to extract information are also conceivable [16]. Although this issue is outside the scope of this chapter, it can be addressed using malware detection methods [17].

9.2.3 Representation of location information

Location information is represented as grid cells on a two-dimensional plane. In this chapter, "location information" and "grid cells" are used interchangeably. The target area is limited to places where users are likely to be present.

9.2.4 Privacy model

We describe the privacy model assumed in this chapter. Privacy information is defined as the information that users provide to the server by disclosing their information. In other words, any information the server can infer about a user, whether or not they participate in anonymous data collection, is not considered privacy information.

To illustrate, consider a survey of birthplace conducted among a group of users. The choices are Tottori Prefecture, Shimane Prefecture, and others. Suppose user A's response is "either Tottori or Shimane," and user B did not respond. If almost all other users respond with "Tottori," it can be inferred that user A and user B are also likely from Tottori. However, the inferred information about non-responding users based on the responses of many others is typically not considered a privacy breach. This is the privacy model assumed in this chapter, similar to the models proposed by Evfimievski et al. [18] and Kasiviswanathan et al. [19].

Based on this model, the privacy protection level is quantified using privacy metrics, which are described in Section 9.3.1.

9.3 Metrics

The privacy metric and the utility metric used in this chapter will be defined in this section.

9.3.1 Privacy metric

A commonly used privacy metric in many papers is k-anonymity [20]. This metric is used under the definition that, in a database containing attribute data of many users, an attacker who knows all but one of user A's attributes can identify user A's record with a confidence of at most $1/k$. This chapter also adopts the k-anonymity metric. Since this chapter focuses on users' location information, k-anonymity is defined as having at least k grid cells as candidates for a user's location. However, some existing studies on k-anonymity for location information aim to obfuscate users' location information so that at least k users are present in a certain area [21],[22]. This approach has the problem that if k users are present at the exact same location, their location information is not obfuscated, and the server receives accurate location information [23]. Additionally, with methods that aim to ensure k users are in a certain area, users cannot achieve k-anonymity on their own and cannot confirm whether there are actually k users in the obfuscated area. On the other hand, the k-anonymity metric used in this chapter has the advantage that users can achieve k-anonymity themselves using the proposed method.

It should be noted that, as with many studies on k-anonymity, it may not be effectively maintained depending on the attacker's prior knowledge.

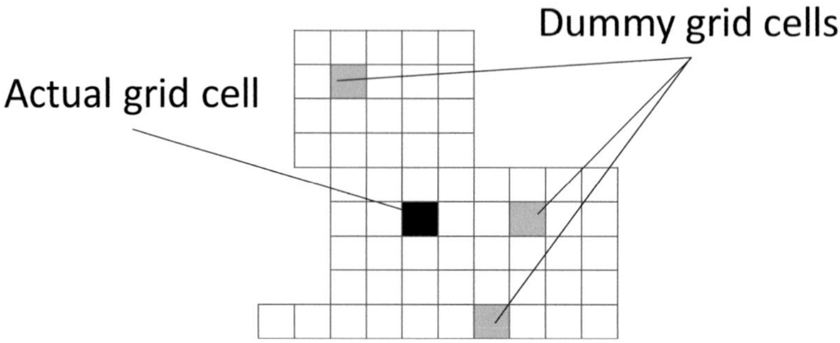

Figure 9.2 Example of 4-anonymity.

For example, consider a situation where the attacker knows that the candidate grid cells for user *U*'s location are $\{X_1,X_2,X_3,X_4\}$. At this point, 4-anonymity is maintained. If the attacker knows that no one is physically present at X_3, the candidate grid cells for user *U*'s location are reduced to $\{X_1,X_2,X_3,X_4\}$, effectively reducing anonymity to 3-anonymity. However, it is generally difficult to determine that no one is present in a grid cell, given that each grid cell has a certain area. Installing surveillance cameras to cover the entire area, including buildings, or deploying a large number of personnel for physical observation would be costly.

Furthermore, even if one person is present in each of the grid cells, the attacker cannot determine if that person is user *U*.

It should also be noted that the potential ineffectiveness of *k*-anonymity due to the attacker's prior knowledge is common to many studies that perform *k*-anonymization on databases. For example, if there are *k* records in a database with identical values for all attributes except the sensitive attribute, and the sensitive attribute values are all different, the attacker can identify the sensitive attribute of an individual if they know which record corresponds to that individual.

In this chapter, it is ensured that each grid cell has a certain area and that there are at least *k* candidate grid cells for the user's location. Many existing studies also attempt to protect user privacy by generating multiple dummy locations [24]–[27].

An example of anonymization that satisfies *k*-anonymity is shown in Figure 9.2. The areas divided by lines represent grid cells. The black grid cell indicates the user's true location. The user informs the data collection server that they are in one of the black or three gray grid cells. This achieves 4-anonymity. In this chapter, the value of *k* is also referred to as the "privacy protection level."

9.3.2 Utility metric

The server estimates the number of users in each grid cell, and the mean squared error between the estimated and true values is used as the utility metric. Many existing studies also use the mean squared error between the estimated and true values to measure estimation accuracy [28]–[30].

Let V_i be the true number of users in grid cell L_i. Let ψ_i be the estimated number of users in grid cell L_i on the server side. Let D be the total number of grid cells and N be the total number of users from whom data is collected. The mean squared error σ^2 is defined as follows:

$$\sigma^2 = \frac{1}{D}\sum_{i=0}^{D-1}\left(\frac{V_i}{N} - \frac{\psi_i}{N}\right)^2. \tag{9.1}$$

9.4 Related Work

In this section, related work will be discussed.

9.4.1 Cyber-physical systems (CPS)

CPS represents a sophisticated convergence of computing and physical elements. In these systems, embedded computers and networks play a crucial role in monitoring and managing physical processes. This interaction typically involves feedback loops where physical phenomena influence computations, and in turn, these computations regulate the physical processes [31],[32]. The advent of CPS technologies is revolutionizing our interaction with the physical world by seamlessly integrating computational power into our everyday environments. As CPS becomes more integrated into our daily lives, the amount of data collected increases exponentially. This data collection, while beneficial for enhancing services and optimizing performance, also raises concerns about privacy. Users may be wary of sharing their location data due to potential misuse. Hence, preserving privacy while maintaining the utility of collected data is a critical challenge in the development and deployment of CPS [33].

Jiang et al. proposed a framework that combines CPS with federated learning [34]. Federated learning allows each client to perform machine learning without sending their training data to the server. However, there is a threat of inference attacks, where an attacker might infer the data held by each client. To address this threat, the framework employs differential privacy techniques to enhance data protection.

9.4.2 Dummy generation for providing services to individual users

Instead of determining the number of users in each grid cell, some methods use dummy location information to protect privacy while providing individual services to users [35],[26],[25]. These methods involve users notifying the service server of not only their true grid cell but also dummy grid cells when they want to use location-aware services. The server responds to all notified grid cells, and users only adopt the responses corresponding to their true grid cells, thus protecting their privacy.

While these studies share the concept of using dummies with this research, they do not aim to estimate the number of users in each grid cell. The method proposed in this study can be combined with these techniques to estimate the number of users in each grid cell.

9.4.3 Obfuscation approach with trusted entity

Many methods have also been proposed where a trusted third party collects location information from k or more users and then sends this information to the service provider [36],[37]. From the perspective of the service provider, k-anonymity is guaranteed because it is impossible to determine which location information belongs to which user among the k users. However, this method is only applicable in scenarios where a trusted third party exists.

9.4.4 Location information collection considering confidentiality

Some methods propose not providing any location information for highly confidential places and only providing location information for less confidential places [38]–[40]. If the proportion of users who set a place as highly confidential is known in advance, it may be possible to estimate the number of users in each location using this method. However, generally, such proportions are unknown, making it difficult to accurately estimate the number of users in each location using these methods.

9.4.5 Negative survey

A negative survey is a technique that protects privacy by ensuring that users never report their true data to the server while the server can infer the true data distribution [10].

In a negative survey, when the true grid cell is L_i, the user reports a grid cell other than L_i to the server. Because users always provide false information, a certain level of privacy is maintained. The server can then infer the true data distribution by collecting information from many users, considering the constraint that users always provide false information. However, a high degree of accuracy requires collecting information from a large number of users.

To improve estimation accuracy on the server side, a method applying a negative survey to location information has been proposed by Forrest et al. [9]. They pre-divide the target area into $2^n \times 2^n$ cells, assigning a unique ID to each cell using only digits 0–3, resulting in an n-digit ID. Each user compares their true cell ID with all $2^n \times 2^n$ cell IDs and creates a set of IDs that differ from their true ID in all digits. For example, if $n = 2$ and the user's true cell ID is 00, the set $\{11,12,13,21,22,23,31,32,33\}$is created. The user then randomly selects one from this set to report to the server. This method is called the Negative Quad Tree (NQT).

Additionally, a method called multidimensional negative survey, which is particularly effective when there are multiple user attributes to be collected, has been proposed [7],[8]. Although not specifically for location information, it can be adapted by considering location information as two attributes: latitude and longitude. This method is called the Multi-Dimensional Analysis (MDA) method. The target area is pre-divided into $x \times y$ cells, and each cell is represented by an X and Y coordinate pair. Thus, each cell is referenced as $(1,1),(1,2),\ldots,(x,y)$. If the user's true cell coordinates are (u_x,u_y), the user creates a set of cells where the X coordinate is not u_x and the Y coordinate is not u_y. For example, if $x = 2$, $y = 3$ and the user's true cell coordinates are (1.2), the set $\{(2,1),(2,3)\}$ is created. The user then randomly selects one from this set to report to the server.

The NQT and MDA methods are compared with the proposed method in Section 9.6.

In both the NQT and MDA methods, users do not notify the server of their true grid cell information, but the server can narrow down the grid cells where users might be. Here, we illustrate MDA as an example. First, consider anonymization for a 4×4 grid. In Figure 9.3(a), assume a user is in the grid cell (b, 2) represented by X. In MDA, the user reports one of the gray grid cells in Figure 9.3(a) to the server. Suppose the user reports (c, 3). The server, upon receiving (c, 3), can infer that the user is in one of the black grid cells in Figure 9.3(b), as these are the cells that could report (c, 3). With 9 black grid cells, $k = 9$, achieving 9-anonymity.

Next, consider anonymization for an 8×8 grid. In Figure 9.4(a), assume a user is in the grid cell (f, 7) represented by X. In MDA, the user reports one of the gray grid cells in Figure 9.4(a) to the server. Suppose the user reports (c, 4). The server, upon receiving (c, 4), can infer that the user is in one of the black grid cells in Figure 9.4(b), as these are the cells that could report (c, 4). With 49 black grid cells, $k = 49$, achieving 49-anonymity.

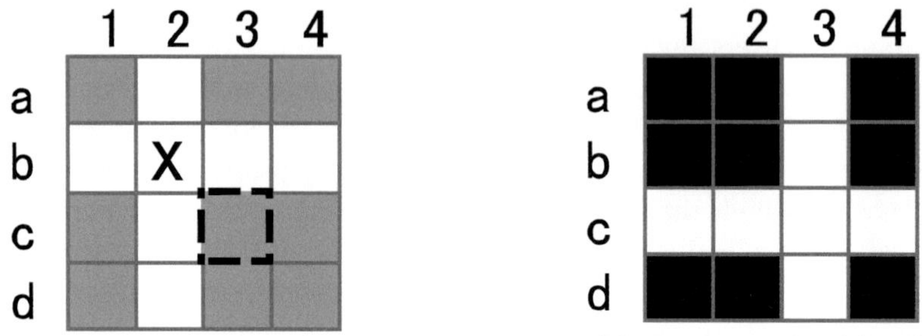

(a) Candidates of grid cells. (b) Estimated grid cells.

Figure 9.3 4×4 in MDA.

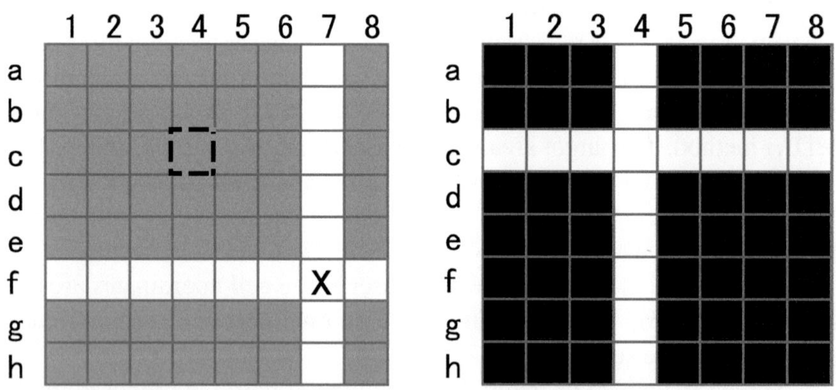

(c) Candidates of grid cells. (d) Estimated grid cells.

Figure 9.4 8×8 in MDA.

Similarly, in NQT, the server can narrow down the grid cells where users might be based on the received information. When this number is k, k-anonymity is achieved.

Table 9.1 shows a comparison between our proposed method and existing methods.

9.5 Proposed Method

We present our proposed method in this section. First, the overview of the proposed method is described in Section 9.5.1. Then, Sections 9.5.2 and 9.5.3 represent the user protocol and the server protocol, respectively. The

Table 9.1 Comparison between existing studies and this work.

	w/o trusted entity	**w/o Considering confidentiality**	**High accuracy**
Obfuscation approach [36][37]	-	✓	✓
Considering confidentiality approach [38]–[40]	✓	-	✓
Negative surveys [7][8]	✓	✓	-
This work	✓	✓	✓

expected utility is discussed in Section 9.5.4. Finally, we show the computational cost in Section 9.5.5.

9.5.1 Overview

Users report a *candidate set* to the server, indicating "I am somewhere within this set." The candidate set includes the actual grid cell L_i where the user is located and k other grid cells. Once enough candidate sets are collected from a sufficient number of users, the server estimates the number of users in each grid cell.

In the following sections, we describe the user protocol and server protocol in sequence, followed by the method for calculating the expected utility value based on the number of users from whom information is collected. Finally, we discuss the computational complexity.

9.5.2 User protocol

The latitude and longitude coordinates of each grid cell, the total number of grid cells D, and the privacy protection level k are predetermined and shared between the user and the server. For simplicity, we assume that all users have the same privacy protection level, but as discussed in Section 9.7, it is possible to extend this method to allow different privacy protection levels for each user. Suppose the true grid cell of user u is L_i The user generates k–1 dummy grid cells randomly and send these k grid cell IDs as the candidate set R_u to the server.

As an example, consider $D = 4$ and k–2. Suppose the true grid cell of user u is L_i. The user's candidate set could be one of {1,0},{1,2},{1,3}, generated randomly.

The user protocol is shown in Algorithm 9.1. Here, *rand*(D) is a function that returns a random integer between 0 and D–1.

Algorithm 9.1 User protocol of user u

Input: Number of grid cells D, Privacy level k, User u's actual grid cell ID i
Output: Candidate set
1: Generate empty set R_u
2: $R_u \leftarrow R_u \cup \{i\}$
3: while |R_u |<k do
4: $r \leftarrow rand(D)$
5: $R_u \leftarrow R_u \cup \{i\}$
6: end while
7: return R_u

9.5.3 Server protocol

The server estimates the number of users in each grid cell L_i. Let V_i be the true number of users in L_i, and let ψ_i be the estimated number of users in L_i by the server. Also, let N be the number of users who reported candidate sets.

Let W_i be the number of candidate sets in the set S that include L_i. That is,

$$W_i = |\{R_j | L_i \in R_j \wedge R_j \in S\}. \tag{9.2}$$

If a user is in grid cell L_{i_1}, L_{i_1} will be included in the user's candidate set with probability 1, and another grid cell L_{i2} where $i_1 \neq i_2$ will be included in the candidate set with probability

$$P_E = \frac{k-1}{D-1}. \tag{9.3}$$

Therefore, assuming the probabilities are distributed as expected, the following equation holds:

$$W_{\mathrm{i}} = N - \sum_{j \neq i} (1 - P_E)\psi_j. \tag{9.4}$$

By constructing this equation for each W_i ($i = 0, \ldots, D{-}1$) , a system of D linear equations with variables ψ_j ($j = 0, \ldots, D{-}1$) is created. Solving this system of equations yields the values of ψ_j. Each ψ_j is the maximum likelihood estimate and an unbiased estimator of .

As an example, consider $D = 4$, $k = 2$, and from eqn (9.2), $W_0 = 35$, $W_1 = 50$, $W_2 = 80$, $W_3 = 35$. Then, from eqn (9.3), $P_E = 1/3$. Thus, from eqn (9.4), the following system of linear equations is generated:

$$\begin{cases} 35 = 100 - \frac{2}{3} \times (\psi_1 + \psi_2 + \psi_3) \\ 50 = 100 - \frac{2}{3} \times (\psi_0 + \psi_2 + \psi_3) \\ 80 = 100 - \frac{2}{3} \times (\psi_0 + \psi_1 + \psi_3) \\ 35 = 100 - \frac{2}{3} \times (\psi_0 + \psi_1 + \psi_2) \end{cases} . \tag{9.5}$$

Solving this system of equations yields $\psi_0 = 2.5$, $\psi_1 = 25$, $\psi_2 = 70$, $\psi_3 = 2.5$.

The server protocol is shown in Algorithm 9.2.

Algorithm 9.2 Server protocol

Input: Number of grid cells D, Privacy level k, Candidate sets S
Generate arrays W and ψ_i
for $i = 0, \ldots, D-1$ do
$W_i \leftarrow$ eqn (9.2) with S
end for
$P_E \leftarrow$ eqn (9.3) with D and k
Calculate eqn (9.4) for all $j = 0, \ldots, D-1$
for $j = 0, \ldots, D-1$ do
$\psi_i \leftarrow$ each result calculated by the linear system of equations
end for
return ψ

9.5.4 Expected utility

To determine the number of users from whom information needs to be collected, it is necessary to calculate the expected utility.

This chapter uses mean squared error (MSE) as the utility metric. Based on the definition of MSE in eqn (9.1), the expected value is expressed as follows:

$$E[\sigma^2] = \frac{1}{D}\sum_{i=0}^{D-1} E\left[\left(\frac{V_i}{N} - \frac{\psi_i}{N}\right)^2\right]. \tag{9.6}$$

Since ψ_i is an unbiased estimator of V_i, $E[\psi_i] = V_i$. Also, $E[(E[\psi_i] - \psi_i)^2$ represents the variance of ψ_i. Therefore, expressing the variance of ψ_i as $Var(\psi_i)$, we get:

$$E\left[\sigma^2\right] = \frac{1}{N^2} \cdot \frac{1}{D} \sum_{i=0}^{D-1} Var\left(\psi_i\right). \tag{9.7}$$

The system of linear equations constructed from eqn (9.4) for all i is equivalent to the following equation after transformations:

$$M \cdot \boldsymbol{V}^{\tau} = \boldsymbol{W}^{\tau},$$

where

$$M = \begin{pmatrix} 0 & 1 - P_E & \dots & 1 - P_E \\ 1 - P_E & 0 & \dots & 1 - P_E \\ \vdots & \vdots & \vdots & \vdots \\ 1 - P_E & 1 - P_E & \dots & 0 \end{pmatrix}, \tag{9.8}$$

and

$$\boldsymbol{V} = (\psi_0, \psi_1, \ldots, \psi_{D-1}),$$

$$\boldsymbol{W} = (N - W_0, N - W_1, \ldots, N - W_{D-1}).$$

Thus,

$$\boldsymbol{V}^{\tau} = \mathrm{M}^{-1} \cdot \boldsymbol{W}^{\tau}. \tag{9.9}$$

Therefore, we get:

$$Var\left(\psi_i\right) = \sum_j \left(M_{i,j}^{-1}\right)^2 Var\left(N - W_j\right) + \sum_{j \neq l} M_{i,j}^{-1} M_{i,l}^{-1} Cov\left(N - W_j, N - W_l\right). \tag{9.10}$$

Consequently, the expected MSE is

$$E\left[\sigma^2\right] = \frac{k\left(D-1\right)^2}{N\left(D-k\right)D^2}. \tag{9.11}$$

9.5.5 Computational complexity

The node protocol generates $k-1$dummy grid cells, so its computational complexity is $O(k)$. As shown in Algorithm 9.1, the node only needs to perform simple calculations.

In the server protocol, solving the system of D linear equations has the highest computational complexity. The system of D linear equations can be solved using matrix operations. Using Gaussian elimination, the order of computational complexity is $O(D^3)$. Using iterative methods such as the Gauss–Seidel method, the order of computational complexity is $O(rD^2)$, where r is the number of iterations.

9.6 Evaluation

In this section, the evaluation settings and the evaluation results will be described.

9.6.1 Evaluation settings

We compare our proposed method with NQT and MDA, as introduced in the related works Section 9.4. Since the values of k for NQT and MDA are fixed depending on the number of grid cells in the target range for collecting location information, the k values cannot be adjusted. Therefore, in the evaluation, when changing the values of k, NQT and MDA were evaluated only within the possible values in that range.

We conducted a mathematical analysis to calculate the expected value of the mean squared error and evaluated it through simulations. For the simulation evaluation, we used the open-source mobility simulator Siafu [41]. Siafu is widely used in research for simulating user movements considering context information. We used the map of Leimen included with the Siafu simulator, adjusted to a size of 4.2 km × 4.2 km. The number of users was set to 96,000, and the number of grid cells was set to 16 × 16 = 256. Users were assumed to travel from home to work either on foot or by car, with the average starting time set at 7 a.m. The simulation started at 5 a.m., and the users' location information at 7 a.m. was used for evaluation.

Additionally, the target range of grid cells needs to be rectangular for MDA and NQT. Specifically, for NQT, the grid cells must be square, meaning the number of grid cells in latitude and longitude must be the same. Although our proposed method can handle any shape of the target range, we set the

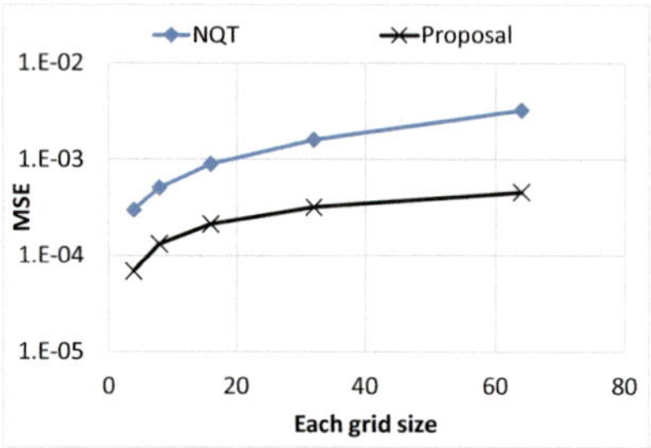

(a) Results of NQT

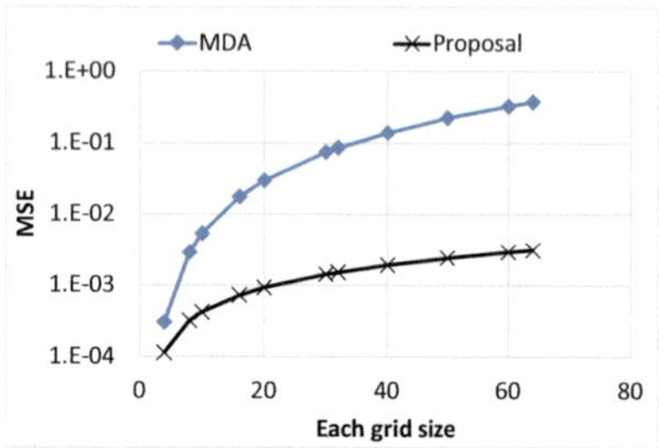

(b) Results of MDA

Figure 9.5 Relationship between the number of grids and MSEs.

environment with the same number of grid cells in latitude and longitude to compare with these existing methods.

9.6.2 Evaluation results

First, we present the results of the mathematical analysis for calculating the expected value of the mean squared error.

The results of calculating the expected value of the mean squared error by changing the number of grid cells in latitude and longitude are shown in Figure 9.5. The number of users was set to 10,000.

Figure 9.5(a) compares the proposed method with NQT, and Figure 9.5(b) compares the proposed method with MDA. In the figures, MSE represents the mean squared error. The horizontal axis represents the number of grid cells in both latitude and longitude. For example, when the horizontal axis is 50, there are a total of 2500 grid cells. The figures show that the proposed method significantly reduces the mean squared error compared to NQT and MDA.

Next, the results of varying the number of users for evaluation are shown in Figure 9.6.

For all methods, the mean squared error is inversely proportional to the number of users. For the proposed method, this relationship is evident from eqn (9.11).

Next, we conducted a simulation evaluation using randomly generated location information. In the simulation, we experimented with the distribution of user densities in each grid cell using gamma distribution, normal distribution, and uniform distribution, each with varying parameters. We repeated the simulation 50 times for each synthetic dataset and took the average value.

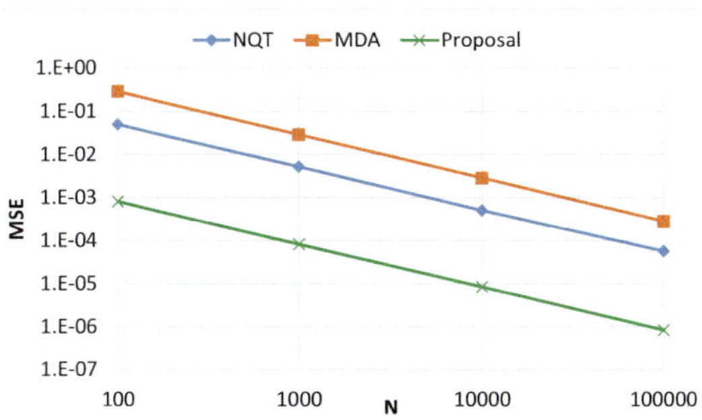

Figure 9.6 The number of users vs. MSEs.

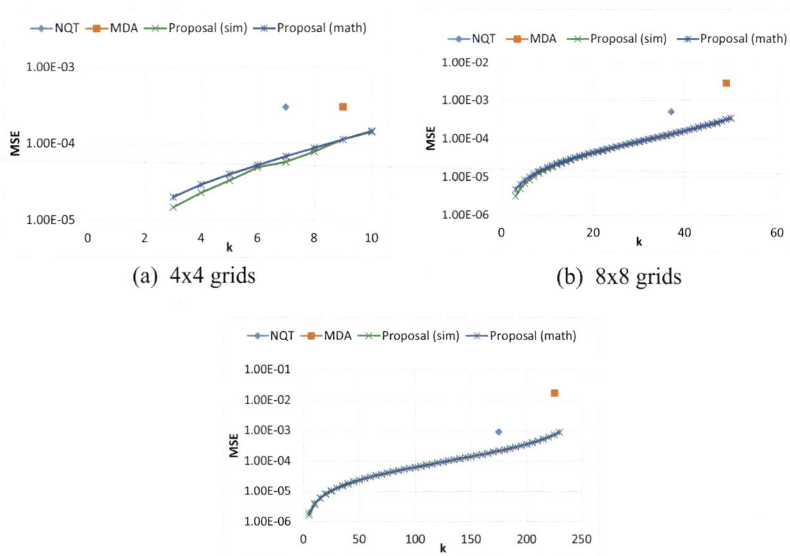

(a) 4x4 grids

(b) 8x8 grids

(c) 6x16 grids

Figure 9.7 The value of *k* vs. MSEs.

The results for the gamma distribution are shown in Figure 9.7. Similar results were obtained for all other distributions.

Proposal (sim) represents the simulation results of the proposed method, while proposal (math) represents the expected value of the mean squared error calculated using eqn (9.11). The figures show that the mean squared

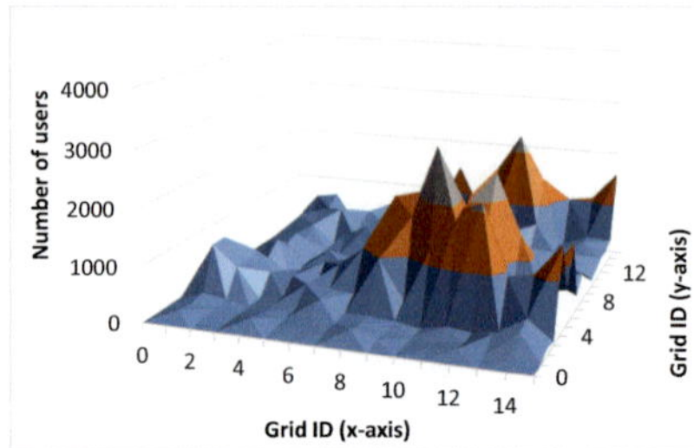

(a) Original

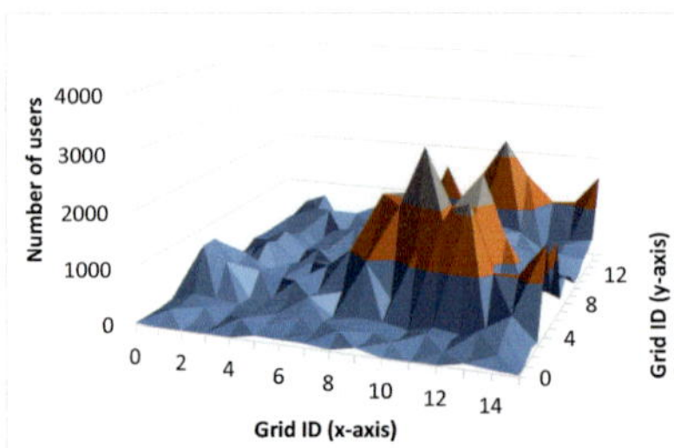

(b) Result of the proposal ($k = 10$)

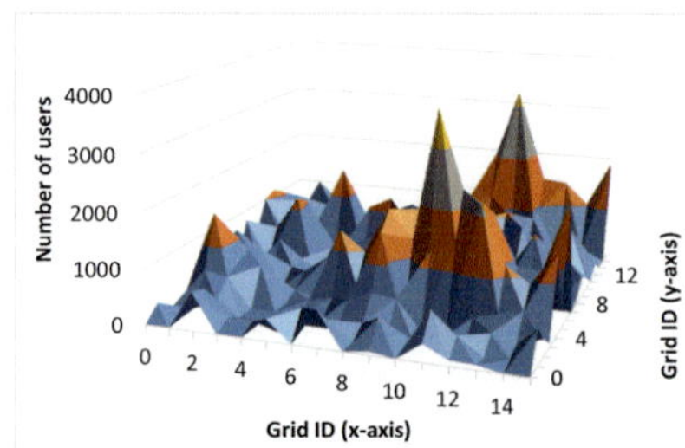

(c) Result of the proposal ($k = 175$)

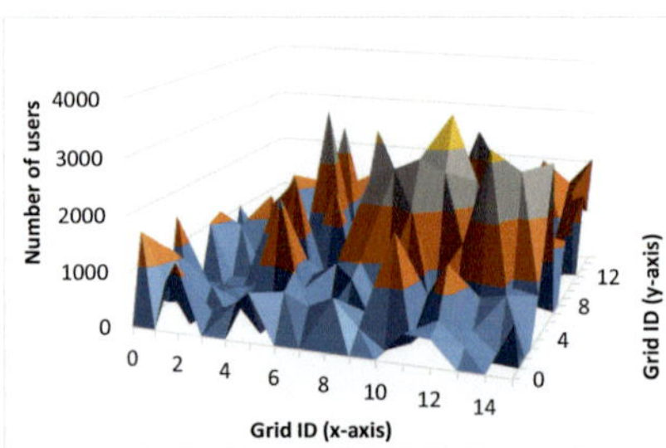

(d) Result of NQT

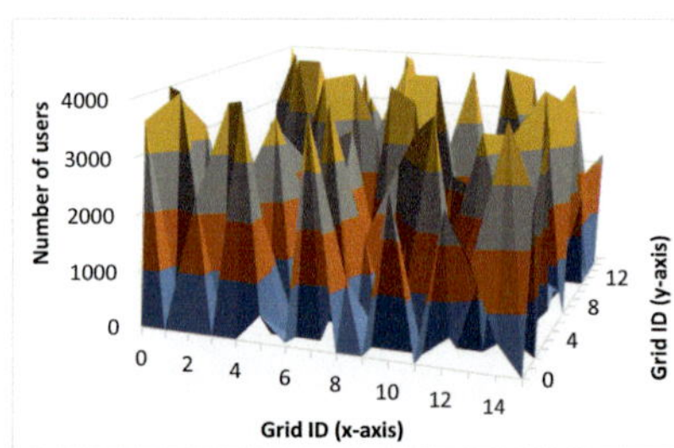

(e) Result of MDA

Figure 9.8 Results of Siafu.

error increases with the value of k. Also, for all values of k and all grid sizes, the proposed method achieves a lower mean squared error than NQT and MDA. Furthermore, eqn (9.11) closely matches the actual mean squared error values obtained.

Next, we evaluated using simulation data generated by Siafu. The distribution of raw data generated by Siafu and the estimated results using each method are shown in Figure 9.8. Figure 9.9(a) shows the original distribution of users. One randomly selected simulation result from 10 simulations using Siafu is shown in Figures 9.8(b)–9.8(e).

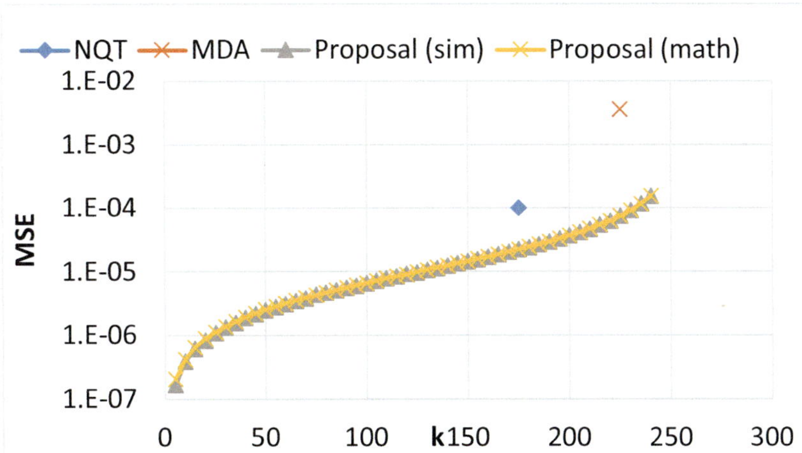

Figure 9.9 The value of k vs. MSEs in Siafu.

Many studies on k-anonymity set the value of k between 3 and 20 [42],[43]. Therefore, we set $k = 10$ for the proposed method results shown in Figure 9.8(b). Additionally, since the NQT method uses $k = 175$, we also show the proposed method results for this value (Figure 9.8(c)). The results show that the proposed method with $k = 10$ almost accurately estimates the original data distribution. Comparing the proposed method with $k = 175$ and NQT (Figure 9.8(d)) with the same k value, the proposed method better estimates the raw data distribution. MDA, however, is almost unable to estimate the raw data distribution (Figure 9.8(e)).

The results of measuring the mean squared error while changing k using Siafu simulation data are shown in Figure 9.9. We repeated the Siafu simulation 10 times and took the average value.

The proposed method achieves the smallest mean squared error, and the calculated expected value of the mean squared error closely matches the actual simulation results.

Finally, we measured the time required for estimation using synthetically generated simulation data. The results are shown in Figure 9.10. We repeated the generation and simulation of synthetic data 50 times and took the average value.

The horizontal axis represents the number of grid cells in latitude and longitude. For example, when this value is 70, there are a total of 4900 grid cells. All methods show a non-linear increase in computation time with the number of grid cells. However, having 4900 grid cells means that estimation can be done in less than an hour for grid cells covering each prefecture in

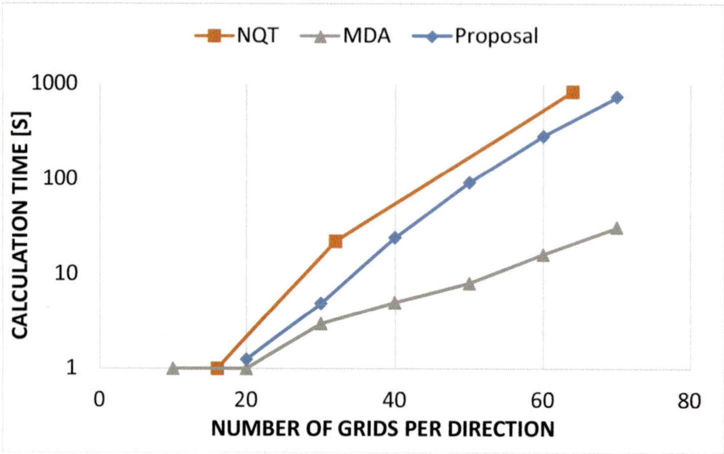

Figure 9.10 Calculation time.

Japan, making the method effective within this range. The time required for estimation was almost the same regardless of how the density distribution of users in each grid cell was changed.

9.7 Discussion

In this chapter, for simplicity, we assume a common privacy protection level for all users. However, it is possible to change the privacy protection level for each user. The procedure is as follows:

1. Group users according to their k values.
2. Use the proposed method to estimate the number of users in each grid cell for each group.
3. Combine the estimation results of each group to obtain the overall estimation.

To verify the effectiveness of this procedure, we conducted additional experiments where each user randomly sets their k value between 5 and 15. The experiments used the location information of 96,000 users, as in the evaluation in Section 9.6. The MSE in this case was 4.0×10^{-7}. For comparison, the MSE was 1.6×10^{-7} when all users set $k = 5$, and 6.1×10^{-7} when all users set $k = 15$. Thus, we confirmed that random setting of k values between 5 and 15 resulted in more accurate estimations than when all users set $k = 15$.

A more accurate calculation method when k values differ for each user remains a future task. Note that we did not compare NQT or MDA here because they do not allow flexible adjustment of k values.

On the server side, estimations are performed for each group of users with the same privacy protection level, and the results are combined to estimate the overall user set. Since the estimation accuracy (mean squared error with the true value) varies depending on the privacy protection level, we believe that weighted summation according to estimation accuracy will enable high-accuracy estimations. Specific verification is a future task.

In the proposed method, $k - 1$ grid cells are selected as dummy location information. It can be intuitively thought that the privacy protection level is higher when these dummy grid cells are widely dispersed rather than clustered near the true grid cell.

In this chapter, since the dummy grid cells are selected completely randomly, we expect some degree of dispersion in the dummy grid cells. However, as a future task, we plan to propose a new metric to measure the degree of dispersion and perform mathematical analysis within the proposed method.

9.7.1 Differential privacy and negative surveys

Our approach is based on the concept of negative surveys. In this method, the user never sends their true location information to the server. The server is aware of this fact and knows that the user must be located somewhere in the set of all candidate cells.

On the other hand, let's consider differential privacy [44],[45], a field that has seen significant research progress in recent years. One technique used in scenarios where data is collected from each user is local differential privacy. In this approach, each user sends their true location information to the server with a certain probability p, and with the remaining probability $1 - p$, they send a random false location. As a result, from the server's perspective, the user's location is indistinguishable across the entire set.

When considering privacy protection purely from this perspective, differential privacy provides a higher degree of privacy protection compared to our proposed method. However, if we consider that users send their true location information with probability p, it becomes clear that, depending on the value of p, our proposed method can offer higher privacy protection.

Additionally, for users who are not familiar with mathematics or statistics, the act of sending their true location to the server, even with a probability

p, might feel like a privacy invasion. This psychological aspect must also be considered alongside the mathematical perspective when evaluating the relationship between our proposed method and differential privacy.

Thus, it is essential to examine both the mathematical and psychological dimensions of the privacy protection provided by differential privacy compared to our proposed approach.

9.7.2 *l*-diversity and negative surveys

In this chapter, we have proposed a method targeting k-anonymity. Given that l-diversity [46],[47] has been suggested as an extension of the k-anonymity privacy metric, we will now discuss l-diversity.

Firstly, it is important to note that both k-anonymity and l-diversity can be applied to any type of privacy information, not just location information. K-anonymity is a metric designed to ensure that it is impossible to determine the target user's value from among k possible candidates. However, if these k candidates happen to all have the same value, then k-anonymity does not provide any actual privacy protection.

In this sense, our proposed method, which ensures that it is unclear in which of the k grid cells the user is located, automatically satisfies l-diversity with $l = k$. By definition, when $k = l$, l-diversity offers a higher degree of privacy protection than k-anonymity. Therefore, our proposed method can be said to provide a higher level of privacy protection than the standard k-anonymity approach.

On the other hand, if the k grid cells selected at random happen to be close to the true grid cell, the user might feel that their privacy is not adequately protected. Although these cells are different, ensuring that they are sufficiently distant from each other can enhance the perceived level of privacy protection. This leads to the concept of semantic l-diversity, which considers the semantic distance between values [48], [49]. Extending our approach to semantic l-diversity remains a future challenge.

9.8 Conclusion

By collecting users' location information from mobile devices such as smartphones, it is possible to perform marketing analyses that link users' consumption behavior to their movement patterns. This capability forms a crucial part of cyber-physical systems (CPS), which integrate computational algorithms with physical processes to enhance automation, precision, and efficiency across various applications. However, while CPS technologies bring significant benefits, they also introduce privacy challenges, particularly concerning the collection and use of sensitive location data.

In this chapter, we consider a scenario where users do not want their exact location information to be known and assume a situation where only information indicating that the user is in one of k grid cells is provided to the server. This scenario is particularly relevant in the context of CPS, where data privacy and security are paramount. Our proposed method addresses this privacy concern by allowing users to randomly generate $k - 1$ dummy grid cells in addition to their true grid cell and report this candidate set to the server. As a result, the server cannot determine the user's exact location among these k grid cells, thereby enhancing privacy protection.

Our method offers a significant advantage over traditional approaches by enabling a flexible setting of k values, unlike existing studies that are constrained by fixed k values. This flexibility allows the system to adapt to varying privacy needs and computational resources, making it more versatile and practical for real-world applications. Moreover, we derived an equation to calculate the expected estimation error, which closely matched the results obtained from our simulations. This demonstrates the robustness and reliability of our method in accurately estimating the number of users in each grid cell with minimal errors.

From a CPS perspective, the integration of our privacy-preserving method into location-based services can significantly improve user trust and data security. By ensuring that the server only receives anonymized and aggregated location data, we can mitigate the risks of data breaches and unauthorized tracking, which are critical concerns in the deployment of CPS. This not only enhances the overall security of the system but also encourages greater user participation, as individuals are more likely to share their data if they are assured of its privacy.

The proposed method also highlights the importance of balancing privacy and utility in CPS. While it is crucial to protect user privacy, the utility of the collected data should not be compromised. Our method achieves a better trade-off between privacy and estimation accuracy compared to existing methods. This balance is essential for the effective functioning of CPS, where accurate data analysis is necessary for optimizing performance and decision-making processes.

Future work will focus on improving the computational speed of the server protocol. Enhancing the efficiency of data processing and analysis in CPS is vital for real-time applications, where quick and accurate responses are required. Additionally, exploring the integration of advanced cryptographic techniques and machine learning algorithms can further enhance the privacy and security of our method. We also aim to extend our approach to consider semantic l-diversity, ensuring that the dummy grid cells are not only numerous but also meaningfully dispersed, thus further improving the perceived and actual privacy protection.

In conclusion, our proposed method provides a robust and flexible solution for collecting and utilizing location information in CPS, ensuring a high level of privacy protection while maintaining data utility. By addressing the privacy concerns inherent in CPS and offering a scalable and efficient solution, our method paves the way for more secure and trustworthy location-based services. The insights and findings from this chapter contribute to the ongoing development and refinement of privacy-preserving techniques in CPS, ultimately enhancing the reliability and user acceptance of these advanced technological systems.

References

[1] M. A. Mohammed *et al.*, "Securing healthcare data in industrial cyber-physical systems using combining deep learning and blockchain technology," *Eng. Appl. Artif. Intell.*, vol. 129, p. 107612, 2024.

[2] R. Yu, X. Zhao, S. Lu, Y.-H. Chen, and C. Li, "Intelligent Game-Theoretic Approach for Resilient Robust Control Design of Cyber-Physical Systems: Application to Intelligent Transportation Systems," *IEEE Trans. Intell. Transp. Syst.*, 2024.

[3] O. M. Ikumapayi, O. T. Laseinde, and E. T. Akinlabi, "Roles of IoT, Big Data Analytics, and Cyber-Physical Systems in a Sustainable Manufacturing," in *E3S Web of Conferences*, 2024, vol. 552, p. 1046.

[4] F. Khan, R. L. Kumar, S. Kadry, Y. Nam, and M. N. Meqdad, "Cyber physical systems: A smart city perspective," *Int. J. Electr. Comput. Eng.*, vol. 11, no. 4, p. 3609, 2021.

[5] A. Pundir, S. Singh, M. Kumar, A. Bafila, and G. J. Saxena, "Cyber-physical systems enabled transport networks in smart cities: Challenges and enabling technologies of the new mobility era," *IEEE Access*, vol. 10, pp. 16350–16364, 2022.

[6] A. H. El-Kady, S. Halim, M. M. El-Halwagi, and F. Khan, "Analysis of safety and security challenges and opportunities related to cyber-physical systems," *Process Saf. Environ. Prot.*, vol. 173, pp. 384–413, 2023.

[7] M. M. Groat, B. Edwards, J. Horey, W. He, and S. Forrest, "Enhancing privacy in participatory sensing applications with multidimensional data," in *Proc. IEEE PerCom*, 2012, pp. 144–152.

[8] M. M. Groat, B. Edwards, J. Horey, W. He, and S. Forrest, "Application and analysis of multidimensional negative surveys in participatory sensing applications," *Pervasive Mob. Comput.*, vol. 9, no. 9, pp. 372–391, 2013.

[9] S. Forrest and M. Groat, "Reconstructing Spatial Distributions from Anonymized Locations," in *Proc. IEEE ICDEW*, 2012, pp. 243–250.

[10] F. Esponda, "Negative surveys," arXiv.org, 2006.

[11] Y. Sei and A. Ohsuga, "An algorithm for privacy-preserving location data collection by probabilistic dummy generation," *IEEJ Trans. Electron. Inf. Syst.*, vol. 135, no. 6, pp. 660–670, 2015, doi: 10.1541/ieejeiss.135.660.

[12] J. A. Burke *et al.*, "Participatory sensing," in *Proc. ACM Sensys Workshop. World Sensor Web*, May 2006, pp. 1–5.

[13] U. Adeel, S. Yang, and J. A. McCann, "Self-Optimizing Citizen-Centric Mobile Urban Sensing Systems," in *Proc. International Conference on Autonomic Computing (CAC)*, 2014, pp. 161–167.

[14] Y. Sei and A. Ohsuga, "Location Anonymization with Considering Errors and Existence Probability," *IEEE Trans. Syst. Man, Cybern. Syst.*, vol. 47, no. 12, pp. 3207–3218, 2017, doi: 10.1109/TSMC.2016.2564928.

[15] R. Isawa, Y. Sei, Y. Tahara, and A. Ohsuga, "Minimizing Noise in Location Privacy Protection Through Equipment Error Consideration," *Int. J. Electr. Comput. Eng. Syst.*, vol. 15, no. 3, pp. 285–296, 2024, doi: 10.32985/ijeces.15.3.7.

[16] M. La Polla, F. Martinelli, and D. Sgandurra, "A Survey on Security for Mobile Devices," *IEEE Commun. Surv. \& Tutorials*, vol. 15, no. 1, pp. 446–471, 2013.

[17] A. Shabtai, U. Kanonov, Y. Elovici, C. Glezer, and Y. Weiss, "'Andromaly': a behavioral malware detection framework for android devices," *J. Intell. Inf. Syst.*, vol. 38, no. 1, pp. 161–190, 2011.

[18] A. Evfimievski, J. Gehrke, and R. Srikant, "Limiting privacy breaches in privacy preserving data mining," in *Proc. ACM PODS*, 2003, pp. 211–222.

[19] S. P. Kasiviswanathan, H. K. Lee, K. Nissim, S. Raskhodnikova, and A. Smith, "What Can We Learn Privately?," *SIAM J. Comput.*, vol. 40, no. 3, pp. 793–826, 2013.

[20] K. LeFevre, D. DeWitt, and R. Ramakrishnan, "Incognito: Efficient full-domain k-anonymity," in *Proc. ACM SIGMOD*, 2005, pp. 49–60.

[21] O. Abul, F. Bonchi, and M. Nanni, "Never Walk Alone: Uncertainty for Anonymity in Moving Objects Databases," in *Proc. IEEE ICDE*, 2008, pp. 376–385.

[22] C.-Y. Chow, M. F. Mokbel, and T. He, “Tinycasper: a privacy-preserving aggregate location monitoring system in wireless sensor networks,” in *Proc. ACM SIGMOD*, 2008, pp. 1307–1310.

[23] R. Shokri, C. Troncoso, C. Diaz, J. Freudiger, and J.-P. Hubaux, “Unraveling an old cloak: k-anonymity for location privacy,” in *Proc. ACM workshop on Privacy in the electronic society*, 2010, pp. 115–118.

[24] H. Kido, Y. Yanagisawa, and T. Satoh, “An anonymous communication technique using dummies for location-based services,” in *Proc. International Conference on Pervasive Services (ICPS)*, 2005, pp. 88–97.

[25] A. Suzuki, M. Iwata, Y. Arase, T. Hara, X. Xie, and S. Nishio, “A user location anonymization method for location based services in a real environment,” in *Proc. ACM SIGSPATIAL GIS*, 2010, pp. 398–401.

[26] T.-H. You, W.-C. Peng, and W.-C. Lee, “Protecting Moving Trajectories with Dummies,” in *Proc. IEEE MDM*, 2007, pp. 278–282.

[27] R. Kato, M. Iwata, T. Hara, Y. Arase, X. Xie, and S. Nishio, “User Location Anonymization Method for Wide Distribution of Dummies,” in *Proc. International Conference on Database and Expert Systems Applications (DEXA)*, 2013, pp. 259–273.

[28] Z. Huang and W. Du, “OptRR: Optimizing Randomized Response Schemes for Privacy-Preserving Data Mining,” in *Proc. IEEE ICDE*, 2008, pp. 705–714.

[29] H. Xie, L. Kulik, and E. Tanin, “Privacy-aware collection of aggregate spatial data,” *Data \& Knowl. Eng.*, vol. 70, no. 6, pp. 576–595, 2011.

[30] J. Horey, M. M. Groat, S. Forrest, and F. Esponda, “Anonymous Data Collection in Sensor Networks,” in *Proc. MobiQuitous*, 2007, pp. 1–8.

[31] V. Lesch, M. Züfle, A. Bauer, L. Iffländer, C. Krupitzer, and S. Kounev, “A literature review of IoT and CPS—What they are, and what they are not,” *J. Syst. Softw.*, vol. 200, p. 111631, 2023.

[32] A. Mishra, A. V Jha, B. Appasani, A. K. Ray, D. K. Gupta, and A. N. Ghazali, “Emerging technologies and design aspects of next generation cyber physical system with a smart city application perspective,” *Int. J. Syst. Assur. Eng. Manag.*, vol. 14, no. Suppl 3, pp. 699–721, 2023.

[33] Z. Yu, H. Gao, X. Cong, N. Wu, and H. H. Song, “A Survey on Cyber–Physical Systems Security,” *IEEE Internet Things J.*, vol. 10, no. 24, pp. 21670–21686, 2023.

[34] S. Jiang, X. Wang, Y. Que, and H. Lin, “Fed-MPS: Federated learning with local differential privacy using model parameter selection for resource-constrained CPS,” *J. Syst. Archit.*, vol. 150, p. 103108, 2024.

[35] R. Kato *et al.*, "A dummy-based anonymization method based on user trajectory with pauses," in *Proc. ACM SIGSPATIAL GIS*, 2012, pp. 249–258.

[36] Y. Zhang, M. Li, D. Yang, J. Tang, G. Xue, and J. Xu, "Tradeoff between location quality and privacy in crowdsensing: An optimization perspective," *IEEE Internet Things J.*, vol. 7, no. 4, pp. 3535–3544, 2020.

[37] F. Buccafurri, V. De Angelis, M. F. Idone, and C. Labrini, "A hierarchical distributed trusted location service achieving location k-anonymity against the global observer," *Comput. Networks*, vol. 243, p. 110301, 2024.

[38] B. Hoh *et al.*, "Enhancing Privacy and Accuracy in Probe Vehicle-Based Traffic Monitoring via Virtual Trip Lines," *IEEE Trans. Mob. Comput.*, vol. 11, no. 5, pp. 849–864, 2012.

[39] T. T. B. Le and T. K. Dang, "Semantic-Aware obfuscation for location privacy at database level," in *Proc. International Conference on Information and Communication Technology*, 2013, vol. 111–120, pp. 111–120.

[40] J. Acharya, K. Bonawitz, P. Kairouz, D. Ramage, and Z. Sun, "Context aware local differential privacy," in *International Conference on Machine Learning*, 2020, pp. 52–62.

[41] M. Martin and P. Nurmi, "A Generic Large Scale Simulator for Ubiquitous Computing," in *Proc. MobiQuitous*, 2006, pp. 1–3.

[42] L. Yao, G. Wu, J. Wang, F. Xia, C. Lin, and G. Wang, "A Clustering K-Anonymity Scheme for Location Privacy Preservation," *IEICE Trans. Inf. Syst.*, vol. E95-D, no. 1, pp. 134–142, 2012.

[43] H. Hu, J. Xu, S. T. On, J. Du, and J. K.-Y. Ng, "Privacy-aware location data publishing," *ACM Trans. Database Syst.*, vol. 35, no. 3, pp. 1–42, 2010.

[44] C. Dwork, K. Kenthapadi, F. McSherry, I. Mironov, and M. Naor, "Our data, ourselves: privacy via distributed noise generation," in *Proc. Eurocrypt*, 2006, vol. 4004, pp. 486–503.

[45] Y. Sei and A. Ohsuga, "Differential Private Data Collection and Analysis Based on Randomized Multiple Dummies for Untrusted Mobile Crowdsensing," *IEEE Trans. Inf. Forensics Secur.*, vol. 12, no. 4, pp. 926–939, 2017.

[46] A. Machanavajjhala, J. Gehrke, D. Kifer, and M. Venkitasubramaniam, "l-diversity: Privacy Beyond k-Anonymity," in *Proc. IEEE ICDE*, 2006, pp. 24:1-24:12.

[47] Y. Sei, H. Okumura, T. Takenouchi, and A. Ohsuga, "Anonymization of Sensitive Quasi-Identifiers for l-Diversity and t-Closeness," *IEEE*

Trans. Dependable Secur. Comput., vol. 16, no. 4, pp. 580–593, 2019, doi: 10.1109/TDSC.2017.2698472.

[48] K. Oishi, Y. Sei, Y. Tahara, and A. Ohsuga, "Semantic diversity: Privacy considering distance between values of sensitive attribute," *Comput. & Secur.*, vol. 94, no. 101823, pp. 1–18, Jul. 2020, doi: 10.1016/j.cose.2020.101823.

[49] K. Oishi, Y. Tahara, Y. Sei, and A. Ohsuga, "Proposal of l-diversity algorithm considering distance between sensitive attribute values," in *2017 IEEE Symposium Series on Computational Intelligence, SSCI 2017 - Proceedings*, 2018, vol. 2018-Janua, doi: 10.1109/SSCI.2017.8280973.

10

Emerging Security and Privacy Schemes for Cyber-physical Systems

Abidemi Emmanuel Adeniyi[1], Rasheed Gbenga Jimoh[2], Joseph Bamidele Awotunde[2], Peace Busola Falola[3], Oluwatobi Blessing Olorunfemi[4] and Agbotiname Lucky Imoize[5]

[1]Department of Computer Science, Bowen University, Nigeria
[2]Department of Computer Science, University of Ilorin, Nigeria
[3]Computer Science Unit, Distance Learning Center, University of Ibadan, Nigeria
[4]Department of Computer Science, Redeemer's University, Nigeria
[5]Department of Electrical and Electronics Engineering, Faculty of Engineering, University of Lagos, Nigeria

Email: abidemi.adeniyi@bowen.edu.ng; jimoh_rasheed@unilorin.edu.ng; awotunde.jb@unilorin.edu.ng; peacefalola@gmail.com; olorunfemib@run.edu.ng; aimoize@unilag.edu.ng

Abstract

The challenges and possibilities in security and privacy are unique due to the rapidly evolving cyber-physical systems (CPS) landscape. Their increasing integration into essential infrastructures like healthcare, transportation, and energy has made it imperative for them to be secure and their data to remain private. This chapter discusses how both CPS digital and physical elements relate, considering sophisticated cyberattacks with physical consequences. Specifically, this chapter analyzes the vulnerabilities resulting from the merger of evermore complex systems with extensive connectivity and cyber-attack sophistication and its impact on privacy in a data-centric world. The chapter underlines the importance of improving security solutions in cyber-space to protect against both present and future attacks. This also touches on advanced technological alternatives, including encryption algorithms for

DOI: 10.1201/9788743801306-10

secure data transformation, machine learning models for threat forecasting and unusual activity detection, and strong user authentication systems that allow only genuine people to get into important machines. Moreover, it highlights how vital privacy-preserving technologies like differential privacy and federated learning are because they enable one to harness all advantages associated with enormous datasets without compromising anybody's confidentiality. This chapter proposes a research agenda that would focus on developing adaptable, integrated security frameworks that are reactive and proactive in identifying and neutralizing threats before they strike. It consists of an ongoing cycle of research, implementation, and refinement of security measures complemented by continuous monitoring of an improving threat landscape so that CPS can remain safe and dependable as the backbone of modern civilization.

10.1 Introduction

Cyber-physical systems (CPS) blend physical and computational operations, integrating them to create a complicated interplay between the digital and physical realms. This has made it vital for industries like healthcare, transportation, or industrial automation to employ strong security measures as these systems grow significantly across various fields. In the last 10 years, linking embedded systems, communications, and controls has formed the centerpiece of research in cyber-physical systems (CPS) to solve problems that arise when merging the cyber and physical worlds [1],[2]. Embedded computers are today common in various sectors such as aerospace, automotive industry, chemical production, civil infrastructure, energy, health care, and others because they have become cheaper and have improved processing power.

Attacks against cyber-physical systems (CPS) can have catastrophic consequences for humans and the environment due to their vital significance in our daily lives. To better comprehend safety-critical cyber-physical systems, attempts have been made to classify assaults and countermeasures. For example, authors in [3] and [4] quantitatively examine the CPS security research trend to identify the distribution of study topics. CPS research is classified based on several application situations, including electricity grids and industrial control systems (ICS) [5]. Some researchers discuss attack detection and secure estimation strategies, whereas others cover automated intrusion detection in CPS [6], [7]. Recent studies have standardized assaults on cyber-physical systems that use physical signals to impact electronic components, particularly sensors [8], [9]. Existing research has not addressed the security and privacy concerns associated with cyber-physical systems' interface with the physical world, one of their distinguishing features. As the cyber and physical worlds become more interwoven, it's crucial to comprehend the security implications of growing threats and technological advancements.

Cyber-physical systems are increasingly interwoven into key infrastructures, making security breaches potentially disastrous [10]. A hacked vehicle-to-vehicle communication network might lead to accidents by transmitting incorrect distance information. Autonomous automobiles have exacerbated the issue by requiring passengers to trust the vehicle's choices. In addition to security problems, CPS privacy is a big issue. Cyber-physical systems collect vast amounts of data for analysis and decision-making, frequently spreading across large geographic regions. The system uses machine learning algorithms to make informed judgments based on collected information. Data breaches can occur at any system level, from collection to transmission, operation, and storage. Again, most current CPS design techniques do not include data protection, putting the obtained data at risk. The CPS comprises two layers that communicate via networks and the cyber-physical layer, which can be further divided into cyber and physical domains (see Figure 10.1).

Cyber-physical systems (CPS) control the world's essential infrastructure. CPS integrates cyber and physical locations, serving as a bridge between the two. Examples include electricity generation, distribution, water treatment, manufacturing, and mining. These systems are highly integrated and tailored to the relevant area [11]. The dangers inherent in the interconnectedness of the cyber and physical realms demand strong protection. Recent research emphasizes the need to detect suspicious activity within the CPS promptly. Advanced machine learning approaches can aid detection, allowing systems to respond quickly to possible threats [12]. However, the issue remains of scaling these security mechanisms across varied IoT settings while retaining system stability and performance. In addition to technological solutions, academic and industrial collaboration is required to develop comprehensive CPS security procedures. This partnership can result in the creation of best practices and standards that improve the overall security posture of these systems. By harnessing the experience of diverse stakeholders, the field may move more quickly toward tackling the multiple security concerns that CPS confronts.

10.1.1 The key contributions of the chapter

CPS security prospects depend on advances in threat identification techniques and resistance methods for emerging cyber threats. Safety protocols

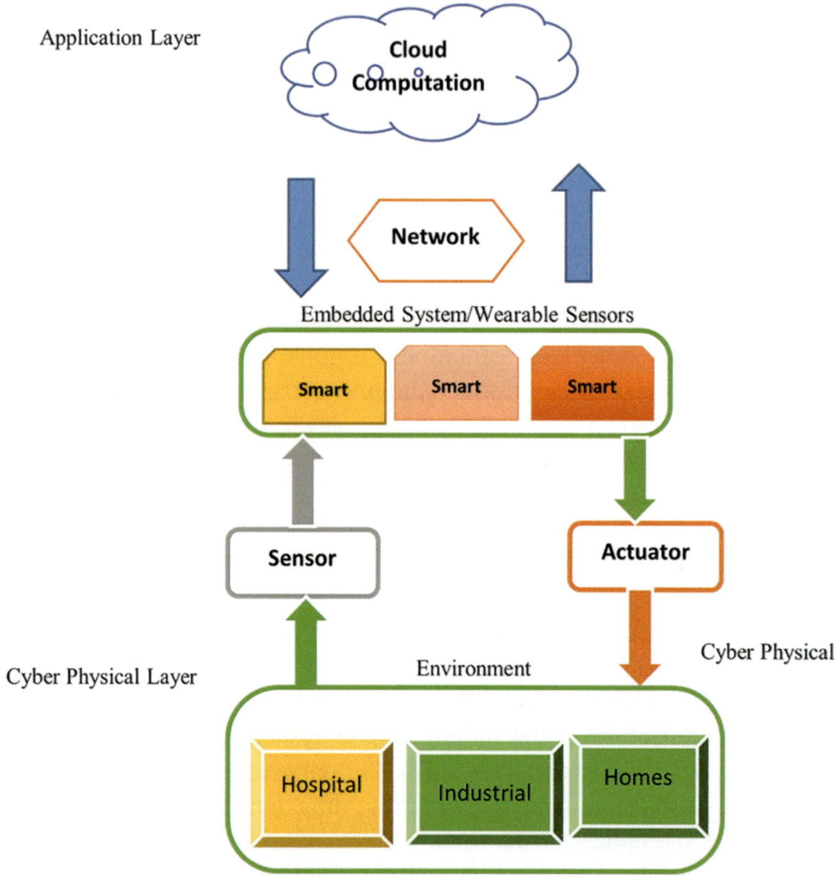

Figure 10.1 CPS architecture.

must adapt as cyber-physical systems change and extend into novel uses. This involves investigating new encryption techniques, such as homomorphic encryption, which allows for the secure computing of encrypted data while maintaining privacy and facilitating data analysis. As CPS becomes more integrated into our everyday lives, the significance of new security and privacy measures cannot be emphasized. The literature discusses various solutions for securing these complex systems, ranging from layered security designs to incorporating machine learning and collaborative frameworks. To address the problems offered by CPS, a multidimensional strategy is required, combining technological innovation with an awareness of human aspects and industry collaboration. As research advances, it is critical to be aware and proactive in building strong security measures to survive the changing environment of cyber threats.

This chapter covers a range of cyber-physical systems with varying complexity and integration scales. Adopting advanced metering infrastructure (AMI) and household energy management systems has led to a transition toward a more dependable and secure grid, known as the smart grid. The growing infrastructure comprises four parts: electricity generation, transmission, distribution, and end-use. End-users are increasingly integrating intelligent control systems, leading to the development of home automation systems. This chapter provides in-depth coverage of these systems. The other section covers the lowest scale of CPS: healthcare systems, including wearable and implanted medical equipment. Healthcare devices can be worn or implanted to regulate various organ functions [13].

Wireless sensor networks facilitate communication among healthcare equipment. They are susceptible to network assaults and device-level compromises. To prevent cyberattacks on critical infrastructure systems (CPSs), it is important to identify weak components that can be exploited through persistent attacks. CPS utilizes various equipment and structures, including sensors, actuators, PLCs, RTUs, and HMIs [14]. These devices communicate with the Internet to perform tasks like measuring and uploading power meter data for analysis. CPSs have several levels, including operations and communications, physical control, supervisory control, and corporate layers [15]. Each layer is described separately because the physical layer consists of sensors and actuators responsible for directly transmitting data to the control system for processing. Programmable logic controllers (PLCs) and remote terminal units (RTUs) are part of the control layer. These units receive information from physical devices and send orders for execution. The control unit provides instructions about specific tasks using numerical values obtained from physical sensors and actuators. The corporate layer, which connects physical, computer, and network components, is prone to security and privacy vulnerabilities in corporate networks [16]. Attackers might exploit cyber threats by employing sophisticated methods and tools to violate the confidentiality, integrity, and availability (CIA) security principles.

10.1.2 Chapter organization

The remaining parts of this chapter are organized as follows: Section 10.2 presents privacy preservation in cyber-physical system environments and discusses differential privacy for cyber-physical systems. Section 10.3 presents cyber-physicals and cyber threats. Section 10.4 introduces the modern security and privacy solution for CPS. Section 10.5 concludes the chapter.

10.2 Privacy Preservation in Cyber-physical System Environments

The need to preserve privacy in cyber-physical system (CPS) environments is critical due to the vast amount of personal and sensitive information these systems handle. The combination of physical and cyber components in these systems complicates issues relating to privacy. Privacy preservation protects sensitive information from unauthorized access while allowing for effective network processing [17]. A study introduced privacy preservation in CPS in 2008 to provide data utility while preventing network advertisers from accessing sensitive data [18]. CPS systems generate large amounts of heterogeneous data from multiple sources, necessitating the development of privacy-preserving methods while maintaining network security measures like anomaly detection [19]. Since CPS systems gradually draw interest of competent hackers with principal objective of gaining access to exfiltration control system data that includes energy information, login details for additional system usage, and an awareness of key node locations to cause important kinetic impact.

An effective and straightforward way to identify privacy-preserving technologies is based on the aim of data transformation [20]. This categorization includes three categories: data generalization, transformation, and aggregation. Generalization techniques protect data security by transforming sensitive attributes into generic values. Transformation methods add new values to the original data and utilize projection to minimize its dimensions. Aggregation methods divide original data into tiny pieces and adjust private variables based on the average of those parts. Other works focused on data aggregation to ensure system security and privacy [21]. These approaches are excellent in protecting sensitive data from unauthorized access. However, data heterogeneity strategies are still in their infancy in CPS research due to the challenge of properly handling many data types. This is not a minor issue given the wide range of data in CPS ecosystems.

An alternative strategy for categorizing privacy preservation strategies is based on their properties. This type includes four categories: heuristic, reconstruction, cryptography, and blockchain-based [22]. These strategies are seen to be successful in data security. Still, they have limitations such as offering little cryptographic information, incurring high computational costs, failing to describe data standards, whether raw or aggregated, and being unable to scale adequately [23]. Numerous techniques involving data mining

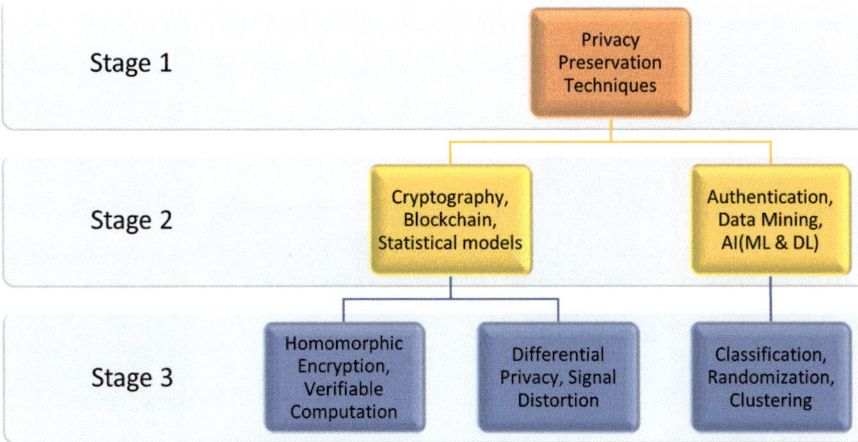

Figure 10.2 Privacy preservation in control systems.

(DM) and machine learning (ML), perturbation (i.e., differentiated privacy (DP)), and encryption were used for transforming, changing, disseminating, and hiding computer data from exposure while analyzing or transferring it through networks. Data in control networks, such as electrical grids, is restricted for safety, confidentiality, and business reasons, making it difficult to access for study purposes [24]. As a result, combating cyber and privacy threats to CPS ecosystems remains an important topic of study, with various studies undertaken specifically to secure CPS physical and network personal data [25-27]. Encryption techniques are typically used to preserve confidential information. However, they still have issues in subsequent evaluation and information management, whereas recently, machine learning, data mining, and statistical methods have been widely utilized [28],[29]. Figure 10.2 illustrates several safeguarding privacy strategies, including their types, methodology, advantages, limitations, and potential improvements.

10.2.1 Differential privacy for cyber-physical systems

Differential confidentiality is an efficient statistical technique that ensures unconditional privacy by making no assumptions about an attacker's knowledge. This assures that perturbed data calculations do not significantly alter when the original data is changed while maintaining data privacy even after access by other parties [30]. The outcomes of any computer are distinct and independent of the initial information in the dataset. Researchers have suggested several privacy-preserving solutions to address specific risks.

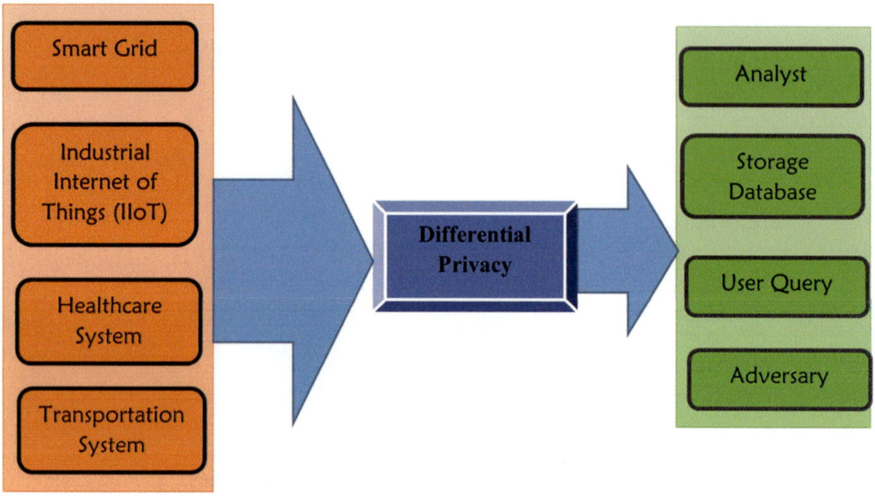

Figure 10.3 Application of differential privacy in the cyber-physical system [36].

Encryption is a fundamental privacy-preserving approach most systems use to secure data from attackers and unknown individuals [31]. It ensures that data is inaccessible to unknown parties. Modern CPSs have limited CPU capability, making encryption difficult to implement [32]. In public key cryptography (also known as asymmetric cryptography), generating and distributing public and private keys is computationally intensive and cannot be effectively carried out on tiny devices with limited resources. Additionally, vulnerabilities in encrypted CPS data can be exploited by brute-force attacks. Encryption techniques in a network of sensors need connections of all nodes to generate and transmit private keys throughout the network. If one node fails in a network of *n* nodes, it becomes almost hard to decrypt and gather data from CPS nodes due to missing keys.

Differential privacy is a simple privacy preservation approach that doesn't require sophisticated hardware [33]. The design and efficiency criteria for CPSs vary depending on their use. The optimality of differential private mechanisms varies based on application requirements. In certain circumstances, maintaining total privacy is the ideal answer, but in others, offering a certain degree of benefit might be considered optimal [34]. Similarly, there is no definition of an optimum differential privacy solution; instead, researchers working in differential privacy use the phrase "approximate optimal solution" to refer to the most suited solution based on the requirements. Moving on to CPS applications, devices that provide differential privacy often communicate time-series data from one destination to another in the smart grid context. Smart grid applications often prioritize point-by-point privacy. The most prevalent energy system assault is non-intrusive load monitoring (NILM), which targets smart home users' appliance usage and routines [35]. Differential privacy solutions in smart grids often aim to prevent assaults. Implementing differential privacy solutions in energy systems aims to provide cost-effective medium-level privacy protection while balancing accuracy and privacy. Figure 10.3 shows the use case possibilities for differential privacy in cyber-physical system applications such as analyst data analysis, storage databases, user query assessment, and attacker query requests.

The true explanation is that the computing cost of differential confidentiality consists solely of noise calculation using an established probability distribution. However, encryption nodes must perform specific duties such as key creation and distribution, data encryption, and decryption. Compared to encryption, differential privacy has lower computational complexity. In differential privacy, CPS users may adjust the amount of privacy based on their needs by changing the noise addition value "ε." Unlike anonymization, differential privacy protects original CPS data during query assessment by perturbation methods, preventing data loss. Differential privacy techniques effectively defend against numerical and non-numerical requests [36]. Differential privacy has been widely used in CPSs to protect individual privacy due to its numerous advantages, mathematical and theoretical foundation, and ease of implementation.

10.2.2 Application of authentication-based privacy preservation for CPS

One critical aspect of cyber-physical systems (CPSs) is that they depend on authentication-based privacy to ensure that only authorized users and devices can access sensitive data or systems [37]. Strong authentication protocols are very important to maintain privacy and security in CPS, which are interconnected networks that are often publicly accessible, with device-to-device (D2D) communication occurring frequently. For example, smart grids, autonomous vehicles, and health monitoring systems are typical CPS environments with several layers of communication and data transmission. Consequently, these interactions may expose private or operational information if appropriate measures are not taken for their protection. One way to safeguard such interactions, therefore, is through strict identification processes that verify the identity of users and machines, thus limiting access to confidential information only to persons with legitimate rights to it.

CPS authentication may come in different forms, such as conventional passwords, hardware tokens, or even more developed biometric systems and digital certificates [38],[39]. Each method has advantages and disadvantages concerning privacy, convenience, and security. For example, although biometrics provide high levels of security due to being unique to an individual, it may have big implications for privacy if any of that person's bodily information is exposed. Public key infrastructures (PKIs) enhanced security within CPSs by enabling authentication through digital certificates. Such certificates guarantee the validity of ownership over public keys while preventing tampering; hence, they act as a trust assurance between devices and systems. Finally, digital certificates help encrypt communications, thus safeguarding privacy when transferring data between parties.

In addition to protecting human–computer interactions, authentication in CPS must consider machine-to-machine (M2M) communications [40]. The challenge here is managing and authenticating many device transactions automatically and safely. Techniques like mutual authentication are critical in such cases, where both parties authenticate each other in a communication. This approach is particularly crucial in industrial applications and critical infrastructure since unauthorized access or manipulation of machines' operations can lead to dire consequences [41]. Another level of privacy protection is provided by integrating context-aware authentication mechanisms that consider the circumstances under which access requests are made. These mechanisms make dynamic authentication decisions based on location, time, and type of access request. Doing so enables CPS to make a trade-off between security requirements and user convenience by adjusting their authentication requirements according to the perceived risk level; this way, they ensure continuity of service but always minimize chances for unauthorized entrance into their systems.

Nonetheless, when applying robust authentication strategies in CPS, attention should also be paid to privacy. For instance, storing and processing authentication data, especially biometric data and personal identifiers, should be a ledge to respect users' privacy while complying with applicable data protection laws. This may involve using privacy-enhancing technologies (PETs) such as zero-knowledge proofs that enable authentication without disclosing the real details, protecting the user's privacy. The issue of protecting privacy through authentication-based means in CPS is complicated by various factors that combine to come up with sophisticated technical solutions, system design considerations, and management practices [42]. Importantly, authentication mechanisms must be enhanced to ensure that as CPS continues evolving and becoming more integrated into daily activities, there is enough privacy protection, hence protecting the complex processes set to run these systems securely.

10.2.3 Application of data mining and machine and deep learning-based privacy preservation in CPS

Data mining, as well as machine learning, is playing a significant role in the advancement of private security techniques within cyber-physical systems [43]. CPS produces immense amounts of information, such as smart grids, health monitoring systems, and urban infrastructure management, which these technologies use to identify patterns, anomalies, and potential hazards – implementing data mining methods with machine learning results in more advanced models aimed at foreseeing privacy violations, thereby protecting personal and business information against unpermitted exposure. The use of machine learning algorithms, especially in pattern recognition and anomaly detection, is important for identifying abnormal behaviors that could indicate intrusions or data leaks in CPS environments [44]. These models are trained on huge amounts of historical data to know what normal means regarding system behavior. They serve as real-time security enhancements and continuously monitor the incoming information for deviations from these norms, making them indispensable for dynamic and complex CPS networks [45]. Furthermore, privacy-preserving data mining techniques are more important than ever in environments where sharing information may put privacy at risk. This is done through differential privacy methods that add some noise or randomness to training datasets for machine learning models, thus preventing others from knowing specific details about any individual entry but leaving just enough accurate detail for meaningful, purposeful analysis. Using such a model allows CPS operators to obtain insights from data while protecting people's personal information they hold on them because otherwise, their lives may be ruined if someone finds out about them.

The creation of federated learning systems is one more significant use for machine learning regarding privacy in CPS [46]. These systems allow the training of machine-learning models on several decentralized devices or servers while keeping their true data intact. For example, utilizing a federated learning approach enables hospitals to enhance their prediction models for patient care without exposing sensitive personal information during that process, hence maintaining confidentiality and compliance with strict medical privacy rules. Moreover, some models could help preserve secrecy by automating data encryption/decryption techniques. Sophisticated models may establish the best possible encryption strategies depending on how much security the data holds and the environments wherein such information is applied, dynamically adapting accordingly as situations change. This flexibility is essential within CPS, where the system states and outside dangers may advance quickly. Nevertheless, applying data mining and artificial intelligence in data safeguarding is a non-terminating headache.

The utmost importance is on ensuring that no data goes out through the machine learning models themselves. Adversaries can only get to sensitive information if they reverse engineer these models; subsequently, it's crucial always to ensure the safety of the model, especially when it comes to inference data they make, and training processes associated with them. Another challenge facing developers of scalable privacy-preserving machine learning algorithms is their complexity [47]. They should not just succeed in hiding something but should also be capable of processing loads of information quickly to meet the real-time processing required by CPS. Although considering privacy and operational efficiency, CPS can use data mining and machine learning as powerful tools. However, great care must be taken when implementing them. There is the possibility that these technologies will become more complex in CPS as time moves on. They would thus become more powerful in countering any privacy issues, even while allowing these systems to have better data mining capabilities, which is what they are built for.

10.2.4 Artificial intelligence in privacy preserving

AI is the science and engineering of creating intelligent machines that think like humans [48]. John McCarthy, dubbed the "father of AI," was the first to present this notion. AI aims to create expert systems capable of intelligent tasks, learning, situational awareness, and human-like behavior. The first AI application was designed for weather forecasting. AI-based apps (e.g., movie recommendations, early illness detection, Google navigators) rely on large amounts of data to make accurate conclusions and suggestions (Figure 10.4). This might compromise data security and privacy.

As systems are interconnected and complex, AI (artificial intelligence) has an important role in transforming privacy protection in cyber-physical systems (CPSs) through innovative methods that fortify the safety of these environments. The deployment of AI technology plays a critical role in solving different privacy difficulties that CPS are confronted with as they become more important to key infrastructures like power grids, transport systems, and healthcare services [49]. One aspect where AI excels is its ability to rapidly analyze huge amounts of information, pick out possible risks to personal data, and automate enforcement processes for data protection regulations. In

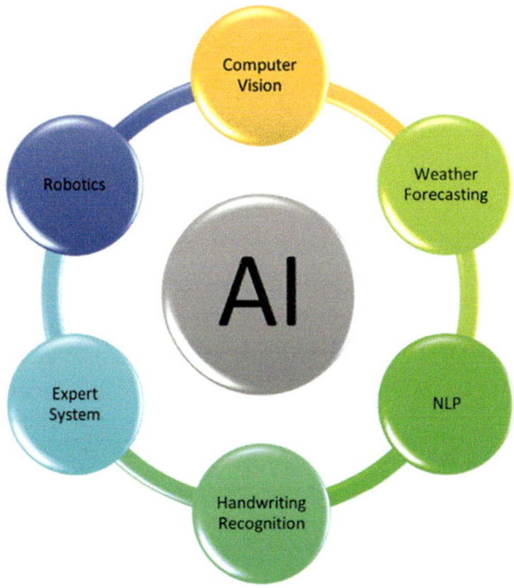

Figure 10.4 Artificial intelligence applications.

CPS, AI may be used to create prediction models that detect privacy breaches before they occur. These models use previous data to understand patterns related to security issues, which allows them to anticipate similar events in the future. This proactive strategy enables system administrators to adopt preventative actions, securing sensitive data. Furthermore, AI-powered systems may automatically alter privacy settings based on real-time data analysis, reacting to new dangers as they emerge without requiring human interaction. This flexibility is critical in contexts where dangerous landscapes are continually shifting. Table 10.1 displays the various AI techniques utilized in the privacy-preserving aspects of CPS.

AI also improves privacy by utilizing powerful anomaly detection techniques. These approaches enable CPS to continually monitor network traffic and user activity, detecting aberrant behaviors that may signal privacy violations. These systems can greatly differentiate near-in-female dissimilarities with negative consequences; they make fewer errors and enhance the speediness of security measures. Further input is that AI supports removing and hiding our data through a process known as privacy-preserving data mining in CPS. Various processes used here include federated learning, which allows the training of an AI model across several separated nodes without having to share any raw information. This approach means important information stays within its locality, lessening the chances of losing such information when using central processing platforms. AI algorithms also assist in executing

Table 10.1 AI in privacy-preserving for CPS.

AI techniques	Application in CPS	Privacy technique	Benefits	Challenges
Federated learning	Distributed learning across multiple CPS devices	Data localization	Enhances privacy by processing data locally	Managing heterogeneous data sources
Differential privacy	Adding noise to data collected from CPS devices	Noise addition	Provides theoretical guarantees of privacy	Balancing privacy with data utility
Homomorphic encryption	Performing computations on encrypted data from CPS	Encryption	Allows data processing while keeping data encrypted	High computational overhead
Secure multi-party computation	Collaborative data analysis without exposing individual inputs	Encryption, secret sharing	Secures data during joint computations	Complexity and scalability issues
Machine learning models	Anomaly detection and predictive maintenance	Model perturbation, data anonymization	Helps in identifying potential threats without revealing sensitive data	Requires continuous model updates

encryption methods such as homomorphic encryption, where the actual data is never revealed. However, it can still be worked on through this type of coding, keeping it safe and ensuring no loss of importance [50]. Using deep learning algorithms, these systems can accurately discern between benign abnormalities and dangerous threats, decreasing false positives and enabling more efficient security responses.

Furthermore, AI helps to maintain privacy in data mining activities inside CPS. Techniques like federated learning, in which AI models are trained across numerous decentralized nodes without exchanging raw data, contribute to data privacy. This technique keeps sensitive information inside its local context, lowering the danger of data leaking during central processing. AI algorithms are also useful in developing encryption techniques such as homomorphic encryption, which allows data to be processed while encrypted, giving security without losing data usefulness. While AI dramatically improves CPS's ability to protect user privacy and security, its deployment must be carefully controlled to balance efficacy, efficiency, and ethical issues. With continued advances in AI research and its application to real-world systems, its role in privacy preservation in CPS is expected to grow more robust and essential, offering a future in which CPS may be both powerful and safe.

10.3 Cyber-physicals and Cyber Threats

A CPS combines physical and communication technologies with cyber, physical, and cyber-physical aspects. A cyber element comprises computing and network components that do not interact directly with the physical world. In contrast, a physical element consists of hardware and industrial components that do not interact directly with the cyber parts. Cyber-physical elements include devices and systems that connect the cyber and physical worlds, such as sensors and actuators [51]. A CPS combines data sources from physical devices and computational and network systems to produce big data. Because of their complexity, big data presents several challenges, particularly regarding system control and data analytics for monitoring and controlling their operations. In a CPS, such as a power system, supervisory control and data acquisition (SCADA) serves as an interface for monitoring and managing activities employing conventional communication and industrial protocols [52]. However, the CPS's interconnectedness of sensors, actuators, and network devices at various power nodes complicates the platform environment (such as a power grid). It generates vast data that must be secured from cyber threats. Table 10.2 shows the variety of cyber threats that can affect CPS.

Table 10.2 Cyber threat and common mitigation strategies.

Cyber threat	Impact on CPS	Common mitigation strategies
Malware	Disruption of operational technology	Regular software updates, anti-malware tools, and network segmentation
Ransomware	Looking for access to critical system	Secure backups, intrusion detection systems, cybersecurity training
Denial of service (DoS)	Overload systems to interrupt services	Distributed denial of service (DDoS) protection, redundancy
Man-in-the-middle attacks	Data interception and manipulation	Encryption, secure communication protocols, VPNs
Data breaches	Unauthorized access to sensitive data	Strong authentication measures, encryption, and access controls
Physical tempering	Direct physical harm to system components	Physical security controls, surveillance systems
Supply chain attacks	Compromise through third-party components	Supplier security assessments and secure software development lifecycle

To detect cyber risks to CPS systems, it's important first to understand their fundamental components. This includes identifying susceptible areas that advanced attackers can exploit. A CPS comprises a variety of sensors, actuators, and components that govern systems and communicate with other networks (including business networks and even Internet connections) to perform CPS tasks [53]. CPSs comprise physical, control, supervisory, and corporate layers. Cyber attackers have produced cyber threats who frequently utilize complex assaulting tactics and tools to violate the confidentiality, integrity, and availability (CIA) security principles. Man-in-the-middle (MITM) attacks and data exfiltration are malicious behaviors that compromise confidentiality [54].

Additional CPS-specific integrity threats include modifying CPS components or registers, exposing system data through fake data injection, data poisoning, and unlawful data or configuration change. This can include data sources such as sensor or device measurements and control commands, which modify the usual occurrences of physical and network devices. Attacks on availability include denial of service (DoS) and distributed DoS. There are other CPS-specific issues in this domain, such as the potential to disrupt the operation of RTUs and PLCs by providing them with incorrect data. This is especially problematic on older systems that lack the processing capability for thorough error checks. Attacks on networks can cause temporary or permanent downtime or physical damage. This can disrupt the regular functioning of

CPSs. Active research is underway to safeguard CPS devices and data against hackers. These measures include preserving privacy, securing original data from unauthorized access, and detecting cyber assaults on CPSs and networks.

10.3.1 Application scenarios of cyber-physical System

Cyber-physical systems (CPSs) combine physical processes, computers, and networking to improve capabilities across various industries, each with its application situations [55]. These systems combine hardware and software with network connectivity to produce responsive environments that vastly increase efficiency, safety, and functionality. The information flow and physical sensing between cyberspace and connected physical devices are described as follows.

A. Industrial sector
In the industrial sector, CPS is key to Industry 4.0, enabling smart production processes. CPS manages physical manufacturing processes using real-time monitoring, data analytics, and autonomous decision-making capabilities [56]. These systems manage complicated industrial processes, adapt operations in response to demand changes, and forecast equipment maintenance requirements before breakdowns occur, reducing downtime and increasing production efficiency.

B. Transportation sector
Transportation is another crucial area that benefits from CPS. Intelligent transportation systems (ITS) use CPS to improve traffic management, road safety, and logistical efficiency [57]. Vehicles outfitted with sensors and communication technology communicate with one another and with road infrastructure, allowing for adaptive traffic control, real-time rerouting to reduce congestion, and early warning systems to avert accidents.

C. Healthcare sector
In the healthcare industry, CPS transforms into complex networks that connect wearable gadgets, implanted sensors, and other medical equipment to continuously monitor patients' health [58]. These systems collect vital data that may be utilized for early diagnosis, individualized treatment regimens, and remote patient monitoring, resulting in considerably improved patient outcomes and healthcare delivery.

D. Energy management
Energy management also heavily relies on CPS through smart grid technologies. These systems optimize the production, distribution, and

consumption of energy. By integrating renewable energy sources, predicting energy demand, and automatically adjusting supply, smart grids help to efficiently manage resources, reduce costs, and improve the reliability and sustainability of energy systems [59].

E. Environmental monitoring
CPS improves environmental monitoring by tracking environmental variables and changes with sensors and networked technologies [60]. These systems can monitor air and water quality, identify dangerous circumstances such as forest fires or floods, and give data to help protect the environment and guide policy choices.

F. Urban planning management
CPS is important in creating smart cities through urban planning and administration. These systems control everything from traffic and waste management to water delivery and public safety [61]. Smart city CPS employs data from many sensors and sources to optimize city operations, improve government services, and improve citizens' quality of life.

G. Agricultural application
CPS-based agricultural applications include precision agriculture approaches that employ sensors and automated systems to monitor crop conditions, optimize water consumption, and manage fertilizers and pesticides [62]. This careful control contributes to higher agricultural yields, less waste, and a lower environmental effect of farming techniques.

10.4 Modern Security and Privacy Solution for CPS

Modern security and privacy solutions for cyber-physical systems (CPSs) are intended to solve the particular issues given by the combination of physical processes, digital networking, and computing. The demand for better security and privacy safeguards rises as these systems become more widespread and critical – from infrastructure to personal devices.

10.4.1 Advanced cryptographic techniques privacy preservation

Securing calculations in different applications might raise privacy problems by allowing one or several parties to exchange and execute functions and analyze data inputs [63]. Users share a public key to send encrypted messages, which protects the system's privacy and integrity while allowing access to message content. Cryptographic procedures are often used among academics to provide system security and privacy. Whether symmetric or asymmetric, encryption techniques aim to convert readable data into unreadable text (ciphertext). Symmetric encryption employs a single key for both parties, whereas asymmetric encryption requires a public key for encryption and a private key for decryption. While efficient, the main issue with these techniques is the trustworthiness of the encrypted keys. MITM attacks can compromise keys and render encryption unusable. A public key infrastructure (PKI) approach to secure devices and facilitate message exchange between users on two edges [64]. The registration authority connects public keys to user identities and implements attestation protocols, firewalls, and authentication to restrict the impacts on disclosed devices. Various cryptographic approaches can secure and safeguard vast clouds or control systems data. Secure multiparty computation (SMC), verifiable computation (VC), and homomorphic encryption (HE) are three effective ways to achieve data privacy in scalable and lightweight calculations. These are explained as follows.

SMC-based privacy preservation has become a common encryption mechanism in various forms of encryption but in different data analysis forms like a distributed PPDM; for example, it employs two well-known techniques: MC garbled circuits and secret sharing [65]. Nevertheless, some studies into SMC have limitations because their strategies are vulnerable to multiple attacks and exhibit high communication complexity, which increases exponentially as the number of participants grows. VC-based privacy preservation is a methodology that enables data owners to examine the safety of operations. An intermediate prover is a strong being with the authority to retrieve demands for computation processes, verify these processes, and pass along the outcomes. In contrast with SMC and HE methods, VC can ensure data integrity but not confidentiality during calculations, hence making it necessary whenever there are parties who might not be trusted or enemies could be present.

HE-based privacy preservation: Rivest introduced HE because common encryption techniques can't operate on encrypted data, so the data should be decrypted first, even if cryptography is often employed to keep sensitive information confidential [66]. This implies that users or parties cannot access these services without compromising their privacy. Privacy based on homomorphic encryption (HE) has been widely studied, mainly due to its ability to perform certain arithmetic operations. Several encryption methods support various homomorphic characteristics, such as multiplicatively homomorphic

(RSA), additively homomorphic (Paillier), and the recently proposed fully homomorphic scheme for complex functions. Many HE techniques remain impractical because their computational overheads impede their efficacy; for instance, there is a framework to aggregate data from smart grids while maintaining customer privacy, where an additive HE method is utilized. They leverage attribute-based encryption to enable access control based on the data that is being held.

10.4.2 Blockchain technology privacy preservation

CPS can use blockchain technology for decentralized protection against hacking and privacy violations using a ledger resistant to manipulation or changes [67]. The technology is used to create safe and open transactions that possess the completeness of information without being subject to control by any one party, making it important in supply chains, smart electrical grids, or even in other kinds of Internet of Things (IoT) [68]. Within a blockchain, something like a message input can be associated with another message that is not more than n bytes long. The key aspects that define a blockchain are addressed below.

Decentralization: all participating parties (i.e., nodes/participants) have the authority to control/add, edit, or validate the appended transactions rather than having them centrally coordinated (peer-to-peer). In a decentralized blockchain network, each user is called a miner, participating in the consensus process and confirming each freshly delivered transaction to grow the chain. This feature lowers the likelihood of a single-point failure or data compromise. Validated transactions on the blockchain are immutable, meaning any changes require verification by other nodes. The consensus protocol ensures the integrity and authenticity of blockchain data by requiring each node to create the same output based on its rules (degree of confidence).

The blockchain network relies on anonymity to ensure integrity among users (miners), with just their addresses necessary. To maintain anonymity and privacy, distinct public keys can be used for each miner. This study topic promises to ensure system security and privacy for users and data transactions. Transparency is the habit of regularly evaluating data in the same miner for self-auditing and preventing corruption. Trustworthiness: data transactions (i.e., records) are continually verified and validated, with their integrity achieved using a cryptographic mechanism (hash) created for each one, which is kept in a block over the blockchain, which guarantees that it cannot be altered or updated (persistence).

10.4.3 Artificial intelligence and machine learning techniques

The new techniques that artificial intelligence (AI) and machine learning (ML) advance are changing privacy and security issues in cyber-physical systems (CPSs) [69]. As cyber-physical systems (CPSs) are critical infrastructures such as smart grids or healthcare systems, using AI and ML for security and privacy is no longer just an option but mandatory. These technologies excel at managing the intricacies of large and interlinked systems and can tackle problems that traditional security systems do not address. Anomaly detection is one of the main application situations for AI and ML in CPS security. With the help of ML algorithms trained on huge datasets, it would be possible to understand what normal system behavior looks like for a specific task; once this knowledge is acquired, live operations can be monitored to find any difference from expected outcomes [70]. These abnormalities may stand for security breaches, for example, an intrusion by a stranger or virus attacks. For example, in the case of a smart grid, ML models can identify atypical power patterns that imply potential cybercrimes or even physical interference with such infrastructures.

Artificial intelligence (AI) and machine learning (ML) are making a revolutionary impact on privacy and security in cyber-physical systems (CPSs) by offering a variety of creative application scenarios. Since CPSs increasingly form the backbone of critical infrastructure, including smart grids and healthcare systems, utilizing AI and ML for security and privacy is no longer just an option but a necessity. These technologies can tackle intricate issues in huge interconnected systems that conventional security measures cannot handle. Anomaly detection is one of the main application scenarios for AI and ML in CPS security. Machine learning algorithms can be trained on large datasets to recognize normal system behavior and then watch for deviations during real-time operations. Such deviations may signal potential threats such as unauthorized access or malware infiltration. For example, within a smart grid, machine learning models may detect abnormal patterns of electricity use which could point to a breach in cybersecurity or physical interference with the infrastructure.

Privacy preservation is another area in which AI and ML have made significant strides. Techniques such as federated learning enable the creation of ML models on decentralized data, allowing learning from sensitive data without any need to centralize it. This tactic is quite beneficial to CPS environments like hospitals, where the privacy of patient information comes first but still undeniably benefits from predictive analytics. Moreover, differential privacy that utilizes machine learning allows adding random noise into datasets or queries, thereby safeguarding individual data points within larger datasets. In this manner, CPS can use data for optimization and performance enhancement without infringing on personal privacy. CPS, AI, and ML also improve security through enhanced cryptographic processes like homomorphic encryption, which permits direct manipulation of encrypted information. To optimize these procedures, ML models can make the CPS more applicable in real-time settings such as banking services where protection against fraud and latency time is a vital consideration. In CPS network security, ML algorithms fine-tune and adapt firewall tactics to changing flow dynamics and risk environments. Moreover, intricate security arrangements may be handled by AI across different CPS elements, thus safeguarding uniformity while minimizing the chances for mistakes in a set-up that would result in a lack of protection.

However massive that potential seems, AI and ML face challenges when transforming CPS privacy and security. To use all these technologies effectively, we should tackle issues related to a lack of transparency in ML models and a tendency to exhibit some form of prejudice or biases over time, thereby compromising its security properties. Consequently, as long as we expect development to be never-ending in terms of more extensive involvement with every aspect of our lives today, AI and ML are going to assume certain important roles when it comes to protecting such systems from new types of threats intended at them while making sure they strictly obey words concerning confidentiality standards set by any people's society these days The multiple range of ways that AI and ML could change the CPS for it to be kept secure and private are vast; however, they come with their problems. To fully utilize the strengths of these technologies, lack of transparency in ML models, possible biases, and even safety issues must be considered seriously. With more advancements to make attachments of CPS at various activities of our societies, they will be strangled up by strict privacy practices together with AI and ML, which are vital in safeguarding them against new threats developed every time.

10.4.4 Challenges and research opportunities

In the sphere of cyber-physical systems (CPSs), there have been a lot of challenges and research opportunities about privacy and security issues owing to the increasing complexity and criticality of these systems. Many believe the most important thing is ensuring that systems have strong security and strict confidentiality, as CPS integrates physical processes with digital networking and control systems. CPSs connect to the Internet with Modus TCP/IP, creating concerns about cybersecurity and data privacy [71]. Cybersecurity needs to find new cyber- and zero-day attacks and secure the cyber and physical components of CPSs. These attacks may change lawfully operational actions and violate availability and confidentiality. Integrity attacks on CPS devices and networks can sniff, steal, or tamper with information, including network traffic and telemetry [72]. The security and privacy challenges are still unresolved in CPSs and their networks.

One of the primary challenges facing CPS security is bringing together devices and systems that are not only heterogeneous but whose security capabilities and standards widely differ [73]. This heterogeneity complicates the deployment of uniform security measures across all components, leading to vulnerabilities that malicious persons can easily exploit. In addition, many CPSs have strict real-time operational requirements, such as driving critical infrastructures or autonomous cars, which impose stringent latencies on security solutions, making it difficult to deploy comprehensive computationally intensive security mechanisms. The scalability of security solutions is also a major challenge. The security mechanisms should grow together with CPS networks, which must become more complex and larger without sacrificing speed or usability. It includes secure and efficient data handling in large quantities, particularly in light of the upcoming Internet of Things (IoT) era, when billions of devices will be communicating nonstop.

The scalability of security solutions is another major challenge. As CPS networks become more complicated, security mechanisms need to be enlarged without hampering efficiency or practicality. This includes the ability to securely and efficiently manage increasing resources, particularly due to the emergence of the Internet of Things (IoT) era in which billions of devices constantly produce and transmit information. It's imperative to consider the complicated nature of CPSs, comprised of physical and communication entities, network protocols, and limited computing power/storage contraptions when considering methods for preserving privacy and detecting intrusions. Thus, every suggested approach should demand significant computing abilities to manage complex protocols/devices, identify new types of invasions, and safeguard sensitive information from unlawful disclosure. In addition, they should adapt themselves and ensure reliability to manage the dynamic conditions within a CPS, such as power networks, by utilizing feature projection and dimensionality reduction schemes on the original dataset. Creating a detailed and complete profile for the unique normal events is not simply feasible, especially if one is collecting data from measurements taken from sensors and network packets since there are always some discrepancies in their distinction between normal and deviant behaviors. There are mistakes on false positive and false negative rates when an ideal case lies within an area of hacking, and the opposite holds for a criminal act violated as lawful. Consequently, this chapter seems significant because it would argue against models that diseased privacy could cause errors of this kind to ascend, thereby making it necessary to maintain high detection levels for effective protection of CPS, which is a deep defense strategy.

Research opportunities in privacy and security within the cyber-physical systems field (CPS) are available. The development of advanced encryption techniques, such as homomorphic encryption and secure multi-party computation, is one area that shows some promise; these enable the processing of encrypted data, thus enhancing their security and user privacy levels. However, more work is needed to optimize these technologies to be computationally efficient for real-time cyber-physical systems (CPSs) applications. An additional major theme of inquiry is the utilization of artificial intelligence (AI) and machine learning (ML) in improving CPS security [74]. Security risks can be forecasted and spotted faster with AI and ML, enabling automated security operations. However, these innovations provide fresh weak points together with their implementation; therefore, they need to undergo careful consideration so as not to violate these systems' integrity. Moreover, a new approach must be in place to construct effective anomaly detection mechanisms that precisely identify and react to unprecedented dangers instantly. Such a system must be able to differentiate between harmless deviations from the normality line and authentic attempts at breaking system security laws. The process requires constant learned behavior pattern adjustments capable of going along with emerging malicious techniques.

Privacy by design is a concept that can be studied further, as it requires that CPS developers consider privacy issues during the design stage [75]. This way, they will not only obey the law but also earn the trust of clients and customers through showing dedication to confidentiality. Finally, given that most CPSs operate in different countries with various legal regimes, research on privacy and security standardization is a priority. It entails examining the impact of regulations such as GDPR on CPS functioning and identifying models that cater to multiple legislative demands while still maintaining strong privacy and safety measures. Tackling these challenges and utilizing these research opportunities requires a multi-disciplinary approach combining cybersecurity, data science, law, and ethics skills. Therefore, CPS privacy and security not only have difficult problems but are also changing places for innovations and improvements.

10.4.5 Lesson learned

Security and privacy issues concerning CPS are properly dealt with in this chapter. In addition, it shows how to combat them through different methods.

It is clear from the chapter that there are many issues in maintaining the security and privacy of CPS. Still, research development can also provide better adapted and stronger solutions than the existing ones. The major takeaways from the chapter are:

i. When CPS integrates various physical and digital components, it can be tricky to achieve uniform security across different systems with different security capabilities. This complexity necessitates adaptable and scalable security solutions.

ii. Many CPSs run under strict real-time constraints, meaning their security must not impede system performance. Thus, we need Africa-focused solutions to balance strong protection against little attack latency.

iii. These companies, such as CPS, usually handle large amounts of sensitive data. Ensuring privacy while allowing such data to be used in operations or decision-making processes becomes a major problem for every organization dealing with such information. Privacy-preserving data mining and federated learning are identified as potential solutions.

iv. This chapter comprehensively examines the evolution of threats facing cyber-physical systems (CPSs), including complex cyberattacks that may have physical implications. Because the threat landscape continues to be dynamic, it also emphasizes continuous improvement of technologies and practices related to security.

v. Machine learning algorithms and artificial intelligence have great potential for enhancing CPS security through better anomaly detection, predictive modeling, and automated response systems. However, this technology integration comes with various challenges, such as ensuring the security of machine learning models themselves.

vi. Addressing security and privacy challenges in cyber-physical systems (CPSs) calls for collaboration among academia, industry, and government to develop new standards, best practices, and fit-for-purpose solutions in developing such systems. This is important since no discipline can advance men's lives within such present-day contexts regarding computer science advancements alone.

10.4.6 Key future research direction

The security and privacy of CPS are dynamic and complex areas with multiple challenges and great opportunities for research and innovation. Tackling these issues calls for a collaborative approach from different fields to improve technologies that protect these vital systems without infringing on users' privacy. CPS security will probably be characterized by fast-paced technological advancements, meaning that flexible and foresighted research strategies are essential. The following are the key areas of research direction to shape the landscape of CPS security and privacy.

i. Investigating cryptographic advancements like homomorphic encryption or algorithms that can resist quantum revolution. This type of technology can potentially protect information traveling and stored safely without being affected by new developments in computer science (like quantum computing).

ii. Predicting and avoiding violations before they occur through improved machine learning algorithms' efficiency also forms a big research area. These systems should focus on decreasing the number of false alarms while increasing immediate reaction capacity.

iii. While AI plays an important role in managing and securing CPS, its integration with privacy-preservation technologies, such as differential privacy and federated learning, will become indispensable. The purpose of this is to guarantee that AI enhances security without compromising on privacy.

iv. Another crucial research area is creating CPS security mechanisms resistant to sophisticated, state-sponsorship attacks. These include technological solutions and regulatory and policy measures that further strengthen these vital systems' security positions.

v. Furthermore, near-future studies must emphasize building interdisciplinary partnerships consisting of specialists from the cybersecurity domain, engineering experts, ethicists, and legal practitioners. All these experts working together would help tackle the multifaceted problems facing CPS and bring forth effective methods that are also lawful or moral.

10.5 Conclusion

The emerging security and privacy challenges threatening these systems are explored in detail in this chapter. These complexities are inherent within these integral systems and are vulnerable to unique and advanced threats. This is because they are the ones that form an interface between cyber technologies and physical processes and, therefore, face new kinds of attacks. The progressive importance of developing robust security and privacy measures cannot be overstated, as they underlie critical infrastructure and profoundly influence daily living. It can be concluded from the chapter that future CPS security will depend on the development of highly advanced collective adaptive security frameworks that can keep pace with fast-changing technology and threats. With the increasing complexity and connectivity of CPS environments, there is a need for flexible security to meet changing conditions while including all possible cyberattack scenarios. Considering that so much data is generated from these systems, attention must be paid to privacy issues, requiring solutions that ensure personal privacy but do not compromise their overall functionalities or efficacy levels.

References

[1] MacCarthy, B. L., & Ivanov, D. (2022). The Digital Supply Chain—emergence, concepts, definitions, and technologies. In The digital supply chain (pp. 3–24). Elsevier.

[2] Vermesan, O., Bröring, A., Tragos, E., Serrano, M., Bacciu, D., Chessa, S., ... & Bahr, R. (2022). Internet of robotic things–converging sensing/actuating, hyperconnectivity, artificial intelligence, and IoT platforms. In Cognitive hyperconnected digital transformation (pp. 97–155). River Publishers.

[3] Giraldo, J., Sarkar, E., Cardenas, A. A., Maniatakos, M., & Kantarcioglu, M. (2017). Security and privacy in cyber-physical systems: A survey of surveys. IEEE Design & Test, 34(4), 7–17.

[4] Lun, Y. Z., D'Innocenzo, A., Malavolta, I., & Di Benedetto, M. D. (2016). Cyber-physical systems security: a systematic mapping study. arXiv preprint arXiv:1605.09641.

[5] He, H., & Yan, J. (2016). Cyber-physical attacks and defenses in the smart grid: a survey. IET Cyber-Physical Systems: Theory & Applications, 1(1), 13–27.

[6] Meshram, C., Imoize, A. L., Jamal, S. S., Alharbi, A. R., Meshram, S. G., & Hussain, I. (2022). CGST: Provably Secure Lightweight Certificateless Group Signcryption Technique Based on Fractional Chaotic Maps. IEEE Access, 10, 39853–39863.

[7] Giechaskiel, I., & Rasmussen, K. (2019). Taxonomy and challenges of out-of-band signal injection attacks and defenses. IEEE Communications Surveys & Tutorials, 22(1), 645–670.

[8] Giechaskiel, I., Zhang, Y., & Rasmussen, K. B. (2019). A framework for evaluating security in the presence of signal injection attacks. In

Computer Security–ESORICS 2019: 24th European Symposium on Research in Computer Security, Luxembourg, September 23–27, 2019, Proceedings, Part I 24 (pp. 512–532). Springer International Publishing.

[9] Yan, C., Shin, H., Bolton, C., Xu, W., Kim, Y., & Fu, K. (2020, May). Sok: A minimalist approach to formalizing analog sensor security. In 2020 IEEE Symposium on Security and Privacy (SP) (pp. 233–248). IEEE.

[10] Rass, S., Schauer, S., König, S., & Zhu, Q. (2020). Cyber-security in critical infrastructures (Vol. 297). Springer International Publishing.

[11] Cortés, J., Dullerud, G. E., Han, S., Le Ny, J., Mitra, S., & Pappas, G. J. (2016, December). Differential privacy in control and network systems. In 2016 IEEE 55th Conference on Decision and Control (CDC) (pp. 4252–4272). IEEE.

[12] Awotunde, J. B., Adeniyi, A. E., Babatunde, A. O., Olagunju, M., Imoize, A. L., & Olanloye, O. D. (2024). 12 An Cryptographic Enhanced Lightweight Algorithm Towards Securing Wireless Networks and Big Data. Computational Modeling and Simulation of Advanced Wireless Communication Systems, 297.

[13] Abdulraheem, M., Adeniyi, E. A., Awotunde, J. B., Imoize, A. L., Jimoh, R. G., Oladipo, I. D., & Falola, P. B. (2024). Artificial Intelligence of Medical Things for Medical Information Systems Privacy and Security. In Handbook of Security and Privacy of AI-Enabled Healthcare Systems and Internet of Medical Things (pp. 63–96). CRC Press.

[14] Paridari,K.,O'Mahony,N.,Mady,A.E.D.,Chabukswar,R.,Boubekeur,M., & Sandberg, H. (2017). A framework for attack-resilient industrial control systems: Attack detection and controller reconfiguration. Proceedings of the IEEE, 106(1), 113–128.

[15] Feng, C., Palleti, V. R., Mathur, A., & Chana, D. (2019, February). A Systematic Framework to Generate Invariants for Anomaly Detection in Industrial Control Systems. In NDSS (pp. 1–15).

[16] Moustafa, N., Creech, G., & Slay, J. (2017). Big data analytics for intrusion detection system: Statistical decision-making using finite Dirichlet mixture models. Data Analytics and Decision Support for Cybersecurity: Trends, Methodologies and Applications, 127–156.

[17] Rajesh, N., Sujatha, K., & Lawrence, A. A. (2016). Survey on privacy preserving data mining techniques using recent algorithms. International Journal of Computer Applications, 133(7), 30–33.

[18] Aggarwal, C. C., & Yu, P. S. (2008). A general survey of privacy-preserving data mining models and algorithms (pp. 11–52). Springer US.

[19] Abiodun, M. K., Imoize, A. L., Awotunde, J. B., Lee, C. C., Adeniyi, A. E., Chioma, U., & Li, C. T. (2023). Analysis of a Double-stage Encryption Scheme Using Hybrid Cryptography to Enhance Data Security in Cloud Computing Systems. Journal of Library & Information Studies, 21(2).

[20] Adeniyi, A. E., Jimoh, R. G., & Awotunde, J. B. (2024). A systematic review on elliptic curve cryptography algorithm for the internet of things: Categorization, application areas, and security. Computers and Electrical Engineering, 118, 109330.

[21] Ferrag, M. A., Maglaras, L. A., Janicke, H., & Jiang, J. (2016). A survey on privacy-preserving schemes for smart grid communications. arXiv preprint arXiv:1611.07722.

[22] Awotunde, J. B., Adeniyi, A. E., Babatunde, A. O., Olagunju, M., Imoize, A. L., & Olanloye, O. D. (2024). 12 An Cryptographic Enhanced Lightweight Algorithm Towards Securing Wireless Networks and Big Data. Computational Modeling and Simulation of Advanced Wireless Communication Systems, 297.

[23] Awotunde, J. B., Farhaoui, Y., Imoize, A. L., Folorunso, S. O., & Adeniyi, A. E. (2023, November). An Enhanced Internet of Medical Things Data Communication Based on Blockchain and Cryptography for Smart Healthcare Applications. In The International Conference on Artificial Intelligence and Smart Environment (pp. 305–313). Cham: Springer Nature Switzerland.

[24] Zhu, T., Xiong, P., Li, G., Zhou, W., & Philip, S. Y. (2020). Differentially private model publishing in cyber-physical systems. Future generation computer systems, 108, 1297–1306.

[25] Zhu, T., Li, G., Zhou, W., & Philip, S. Y. (2017). Differential privacy and applications. Cham, Switzerland: Springer International Publishing.

[26] Habibzadeh, H., Nussbaum, B. H., Anjomshoa, F., Kantarci, B., & Soyata, T. (2019). A survey on cybersecurity, data privacy, and policy issues in cyber-physical system deployments in smart cities. Sustainable Cities and Society, 50, 101660.

[27] Imoize, A. L., Balas, V. E., Solanki, V. K., Lee, C. C., & Obaidat, M. S. (Eds.). (2023). Handbook of Security and Privacy of AI-Enabled Healthcare Systems and Internet of Medical Things. CRC Press.

[28] Adeniyi, A. E., Abiodun, K. M., Awotunde, J. B., Olagunju, M., Ojo, O. S., & Edet, N. P. (2023). Implementation of a block cipher algorithm for medical information security on cloud environment: using modified advanced encryption standard approach. Multimedia Tools and Applications, 82(13), 20537–20551.

[29] AbdulRaheem, M., Awotunde, J. B., Chakraborty, C., Adeniyi, E. A., Oladipo, I. D., & Bhoi, A. K. (2023). Security and privacy concerns in the smart healthcare system. In Implementation of Smart Healthcare Systems using AI, IoT, and Blockchain (pp. 243–273). Academic Press.
[30] Hassan, M. U., Rehmani, M. H., & Chen, J. (2019). Differential privacy techniques for cyber-physical systems: A survey. IEEE Communications Surveys & Tutorials, 22(1), 746–789.
[31] Boulemtafes, A., Derhab, A., & Challal, Y. (2020). A review of privacy-preserving techniques for deep learning. Neurocomputing, 384, 21–45.
[32] Li, C. T., Weng, C. Y., Chen, C. L., Lee, C. C., Deng, Y. Y., & Imoize, A. L. (2022). An efficient authenticated key agreement scheme supporting privacy-preservation for internet of drones communications. Sensors, 22(23), 9534.
[33] Raisaro, J. L., Choi, G., Pradervand, S., Colsenet, R., Jacquemont, N., Rosat, N., ... & Hubaux, J. P. (2018). Protecting privacy and security of genomic data in i2b2 with homomorphic encryption and differential privacy. IEEE/ACM transactions on computational biology and bioinformatics, 15(5), 1413–1426.
[34] Abi Sen, A. A., Eassa, F. A., Jambi, K., & Yamin, M. (2018). Preserving privacy in the internet of things: a survey. International Journal of Information Technology, 10, 189–200.
[35] Ramadan, R., Huang, Q., Zalhaf, A. S., Bamisile, O., Li, J., Mansour, D. E. A., ... & Yehia, D. M. (2024). Energy Management in Residential Microgrid Based on Non-Intrusive Load Monitoring and Internet of Things. Smart Cities, 7(4), 1907–1935.
[36] Hassan, M. U., Rehmani, M. H., & Chen, J. (2019). Differential privacy techniques for cyber-physical systems: A survey. IEEE Communications Surveys & Tutorials, 22(1), 746–789.
[37] Sain, M., Normurodov, O., Hong, C., & Hui, K. L. (2021, February). A survey on the security in cyber-physical systems with multi-factor authentication. In 2021 23rd International Conference on Advanced Communication Technology (ICACT) (pp. 1–8). IEEE.
[38] Sudarsan, S. V., Schelén, O., & Bodin, U. (2021). Survey on delegated and self-contained authorization techniques in CPS and IoT. IEEE Access, 9, 98169–98184.
[39] Adeniyi, J. K., Ajagbe, S. A., Adeniyi, E. A., Mudali, P., Adigun, M. O., Adeniyi, T. T., & Ajibola, O. (2024). A biometrics-generated private/public key cryptography for a blockchain-based e-voting system. Egyptian Informatics Journal, 25, 100447.

[40] Mishra, A., Jha, A. V., Appasani, B., Ray, A. K., Gupta, D. K., & Ghazali, A. N. (2023). Emerging technologies and design aspects of a next-generation cyber-physical system with a smart city application perspective. International Journal of System Assurance Engineering and Management, 14(Suppl 3), 699–721.

[41] Dafflon, B., Moalla, N., & Ouzrout, Y. (2021). The challenges, approaches, and used techniques of CPS for manufacturing in Industry 4.0: a literature review. The International Journal of Advanced Manufacturing Technology, 113, 2395–2412.

[42] Habibzadeh, H., Nussbaum, B. H., Anjomshoa, F., Kantarci, B., & Soyata, T. (2019). A survey on cybersecurity, data privacy, and policy issues in cyber-physical system deployments in smart cities. Sustainable Cities and Society, 50, 101660.

[43] Mohammed, A. S., Reinecke, P., Burnap, P., Rana, O., & Anthi, E. (2022). Cybersecurity challenges in the offshore oil and gas industry: an industrial cyber-physical systems (ICPS) perspective. ACM Transactions on Cyber-Physical Systems (TCPS), 6(3), 1–27.

[44] Jeffrey, N., Tan, Q., & Villar, J. R. (2023). A review of anomaly detection strategies to detect threats to cyber-physical systems. Electronics, 12(15), 3283.

[45] Yaacoub, J. P. A., Salman, O., Noura, H. N., Kaaniche, N., Chehab, A., & Malli, M. (2020). Cyber-physical systems security: Limitations, issues, and future trends. Microprocessors and Microsystems, 77, 103201.

[46] Agrawal, S., Sarkar, S., Aouedi, O., Yenduri, G., Piamrat, K., Alazab, M., ... & Gadekallu, T. R. (2022). Federated learning for intrusion detection system: Concepts, challenges, and future directions. Computer Communications, 195, 346–361.

[47] So, J., Guler, B., & Avestimehr, S. (2020). A scalable approach for privacy-preserving collaborative machine learning. Advances in Neural Information Processing Systems, 33, 8054–8066.

[48] Cao, L. (2022). AI science and engineering: a new field. IEEE Intelligent Systems, 37(1), 3–13.

[49] Rani, S., Kataria, A., Chauhan, M., Rattan, P., Kumar, R., & Sivaraman, A. K. (2022). Security and privacy challenges in the deployment of cyber-physical systems in smart city applications: State-of-art work. Materials Today: Proceedings, 62, 4671–4676.

[50] Su, G., Wang, J., Xu, X., Wang, Y., & Wang, C. (2024). The Utilization of Homomorphic Encryption Technology Grounded on Artificial Intelligence for Privacy Preservation. International Journal of Computer Science and Information Technology, 2(1), 52–58.

[51] Greer, C., Burns, M., Wollman, D., & Griffor, E. (2019). Cyber-physical systems and Internet of things.

[52] Balla, A., Habaebi, M. H., Islam, M. R., & Mubarak, S. (2022). Applications of deep learning algorithms for Supervisory Control and Data Acquisition intrusion detection system. Cleaner Engineering and Technology, 9, 100532.

[53] Pivoto, D. G., De Almeida, L. F., da Rosa Righi, R., Rodrigues, J. J., Lugli, A. B., & Alberti, A. M. (2021). Cyber-physical systems architectures for industrial Internet of things applications in Industry 4.0: A literature review. Journal of manufacturing systems, 58, 176–192.

[54] Alkofahi, H., Alawneh, H., & Skjellum, A. (2024). MitM attacks on intellectual property and integrity of additive manufacturing systems: A security analysis. Computers & Security, 140, 103810.

[55] Wang, L., & Haghighi, A. (2016). The combined strength of holons, agents, and function blocks in cyber-physical systems. Journal of Manufacturing Systems, 40, 25–34.

[56] Antons, O., & Arlinghaus, J. C. (2022). Data-driven and autonomous manufacturing control in cyber-physical production systems. Computers in Industry, 141, 103711.

[57] Liu, Y., Tao, X., Li, X., Colombo, A. W., & Hu, S. (2023). Artificial intelligence in smart logistics cyber-physical systems: State-of-the-art and potential applications. IEEE Transactions on industrial cyber-physical systems, 1, 1–20.

[58] Shaikh, T. A., Rasool, T., & Verma, P. (2023). Machine intelligence and medical cyber-physical system architectures for smart healthcare: Taxonomy, challenges, opportunities, and possible solutions. Artificial Intelligence in Medicine, 102692.

[59] Alotaibi, I., Abido, M. A., Khalid, M., & Savkin, A. V. (2020). A comprehensive review of recent advances in smart grids: A sustainable future with renewable energy resources. Energies, 13(23), 6269.

[60] Adedeji, K. B., & Hamam, Y. (2020). Cyber-physical systems for water supply network management: Basics, challenges, and roadmap. Sustainability, 12(22), 9555.

[61] Juma, M., & Shaalan, K. (2020). Cyber-physical systems in the smart city: Challenges and future trends for strategic research. In Swarm Intelligence for Resource Management in the Internet of Things (pp. 65–85). Academic Press.

[62] Peladarinos, N., Piromalis, D., Cheimaras, V., Tserepas, E., Munteanu, R.A., & Papageorgas, P. (2023). Enhancing smart agriculture by implementing digital twins: A comprehensive review. Sensors, 23(16), 7128.

[63] Feng, Q., He, D., Zeadally, S., Khan, M. K., & Kumar, N. (2019). A survey on privacy protection in the blockchain system. Journal of network and computer applications, 126, 45–58.

[64] Marino, F., Moiso, C., & Petracca, M. (2019). PKIoT: A public key infrastructure for the Internet of Things. Transactions on Emerging Telecommunications Technologies, 30(10), e3681.

[65] Gunawan, D. (2020). Classification of privacy preserving data mining algorithms: a review. Jurnal Elektronika dan Telekomunikasi, 20(2), 36–46.

[66] Matta, P., Arora, M., & Sharma, D. (2021). A comparative survey on data encryption Techniques: Big data perspective. Materials today: proceedings, 46, 11035–11039.

[67] Maleh, Y., Lakkineni, S., Tawalbeh, L. A., & AbdEl-Latif, A. A. (2022). Blockchain for cyber-physical systems: Challenges and applications. Advances in blockchain technology for cyber-physical systems, 11–59.

[68] Azizi, N., Malekzadeh, H., Akhavan, P., Haass, O., Saremi, S., & Mirjalili, S. (2021). IoT–blockchain: Harnessing the power of the Internet of Things and blockchain for the smart supply chain. Sensors, 21(18), 6048.

[69] Salau, B. A., Rawal, A., & Rawat, D. B. (2022). Recent advances in artificial intelligence for wireless internet of things and cyber-physical systems: A comprehensive survey. IEEE Internet of Things Journal, 9(15), 12916–12930.

[70] Jamal, A. A., Majid, A. A. M., Konev, A., Kosachenko, T., & Shelupanov, A. (2023). A review on security analysis of cyber-physical systems using Machine learning. Materials today: proceedings, 80, 2302–2306.

[71] Luo, L., Morales-Gonzalez, C., Wang, S., Ling, Z., & Fu, X. (2024, February). Unified View of IoT and CPS Security and Privacy. In 2024 International Conference on Computing, Networking, and Communications (ICNC) (pp. 495–499). IEEE.

[72] Omolara, A. E., Alawida, M., & Abiodun, O. I. (2023). Drone cybersecurity issues, solutions, trend insights, and future perspectives: a survey. Neural computing and applications, 35(31), 23063–23101.

[73] Wang, Z., Xie, W., Wang, B., Tao, J., & Wang, E. (2021). A survey on recent advanced research of CPS security. Applied Sciences, 11(9), 3751.

[74] Abdulhussein, M. (2024). The Impact of Artificial Intelligence and Machine Learning on Organizations Cybersecurity. Liberty University.

[75] Horváth, I. (2022). Designing next-generation cyber-physical systems: Why is it an issue? Journal of Integrated Design and Process Science, 26(3–4), 317–349.

11

Security and Privacy Concerns and Risks in Modern Cyber-physical Systems

Joseph Bamidele Awotunde[1], Agbotiname Lucky Imoize[2], Abidemi Emmanuel Adeniyi[3], Peace Busola Falola[4], Kannan Srinivasan[5], Guman Singh Chauhan[6] and Rahul Jadon[7]

[1]Department of Computer Science, University of Ilorin, Nigeria
[2]Department of Electrical and Electronics Engineering, Faculty of Engineering,
University of Lagos, Nigeria
[3]Department of Computer Science, Bowen University, Nigeria
[4]Computer Science Unit, Distance Learning Center, University of Ibadan, Nigeria
[5]Saiana Technologies Inc., USA
[6]John Tesla Inc., USA
[7]CarGurus Inc., USA

Email: awotunde.jb@unilorin.edu.ng; aimoize@unilag.edu.ng; abidemi.adeniyi@bowen.edu.ng; pb.falola@ui.edu.ng; kannansrinivasan@ieee.org; gumansinghchauhan@ieee.org; rahuljadon@ieee.org

Abstract

As cyber-physical systems (CPSs) become increasingly prevalent in various sectors, including healthcare, agriculture, industries and manufacturing, transportation, and smart cities, the vulnerabilities inherent in their interconnected nature pose significant risks to individual privacy and overall system integrity. Therefore, this chapter explores the critical security and privacy concerns associated with modern CPS, which integrates computational elements with physical processes. The study examines the diverse threats these systems face, including unauthorized access, data breaches, and operational

DOI: 10.1201/9788743801306-11

disruptions, while also considering the implications of these risks on user trust and societal acceptance. The chapter identifies gaps in current practices through a comprehensive analysis of existing security frameworks and privacy regulations. It proposes recommendations to enhance CPS's resilience against emerging threats. Ultimately, this research underscores the necessity for a multidisciplinary approach to security and privacy that incorporates technological, regulatory, and human factors to safeguard the future of cyber-physical systems.

11.1 Introduction

Cyber-physical systems (CPSs) integrate computation, networking, and physical processes, creating environments where software systems monitor and control physical entities in real time [1]. CPS represents a crucial evolution in embedded systems, combining cyber capabilities with physical operations to interact with the real world through feedback loops [2]. These systems, which integrate hardware and software for monitoring, automation, and control, are used across various domains, including critical infrastructures, healthcare, transportation, smart grids, energy, and industrial automation [3]. Hence, it allows for the monitoring, controlling, and optimizing of complex systems in areas. Cyber-physical systems form the foundation for many advanced applications in automation and smart environments by tightly integrating these components [4]. Their development addresses interoperability, scalability, and security challenges, which are critical for reliable and efficient operation [5].

While CPS enhances convenience, efficiency, and functionality, it also introduces complex security and privacy risks. In today's interconnected world, these risks have become increasingly significant due to the sensitive nature of CPS data, potential access vulnerabilities, and the high stakes associated with breaches [6]. Modern CPS is central to industries such as healthcare, where they assist in monitoring patients; in transportation, where they optimize logistics; and in smart grids, where they manage energy distribution [7]. These systems rely on sensor networks, embedded systems, and software applications to collect and process data, perform operations, and control physical devices. The interdependent nature of CPS components and real-time data exchange between the cyber and physical realms introduce specific vulnerabilities [8].

Since CPS often controls critical functions, unauthorized access can have significant consequences, such as manipulating traffic signals, overriding medical device settings, or disabling power grid components. Remote and physical access points in CPS may allow malicious actors to breach the system, allowing them to control or alter functionalities. Attackers might exploit this to disrupt services or manipulate the data that CPS generates or acts upon. Data generated and exchanged in CPS are often used for real-time decision-making; hence, its integrity and authenticity are critical. If attackers manipulate this data, altering sensor readings or injecting false data, it can lead to incorrect decisions, jeopardizing safety and efficiency. An example of this risk is in autonomous vehicles, where falsified sensor data could lead to dangerous situations, like incorrect object detection, potentially causing accidents.

Physical aspects of CPS, like sensors or controllers, are vulnerable to direct attacks due to their exposure to the real world [9]. For example, sensors embedded in critical infrastructure could be tampered with, leading to incorrect readings or malfunctioning. Attackers with physical access to these devices can extract sensitive data, inject malware, or render the devices inoperative. This represents a significant risk since physical security is traditionally weaker in CPS than digital security. CPS is vulnerable to specialized attacks, such as side-channel attacks that exploit power consumption, electromagnetic leaks, or even acoustic signals to gain information about the system [10]. Furthermore, CPSs are highly susceptible to denial-of-service (DoS) attacks, where attackers overwhelm the system, leading to performance degradation or even complete shutdown [11]. For example, DoS attacks on a smart grid could disrupt energy distribution, causing widespread power outages.

The widespread deployment of CPS in domains like healthcare and smart homes means they gather significant amounts of personal data [12]. For instance, a healthcare CPS may collect data about a patient's vital signs, location, or health history, while a smart home CPS might collect data on residents' routines and preferences. Unauthorized access to or misuse of this data could lead to severe privacy violations. In addition to real-time data, CPS often collects metadata, such as timestamps and usage patterns, which can be exploited to profile individuals or monitor behaviors without consent [13]. This information can be sensitive, revealing personal habits, health conditions, or work routines, raising significant ethical and privacy concerns [14]. For instance, a smart grid system might inadvertently reveal a household's energy consumption patterns, indicating whether occupants are home or away.

Threat modeling is essential in understanding and mitigating security and privacy risks in CPS. It involves identifying potential threat actors, assessing their motivations and capabilities, and mapping out possible attack vectors. This process is complicated in CPS by its hybrid nature, requiring a model that includes both cyber and physical elements [15]. For example, an effective threat model for a transportation CPS might consider risks posed by remote attackers, such as data manipulation, and physical risks, such as tampering with GPS equipment. Applying risk management frameworks like NIST's Cybersecurity Framework to CPS can be complex but essential [16]. These frameworks help organizations identify, protect, detect, respond to, and recover from cyber threats. Implementing such a framework in CPS requires adapting it to handle physical threats, operational constraints, and data privacy concerns [17]. For instance, a risk management framework for a smart grid CPS should consider IT-related risks and the physical security of substations and distributed components.

Data encryption, both in transit and at rest, is fundamental to protecting sensitive information within CPS. However, due to CPS's real-time operational requirements, encryption methods must balance security with computational efficiency [18]. Lightweight cryptographic solutions are being developed to secure CPS without compromising performance [19]. Anonymization techniques are also critical in cases where CPS must share or process personal data. By removing identifiable information, these techniques can help to protect privacy, though they require careful implementation to avoid compromising data utility [20]. Artificial intelligence (AI) and machine learning (ML) are increasingly used to detect unusual patterns that may indicate security threats in CPS [21]. By analyzing sensor data and system logs, AI-based solutions can flag potential issues, such as abnormal network traffic, unusual device activity, or environmental irregularities [22]. In industrial CPS, for example, AI-driven solutions can monitor equipment performance data to identify early indicators of tampering or malfunction. Blockchain technology offers potential solutions for CPS security by providing a decentralized, immutable ledger for recording transactions or data exchanges. In a smart grid, CPS, for example, blockchain can track energy distribution and consumption data tamper-proof, ensuring data integrity and transparency [23]. However, scalability and energy consumption issues must be addressed for effective blockchain integration in CPS.

Cyber-physical systems are revolutionizing industries by blending physical and digital interactions, but they also introduce significant security and privacy challenges. CPS faces diverse threats, from unauthorized access and data integrity risks to physical security vulnerabilities and privacy concerns. Effective management of these risks requires a comprehensive approach, including threat modeling, risk management frameworks, encryption, AI, and blockchain technology. With these solutions, CPS can enhance its resilience against potential threats, enabling safer and more secure social integration.

As CPS grows in scope and functionality, so must our approach to securing them evolve, ensuring these systems are reliable, resilient, and trustworthy in an increasingly interconnected world.

11.1.1 Key contributions of the chapter

The following are the significant contributions of this chapter:

i. The chapter examines the major security threats in CPS, where integrating physical and digital components leads to potential security breaches.

ii. The chapter discusses threats specific to CPS in general; these threats are often more complex due to CPS's real-time data requirements and critical nature.

iii. Since CPS often handles sensitive data, the chapter explored the privacy concerns of CPS

iv. The chapter concludes by discussing future trends and challenges, including the increasing complexity of CPS and the rise of IoT integration.

11.1.2 Chapter organization

Section 11.2 presents the major security threats in CPS, which are divided into three categories according to their types of threats within the CPS. Section 11.3 discusses the privacy concerns and risks in modern cyber-physical systems. Section 11.4 presents risk assessment and threat modeling in cyber-physical systems. Section 11.5 discusses the future directions and emerging trends in cyber-physical systems, and finally, Section 11.6 concludes the chapter with future direction.

11.2 The Main Security Threats in Cyber-physical Systems

Cyber-physical systems integrate physical processes with networked digital components, making them vulnerable to various security threats. Compared to most networking systems, CPS systems were not designed with security services in mind, which allowed attackers to take advantage of several vulnerabilities and loopholes to initiate security attacks. This is also because CPS devices are heterogeneous, using multiple technologies and protocols to interact and function across various Internet of Things (IoT) domains. The security threats in CPS can be divided into three, namely: (i) cyber, (ii) physical, and (iii) hybrid security threats; and these can combine to create cyber-physical potential dangers. These threats are especially concerning in critical infrastructure, where compromised CPS can lead to safety hazards.

11.2.1 Cyber security threats in cyber-physical systems

Cyber-physical systems integrate computing, networking, and physical processes to create systems central to modern infrastructure, including power grids, healthcare, transportation, and manufacturing [4], [24]. As these systems are increasingly interconnected, they become more susceptible to cybersecurity threats, leading to significant disruption, economic loss, and safety concerns [25], [26]. Cybersecurity threats in CPS are unique due to the interaction between physical and digital components, where a cyberattack can directly affect physical operations. According to Alguliyev et al. [27], there were numerous reasons why cyber risks received more attention than physical ones when it came to industrial IoT security. This pertains to the transition of the electrical grid to advanced metering infrastructure (AMI), which led to the emergence of previously unidentified threats from hackers in addition to SCADA issues [28], [29]. Unlike physical attacks, which necessitate actual presence and tangible instruments, electronic attacks can now be launched from any device.

11.2.1.1 Malware attacks

Malware can infect CPS to disrupt or compromise control systems. Common forms include viruses, worms, and ransomware, leading to unauthorized access, data loss, or manipulation of physical processes. For example, a ransomware attack on a hospital's medical devices could disrupt critical healthcare services. Malware attacks, including ransomware, can disrupt CPS operations by taking control of crucial components. In a CPS environment, ransomware can halt physical systems, making industries like manufacturing and healthcare vulnerable to extortion [30]. Malware poses a significant cybersecurity threat to CPS, which integrates computing, networking, and physical processes (like smart grids or industrial systems). Malware in CPS can disrupt operations, steal data, or damage physical assets, causing safety, privacy, and economic impacts. Due to the critical nature of CPS, malware attacks such as ransomware, trojans, or worms can lead to severe consequences like shutting down critical infrastructure or manipulating sensor data. Protecting CPS from malware involves robust security measures like network segmentation, anomaly detection, and system hardening, ensuring these systems remain resilient to evolving cybersecurity threats and operational disruptions [31].

11.2.1.2 Denial of service (DoS) attacks

DoS attacks aim to overload CPS networks, rendering systems unavailable. This attack is particularly dangerous in CPS as it can prevent operators from monitoring and controlling physical processes. A DoS attack could disrupt traffic flow by blocking real-time data from traffic lights or signaling systems in a transportation system. DoS attacks can overload the system's computational resources, rendering CPS components temporarily inoperable. For example, DoS attacks can result in significant service disruptions or even accidents in smart grids or traffic management systems. Denial of service (DoS) attacks are significant cybersecurity threats to CPS, which integrate computational and physical elements, such as in smart grids or industrial automation [32]. In a DoS attack, an attacker overwhelms the system with excessive requests or exploits vulnerabilities, making it temporarily or permanently unavailable to legitimate users. This disruption can have severe consequences, halting critical infrastructure, damaging physical assets, or risking human safety. CPS relies on real-time communication and control; therefore, any delay or unavailability induced by DoS attacks undermines reliability, impeding the system's intended functionality and security integrity [33], [34]. Effective defense mechanisms are essential to safeguard CPS.

11.2.1.3 Man-in-the-middle (MitM) attacks

In a MitM attack, the attacker intercepts communication between components of the CPS, enabling them to eavesdrop, alter, or inject malicious data. This can be particularly harmful in systems with sensitive information, such as healthcare or military operations, where unauthorized changes can have severe consequences. In CPS, MitM attacks pose a severe cybersecurity threat. During a MitM attack, a malicious actor intercepts communication between two entities, often manipulating or stealing data. In CPS, this could involve intercepting sensor data or commands in real-time, causing equipment to malfunction or creating safety risks [9]. By pretending to be a legitimate participant, the attacker can alter data to disrupt operations, spy on sensitive information, or inject false commands. Given the critical nature of CPS in sectors like healthcare, energy, and transportation, MitM attacks can lead to significant damage, financial loss, and compromised safety.

11.2.1.4 Insider threats

CPS often relies on a complex web of employees and third-party vendors, creating vulnerabilities from within. Insiders accessing CPS can misuse their privileges to sabotage operations, steal data, or introduce vulnerabilities. Unauthorized access can lead to data theft, manipulation, or damage. Insider threats, where authorized individuals exploit their access, are particularly dangerous in CPS due to the direct interaction with critical physical processes. Insider threats in CPS pose significant cybersecurity risks as trusted individuals such as employees, contractors, or partners have access to sensitive systems and data. These insiders may exploit this privileged access, either maliciously or unintentionally, compromising system integrity, availability, or confidentiality. In CPS, insider threats can disrupt essential services by tampering with operational technology, leaking critical information, or launching cyberattacks that impact physical and digital infrastructures [35]. Since CPS underpins critical sectors like energy, healthcare, and transportation, insider threats can have devastating effects, making it essential for organizations to implement strict access controls, continuous monitoring, and comprehensive insider risk management strategies [36].

11.2.1.5 Data integrity and manipulation attacks

Cyber-physical systems rely on accurate data from sensors to make decisions. Attackers can manipulate sensor data, leading to incorrect decisions. For example, in an industrial setting, manipulated data could cause machines to operate unsafely, risking equipment and human lives. Data integrity and manipulation attacks in CPS involve malicious actions that alter or corrupt the data exchanged between physical devices and their digital counterparts [37]. These attacks compromise data reliability, leading to incorrect decision-making or system malfunctions. For instance, attackers might inject false sensor readings or manipulate control signals, causing physical systems (e.g., industrial machines and medical devices) to behave erratically [38]. Such attacks undermine the safety and functionality of CPS, potentially resulting in catastrophic consequences. Protecting data integrity through encryption, secure communication protocols, and real-time monitoring is essential to mitigate these risks [39].

Data integrity is critical in CPS, as these systems rely on accurate sensor data for decision-making. Attackers can intercept and alter sensor data, leading to incorrect responses in physical processes [40]. For instance, manipulating temperature sensor data in a smart grid could cause power outages or damage equipment. Data manipulation and spoofing are significant cybersecurity threats in CPS, which integrate physical processes with computing and networking. Data manipulation involves altering legitimate data and disrupting the accuracy of real-time data streams crucial for CPS operations, like those in power grids or autonomous vehicles. Spoofing, on the other hand, entails sending false data to deceive the system, potentially misleading it to perform unsafe actions. These attacks can lead to malfunctions, physical damages, or unauthorized control over critical infrastructures, emphasizing the need for robust security measures to authenticate data sources and ensure data integrity in CPS environments [41].

11.2.1.6 Spoofing attacks

Attackers can trick the system by feeding it false information, often through sensor spoofing. In CPS, this can lead to actuators' incorrect actions, potentially causing physical harm or operational disruptions. Spoofing attacks in CPS occur when an attacker impersonates a legitimate device or user to gain unauthorized access or control. The attacker can deceive the system into accepting malicious inputs by falsifying signals, such as sensor data or control commands. This can lead to incorrect actions, like misdirected processes or manipulated physical systems. For example, spoofing could cause a power plant to malfunction in a smart grid by sending fake data to control systems. These attacks undermine the trust and security of CPS, highlighting the need for robust authentication and verification mechanisms to prevent unauthorized access.

11.2.1.7 Supply chain vulnerabilities

Components of CPS often come from multiple vendors, creating vulnerabilities if any component is compromised. A compromised part in a supply chain could introduce backdoors, which attackers can exploit to infiltrate the system. Supply chain vulnerabilities in CPS are a significant cybersecurity concern. As CPS integrates physical processes with digital systems, attacks targeting the supply chain can compromise both. These vulnerabilities arise from third-party suppliers, hardware/software components, and network connections, where malicious actors exploit weak links to gain unauthorized access or introduce malicious code. Attacks on CPS can disrupt production, damage infrastructure, and jeopardize sensitive data. Furthermore, the interconnected nature of CPS increases the complexity of securing every point in the supply chain, making it more difficult to detect and mitigate threats, leading to potential cascading failures.

11.2.1.8 Communication interception and replay attacks

CPS relies on real-time data exchange between sensors, actuators, and controllers. Attackers can intercept, alter, or replay communication, tricking the system into repeating or reversing critical actions. Communication interception and replay attacks are significant cybersecurity threats in CPS. In communication interception, malicious actors eavesdrop on data exchanges between devices or systems, gaining unauthorized access to sensitive information. Replay attacks involve capturing valid communication messages and retransmitting them to deceive the system, often causing unauthorized actions or disrupting operations. Both attacks compromise data integrity, confidentiality, and system availability, making CPS vulnerable to manipulation, unauthorized control, and service disruptions. Securing CPS requires robust encryption, authentication, and anomaly detection mechanisms to protect against these risks and ensure safe, reliable system performance.

11.2.1.9 Side-channel attacks

Attackers might exploit indirect data such as power consumption or electromagnetic emissions to deduce sensitive information or inject false signals into the system, bypassing traditional network security defenses. Side-channel attacks are a cybersecurity threat to CPS, where attackers exploit physical characteristics of a system, such as power consumption, electromagnetic radiation, or timing variations, to extract sensitive information. Unlike traditional attacks that target software vulnerabilities, side-channel attacks focus on indirect data leakage through physical outputs. By analyzing these signals, attackers can uncover encryption keys, passwords, or other confidential information. These attacks can be difficult to detect and mitigate, making CPS, especially those involving embedded devices, highly vulnerable. Effective countermeasures include shielding, noise generation, and advanced cryptographic techniques to minimize side-channel information leakage.

11.2.1.10 Zero-day vulnerabilities

CPS frequently operates with legacy systems or software that may have unpatched vulnerabilities. Zero-day exploits targeting these unpatched vulnerabilities can be especially dangerous, as CPS systems are often challenging to update without downtime. Zero-day vulnerabilities are a significant cybersecurity threat to CPS. These are flaws or weaknesses in software or hardware that are unknown to the vendor or public, leaving systems unprotected until discovered and patched. Attackers exploit these vulnerabilities before developers can release a fix, often leading to unauthorized access, data breaches, or system manipulation. In CPS, zero-day exploits can disrupt critical infrastructure, compromise safety, or cause physical damage. Because of the lack of pre-existing defenses, zero-day attacks are particularly dangerous, making proactive monitoring, vulnerability assessment, and rapid patch

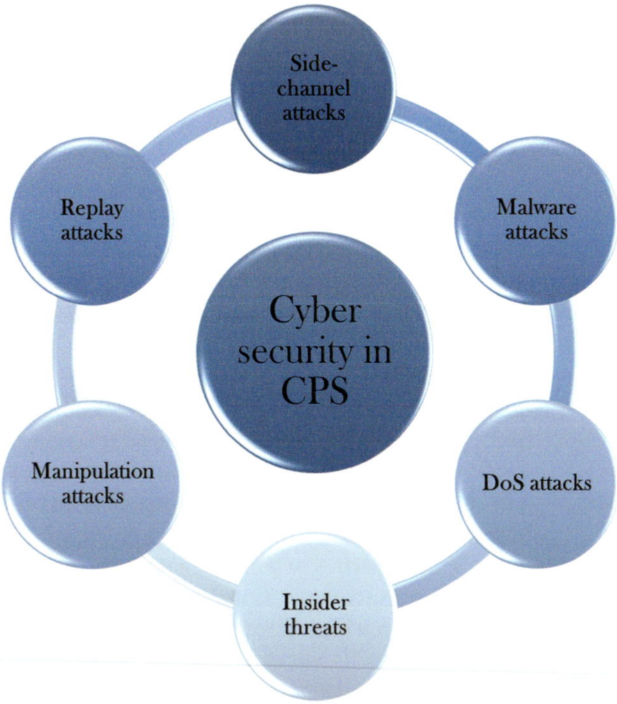

Figure 11.1 The cybersecurity threats in cyber-physical systems.

deployment essential for CPS security. Figure 11.1 shows the cybersecurity threats in cyber-physical systems.

11.2.2 The major issues of cybersecurity threats in cyber-physical systems

Cyber-physical systems (CPSs), which integrate computational and physical components to monitor and control physical processes, face unique cyber threats that make them especially vulnerable. Table 11.1 summarizes the major issues of cybersecurity threats in CPS.

11.2.3 Physical security threats in cyber-physical systems

11.2.3.1 Physical damage

Physical damage is a critical threat to the security of CPS because it directly impacts the hardware components, leading to potential failures in functionality and safety. CPS often integrates software with physical components

Table 11.1 The major issues of cybersecurity threats in cyber-physical systems.

The major issues	Descriptions
System integrity and safety	Many CPS applications, such as those in transportation, healthcare, and energy, are highly sensitive to data integrity. Attacks that compromise data accuracy can lead to incorrect system responses, causing physical harm, equipment damage, or even loss of life. For example, an attack on an autonomous vehicle's sensors could lead to dangerous navigation errors.
Authentication and access control weaknesses	CPS often connects to multiple networks and devices, creating vulnerabilities if access control is not rigorously enforced. Unauthorized access could allow attackers to take control of the system or insert malicious commands. For instance, a compromised medical device could put patients at risk by delivering incorrect dosages or collecting faulty data.
Data confidentiality	CPS typically transmits sensitive information about the physical environment and system status. Cyber threats targeting data confidentiality can lead to data leaks, allowing unauthorized parties to gain insight into critical infrastructure details or sensitive operational data, such as patient information in a healthcare CPS.
Physical manipulation	Since CPS directly interacts with the physical world, attackers can manipulate actuators or sensors to produce incorrect physical states. This can lead to dangerous outcomes in applications like industrial control systems, where machinery may be damaged or manipulated to cause unsafe conditions.
Interdependency of components	CPS systems often involve multiple interconnected components that depend on each other. A compromise in one part of the system can have cascading effects on the entire network, making it difficult to isolate and mitigate attacks. This interdependency is common in smart cities, where the failure of one system (e.g., power supply) could disrupt others (e.g., transportation or healthcare)
Limited cybersecurity for legacy systems	Many CPS rely on legacy systems with limited cybersecurity capabilities due to processing power, memory, or outdated design constraints. Such systems often lack built-in security features, making them easy targets for cyberattacks, particularly in critical infrastructure settings like water treatment facilities and transportation networks.
Difficulty in real-time detection and response	Since CPS often requires real-time operations, detecting and mitigating cyber threats without disrupting essential functions is challenging. Traditional cybersecurity approaches may be too slow or interfere with system performance, making CPS an easy target for sophisticated, quick, and covert attacks.

like sensors, actuators, and controllers that monitor or manipulate real-world operations. Physical threats, such as tampering, sabotage, or environmental hazards (e.g., fires, floods, earthquakes), can damage these components, interrupting data flow or corrupting system performance. This can compromise the reliability of operations in sectors like energy, transportation, and healthcare, where CPSs are widely used. Physical attacks may expose the system to unauthorized access, allowing attackers to manipulate or disable key processes. Therefore, securing CPSs from physical damage is essential to maintain operational integrity, safety, and trustworthiness. This often involves layered defenses, including restricted access, tamper-resistant designs, environmental protection, and constant monitoring of system integrity.

11.2.3.2 Physical tampering with hardware

Physical tampering with hardware is a significant security threat in CPS. It involves unauthorized physical interaction with a system's hardware components, aiming to disrupt operations, alter data, or insert malicious elements. Attackers may exploit CPS sensors, controllers, or communication module vulnerabilities to manipulate system behavior. Such tampering can compromise data integrity, leading to erroneous outputs or triggering unintended actions. For example, tampering can result in severe safety risks in critical infrastructures like power grids or medical devices. Effective physical security measures, such as access control, tamper-proofing, and real-time monitoring, are essential to prevent these threats. Attackers can physically access devices such as sensors, actuators, controllers, and communication hardware, manipulating or damaging them to disrupt the system's operation. This can lead to the malfunction of the entire system, potentially causing physical damage to critical infrastructure (e.g., power grids and transportation systems), and tampering with industrial robots causes them to perform unintended actions or attack sensor nodes to distort collected data.

11.2.3.3 Side-channel attacks

Side-channel attacks in CPS exploit unintentional information leaks from a system's physical properties, such as power consumption, electromagnetic emissions, or timing information, to infer sensitive data. These attacks threaten physical security by bypassing traditional cybersecurity measures and gaining unauthorized access to critical information without directly intruding into the system. For example, attackers might monitor power fluctuations in a device to deduce cryptographic keys. Given CPS's integration into critical infrastructure, from healthcare to power grids, side-channel vulnerabilities pose significant risks, potentially compromising safety, privacy, and functionality, especially as CPS expands in scope and interconnectivity. Attackers may exploit the physical characteristics of a system, such as power consumption, electromagnetic radiation, or timing patterns, to infer sensitive information or compromise security. This can allow attackers to reverse-engineer system behavior or extract cryptographic keys or sensitive data, compromising the confidentiality and integrity of the CPS. An attacker might use a differential power analysis attack to extract cryptographic keys from an embedded device.

11.2.3.4 Repair

In CPS, physical security threats arise when unauthorized individuals or devices attempt to interfere with system components like sensors, actuators, or network connections. Repairing physical security threats in CPS involves identifying vulnerabilities, isolating compromised hardware, and replacing or repairing damaged components. Strategies often include reinforcing access control, utilizing tamper-resistant hardware, and implementing real-time monitoring to detect anomalies. Repairs may also involve recalibrating sensors, patching software, and enhancing encryption for communication channels. An ongoing evaluation of physical safeguards ensures the system remains resilient against future threats, minimizing downtime and maintaining the integrity and safety of the CPS.

11.2.3.5 Loss

Physical security threats like tampering, unauthorized access, and sabotage in CPS can lead to severe losses. These include compromised data integrity, disrupted services, and damaged equipment, as physical components are directly connected to the system's digital layer. For example, an attacker could manipulate sensors or actuators to alter system behaviors, causing safety hazards, operational disruptions, and financial losses. Such breaches can also erode trust, particularly in sectors like healthcare, manufacturing, and critical infrastructure, where CPS plays a vital role. Addressing these threats requires robust physical security, continuous monitoring, and effective cyber-physical security integration to minimize risk. The most concerning situation in cybersecurity for smart grids is when multiple substations fail due to a malicious attack [42]. Such failures could cause widespread blackouts across major metropolitan areas for extended hours. A historical example includes the massive blackout in the U.S. on August 14, 2003 [43]. Some sources speculate this event may have been influenced by the People's Liberation Army (PLA), a politically motivated group based in China, highlighting the risks posed by coordinated cyber-physical attacks [44]. Figure 11.2 gives the physical security threats in cyber-physical systems.

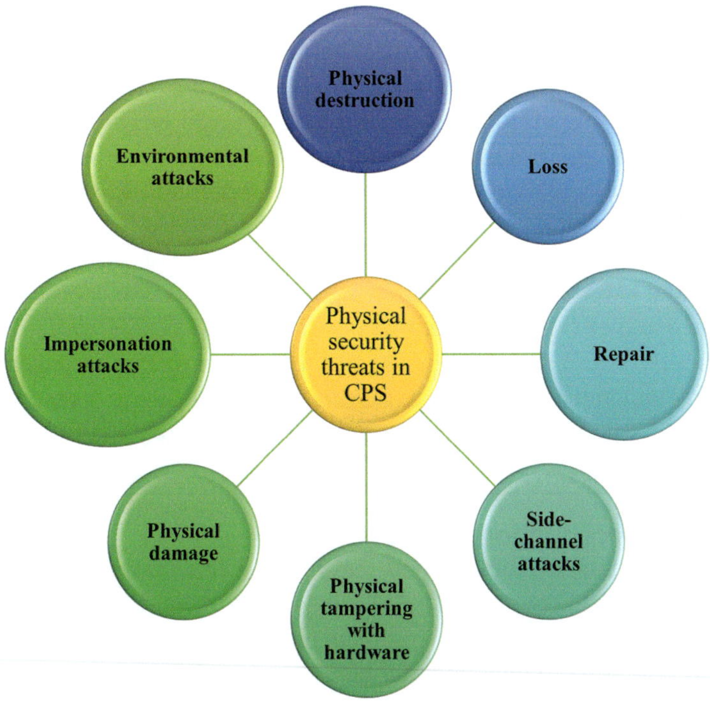

Figure 11.2 The physical security threats in cyber-physical systems.

11.2.3.6 Physical destruction or sabotage

Physical destruction or sabotage is a significant security threat in CPS, involving deliberate damage to hardware components critical to system functionality. Attackers may target sensors, actuators, or network devices, disrupting the real-time data flows and processes these systems rely on. Such interference can lead to system malfunctions, degraded performance, or complete system shutdown. Examples include tampering with power grids, transportation systems, or healthcare devices, often resulting in severe consequences. Effective physical security measures are essential to prevent unauthorized access and protect these systems against direct physical attacks that could jeopardize their reliability and safety. Attackers can physically destroy components of a CPS to cause permanent damage or operational disruption. This can result in significant financial and operational losses, particularly for systems operating in critical infrastructure sectors like transportation, energy, and healthcare sabotaging power grid transformers, causing widespread blackouts, or disabling critical machinery in a manufacturing plant.

11.2.3.7 Environmental attacks

Environmental attacks in CPS exploit natural factors – temperature, humidity, or electromagnetic interference to degrade performance or damage components. By manipulating or amplifying these environmental conditions, attackers can cause malfunctions in sensors, controllers, or communication channels, leading to system failures. Such attacks are particularly concerning in critical infrastructures like power grids or water systems, where physical and digital vulnerabilities merge, compromising overall security and safety. Environmental factors, such as temperature, humidity, or electromagnetic interference, can be used maliciously to disrupt CPS components. These attacks can degrade the performance or cause failure of sensors and actuators, leading to system errors. Using extreme temperatures to overheat or freeze a sensor causes inaccurate readings and incorrect system responses.

11.2.3.8 Impersonation attacks

Impersonation attacks in cyber-physical systems (CPSs) are critical security threats where attackers replicate authorized users' identities, allowing unauthorized access to control and manipulate physical components. Such attacks, often leveraging AI to generate highly realistic credentials or mimicry, pose severe risks in sectors like industrial control and medical systems, leading to potential physical disruptions. Countering these attacks requires robust authentication, real-time monitoring, and AI-driven anomaly detection mechanisms to enhance CPS resilience and prevent unauthorized physical actions (e.g., in smart grids and healthcare devices) [45]. Attackers may physically take control of devices or impersonate authorized users to gain unauthorized access to CPS components. Once the attacker gains control, they can manipulate the system, steal data, or damage components using a compromised key card to access secure areas of a facility or impersonating an operator to issue commands to control systems.

11.2.3.9 Jamming and interference with wireless communications

Jamming and interference pose significant threats to wireless communication in CPS. Jamming attacks disrupt signal transmission by overwhelming communication channels with noise, hindering data flow between devices. This interference can lead to critical failures in CPS environments like healthcare, transportation, and power grids, where real-time data exchange is essential for safe operation. Modern CPS security strategies incorporate resilient control mechanisms, cooperative jamming, and signal-detection protocols to counter such disruptions. Research highlights the need for robust, adaptive techniques as CPS threats evolve alongside advancements in AI and ML-based attacks and defenses [46]. Many CPS devices rely on wireless communication for data transmission. Physical jamming or interference can disrupt this communication, causing a denial of service or incorrect system behavior. Jamming can isolate devices from critical communication, causing delays, incorrect readings, or complete failure of a CPS network and attacking communication between smart grid components by jamming radio frequencies for transmitting control signals.

11.2.3.10 Malicious firmware and software installation

In CPS, malicious firmware and software installation pose significant physical security risks. Attackers exploit vulnerabilities by installing unauthorized firmware updates or tampering with software to control critical system operations. These malicious modifications can lead to data breaches, disrupted operations, or physical damage to infrastructure, as demonstrated in high-profile attacks like Stuxnet. Physical access to systems or insufficiently secured updates often enables these attacks, threatening essential sectors like healthcare, energy, and transport. Improved CPS resilience demands secure firmware updates, cryptographic verification, and robust physical security practices to mitigate these risks and ensure system integrity [47], [48]. Attackers may gain physical access to a CPS device and load malicious firmware or software during manufacturing or through physical intervention in the field. Malicious code can be used to take control of the system, disable safety features, or cause system malfunction. This threat can be particularly dangerous if the firmware is not easily detected or updated. Inserting malware into programmable logic controllers (PLCs) used in industrial automation systems to control production lines or safety features.

11.2.4 The mitigation strategies for physical security threats in cyber-physical systems

Physical security in CPS is an ongoing challenge, as these systems often operate in open, distributed, and sometimes hostile environments. Thus, physical threats must be addressed alongside digital security considerations to ensure robust, secure operations. Mitigating physical security threats in CPS is crucial, especially given their role in critical infrastructure, transportation, and healthcare systems. Table 11.2 summarizes the physical security threats in cyber-physical systems.

Table 11.2 The physical security threats in cyber-physical systems.

Mitigations	Descriptions
Risk assessment and asset prioritization	A comprehensive risk assessment framework helps identify critical assets and potential threats, allowing organizations to focus their resources on the most vulnerable components. This approach also assesses how different threats could impact the CPS's operations and enables the development of targeted security plans.
Access control and physical barriers	Implementing strict access control mechanisms (e.g., biometric systems and ID cards) ensures that only authorized personnel can interact with sensitive CPS areas. Adding physical barriers, such as fences and locked doors, further reduces unauthorized access to critical components, lowering the risk of sabotage or tampering.
Intrusion detection systems (IDS)	IDSs are valuable for monitoring real-time threats in CPS environments. By using sensors and video surveillance, IDS detects unusual activities and alerts security teams to potential threats, allowing quick responses to prevent intrusions from escalating into significant breaches.
Redundancy and resilient architecture	Redundant systems and resilient network design are crucial for CPS. Implementing backup components and diversified network paths ensures that, if one component fails or is compromised, the system can continue to operate with minimal disruption, which is critical in preventing cascading failures. Use redundant systems to ensure reliability even if one part of the system is compromised.
Data encryption and secure communication protocols	Encryption and secure communication protect data integrity and confidentiality within CPS networks. Techniques such as transport layer security (TLS) and end-to-end encryption safeguard data exchanges and prevent physical or cyber tampering with transmitted data, especially in CPS that rely on wireless communication.
Incident response and recovery planning	Effective incident response protocols are essential to managing threats quickly and minimizing damage. A well-defined recovery plan helps restore operations after an attack and includes regular drills to ensure readiness. This strategy also integrates cross-departmental collaboration, vital in large CPS infrastructures.
Regular training and awareness programs	Educating staff about CPS security policies, potential physical threats, and response procedures enhances security. Training programs keep personnel updated on emerging threats and best practices, making them more likely to proactively identify and prevent security risks.

Mitigations	Descriptions
Tamper detection	Tamper detection in CPS involves monitoring devices for signs of physical interference, such as unauthorized access or hardware manipulation. By employing sensors, alarms, or cryptographic methods, this strategy identifies and responds to potential breaches, ensuring the system's integrity. It helps prevent malicious attacks that could compromise data, control systems, or safety mechanisms. Utilize sensors and mechanisms to detect tampering or physical attacks.
Firmware integrity checking	Firmware integrity checking is crucial in mitigating physical security threats to CPS. By ensuring the authenticity and integrity of firmware, systems can defend against unauthorized modifications, which could otherwise compromise both software and hardware. This strategy includes secure boot mechanisms, real-time monitoring, and cryptographic checks, offering proactive protection against firmware attacks that target vulnerabilities in embedded systems. Regularly verify and update the firmware to protect against malware and unauthorized modifications.
Secure supply chain practices	Secure supply chain practices in cyber-physical systems (CPSs) mitigate physical security threats by ensuring the integrity and reliability of components from suppliers. This includes vetting vendors, implementing encryption, and conducting regular audits to detect tampering or counterfeiting. Robust tracking, authentication, and secure delivery methods are also employed to protect CPS from vulnerabilities introduced through external supply chain risks. Monitor and secure the supply chain to ensure components are not tampered with before installation.

11.2.5 Hybrid security threats in cyber-physical systems

Hybrid security threats in CPS arise from integrating physical and cyber domains, exploiting vulnerabilities in both realms. These threats combine traditional cyberattacks, like hacking or malware, with physical disruptions, such as sabotage or sensor tampering. For example, an attacker might compromise a smart grid's control system (cyber) to cause equipment failures (physical). CPS hybrid threats are particularly dangerous because they can have cascading effects; a small cyber intrusion could lead to widespread physical damage, risking human safety, infrastructure stability, and data integrity. Adversaries may use these attacks to disrupt critical sectors, including healthcare, transportation, and energy. Key challenges include the complexity of CPS environments, system interdependence, and difficulty detecting blended attacks. Addressing these threats requires robust security strategies, integrating advanced monitoring, real-time threat detection, and collaborative frameworks between physical and digital defense teams.

11.2.5.1 Cyber-physical interaction threats

Cyber-physical systems integrate physical processes with computational elements, creating vulnerabilities where cyberattacks can influence physical outcomes. Physical security threats in CPS arise when malicious actors exploit these interactions, potentially causing harm to both systems and individuals. Cyber threats, like hacking or malware, can compromise sensors, actuators, and control systems, manipulating physical processes such as industrial equipment operations, transportation systems, or healthcare devices. These threats may lead to physical damage, safety risks, financial losses, or even loss of life. Protecting CPS requires securing both the cyber and physical layers to prevent malicious interference and ensure safety. CPS relies on real-time data from physical processes (sensors, actuators) to perform computations and control actions in the physical world. A hybrid attack can simultaneously exploit vulnerabilities in both these domains.

Examples:

Sensor manipulation: Attackers can manipulate sensor readings (such as temperature, pressure, or speed) to affect control algorithms. This can mislead the system's software, causing incorrect decisions that impact the physical system.

Actuator control: Attackers can control actuators (e.g., motors, valves, robotic arms) to cause physical damage, such as shutting down industrial machines or accelerating a vehicle uncontrollably.

11.2.5.2 Communication network attacks

In CPS, communication network attacks targeting physical security involve exploiting vulnerabilities in integrating physical processes and computational elements. These attacks can disrupt critical systems such as smart grids, autonomous vehicles, and industrial control systems. Threats include jamming, eavesdropping, spoofing, and denial-of-service (DoS) attacks on communication channels, leading to unauthorized access or manipulation of physical devices. Malicious actors can compromise sensors, actuators, and communication links, causing malfunction, data manipulation, or system shutdowns, endangering public safety, privacy, and operational continuity. Effective security measures are crucial for safeguarding both the digital and physical components. CPS often relies on communication networks to transmit data between sensors, actuators, and control centers. Cyber threats can compromise the network, intercepting, altering, or injecting malicious data.

Examples:
Man-in-the-middle (MITM) attacks: Cyber attackers intercept and manipulate data transmitted between sensors and control systems, leading to incorrect physical actions.

Denial of service (DoS) attacks involve overloading communication channels to disrupt data flow. This could cause systems to operate with outdated or incomplete information, leading to physical consequences such as grid failure or transportation delay.

11.2.5.3 Control system exploits

CPS typically uses complex control systems (such as SCADA and DCS) to manage the physical processes. These systems can be vulnerable to cyberattacks, which can lead to unsafe conditions in the physical domain. CPS control systems are increasingly targeted by cyberattacks due to their integration of computing, communication, and physical processes [46]. Vulnerabilities within these systems allow adversaries to exploit control algorithms, often leading to unsafe operations, data theft, or even physical damage. Exploits may involve manipulating sensor data, overloading communication channels, or injecting faulty commands to disrupt physical processes. Recent studies emphasize the growing sophistication of threats such as malware and denial-of-service attacks, highlighting the need for advanced security measures. Protecting CPS involves a combination of intrusion detection, real-time monitoring, and robust encryption for both hardware and software components [49].

Examples:
Malware injection: Cyber adversaries can infect the software controlling critical infrastructure (like power grids or manufacturing facilities) to cause the system to behave erratically, leading to physical damage or failure.

Command spoofing: By injecting fake commands into the system, attackers can alter the physical process, such as causing machinery to malfunction or malfunctioning industrial robots to harm workers.

Figure 11.3 displays the hybrid security threats in CPSs.

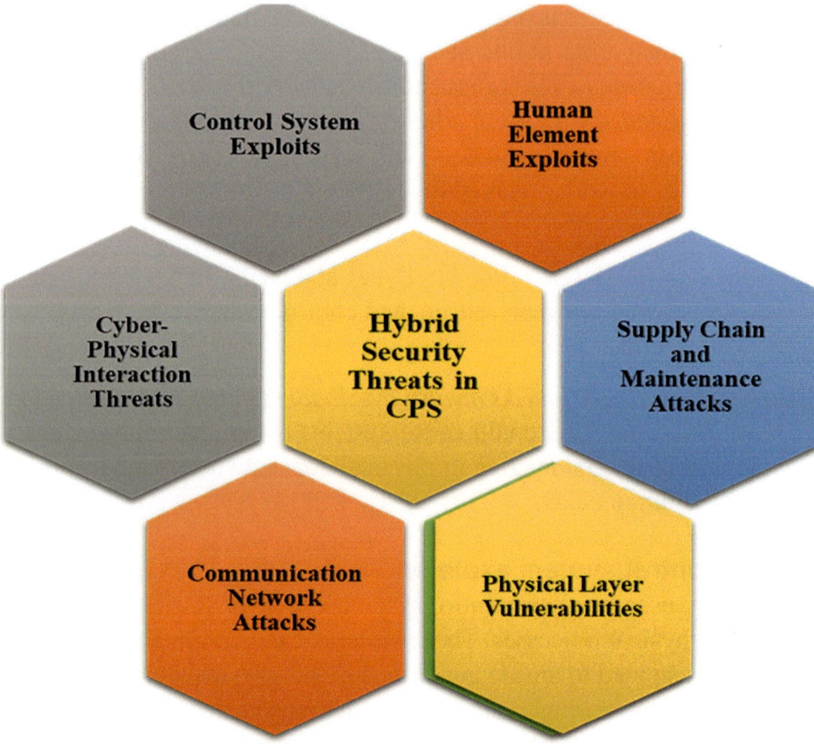

Figure 11.3 The hybrid security threats in cyber-physical systems.

11.2.5.4 Data integrity and authentication vulnerabilities

The reliability of data, which drives physical systems' decisions, is critical. Hybrid threats can target both data integrity and the authentication of users and devices within the system. CPS faces significant data integrity and authentication vulnerabilities, particularly when physical security is compromised. Integrating IoT devices and sensors in CPS increases their exposure to attacks, where adversaries can manipulate data or interfere with sensor-actuator networks. For instance, attackers may exploit vulnerabilities in smart grid communications or medical devices to alter crucial data, jeopardizing safety or privacy [50]. Malicious insiders and physical attacks on the hardware components, such as sensors or controllers, can bypass security mechanisms, compromising sensor data authenticity [51]. Effective countermeasures, such as cryptographic protocols and real-time anomaly detection, are essential to mitigate these risks.

Examples:
Data tampering: An attacker alters the sensor data (e.g., temperature or pressure) sent to control systems, affecting decision-making algorithms. This could result in faulty products in manufacturing, while critical infrastructures like nuclear plants could cause catastrophic physical outcomes.

Spoofing device identity: Attackers can impersonate legitimate devices in the system, allowing them to inject incorrect data, disable legitimate devices, or cause malicious behaviors in both the cyber and physical domains.

11.2.5.5 Physical layer vulnerabilities

Cyber-physical systems are vulnerable to various physical-layer security threats, primarily due to their reliance on real-time data exchange between cyber and physical components. These vulnerabilities can be exploited in several ways, including physical attacks on sensors, communication channels, and control systems. For instance, attacks targeting sensor devices can corrupt the data, leading to actuators' incorrect actions. Additionally, physical tampering with communication infrastructure or the physical environment (e.g., environmental disruptions) can affect system performance. Threats like insider attacks, improper change management, and inadequate encryption mechanisms further exacerbate security risks [52]. Attacks targeting a CPS's physical devices and infrastructure can have immediate, real-world consequences. Addressing these challenges requires robust security protocols, such as real-time monitoring, cryptographic solutions, and secure integration of new components to safeguard critical infrastructure [53].

Examples:
Tampering with physical sensors: Physical damage to sensors (e.g., placing objects over them or damaging wiring) can send incorrect data to control systems, which could cause faulty system responses.

Jamming or spoofing sensors: In CPS involving GPS (e.g., autonomous vehicles or drones), attackers can jam or spoof GPS signals, leading to misdirection and physical harm, such as vehicle crashes or drone malfunctions.

11.2.5.6 Supply chain and maintenance attacks

Supply chain and maintenance attacks on CPS target integrating physical processes with digital networks. These attacks exploit vulnerabilities at various stages, from raw material procurement to final product assembly. For instance, malicious actors may insert counterfeit components or compromise firmware during production or maintenance phases, impacting the system's security. The interconnectedness of CPS across industries increases the attack surface, facilitating unauthorized access and disruption of both physical and cyber functionalities. Such attacks can severely disrupt operations in sectors like energy and healthcare, emphasizing the need for robust supply chain security measures. CPS is highly dependent on diverse suppliers for hardware, software, and firmware [54]. Security breaches in the supply chain can introduce cyber and physical risks into the system.

Examples:
Compromised software updates: Attackers could infiltrate the software update process, introducing malware or backdoors that compromise CPS devices' cybersecurity and physical operations.

Infected hardware components: Malicious actors could insert compromised hardware into the supply chain, which would go undetected, allowing them to take control of a physical process.

11.2.5.7 Human element exploits

In CPS, human factors represent a significant vulnerability in physical security. Humans can intentionally or unintentionally compromise system integrity, often through misconfigurations or exploitation of psychological vulnerabilities like social engineering. Recent research highlights the role of human error in numerous security breaches, such as the WannaCry ransomware attack and data leaks at companies like Equifax [55]. Human factors remain a major vulnerability in CPS security, where operators, engineers, or maintenance personnel may inadvertently or maliciously introduce threats [56]. Moreover, human involvement in interacting with physical and digital infrastructures amplifies risks, requiring comprehensive training and awareness strategies to mitigate these threats [57]. Ensuring robust human-centered security protocols is vital to the resilience of CPS.

Examples:
Insider attacks: Disgruntled employees or contractors may manipulate the system's cyber and physical components, either by providing false inputs or directly damaging physical assets.

Social engineering: Attackers could use social engineering tactics to trick operators into providing access to sensitive systems or installing malicious software that targets both cyber and physical vulnerabilities.

11.2.5.8 Lack of real-time response mechanisms

The lack of real-time response mechanisms in CPS is a significant challenge due to the intricate interaction between cyber and physical layers.

These systems often rely on complex feedback control mechanisms like PID and LQG controllers to manage real-time physical processes. However, the increasing sophistication and scale of CPS and vulnerabilities to cross-layer attacks complicate swift threat detection and mitigation. Real-time detection remains problematic, especially when cyberattacks manipulate physical and digital components, leading to substantial damage. Recent studies suggest that better integration of automated resilience frameworks is critical to enhancing CPS security [48], [58]. CPS must respond to physical changes in real time. Still, hybrid attacks may create delays or errors in these responses, allowing physical damage to occur before corrective actions can be taken.

Examples:
Real-time control failures: In autonomous systems, delays caused by cyberattacks on control algorithms (e.g., through data overloads or altered logic) may prevent quick responses to sudden physical threats like equipment failure or environmental hazards, causing catastrophic outcomes.

11.2.5.9 Interdependencies between cyber and physical components

Cyber-physical systems are highly interdependent, where cyber components (software, networks) and physical components (hardware, sensors, actuators) work together to control and monitor processes. Security threats exploit these interdependencies, as a cyberattack on the digital layer can directly impact physical operations, leading to system failures, safety hazards, or resource damage. For example, disruptions in communication protocols (like DNP3) can impair physical components such as power grids or industrial systems. Understanding these links is crucial for effective risk management and ensuring the resilience of CPS in the face of cyber and physical threats [59]. In CPS, the cyber and physical elements are tightly coupled. A vulnerability in one domain often translates to a vulnerability in the other.

Example:
Cascading failures: A cyberattack on one part of the system could cascade and cause failures in other parts, resulting in physical and operational consequences. For instance, an attack on a software component controlling traffic lights could cause traffic congestion, accidents, and delays that physically disrupt a city's operations.

Hybrid security threats in CPS refer to a complex combination of traditional cyber threats and physical attacks that jointly compromise a system's digital and physical components. CPS integrates physical processes, such as sensors, actuators, and control systems, with computational resources, networks, and software. This interconnectedness creates vulnerabilities that attackers can exploit, targeting either the cyber (computational) or physical (real-world) elements. Hybrid security threats in CPSs are a significant concern due to the complex interdependencies between digital and physical components. Considering the traditional cyber vulnerabilities and the specific risks introduced by physical elements, these systems must be secured holistically. Addressing these threats requires a combination of advanced cybersecurity measures, physical security protocols, and real-time monitoring to mitigate potential risks and ensure safe, reliable system operation.

11.3 The Privacy Concerns and Risks in Modern Cyber-physical Systems

Cyber-physical systems integrate physical components with digital networks, creating interdependent systems that monitor and control critical infrastructures like healthcare, smart cities, and autonomous vehicles [60], [61]. However, this connectivity introduces significant privacy concerns. CPS collects vast amounts of data, often involving sensitive information like location, health, and behavior, which can be intercepted, exposed, or misused if improperly secured. Unauthorized access or data breaches can lead to privacy invasions, identity theft, and other malicious actions. Privacy risks are exacerbated by the limited security measures in some CPS devices, making them vulnerable to cyberattacks [62]. Further, the interconnected nature of CPS means that a single compromised device can cascade security breaches across the network.

The CPS integrates physical components with digital computation and communication to enable functions in fields like healthcare, manufacturing, transportation, and critical infrastructure [4]. While this convergence enhances efficiency, it raises significant privacy concerns due to the inherent risks of data breaches, unauthorized access, and misuse of sensitive information. Moreover, CPS often relies on real-time data processing, which, if intercepted or manipulated, could jeopardize user safety and system integrity, emphasizing the need for robust security and privacy protections [63]. Here's a detailed look at the privacy concerns and risks involved:

11.3.1 Data collection and surveillance risks

Data collection and surveillance in CPS pose privacy risks due to extensive user data monitoring across both digital and physical realms. Modern CPS collects real-time data from interconnected devices, often without explicit user consent, raising risks of identity tracking and unauthorized data sharing. Enhanced data protection regulations, such as those recently enacted in various U.S. states, aim to limit unauthorized data processing, highlighting the need for robust privacy standards in evolving CPS environments [64]. CPS often relies on continuous data collection from sensors, cameras, and IoT devices. This data includes sensitive information about people's location, health, and behavior, creating detailed profiles of individuals or groups. CPSs in smart cities, homes, or healthcare environments are designed to monitor activities 24/7. This level of surveillance raises privacy concerns as individuals may not fully understand or consent to the extent of monitoring. It's often unclear to users what data is collected, how it's stored, who has access, and for what purposes. This lack of transparency creates uncertainty and erodes trust.

11.3.2 Unauthorized data access and cybersecurity threats

Unauthorized data access in CPS creates privacy and security risks by exposing sensitive data to unauthorized parties, which may lead to identity theft, data manipulation, or sabotage of physical components. Cyber threats such as phishing, weak authentication, and insider attacks are common entry points, risking data integrity and physical safety. Effective mitigation involves multi-layered security practices, including stringent access controls, user authentication, and incident response plans [65]. CPSs have multiple entry points due to their reliance on IoT devices, sensors, and networks, making them vulnerable to cyberattacks. Hackers can gain unauthorized access, steal data, or take control of physical systems. Many CPS components, especially IoT devices, lack robust access control and encryption measures, making it easier for attackers to compromise them and gain access to sensitive information. A breach in CPS can expose digital data and lead to physical safety risks, especially in systems that control critical infrastructure like power grids, transportation, and healthcare systems.

11.3.3 Interconnectedness and third-party risks

Interconnectedness in CPS enhances operational efficiency but increases exposure to third-party risks, as each connected entity can become a potential vulnerability. Privacy concerns arise due to unauthorized access or misuse of data by third-party suppliers. Recent European frameworks like GDPR and NIS2 enforce stricter controls, emphasizing risk assessments and monitoring to protect data across complex supply chains [66]. CPS systems are interconnected and often share data with other networks or third-party services. This interconnectedness increases the attack surface and can lead to unauthorized data sharing, making it difficult to track and control where sensitive information goes. CPS frequently relies on third-party vendors and service providers for components or maintenance. These vendors may not prioritize security or have adequate protections, creating potential entry points for attackers.

11.3.4 Privacy risks related to real-time data processing

In CPS, real-time data processing poses privacy risks due to the continuous flow of sensitive information between physical and digital components. Challenges include preventing unauthorized access, managing data accurately under time constraints, and balancing utility with privacy through differential privacy and data anonymization to reduce data traceability. These systems face unique vulnerabilities due to the large-scale integration of IoT devices and big data analytics, which can increase attack surfaces and invite cyber threats targeting personal and operational data, particularly in smart cities, healthcare, and transportation sectors [50]. CPS systems that process real-time data, such as traffic systems or healthcare monitoring, can create detailed behavioral profiles. While this can improve services, it also risks exposing personal data that can be misused if not adequately protected. Even if CPS data is anonymized, real-time data analysis can enable inference attacks, where attackers deduce identities or private information by correlating data points, such as location and behavior patterns.

11.3.5 Physical safety risks due to privacy violations

CPSs in transportation or smart cities often track users' locations, posing risks if this data is accessed or misused. Stalking, location-based targeting, and other physical threats become possible if location privacy is compromised. Unauthorized access to CPS that control physical systems (e.g., autonomous vehicles, healthcare devices) can endanger lives. Hackers could manipulate devices to create dangerous conditions or disrupt essential services.

11.3.6 Legal and regulatory challenges

Many existing privacy laws were not designed for the unique complexities of CPS, leading to gaps in protections. For instance, regulatory frameworks may not fully address data ownership and usage in CPS environments, leading to potential misuse. CPS often operates across regions and countries, which means it is subject to multiple privacy regulations. Navigating compliance across jurisdictions is challenging and can lead to privacy risks due to inconsistent protections.

11.3.7 User awareness and consent issues

Users interacting with CPS may not be fully aware of the data collected about them, especially in environments like smart cities or buildings where data collection is passive. This lack of consent can lead to privacy breaches if data is shared or used unexpectedly. Unlike traditional digital systems, CPS often does not offer users easy ways to control their data, view what's collected, or opt out of data collection. This loss of control over personal data creates a sense of privacy intrusion and may result in user distrust.

11.3.8 Risks of data misuse and secondary uses

Data collected for one purpose in CPS (e.g., location data for traffic management) may be repurposed for another (e.g., advertising), a phenomenon known as function creep. This type of secondary data usage often occurs without user consent and raises ethical and legal concerns. Data collected by CPS can be used to create profiles that lead to discrimination in areas like insurance, hiring, or creditworthiness. Predictive analytics can exacerbate biases if not carefully managed, resulting in privacy violations and unfair treatment of individuals.

11.3.9 Difficulty of implementing robust privacy protections

Many CPS components, particularly IoT devices, have limited processing power, restricting their ability to implement strong encryption and privacy-preserving measures. Ensuring data privacy while maintaining CPS operational efficiency is challenging. Privacy-preserving methods like data anonymization or differential privacy can reduce real-time data accuracy, which may affect critical services. Many CPSs rely on legacy infrastructure that may not support modern privacy standards or is challenging to update, leaving these systems more vulnerable to privacy breaches.

11.3.10 The combined cyber-physical attacks and advanced persistent threats (APTs)

Combined cyber-physical attacks and advanced persistent threats (APTs) represent a sophisticated and dangerous category of security threats that target both the digital (cyber) and physical layers of critical infrastructure. These attacks are increasingly concerning as they focus not only on data theft or disruption but also on influencing or sabotaging physical systems.

The cyber-physical attacks involve breaches that cross the boundary between cyber (digital) and physical domains. Attackers exploit vulnerabilities in digital systems that control physical devices, machinery, or infrastructure, such as power grids, water treatment plants, transportation networks, and manufacturing systems. For example, by hacking into the control systems of a power plant, an attacker might disrupt operations, causing power outages or even physical damage. APTs are long-term, stealthy, and well-coordinated attack campaigns often attributed to highly skilled attackers, like state-sponsored groups or organized cybercriminal organizations. APTs aim to infiltrate systems without immediate detection, allowing attackers to gather intelligence, manipulate processes, or remain dormant until a strategic moment arises. APTs often target critical infrastructure, government agencies, or large corporations where prolonged access can yield high rewards or inflict significant damage.

Advanced persistent threats in CPS are sophisticated, prolonged cyber-attacks that aim to infiltrate and exploit critical infrastructures, often without immediate detection [67]. CPS includes systems like power grids, transportation, healthcare, and manufacturing, which blend computational resources with physical components to deliver essential services. APTs against CPS are particularly dangerous because they target vulnerabilities within both digital and physical layers, potentially disrupting operations and even causing physical harm. APTs are typically orchestrated by skilled adversaries, often funded by nation-states or organized cybercriminal groups. These threats unfold in stages: reconnaissance, gaining initial access, establishing a foothold, privilege escalation, and then exfiltrating data or sabotaging operations. Once inside a CPS, attackers may lie dormant, observing and mapping the system's behaviors to identify weak points. Due to CPS's interconnectivity and reliance on legacy technologies, they are highly susceptible to these threats, which can exploit outdated protocols or insecure communication channels [68]. Detection and mitigation of APTs in CPS are challenging due to their stealthy nature and the complex, interconnected architecture of CPS. Advanced monitoring, anomaly detection, and robust cybersecurity frameworks are essential for reducing the risks posed by APTs in these critical systems.

In a combined attack, the digital and physical domains are exploited in tandem over an extended period, leveraging APT tactics to ensure stealth and persistence. Attackers may penetrate cyber systems controlling physical infrastructure, manipulate data or device functionality, and even alter physical equipment's performance or safety settings. For instance, attackers might subtly alter readings on an industrial control system to make equipment appear stable, even as they push it toward unsafe conditions. Stuxnet, one of the most famous cases, is often cited as an early example where a cyberattack affected physical systems, targeting centrifuges in Iran's nuclear facilities [69]. Today's combined cyber-physical APTs could, for example, involve an attacker compromising the digital systems of a dam to release water unexpectedly, potentially causing downstream flooding.

Defending against these threats is particularly challenging due to their complexity and the overlap of IT and operational technology (OT) domains. Security measures must account for cybersecurity and physical safety protocols, requiring collaboration across different sectors and integrating advanced threat detection systems. Combined cyber-physical APTs are especially critical because their impact extends beyond the virtual realm into real-world safety and stability, demanding enhanced multi-layered defense strategies.

11.3.11 The major issues of privacy concerns and risks in modern Cyber-physical systems

Cyber-physical systems face significant privacy issues due to extensive data collection and connectivity with physical processes. The primary risks involve unauthorized access to sensitive data and vulnerability to cyberattacks, such as data interception and injection attacks. These systems are complex, and managing data access across various stakeholders can lead to insider threats, whether intentional or accidental [70]. Balancing security with system usability, especially in resource-limited environments like healthcare, further complicates privacy protection, as it can reduce safeguards in critical scenarios. Additionally, CPS's dynamic nature exposes them to evolving cyber threats, demanding continuous updates and advanced, adaptive security measures. Addressing these challenges requires secure data-sharing protocols, robust access control, and tailored security solutions to maintain privacy and safeguard sensitive information [71]. Privacy concerns in CPS, which integrate cyber components with physical processes, arise from the large-scale data collection, connectivity, and control these systems employ. As CPS become integral to areas like smart grids, industrial automation, healthcare, and autonomous vehicles, they are increasingly susceptible to cyber risks that threaten security and privacy. Table 11.3 summarizes the major issues of cybersecurity threats in CPSs.

Table 11.3 The major issues of cybersecurity threats in cyber-physical systems.

The major issues	Descriptions
Data privacy and unauthorized access	CPS collects massive amounts of sensitive data from sensors and interconnected devices. Without robust privacy protections, this data is at risk of exposure and misuse. For example, smart grids require detailed usage data, which can reveal personal patterns. Encryption and anonymization are essential but are often insufficient alone due to CPS's real-time data-sharing requirements.
Vulnerability to cyberattacks	CPS relies on extensive networks that cyberattacks can breach, including eavesdropping, data interception, and denial-of-service (DoS) attacks. In industrial control systems (ICS), unauthorized access can disrupt operations, and attacks like data injection or manipulation can corrupt control processes. This risk is exacerbated by legacy systems that lack updated security protocols.
Insider threats and system complexity	The complexity of CPS and the involvement of various stakeholders increase the risk of insider threats. Malicious insiders or unintentional mishandling of data can compromise privacy and security, especially when device-level access control is insufficient. Coordinated management is crucial to protect sensitive information, particularly in critical infrastructures like medical devices or industrial applications.
Balance between security and usability	In applications like healthcare, CPS devices must be accessible in emergencies, yet this accessibility often reduces security measures, making privacy vulnerabilities more prominent. Designing CPS to balance robust security with usability remains a significant challenge, especially under resource constraints.
Evolving attack surfaces and need for adaptive security	CPSs are dynamic and interact in real-time with their environment, exposing them to a constantly evolving cyber threat landscape. Traditional security measures may not be sufficient against newer attack methods targeting CPS, necessitating continuous updates and adaptive security measures to mitigate privacy risks.

Recent research highlights the importance of security measures tailored to CPS, such as lightweight cryptographic solutions and anomaly detection in data collection, to address privacy concerns. Strengthening CPS privacy demands improved device-level security, data protection protocols, and secure integration practices in complex systems.

11.4 The Risk Assessment and Threat Modeling in Cyber-physical Systems

Risk assessment and threat modeling are critical processes in ensuring the security and resilience of CPS. CPS integrates computational elements with physical processes, often found in industrial control systems, smart cities, healthcare, transportation, and energy grids. These systems rely on a tight integration between the physical and digital worlds, making them particularly vulnerable to various threats and attacks [68]. Risk assessment and threat modeling in CPS involve identifying, analyzing, and prioritizing potential security risks that could compromise the system‘s functionality, safety, and data integrity [72].

Risk assessment is identifying and evaluating risks associated with a system, helping prioritize resources to mitigate the most critical threats. For CPS, risk assessment requires understanding the interdependencies between digital and physical components. This involves examining system vulnerabilities, identifying potential threat actors (such as hackers, insiders, or natural events), and evaluating the possible impact of different attacks on system operations [73]. Risk assessment typically begins with asset identification, defining what aspects of the CPS are critical to its operations. This could include sensors, actuators, communication channels, or data storage units. Once assets are identified, the next step is to assess their vulnerabilities by analyzing how they might be exploited through software weaknesses, hardware malfunctions, or user errors [74]. Impact analysis then helps estimate the potential consequences of an attack, such as operational downtime, physical damage, or safety risks, allowing prioritization of threats based on likelihood and potential severity.

Threat modeling is the systematic approach to identifying and analyzing threats that could compromise CPS. This process includes creating a comprehensive understanding of the system's attack surface, or the sum of all points where an attacker could attempt to enter or exploit the system. This typically involves identifying potential attack vectors, defining adversarial capabilities, and mapping out how an adversary might move through the system. Common threat modeling frameworks like spoofing, tampering, repudiation, information disclosure, denial of service, and elevation of privileges (STRIDE) or damage, reproducibility, exploitability, affected users, and discoverability (DREAD) can be applied to CPS to categorize and analyze potential threats [75], [76], For example, in a smart grid CPS, a tampering attack could manipulate sensor data to mislead control decisions, leading to blackouts or system malfunctions. By combining risk assessment and threat modeling, CPS developers and administrators can develop a security strategy that addresses immediate and long-term threats [77]. This might include implementing real-time monitoring, designing fail-safe mechanisms, establishing strict access controls, and routinely updating the system based on emerging threats.

11.4.1 The risk assessment in cyber-physical systems

In CPS, risk assessment is a systematic approach to identifying, analyzing, and mitigating potential risks that could impact the system's performance, security, and safety. CPS combines computational and physical components, making it critical to evaluate risks that can arise both from the digital (cyber) and physical domains. Risk assessment in CPS typically involves several steps. The first step is identifying potential threats, which may include cyber threats like hacking, malware, and unauthorized access, as well as physical threats like hardware malfunctions or environmental hazards. The next step is analyzing vulnerabilities within the system, assessing which components are most at risk of these threats and how susceptible they are to compromise.

Following this, risk evaluation is conducted, quantifying each identified risk's likelihood and potential impact on the system's operations and safety. This includes assessing the potential harm to data integrity, physical damage, and the possibility of cascading failures across interconnected components. The final step is mitigation planning, where measures are devised to reduce or eliminate high-risk threats. These may include implementing cybersecurity protocols, reinforcing physical components, or creating contingency plans for system recovery. This proactive approach to identifying, evaluating, and controlling risks is essential to ensure that CPS operates reliably, securely, and safely, especially in environments where failures can have severe consequences, like healthcare, energy, or transportation.

CPS risk assessment involves identifying, analyzing, and evaluating potential risks impacting the system's operation, safety, and security. The assessment covers physical and cyber components for CPS, often including complex machinery, sensors, networks, and software. Figure 11.4 displays the general steps of risk assessment in CPSs. The steps in risk assessment are outlined as follows.

11.4.1.1 Identify assets

Determine the critical assets within the CPS (e.g., sensors, controllers, data). In modern CPS, identifying assets is a crucial step in risk assessment, aiming

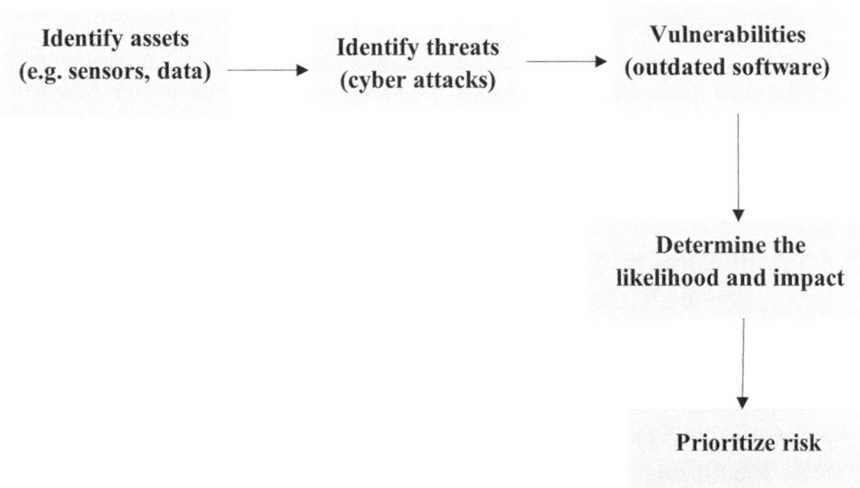

Figure 11.4 The general steps of risk assessment in cyber-physical systems.

to safeguard interconnected digital and physical components. This phase involves creating a comprehensive inventory of all assets critical to the operation of CPS, such as hardware, software, data, communication interfaces, and even the physical environment in some cases. These assets are classified based on their role and importance within the system and their vulnerability to specific risks, including cyber-attacks, environmental factors, and operational failures. Identifying assets helps establish the scope of protection efforts, guiding organizations in allocating resources and prioritizing security controls for higher-value components. For instance, high-value assets like control systems in energy grids or autonomous maritime vessels require stringent cybersecurity due to the severe consequences of failure or compromise. This prioritization allows for a more targeted and cost-effective deployment of resources, focusing on assets that, if compromised, could disrupt system operations or lead to financial or reputational damage.

Recent frameworks such as the FMECA-ATT&CK method extend traditional risk assessment models by incorporating adversarial techniques, particularly relevant for CPSs in critical infrastructure like energy and maritime sectors [78]. These frameworks leverage models such as the MITRE ATT&CK to assess threats specific to CPS components, aligning with industry-specific standards to achieve a more systematic evaluation of risk [79]. Experts recommend regularly updating asset inventories and adjusting priorities to reflect emerging threats as cyber-physical environments continuously evolve and face new security challenges. Overall, identifying and categorizing assets forms a foundation for risk assessment, enabling CPS operators to mitigate threats efficiently and effectively while also adapting to regulatory requirements and industry standards. By keeping this inventory current and aligning it with comprehensive threat models, organizations can strengthen resilience in their cyber-physical systems, especially in critical industries where security is paramount.

11.4.1.2 Identify threats

Recognize threats like cyberattacks, natural disasters, or equipment failure. In modern CPS, the risk assessment involves identifying various security threats that could disrupt interconnected networks and autonomous systems. CPS faces unique and evolving risks due to their integration with critical infrastructure like energy grids, industrial control systems, and healthcare devices. Identifying these threats as part of risk assessment is crucial for establishing effective security measures.

One primary threat is the potential for malicious intrusions that exploit vulnerabilities in network connections, often facilitated by weak authentication or outdated software in CPS components. These intrusions can lead to unauthorized control or disruption, particularly in autonomous systems where decision-making relies on real-time data integration. For instance, manipulating sensor data in smart grids can mislead system operations, affecting energy distribution or causing blackouts if left unchecked [80]. Another significant threat is insider attacks malicious activities from individuals within the organization, often difficult to detect due to their access privileges. These threats are especially problematic in complex CPS environments, where human operators oversee various automated processes. Effective risk assessments in these systems must account for insider threats and include strict access controls and behavioral monitoring to reduce risks [81], [82].

11.4.1.3 Vulnerability analysis

Vulnerabilities are analyzed through testing tools, configuration audits, and penetration testing. For CPS, vulnerabilities may arise from outdated software, unpatched hardware, or inadequate network segmentation. Automation and remote connectivity in CPS increase exposure, making this step critical. Tools like vulnerability scanners and threat intelligence platforms support this stage, enabling comprehensive insights into system weaknesses. Vulnerability analysis in CPS is a crucial risk assessment component, particularly as these systems underpin critical infrastructures. The primary goal is identifying and addressing vulnerabilities before adversaries exploit them, leading to significant consequences such as system failures or security breaches. The process starts with identifying vulnerabilities, which includes scanning for weak spots in the system's cyber and physical components. These vulnerabilities can stem from outdated software, poorly configured hardware, or inadequate communication protocols. Tools like vulnerability management systems (VMS) and databases like the common vulnerabilities and exposures (CVE) are used to monitor emerging threats.

Next, risk assessment evaluates the potential impact and likelihood of exploiting these vulnerabilities. This step involves classifying the severity of identified weaknesses in terms of their potential to disrupt system operations, including data loss, integrity breaches, or system downtime. Key metrics such as the confidentiality, integrity, and availability (CIA) triad are applied to assess the risks [83]. Following risk evaluation, prioritization helps to focus on the most critical vulnerabilities. High-impact, easily exploitable vulnerabilities are prioritized, while lower-risk vulnerabilities are dealt with later or monitored for changes [84]. Once prioritized, security measures, including preventive, detective, and corrective actions, are implemented to mitigate the risks. Finally, continuous monitoring is essential as new vulnerabilities emerge regularly. This ongoing process ensures that CPS remains resilient against evolving cyber threats and that corrective actions are promptly taken to secure vulnerable components [83], [84]. By integrating these steps, identification, assessment, prioritization, and mitigation, CPS can be better protected from attacks and maintain both security and operational continuity.

11.4.1.4 Determine likelihood and impact

Analyze the probability of each threat exploiting a vulnerability and its potential impact. In the context of CPS, risk assessment involves evaluating the likelihood of threats and their potential impacts, which is crucial for securing interconnected cyber and physical environments. Determining likelihood and impact begins by assessing potential vulnerabilities in a system's cyber and physical layers. The likelihood is influenced by the system's exposure to cyberattacks, such as those exploiting weak points in communication protocols or software vulnerabilities. For example, an attack's likelihood might increase if the system lacks robust authentication mechanisms. Impact assessment evaluates the severity of an event if a vulnerability is exploited, considering the effects on confidentiality, integrity, and availability of both cyber and physical elements [85]. These factors are crucial in prioritizing risks; high-likelihood, high-impact threats, such as critical infrastructure failures, require immediate attention. New methodologies like the cyber loss of protection analysis (CPS LOPA) integrate security and safety to ensure dependable system design [85].

11.4.1.5 Prioritize risks

Rank risks based on severity, focusing on the most critical ones for mitigation. In modern CPS, risk assessment involves several critical steps, with risk prioritization as a key component. The first step is identifying and assessing potential risks, including cyber and physical threats, which could harm system integrity, confidentiality, or availability. Once identified, risks are analyzed for potential impacts on system functionality, safety, and data security. The risk prioritization process then considers the likelihood of these threats occurring and the severity of their consequences. This step often involves using a risk matrix to rank risks based on their likelihood and potential impact. Prioritizing risks based on their severity and the resources needed to address them is essential. This involves a risk matrix, where risks are rated on their likelihood and potential damage. Cyber threats that could cause significant disruption, such as attacks targeting critical medical devices or industrial control systems, typically demand more urgent attention. The prioritization helps guide decisions about where to allocate resources for mitigation efforts, such as implementing stronger access controls, more frequent updates, or additional personnel training.

Focusing on high-priority risks that could disrupt critical operations or lead to significant financial or reputational losses is essential for CPS. Risk mitigation measures, such as deploying encryption, firewalls, and intrusion detection systems, are implemented to address these prioritized threats. Monitoring and reevaluation are necessary to ensure the system adapts to evolving threats. These assessments are foundational for building resilient, secure CPS that can withstand cyber and physical vulnerabilities.

11.4.2 The threat modeling in cyber-physical systems

In CPS, threat modeling is essential to identifying and mitigating risks to the interconnected digital and physical components that control critical infrastructure, such as power grids, transportation, and healthcare systems. CPS threat modeling involves understanding the system's architecture and data flow and identifying assets, potential threats, vulnerabilities, and security requirements. Given CPS's reliance on sensors, actuators, and networks, threats can arise from both cyber and physical domains, making considering a wide range of attack vectors crucial.

The threat modeling process in CPS typically involves defining potential adversaries (e.g., hackers, insider threats, or state-sponsored actors),

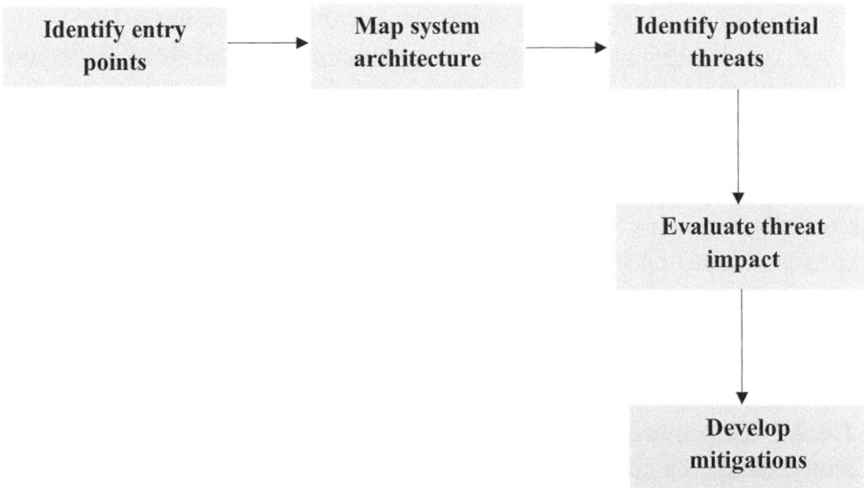

Figure 11.5 The general steps of threat modeling in cyber-physical systems

assessing their capabilities and motives, and determining likely attack paths. Common threats include denial of service, data breaches, sensor manipulation, and malicious software that can disrupt operations or cause safety hazards. This approach enables designers to prioritize security measures based on risk and impact. By evaluating and addressing these threats early in the design phase, CPS threat modeling helps enhance resilience, ensuring that systems remain secure and reliable despite evolving cyber and physical threats. Threat modeling is a structured approach to identifying and evaluating potential threats to a CPS. This process focuses on understanding possible attack vectors, the pathways through which attackers could breach security, and what protections are in place or needed. Figure 11.5 shows the general steps of threat modeling in CPSs. The general steps in threat modeling as described as follows.

11.4.2.1 Identify entry points

Determine where an attacker could gain access (e.g., network access points). Identifying entry points for threat modeling in CPS requires a multifaceted approach, especially given the interconnected nature of physical and digital components. Key entry points include system architecture, data flows, and the interactions between cyber and physical elements. Analyzing data flows, for instance, can reveal vulnerabilities at interfaces, where communication between subsystems might be susceptible to attacks such as spoofing, tampering, or denial of service. Frameworks like STRIDE and common vulnerability scoring system (CVSS) are commonly used to classify and assess these threats.

Modeling tools like attack trees and discrete event systems (DES) simulation enable structured analysis by visualizing potential threat paths and simulating attack scenarios, allowing cybersecurity teams to predict and mitigate impacts on CPS safety. For example, a DES-based model can simulate the propagation of an attack through CPS layers, assessing the impact on both physical processes and cyber responses, as demonstrated in research on autonomous systems [86]. Testbed environments are also essential for safe experimentation, enabling security evaluations without affecting live systems. These testbeds can simulate CPS environments for validating controls, training personnel, and testing intrusion prevention and detection systems, which strengthens preparedness for real-world cyber threats [87].

11.4.2.2 Map system architecture

Create a detailed model of CPS architecture, including communication paths, data flows, and device relationships. The map system architecture in modern CPS is crucial for threat modeling, identifying, and mitigating vulnerabilities within interconnected physical and digital infrastructures. CPS typically integrates hardware, software, and network components to manage and monitor physical processes like industrial systems and smart cities in real-time environments. These systems are prone to security threats due to their complex interdependencies and open connectivity.

Threat modeling for CPS involves using frameworks like STRIDE and data flow diagrams (DFDs) to map potential attack vectors and their impact on system components. By defining critical nodes (sensors, gateways, and central control units) within a CPS, these methods assess risks related to data transmission, control processes, and environmental interaction. Recent methodologies emphasize combining threat models to address CPS-specific challenges like physical tampering and cross-system malware propagation. Tools like the generic modeling environment (GME) allow for domain-specific adaptation, automating threat analysis based on model attributes and constraints tailored to CPS architectures (e.g., monitoring wireless communication in sensor networks) [88]. Through this structured approach, the map system architecture supports both threat detection and the design of robust security protocols to ensure resilience against potential cyber-physical threats.

11.4.2.3 Identify potential threats

Use frameworks like STRIDE to categorize threats. In CPS, threat modeling is essential due to the interconnectedness of physical and cyber domains, presenting a range of potential vulnerabilities. Key threats include those targeting data confidentiality, integrity, and availability, which are particularly important as these systems often manage critical infrastructure, such as industrial controls or smart grids. Common threat modeling approaches, like STRIDE or PASTA, identify system-level vulnerabilities and account for both cyber and physical risks, especially when combined with methods like fault tree analysis (FTA) and failure mode and effects analysis (FMEA) for more thorough risk assessments [76]. Physical threats such as sensor tampering or device manipulation pose unique challenges.

Cyberattacks exploiting software vulnerabilities can trigger physical consequences, making safety a top priority. Compromised components can result in system malfunctions, potentially affecting human safety, financial losses, or reputational harm for organizations [89]. Additionally, the adaptability of threat modeling methods varies, impacting their integration within development cycles. Hybrid approaches incorporating safety analysis tend to be more effective for CPS as they comprehensively address cross-domain risks [88]. Understanding and mitigating these multifaceted threats requires a systematic and continuous approach to keep up with evolving system designs and threat landscapes.

11.4.2.4 Evaluate threat impact

Analyze the potential damage each threat could cause. Evaluating threat impact in CPS is critical due to their complex integration of software, hardware, and physical processes, often in high-stakes domains like transportation, energy, and healthcare. Threat modeling in CPS generally combines multiple methods to address diverse threat vectors affecting the cyber and physical layers. For example, methodologies like process for attack simulation and threat analysis (PASTA) provide structured guidance, while combining it with STRIDE and LINDDUN can enhance coverage by accounting for software, hardware, and environmental risks. This hybrid approach helps identify high-impact attack paths and enables recursive analysis from the system level to specific subsystems, a necessity in complex CPS [89]. Cyber-physical threats often propagate through interconnected subsystems, meaning a single compromised component can have cascading effects. Therefore, an impact assessment in CPS must account for dependencies across these subsystems, often using models like attack trees and scenario-based risk assessments. Such methods help prioritize vulnerabilities based on their potential impact, ensuring that defenses are concentrated where they are most critical to overall system resilience [90].

11.4.2.5 Develop mitigations

Create security controls to address identified threats. Mitigating threats in CPS involves a comprehensive approach to threat modeling, integrating methods tailored to these systems' unique cyber and physical vulnerabilities. Methods like STRIDE and LINDDUN are effective in CPS for assessing system confidentiality, integrity, and availability threats. At the same time, the method PASTA is valuable for its adaptability across CPS components, allowing for risk and impact analysis at multiple subsystem levels. By combining methods, analysts can more thoroughly account for both cyber vulnerabilities and physical risks, such as hardware tampering or malware infiltration in CPS components like medical devices or industrial control systems [89], [90]. Given CPS's complex, interconnected nature, an effective mitigation strategy incorporates automation tools for real-time monitoring and threat response. Methods that allow for recursive application across subsystems support continuous security adjustments across the development lifecycle, which is essential for sustaining CPS resilience. Tailoring these methods to organizational needs and incorporating them into development practices, such as Agile, ensures they remain effective and manageable, even for large-scale CPS implementations.

11.5 The Future Directions and Emerging Trends in Cyber-physical Systems

Modern CPSs are evolving rapidly, with emerging trends focusing on advanced integration, security, and societal impact. A key direction involves the incorporation of AI to enhance system autonomy, decision-making, and adaptability. AI integration enables innovations such as predictive maintenance, real-time optimization, and autonomous operation across domains like manufacturing and healthcare. Additionally, blockchain technologies are being explored to ensure secure data sharing and transaction verification within CPS environments. Another significant trend is edge computing, which enables real-time processing closer to data sources. This minimizes latency and supports applications requiring instantaneous feedback, such as autonomous vehicles.

However, it also raises security concerns, driving advancements in encryption, authentication, and intrusion detection systems. Interoperability is becoming increasingly vital, with efforts to establish cross-industry standards that facilitate seamless communication between CPS components. For instance, smart cities and precision agriculture benefit from integrating data from diverse systems like transportation networks and meteorological sensors. Ethical and regulatory challenges are gaining attention, especially in ensuring CPS aligns with societal values while safeguarding against cyber threats. Future developments will likely balance innovation with security, reliability, and inclusivity. Future directions in CPS are driven by integrating artificial intelligence, enhanced cybersecurity, digital twins, and cross-domain interoperability. Here are some emerging trends and their implications:

11.5.1 AI integration and autonomy

AI is increasingly embedded within CPS for decision-making and real-time data processing. For example, AI-driven CPS systems in autonomous vehicles and smart manufacturing allow these systems to adapt to new data, improve response times, and operate independently with minimal human intervention. AI enables predictive maintenance, anomaly detection, and optimization in various sectors, boosting productivity and reducing costs. The integration of AI in CPS is driving transformative advancements, making these systems increasingly autonomous and efficient. AI enables CPS to manage complex tasks by providing advanced cognition, real-time data analysis, and adaptive decision-making.

For instance, AI is critical in fault detection, system optimization, and predictive maintenance, enhancing reliability across healthcare, agriculture, and transportation industries. Emerging trends highlight the role of AI in creating autonomous systems that balance human-in-the-loop interactions and full automation [91]. These systems are designed to self-adapt, reconfigure, and mitigate faults without human intervention. For example, AI ensures situational awareness and real-time response to environmental changes in autonomous vehicles. Similarly, CPS integrated with AI in healthcare supports remote monitoring and adaptive care for the elderly, enhancing safety and efficiency. Despite these advancements, challenges persist, including ensuring system safety, managing complexity, and addressing trust in AI-driven decisions [92]. Tools like the architecture analysis and design language (AADL) are being developed to ensure fault tolerance and robust system design in safety-critical applications. AI-driven CPS is poised to revolutionize industries by integrating IoT, digital twins, and advanced analytics, fostering more resilient and intelligent systems [93].

11.5.2 Digital twins

One prominent trend is digital twins, which create virtual models of physical systems to simulate real-time data, predict future scenarios, and enhance system optimization. This technology is particularly transformative in energy manufacturing, healthcare, and energy fields, enabling real-time monitoring, predictive maintenance, and process optimization to enhance operational efficiency. Digital twins (DTs) are revolutionizing modern CPS by serving as dynamic, virtual counterparts to physical entities. Future directions emphasize integrating emerging technologies like edge computing, AI, and 5G/6G networks to enable real-time synchronization, predictive maintenance, and intelligent decision-making. Trends include leveraging the Internet of digital twins (IoDT) for interconnected virtual twins, facilitating smart city applications, autonomous systems, and advanced manufacturing processes. Enhanced interoperability, security, and privacy mechanisms remain crucial for widespread adoption and scalability in diverse sectors.

11.5.3 Cross-domain interoperability and standardization

Ensuring seamless communication among devices across different sectors is essential for CPS, enabling collaboration across industries like transportation, energy, and smart cities. Industry-specific standards (e.g., HL7 in healthcare) and cross-domain frameworks allow CPS to integrate with diverse systems while meeting regulatory requirements. This approach promotes efficiency and enhances the potential for innovative applications, such as precision agriculture, by integrating meteorology and agricultural CPS data. Cross-domain interoperability and standardization are crucial for advancing CPS, which integrates physical and digital components to create intelligent, interconnected environments. The shift toward system-of-systems frameworks highlights the need for unified data models and standards to enable seamless interaction between diverse components. Standardized approaches, such as model-based systems engineering and ontologies, facilitate communication and data sharing across domains, which are critical for dynamic environments like smart cities, healthcare, and autonomous systems. Emerging trends include the increasing adoption of digital twins, which simulate CPS components to enhance predictability and adaptability.

Advanced machine learning algorithms, particularly deep and transfer learning, are pivotal in optimizing system operations and enabling real-time decision-making. The IoT integration further enriches CPS capabilities by offering enhanced sensor networks and data analysis tools. Simultaneously, robust cybersecurity frameworks are necessary to mitigate risks from interconnected operations, especially given the rapid growth of IoT-based systems. Future directions involve addressing challenges such as scalability, real-time processing, and ensuring interoperability among heterogeneous systems. Initiatives like the Digital Twin Consortium and CPS frameworks underscore the importance of multidisciplinary collaboration to establish standardized protocols for system design and operation [94].

11.5.4 Cybersecurity enhancements

Ensuring cybersecurity is critical as CPS systems become more connected. Cybersecurity trends include securing edge devices, using encryption, implementing intrusion detection, and leveraging network segmentation. These measures protect against malware, data breaches, and physical cyberattacks. Additionally, insider threats are mitigated with strict access controls and cybersecurity training for personnel. Cybersecurity in modern CPS is evolving rapidly to address emerging threats and vulnerabilities. Key trends for 2024 and beyond focus on integrating advanced technologies and adaptive strategies to enhance system resilience and security [95].

AI and ML-based models are becoming central to detecting anomalies, predicting attacks, and automating responses [96], [97]. They enable CPS to defend against threats proactively and pose risks as adversaries exploit these tools to craft sophisticated attacks. With the decentralization of systems and the rise of IoT, Zero Trust models are gaining traction. These require strict identity verification for every access request, bolstering the security of interconnected CPS components. As CPS increasingly relies on cloud-based platforms, secure cloud architectures and regulatory compliance are critical. Addressing cloud vulnerabilities ensures the integrity of CPS operations. Governments and organizations are introducing stringent data privacy and security regulations, such as those concerning AI ethics and critical infrastructure protection, to ensure safe CPS integration [98]. Continuous assessment and mitigation of vulnerabilities across the digital ecosystem are essential. Cybersecurity strategies now prioritize resilience over exhaustive remediation, focusing on maintaining critical operations during attacks [99].

11.5.5 Edge computing and IoT

The move toward edge computing in CPS supports decentralized data processing close to the data source, reducing latency and enhancing response times. This trend is particularly valuable in applications that require immediate feedback, such as autonomous driving and industrial automation. With IoT integration, edge computing also boosts CPS functionality by enabling real-time, localized data analysis without relying heavily on centralized servers [100]. Edge computing and IoT are pivotal in the evolution of modern

CPS, enabling decentralized, efficient, and intelligent interactions between the physical and digital realms. The integration of edge computing with IoT allows data processing at or near the source, reducing latency and enhancing real-time decision-making. Future directions highlight trends like Edge AI, which combines artificial intelligence with edge devices for autonomous operations, and advancements in 5G connectivity, facilitating seamless communication between edge and cloud systems [101].

Emerging trends include blockchain to secure distributed IoT networks, multi-access edge computing to handle growing data volumes, and fog computing, which bridges gaps between cloud and edge. These innovations reshape applications like autonomous systems, smart cities, and healthcare. Additionally, cybersecurity remains a critical focus, as increasing IoT adoption raises risks that require robust defenses. These advancements position CPS as integral to building responsive and resilient digital ecosystems.

11.5.6 Sustainability and energy efficiency

A growing focus is on creating sustainable CPS, particularly through smart grid applications that optimize energy distribution and incorporate renewable resources. These systems improve energy efficiency and align with broader environmental goals by reducing carbon footprints and supporting sustainable urban infrastructure development. Sustainability and energy efficiency are pivotal in shaping the future of CPS. Emerging trends highlight integrating advanced technologies like AI and renewable energy sources to reduce the environmental impact and enhance operational efficiency. For example, AI is being leveraged to optimize energy usage in real-time, particularly in managing complex systems like smart grids and autonomous transportation, reducing carbon footprints and operational costs.

Moreover, CPS designs increasingly incorporate renewable energy solutions, such as integrating solar and wind power, while employing energy storage technologies like batteries to ensure stability. These advancements are complemented by regulatory frameworks mandating sustainability reporting, such as the EU's Corporate Sustainability Reporting Directive, which drives transparency and accountability in energy usage and environmental impacts. The focus on sustainable supply chains and circular economy principles will continue to grow. Companies aim to reduce waste, enhance resource efficiency, and adopt sustainable production practices. Technology like IoT sensors in CPS facilitates monitoring and optimization across industrial processes, contributing to overall sustainability efforts. These trends align with global decarbonization goals, marking a transformative era for CPS in addressing environmental challenges while maintaining technological progress.

These trends indicate a shift toward more adaptive, secure, and interoperable CPS frameworks that can meet the demands of various industries while advancing operational resilience and sustainability. Future directions in modern CPS emphasize seamless AI, IoT, and edge computing integration for real-time decision-making. Key trends include enhancing system resilience, ensuring cybersecurity, leveraging digital twins for predictive analytics, and advancing autonomous systems. Sustainability, ethical AI, and human-CPS collaboration are central to creating smarter, adaptive, and sustainable solutions for industries and society.

11.6 Conclusions and Future Scope

Modern CPSs have revolutionized industries by integrating computation, communication, and control into physical processes. However, this interconnectivity has amplified security and privacy risks, making them critical concerns. Vulnerabilities in CPS can lead to significant consequences, including data breaches, system failures, and physical damage. Ensuring robust security measures and privacy safeguards is essential to protecting sensitive data and critical infrastructures. This requires a multi-faceted approach, combining cryptographic techniques, secure communication protocols, and real-time threat detection systems. Additionally, regulatory frameworks and standards are vital in addressing these challenges. Future research and development in CPS security and privacy can explore various dimensions. Integrating AI and ML models can enhance threat detection, anomaly analysis, and predictive maintenance. Secondly, blockchain technology could provide decentralized and tamper-proof data integrity and access control solutions. Thirdly, advancing hardware security measures, such as trusted execution environments, can mitigate risks at the device level. Further, with the rise of quantum computing, post-quantum cryptographic algorithms need to be developed to counteract emerging threats. Collaboration among researchers, industry stakeholders, and policymakers will be crucial to creating secure and privacy-aware CPS. Education and awareness programs are equally important to equip users and administrators with the knowledge to mitigate risks effectively. By prioritizing proactive measures and innovative solutions, CPS can evolve into more resilient systems, ensuring safety and privacy in increasingly interconnected environments.

References

[1] Molina, E., & Jacob, E. (2018). Software-defined networking in cyber-physical systems: A survey. *Computers & electrical engineering*, *66*, 407–419.

[2] Lee, E. A. (2008, May). Cyber physical systems: Design challenges. In *2008 11th IEEE international symposium on object and component-oriented real-time distributed computing (ISORC)* (pp. 363–369). IEEE.

[3] Sarker, I. H., Janicke, H., Ferrag, M. A., & Abuadbba, A. (2024). Multi-aspect rule-based AI: Methods, taxonomy, challenges and directions toward automation, intelligence and transparent cybersecurity modeling for critical infrastructures. *Internet of Things*, 101110.

[4] Javaid, M., Haleem, A., Singh, R. P., & Suman, R. (2023). An integrated outlook of Cyber–Physical Systems for Industry 4.0: Topical practices, architecture, and applications. *Green Technologies and Sustainability*, *1*(1), 100001.

[5] Rajkumar, R., Lee, I., Sha, L., & Stankovic, J. (2010, June). Cyber-physical systems: the next computing revolution. In *Proceedings of the 47th design automation conference* (pp. 731–736).

[6] Awotunde, J. B., Oguns, Y. J., Amuda, K. A., Nigar, N., Adeleke, T. A., Olagunju, K. M., & Ajagbe, S. A. (2023). Cyber-physical systems security: analysis, opportunities, challenges, and future prospects. *Blockchain for Cybersecurity in Cyber-Physical Systems*, 21–46.

[7] Abikoye, O. C., Bajeh, A. O., Awotunde, J. B., Ameen, A. O., Mojeed, H. A., Abdulraheem, M., ... & Salihu, S. A. (2021). Application of internet of thing and cyber physical system in Industry 4.0 smart manufacturing. In *Emergence of Cyber Physical System and IoT in Smart Automation and Robotics: Computer Engineering in Automation* (pp. 203–217). Cham: Springer International Publishing.

[8] Alvarez-Alvarado, M. S., Apolo-Tinoco, C., Ramirez-Prado, M. J., Alban-Chacón, F. E., Pico, N., Aviles-Cedeno, J., ... & Rengifo, J. (2024). Cyber-physical power systems: A comprehensive review about technologies drivers, standards, and future perspectives. *Computers and Electrical Engineering*, *116*, 109149.

[9] Yaacoub, J. P. A., Salman, O., Noura, H. N., Kaaniche, N., Chehab, A., & Malli, M. (2020). Cyber-physical systems security: Limitations, issues and future trends. *Microprocessors and microsystems*, *77*, 103201.

[10] Kacmarcik, A. N. D. R. E. W., & Prvulovic, M. I. L. O. S. (2024). Securing CPS through Simultaneous Analog Side-Channel Monitoring of Cyber and Physical Domains. *IEEE Access*.

[11] Cai, T., Jia, T., Adepu, S., Li, Y., & Yang, Z. (2023). ADAM: an adaptive DDoS attack mitigation scheme in software-defined cyber-physical system. *IEEE Transactions on Industrial Informatics*, *19*(6), 7802–7813.

[12] Ayo, F. E., Awotunde, J. B., Ogundele, L. A., Solanke, O. O., Brahma, B., Panigrahi, R., & Bhoi, A. K. (2024). Ontology-Based Layered

Rule-Based Network Intrusion Detection System for Cybercrimes Detection. *Knowledge and Information Systems*, 1–38.

[13] Keshk, M., Turnbull, B., Sitnikova, E., Vatsalan, D., & Moustafa, N. (2021). Privacy-preserving schemes for safeguarding heterogeneous data sources in cyber-physical systems. *IEEE Access*, *9*, 55077–55097.

[14] Awotunde, J. B., Adeniyi, A. E., Falola, P. B., Adigun, M. O., Ayo, F. E., Imoize, A. L., & Rodríguez, D. Z. (2024). Cybersecurity in centralized healthcare systems: overview, design framework, challenges, and research trends.

[15] Hu, F., Lu, Y., Vasilakos, A. V., Hao, Q., Ma, R., Patil, Y., ... & Xiong, N. N. (2016). Robust cyber–physical systems: Concept, models, and implementation. *Future generation computer systems*, *56*, 449–475.

[16] Szczepaniuk, E. K., & Szczepaniuk, H. (2024). Cybersecurity Risk Management Framework for Cyber-physical Systems. In *Emerging Trends for Securing Cyber Physical Systems and the Internet of Things* (pp. 114–134). CRC Press.

[17] Möller, D. P. (2023). NIST cybersecurity framework and MITRE cybersecurity criteria. In *Guide to Cybersecurity in Digital Transformation: Trends, Methods, Technologies, Applications and Best Practices* (pp. 231–271). Cham: Springer Nature Switzerland.

[18] Jimoh, R. G., Awotunde, J. B., Ogundokun, R. O., & Adeoti, D. S. (2024). A randomized encryption algorithm for the MPEG-DASH digital rights management. *Information Security Journal: A Global Perspective*, 1–13.

[19] Jan, M. A., Khan, F., Khan, R., Mastorakis, S., Menon, V. G., Alazab, M., & Watters, P. (2020). Lightweight mutual authentication and privacy-preservation scheme for intelligent wearable devices in industrial-CPS. *IEEE transactions on industrial informatics*, *17*(8), 5829–5839.

[20] Domingo-Ferrer, J., Farras, O., Ribes-González, J., & Sánchez, D. (2019). Privacy-preserving cloud computing on sensitive data: A survey of methods, products and challenges. *Computer Communications*, *140*, 38–60.

[21] Awotunde, J. B., Imoize, A. L., Adeniyi, E. A., AbdulRaheem, M., Oladipo, I. D., Jimoh, R. G., & Falola, P. B. (2023). Artificial intelligence-enabled security systems for 6G wireless networks: algorithms, strategies, and applications.

[22] Himeur, Y., Ghanem, K., Alsalemi, A., Bensaali, F., & Amira, A. (2021). Artificial intelligence based anomaly detection of energy consumption in buildings: A review, current trends and new perspectives. *Applied Energy*, *287*, 116601.

[23] Awotunde, J. B., Gaber, T., Prasad, L. N., Folorunso, S. O., & Lalitha, V. L. (2023). Privacy and security enhancement of smart cities using hybrid deep learning-enabled blockchain. *Scalable Computing: Practice and Experience*, *24*(3), 561–584.

[24] Pundir, A., Singh, S., Kumar, M., Bafila, A., & Saxena, G. J. (2022). Cyber-physical systems enabled transport networks in smart cities: Challenges and enabling technologies of the new mobility era. *IEEE Access*, *10*, 16350–16364.

[25] Atıcı, S., & Tuna, G. (2025). Impact of cybersecurity attacks on electrical system operation. In *Cyber Security Solutions for Protecting and Building the Future Smart Grid* (pp. 117–160). Elsevier.

[26] Li, Y., & Liu, Q. (2021). A comprehensive review study of cyber-attacks and cyber security; Emerging trends and recent developments. *Energy Reports*, *7*, 8176–8186.

[27] Alguliyev, R., Imamverdiyev, Y., & Sukhostat, L. (2018). Cyber-physical systems and their security issues. *Computers in Industry*, *100*, 212–223.

[28] Ten, C. W., Liu, C. C., & Manimaran, G. (2008). Vulnerability assessment of cybersecurity for SCADA systems. *IEEE Transactions on Power Systems*, *23*(4), 1836–1846.

[29] Coffey, K., Smith, R., Maglaras, L., & Janicke, H. (2018). Vulnerability analysis of network scanning on SCADA systems. *Security and Communication Networks*, *2018*(1), 3794603.

[30] Malik, M. I., Ibrahim, A., Hannay, P., & Sikos, L. F. (2023). Developing resilient cyber-physical systems: a review of state-of-the-art malware detection approaches, gaps, and future directions. *Computers*, *12*(4), 79.

[31] Adeniyi, A. E., Jimoh, R. G., & Awotunde, J. B. (2024). A systematic review on elliptic curve cryptography algorithm for internet of things: Categorization, application areas, and security. *Computers and Electrical Engineering*, *118*, 109330.

[32] Kayan, H., Nunes, M., Rana, O., Burnap, P., & Perera, C. (2022). Cybersecurity of industrial cyber-physical systems: A review. *ACM Computing Surveys (CSUR)*, *54*(11s), 1–35.

[33] Ribas Monteiro, L. F., Rodrigues, Y. R., & Zambroni de Souza, A. C. (2023). Cybersecurity in Cyber–Physical Power Systems. *Energies*, *16*(12), 4556.

[34] AbdulRaheem, M., Oladipo, I. D., Imoize, A. L., Awotunde, J. B., Lee, C. C., Balogun, G. B., & Adeoti, J. O. (2024). Machine learning assisted snort and zeek in detecting DDoS attacks in software-defined networking. *International Journal of Information Technology*, *16*(3), 1627–1643.

[35] Al-Mhiqani, M. N., Alsboui, T., Al-Shehari, T., hameed Abdulkareem, K., Ahmad, R., & Mohammed, M. A. (2024). Insider threat detection in cyber-physical systems: a systematic literature review. *Computers and Electrical Engineering*, *119*, 109489.

[36] Djenna, A., Harous, S., & Saidouni, D. E. (2021). Internet of things meet internet of threats: New concern cyber security issues of critical cyber infrastructure. *Applied Sciences*, *11*(10), 4580.

[37] Khalaf, M., Ayad, A., Tushar, M. H. K., Kassouf, M., & Kundur, D. (2024). A Survey on Cyber-Physical Security of Active Distribution Networks in Smart Grids. *IEEE Access*.

[38] Sun, Y., Lo, F. P. W., & Lo, B. (2019). Security and privacy for the internet of medical things enabled healthcare systems: A survey. *IEEE Access*, *7*, 183339–183355.

[39] AbdulRaheem, M., Awotunde, J. B., Chakraborty, C., Adeniyi, E. A., Oladipo, I. D., & Bhoi, A. K. (2023). Security and privacy concerns in smart healthcare system. In *Implementation of Smart Healthcare Systems using AI, IoT, and Blockchain* (pp. 243–273). Academic Press.

[40] Sheikh, Z. A., Singh, Y., Singh, P. K., & Ghafoor, K. Z. (2022). Intelligent and secure framework for critical infrastructure (CPS): Current trends, challenges, and future scope. *Computer Communications*, *193*, 302–331.

[41] Gubbi, K. S., & Murthy, J. S. (2024). CloudSec Dynamics: Safeguarding Interconnected Realms–From Cyber-Physical Systems to Vehicular Networks in the Cloud Age. In *Cloud Security* (pp. 275–295). Chapman and Hall/CRC.

[42] Amin, S. M. (2010). Securing the electricity grid. *The Bridge*, *40*(1), 19–20.

[43] Muir, A., & Lopatto, J. (2004). Final report on the August 14, 2003 blackout in the United States and Canada: causes and recommendations.

[44] Eun, Y. S., & Aßmann, J. S. (2016). Cyberwar: Taking stock of security and warfare in the digital age. *International Studies Perspectives*, *17*(3), 343–360.

[45] Jbair, M., Ahmad, B., Maple, C., & Harrison, R. (2022). Threat modelling for industrial cyber physical systems in the era of smart manufacturing. *Computers in Industry*, *137*, 103611.

[46] Duo, W., Zhou, M., & Abusorrah, A. (2022). A survey of cyber attacks on cyber physical systems: Recent advances and challenges. *IEEE/CAA Journal of Automatica Sinica*, *9*(5), 784–800.

[47] Xu, Z., & Baykal-Gürsoy, M. (2022). Power allocation for cooperative jamming against a strategic eavesdropper over parallel channels. *IEEE Transactions on Information Forensics and Security*, *18*, 846–858.

[48] Humayed, A., Lin, J., Li, F., & Luo, B. (2017). Cyber-physical systems security—A survey. *IEEE Internet of Things Journal*, *4*(6), 1802–1831.
[49] Hammoudeh, M., Epiphaniou, G., & Pinto, P. (2023). Cyber-physical systems: security threats and countermeasures. *Journal of Sensor and Actuator Networks*, *12*(1), 18.
[50] Sharma, M. (2024, January). Enhancing Security and Privacy in Cyber-Physical Systems: Challenges and Solutions. In *2024 IEEE 14th Annual Computing and Communication Workshop and Conference (CCWC)* (pp. 0682–0686). IEEE.
[51] Ashibani, Y., & Mahmoud, Q. H. (2017). Cyber physical systems security: Analysis, challenges and solutions. *Computers & Security*, *68*, 81–97.
[52] Huang, S., Poskitt, C. M., & Shar, L. K. (2024). Security Modelling for Cyber-Physical Systems: A Systematic Literature Review. *arXiv preprint arXiv:2404.07527.*
[53] Wurm, J., Jin, Y., Liu, Y., Hu, S., Heffner, K., Rahman, F., & Tehranipoor, M. (2016). Introduction to cyber-physical system security: A cross-layer perspective. *IEEE Transactions on Multi-Scale Computing Systems*, *3*(3), 215–227.
[54] Zhang, T., Shi, S., Rahman, M. H., Varshney, N., Kulkarni, A., Farahmandi, F., & Tehranipoor, M. (2024). INSPECT: Investigating Supply Chain and Cyber-Physical Security of Battery Systems. *Cryptology ePrint Archive*.
[55] Klein, G., & Zwilling, M. (2024). The weakest link: employee cyber-defense behaviors while working from home. *Journal of Computer Information Systems*, *64*(3), 408–422.
[56] Mazhar, T., Shah, S. F. A., Inam, S. A., Awotunde, J. B., Saeed, M. M., & Hamam, H. (2024). Analysis of integration of IoMT with blockchain: issues, challenges and solutions. *Discover Internet of Things*, *4*(1), 1–36.
[57] Yu, Z., Gao, H., Cong, X., Wu, N., & Song, H. H. (2023). A Survey on Cyber–Physical Systems Security. *IEEE Internet of Things Journal*, *10*(24), 21670–21686.
[58] Ayo, F. E., Awotunde, J. B., Folorunso, S. O., Panigrahi, R., Garg, A., & Bhoi, A. K. (2024). Bot-FFX: A Robust and Efficient Framework for Fast Flux Botnet (FFB) Detection. *Wireless Personal Communications*, 1–24.
[59] Al Homoud, L., Davis, K., Hossain-McKenzie, S., & Jacobs, N. (2024, April). CyberDep: Towards the Analysis of Cyber-Physical Power System Interdependencies Using Bayesian Networks and Temporal

Data. In *2024 IEEE Kansas Power and Energy Conference (KPEC)* (pp. 1–6). IEEE.

[60] Möller, D. P., & Möller, D. P. (2016). Introduction to cyber-physical systems. *Guide to Computing Fundamentals in Cyber-Physical Systems: Concepts, Design Methods, and Applications*, 81–139.

[61] Guo, L. (2024). IoT-enabled Adaptive Control Systems for Cyber-Physical Security in Autonomous Vehicles. *Journal of Artificial Intelligence Research and Applications*, *4*(1), 260–283.

[62] Habibzadeh, H., Nussbaum, B. H., Anjomshoa, F., Kantarci, B., & Soyata, T. (2019). A survey on cybersecurity, data privacy, and policy issues in cyber-physical system deployments in smart cities. *Sustainable Cities and Society*, *50*, 101660.

[63] Simonthomas, S., Subramanian, R., & Balakrishnan, S. (2024). A Novel Approach For Enhancing Cyber Physical System Security And Attack Detection Techniques In Smart Grid System. *Nanotechnology Perceptions*, 277–315.

[64] Jiang, Y., Rezazadeh Baee, M. A., Simpson, L. R., Gauravaram, P., Pieprzyk, J., Zia, T., ... & Le, Z. (2024). Pervasive User Data Collection from Cyberspace: Privacy Concerns and Countermeasures. *Cryptography*, *8*(1), 5.

[65] Darbar, A., Reddy, A. S. K., Lohith, P. V. S. N., Kumar, P. S., & Tata, R. K. (2024, August). A Study on Automating SOS Alerts for Unauthorized Access Detection and Home Security. In *2024 Second International Conference on Intelligent Cyber Physical Systems and Internet of Things (ICoICI)* (pp. 524–527). IEEE.

[66] Isakov, A., Urozov, F., Abduzhapporov, S., & Isokova, M. (2024). Enhancing Cybersecurity: Protecting Data In The Digital Age. *Innovations in Science and Technologies*, *1*(1), 40–49.

[67] Ojo, B., Ogborigbo, J. C., & Okafor, M. O. (2024). Innovative solutions for critical infrastructure resilience against cyber-physical attacks. *World Journal of Advanced Research and Reviews*, *22*(03), 1651–1674.

[68] Mallick, M. A. I., & Nath, R. (2024). Navigating the Cyber security Landscape: A Comprehensive Review of Cyber-Attacks, Emerging Trends, and Recent Developments. *World Scientific News*, *190*(1), 1–69.

[69] Çetinkaya, Ş., & Terzi, S. (2024). Analysing the Effects of Cyber Security on National Security from a Realist Perspective:" Stuxnet" Example. *Güvenlik Çalışmaları Dergisi*, *26*(1), 38–51.

[70] Gaggero, G. B., Armellin, A., Portomauro, G., & Marchese, M. (2024). Industrial Control System-Anomaly Detection Dataset (ICS-ADD) for

Cyber-Physical Security Monitoring in Smart Industry Environments. *IEEE Access*.

[71] Falola, P. B., Adeniyi, E. A., Awotunde, J. B., Jimoh, R. G., & Imoize, A. L. (2023). Security challenges and prospects of 6G network in cloud environments.

[72] Noor, M. M., Selamat, A., Husain, N. A., & Krejcar, O. (2024). Security and Safety in Cyber-Physical System (CPS): An Inclusive Threat Model. *Journal of Advanced Research in Applied Sciences and Engineering Technology*, *40*(2), 176–202.

[73] Abdelkader, S., Amissah, J., Kinga, S., Mugerwa, G., Emmanuel, E., Mansour, D. E. A., ... & Prokop, L. (2024). Securing modern power systems: Implementing comprehensive strategies to enhance resilience and reliability against cyber-attacks. *Results in Engineering*, 102647.

[74] Jimmy, F. N. U. (2024). Cyber security Vulnerabilities and Remediation Through Cloud Security Tools. *Journal of Artificial Intelligence General science (JAIGS) ISSN: 3006–4023*, *2*(1), 129–171.

[75] Saßnick, O., Rosenstatter, T., Schäfer, C., & Huber, S. (2024, May). STRIDE-based Methodologies for Threat Modeling of Industrial Control Systems: A Review. In *2024 IEEE 7th International Conference on Industrial Cyber-Physical Systems (ICPS)* (pp. 1–8). IEEE.

[76] Jamil, A. M., Ben Othmane, L., & Valani, A. (2021, November). Threat modeling of cyber-physical systems in practice. In *International Conference on Risks and Security of Internet and Systems* (pp. 3–19). Cham: Springer International Publishing.

[77] Zahid, S., Mazhar, M. S., Abbas, S. G., Hanif, Z., Hina, S., & Shah, G. A. (2023). Threat modeling in smart firefighting systems: Aligning MITRE ATT&CK matrix and NIST security controls. *Internet of Things*, *22*, 100766.

[78] Yousaf, A., Amro, A., Kwa, P. T. H., Li, M., & Zhou, J. (2024). Cyber risk assessment of cyber-enabled autonomous cargo vessel. *International Journal of Critical Infrastructure Protection*, *46*, 100695.

[79] Badawy, M., Sherief, N. H., & Abdel-Hamid, A. A. (2024). Legacy ICS Cybersecurity Assessment Using Hybrid Threat Modeling—An Oil and Gas Sector Case Study. *Applied Sciences*, *14*(18), 8398.

[80] Amro, A., Gkioulos, V., & Katsikas, S. (2023). Assessing cyber risk in cyber-physical systems using the ATT&CK framework. *ACM Transactions on Privacy and Security*, *26*(2), 1–33.

[81] Saxena, N., Hayes, E., Bertino, E., Ojo, P., Choo, K. K. R., & Burnap, P. (2020). Impact and key challenges of insider threats on organizations and critical businesses. *Electronics*, *9*(9), 1460.

[82] Rosado, D. G., Santos-Olmo, A., Sánchez, L. E., Serrano, M. A., Blanco, C., Mouratidis, H., & Fernández-Medina, E. (2022). Managing cybersecurity risks of cyber-physical systems: The MARISMA-CPS pattern. *Computers in Industry*, *142*, 103715.

[83] Northern, B., Burks, T., Hatcher, M., Rogers, M., & Ulybyshev, D. (2021). Vercasm-cps: Vulnerability analysis and cyber risk assessment for cyber-physical systems. *Information*, *12*(10), 408.

[84] Aslan, Ö., Aktuğ, S. S., Ozkan-Okay, M., Yilmaz, A. A., & Akin, E. (2023). A comprehensive review of cyber security vulnerabilities, threats, attacks, and solutions. *Electronics*, *12*(6), 1333.

[85] Tantawy, A., Abdelwahed, S., & Erradi, A. (2022). Cyber lopa: An integrated approach for the design of dependable and secure cyber-physical systems. *IEEE Transactions on Reliability*, *71*(2), 1075–1091.

[86] Serru, T., Nguyen, N., Batteux, M., & Rauzy, A. (2022). Modeling cyberattack propagation and impacts on cyber-physical system safety: An experiment. *Electronics*, *12*(1), 77.

[87] Shevchenko, N., Chick, T. A., O'Riordan, P., Scanlon, T. P., & Woody, C. (2018). Threat modeling: a summary of available methods. *Software Engineering Institute| Carnegie Mellon University.*

[88] Martins, G., Bhatia, S., Koutsoukos, X., Stouffer, K., Tang, C., & Candell, R. (2015, August). Towards a systematic threat modeling approach for cyber-physical systems. In *2015 Resilience Week (RWS)* (pp. 1–6). IEEE.

[89] Shevchenko, N., Frye, B. R., & Woody, C. (2018). Threat modeling for cyber-physical system-of-systems: Methods evaluation. *Software Engineering Institute: Pittsburgh, PA, USA.*

[90] Shevchenko, N. (2019, February). *Evaluating threat modeling methods for cyber-physical systems.*

[91] Radanliev, P., De Roure, D., Van Kleek, M., Santos, O., & Ani, U. (2021). Artificial intelligence in cyber physical systems. *AI & society*, *36*, 783–796.

[92] Oliveira, L. M., Dias, R., Rebello, C. M., Martins, M. A., Rodrigues, A. E., Ribeiro, A. M., & Nogueira, I. B. (2021). Artificial intelligence and cyber-physical systems: A review and perspectives for the future in the chemical industry. *AI*, *2*(3), 27.

[93] Mhapsekar, R. U., Umrani, M. I., Faizan, M., Ali, O., & Abraham, L. (2024). Building Trust in AI-Driven Decision Making for Cyber-Physical Systems (CPS): A Comprehensive Review. *arXiv preprint arXiv:2405.06347.*

[94] Chui, K. T., Gupta, B. B., Liu, J., Arya, V., Nedjah, N., Almomani, A., & Chaurasia, P. (2023). A survey of internet of things and cyber-physical systems: standards, algorithms, applications, security, challenges, and future directions. *Information*, *14*(7), 388.

[95] Akinsanya, M. O., Ekechi, C. C., & Okeke, C. D. (2024). The evolution of cyber resilience frameworks in network security: a conceptual analysis. *Computer Science & IT Research Journal*, *5*(4), 926–949.

[96] Ajibade, S. S. M., Alhassan, G. N., Zaidi, A., Oki, O. A., Awotunde, J. B., Ogbuju, E., & Akintoye, K. A. (2024). Evolution of machine learning applications in medical and healthcare analytics research: A bibliometric analysis. *Intelligent Systems with Applications*, 200441.

[97] Adeniyi, A. E., Jimoh, R. G., & Awotunde, J. B. (2024). A systematic review on elliptic curve cryptography algorithm for internet of things: Categorization, application areas, and security. *Computers and Electrical Engineering*, *118*, 109330.

[98] Volk, M. (2024). A safer future: Leveraging the AI power to improve the cybersecurity in critical infrastructures. *Electrotechnical Review/ Elektrotehniski Vestnik*, *91*(3).

[99] Petrovic, N., & Jovanovic, A. (2023). Towards Resilient Cyber Infrastructure: Optimizing Protection Strategies with AI and Machine Learning in Cybersecurity Paradigms. *International Journal of Information and Cybersecurity*, *7*(12), 44–60.

[100] Cao, K., Hu, S., Shi, Y., Colombo, A. W., Karnouskos, S., & Li, X. (2021). A survey on edge and edge-cloud computing assisted cyber-physical systems. *IEEE Transactions on Industrial Informatics*, *17*(11), 7806–7819.

[101] Sánchez, J. M. G., Jörgensen, N., Törngren, M., Inam, R., Berezovskyi, A., Feng, L., ... & Tan, K. (2022). Edge computing for cyber-physical systems: A systematic mapping study emphasizing trustworthiness. *ACM Transactions on Cyber-Physical Systems (TCPS)*, *6*(3), 1–28.

12

The Ethics of Security and Privacy of Cyber-physical Systems: Emerging Trends, Technology, and Applications

Richard Govada Joshua[1], Peter Anuoluwapo Gbadega[2], Samuel Oluwatobi Tofade[3] and Agbotiname Lucky Imoize[4]

[1]Comprobase Inc, United States
[2]Department of Electrical and Electronic Engineering Science, University of Johannesburg, South Africa
[3]CleanTech Renewable Energy, Nigeria
[4]Department of Electrical and Electronics Engineering, Faculty of Engineering, University of Lagos, Nigeria

Email: joshuarichardgovada@ieee.org; perosman4real1987@gmail.com; tofade.samuel@gmail.com; aimoize@unilag.edu.ng

Abstract

Cyber-physical systems (CPS) are becoming indispensable across industries such as healthcare and energy, but their security and privacy vulnerabilities pose critical ethical issues. This study investigates these concerns, identifying three main types of security threats: hardware, software, and network attacks. Hardware attacks target physical components like sensors, compromising data integrity through direct or remote manipulation. Network threats, such as man-in-the-middle and denial-of-service (DoS) attacks, disrupt data transmission and critical system operations. Software vulnerabilities often arise from malicious code injections in CPS devices, particularly affecting machine learning (ML) algorithms used for data processing. Privacy is equally crucial, especially in CPS applications that generate sensitive data, such as healthcare information. This research emphasizes the need for robust data ownership, consent protocols, and legal frameworks to

DOI: 10.1201/9788743801306-12

safeguard user privacy and ensure responsible data sharing. Advanced technologies like ML and blockchain show potential for mitigating these issues. ML algorithms require regular updates with new data to prevent manipulation, while blockchain technology offers a secure, decentralized structure to enhance data transparency and security. This study highlights the necessity for an integrated, end-to-end security and privacy approach for CPS, which is foundational for their reliable use and widespread adoption in critical sectors.

12.1 Introduction

Cyber-physical systems (CPS) combine digital and physical processes to seamlessly integrate networking, computation, and physical components across various disciplines. These systems have ushered in an era of automation, efficiency, and comfort, which oversees everything from medical gadgets to vital infrastructure. With their revolutionary real-time monitoring, decision-making, and control capabilities, CPS has revolutionized several industries, including transportation, healthcare, manufacturing, energy, and defense. However, there are also more risks associated with these developments, especially when it comes to privacy and security ethics. The ethical issues raised by the creation and application of CPS have come under renewed scrutiny as a result of its broad adoption [1]. Due to their intrinsic digital connection, CPSs are vulnerable to a variety of threats, including data exploitation, privacy violations, and cyberattacks. Simultaneously, the development of Internet of Things (IoT) technologies, artificial intelligence (AI), and machine learning (ML) have increased the size and complexity of these systems. The usefulness and intelligence of CPS have greatly increased thanks to these technologies, but they have also opened up new ethical questions, particularly concerning security and privacy.

Security in CPS encompasses the protection of both the digital and physical components of the system from threats such as cyberattacks, unauthorized access, and data breaches. CPSs are often deployed in environments where failure or compromise, such as power grids, autonomous vehicles, and medical devices, can have dire consequences. Thus, securing CPS is not only a technical requirement but also an ethical imperative. Ensuring the reliability and safety of these systems is critical to protecting human lives and maintaining public trust in technology. On the other hand, privacy in CPS pertains to the protection of personal and sensitive data generated and processed by these systems. As CPSs collect vast amounts of data in real time from sensors, cameras, and other devices, questions arise regarding who has access to this data, how it is stored, and for what purposes it is used [2, 3].

Unauthorized collection, misuse, or breach of personal data can lead to significant ethical violations, particularly when individuals are unaware of the extent of data collection or when their consent has not been adequately obtained. Addressing the ethical concerns surrounding CPS is further complicated by the fact that these systems operate across a wide range of industries, each with its own unique security and privacy requirements. For instance, the security needs of CPS in healthcare, where patient data and life-critical devices are involved, differ significantly from the security requirements of CPS in transportation or industrial automation. Similarly, privacy concerns in smart homes and consumer IoT devices vary from those in military or government CPS, where national security may be at stake. Thus, the ethics of security and privacy in CPS must be considered in a context-specific manner [4].

The rapid evolution of cyber-physical systems (CPS), which integrate computational, networking, and physical processes, has revolutionized critical sectors, including healthcare, transportation, energy, and industrial automation. However, alongside these advancements, significant concerns related to the security and privacy of these systems have emerged, necessitating thorough examination. Modern societies have become highly dependent on CPS for essential services. The integration of digital and physical realms means that security breaches or privacy violations in CPS can lead to catastrophic real-world consequences, ranging from economic loss to risks to human safety. With the stakes so high, there is a growing need to safeguard these systems from potential vulnerabilities.

Cyberattacks may jeopardize physical infrastructure security, which is more likely to occur as CPSs get more advanced. Traditional security techniques are no longer adequate to safeguard these networked systems because of the special difficulties in combining the physical and cyber layers. There are emerging new attack vectors, such as AI-driven decision-making, autonomous systems, and connected gadgets (IoT). The goal of this study is to discuss how to protect CPS against these changing risks. CPSs collect and process massive amounts of data, much of which is sensitive or personal. This data is often shared across multiple platforms, leading to concerns about data ownership, consent, and sharing practices. Privacy violations in CPS can have profound implications for individuals and organizations [5, 6]. Understanding how to design CPS with privacy as a core consideration is crucial to maintaining trust in these systems. Beyond technical challenges, the ethical implications of deploying CPS, particularly in areas like AI-driven decision-making and autonomous systems, need to be addressed.

Decisions made by machines in real time can directly affect human lives. There is a growing need to develop frameworks that ensure ethical governance in CPS, transparency, accountability, and fairness. Emerging technologies such as blockchain, artificial intelligence (AI), and machine learning offer new opportunities to improve CPS security and privacy. However, these technologies also introduce new challenges, including algorithmic bias, data security, and ethical AI usage concerns. This study is motivated by the need to explore how these emerging technologies can be harnessed to address the security and privacy concerns of CPS [7].

12.1.1 Ethical imperative of security in cyber-physical systems

Complex networks that combine physical operations and computing algorithms are known as cyber-physical systems. In contrast to conventional information systems, which function only digitally, CPS functions at the nexus of the digital and physical domains. Physical processes can be seen and controlled, frequently in real time, by combining sensors, actuators, and embedded systems. Critical infrastructures, including electricity grids, transportation networks, and industrial control systems, are common places to find these systems. Consumer applications like wearable health gadgets and smart homes are frequently used. The defining feature of CPS is the ability to autonomously make decisions based on data collected from the physical environment. For example, in smart grid applications, CPS can dynamically adjust energy distribution based on real-time consumer and power generator data. Similarly, in healthcare, CPS can monitor patients' vital signs and adjust life-support systems as needed. This autonomous decision-making capability highlights the importance of ensuring that CPSs are secure and that the data they generate is kept private and used ethically [8, 9].

The security of CPS is a multifaceted issue that encompasses both physical and cyber threats. Physical components of CPS, such as sensors, actuators, and control systems, are susceptible to manipulation, tampering, or physical damage, which can have catastrophic effects. On the cyber side, CPSs are vulnerable to various forms of attacks, including denial-of-service (DoS), malware infections, and unauthorized access. The impact of these cyberattacks on CPS can be far-reaching, potentially disrupting critical services, causing economic losses, and even endangering human lives. From an ethical perspective, the security of CPS is tied to the duty to protect the public from harm. CPS are often deployed in environments where failure can result in loss of life, physical damage, or significant disruption to society. For instance, a cyberattack on a smart grid could cause widespread blackouts, impacting hospitals, transportation, and other essential services. Similarly, an attack on autonomous vehicles could lead to accidents and fatalities [10].

Ensuring that CPSs are resilient to attacks and can operate safely even in the presence of malicious activity is, therefore, a critical ethical responsibility for developers, operators, and regulators. However, ensuring security in CPS is not without its challenges. CPS are often designed to operate in distributed environments, with components located in different physical locations and connected through public or private networks. This distributed nature makes it difficult to monitor and secure every component of the system. Furthermore, many CPSs are deployed in resource-constrained environments with limited computational power, memory, and bandwidth. As a result, traditional security mechanisms, such as encryption and firewalls, may not be feasible. Accountability is a further ethical consideration regarding CPS security. It might be challenging to identify the perpetrator of a security breach. Device makers, network operators, and service providers are just a few of the many parties involved in CPS, and each may have varying degrees of control over the system. It is crucial to establish clear lines of accountability to ensure that security breaches are appropriately handled and that the people who caused the breach are held accountable [11, 12].

12.1.2 Privacy concerns in cyber-physical systems

Privacy is concerned with safeguarding the sensitive and personal information that CPS generates and processes, whereas security is concentrated on defending the CPS against outside attacks. Many CPSs gather a lot of personal data from people, especially those that are utilized in consumer applications. Information regarding a person's location, routines, health, and interactions with their surroundings may be included in this data. Significant ethical questions are raised by the gathering and use of this data, especially when people are not informed about the scope of the collection or when their consent has not been acquired [13]. The continuous and real-time collection of data in CPS frequently makes privacy concerns worse. For instance, during the day, an individual's activities, habits, and preferences may be recorded by smart home devices. Likewise, information on a person's heart rate, amount of exercise, and sleeping habits may be gathered by wearable medical technology. Constantly gathering data can result in comprehensive profiles of people that can be utilized for nefarious, as well as beneficial purposes.

One of the key ethical concerns related to privacy in CPS is the issue of consent. In many cases, individuals may not be fully aware of the extent of data collection or how their data are being used [14]. For example, individuals may consent to the collection of data for a specific purpose, such as monitoring their energy usage, without realizing that their data may also be used for other purposes, such as targeted advertising or selling to third parties. Ensuring that individuals are fully informed about the data collection process and that their consent is obtained is a critical ethical responsibility for CPS developers and operators. Data ownership and control are further privacy concerns in CPS. A lot of the time, third-party service providers who can have different privacy practices than the individual collect and keep the data created by CPS. This poses the question of who is entitled to access the data and who owns it. After personal data has been gathered, people can lose control over it, which can result in misuse or unwanted access. Moreover, privacy issues may arise from data sharing between many CPS stakeholders and components. For instance, governmental organizations, utility corporations, and other third parties may receive access to the data gathered by a smart grid system. Protecting people's privacy and averting data breaches require making sure that data are shared securely and privately [15, 16].

12.1.3 Emerging trends in CPS security and privacy

The security and privacy issues that CPSs deal with are always changing. The use of machine learning (ML) and artificial intelligence (AI) to quickly identify and address security issues is one of the major new trends in CPS security. A security breach may be indicated by patterns and abnormalities in the massive volumes of data created by CPS, which can be analyzed using AI and ML. AI can be used, for instance, to track down indications of a denial-of-service attack in network traffic or to spot anomalous activity in CPS components that would point to manipulation. Blockchain technology is another new development that is being used to improve CPS security and privacy [17].

Blockchain is a desirable option for safeguarding CPS data because it offers a decentralized, tamper-proof database for recording transactions. Blockchain, for instance, can be used to protect the integrity of data gathered by CPS sensors from unwanted manipulation or change. Blockchain can also be used to enable data sharing between various CPS stakeholders and components securely and privately. One of the main new developments in privacy is the use of technologies that safeguard sensitive data while enabling data analysis, such as homomorphic encryption and differential privacy. The privacy of individuals is protected while yet allowing insightful conclusions to be drawn from the data thanks to these technologies, which enable data to be examined in aggregate without disclosing individual data points [18, 19].

12.1.4 Key contributions of the chapter

The key contributions of this chapter are as follows:

1. A comprehensive review of the ethical challenges in securing CPS and ensuring privacy

   A comprehensive review of the ethical challenges in securing cyber-physical systems (CPS) and ensuring privacy delves into the moral complexities and responsibilities that arise in safeguarding these interconnected systems. As CPS integrates physical and digital components, such as healthcare devices, transportation networks, and smart grids, the ethical stakes are high. This review examines key issues like data ownership, consent, and the potential for harm from security breaches, which can directly impact individuals' privacy and safety. By identifying and analyzing these ethical challenges, the review highlights the need for a balanced approach to protecting both the functionality of CPS and the rights of individuals, ultimately guiding stakeholders toward more responsible and secure implementations.

2. Investigation of emerging trends and technologies, including AI, blockchain, and privacy-preserving techniques, to enhance the security and privacy of CPS

   The investigation into emerging trends and technologies such as artificial intelligence (AI), blockchain, and privacy-preserving techniques focuses on their potential to strengthen the security and privacy of cyber-physical systems (CPS). AI offers advanced capabilities in real-time monitoring and predictive threat detection, enabling CPS to respond swiftly to potential cyber threats. Blockchain technology, with its decentralized and transparent data management framework, provides a secure way to manage and verify information exchanges within CPS, reducing the risk of data tampering. Additionally, privacy-preserving techniques, like differential privacy, are explored for their ability to protect individual data without compromising the functionality and utility of CPS. By examining these technologies, this investigation aims to identify innovative solutions that can adapt to the evolving security and privacy challenges facing CPS.

3. Discussion of real-world applications of CPS, highlighting ethical dilemmas related to security breaches and privacy violations

   The discussion of real-world applications of cyber-physical systems (CPS) reveals complex ethical dilemmas, particularly when it comes to security breaches and privacy violations. In sectors like healthcare, transportation, and smart cities, CPS integrates physical and digital systems, gathering vast amounts of data to optimize services and improve efficiency. However, this data collection raises serious ethical concerns. For instance, in healthcare, unauthorized access to CPS can lead to data breaches, risking patient confidentiality and potentially jeopardizing lives if medical devices are compromised. Similarly, in smart cities, surveillance systems intended to enhance safety could infringe on personal privacy if data are misused or inadequately protected. These scenarios underscore the need for a careful balance between leveraging CPS for societal benefits and safeguarding individual rights to privacy and security.

4. Exploration of the balance between ensuring the security of CPS and protecting the privacy of individuals and organizations

   Exploring the balance between securing cyber-physical systems (CPS) and protecting individual and organizational privacy is crucial, as both aspects are often at odds. On the one hand, robust security measures are essential to protect CPS from cyber threats that could disrupt operations, cause physical harm, or lead to data breaches. However, heightened security protocols can sometimes encroach on privacy by enabling extensive data collection, surveillance, or restrictive access controls. Finding this balance requires a careful ethical and technical approach, where security measures are strong enough to prevent attacks yet mindful of users' privacy rights. By developing strategies that respect security and privacy, organizations can foster trust and ensure that CPS enhances, rather than infringes upon, the rights of individuals and entities.

12.1.5 Chapter organization

This chapter is structured as follows: Section 12.2 explores the ethical challenges of CPS security, focusing on physical and cyber threats. Section 12.3 delves into the privacy concerns in CPS, discussing issues such as consent, data ownership, and data sharing. Section 12.4 examines emerging technologies and trends in CPS security and privacy, including AI, blockchain, and privacy-preserving techniques. Section 12.5 provides case studies of real-world CPS applications, highlighting ethical dilemmas and potential solutions. Finally, Section 12.6 concludes with recommendations for future research and best practices for addressing the ethical challenges of CPS security and privacy.

12.2 Context and Literature Review

The rapid proliferation of cyber-physical systems (CPS), which integrate computational, physical, and networking elements to create interconnected systems, has significantly transformed various sectors such as healthcare, energy, transportation, and manufacturing. Despite their tremendous benefits, CPSs face growing concerns over security, privacy, and ethical implications. The literature on these topics highlights several key areas of research, including the identification of vulnerabilities, privacy-preserving mechanisms, the role of emerging technologies like blockchain and artificial intelligence (AI), and the ethical considerations of deploying CPS. The security and privacy of CPS are critical challenges that demand a multifaceted approach encompassing technical, legal, and ethical perspectives.

While significant progress has been made in identifying vulnerabilities and proposing mitigation strategies, the rapidly evolving nature of CPS requires continuous innovation in both security technologies and privacy-preserving techniques. Furthermore, addressing the ethical implications of CPS, particularly in the context of AI and autonomous systems, is crucial for ensuring the responsible development and deployment of these systems. This literature review surveys the most relevant studies to date, focusing on the ethical, security, and privacy challenges posed by CPS, as well as the strategies proposed to mitigate them.

12.2.1 Security challenges in cyber-physical systems

Cyber-physical systems are characterized by the tight integration of cyber components (software, data) with physical infrastructure (sensors, actuators). This interconnected nature creates a significant attack surface for malicious entities. Traditional cybersecurity measures, designed for either purely physical or cyber systems, often fall short in CPS due to the interaction between the two domains. A broad body of literature has explored the unique security vulnerabilities in CPS. [20] classify the security threats in CPS into three categories: hardware attacks, software attacks, and network-based attacks. Hardware attacks target physical components, such as sensors or actuators, while software attacks focus on exploiting vulnerabilities in control systems or operating software.

Network-based attacks, such as denial of service (DoS) and man-in-the-middle (MitM) attacks, target the communication channels between system components. Stuxnet, a well-documented case in the literature, illustrates how a cyberattack on a CPS can cause real-world physical damage. In this case, Farwell and Rohozinski [21] highlight the sophistication of the malware, which exploited several zero-day vulnerabilities to control the industrial control systems of an Iranian nuclear facility, causing physical damage to its centrifuges. The Stuxnet attack exposed the potential risks to critical infrastructure posed by inadequately secured CPS. [22] examines the cybersecurity risks associated with the application of AI and machine learning in critical infrastructure sectors such as supply chain management and project management, highlighting how these vulnerabilities could be leveraged for exploitation.

Additionally, we explore how cybersecurity weaknesses in various industries can target AI and machine learning systems, potentially compromising sensitive data and valuable resources. In the context of remote estimation for cyber-physical systems (CPSs), sensor data transmitted via networks can be compromised by adversaries, resulting in potential privacy breaches (such as the exposure of the system's state) and/or the malfunctioning of the remote estimator. [23] propose a chaotic masking protocol aimed at safeguarding the transmission of sensor measurements.

Recent studies have explored the role of autonomous systems and artificial intelligence in expanding the attack surface of CPS. [24] identifies that the increasing reliance on autonomous decision-making in CPS introduces new security risks, particularly in autonomous vehicles, drones, and industrial robots. These systems often rely on sensors and machine learning models that can be manipulated or spoofed to cause unintended physical consequences. Zhou et al. [25] explore how adversarial machine learning can be used to attack AI-driven CPS by subtly altering input data to trick the system into making incorrect decisions. This could have severe consequences in contexts like self-driving cars, where adversarial attacks on the vehicle's sensors could lead to accidents. The ethical challenge of ensuring the security of such systems while allowing them to make autonomous decisions remains an ongoing area of research.

12.2.2 Privacy concerns in CPS

Privacy concerns in CPS arise primarily from the massive amount of data collected by sensors and other input devices. Data ownership, consent, sharing, and storage have become critical areas of concern. Mirchev et al. [26] emphasize the need for clear guidelines on data ownership in CPS. Since these systems often collect sensitive data, such as health information in smart medical devices or geolocation data in autonomous vehicles, determining who owns and controls this data is critical. The absence of well-defined data ownership rights creates ambiguity, particularly when multiple stakeholders are involved, such as manufacturers, service providers, and end users. Wright and Friedewald [27] discuss the implications of pervasive data collection in smart grids, where energy consumption data can be analyzed to infer personal habits.

They argue for greater transparency and user control over the data collected, advocating for policies that enforce the right to be informed and to consent to data usage. Several techniques have been proposed to protect the privacy of data within CPS. Differential privacy is a method frequently cited in the literature, designed to allow statistical analysis of large datasets while protecting the privacy of individuals. Wang et al. [28] present differential privacy as a robust solution for preventing reidentification in datasets by introducing noise into the data, making it difficult for attackers to identify specific individuals. Another promising approach is homomorphic encryption, which allows computations to be performed on encrypted data without needing to decrypt it first. Keshk et al. [29] propose that this method could be used in CPS to ensure that sensitive data are kept secure, even when processed by third-party systems.

Homomorphic encryption can help mitigate risks in smart cities, industrial CPS, and medical CPS, where sensitive data are routinely processed. The ethics of data sharing in CPS also require careful consideration. Jaiman and Urovi [30] suggest that CPS must adopt user-centric models for data sharing, where users have greater control over how their data are shared and with whom. They emphasize that informed consent should be a fundamental principle guiding data sharing in CPS. Ensuring that users understand what data are collected, how it is used, and what risks are involved is critical to maintaining trust in CPS applications.

12.2.3 Emerging technologies in CPS security and privacy

Emerging technologies such as blockchain, artificial intelligence (AI), and machine learning have been increasingly explored as tools to enhance the security and privacy of CPS. Blockchain technology, with its decentralized and immutable ledger, has been proposed as a promising solution for ensuring the integrity and security of data in CPS. Dorri et al. [31] argue that blockchain can mitigate security risks by ensuring tamper-proof data exchanges between CPS components. The decentralized nature of blockchain reduces the risk of a single point of failure, while its cryptographic foundation ensures that data cannot be altered once recorded. In the context of smart grids, Liu et al. [32] highlight how blockchain can enable secure peer-to-peer energy trading while protecting the privacy of energy consumption data. The authors suggest that blockchain can ensure that transactions are transparent and auditable while still maintaining the privacy of individual users.

AI and machine learning have also been investigated as tools for improving the security of CPS. Fei and Shen [33] propose using machine learning algorithms to detect anomalous behavior in CPS, such as unusual patterns in network traffic that may indicate an ongoing attack. AI-driven systems can offer real-time threat detection and response, providing a significant advantage over traditional static security measures. However, as noted by McDermid et al. [34], the use of AI in CPS also introduces ethical concerns, particularly regarding algorithmic bias and the transparency of AI decision-making processes. The black-box nature of many machine learning models can make it difficult to understand how decisions are made, raising questions about accountability when AI-driven systems cause harm.

Comparative analysis from different studies, including the scope, methods, findings, strengths, and limitations, is conducted to critically analyze past literature effectively. Table 12.1 depicts the comparative analysis of past literature on security and privacy in cyber-physical systems.

The bibliometric analysis of The Ethics of Security and Privacy of Cyber-Physical Systems reveals a rising trend in publications, especially in the past decade, reflecting increased academic and industrial interest in the ethical aspects of CPS. Leading countries in this research include the United States, China, and Germany, with substantial contributions from institutions like MIT, Stanford University, and Tsinghua University. The primary focus areas include data privacy, ethical AI in CPS, and regulatory frameworks. Publications are predominantly found in IEEE journals and conferences, underscoring the technology-focused nature of the topic. Figure 12.1 gives the annual publication trends in CPS ethics. Figure 12.2 shows the annual publications by country on CPS ethics. Figure 12.3 provides a network map of keywords based on assumed co-occurrence relationships.

Figure 12.1 depicts the annual publication trends in CPS ethics. This graph shows the yearly publication count on the topic, which shows that the interest in the ethics of security and privacy in cyber-physical systems (CPS) has increased over time. A sharp rise in recent years suggests a growing interest in ethical issues tied to CPS security and privacy. Figure 12.2 shows the annual publications by country on CPS ethics. The chart includes hypothetical data for 10 countries, with countries like the United States, China, and Germany prominently displayed due to their higher publication counts. The bar chart indicates a strong research focus on CPS ethics in the United States, China, and Germany, while other countries like Japan, South Korea, and

Table 12.1 Comparative analysis of past literature on security and privacy in cyber-physical systems.

Ref.	Year	Focus area	Methodology	Key findings	Strengths	Limitations
Squillace et al. [22]	2024	AI and ML vulnerabilities in CPS for supply chain management	Case study analysis	AI and ML systems can be exploited to compromise data and resources	Highlights specific vulnerabilities in critical infrastructure	Limited scope to supply chain and project management
Chen et al. [23]	2024	Privacy and security in CPS remote estimation	Chaotic masking protocol	Chaotic masking enhances the security of sensor data transmission	Offers a novel protocol to protect against adversarial attacks	Requires further validation in real-world scenarios
Fathy et al. [35]	2024	Optimal reactive power dispatch with RER integration	Enhanced Artificial Gorilla Troops Optimizer (EGTO)	Improved voltage profile and system stability under uncertainty	Incorporates stochastic behavior of RERs in optimization	Lack of application in larger, more complex power systems
Wang et al. [36]	2019	Cybersecurity vulnerabilities in smart grids	Simulation-based analysis	Identified major weaknesses in smart grid communication protocols	Comprehensive analysis of smart grid security	Limited focus on communication protocols without hardware integration
Kayan et al. [37]	2022	Security threats in industrial IoT	Risk-based assessment model	Industrial IoT systems are highly vulnerable to cyberattacks	Focuses on practical industry scenarios	It does not address mitigation strategies in detail
Hu et al. [38]	2018	Intrusion detection in CPS networks	Hybrid intrusion detection system (IDS)	Proposed a hybrid IDS combining anomaly and signature-based detection methods to enhance CPS security	Effectively reduces false positives in intrusion detection	Computationally intensive, may be impractical for real-time application
Rahman et al. [39]	2021	Data integrity and confidentiality in CPS	Blockchain-based CPS security	Blockchain technology provides a secure method for maintaining data integrity and confidentiality in CPS networks	High-level security is provided through the blockchain's decentralized nature	High computational power requirements, scalability issues
Genge et al. [40]	2019	Secure communication in industrial CPS	Cryptography and secure communication protocols	Proposes an encryption-based communication protocol to protect sensitive data in industrial CPS	Ensures confidentiality and integrity in industrial environments	High complexity, difficult to implement in resource-constrained systems

(Continued)

Table 12.1 Continued

Ref.	Year	Focus area	Methodology	Key findings	Strengths	Limitations
Adil et al. [41]	2022	Privacy protection in Smart Grid CPS	Differential privacy mechanisms	Differential privacy is effective in protecting user data without compromising system performance in smart grids	Maintains a balance between data utility and privacy	Limited application to smaller smart grid scenarios, needs broader validation
Anand et al. [42]	2020	Security vulnerabilities in autonomous vehicle CPS	Threat model analysis	Identified key vulnerabilities in the communication and control systems of autonomous vehicles	Comprehensive threat model for automotive CPS	Limited focus on mitigation techniques, lacks practical implementation examples
Zhou et al. [43]	2023	Real-time attack detection in CPS	A model-based and data-driven hybrid approach	Model-based methods combined with machine learning improve real-time attack detection accuracy in CPS	High detection rates and low false alarms	High computational cost and data dependency may limit real-world application
Mtukushe et al. [44]	2023	Secure monitoring in industrial CPS	Cyber resilience strategy	A resilient monitoring framework is proposed to enhance the robustness of industrial CPS against cyberattacks	Focuses on enhancing system resiliency and postattack recovery	Needs extensive testing in diverse industrial CPS settings
Raza et al. [45]	2022	Machine learning-based anomaly detection in CPS	Unsupervised learning techniques	Unsupervised machine learning methods outperform traditional techniques in detecting anomalies in CPS	Reduced reliance on labeled data, adaptable to various CPS	May struggle with new or sophisticated attacks, high false positives possible
Guo [46]	2024	Adaptive control for CPS security	Adaptive control framework for security	Adaptive control strategies can dynamically mitigate security risks in CPS environments	Real-time adaptability enhances security against evolving threats	Complexity in implementation for large-scale CPS environments
Stellios et al. [47]	2021	Security and privacy in healthcare CPS	IoT-based healthcare CPS security framework	IoT-enabled CPS can improve healthcare services but pose significant security and privacy risks	Proposes a robust security framework for IoT-based healthcare systems	Scalability issues and high maintenance costs in large healthcare systems

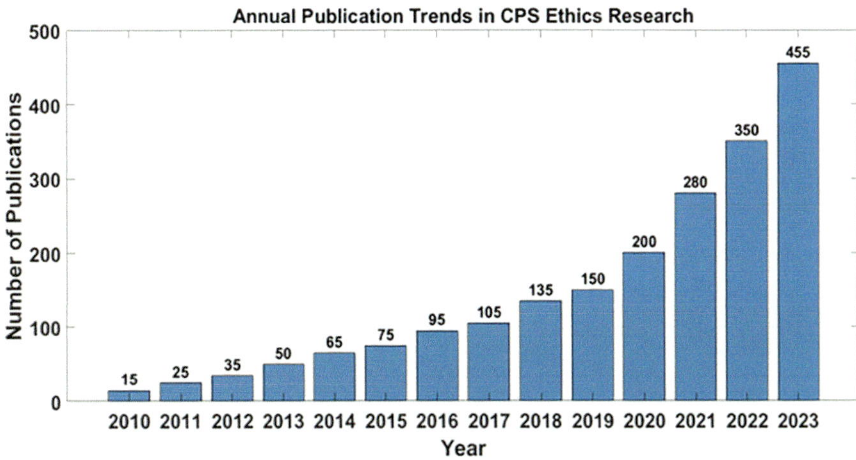

Figure 12.1 Annual publication trends in CPS ethics.

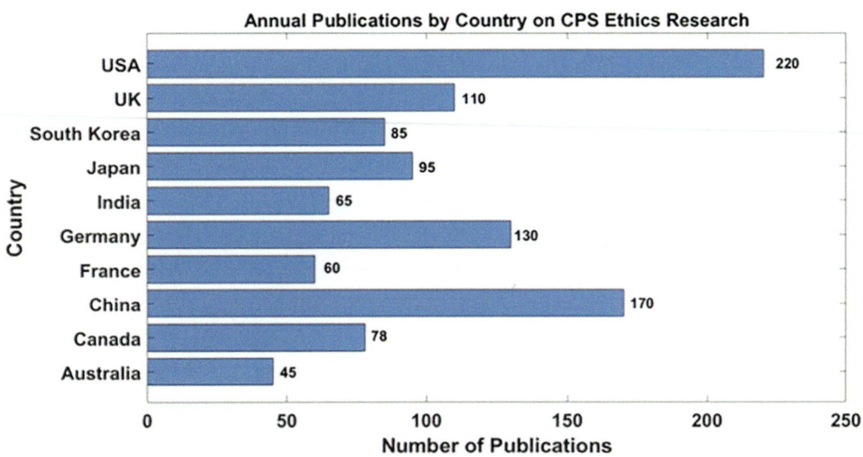

Figure 12.2 Annual publications by country on CPS ethics.

the United Kingdom also contribute significantly. This geographical spread shows the global relevance of CPS ethics, with leading nations likely playing a key role in advancing policies and technologies related to CPS privacy and security. Figure 12.3 provides a basic visualization of co-occurrences and clusters. Keywords represent the key terms, and the connection is an adjacency matrix where 1 represents a co-occurrence between two keywords. This network map visualizes frequently occurring keywords (e.g., cybersecurity, data privacy, ethics, and IoT) and how they interconnect. Clusters reveal

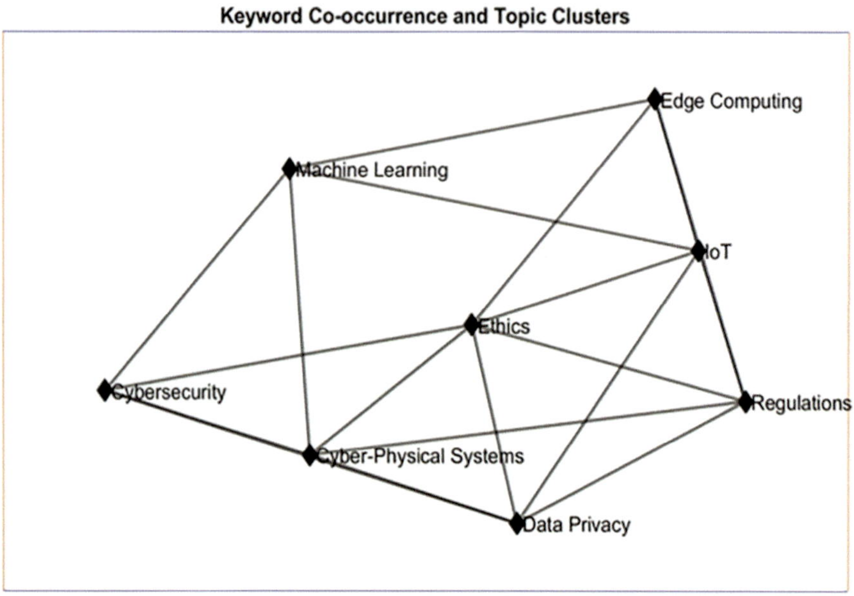

Figure 12.3 Network map of keywords based on assumed co-occurrence relationships.

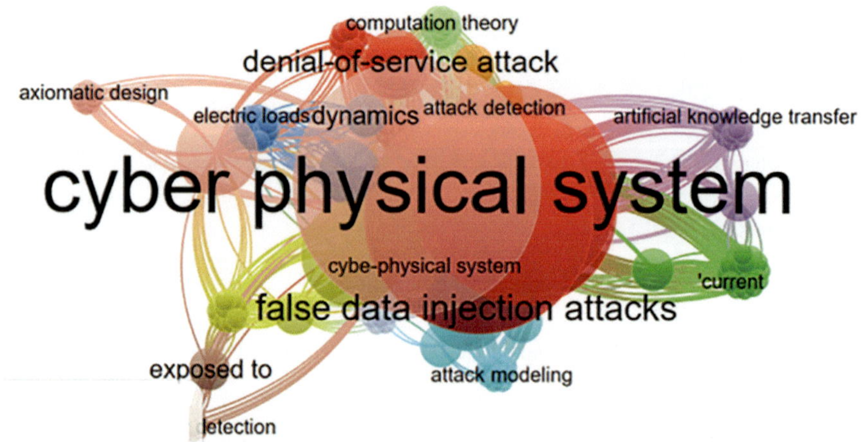

Figure 12.4 Network visualization of the co-occurrence of keywords.

subtopics, such as ethics of autonomous systems or privacy in industrial IoT, which show dominant themes and emerging trends within the field. Figures 12.4–12.7 depict the VOSviewer network and density visualizations generated from data gathered from 36,598 Scopus documents.

Figure 12.4 shows a network visualization that represents the co-occurrence of keywords within the dataset. Keywords that frequently appear

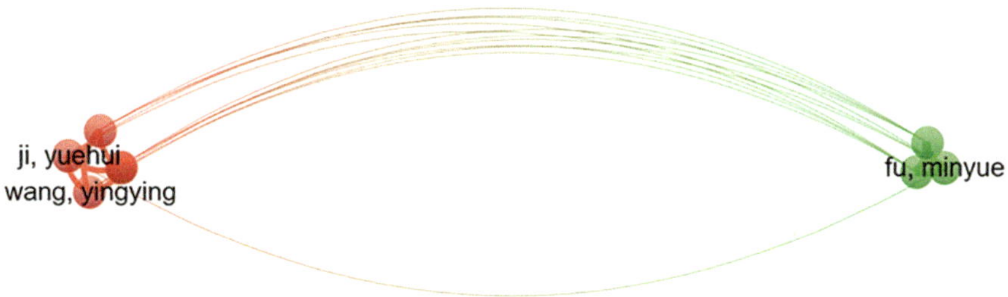

Figure 12.5 The bibliographic coupling network diagram of the authors.

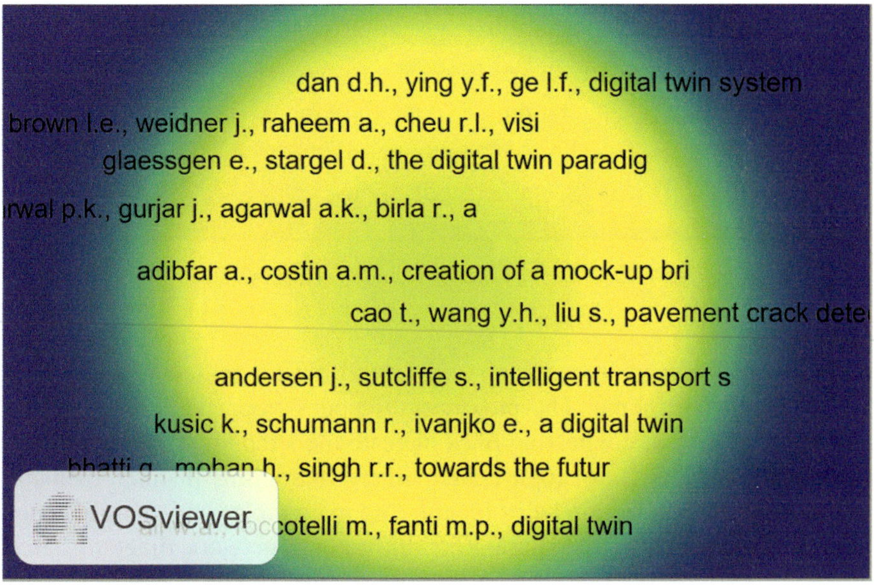

Figure 12.6 Density visualization of cocitation by cited references.

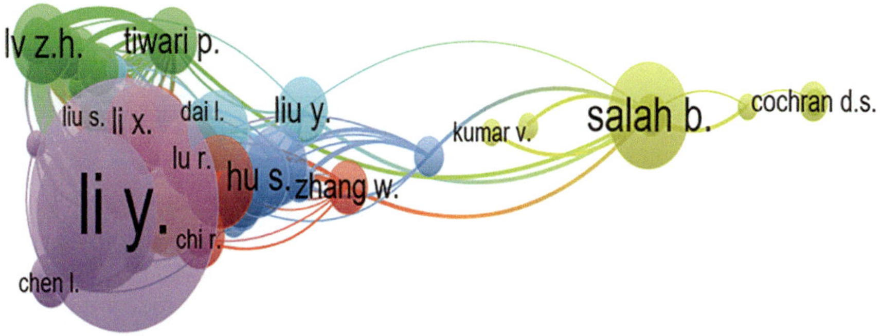

Figure 12.7 The cocitation network diagram of cited authors.

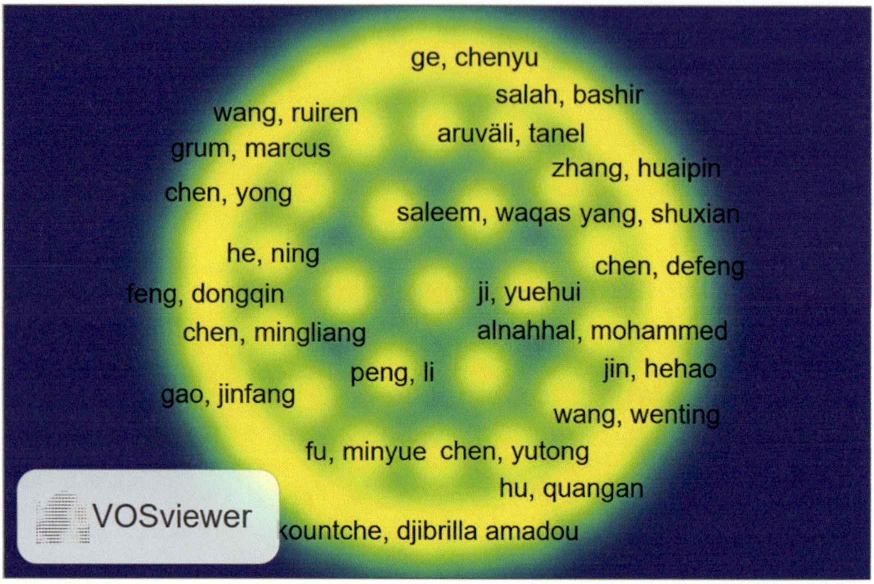

Figure 12.8 Density visualization of citation by authors.

together are grouped into clusters, with each cluster indicating a specific research topic or theme. The proximity of nodes (representing keywords) and the thickness of connecting lines indicate the strength of co-occurrence relationships. Nodes are color-coded, likely signifying distinct thematic clusters. This visualization helps identify the main topics and areas of focus within the research field. Figure 12.5 illustrates a network diagram based on bibliographic coupling among authors. Bibliographic coupling occurs when two authors cite the same third-party sources, implying a thematic or research-methodology similarity. The visualization groups enter clusters where they share a significant number of bibliographic connections, highlighting collaborative research groups or research areas with a shared foundation. The network's structure reveals key contributors and suggests possible research collaborations or influences within the field. Figure 12.6 shows the cocitation network diagram which represents relationships between references based on how often they are cited together in the dataset. References that frequently appear in the same bibliographies form clusters, which may reflect foundational research or commonly referenced works within specific research themes. The network shows clusters of seminal works that influence various research subfields, offering insights into the foundational literature that underpins the body of research. Figure 12.7 shows the cocitation network diagram of cited authors. Figure 12.8 presents a density visualization

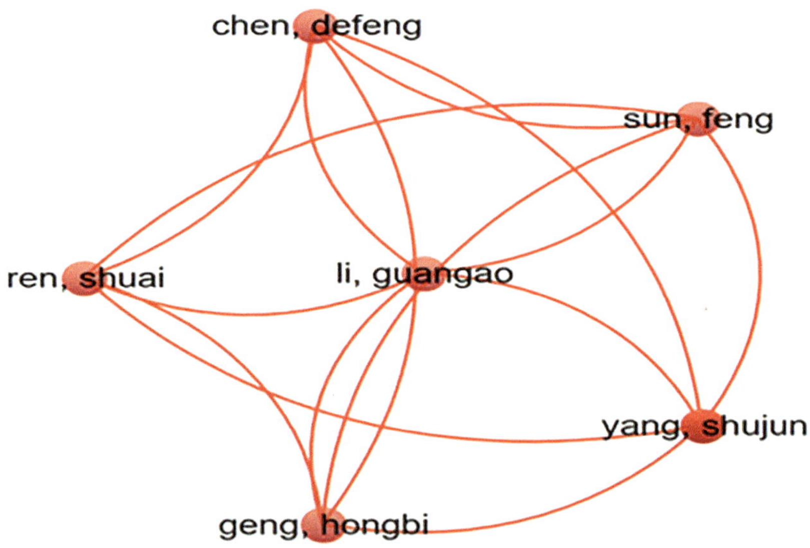

Figure 12.9 Coauthorship network diagram by author.

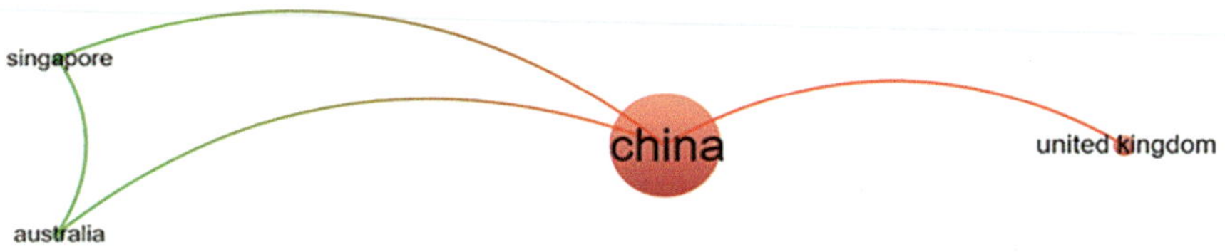

Figure 12.10 Coauthorship network diagram by countries.

of citations per author. Areas with a higher density (indicated by warmer colors) represent authors with more frequent citations, signifying their influence or prominence in the research field. This density map helps in identifying the most highly cited authors, offering a quick overview of the field's most impactful contributors based on citation frequency. Figure 12.9 depicts the coauthorship network diagram by authors. Figure 12.10 illustrates the coauthorship network diagram by country.

12.3 Methodology

This section provides a comprehensive description of the methods employed to conduct the research presented in this chapter. It outlines the steps taken in the literature review, the criteria used for selecting relevant studies, the comparative analysis framework developed to evaluate key findings from prior research, and the methodological approaches used to understand the security, privacy, and ethical challenges of cyber-physical systems (CPS). The goal of this methods section is to demonstrate how the information gathered and analyzed was synthesized to derive insights on CPS vulnerabilities, privacy risks, emerging technologies, and the associated ethical implications [48].

12.3.1 Research design: Literature review framework

The research adopted an extensive literature review methodology, which is a well-established approach for synthesizing prior research and identifying gaps or trends in a particular field. The literature review was performed in two main phases:

- *Phase 1*: Initial exploratory review of the most widely cited articles in the field of CPS, focusing on foundational studies related to security, privacy, and ethical concerns.
- *Phase 2*: In-depth systematic review of more specific topics such as the application of blockchain, artificial intelligence (AI), and machine learning in CPS security, privacy-preserving techniques, and ethical frameworks.

A literature review is particularly well-suited for this study because the research questions are multifaceted and demand an understanding of technical, legal, and ethical perspectives across a broad range of disciplines. CPS itself is an interdisciplinary field that bridges computer science, electrical engineering, mechanical engineering, and cybersecurity, among other areas [48]. Thus, a literature review provides the flexibility to cover the breadth and depth necessary to discuss CPS vulnerabilities, the solutions proposed in the literature, and the technologies being integrated into CPS environments.

The research questions that guided the literature review include:

1. What are the main security challenges faced by CPS?
2. How does CPS impact user privacy, and what solutions have been proposed to preserve it?
3. How do emerging technologies like blockchain and AI contribute to or mitigate CPS security and privacy challenges?
4. What are the ethical considerations surrounding CPS, particularly in relation to autonomous systems and AI?

These questions structured the review process and ensured that the study remained focused on the most relevant and impactful findings.

12.3.2 Data collection: Identifying relevant literature

A structured data collection process was followed to build a comprehensive understanding of CPS security, privacy, and ethical issues. This involved identifying relevant literature from academic databases and systematically reviewing each study to ensure it aligned with the research questions.

12.3.2.1 Selection of databases

The process of conducting a comprehensive literature search is crucial for any research endeavor, particularly when exploring complex and interdisciplinary fields such as cyber-physical systems (CPS) [48]. To facilitate a thorough understanding of the subject matter, several databases were strategically chosen based on their unique strengths and the specific needs of this research. The first database selected was IEEE Xplore, renowned for its vast repository of research papers focused on engineering and technology. Given the highly technical nature of CPS, which blends physical processes with computational algorithms and networking, IEEE Xplore proved to be an invaluable resource. It houses a plethora of peer-reviewed articles, conference papers, and technical standards that are central to the field of CPS.

The advanced search capabilities of IEEE Xplore allow for targeted queries using keywords that align with the specific facets of CPS being investigated, such as security measures, design frameworks, and system architectures [49]. By leveraging this database, the research was able to extract cutting-edge studies and technical documentation that reflect the latest advancements and methodologies in CPS, thereby ensuring a solid foundation of technical knowledge.

The second database utilized was ScienceDirect, which offers a more interdisciplinary approach to literature searching. Unlike IEEE Xplore, which primarily focuses on engineering and technology, ScienceDirect encompasses a wide range of academic disciplines, including ethics, social sciences, and information technology. This broader scope was particularly beneficial for examining the ethical implications and privacy concerns associated with CPS, as these elements are critical in understanding the broader societal impacts of technology. ScienceDirect hosts a multitude of articles that delve into the ethical considerations surrounding AI and blockchain technologies within CPS, allowing research to explore how these technologies intersect with societal values and regulatory frameworks. The database's user-friendly interface and rich collection of review articles facilitated a deeper exploration of existing literature, enabling the research team to synthesize diverse perspectives and establish a nuanced understanding of the ethical dimensions of CPS [49]. Furthermore, the inclusion of case studies and empirical research available in ScienceDirect provided concrete examples of how theoretical concepts are applied in real-world scenarios, enhancing the applicability of the findings.

In addition to IEEE Xplore and ScienceDirect, Google Scholar served as a supplementary tool in the literature search process. Google Scholar is widely recognized for its ability to index a vast array of academic literature, including books, theses, conference papers, and reports from various sources, both prominent and lesser-known. This breadth made it an ideal platform for capturing grey literature, which often contains valuable insights that may not be published in traditional academic journals [49]. Utilizing Google Scholar allowed for the identification of relevant conference proceedings that might not have been accessible through more specialized databases. Furthermore, Google Scholar's robust citation tracking features enabled the research team to monitor citation patterns, ensuring that seminal works and highly cited studies were included in the analysis. This was particularly important for establishing a comprehensive literature base that reflects the evolving nature of CPS research. By using Google Scholar, the research benefited from a more holistic view of the existing literature, including diverse contributions from various authors and institutions, thus enriching the overall understanding of the field.

The combination of these three databases – IEEE Xplore, ScienceDirect, and Google Scholar – provided a well-rounded foundation for literature search. Each database contributed unique strengths that collectively enhanced the research quality. IEEE Xplore ensured a technical depth with high-quality engineering and technological papers, while ScienceDirect broadened the scope to include ethical, social, and interdisciplinary perspectives [50]. Google Scholar's ability to capture grey literature and track citation patterns complemented the findings by incorporating a wider range of scholarly contributions. Together, these databases enabled the research to address the technical aspects of CPS and the ethical and societal implications, resulting in a comprehensive examination of the topic. This methodological rigor underscores the importance of utilizing multiple databases in literature searches to ensure a well-rounded understanding of complex subjects like cyber-physical systems.

12.3.2.2 Search keywords

In the realm of cyber-physical systems (CPS), a comprehensive understanding of the intersecting dimensions of security and privacy is paramount. To effectively explore these areas, a well-structured keyword strategy is essential, as explained in Figure 12.3. The keywords identified for this research focus on critical dimensions, guiding the search toward relevant literature and insights. The first pair, "Cyber-Physical Systems" and "Security," serves as a foundational entry point into the discourse surrounding the protection of interconnected systems [50]. This combination reflects the dual nature of CPS, which integrates computational processes with physical entities, creating unique vulnerabilities and challenges. The need for security in CPS is amplified by the growing integration of these systems into critical infrastructures such as transportation, healthcare, and energy. Therefore, the implications of security breaches are significant, warranting in-depth exploration of the methodologies and technologies designed to safeguard these systems.

Moreover, the keyword combination "CPS" and "Privacy" or "Privacy-preserving" highlights the importance of protecting user data in these interconnected environments. As CPS becomes increasingly ubiquitous, the potential for data collection and surveillance rises, necessitating robust privacy measures. This search term directs focus toward literature that discusses privacy-preserving technologies and frameworks designed to mitigate risks associated with data breaches. In the context of CPS, privacy is not merely about protecting individual information; it also involves ensuring the integrity and reliability of the systems that rely on this data. By exploring this dimension, researchers can uncover best practices, emerging technologies, and policy recommendations aimed at safeguarding privacy in a landscape where the convergence of physical and digital systems blurs traditional boundaries [50].

Another critical area of focus is captured by the keywords "CPS vulnerabilities" and "Attack surfaces." This combination is essential for identifying the specific weaknesses within CPS that adversaries might exploit. Understanding the attack surfaces of CPS is crucial for developing strategies that enhance system resilience. The exploration of vulnerabilities encompasses a wide range of factors, including software flaws, hardware limitations, and operational weaknesses. By searching for this combination, researchers can gain insights into various types of threats that may compromise the functionality and safety of CPS, ranging from malicious attacks to unintentional failures [50]. This focus not only aids in identifying existing vulnerabilities but also facilitates the development of proactive measures to fortify systems against potential threats.

Incorporating "Blockchain" and "Cyber-Physical Systems" as keywords reflects the growing recognition of blockchain technology's potential to enhance security and privacy in CPS. Blockchain provides a decentralized, tamper-proof framework that can address some of the inherent vulnerabilities in CPS. Researchers can explore how blockchain applications can secure data transactions, authenticate devices, and ensure integrity in CPS environments by searching for literature related to these keywords. This intersection of blockchain and CPS opens avenues for innovative solutions that leverage distributed ledger technology to create more robust and trustworthy systems. Additionally, the implications of integrating blockchain into CPS extend beyond security; they encompass broader discussions about governance, accountability, and transparency in the management of interconnected systems [50].

The keywords "Artificial Intelligence" and "Machine Learning" in "CPS security" highlight the transformative potential of AI technologies in enhancing CPS security frameworks. The application of machine learning algorithms can significantly improve threat detection, response capabilities, and anomaly detection within these systems. By searching for this combination, researchers can delve into various AI-driven approaches that bolster CPS security, such as predictive analytics for identifying potential threats before they manifest. The integration of AI in CPS security not only enhances protection mechanisms but also raises important questions regarding the ethical implications of autonomous decision-making processes. Consequently, examining this intersection enables a deeper understanding of how AI technologies can be ethically employed in CPS, balancing security needs with the principles of fairness, accountability, and transparency.

Moreover, the exploration of "Ethical considerations" in "Autonomous systems" and "CPS" brings to the forefront the moral dilemmas associated with the deployment of autonomous technologies. As CPS increasingly incorporates autonomous functionalities, addressing ethical concerns becomes imperative [50]. This keyword combination invites researchers to examine the implications of decision-making algorithms, liability in the event of failures, and the societal impact of deploying autonomous systems. Ethical considerations in CPS extend to issues such as ensuring equitable access to technology, protecting user rights, and addressing biases inherent in machine learning models. By focusing on this dimension, researchers can contribute to the development of ethical guidelines and frameworks that guide the responsible implementation of CPS technologies, ensuring that security measures do not come at the expense of fundamental ethical principles. Figure 12.11 depicts cyber-physical systems bridging AI, privacy, and ethical innovation.

The final set of keywords, "Adversarial attacks" in "CPS," underscores the importance of understanding how adversaries can exploit vulnerabilities within these systems. This search term directs researchers to literature that

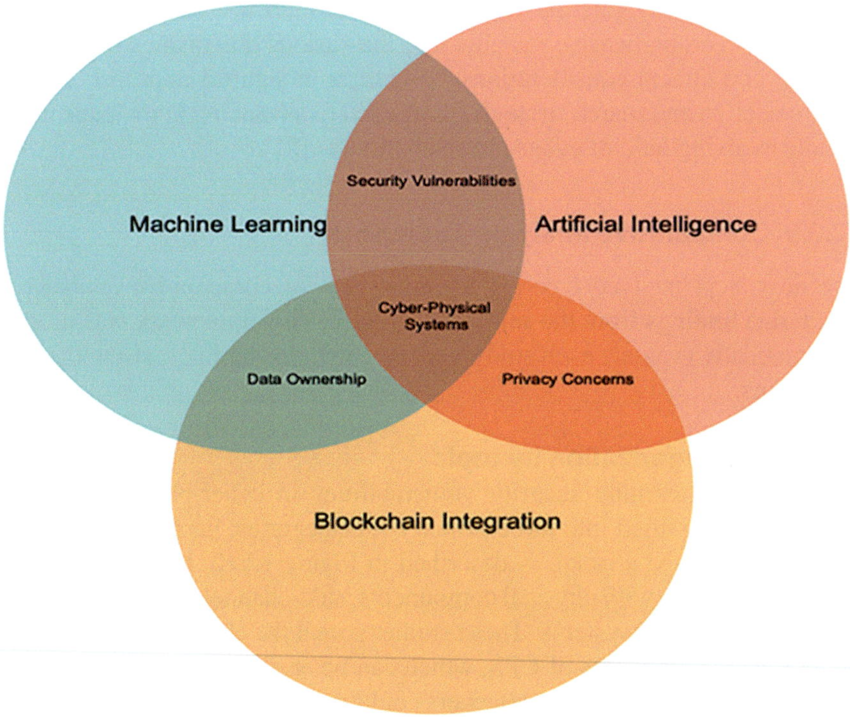

Figure 12.11 Cyber-physical systems bridging AI, privacy, and ethical innovation.

discusses specific strategies employed by attackers, including methods for manipulating machine-learning models and disrupting the functionality of CPS. Understanding adversarial attacks is essential for developing effective defense mechanisms, as it enables the identification of potential threats and the implementation of countermeasures. Furthermore, the complexity of CPS necessitates a nuanced approach to security, requiring continuous adaptation to evolving threats [51]. By investigating adversarial attacks, researchers can contribute to the development of robust security protocols that enhance the resilience of CPS against malicious activities.

To refine search results and ensure the retrieval of relevant literature, the use of boolean operators such as AND, OR, and NOT is essential. For instance, utilizing the combination of "CPS" AND "security" AND "autonomous vehicles" yields more specific and focused results compared to searching for each term independently. Boolean operators facilitate the construction of precise queries that align with the research objectives, allowing for more efficient exploration of existing literature. By strategically combining keywords, researchers can navigate the vast landscape of CPS research, ensuring that they gather comprehensive insights into the various dimensions of security, privacy, and ethical considerations. Overall, a thoughtful approach to keyword selection and search strategies is integral to advancing knowledge in the rapidly evolving field of cyber-physical systems [51].

12.3.3 Comparative analysis framework

The next step involved creating a framework for comparative analysis to synthesize findings from the selected literature. This framework was used to systematically evaluate each study's scope, methods, findings, strengths, and limitations.

12.3.3.1 Categorization by topic

The studies examining security vulnerabilities in cyber-physical systems (CPS) were classified into three primary subcategories: hardware, software, and network-based attacks, as described in Figure 12.12. Hardware attacks include tampering with physical components, side-channel attacks, and direct access to embedded systems. These studies reveal the challenges in securing the physical components of CPS, which can be easily exploited due to their tangible nature. For instance, attackers could manipulate sensors or actuators in critical infrastructure such as energy grids or healthcare devices, leading to potentially catastrophic consequences. The research highlights the importance of designing robust physical components with tamper-proof features and hardware-level encryption techniques [51]. Some studies further emphasize the difficulty of monitoring hardware vulnerabilities remotely, requiring advancements in real-time anomaly detection to ensure rapid response to physical threats.

Software-based attacks, on the other hand, exploit vulnerabilities in the code running on CPS devices, such as through malware or malicious code injections. Studies in this category discuss a wide range of security flaws, including buffer overflow vulnerabilities, race conditions, and backdoors in firmware that allow hackers to hijack CPS functions. Researchers argue that due to the complexity of CPS software, which often integrates legacy systems with newer technologies, traditional security measures like firewalls and antivirus programs are insufficient. Instead, they advocate for dynamic threat detection systems, patch management protocols, and regular software audits to mitigate these risks [51]. Moreover, ensuring that software updates can be securely and reliably deployed across large, decentralized CPS networks remains a critical challenge.

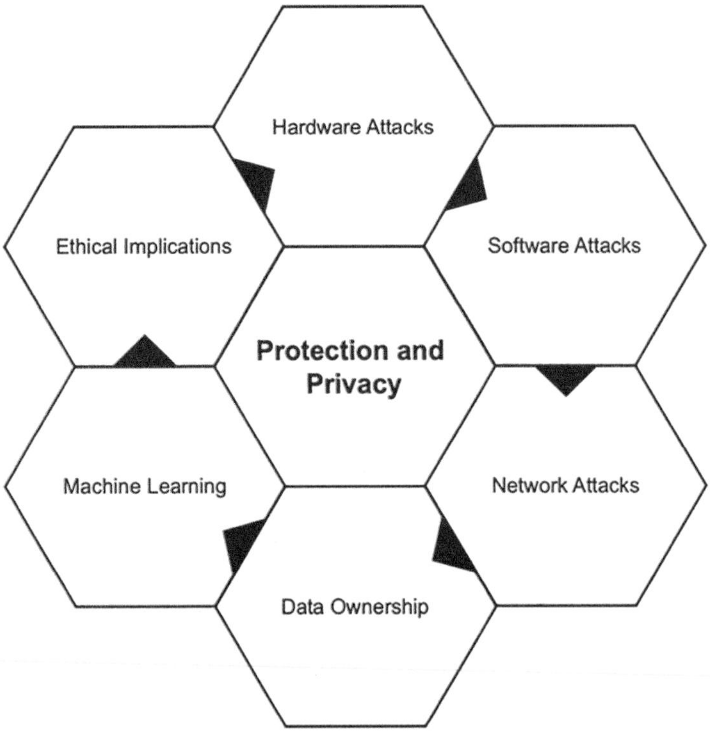

Figure 12.12 Security and ethical safeguards in cyber-physical systems.

Finally, network-based attacks were heavily studied due to the interconnected nature of CPS. These systems rely on communication networks to transmit data between sensors, actuators, and control units, making them susceptible to man-in-the-middle attacks, denial of service (DoS), and eavesdropping. Researchers particularly focused on the vulnerabilities introduced by wireless networks, which are more prone to interception and interference [51]. Encryption protocols such as SSL/TLS are commonly used to protect data in transit; however, many studies have highlighted their inadequacy in real-time environments where speed and low latency are critical. Some researchers propose using decentralized network architectures and blockchain technology to secure CPS communications, which can reduce the attack surface and improve resilience against network-based threats.

Privacy is another significant area of concern in CPS, and the studies reviewed cover various aspects such as data ownership, consent, and encryption techniques. With the widespread deployment of CPS in sensitive sectors like healthcare, transportation, and smart cities, these systems generate massive amounts of data that need to be carefully protected. Data ownership emerged as a key theme, with multiple studies questioning who has the right to access and control the information generated by CPS [52]. For example, in a healthcare setting, does the patient own the data collected by wearable devices, or does ownership transfer to the healthcare provider? Researchers argue that a clear framework for data ownership is necessary to ensure that individuals retain control over their personal information, especially as CPS becomes more pervasive.

Consent is another area of interest, particularly concerning the use of CPS in public spaces where data collection often occurs without explicit user permission. For example, smart city infrastructure can gather data on citizens' movements, behaviors, and interactions without them being fully aware of the data being collected. Studies in this area suggest that current consent models, such as opt-in or opt-out mechanisms, are inadequate for dealing with the real time, continuous data collection characteristic of CPS [52]. Researchers advocate for more transparent data collection policies and dynamic consent models that allow individuals to manage their privacy preferences in real time. Public awareness campaigns could also help educate users about how their data are collected and used by CPS, promoting more informed consent practices.

In the realm of encryption techniques, many studies focus on the application of advanced cryptographic methods to protect data generated and processed by CPS. Traditional encryption protocols like AES and RSA are commonly used. Still, several studies explored newer techniques like differential privacy and homomorphic encryption, which allow data to be processed without revealing sensitive information. Differential privacy has gained traction due to its ability to protect individual data points while allowing aggregate analysis, making it ideal for smart city applications where large datasets are necessary for decision-making. However, researchers note that while these encryption methods enhance privacy, they also introduce challenges in terms of computational overhead and latency, which can be problematic in real-time CPS environments. As a result, ongoing research aims to balance strong privacy protections with the need for efficient, low-latency processing.

The role of emerging technologies like blockchain, artificial intelligence (AI), and machine learning in securing CPS was a major focus of the reviewed studies. Blockchain technology is seen as a promising solution for decentralized security in CPS, offering a tamper-resistant ledger for recording transactions and data exchanges [52]. This is especially useful in sectors like supply chain management, where transparency and traceability are critical.

By leveraging smart contracts, CPS can automate security protocols, ensuring that only authorized actions are executed. Studies also examined how AI and machine learning algorithms can enhance CPS security by enabling systems to learn from previous attacks and adapt to new threats in real time. These technologies can be employed for anomaly detection, where AI models analyze vast amounts of data to identify deviations from normal behavior, flagging potential security breaches.

However, these advancements also raise ethical concerns, particularly around autonomous decision-making and data sharing. As CPS becomes more intelligent and capable of making decisions without human intervention, ethical questions arise regarding accountability. For instance, in the case of autonomous vehicles, if a CPS malfunctions and causes harm, who is responsible: the manufacturer, the software developer, or the AI system itself? The studies suggest that regulatory frameworks must evolve to address these new challenges, ensuring that clear lines of responsibility are established [52]. Moreover, as AI and machine learning models are trained on large datasets, concerns about data bias and discrimination were frequently mentioned. Biased algorithms can lead to unfair outcomes, particularly in areas like healthcare or law enforcement, where CPS may be used to make critical decisions about individuals' lives.

Lastly, the ethical implications of data sharing within CPS networks were discussed extensively. While data sharing is crucial for the effective operation of CPS, particularly in collaborative environments like smart cities or autonomous transportation systems, it also raises privacy and security risks. For example, sharing data between autonomous vehicles and traffic management systems can improve safety and efficiency, but it also creates opportunities for hackers to intercept sensitive information or manipulate system behavior [52]. Some studies advocate for stricter data governance policies and enhanced data anonymization techniques to mitigate these risks. Furthermore, there is a growing consensus that ethical guidelines need to be integrated into the design and development of CPS from the outset, ensuring that these systems are secure, efficient, and aligned with societal values and ethical principles.

12.3.3.2 Analysis of methods and findings

In the realm of cyber-physical systems (CPS), security is an essential aspect that demands rigorous examination. The methodological approaches taken by various research groups have shown a wide spectrum of strategies to address the vulnerabilities inherent in CPS. One notable study by Humayed et al. [20] focused on classifying CPS vulnerabilities, offering a structured framework that sheds light on the multifaceted nature of security threats [53]. This classification was instrumental in juxtaposing theoretical models with practical applications. For instance, when compared with case studies of real-world cyberattacks like the infamous Stuxnet incident, a significant gap in the literature became evident. While Humayed et al. [20] outlined various vulnerabilities, their framework lacked a focus on dynamic and real-time defense mechanisms capable of countering the sophisticated and adaptive strategies employed by modern adversaries. This highlights a critical area for future research: the development of proactive security measures that can evolve alongside emerging threats in CPS environments. Moreover, the findings suggest that existing security frameworks must incorporate continuous monitoring and adaptive responses to remain effective against attacks that are not only complex but also rapidly changing.

Furthermore, the analysis of privacy-preserving techniques within CPS reveals a crucial interplay between theoretical robustness and practical applicability [52]. Differential privacy and homomorphic encryption, two widely cited methodologies, were scrutinized to evaluate their feasibility in real-world implementations. Despite their strong theoretical foundations, challenges pertaining to scalability and computational efficiency were identified. For example, while differential privacy offers a mathematical guarantee for the protection of individual data points, its application in large-scale CPS contexts may lead to significant data utility trade-offs. On the other hand, the computational overhead associated with homomorphic encryption poses challenges in processing speed and resource consumption, particularly in resource-constrained environments typical of CPS applications. This comparative analysis underscores the need for further investigation into optimizing these techniques, potentially through hybrid approaches that balance security, efficiency, and scalability. Additionally, exploring alternative privacy-preserving mechanisms tailored for specific CPS applications could contribute significantly to advancing privacy in this domain.

Emerging technologies, particularly blockchain and artificial intelligence (AI), represent another significant focus in comparing CPS methodologies. The examination of blockchain studies, categorized by their implementation methods – public versus private blockchains – and their specific use cases, such as smart grids and autonomous vehicles, revealed diverse perspectives on security and efficiency [53]. For instance, while public blockchains offer transparency and decentralization, private blockchains may provide better control and scalability for specific applications. This dichotomy indicates a gap in the literature regarding the optimal conditions for deploying each type of blockchain in CPS environments. Furthermore, the comparative evaluation of AI-based threat detection systems illustrated the challenges associated with detecting new and previously unknown threats. Many of these systems rely on machine learning algorithms trained on historical attack data, raising concerns about their adaptability to novel threats that do not fit established patterns. Therefore, this comparative study points to the necessity for future research to focus on developing AI models that can better generalize across various attack vectors and improve their responsiveness to evolving security threats in CPS.

Lastly, the ethical dimensions of CPS technologies cannot be overlooked, as they intersect with security and privacy considerations. The methodologies employed in ethical analyses often vary widely, from normative frameworks that assess the implications of technology use to empirical studies that examine stakeholder perceptions. This comparative approach reveals a pressing need for a cohesive framework that integrates ethical considerations into the design and implementation of CPS technologies [53]. For instance, while some studies advocate for ethical guidelines to govern the development of autonomous systems, others emphasize the need for ongoing ethical education for engineers and developers in the field. This divergence indicates that while ethical frameworks exist, their application in practice remains inconsistent, leading to gaps in addressing ethical dilemmas as they arise in CPS. By identifying these inconsistencies, the comparative analysis highlights the importance of establishing robust ethical guidelines that govern technology and consider the societal implications of its use, thereby ensuring a more responsible and comprehensive approach to CPS security, privacy, and ethical challenges.

12.3.4 Evaluation of ethical considerations

Given the interdisciplinary nature of cyber-physical systems (CPS), the ethical dimensions of deploying AI and autonomous systems necessitate a qualitative approach to understand their societal impacts thoroughly. CPS integrates computing, networking, and physical processes, creating systems where digital and physical elements coexist and interact seamlessly [53]. This complexity raises significant ethical considerations, particularly in sectors where decisions can have profound consequences, such as healthcare and transportation. Therefore, it is crucial to evaluate these ethical implications through established frameworks. Various frameworks, including deontological ethics, consequentialism, and user-centric models, provide valuable lenses for assessing the responsibilities of engineers, developers, and organizations involved in CPS.

Deontological ethics emphasizes the inherent duties and responsibilities of engineers and developers to ensure that CPS technologies do no harm. This framework posits that certain actions are morally obligatory, irrespective of their outcomes. In the context of CPS, this translates to a commitment to safety, security, and ethical design principles. For instance, engineers must prioritize user safety when designing autonomous vehicles, ensuring that the systems are equipped to handle a variety of scenarios, including emergencies. Adopting deontological ethics can serve as a foundation for creating robust ethical guidelines that govern the development and deployment of CPS technologies. This framework not only focuses on the technical competencies required but also addresses the moral obligations that engineers must uphold, such as thorough testing, accountability, and transparency [53]. Moreover, it encourages professionals to foster a culture of ethical responsibility within organizations, promoting ongoing dialogue about the implications of their work on society.

Consequentialism, another critical ethical framework, focuses on the outcomes of deploying autonomous systems and AI in critical sectors like healthcare and transportation. This perspective evaluates the morality of an action based on the results it produces, making it essential for assessing the real-world impacts of CPS technologies. For example, in healthcare, the deployment of AI systems for diagnostics and treatment planning could lead to improved patient outcomes but may also introduce risks related to accuracy and data privacy [54]. Thus, analyzing the potential benefits against the possible harms is crucial for responsible decision-making. Additionally, in transportation, autonomous vehicles promise to reduce accidents and improve traffic efficiency, yet they also raise ethical questions about liability and accountability in the event of malfunctions or accidents. By applying consequentialist principles, researchers and practitioners can systematically evaluate the trade-offs associated with CPS deployment, fostering more informed and ethically sound decisions that prioritize overall societal well-being.

User-centric models further emphasize the importance of prioritizing user consent, transparency, and privacy in CPS, particularly regarding data sharing and AI decision-making. As CPS often relies on collecting and processing vast amounts of personal data, ensuring that users are informed and consenting participants in this process is vital. This framework encourages the development of technologies that empower users, allowing them to control their data and understand how it is used within autonomous systems [54]. Transparency is a core component of this approach, as it fosters trust between users and technology providers. For instance, when individuals are aware of how their data are utilized and how AI systems make decisions, they are more likely to accept and engage with these technologies. Furthermore, this user-centric perspective highlights the need for ethical standards that govern data protection and privacy, ensuring that CPS developers prioritize user rights and preferences. By integrating user-centric models into the development of CPS, engineers can create more ethical and responsible technologies that genuinely serve the needs and interests of society.

The application of these ethical frameworks to the existing literature reveals a pressing need for further exploration of the potential harms associated with CPS, especially in scenarios where autonomous systems might make decisions with unintended consequences [54]. For instance, studies exploring the implications of self-driving cars often emphasize their potential to reduce traffic fatalities, yet there remains a lack of comprehensive analysis on how these systems might respond in complex and unpredictable environments. Similarly, AI applications in healthcare have the potential to revolutionize patient care, yet ethical discussions surrounding data privacy, algorithmic bias, and accountability in decision-making are often underrepresented. By critically engaging with these ethical frameworks, researchers can identify gaps in the current literature and advocate for a more nuanced understanding of the societal impacts of CPS technologies. Ultimately, integrating deontological ethics, consequentialism, and user-centric models into the discourse surrounding CPS can lead to more ethically sound practices and policies, ensuring that the benefits of these technologies are realized while minimizing potential harm.

12.4 Key Takeaways from the Study

The literature review highlighted several key findings regarding the security challenges, privacy concerns, and the role of emerging technologies in cyber-physical systems (CPS). Each of these aspects is interconnected and underscores the complexity of managing CPS effectively. Below, we delve into a detailed examination of these findings.

12.4.1 Challenges in cyber-physical systems

12.4.1.1 Security challenges in cyber-physical systems

The integration of cyber components with physical infrastructure in cyber-physical systems (CPS) presents a unique set of security challenges. As noted by Humayed et al. [20], security threats can be broadly categorized into three primary types: hardware attacks, software attacks, and network-based attacks. Each of these categories poses distinct challenges that necessitate tailored mitigation strategies, highlighting the complexity of securing CPS in an increasingly interconnected environment. Understanding these categories is essential for developing comprehensive security frameworks that can effectively address the vulnerabilities inherent in CPS.

Hardware attacks specifically target the physical components of CPS, such as sensors, actuators, and embedded systems. Since hardware is often the first line of defense, any compromise can have severe and far-reaching consequences. For instance, an attacker could manipulate a sensor to provide false data, leading to incorrect decisions by the CPS. The implications of hardware attacks are particularly profound in critical sectors such as manufacturing and healthcare, where sensor integrity is vital for safety and operational efficiency [53]. Tampering with sensors in an industrial setting could trigger catastrophic failures, potentially endangering lives and causing significant financial losses. Moreover, studies have demonstrated that hardware attacks can exploit vulnerabilities throughout the manufacturing process, supply chains, and even during the design phase of CPS. By targeting the foundational elements of a system, attackers can undermine the entire operational framework, making it crucial for organizations to implement robust security measures at the hardware level.

In contrast, software attacks predominantly focus on vulnerabilities within the control systems, application software, or communication protocols that govern CPS operations. These vulnerabilities are often exploited to gain unauthorized access or disrupt system functionality. A prominent example is the malware known as Stuxnet, which illustrated how software vulnerabilities could be leveraged to cause physical damage. Specifically targeting the control systems of Iran's nuclear facilities, Stuxnet demonstrated that malware could manipulate physical processes by taking control of industrial control systems, resulting in extensive damage to critical infrastructure [54]. This incident underscores the potential for devastating effects when software vulnerabilities remain unaddressed. As CPS becomes more reliant on complex software systems, the need for rigorous software security practices, including regular updates, patch management, and vulnerability assessments, becomes increasingly imperative to mitigate the risks posed by potential exploits.

Finally, network-based attacks present additional challenges to CPS security by exploiting vulnerabilities in communication networks. These vulnerabilities can expose CPS to various attacks, including denial of service (DoS) and man-in-the-middle (MitM) attacks. Such attacks disrupt communication between different components of CPS, potentially leading to loss of control or critical failures. For example, a DoS attack targeting an autonomous vehicle's communication network could prevent it from receiving real-time data, jeopardizing its ability to operate safely and effectively. Additionally, network-based attacks can facilitate data breaches, exposing sensitive information that could be exploited for malicious purposes, such as identity theft or industrial espionage [54]. As CPS increasingly depends on reliable and secure communication channels, organizations must prioritize the implementation of robust network security measures, including intrusion detection systems, encryption, and traffic monitoring, to safeguard against these potential threats.

The integration of cyber components with physical infrastructure in CPS introduces complex security challenges that require a multifaceted approach to risk mitigation. By understanding the unique characteristics of hardware, software, and network-based attacks, organizations can develop targeted security strategies that address the vulnerabilities within their CPS frameworks. This proactive stance not only enhances the resilience of CPS against potential threats but also ensures the safety and reliability of critical infrastructure as it becomes increasingly interconnected in a digital world. The ongoing evolution of CPS necessitates a continuous assessment of security practices to keep pace with emerging threats, reinforcing the need for collaborative efforts among stakeholders to establish comprehensive security protocols that protect against the myriad challenges posed by this dynamic landscape [54].

12.4.1.2 Emerging vulnerabilities due to AI and machine learning

The growing reliance on artificial intelligence (AI) and machine learning technologies in cyber-physical systems (CPS) is transforming the landscape of automation and efficiency across various sectors. However, this increasing integration has also introduced a new array of vulnerabilities that demand urgent attention. Squillace et al. emphasize that AI systems are often deployed in environments where they are susceptible to a multitude of security threats. The inherent complexity of machine learning algorithms creates potential weak points that malicious actors can exploit. For example, adversarial machine learning techniques allow attackers to subtly manipulate input data, tricking AI systems into making incorrect predictions or decisions [54]. Such vulnerabilities highlight the necessity for robust security measures to safeguard these systems from external threats, particularly as they become integral to critical infrastructures such as transportation, healthcare, and manufacturing.

One significant area of concern lies in autonomous systems, including drones and self-driving cars, which are particularly susceptible to these new vulnerabilities. For instance, an attacker could spoof sensor data – misleading the system into interpreting its environment inaccurately. By manipulating the data that feeds into machine learning models, malicious actors can induce erratic behavior in autonomous systems, potentially resulting in accidents or operational failures. This not only poses significant safety risks but also raises critical questions about accountability and liability when such incidents occur [21]. As CPS increasingly relies on AI for critical decision-making, ensuring the integrity and security of these systems becomes paramount.

The implications of these vulnerabilities extend beyond mere technical failures; they encompass broader societal concerns. For example, the potential for malicious manipulation of autonomous systems can undermine public trust in technology, particularly in sectors such as transportation and healthcare, where safety is paramount. As CPS becomes more interconnected and reliant on AI, the consequences of a security breach could be catastrophic, leading to loss of life, damage to property, erosion of consumer confidence property damage, and consumer confidence erosion. This necessitates a multifaceted approach to security that includes not only technological solutions but also regulatory frameworks and ethical guidelines to govern the development and deployment of AI in CPS. Stakeholders must engage in collaborative efforts to create robust security standards that address the unique challenges posed by AI-driven systems [55].

To mitigate the risks associated with AI and machine learning in CPS, it is essential to adopt proactive measures that emphasize resilience and adaptability. This includes investing in advanced security protocols to detect and respond to adversarial attacks in real time. Additionally, integrating diverse data sources and redundancy in sensor inputs can help create a more robust system capable of identifying anomalies and resisting manipulation. Continuous monitoring and updating machine learning models are also critical to ensure they can adapt to evolving threats. As CPS becomes increasingly complex and intertwined with AI technologies, fostering a culture of security awareness and preparedness will be essential for safeguarding these systems against potential vulnerabilities and ensuring their safe and reliable operation in the future.

12.4.1.3 Case studies of cyberattacks on CPS

Numerous case studies illustrate the potential risks posed by inadequate security in cyber-physical systems (CPS), with the Stuxnet attack standing out as one of the most cited examples. This sophisticated cyberattack, which occurred in 2010, showcased how vulnerabilities within CPS could be exploited to create significant physical damage. By leveraging multiple zero-day vulnerabilities, the Stuxnet malware managed to infiltrate the control systems of an Iranian nuclear facility. Once inside, it manipulated the centrifuges used for uranium enrichment, causing them to spin out of control and ultimately destroying them. This incident not only demonstrated the capabilities of state-sponsored cyber warfare but also highlighted the vulnerabilities inherent in the integration of cyber systems with physical processes [55]. The consequences of Stuxnet were profound, emphasizing that cyberattacks can have real-world repercussions, including disruption of critical operations and safety risks. This attack underlined the urgent need for robust security measures in CPS to safeguard against similar threats.

Beyond the Stuxnet incident, several other high-profile attacks have further underscored the vulnerabilities present in CPS. A notable example is the 2015 cyberattack on Ukraine's power grid, which resulted in a significant disruption of electrical supply to over 200,000 residents. This attack demonstrated how cyber threats could be directed at critical infrastructure, leading to substantial service outages and public safety concerns [55]. The malware used in this incident compromised the control systems of the utility provider, allowing the attackers to take control of operational processes and shut down power to various regions. This event showcased the direct impact of cyberattacks on public utilities and highlighted the broader implications for national security and the economy. The ability to manipulate essential services raises alarms about the resilience of CPS in the face of cyber threats, further accentuating the necessity for enhanced security protocols.

These incidents serve as critical reminders of the importance of understanding the evolving security landscape of CPS. The nature of these systems, which often combine operational technology with information technology, makes them particularly susceptible to cyber threats. As demonstrated by both the Stuxnet attack and the Ukraine power grid incident, the consequences of inadequate security can be dire, affecting not only individual organizations but society. A comprehensive security strategy is essential for protecting CPS from potential cyberattacks. This strategy should involve risk assessment, threat modeling, and the implementation of multilayered security measures that include both proactive and reactive approaches [55]. Organizations must remain vigilant and continually assess their security posture to adapt to the dynamic nature of cyber threats.

Moreover, the lessons learned from these case studies highlight the need for collaboration among various stakeholders in the field of CPS security. Government agencies, private sector organizations, and academia must work together to develop best practices and share information on emerging threats. Such collaboration can lead to the creation of more resilient systems and foster a culture of security awareness across industries. Education and training programs should also be prioritized to ensure that individuals working within CPS understand the risks and are equipped to implement effective security measures [56]. By taking a proactive stance and learning from past incidents, stakeholders can better prepare for the challenges posed by cyber threats, ultimately enhancing the security and reliability of cyber-physical systems.

12.4.2 Privacy concerns in cyber-physical systems

12.4.2.1 Data collection and ownership issues

Cyber-physical systems (CPS) are characterized by their reliance on extensive data collection from a multitude of sources, including sensors, actuators, and user interactions. This data serves as the backbone for the effective functioning of these systems, enabling them to operate seamlessly and respond to real-time changes in their environment. However, the extensive data gathering inherent in CPS raises significant privacy concerns that cannot be overlooked. For example, in the case of smart medical devices, the health data collected from users may be claimed by various parties, including manufacturers, service providers, and the users themselves [56]. This ambiguity can lead to conflicts regarding the usage and control of the data, making it imperative to address these ownership issues to safeguard users' privacy.

The lack of clear guidelines on data ownership in CPS complicates the establishment of trust between users and service providers. Trust is a fundamental component in the relationship between users and the technology they interact with, especially in systems that handle sensitive data. When users are unsure about who owns their data and how it will be used, their willingness to engage with CPS diminishes. This is particularly critical in applications like healthcare, where personal health information is often collected and processed [56]. The potential for misuse of this sensitive information can lead to significant adverse outcomes, not just for individual privacy but also for public trust in CPS. As such, stakeholders involved in the development and deployment of CPS must prioritize the establishment of clear ownership rights and usage guidelines to foster user confidence.

To mitigate privacy concerns effectively, stakeholders must engage in collaborative discussions to clarify data ownership rights. This process involves defining who has the right to access, share, and utilize the data collected by CPS. Involving users in these discussions is essential, as their perspectives and concerns must be considered to ensure that the resulting guidelines are comprehensive and considerate of individual privacy. Furthermore, regulatory frameworks may need to be established or updated to reflect the unique challenges posed by CPS, especially in terms of data ownership and user consent. By implementing transparent policies that delineate data ownership, stakeholders can create an environment where users feel empowered to engage with CPS without fear of exploitation or privacy breaches [56].

12.4.2.2 Implications of pervasive data collection

The pervasive nature of data collection in cyber-physical systems (CPS) has sparked considerable ethical concerns surrounding the analysis and sharing of this data. As these systems become increasingly integrated into our daily lives, they gather vast amounts of information from various sources, including sensors and user interactions. This data can reveal sensitive details about individuals, particularly when it comes to energy consumption patterns in smart grids. For instance, if a smart grid can determine when individuals are home based on their energy usage, it opens the possibility of profiling and targeting users without their consent. Therefore, the ethical implications of such analyses demand careful consideration and robust safeguards to protect user privacy [56].

As data analytics techniques evolve and become more sophisticated, the risk of reidentification grows. Reidentification refers to the process by which anonymized data can be matched with publicly available information to uncover the identity of individuals. This risk poses a significant challenge for CPS, particularly in environments where data are continuously collected and analyzed. For example, even if energy consumption data are anonymized, patterns and behaviors can still be discerned that may reveal the identities of individuals or their specific lifestyles. This situation necessitates the need for CPS to adopt effective privacy-preserving mechanisms to mitigate these risks. Without such measures, users may become increasingly hesitant to engage with these systems, ultimately hindering the potential benefits of data-driven technologies.

Several techniques have been proposed to address privacy risks associated with data collection in CPS. One of the most promising approaches is differential privacy, which aims to protect individual identities while still allowing for meaningful data analysis [57]. Differential privacy introduces a controlled amount of noise into datasets, making it challenging to trace data back to specific individuals. By altering the data to mask individual contributions, differential privacy ensures that the insights gleaned from the data are statistically valid without compromising personal privacy. Wang et al. have presented differential privacy as a robust solution for preventing reidentification, emphasizing its effectiveness in preserving user privacy while enabling organizations to derive actionable insights from the data collected. This approach balances the need for data-driven decision-making with the imperative of safeguarding individual privacy.

The importance of implementing privacy-preserving mechanisms like differential privacy cannot be overstated, especially as CPS continues to proliferate across various sectors, including healthcare, transportation, and energy. As these systems evolve, organizations need to prioritize ethical data practices that respect user privacy [57]. This commitment not only builds trust between users and CPS providers but also fosters a more sustainable and responsible approach to data utilization. By embracing techniques like differential privacy, stakeholders can navigate the complex landscape of data collection while ensuring that individual rights are upheld. Ultimately, the ethical implications of data analysis in CPS highlight the necessity for continuous dialogue, research, and innovation in the pursuit of privacy-preserving technologies that align with societal values and expectations.

12.4.2.3 Data sharing and informed consent

The ethical dimensions of data sharing in cyber-physical systems (CPS) play a pivotal role in maintaining user trust, which is essential for the successful implementation and acceptance of these technologies. In a landscape where data are constantly collected from various sensors and devices, users must be well-informed about what specific data are being gathered, the purpose behind its collection, and the potential risks associated with its use. This transparency is crucial for fostering trust and encouraging users to engage more actively with CPS technologies, as it empowers them to make informed decisions regarding their data [57].

Moreover, the concept of informed consent in data sharing must extend beyond the initial stages of data collection. Users should have the ability to modify their consent preferences over time, reflecting the dynamic nature of their data and how it is utilized. This ongoing dialogue regarding consent is vital, especially given that data usage practices are continually evolving with technological advancements and changes in privacy regulations. Allowing users to adjust their consent preferences ensures that they maintain a sense of agency over their personal information, which is crucial in a digital landscape where data privacy concerns are increasingly prominent.

Implementing adaptive consent models enhances user control and aligns with ethical best practices in data governance. Organizations can demonstrate a commitment to ethical data stewardship and respect for user autonomy by providing mechanisms for users to revisit and revise their consent agreements. This adaptability is particularly important in the context of CPS, where the stakes can be high, and the implications of data misuse or mismanagement can have real-world consequences. In this way, fostering a culture of informed consent can lead to more responsible data practices that prioritize user well-being and trust [57].

Ultimately, cultivating user trust through ethical data-sharing practices is not merely a regulatory obligation but a strategic advantage for organizations operating in the CPS domain. When users feel confident that their data are being handled ethically and transparently, they are more likely to embrace these technologies, thereby enhancing the overall efficacy and success of CPS initiatives. As the field continues to evolve, prioritizing user-centric approaches to data sharing will be crucial for sustaining long-term engagement and trust in cyber-physical systems.

12.4.3 Advancements in security and privacy technologies for cyber-physical systems

12.4.3.1 The role of blockchain technology

Emerging technologies, particularly blockchain, have garnered significant attention for their potential to enhance the security and privacy of cyber-physical systems (CPS). The decentralized architecture of blockchain provides a tamper-proof mechanism for data exchange between various CPS components. This characteristic is vital for ensuring the integrity of data, which is especially important in critical applications like smart grids and healthcare systems [58]. This property is crucial in environments where maintaining accurate and trustworthy data is essential for operational success and safety.

In the context of smart grids, the application of blockchain technology demonstrates its capability to facilitate secure peer-to-peer energy trading among consumers. By allowing users to trade energy directly with one another without the need for centralized authority, blockchain empowers consumers and enhances the efficiency of energy markets. This innovative approach not only streamlines transactions but also reduces costs associated with intermediaries, benefiting buyers and sellers.

Moreover, the dual capability of blockchain to ensure transparency while protecting user privacy plays a significant role in building trust among stakeholders in energy markets. Transparency is essential in fostering confidence in the system, as participants can verify transactions independently.

This trust is crucial in encouraging the wider adoption of decentralized energy trading platforms, which can lead to more resilient and sustainable energy systems. By allowing users to monitor their energy transactions without compromising personal information, blockchain technology addresses the growing concerns regarding data privacy and security in the digital age.

12.4.3.2 Artificial intelligence and machine learning in CPS security

Artificial intelligence (AI) and machine learning technologies are increasingly vital in bolstering the security of cyber-physical systems (CPS). This advanced capability marks a significant improvement over traditional static security measures, which often struggle to adapt to the fluid and dynamic nature of modern threats. By utilizing machine learning, CPS can continually learn from data, enabling them to identify unusual patterns or behaviors that may indicate a security breach [58]. This proactive approach allows for immediate remediation, thus minimizing potential damage and enhancing the overall resilience of the system.

Despite the advantages of integrating AI into CPS, there are notable challenges that must be addressed. The black-box nature of many machine learning models poses significant difficulties in understanding how decisions are made. This lack of transparency complicates accountability, as stakeholders may struggle to ascertain the rationale behind the actions of AI systems. Such opacity can foster mistrust among users and operators, particularly in high-stakes applications where decisions can have serious consequences.

The implications of algorithmic bias are especially concerning in applications such as autonomous vehicles. If the algorithms driving these systems are biased, they could lead to unsafe decision-making processes, potentially resulting in accidents and endangering lives. For example, if an autonomous vehicle's perception system misinterprets the behavior of pedestrians due to skewed training data, it might fail to react appropriately in a critical situation. This underscores the necessity of ensuring fairness and accuracy in machine learning models, as biased algorithms could undermine the safety and reliability of CPS in real-world scenarios [59].

To address these challenges, it is crucial to implement strategies that enhance the transparency and accountability of AI systems used in CPS. This includes developing explainable AI models that can clarify how decisions are made and establishing robust protocols for auditing and monitoring algorithms to identify and mitigate bias[58]. Moreover, fostering collaboration between technologists, ethicists, and regulators can facilitate the development of guidelines and standards that prioritize ethical considerations in the deployment of AI in CPS. By addressing these challenges, the benefits of AI and machine learning can be fully realized, ensuring that CPS is not only secure but also fair and trustworthy.

12.4.3.3 Future directions for emerging technologies in CPS

The exploration of emerging technologies in cyber-physical systems (CPS) is still in its infancy, and there is a pressing need for further research to fully understand their implications for security and privacy. As CPS increasingly intertwines with daily life, the need to address the vulnerabilities that arise becomes paramount. Current literature indicates that while significant advancements have been made, the complexities inherent in CPS call for more rigorous investigation into how emerging technologies can mitigate these challenges. By deepening our understanding of these technologies, we can develop more effective strategies to protect both the cyber and physical components of these systems [60].

One of the most promising intersections in the realm of CPS is the combination of blockchain and artificial intelligence (AI). This synergy presents exciting opportunities for enhancing the resilience of CPS. Blockchain's inherent data integrity features can provide a secure framework for transactions and data exchanges within CPS, ensuring that data remains untampered and verifiable. When paired with AI's analytical capabilities, which can process vast amounts of data and identify patterns, the potential for more secure and efficient CPS environments increases significantly [27]. This integration could lead to real-time monitoring and anomaly detection, allowing for quicker responses to potential security threats. As researchers explore these intersections, the focus must also be on developing scalable solutions that can be implemented across various CPS applications.

In addition to blockchain and AI, the potential of edge computing represents another avenue for enhancing the security and privacy of CPS. Edge computing allows data to be processed closer to its source, which can significantly reduce the risks associated with data transmission and storage. By minimizing the distance that data must travel, edge computing can lower the chances of interception or tampering during transmission. Furthermore, processing data at the edge can improve response times and reduce latency, critical factors in applications where real-time decision-making is essential [60]. This localized approach strengthens security and enhances privacy by limiting the exposure of sensitive data to centralized storage systems, which can be vulnerable to breaches.

The integration of these emerging technologies, blockchain, AI, and edge computing into CPS underscores the importance of an innovative approach to security and privacy. As researchers and practitioners collaborate to explore these technologies, the focus should be on creating robust frameworks that leverage their strengths while addressing the unique challenges CPS poses. A proactive stance in research and development can ensure that as CPS continues to evolve, they do so with a solid foundation in security and privacy, ultimately leading to more resilient and trustworthy systems that enhance the quality of life for users.

12.4.3.4 Comparative analysis of related works

A comparative analysis of past literature reveals key insights and gaps in the existing research landscape. Table 12.2 summarizes the findings from various studies, highlighting their scope, methodologies, strengths, and limitations.

Table 12.2 provides a snapshot of the diverse approaches taken in the literature to address the security and privacy challenges in CPS. While significant strides have been made, gaps remain in terms of empirical validation, practical implementations, and comprehensive frameworks for addressing the complexities of CPS security and privacy.

12.5 Discussion of Key Findings from the Study

The findings from this literature review emphasize the multifaceted and interrelated nature of the security, privacy, and ethical challenges facing cyber-physical systems (CPS). As these systems become more prevalent across various sectors, including healthcare, transportation, and manufacturing, the need for robust frameworks that address their vulnerabilities becomes increasingly urgent [55]. This section delves into the implications of the findings, the interplay between emerging technologies and their associated challenges, and the necessity for a collaborative approach to secure and ethical CPS deployment. The integration of cyber and physical components in CPS inherently increases the complexity of security measures. Traditional cybersecurity approaches, often designed for either cyber or physical domains, frequently fall short in addressing the unique vulnerabilities presented by CPS. The literature highlights a pressing need for a holistic security framework that can effectively manage risks across these intertwined domains. However, the security of CPS cannot be effectively addressed by simply categorizing threats; instead, there must be a focus on developing comprehensive strategies that consider the interactions between these categories [57].

One of the most critical aspects of CPS security is the need for continuous monitoring and adaptive security measures. Given the rapid evolution of technology, security solutions must be dynamic and responsive to

Table 12.2 Summary of the findings from various studies.

Study	Focus area	Methodology	Key findings	Strengths	Limitations
Humayed et al. [20]	Security threats	Literature review	Identified categories of attacks	Comprehensive categorization	Lacks empirical data
Farwell and Rohozinski [21]	Case study	Case analysis	Stuxnet's impact on CPS security	Real-world implications	Limited generalizability
Squillace et al. [22]	AI vulnerabilities	Theoretical analysis	AI can be exploited in CPS	Highlights AI-related risks	Lacks practical examples
Mirchev et al. [26]	Data ownership	Conceptual framework	Ownership issues in CPS data	Clear framework	Limited focus on implementation
Wright and Friedewald [27]	Data privacy	Survey	Ethical implications of data collection	Broad ethical perspective	Lacks specific case studies

emerging threats. For instance, the Stuxnet attack serves as a stark reminder of how sophisticated cyberattacks can exploit vulnerabilities in CPS to cause physical harm [61]. This incident not only underscores the need for rigorous security assessments and updates but also emphasizes the importance of threat intelligence sharing among organizations. Establishing collaborative platforms for sharing information about emerging threats and vulnerabilities can help organizations stay one step ahead of potential attackers [58].

Moreover, the increasing use of AI and machine learning in CPS introduces a new layer of complexity to security challenges. While these technologies can enhance the capabilities of CPS, they also create additional attack surfaces. Adversarial machine learning, as discussed in Zhou et al.'s [25] research, poses significant risks, particularly in safety-critical applications like autonomous vehicles. The potential for attackers to manipulate input data to mislead AI systems necessitates the development of robust defenses that can identify and mitigate such threats. Research must continue to explore methods for enhancing the resilience of AI models against adversarial attacks while maintaining their performance and accuracy in real-world scenarios.

Privacy remains a paramount concern in the deployment of CPS, particularly due to the extensive data collection inherent in these systems. The literature highlights several key areas that require attention, including data ownership, consent, and the implications of pervasive data collection. As CPS often involves multiple stakeholders, such as manufacturers, service providers, and end-users, establishing clear guidelines for data ownership is critical [60]. The ambiguity surrounding data ownership can lead to conflicts and mistrust among stakeholders, undermining the effectiveness of CPS.

To address these challenges, a user-centric approach to data sharing and privacy must be prioritized. This approach involves empowering users with greater control over their data, including the ability to provide informed consent regarding its collection and use. Policymakers and practitioners should work collaboratively to develop regulations that protect users' rights while promoting innovation in CPS [60]. Furthermore, the implementation of privacy-preserving techniques such as differential privacy and homomorphic encryption offers promising solutions to mitigate privacy risks. However, their effectiveness in practical applications remains an area of active research. For instance, while differential privacy provides a robust framework for preventing reidentification in datasets, its practical deployment in real-time CPS applications requires further exploration. Similarly, homomorphic encryption, which allows computations to be performed on encrypted data, holds great potential for enhancing privacy, but its computational overhead and efficiency in large-scale CPS must be addressed [62].

Additionally, as CPS continues to evolve, new privacy challenges may emerge. For example, the increasing use of interconnected devices in smart cities and the Internet of Things (IoT) raises concerns about the potential for surveillance and the aggregation of personal data. Researchers must remain vigilant in identifying and addressing these emerging privacy issues, ensuring that privacy considerations are integrated into the design and deployment of CPS from the outset [62].

The exploration of emerging technologies such as blockchain and AI reveals their potential to enhance the security and privacy of CPS but also highlights the complexities and ethical considerations accompanying their use. With its decentralized and tamper-proof characteristics, blockchain technology offers a promising solution for securing data exchanges within CPS. For example, in the context of smart grids, blockchain can facilitate secure energy trading while ensuring the privacy of individual users' energy consumption data. However, the scalability and integration of blockchain into existing CPS infrastructure remain significant challenges [63]. Researchers must continue to explore practical solutions for implementing blockchain technology in diverse CPS environments.

AI and machine learning also present opportunities for improving CPS security through real-time threat detection and anomaly recognition. Fei and Shen's proposal for using machine learning algorithms to identify unusual patterns in network traffic highlights these technologies' potential to enhance CPS's security posture. However, the ethical implications of AI use in CPS cannot be overlooked. Concerns about algorithmic bias, transparency, and accountability must be addressed to ensure that AI-driven systems do not inadvertently exacerbate existing inequalities or lead to unintended consequences [63].

The black-box nature of many machine learning models raises questions about the transparency of AI decision-making processes. When AI systems are used in critical applications, such as autonomous vehicles, it is essential to ensure that the decision-making processes are interpretable and accountable. Researchers should explore methods for improving the transparency and explainability of AI algorithms to enhance user trust and enable meaningful oversight.

Addressing the complex challenges posed by CPS requires a collaborative and interdisciplinary approach that spans technical, legal, and ethical domains. Stakeholders, including researchers, practitioners, policymakers, and users, must work together to develop comprehensive frameworks that integrate security, privacy, and ethical considerations [64]. This collaboration is essential for creating CPS that is not only technologically advanced but also socially responsible.

Furthermore, fostering public awareness and understanding of CPS is critical for building trust among users and stakeholders. Educational initiatives aimed at informing users about the implications of CPS and their rights regarding data privacy can empower individuals to make informed decisions and participate in discussions about the ethical deployment of these systems [65].

In conclusion, the rapid proliferation of CPS presents both opportunities and challenges that require ongoing research, innovation, and collaboration. The security and privacy concerns identified in the literature highlight the necessity for continuous adaptation and improvement of strategies to mitigate risks. By addressing these challenges holistically and ethically, stakeholders can ensure the responsible development and deployment of CPS that enhance societal well-being while safeguarding individual rights and freedoms. Future research should continue to explore the evolving landscape of CPS technologies and their implications, striving for a balance between technological advancement and ethical responsibility [66].

12.6 Conclusion and Future Scope

The importance of cyber-physical systems (CPS) continues to grow as industrial and commercial processes become more complex. There are security concerns and a novel solution as failures in industries such as power systems and healthcare that require novel solutions as failures in industries such as power systems and healthcare, where CPS is rapidly being adopted, are often catastrophic. The security threats have been classified as hardware, software, and network attacks. Hardware attacks occur when the tangible components, usually the edge devices such as sensors and actuators, are physically or remotely manipulated by attackers. The data collected by these edge devices can be temporarily stored on them and processed for decision-making before being transferred to a database and more powerful servers for more processing. Network attack occurs when the data are intercepted in a man-in-the-middle attack case, or the master or server cannot communicate with the edge devices in a case called denial of service (DoS). The code on the edge devices, usually machine learning (ML)-based, can also be of interest to attackers by injecting malicious code. This is a software attack. Security strategies should address each category of threat, work together as a comprehensive security protocol, and continuously evolve to prevent new forms of attack.

Another challenge addressed in this chapter is privacy related to CPS deployment and adoption. Ownership and consent are the two main legs of privacy. The sensors, actuators, and other edge devices of the CPS generate a large amount of data. Privacy is essentially important in healthcare and third-party asset monitoring CPS deployments. Individuals in healthcare, CPS, and asset owners are the default owners of the data. Still, the service providers need access to these data to serve these individuals better and provide real-time insights. However, consent must be sought before sharing users' data with third parties to avoid conflict and build trust. It is also noted that policies and legal frameworks that ensure users' privacy is protected need to be developed.

The codes deployed on edge devices and the more powerful servers to derive insights from the gathered data are predominantly machine learning (ML) algorithms, a subfield of artificial intelligence (AI). The models trained by the algorithms are as smart as the training data. Attackers have found a way to deceive the models and cause them to malfunction by feeding them false data based on the knowledge of the training data. Therefore, it is advised that these models must be retrained periodically as new parameters and new categories of data become available to prevent possible software exploitation.

Ultimately, this chapter brings to limelight the security and privacy challenges that must be addressed as the deployment and adoption of cyber-physical systems (CPS) rises. Hence, any deployment of CPS in any industry must be viewed as an end-to-end system, starting from the physical end sensors that can be seen and touched to the backend servers that will analyze the data for inference and decision-making. It has also been shown that solutions to these security and privacy challenges will continue evolving as attackers seek CPS vulnerabilities and users continue to know how their data are being used. Also, new technologies such as blockchain may be explored and adapted for CPS. Due to the enormous economic, health, and environmental benefits of autonomous systems, healthcare, and net-zero power systems, respectively, CPS adoption and deployment will continue to grow rapidly, provided the security and privacy challenges are addressed adequately.

References

[1] Vangala, A., Das, A.K., Dedeoglu, V. and Jurdak, R., Security and Privacy of Cyber-Physical Systems, in Cyber-Physical Systems for Industrial Transformation. 2023, CRC Press. p. 97–113.

[2] Bala, I., Pindoo, I., Mijwil, M.M., Abotaleb, M. and Yundong, W., Ensuring security and privacy in Healthcare Systems: a Review Exploring challenges, solutions, Future trends, and the practical applications of Artificial Intelligence. Jordan Medical Journal, 2024. **58**(2).

[3] Yaacoub, J.P.A., Salman, O., Noura, H.N., Kaaniche, N., Chehab, A. and Malli, M., Cyber-physical systems security: Limitations, issues and future trends. Microprocessors and microsystems, 2020. **77**: p. 103201.
[4] Liao, W., Security and Privacy of Cyber-Physical Systems. 2018: Case Western Reserve University.
[5] Khalaf, M., Ayad, A., Tushar, M.H.K., Kassouf, M. and Kundur, D., A Survey on Cyber-Physical Security of Active Distribution Networks in Smart Grids. IEEE Access, 2024.
[6] Saeed, M.M. and M. Alsharidah, Security, privacy, and robustness for trustworthy AI systems: A review. Computers and Electrical Engineering, 2024. **119**: p. 109643.
[7] Yu, Z., Kaplan, Z., Yan, Q. and Zhang, N., Security and privacy in the emerging cyber-physical world: A survey. IEEE Communications Surveys & Tutorials, 2021. **23**(3): p. 1879–1919.
[8] Bindra, S.S. and A. Aggarwal, Security in cyber physical systems: Transformation and challenges. Journal of Autonomous Intelligence, 2024. **7**(4).
[9] Salam, A., Internet of things for sustainability: perspectives in privacy, cybersecurity, and future trends, in Internet of things for sustainable community development: wireless communications, sensing, and systems. 2024, Springer. p. 299–326.
[10] Kaushik, K., Ethical Considerations in AI-Based Cybersecurity, in Next-Generation Cybersecurity: AI, ML, and Blockchain. 2024, Springer. p. 437–470.
[11] Kumar, S. and B. Bhowmik. Emergence, Evolution, and Applications of Cyber-Physical Systems in Smart Society. in 2024 Fourth International Conference on Advances in Electrical, Computing, Communication and Sustainable Technologies (ICAECT). 2024. IEEE.
[12] Kandasamy, M., Shanmugam, R., Patel, V., Patel, U., Bulchandani, A. and Bhardwaj, A., Design challenges in cyber-physical systems: An overview of privacy threats in ubiquitous computing. Ubiquitous and Transparent Security, 2024: p. 207–235.
[13] Gaba, S., Budhiraja, I., Kumar, V., Martha, S., Khurmi, J., Singh, A., Singh, K.K., Askar, S.S. and Abouhawwash, M., A systematic analysis of enhancing cyber security using deep learning for cyber physical systems. IEEE Access, 2024.
[14] Sharma, M., Enhancing Security and Privacy in Cyber-Physical Systems: Challenges and Solutions. in 2024 IEEE 14th Annual Computing and Communication Workshop and Conference (CCWC). 2024. IEEE.

[15] Oudina, Z., Derdour, M., Dib, A. and Yaakoubi, M.A., Identifying and Addressing Trust Concerns in Cyber-Physical Systems for the Oil and Gas Industry. Ingénierie des Systèmes d'Information, 2024. **29**(2).

[16] Mohammed, M.A., Lakhan, A., Zebari, D.A., Abd Ghani, M.K., Marhoon, H.A., Abdulkareem, K.H., Nedoma, J. and Martinek, R., Securing healthcare data in industrial cyber-physical systems using combining deep learning and blockchain technology. Engineering Applications of Artificial Intelligence, 2024. **129**: p. 107612.

[17] Mallick, M.A.I. and R. Nath, Navigating the Cyber security Landscape: A Comprehensive Review of Cyber-Attacks, Emerging Trends, and Recent Developments. World Scientific News, 2024. **190**(1): p. 1–69.

[18] Chakraborty, S., Jha, S., Samii, S. and Mundhenk, P., Introduction to the Special Issue on Automotive CPS Safety & Security: Part 2. ACM Transactions on Cyber-Physical Systems, 2024. **8**(2): p. 1–17.

[19] Prince, N.U., Al Mamun, M.A., Olajide, A.O., Khan, O.U., Akeem, A.B. and Sani, A.I., Emerging Trends for Securing Cyber Physical Systems and the Internet of Things. 2024.

[20] Humayed, A., Lin, J., Li, F. and Luo, B., Cyber-physical systems security—A survey. IEEE Internet of Things Journal, 2017. **4**(6): p. 1802–1831.

[21] Farwell, J.P. and R. Rohozinski, Stuxnet and the future of cyber war. Survival, 2011. **53**(1): p. 23–40.

[22] Squillace, J., J. Cappella, and A. Sepp. User Vulnerabilities in AI-Driven Systems: Current Cybersecurity Threat Dynamics and Malicious Exploits in Supply Chain Management and Project Management. in 2024 ASU International Conference in Emerging Technologies for Sustainability and Intelligent Systems (ICETSIS). 2024. IEEE.

[23] Chen, T., Cecilia, A., Astolfi, D., Wang, L., Liu, Z. and Su, H., Chaotic Masking Protocol for Secure Communication and Attack Detection in Remote Estimation of Cyber-Physical Systems. arXiv preprint arXiv:2403.09076, 2024.

[24] He, H., Gray, J., Cangelosi, A., Meng, Q., McGinnity, T.M. and Mehnen, J., The challenges and opportunities of human-centered AI for trustworthy robots and autonomous systems. IEEE Transactions on Cognitive and Developmental Systems, 2021. **14**(4): p. 1398–1412.

[25] Zhou, S., Liu, C., Ye, D., Zhu, T., Zhou, W. and Yu, P.S., Adversarial attacks and defenses in deep learning: From a perspective of cybersecurity. ACM Computing Surveys, 2022. **55**(8): p. 1–39.

[26] Mirchev, M., I. Mircheva, and A. Kerekovska, The academic viewpoint on patient data ownership in the context of big data: scoping review. Journal of Medical Internet Research, 2020. **22**(8): p. e22214.
[27] Wright, D. and M. Friedewald, Integrating privacy and ethical impact assessments. Science and Public Policy, 2013. **40**(6): p. 755–766.
[28] Wang, Y., Wang, Q., Zhao, L. and Wang, C., Differential privacy in deep learning: Privacy and beyond. Future Generation Computer Systems, 2023. **148**: p. 408–424.
[29] Keshk, M., Turnbull, B., Sitnikova, E., Vatsalan, D. and Moustafa, N., Privacy-preserving schemes for safeguarding heterogeneous data sources in cyber-physical systems. IEEE Access, 2021. **9**: p. 55077–55097.
[30] Jaiman, V. and V. Urovi, A consent model for blockchain-based health data sharing platforms. IEEE access, 2020. **8**: p. 143734–143745.
[31] Dorri, A., Steger, M., Kanhere, S.S. and Jurdak, R., Blockchain: A distributed solution to automotive security and privacy. IEEE communications magazine, 2017. **55**(12): p. 119–125.
[32] Liu, Y., L. Wu, and J. Li, Peer-to-peer (P2P) electricity trading in distribution systems of the future. The Electricity Journal, 2019. **32**(4): p. 2–6.
[33] Fei, C. and J. Shen, Machine learning for securing Cyber–Physical Systems under cyber attacks: A survey. Franklin Open, 2023: p. 100041.
[34] McDermid, J.A., Jia, Y., Porter, Z. and Habli, I., Artificial intelligence explainability: the technical and ethical dimensions. Philosophical Transactions of the Royal Society A, 2021. **379**(2207): p. 20200363.
[35] Fathy, A., D. Yousri, and E.F. El-Saadany, A novel memory-based artificial gorilla troops optimizer for installing biomass distributed generators in unbalanced radial networks. Sustainable Energy Technologies and Assessments, 2024. **68**: p. 103885.
[36] Wang, H., Zhao, H., Zhang, J., Ma, D., Li, J. and Wei, J., Survey on unmanned aerial vehicle networks: A cyber physical system perspective. IEEE Communications Surveys & Tutorials, 2019. **22**(2): p. 1027–1070.
[37] Kayan, H., Nunes, M., Rana, O., Burnap, P. and Perera, C., Cybersecurity of industrial cyber-physical systems: A review. ACM Computing Surveys (CSUR), 2022. **54**(11s): p. 1–35.
[38] Hu, Y., Yang, A., Li, H., Sun, Y. and Sun, L., A survey of intrusion detection on industrial control systems. International Journal of Distributed Sensor Networks, 2018. **14**(8): p. 1550147718794615.
[39] Rahman, Z., Khalil, I., Yi, X. and Atiquzzaman, M., Blockchain-based security framework for a critical industry 4.0 cyber-physical system. IEEE Communications Magazine, 2021. **59**(5): p. 128–134.

[40] Genge, B., P. Haller, and A.-V. Duka, Engineering security-aware control applications for data authentication in smart industrial cyber–physical systems. Future Generation Computer Systems, 2019. **91**: p. 206–222.

[41] Adil, M., Jan, M.A., Liu, Y., Abulkasim, H., Farouk, A. and Song, H., A systematic survey: Security threats to UAV-aided IoT applications, taxonomy, current challenges and requirements with future research directions. IEEE Transactions on Intelligent Transportation Systems, 2022. **24**(2): p. 1437–1455.

[42] Anand, P., Singh, Y., Selwal, A., Alazab, M., Tanwar, S. and Kumar, N., IoT vulnerability assessment for sustainable computing: threats, current solutions, and open challenges. IEEE Access, 2020. **8**: p. 168825–168853.

[43] Zhou, X., Ahmed, B., Aylor, J.H., Asare, P. and Alemzadeh, H., Hybrid knowledge and data driven synthesis of runtime monitors for cyber-physical systems. IEEE Transactions on Dependable and Secure Computing, 2023. **21**(1): p. 12–30.

[44] Mtukushe, N., Onaolapo, A.K., Aluko, A. and Dorrell, D.G., Review of cyberattack implementation, detection, and mitigation methods in cyber-physical systems. Energies, 2023. **16**(13): p. 5206.

[45] Raza, A., Memon, S., Nizamani, M.A. and Shah, M.H., Machine learning-based security solutions for critical cyber-physical systems. in 2022 10th International Symposium on Digital Forensics and Security (ISDFS). 2022. IEEE.

[46] Guo, L., IoT-enabled Adaptive Control Systems for Cyber-Physical Security in Autonomous Vehicles. Journal of Artificial Intelligence Research and Applications, 2024. **4**(1): p. 260–283.

[47] Stellios, I., P. Kotzanikolaou, and C. Grigoriadis, Assessing IoT enabled cyber-physical attack paths against critical systems. Computers & Security, 2021. **107**: p. 102316.

[48] Lee, E.A. Cyber physical systems: Design challenges. in 2008 11th IEEE international symposium on object and component-oriented real-time distributed computing (ISORC). 2008. IEEE.

[49] Alaba, F.A., Othman, M., Hashem, I.A.T. and Alotaibi, F., Internet of Things security: A survey. Journal of Network and Computer Applications, 2017. **88**: p. 10–28.

[50] Ashok, M., Madan, R., Joha, A. and Sivarajah, U., Ethical framework for Artificial Intelligence and Digital technologies. International Journal of Information Management, 2022. **62**: p. 102433.

[51] Bonawitz, K., Towards federated learning at scale: System design (2019). CoRR abs/1902.01046. 1902.

[52] Christidis, K. and M. Devetsikiotis, Blockchains and smart contracts for the internet of things. IEEE access, 2016. **4**: p. 2292–2303.

[53] Dautenhahn, K., Socially intelligent robots: dimensions of human–robot interaction. Philosophical transactions of the royal society B: Biological sciences, 2007. **362**(1480): p. 679–704.

[54] Eibl, G. and D. Engel, Differential privacy for real smart metering data. Computer Science-Research and Development, 2017. **32**: p. 173–182.

[55] Gupta, R., Tanwar, S., Al-Turjman, F., Italiya, P., Nauman, A. and Kim, S.W., Smart contract privacy protection using AI in cyber-physical systems: tools, techniques and challenges. IEEE access, 2020. **8**: p. 24746–24772.

[56] He, D., S. Chan, and M. Guizani, Security in the Internet of Things supported by mobile edge computing. IEEE Communications Magazine, 2018. **56**(8): p. 56–61.

[57] Javaid, M., Haleem, A., Singh, R.P. and Suman, R., Towards insighting cybersecurity for healthcare domains: A comprehensive review of recent practices and trends. Cyber Security and Applications, vol 1, pp. 100016.

[58] Khan, M.A. and K. Salah, IoT security: Review, blockchain solutions, and open challenges. Future generation computer systems, 2018. **82**: p. 395–411.

[59] Zhang, Q., Ethics in the autonomous vehicle (AV) development process: How does the person-organization ethics fit influence the ethical performance of AV? 2023: The University of Memphis.

[60] Kshetri, N., Can blockchain strengthen the internet of things? IT professional, 2017. **19**(4): p. 68–72.

[61] Stergiou, C., Psannis, K.E., Gupta, B.B. and Ishibashi, Y., Security, privacy & efficiency of sustainable cloud computing for big data & IoT. Sustainable Computing: Informatics and Systems, 2018. vol **19**: p. 174–184.

[62] Lin, P., Robots in War: Issues of Risk and Ethics. Ethics and Robotics/ Akademische Verlagsgesellschaft AKA GmbH, 2009.

[63] Manulis, M., Bridges, C.P., Harrison, R., Sekar, V. and Davis, A., Cyber security in new space: analysis of threats, key enabling technologies and challenges. International Journal of Information Security, 2021. vol **20**: p. 287–311.

[64] Mollah, M.B., et al., Blockchain for the internet of vehicles towards intelligent transportation systems: A survey. IEEE Internet of Things Journal, 2020. **8**(6): p. 4157–4185.

[65] Roman, R., J. Zhou, and J. Lopez, On the features and challenges of security and privacy in distributed internet of things. Computer networks, 2013. **57**(10): p. 2266–2279.
[66] Shi, Weisong, Jie Cao, Quan Zhang, Youhuizi Li, and Lanyu Xu. "Edge computing: Vision and challenges." IEEE internet of things journal, 2016. vol 3, **3**(5): p. 637–646.

13

Intrusion Detection Techniques for Cyber-physical Systems

Comfort Oluwaseyi Folorunso[1], Lateef Adesola Akinyemi[2,3], Wasiu Adewale Raheem[1], Olumide Francis Odeyinka[1], Eniola Sodiq Olaleye[1] and Oluwafemi Ipinnimo[1]

[1]Department of Systems Engineering, Faculty of Engineering, University of Lagos, Nigeria
[2]Department of Electronic and Computer Engineering, Faculty of Engineering, Lagos State University, Nigeria
[3]Centre for Augmented Intelligence and Data Science (CAIDS), School of Computing, CSET University of South Africa, South Africa

Email: cfolorunso@unilag.edu.ng; akinyla@unisa.ac.za; lateef.akinyemi@lasu.edu.ng; wraheem@unilag.edu.ng; oodeyinka@unilag.edu.ng; eniolaolaleye426@gmail.com; oipinnimo@unilag.edu.ng

Abstract

The dynamic nature of cyber security threats necessitates innovative approaches to safeguard networks and systems. This work examines intrusion detection techniques to prevent attacks that can harm cyber-physical systems (CPS). Intrusion detection techniques for CPS employ cutting-edge detection methods such as behavior analysis and anomaly detection algorithms to identify and prevent infiltration attempts. This work emphasizes achieving optimization, digital operation, and safety in a CPS using a power generation plant case study. Nine different machine learning algorithms, including CatBoost, decision tree, XGBoost, lightGBM, random forest, AdaBoost, XGBoost, logistic regression, k-nearest neighbors (KNN), and naive Bayes were employed in this study and their performance on attack detection have been examined. The HIL-based augmented ICS (HAI) security dataset is used. The random

DOI: 10.1201/9788743801306-13

forest gave the best results with AUC, sensitivity, accuracy, precision, and F1 of over 99.31%, followed by the CatBoost (over 99.1%) and the XGBM (over 98.86%). The lessons learned and future directions are presented.

13.1 Introduction

A cyber-physical system (CPS) combines cyberspace and the physical environment by installing systems, sensors, computational processes, and actuators to monitor the physical process in real time. These systems are usually intended to run either fully or semi-fully themselves and are often used in sectors such as energy, healthcare, transportation, industrial, control, and smart cities. It must be noted that all CPSs possess at least one shared characteristic: they can alter physical contexts based on digital computations, thereby optimizing operations. Some examples of CPS include smart grids, self-driving cars, industrial robots, and other healthcare applications like pacemakers and infusion pumps [1].

CPSs are designed to operate in very specific and demanding conditions. Thus, the flows between the software and the hardware modules must be fully integrated to achieve real-time operation, precision, and reliability. Sensors in a CPS gather information from the physical environment, while outputs and controllers transform the information. For instance, in the industrial environment, it is possible to use CPS to assess the health status of the equipment and other systems, diagnose any abnormalities, and even correct them through intelligent reconfiguring machinery to prevent potential breakdown, thereby increasing production efficiency. In healthcare, CPS will enable constant patient vital assessment and treatment without human intervention, enhancing the quality of services. This integration of physical and digital components in CPS brings out increased efficiency and capabilities, but at the same time, poses great dangers in terms of security. These systems are normally interfaced with larger networks and the internet, and therefore, are susceptible to hacking. Since the CPS applications are used in scenarios where their failure is fatal, a successful attack may cause severe damage, including power blackouts, transportation systems breakdown, or disruption of the healthcare system. Therefore, securing the CPS is critical, wherein intrusion detection plays a significant role in protection.

Intrusion detection systems (IDS) are programs or security tools structured to check network activity and system performance for signs of malicious behavior or unauthorized access. In the context of CPS, IDSs play a fundamental role in defending the reliability and accessibility of the system. CPS protection requires IDS because it detects incoming exploits and other strange behaviors. The fundamental characteristics of CPS include interconnectedness, real-time constraints, physical implications, and heterogeneous components [2].

a. *Interconnectedness:* CPS components are frequently distributed and connected, which brings about the problem of component failure propagation.
b. *Real-time constraints:* many CPS systems and applications have time constraints for responding, so the intrusion detection mechanisms have to be efficient and low-latency.
c. *Physical implications:* CPS cyberattacks can include physical deprivations like causing blackouts or industrial disasters.
d. *Heterogeneous components:* CPSs comprise hardware, software, and physical parts, making security management complex.

A CPS is made up of various components. It defines smart cities, operation technology, IT infrastructure, and the Internet of Things (IoT). It is critical for organizations' security networks. These structures may be vulnerable and exposed to cyber threats if the appropriate cyber security measures are not implemented and integrated into the security policies. Expanding the risk view to incorporate CPSs helps to experience smoother business flows in the organization. IDSs are uniquely suited for enhancing the safety of CPS as they are meant to monitor and detect unlawful intrusion. IDSs are important control mechanisms that can help CPS deal with cyber threats. It plays an important role in enabling organizations to prevent attacks on their systems, thus guaranteeing their operations and services' effectiveness, reliability, and integrity. Some of these important roles are summarized in Figure 13.1.

Due to the current trend toward using CPS in infrastructure, it is now possible to increase the protection of these systems. IDSs are critical in providing security to these systems against intruders' access, malicious activities, and other related risks. Unlike regular information technologies designed, among other things, to ensure data protection, CPS addresses the issue of securing both electronic parts of systems and processes. In those systems, penetration can be linked to physical impact and thus may have drastic consequences [2]. For instance, an attack on the smart grid may disempower various communities of power or lead to disjointed power networks. In contrast, an attack on the autonomous vehicle system may lead to loss of control and random crashes.

In CPS, the loss does not only mean that data have been stolen or manipulated but there are various effects of intrusions. Since their computation and

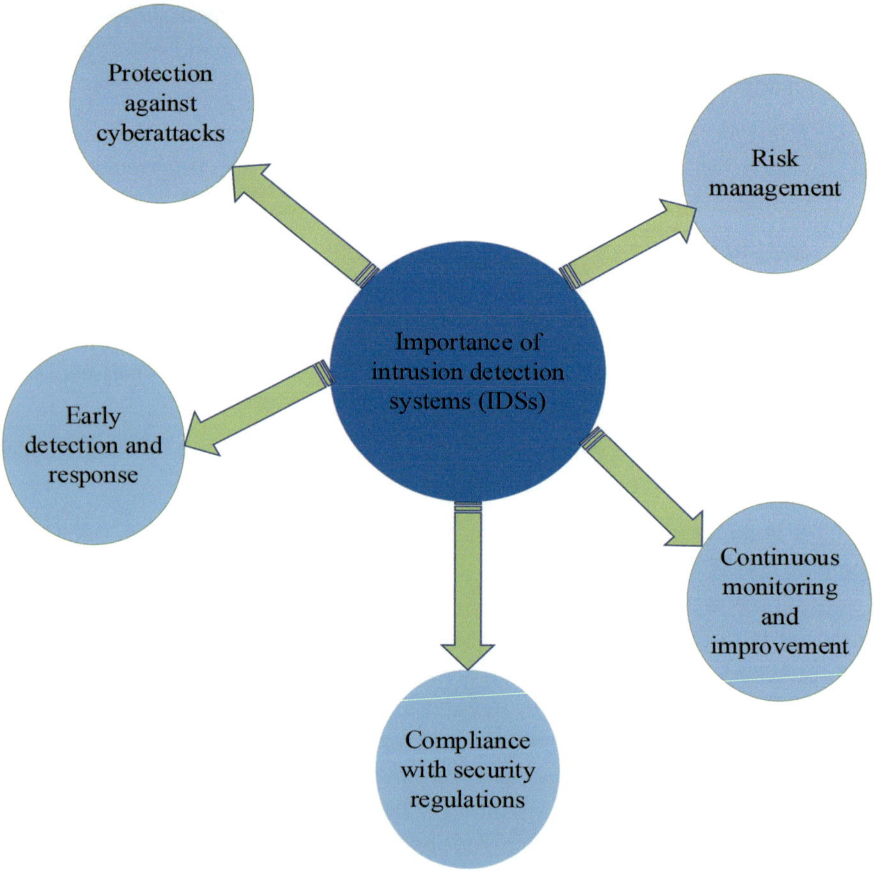

Figure 13.1 Importance of intrusion detection systems (IDS) in cyber-physical systems (CPS).

physical system strongly connect such processes, any violation in the cyber domain has a direct and measurable impact on the physical environment. This is even the case for CPS used in high-risk applications for which real-time operation and decision-making are critical to the system's functionality [2]. For instance, in industrial control systems, a cyberattack can change how machinery is run by causing production breakdowns or physical destruction of equipment or endangering the lives of those operating them. Therefore, intrusion detection in CPS has an important function of determining threats that need to be prevented from resulting in danger. Thus, the IDS for CPS has to identify unauthorized actions in cyberspace and physical space.

For instance, while traditional IDS may look at log traffic for suspicious activity in the network, IDS in CPS may also have to look for variations in sensor data and physical processes that might have been interfered with or tampered with. This twofold concern makes the intrusion detection problem more challenging, although it is crucial for ensuring the CPS's confidentiality, accuracy, and security [2].

13.1.1 Challenges unique to intrusion detection in CPS

Intrusion detection for CPS proposes a set of problems that differ from those encountered in intrusion detection in conventional IT systems. These problems arise from the CPS architecture, the dissimilarities between conventional computing systems, and the requirements essential for CPS applications [3]. Some of the challenges include the following:

1. *Real-time requirements:* CPSs are well applied in real-time applications where any delay in intrusion detection or response can pose threats. For instance, in an automobile self-driving car, any sign of delayed discovery of a cyberattack that affects the control system may lead to accidents. This need for immediate detection of intrusions reduces the applicability of conventional IDS methodologies that may cause latency or involve analysis that may take quite some time. IDS for CPS must be both timely and precise in order not to miss an emergent attack and, at the same time, avoid interfering with other vital processes [4], [5].

2. *Resource constraints:* some CPS components, especially those employed in areas like industrial control or healthcare, are often constrained in their resources. In general, sensors, actuators, and embedded systems have low computing capabilities and limited memory and power availability in CPS. This restricts the types of algorithms that can be used in intrusion detection since traditional IDS, which are computationally intensive, may not be possible. One of the significant research problems in CPS security is to build compact IDS that can run on low-power hardware [4], [5].

3. *Heterogeneity and scalability:* thus, CPSs are usually made of heterogeneous devices and systems that have different functionalities, protocols of interaction, and security demands. No uniform approach is possible when deploying an intrusion detection solution. An IDS should be capable of running on various platforms, including rack servers and endpoints, cutting across the high-end to low-end technologies, and must support multiple protocols. Further, CPSs are normally large-scale, with extensive numbers of devices ranging in thousands or even millions, all functioning in coordination. Extending intrusion detection

to accommodate such large and heterogeneous networks without compromising on the same is major [4], [5].

4. *Physical and cyber integration:* another critical problem in CPS is the physical and cyber interrelation, or in other words, the integration of physical and cyber layers that are intimately connected. Intrusion detection systems are not just supposed to input some number derived from analyzing a set of signals obtained from analyzing the cyber activities of the network traffic, system logs, and the like; they also have to understand physical processes such as sensor readings and actuator outputs. This is something that IDS needs to understand well, specifically the physical processes they are trying to monitor, along with being able to discern between subtler changes in the physical layer data and more profound fluctuations that could signal the possibility of an attack. For instance, a slight variation in temperature in a smart grid system may be insignificant. Still, if the temperature suddenly drops or rises to very high levels, this may indicate tampering. This is a critical aspect in the detection of intrusions in CPS, especially because these may be minimal but play a significant role in intrusion detection [4], [5].

5. *Sophisticated and hybrid attacks:* CPSs are especially exposed to more complex cyberattacks that exploit online and offline weaknesses. These are also referred to as hybrid attacks, and they pose a more significant threat since they use different methods and phases and are generally hard for IDS to identify. For instance, an attacker may initially gain entry into a CPS's network, and from there, interfere with sensor data to make the CPS act abnormally. IDS must also be able to identify the first phase of the network intrusion, as well as the second phase, when physical access is gained [4], [5].

13.1.2 Research gaps and motivations for IDS techniques

CPSs are exposed to numerous security vulnerabilities. However, current and future efforts have revealed research gaps in designing efficient IDS for CPS. Many conventional IDS solutions do not consider the requirements and peculiarities of CPS and are initially developed to protect general-purpose IT systems. Due to this, a tendency has been developing over the years to design new intrusion detection techniques that will solve the problems of CPS [6].

Another area of research that requires addressing is the absence of context-aware intrusion detection in CPS. As described later, conventional IDS mainly operates on cyber data, such as network traffic or system logs, while ignoring the physical data the system controls. However, in the case of CPS, physical context is used to recognize attacks. For instance, when IDS monitors a smart grid system, it must be able to correlate signals observed over the network with physical ones such as voltage or frequency that may point to a cyberattack.

Computation of attributes in a CSP environment can only be done by contextual IDS incorporating physical and cyber data to facilitate timely and accurate identification of threats in CPS [7]. Another central area of study is more lightweight and adaptive intrusion detection. Due to the limited resources available in many CPS devices, IDS must be implemented with low computational and energy requirements. Moreover, CPS environments are open and often have variable or unpredictable characteristics, such as the topology of the layers in the CPS system, the devices' configuration, and the operational status of the CPS system.

IDS needs to adapt to these changes in a way that does not affect detection capabilities. One requires an adaptive IDS that can learn from the system's behavior over time and adjust its detection strategies accordingly, especially in the existing CPS environment, which has always been changing. Finally, IDS must be designed to operate with large-scale CPS networks effectively and efficiently. Most CPS includes hundreds, thousands, or millions of interconnected devices, especially in smart city or industrial sectors. Intrusion control, especially in such extensive networks, without considerably increasing latency or overhead, is a difficult issue that demands techniques for distributed and hierarchical intrusion detection. From a research perspective, addressing these gaps will lead to the development of novel IDS that will boost CPS security, and thereby, the resistance against cyberattacks on critical infrastructures.

This chapter aims to explore and address these research gaps by outlining intrusion detection techniques specifically designed for CPS. These techniques are expected to provide robust, context-aware, and efficient methods for detecting intrusions in CPS's cyber and physical domains, ensuring the security and reliability of these vital systems facing increasingly sophisticated cyber threats.

13.1.3 Chapter organization

Section 13.1 introduces CPS, its importance, and the challenges of IDS for CPS. The contributions of this book chapter are also outlined here. Section 13.2 discusses related works on intrusion techniques for CPS. A summary of the reviewed works with different machine learning algorithms and intrusion datasets is presented herewith. An overview of different IDS techniques for CPS is provided in Section 13.3. The CPS architecture and fundamental challenges of CPS are also analyzed. Section 13.4 focuses on the applications of CPS, while Section 13.5 outlines the future direction of CPS. Section 13.6 focuses on the problem and methods of intrusion detection and various machine algorithms used in CPS. The results obtained are discussed in Section 13.7. The lessons learned from this work are presented and discussed.

13.2 Related Works on the IDS for CPSs

IDSs have been described as systems that observe and assess data to detect any intrusion in a network [8]. IDSs for CPSs are classified based on audit material and detection techniques [2]. The audit material describes the way the system gathers data before analyzing it. This is done either through the host or network-based audit methods. The detection techniques describe approaches that analyze the behavior of runtime features. These approaches are either based on a particular behavior pattern (knowledge-based) or patterns that are not regular (behavior-based) [7]. The behavior-specification-based approach describes intrusion detection which does not consider users, groups, or data profiling [2]. Different intrusion detection approaches have been employed in the literature, as shown in Figure 13.2.

Securing CPSs has been of utmost interest to everyone, including governments at all levels, due to their importance in data generation, retrieval, and storage. So much emphasis has been placed on developing novel techniques that improve the performance of IDS for CPSs. Most of the popular approaches for developing IDS for CPS are deep learning-based. The application of deep learning in developing intrusion techniques was first proposed by [7]. One of its advantages over other IDS techniques is its strong feature learning ability during unsupervised training layer by layer. The applications of deep learning methods for IDS abound in the literature.

For example, the work [9] implemented a split learning approach for a smart meter IDS in software-defined networks (SDN). Results indicated an accuracy of over 81.1% and F1-score of 79.9. The authors compared their results with that of a federated learning-based model with an F1-score of 78.9 with over 80.3% classification accuracy, and the split learning technique method exhibited a better accuracy. Sadaf and Sultana [10] developed an Auto-IF method based on deep learning using Autoencoder (AE) and Isolation Forest (IF) for a fog environment. The method pointed at the binary groups of incoming packets as fog devices, differentiating attacks in normal

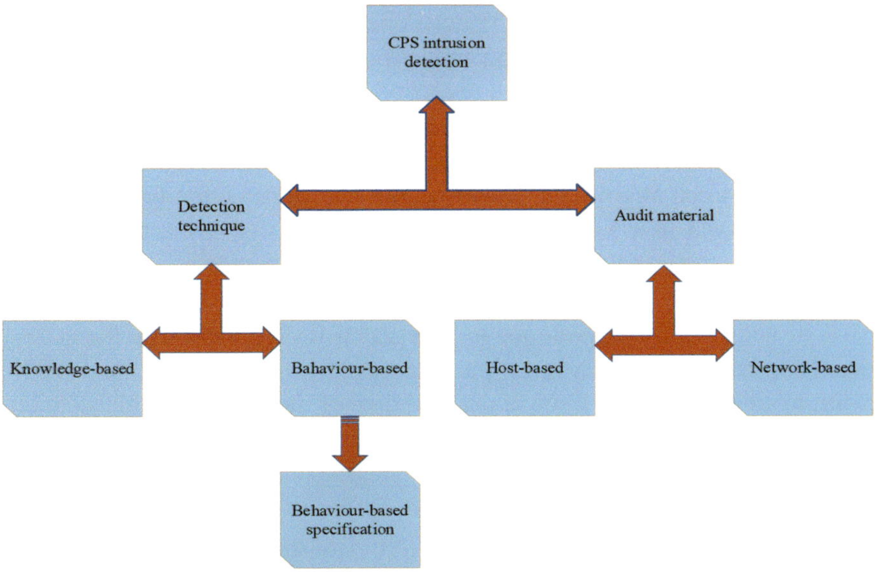

Figure 13.2 Classification of intrusion detection approaches.

real-time packets. The technique was tested on the NSL-KDD dataset, and 95.4% accuracy was obtained.

Similarly, [11] used an innovative CPS-GUARD centered on a single semisupervised auto-encoder and a method to set the threshold to differentiate normal operations from attacks. CPS-GUARD is estimated using direct experiments with normal and intrusion data points about individual sensing devices, an HTTP server, and four full-fledged systems comprising CPSs. The recall of 0.95–1.00, precision of 0.96–0.9, and false positive rate of 0.006–0.027 were obtained based on the type of the system. In addition, [12] used a generic-specific auto-encoder framework that learns generic and specific features common to a particular domain.

Moreso, the work [13] modified a federated learning IDS model using real-time network traffic. A heterogeneous nondistributed dataset was obtained, and the performance of a deep belief network (DBN) based IDS was evaluated. Results from this model were compared with those of a deep neural network-based IDS and a centralized IDS method, and a performance improvement of over 20% (F1-score) resulted. Using deep neural networks, [14] focused on identifying the best algorithm that can effectively detect future attacks. Experimental results of DNNs on the KDDCup 99 dataset indicated a learning rate range of (0.01–0.5) and a better accuracy than other machine learning models.

Furthermore, the study [15] developed an IDS based on a convolutional neural network. Dimension reduction methods were used to remove unwanted features in the network data, and data features were extracted via CNN. The KDD-CUP99 dataset was used to validate the model performance, with evidence showing that the accuracy of 94% and recall are better than that of traditional algorithms. However, the rate of detection for remote-to-local (R2L) and user-to-root (U2R) attacks are low (20.61% and 18.96%, respectively), thus indicating that the model developed possesses practical relevance.

In addition, [16] developed an integrated IDS model using the staked denoising autoencoders extreme learning machine (SDAE-ELM) and DBN-Softmax to surmount the issue of delayed time of training and small accuracy of classification of traditional deep neural network models, thus enhancing response to attacks and intrusions. The integrated model aimed to improve the detection accuracy of host intrusion traffic, training effectiveness, and overall detection performance. The gradient descent technique was used to train and optimize the network while validation was done using five datasets – CIDDS-001, NSL-KDD, UNSW-NB15, ADFA-LD, and KDD CUP99. Results indicated that the integrated IDS models performed better than traditional IDS models.

Also, [17] analyzed the performance of a model based on DBN to identify intrusion in the connection of devices. Validation was done on the CICIDS2017 dataset using different class balancing methods. The model was compared to a conventional multilayer perceptron (MLP) model. The results showed that the DBN approach performed better, with a major improvement in intrusion detection in the training dataset.

In addition, [18] built an attack detection system using feed-forward neural networks with low false negative and positive rates. One of the feed-forward neural networks was used for the nonfuzzified data, while the other analyzed the fuzzy data. Analyses of both networks in detecting network intrusions were carried out, and it was observed that the IDS system developed could differentiate between a normal intrusion and an attack.

Moreso, [8] considered the impact of big data generated in a network and its effect on detecting attacks. Thus, the authors developed a Spark-Chi-support vector machine model for detecting attacks using a ChiSqSelector for feature selection and a support vector machine (SVM) as a classifier on the Apache Spark Big Data platform. The KDD99 dataset was employed for training and testing. The analyses compared the Chi-SVM classifier and a Chi-logistic regression classifier, and results indicated the Spark-Chi-SVM model outperformed others. At the same time, the training period was abridged, making it suitable for big data.

Several studies have outlined the use of machine learning-based methods. For example, [19] developed a fuzzy-based semisupervised learning IDS by using unlabeled samples with a classification algorithm to improve the performance of the IDS. A hidden layer feed-forward neural network was trained to give a fuzzy membership vector, and unlabeled samples were categorized into low, mid, and high fuzzy categories. The classifier was retrained by fusing each category into the original training set. The NSL-KDD dataset was used for validation, and the results revealed that the low and high fuzzy unlabeled samples made a major contribution to improving the performance of the classifier compared to other classifiers. In addition, [20] developed a similar supervised machine learning-based IDS to detect four different intrusions. Their results indicated a 99.97% classification accuracy for known attack detection and 85% classification accuracy for new attacks.

Other methods have been developed to address network intrusion and increase classification accuracy. For instance, [21] developed an IDS for detecting two types of smart grid attacks – price manipulation attacks and denial of service (DoS) attacks. The first problem was addressed by developing a Cumulative Sum (CUSUM) algorithm that detects manipulation even with granular price changes. The denial of service issue was tackled by efficient monitoring of abnormal nodes. Results revealed the robustness of the IDS system compared to traditional methods, with over 95% detection rate and a false positive rate below 5%.

Also, [22] developed IDS based on novel honey token-based encrypted pointers to restrict attacks on infrastructure networks. The honey tokens inside the frame served as a trap for the attacker, with the nodes working inside the four different operating pools of the infrastructure network. The pool divisions were done according to their computing ability and vulnerability level and were given their security measure inside the network. Using network penetration testing, 64 nodes were used for simulations of the model, and performance was analyzed as either false negative or true positive alarms. Evidence from the simulations indicated a high accuracy in detecting intrusion and attacks.

In conclusion, different machine learning-based approaches and deep learning methods have been used to develop the IDS model, and different intrusion datasets have been used to validate such models. Table 13.1 summarizes the various methods used, while Table 13.2 shows the various datasets employed for intrusion detection in the literature. The next section discusses a comprehensive description of the CPS system.

Table 13.1 Summary of different IDS methods.

	Method	Techniques	Author(s)
1	Deep learning	Deep belief networks	[17]
		Federated learning based	[13], [23]
		Self-taught learning (STL) framework	[24]
		Deep neural network	[12], [14], [25]
		Convolutional neural network	[15]
		Hybrid methods	[27], [28], [29]
2	Machine learning-based methods	Fuzziness-based semisupervised learning	[18], [19], [20]
		Support vector machine (SVM)	[8], [30]
		KNN	[48]
		Decision trees	[33], [34], [35], [36]
		ANN	[37], [38], [39]
		Random forest	[40], [41], [42]
		Linear regression, naïve Bayes	[43]
		Logistic regression	[44]
3	Optimization based	Whale optimization	[45]
		Grey wolf optimization	[46], [47]
		Binary golden jackal optimization	[48], [49]
		Bird swarm optimization	[27]
		Particle swarm optimization	[50], [51]
4	Other methods	Honey token-based encrypted pointers	[22]
		Cumulative sum (CUSUM) algorithm	[21]
		gravitational search algorithm	[35]

Table 13.2 Common datasets for intrusion detection models.

	Dataset	Attributes	Authors used	Comment
1	UNSW-NB15	Over two million records with 49 features.	[52]; [44]; [34]; [47]	It is mostly used as a benchmark dataset for IDS
2	KDDC99	About five million records with 30 features		Common
3	CIC-IDS-2017	Well-used dataset with a usability score of 10.		Popularly used
4	NSL-KDD	Well-used dataset with a usability score of 6.25	[25], [33], [34]	Not common
5	CSE-CIC IDS-2018	83 features with a usability score of 9.71.	[54]	
6	N-BaIoT	115 Attributes, 7,062,606 records, usability score of 5.88	[33]	
7	HIKARI-2021	Usability score of 3.53	[34]	
8	DARPA 1998	Over 4.9 million records	[37]	Not common

13.3 Intrusion Detection Techniques for Cyber-physical Systems

CPSs are systems that automate, model, and control the device of a physical system in a digital environment. They are massive-scale, geographically distributed, federated, and heterogeneous. They are crucial systems that contain actuators, sensors, networking, and control elements. According to [55], a CPS is "an engineered method that incorporates the components of computation, sensing, networking and control into physical entities and facilities as interconnected to the internet and other similar systems."

A CPS enables users to model the physical system in the real world in a virtual environment. Subsequently, the real-time behavior of a physical system over both the temporal and spatial domains is understood and encoded in algorithms by the software and then represented visually and interactively in a digital user interface [56]. CPSs are becoming increasingly part of our environment in homes, offices, industries, and infrastructures.

Examples of CPSs that have become almost thoroughly embedded in today's world include, for instance, unmanned aircraft systems [57], [58], smart grids [67], industrial processes [61], [62], and continuous healthcare systems [63], [64]. They are complex control systems that have several control loops, tight timing constraints, low variability in the traffic over the communication networks, and systems that might be rather old and might integrate wireless network sections. CPSs integrate cyber (network components and off-the-shelf servers) and physical (sensors and actuators).

With this integration becoming more and more prevalent, protecting these systems also becomes more and more vital. Although such systems present benefits that have been unprecedented, they are hugely at risk of hacks. The risk attack model that defines CPS also comprises short and long-duration attacks. Unfortunately, a ruthless competitor may take his or her place in the system and expunge the concerned processes to cause a calamity. A more advanced opponent, on the other hand, will be careful not to send traffic that will interfere with normal system functions to establish the propagation and setup for a synchronized attack at a particular time [2].

13.3.1 Typical CPS architecture

The generic CPS model may be derived by evaluating the components broadly defined as CPS components. CPS could be very large-scale, more complex, and probably highly application-specific. Like any current large-scale networked system, CPS architecture will have a physical stratum, sensor/

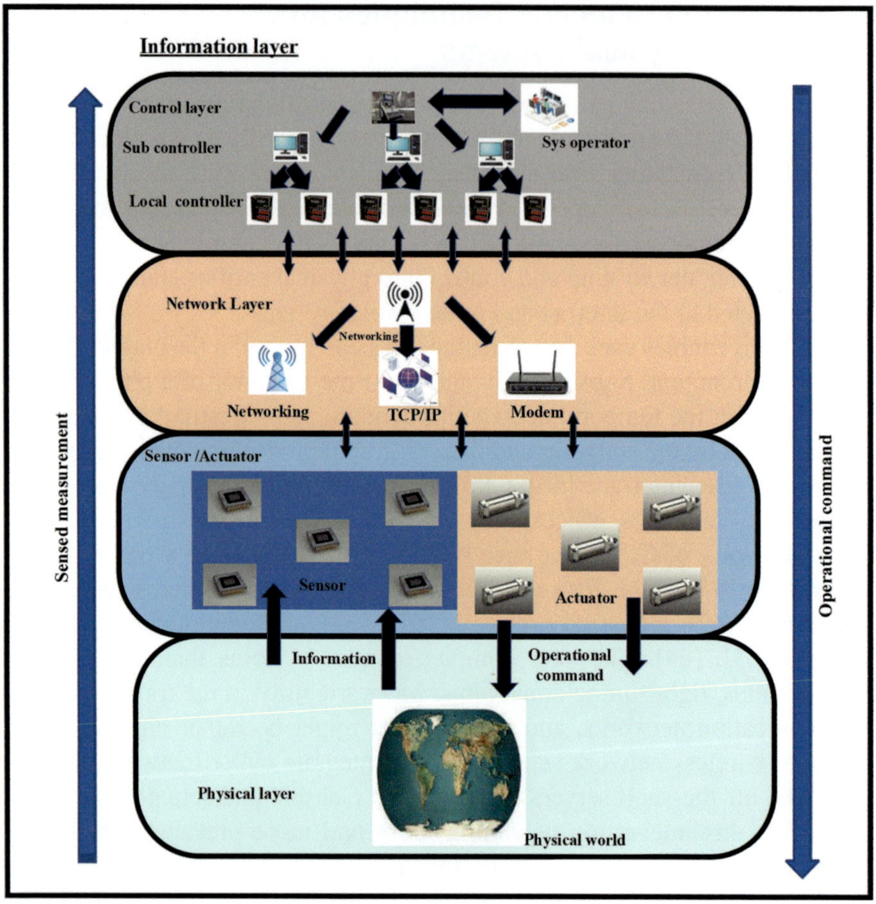

Figure 13.3 CPS architecture.

actuator stratum, network stratum, and control stratum. CPS obtains the properties from each component, including distributed control systems (DCS), real-time embedded systems, and communication devices. Specifically, some features that dominate include heterogeneity, real-time processes, autonomy, distributed control, and management. The architecture of CPS is illustrated in Figure 13.3. This architecture comprises five layers [65].

1. *Physical layer:* this is the real-world environment in which the system is built. Hence, it is the base of the system. As physical entities, it comprises physical objects, sensors, and actuators. Sensors collect data from the physical environment, while actuators execute actions responding to the information received.

2. *Sensor/actuator layer:* this is the outermost layer associated with the physical layer. It is connected to sensors and actuators. On this layer, physical signals are converted to digital signals and vice versa.
3. *Network layer:* this layer offers a means of connecting different aspects of the CPS. It comprises routers, switches, modems, and communication standards such as TCP/IP and wireless technology.
4. *Control layer:* this layer also comprises decision-making and control. It comprises controllers that analyze data from the lower layers and produce control signals. These controllers can, in turn, be centralized or distributed.
5. *Information layer:* this layer concerns data processing, storage, and presentation. This is in the form of databases, software applications, and interfaces that users shall interact with. This layer is designed to provide information feedback to the human operators and record past events.

The overall flow of information in the CPS is as follows.

In the physical layer, sensors acquire data feeds from the physical environment. The data passes to the sensor/actuator layer, where data is then converted to the digital format. The digital data is then forwarded to the network layer and sent to other system components. The control layer takes the data received, processes this data, and forms control commands for it. These control commands are then passed back through the network layer to the sensor/actuator layer. The sensor/actuator layer interprets the control signals to produce physical outputs, including the actuation of certain devices or modification of certain sensors.

The information layer is concerned with data analysis and acts as a data warehouse. This architecture enables the observation, regulation, and optimization of the physical systems in real time. For instance, the generation utility, the electricity transmission through the transmission lines into residences and enterprises forms the physical layer in the electrical distribution network CPS [66]. The physical layer directly interfaces with the actuator/sensor layer; the sensors measure the physical system, and then the actuators implement actions. In the generation utility example, the system measurements are denoted as voltage, current, and phase angle, and they are in phase with each other [66].

The summary layer focuses on networking sensors and actuators, in addition to connecting the sensor/actuator layer and supervisory layer using multiple communication devices and protocols. More specifically, the protocols used in this layer are RS-232, Ethernet, TCP/IP, DNP, dial-up modem,

MODBUS, and other exclusive mobile protocols [65], [66]. The real measurement data acquired by one or more sensors will be transmitted to the control layer via the network layer for problem-solving. Conversely, the control layer's operational commands, which have been generated, will be conveyed to the actuators via the network layer [65].

The control layer can be segmented into the locally distributed control action level, the supervisory subcontrol level, and the supervisory higher control level. It depends on intelligence, such as electronic devices, microcomputers, electrical equipment, programmable logic controllers, and remote terminal units. The local distributed control action level generates a local feedback control system where distributed control decisions are made. The system level control is derived from the monitoring subcontrol level feedback control loops where the overall measured data from different locations in the network are aggregated [65].

Lastly, the supervisory higher control level enables the system to initiate human-assisted control. The measured data is mainly transferred to human operators through the CPS user interface. These operators manage the system's status worldwide and may respond as soon as necessary. The information layer is conceptual but connects all the other layers in the CPS from top to bottom [65]. The next two sections discuss the various approaches employed for intrusion detection in the CPS architecture and the areas where the CPS system can be applied.

13.3.2 Overview of different IDS approaches

Generally, intrusion detection processes are divided into four approaches, which are discussed in this section. The approaches include anomaly-based, signature-based, hybrid (anomaly and signature), and data-driven.

13.3.2.1 Anomaly-based detection or behavioral-based detection

It is a method in the CPS in which an algorithm or model detects anything that deviates from what is normal. This could be an abnormal shift from normal conditions due to a security breach or system failure. It functions in the way that it first acknowledges normal behavior and then looks for variation in that same behavior. There are different types of anomaly-based detection techniques, including deep learning approaches, machine learning techniques, and statistical techniques [67].

One of the advantages of anomaly-based detection is that it efficiently detects evolving threats and subtle anomalies. In addition, it requires adaptive and minimal prior knowledge. However, the system may experience false positives, difficulty setting thresholds, and high computational overhead as part of its challenges. The anomaly-based detection in CPS can be applied in network intrusion detection, sensor data anomalies, system performance degradation, autonomous systems, and industrial process monitoring [68].

13.3.2.2 The signature-based detection

This is one of the methods used in CPS to identify threats, which is carried out based on certain patterns already familiar to the system. This is usually formulated based on the known attack patterns, the vulnerabilities, or the malicious activity observed. Different types of signature-based detection include network traffic signatures, system call signatures, sensor data signatures, and behavioral signatures [67]. Some benefits of signature-based detection mechanisms are that they are effective for known threats, easy to implement, and have low false favorable rates. However, the system may be limited to known threats, vulnerable to evasion techniques, and requires constant updates. Signature-based detection can be used in detection systems, malware detection, system anomaly detection, and industrial process monitoring [69].

13.3.2.3 Hybrid approaches

The hybrid technique is a combination of anomaly-based detection and signature-based detection techniques. As a result, the benefits of each technique are captured while avoiding the disadvantages of the two. Thus, developing a synergistic effect and having a more adequate and efficient detection system can be possible using all these approaches. The different types of hybrid approaches include sequential approach, parallel approach, and hierarchical approach [67]. Some key benefits of the hybrid approaches include enhanced detection capabilities, reduced false positives, improved adaptability, and increased resilience. However, the system may be complex, it requires fine-tuning to produce the best results, and it also requires some resource requirements [70].

13.3.2.4 Data-driven approaches

Big data techniques in the CPS involve analyzing large amounts of information produced by the CPS to make findings, optimize performance, and strengthen security. In this method, an organization can be able to conclude, improve the functionality of a particular system, and even detect a deviation [67]. The key components of data-driven approaches include data collection, preprocessing, data analysis, modeling, decision-making, and optimization.

It is better applied in predictive maintenance, energy optimization, process control, anomaly detection, and autonomous systems. However, it requires high data quality, privacy and security. It also requires high computational resources and model interpretability [71].

13.4 Applications of CPS

CPS can transform several sectors by incorporating computing and networking technologies with physical world phenomena. Figure 13.4 summarizes CPS applications.

1. *Smart cities:* a smart city in the framework of CPS is a metropolitan environment that uses cutting-edge technology to enhance resource optimization, advance the standard of living, and foster sustainability. Smart traffic signals, driverless cars, and traffic control to enhance traffic signal timings [72]. Applications include advanced utility management systems for effective distribution and utilization of electric energy with consideration of distributed power resources, smart waste bins for proper collection and disposal of wastes with a proper channel toward recycling [73], and sensors for monitoring air quality, water quality, and noise level sensors [74].
2. *Healthcare:* CPSs are transforming the healthcare sector by incorporating digital tools with physical procedures to advance medical care, improve productivity, and decrease overheads. Examples include smart clothes and biosensors to monitor a patient's condition from a distance [72]; intelligent medical diagnostic and therapeutic instruments, as well as rehabilitation aids [75]; application of electronic health records (EHRs) and data technology to enhance the quality of patient care [72].
3. *Manufacturing:* robotics and automation of control systems have improved the performance of assembly line operations [76]. Other applications in manufacturing include predicting equipment lifecycle, repair and replacement [73], mechanized inspection, and quality control measures [77].
4. *Transportation:* CPS is deployed in self-driven cars and trucks to transport people and goods, unmanned aerial vehicles or drones for distribution, etc. [75], as well as in traffic, parking, and public transportation [78].
5. *Energy:* energy supply and demand management networks use integrated renewable energy [79]. Electrical and electronic civil infrastructures such as smart buildings use energy management applications [74].

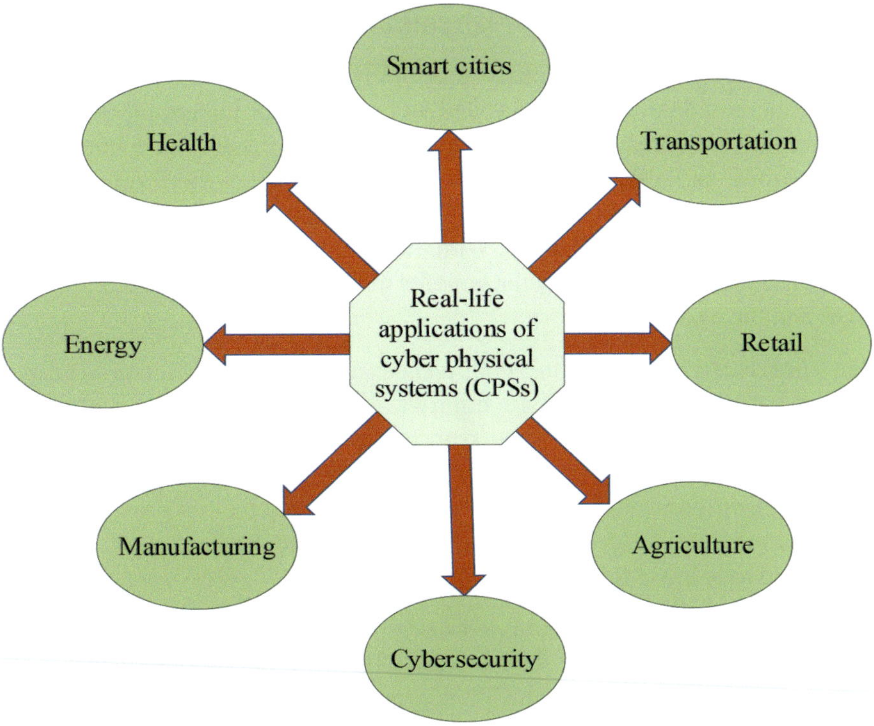

Figure 13.4 Real-life applications of cyber-physical systems.

6. *Agriculture:* CPS is used to optimize crop management, irrigation, and pest control with the help of sensors, drones, and data analytics. They have also applied equipment for farming with the help of technologies for better production and utilization of resources [80].

7. *Retail:* CPS uses scanners for self-checkout, recommendation programs, and commodity storage and logistics [81]. Exploring the means and ways through which the idea of supply chain management can be effective if data analytics is incorporated into the firm's supply chain [78].

8. *Cybersecurity:* applying CPS to perform the traffic analysis detects the anomalies from the network and takes action against threats [73]. Security of IoT devices and the connections among them from susceptibilities and invasions [82].

These are a few examples of the many potential applications of CPS. We can expect to see even more innovative and impactful use cases as technology advances. Hence, the next section discusses the potential future direction of the CPS system.

13.5 The Future of Cyber-physical Systems

CPS is dynamic and continuously developing due to technological enhancements, increased system intricacy, and high demand for interconnectivity and autonomous systems. In the future, CPS is expected to be more intelligent, autonomous, and adaptive to the environment. Although these future directions will further define CPS's capabilities, applications, and impacts on society, they present new challenges. With these odds and opportunities in mind, it gives a clear pointer on how the benefits of CPS can be maximized to better lives and the environment.

1. *Enhanced autonomy and intelligence:* artificial intelligence (AI) algorithms will allow CPS to improve its decision-making capabilities, learn from experience, and respond more to situational occurrences [83]. Storing and processing data near the source will minimize the time taken to convey results, hence, real-time outcomes. AI and machine learning (ML) algorithms [84], as well as edge computing [85], can be used to achieve this purpose.

2. *Increased interoperability and integration:* standardizing the interface and protocol will help to integrate CPS with the various systems and gadgets easily [86]. When CPS is connected to IoT, more devices can be connected, and more data can be exchanged [87]. The use of blockchain technology can establish a reliable and highly transparent mechanism of information exchange and transaction processing [87].

3. *Enhanced security and resilience:* encryption, intrusion, and anomalous detection measures should be adopted, which make CPS secure [88]. The design of CPS to operate efficiently in the failure and disruption environment will guarantee their operation [89]. Data protection and data security, as well as data integrity issues, will have to be considered and resolved ethically [87], [90].

4. *Human–machine collaboration:* combining augmented reality (AR) and virtual reality (VR) will improve the organizational and interactional relationships between humans and machines and give original interfaces. The ability to create sociocognitive robots that can learn to perform tasks in symbiosis with human beings will increase performance rates [32].

5. *Sustainability and environmental impact:* the most important strategic objectives of managing energy systems will be energy efficiency and environmental considerations. The disclosure to recycle and use

recyclable material and natural fiber will help in creating a better environment in the future [91]. Integration of circular economy strategies within production processes with a view of minimizing wastage and optimizing the utilization of resources [92].

6. *Ethical considerations:* selecting correct features and properties will also be crucial for the CPS algorithms to be nondiscriminative and fair for human beings [93]. It will be important to devise ways of making accountability for the choices of the autonomous CPS. Security and privacy of the user's personal information will be another crucial consideration [93].

13.6 Problem Formulation and Techniques for Intrusion Detection in Cyber-physical Systems

The problem formulation and methods employed in this book chapter are discussed in this section.

a. *Problem formulation:* a scenario of power generation.
Suppose we have a CPS system represented with a discrete-time linear state-space model. This can be mathematically formulated as shown in eqn (13.1) and (13.2)

$$x(k+1) = \alpha x(k) + \beta u(k) + \gamma(k), \tag{13.1}$$

$$y(k) = \omega x(k) + \kappa(k), \tag{13.2}$$

where $x(k) \in R^n$, $u(k) \in R^m$, $y(k) \in R^p$, $\alpha \in R^{n \times n}$, $\beta \in R^{n \times m}$, $\omega \in R^{p \times n}$, $\gamma(k) \in R^n$, and $\kappa(k) \in R^p$ denote the state vector at the time k, $u(k)$ is the control time, $y(k)$ is the output measurement, α is the state transition matrix, β is the control input matrix, ω is the output matrix, and $\gamma(k)$ is the process and measurement noise, correspondingly.

The aim is to detect cyberattacks or intrusions into the CPS. The attacks can be represented as abnormalities in measurement data or control inputs. One way to phrase an intrusion is as an additive term shown in eqn (13.3)

$$y(k) = \omega x(k) + \kappa(k) + a(k), \tag{13.3}$$

where $a(k) \in R^p$ denotes the intrusion signal in the system.

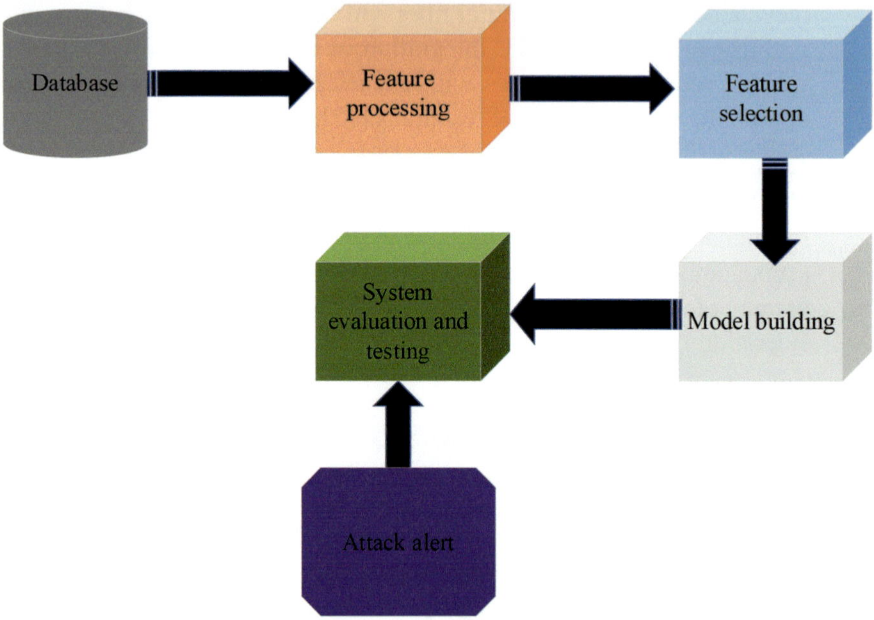

Figure 13.5 Flow diagram of the method employed in this study.

b. *Method employed in this study:* a supervised ML model trains a dataset. The training dataset contains cases of the normal network traffic and times when there is an intrusion into the network. Figure 13.5 is a flow diagram of the method used in this study.

13.6.1 Dataset

Data is collected from the HIL-based augmented ICS (HAI) security dataset, after which feature engineering is carried out on the data. Both feature processing and feature selection are done to get an optimal feature subset. The HAI security dataset was collected from an industrial control system (ICS) test bed augmented with a hardware-in-the-loop (HIL) simulator. The dataset includes ICS operational data from normal and abnormal situations, covering 38 attack scenarios.

The test bed consists of components like a boiler, a turbine, and a water treatment system, working together to emulate a power generation plant [94]. The attack data was generated by injecting a simulated cyberattack targeting the control system. These attacks were designed to disrupt normal operations by manipulating sensor inputs, altering control set points, or overriding

Table 13.3 The sixty-eight (68) features that were selected.

[“p1_b2004,” “p1_b2016,” “p1_b3004,” “p1_b3005,” “p1_b4002,” “p1_b4005,” “p1_b400b,” “p1_b4022,” “p1_fcv01d,” “p1_fcv01z,” “p1_fcv02d,” “p1_fcv02z,” “p1_fcv03d,” “p1_fcv03z,” “p1_ft01,” “p1_ft01z,” “p1_ft02,” “p1_ft02z,” “p1_ft03,” “p1_ft03z,” “p1_lcv01d,” “p1_lcv01z,” “p1_lit01,” “p1_pcv01d,” “p1_pcv01z,” “p1_pcv02d,” “p1_pcv02z,” “p1_pit01,” “p1_pit02,” “p1_pp01ad,” “p1_pp01ar,” “p1_pp01bd,” “p1_pp01br,” “p1_pp02d,” “p1_pp02r,” “p1_stsp,” “p1_tit01,” “p1_tit02,” “p2_24vdc,” “p2_autogo,” “p2_emerg,” “p2_manualgo,” “p2_onoff,” “p2_rtr,” “p2_sit01,” “p2_tripex,” “p2_vt01,” “p2_vtr01,” “p2_vtr02,” “p2_vtr03,” “p2_vtr04,” “p3_fit01,” “p3_lcp01d,” “p3_lcv01d,” “p3_lit01,” “p3_pit01,” “p4_ht_fd,” “p4_ht_po,” “p4_ht_ps,” “p4_ld,” “p4_st_fd,” “p4_st_gov,” “p4_st_ld,” “p4_st_po,” “p4_st_ps,” “p4_st_pt01,” “p4_st_tt01,” “attack”]

actuator commands. Various attack types were simulated, including manipulating process variables (e.g., temperature and pressure), controlling logic tampering, and actuator malfunction [94]. The data used in this study consists of 60,977 samples, with 40,000 instances of normal (nonattack) operations and 20,977 instances of cyberattacks.

13.6.2 Feature processing and selection

To reduce dimensionality and focus on the most relevant features for detecting anomalies, recursive feature elimination (RFE) was employed using a RandomForestClassifier as the base model. The RFE process helped to iteratively eliminate less important features until a subset of the most significant variables was identified. Sixty-eight features were selected, and they are the primary sensor readings and actuator statuses that play a key role in distinguishing between normal and attack states. These features are shown in Table 13.3.

13.6.3 Model building and hyperparameter tuning

Nine machine learning models were evaluated, including k-nearest neighbors (KNN), logistic regression, decision tree, random forest, XGBoost, lightGBM, AdaBoost, CatBoost, and naive Bayes. These classifiers were selected because they have proven effective on similar classification problems and they are not computationally intensive. Hyperparameter tuning was conducted using “Optuna,” which involved defining objective functions for each model and exploring a range of parameters to optimize model performance. The sci-kit-learn and eleven other relevant libraries in Python were used to achieve this.

13.6.3.1 The k-nearest neighbor (KNN)

It is a supervised machine learning algorithm that is used for classification and regression tasks. It is a nonparametric algorithm that does not make any assumptions about the underlying distribution of the data [24]. The dataset was prepared by ensuring it has features and corresponding labels (since we are dealing with classification problems). The features were then normalized to avoid bias. K represents the number of neighbors considered when making predictions. The optimal value of k was chosen according to the dataset being used. The distance between each test point and all training points was calculated. The Minkowski distance metrics were used and are shown in eqn (13.4). The distances were sorted from smallest to largest, while the dominant class among the k nearest neighbors was determined, and the test point was assigned to that class. The KNN algorithm is defined in eqn (13.5).

$$d(p,q) = \left(\sum |p_i - q_i|^r\right)^{\frac{1}{r}}, \tag{13.4}$$

where p_i, q_i and r are the ith coordinates of the points and positive real number, respectively.

$$\text{KNN}(x) = \text{argmax}_y \sum_{i=1}^{n} I(y_i = y), \tag{13.5}$$

where argmax is a function that finds the value of y that maximizes the following expression. It identifies the class label that occurs most frequently among the nearest neighbors. y represents a potential class label. $I(y_i = y)$ is an indicator function that returns 1 if the class label y_i of the ith neighbor equals y, and 0 otherwise. Essentially, it counts how many of the nearest neighbors belong to classy. The n refers to the number of nearest neighbors being considered.

13.6.3.2 Logistic regression

It is a linear model that predicts probabilities for binary classification problems. This model takes a set of predictor variables (features) as input. These features are combined linearly using weights or coefficients [24]. The core of logistic regression is the sigmoid function (also known as the logistic function), which maps any real value to a value between 0 and 1. The sigmoid function is described in eqn (13.6).

$$\sigma(z) = \frac{1}{1 + e^{-z}}, \tag{13.6}$$

where $\sigma(z)$ is the sigmoid function's output (the probability). e is Euler's number (approximately 2.71828). z is a linear combination of the predictor variables and their corresponding coefficients shown in eqn (13.7).

$$z = \beta_0 + \beta_1 + \beta_2 x_2 + \cdots + \beta_p x_p, \tag{13.7}$$

where $\beta_0, \beta_1, \ldots \beta_p$ are the model's coefficients or weights and are estimated using maximum likelihood estimation. Also, $x_1, x_2, \ldots x_p$ are the predictor variables.

Therefore, the logistic regression model predicts the probability of a positive outcome (e.g., $y = 1$) as shown in eqn (13.8)

$$p(y = 1|x) = \hat{}\sigma(z). \tag{13.8}$$

13.6.3.3 Decision tree

This model splits data into subsets based on feature values, making decisions at each branch. The tree starts with a root node, which represents the entire dataset. At each internal node, an attribute is selected to split the data. The attribute choice is typically based on a metric that measures the information gain or impurity reduction. The node is divided into branches, one for each possible value of the selected attribute. This process is repeated for each branch until all data points belong to the same class (leaf node). The Gini impurity measures how often a random element from the set would be incorrectly labeled if it was randomly labeled according to the distribution of labels in the subset. The Gini impurity is calculated using the formula in eqn (13.9). The decision tree aims to choose the splits that maximize information gain or minimize the Gini impurity, leading to more homogeneous subsets.

$$\text{Gini}(D) = 1 - \sum_{i=1}^{c} p_i^2, \tag{13.9}$$

where p_i is the probability of an element being classified into class i and c is the number of classes.

13.6.3.4 Random forest

An ensemble of decision trees reduces overfitting by averaging multiple trees. Random forest creates multiple decision trees by randomly sampling the training data with replacement. This process is known as bootstrapping. Each tree is trained on a different subset of the data. A random subset of features is selected at each tree node to determine the split. This helps to reduce the correlation between trees and improve generalization. To make predictions, the forest "votes" on the class or value for a new data point. For classification tasks, the majority vote is used. The average of the predictions from all trees is taken for regression tasks. A decision tree model is shown in eqn (13.10).

$$f(x) = \frac{1}{B}\sum_{b=1}^{B} f_{\mathrm{b}}(x), \tag{13.10}$$

where B denotes the total number of functions being averaged. $f_b(x)$ represents the individual functions indexed by b, where b ranges from 1 to B, and each function of f_b takes the same input x.

13.6.3.5 XGBoost (eXtreme gradient boosting)

This is a gradient-boosting algorithm that iteratively improves model accuracy by optimizing errors from previous trees. XGBoost typically uses decision trees as base learners. The algorithm starts with a base model and iteratively adds new models to improve the prediction. Each new model is trained to correct the errors of the previous models. The algorithm uses gradient descent to find the optimal weights for each base learner. It calculates the gradient of the loss function for the predictions and updates the weights accordingly. XGBoost incorporates regularization techniques (L1 and L2 regularization) to prevent overfitting and improve generalization. The decision tree model is represented in eqn (13.11).

$$y_{\mathrm{i}} = \sum_{k=1}^{k} F_{\mathrm{k}}(x_{\mathrm{i}}), \tag{13.11}$$

where $F_{\mathrm{k}}(x_{\mathrm{i}})$ are individual functions or models indexed by k, evaluated at the input x_{i}. K is a positive integer comprising the total number of functions being summed.

13.6.3.6 LightGBM

It is a fast gradient-boosting algorithm that uses histogram-based learning for better efficiency. LightGBM divides the feature values into bins and creates histograms. This reduces the memory footprint and computational cost. It grows tree leaf-wise and splits the leaf node with the largest gain at each iteration. This can lead to more accurate models compared to level-wise growth, which splits all nodes simultaneously. It can bundle exclusive features together, which means features that rarely appear together can be combined into a single feature. This reduces the number of features and improves training speed. It can directly handle categorical features without requiring one-hot encoding. It uses gradient boosting to add new models to improve the prediction iteratively. Each new model is trained to correct the errors of the previous models. This algorithm is represented in eqn (13.12).

$$y = f(x) = \sum_{i=1}^{M} \text{leaf}_{\text{i}}(x), \tag{13.12}$$

where M indicates the total number of leaf nodes being considered. $\text{leaf}_{\text{i}}(x)$ is the value associated with the ith leaf node evaluated at some input x. Each leaf node typically contains a value that contributes to the overall output.

13.6.3.7 AdaBoost

It is a boosting algorithm that iteratively trains a series of weak classifiers (e.g., decision trees) and then combines their predictions to create a strong classifier. It assigns weights to each training instance based on their contribution to the prediction error. The algorithm is represented in eqn (13.13).

$$F(x) = \sum_{m=1}^{M} \alpha_{\text{m}} h_{\text{m}}(x), \tag{13.13}$$

where M indicates the total number of functions being summed. α_{m} are the coefficients or weights associated with each function $h_{\text{m}}(x)$. They determine how much influence each function has on the final output. $h_{\text{m}}(x)$ are the individual functions indexed by m, evaluated at the input x. Depending on the context, each function can represent different models, transformations, or basis functions.

13.6.3.8 CatBoost

This is a gradient-boosting algorithm tailored for categorical features without extensive preprocessing. CatBoost uses a special encoding technique called target encoding. Instead of converting categorical features into numerical values using one-hot encoding or other methods, it directly encodes them based on the target variable. This helps to capture the relationship between categorical features and the target. This model is represented with eqn (13.14).

$$y = \sum_{i=1}^{N} \lambda_{\text{i}} f(x_{\text{i}}), \tag{13.14}$$

where N indicates the total number of terms in the summation. λ_{i} is the coefficients associated with each function evaluation. They determine how much influence each term has on the final output y. $f(x_{\text{i}})$ denotes the value of the function f, evaluated at the specific input point x_i. Each input point represents different data points in the dataset.

13.6.3.9 Naive Bayes

It is a probabilistic model assuming feature independence and is used for simple and fast classification. It is based on Bayes' theorem, which calculates the likelihood of an event (e.g., attack or not attack) given evidence (i.e., any of the features, e.g., "p1_b2004"). The model is represented in eqn (13.15).

$$p(y|x) = \frac{P(y)\prod_{i=1}^{n} P(x_i \mid y)}{p(x)}, \tag{13.15}$$

where $P(y)$ is the prior probability of event y, representing how likely y is before considering any information about x. $P(x_i|y)$ represents the conditional probability of each observation x_i, given that y has occurred. $\Pi_{i=1}^{n} P(x_i \mid y)$ is the product, which indicates that multiple features are being considered, that is, $x_i, x_2, \ldots x_n$ which are multiplied by their probability under the assumption that they are conditionally independent given y. $p(x)$ is the marginal probability of event x, which serves as a normalizing constant to ensure that the probabilities sum to 1. It can be computed using the law of total probability, given in eqn (13.16)

$$P(x) = \sum_{y} P(y) P(x \mid y). \tag{13.16}$$

13.7 Results and Discussion

This section presents the numerical results and discusses the results regarding the present study. The numerical and performance analysis was conducted and achieved in a PYTHON environment. Furthermore, feature selection was performed to identify the most relevant features for the model. Initially, all features except the target variable (attack) were considered. Recursive feature elimination (RFE) was used with a RandomForestClassifier to select the top features.

Table 13.4 compares many machine learning models by examining five performance metrics – accuracy, precision, recall (sensitivity), F1-score, and area under the curve (AUC) – on the test dataset. These measurements shed light on the models' capacity to reconcile accurate positive and negative classifications with a tendency to generalize to previously unreported data. Concerning more sophisticated techniques like Random Forest, XGBoost,

Table 13.4 Summary of results of different algorithms employed in this study.

Model	Accuracy (test)	Precision (test)	Recall sensitivity (test)	F1 (test)	AUC (test)
KNN	0.971958	0.956791	0.961526	0.959153	0.983713
Logistic regression	0.703783	0.996475	0.135377	0.238370	0.766227
Decision tree	0.976222	0.959773	0.971264	0.965484	0.974996
Random forest	0.995682	0.993143	0.994253	0.993698	0.999822
XGBM	0.993768	0.988561	0.993295	0.990922	0.999490
AdaBoost	0.825134	0.877742	0.568487	0.690049	0.896866
Light GBM	0.983492	0.984243	0.967273	0.975684	0.998186
CatBoost	0.995190	0.990938	0.995051	0.992990	0.999680
Naive Bayes	0.568219	0.413318	0.622286	0.496719	0.610174

LightGBM, and CatBoost, the outcomes provide a noticeable differentiation from more basic models like logistic regression and naive Bayes.

With an accuracy of 97.2%, precision of 95.7%, and recall of 96.2%, KNN produces excellent results in every category. With a harmonic mean of precision and recall of 95.9%, the F1-score indicates a balanced performance regarding positive and negative categorization. The AUC of 0.98 adds more evidence to the effectiveness of KNN's class differentiation. Though it could be computationally costly when used on larger datasets, KNN's straightforwardness and adaptability are responsible for its excellent performance. More importantly, with a substantially lower accuracy of 70.4%, logistic regression accomplishes worse than the other models. Recall has a 13.5%, which is the price paid for its practically flawless precision of 99.6%. This model fails to balance precision and recall, as evidenced by its very low F1-score of 0.24, which reflects its ineffectiveness in capturing positive examples.

Despite being a widely used baseline model, logistic regression's poor recall and AUC of 0.77 indicate that it may have trouble handling more complicated patterns or unbalanced datasets. The decision tree exhibits remarkable performance, balancing precision (95.9%) and memory (97.1%), with an accuracy of 97.6%. Its F1-score (96.5%) and AUC (0.97) further highlight its excellent performance. While decision trees are excellent at discovering trends in smaller datasets, overfitting is a potential problem. It performs better in this comparison than logistic regression because of its poorer generalization capabilities. With an accuracy of 82.5%, AdaBoost, another boosting technique, fares inadequately.

Although its recall (56.8%) and F1-score (0.69) indicate that it might not be the best choice for this dataset, its precision (87.8%) is relatively high. Although AdaBoost's AUC (0.90) suggests a respectable level of classification capacity, it performs worse than more advanced models like XGBoost and RF. LightGBM achieves 98.3% accuracy with high precision (98.4%) and recall (96.7%), matching XGBoost's performance.

According to the F1-score (97.6%) and AUC (0.998), this model is ranked among the best in this assessment. LightGBM performs admirably in this situation, as seen by its reputation for speed and effectiveness, particularly when working with huge datasets. With accuracy (99.5%), precision (99.1%), recall (99.5%), and F1-score (99.3%), CatBoost produces some of the greatest results. It is further evidence that it is well-suited for the dataset, and its AUC (0.9997) is among the highest. Like other gradient-boosting techniques, CatBoost is particularly effective in managing complicated information distributions and is specifically designed for categorical data.

The naive Bayes shows 56.8% accuracy, 41.3% precision, and 62.2% recall, naive Bayes falls short in nearly every category. It struggles to produce accurate and balanced predictions, as seen by its F1-score of 0.50 and AUC of 0.61. Its inadequate performance on this dataset, particularly when correlated features are present, may be attributed to naive Bayes' oversimplified expectation of feature independence. The best-performing model is the random forest, which has near-perfect accuracy (99.57%), precision (99.31%), recall (99.43%), and AUC (0.9998). The model's 99.37% F1-score demonstrates how well it can balance recall and precision.

The advantage of random forest is that it reduces overfitting by averaging the predictions of several trees, which is an ensemble approach. According to this finding, it performs better than individual models like the decision tree or KNN when handling complicated and potentially noisy data. With accuracy, precision, recall, and AUC values all above 99%, XGBoost produces excellent results. The F1-score of 99.1% and the AUC of 0.9995 demonstrate how well XGBoost handles recall and precision. XGBoost is one of the most dependable models in our comparison because, as a gradient-boosting technique, it is excellent at capturing intricate relationships within the data by creating sequential models to fix the flaws of the prior ones.

To summarize, ensemble models like random forest, XGBoost, lightGBM, and CatBoost outperform the competition with almost flawless results in every metric, which makes them ideal for predicting attacks on intricate datasets. Less complex models, such as logistic regression and naive Bayes, perform worse overall and have poorer recall, which highlights their limitations when dealing with complex data trends. For this classification problem, the advanced ensemble methods are the best option due to their greater capacity for prediction, reliability, and generalization capabilities. Plotting the true positive rate versus the false positive rate allows the area

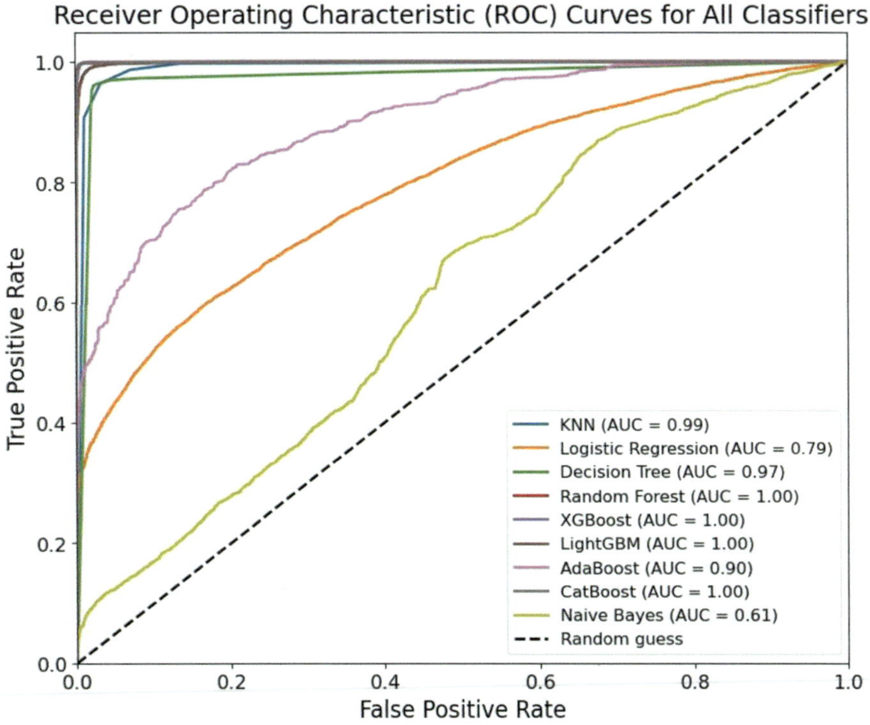

Figure 13.6 The ROC curves for all the classifiers in the study.

under the ROC curve to be used to assess the effectiveness of different classifiers as depicted in Figure 13.6.

From Figure 13.6, the classifier effectiveness is measured by the area under the curve (AUC), where higher AUC values correspond to improved discrimination between classes. With an AUC of 1.0, XGBoost, random forest, lightGBM, and CatBoost all attain perfect classification. They are highly effective at accurately differentiating between positive and negative classes. K-nearest neighbors (KNN) demonstrate near-perfect classification accuracy with an AUC of 0.99, demonstrating strong performance. With an AUC of 0.97, the decision tree model trails closely behind the ensemble models, indicating a marginally lower level of accuracy.

With an AUC of 0.90, AdaBoost's performance is mediocre at best, demonstrating its ability but lacking the robustness of its ensemble competitors. Logistic regression performs worse, especially regarding false positives, with an AUC of 0.79. The least successful classifier is naive Bayes, which has an AUC of 0.61 and slightly outperforms random guessing (shown by the

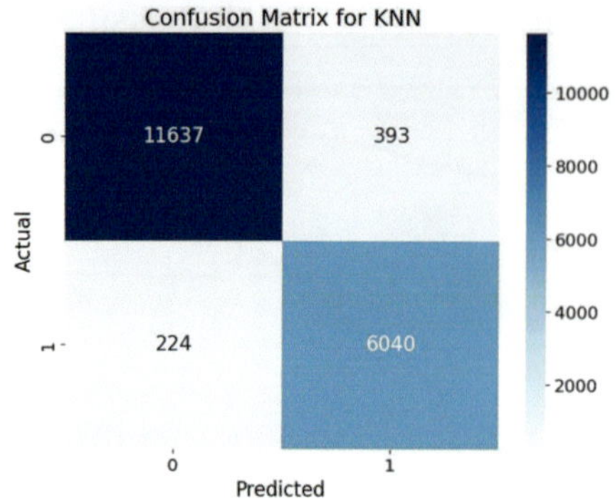

Figure 13.7 The confusion matrix for KNN in the study.

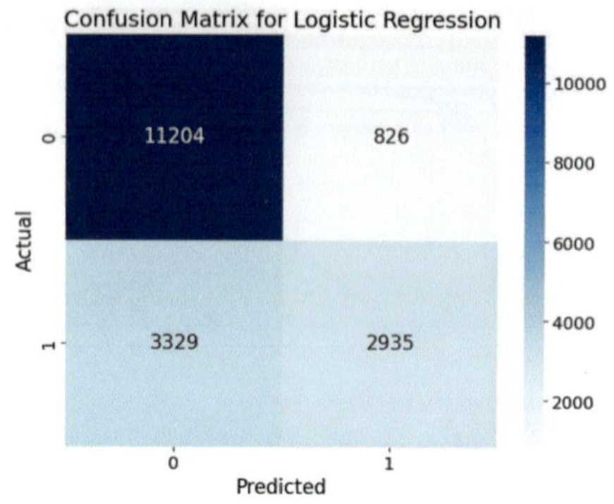

Figure 13.8 The confusion matrix for logistic regression in the study.

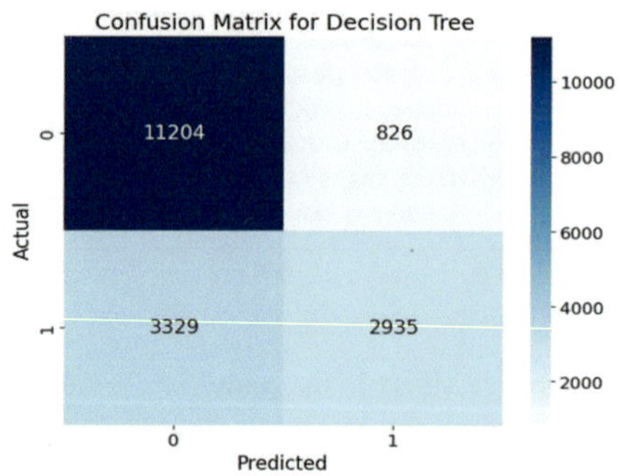

Figure 13.9 The confusion matrix for the decision tree in the study.

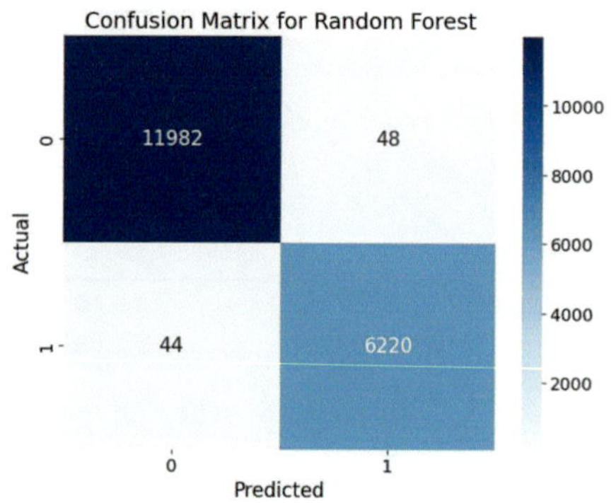

Figure 13.10 The confusion matrix for the random forest in the study.

diagonal line). The ensemble approaches, particularly XGBoost, random forest, LightGBM, and CatBoost, perform noticeably better than more straightforward algorithms like logistic regression and naive Bayes, making them more appropriate for this classification challenge. The performance of each model was summarized based on the evaluation metrics. The best-performing model was identified based on the highest test accuracy and other relevant metrics. Additionally, the confusion matrix for each classifier employed in this study is shown in Figures 13.7–13.14.

Figure 13.7 shows that 11,637 data were rightly classified as negative (true negative), and 6040 data were rightly classified as positive (true positive) using KNN. However, 393 data were wrongly classified as positive (false positive), and 224 were wrongly classified as negative (false negative). In addition, Figure 13.8 shows that 11,204 were rightly classified as negative,

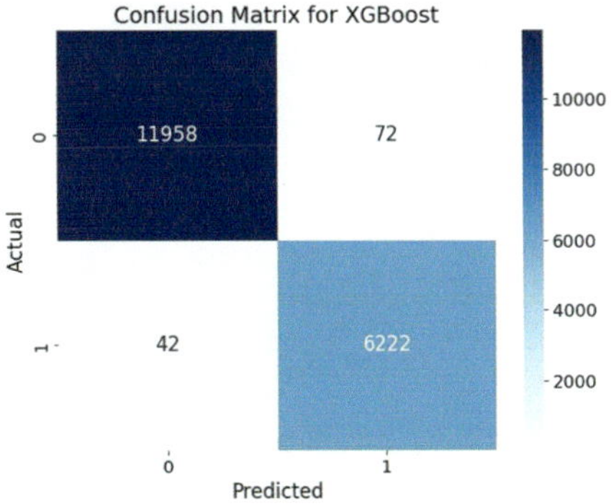

Figure 13.11 The confusion matrix for the XGBoost in the study.

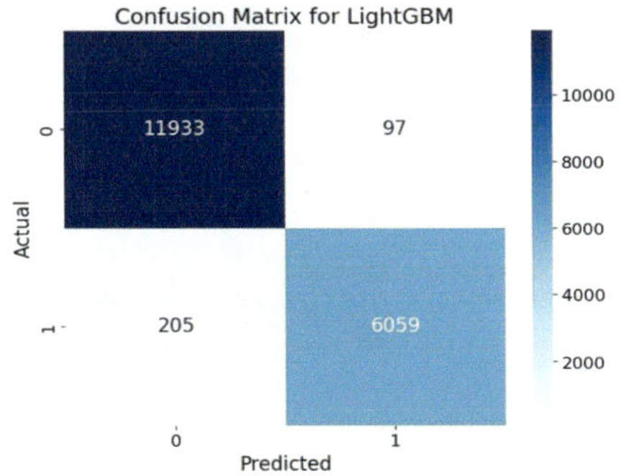

Figure 13.12 The confusion matrix for the LightGBM in the study.

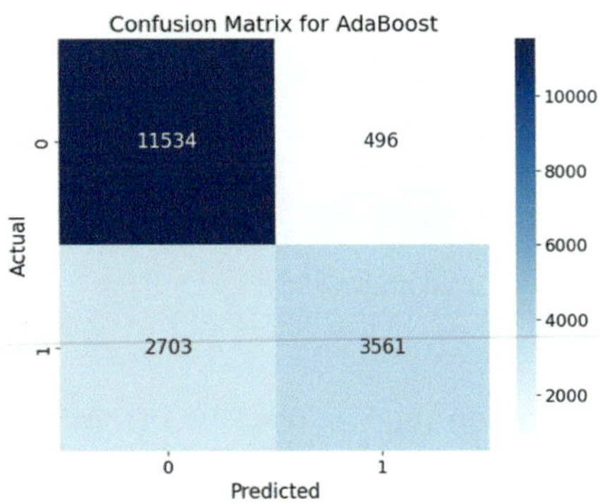

Figure 13.13 The confusion matrix for the AdaBoost in the study.

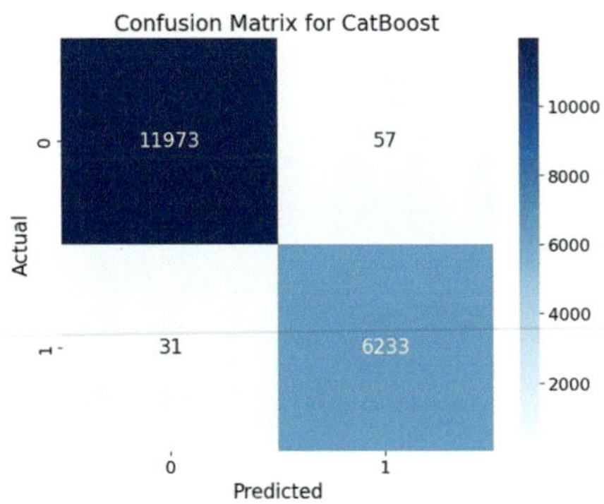

Figure 13.14 The confusion matrix for the CatBoost in the study.

and 2,935 were rightly classified as positive using the logistic regression. However, 3,329 were wrongly classified as positive, and 826 were wrongly classified as negative. The increased false-negative rate suggests that while the model forecasts class 0 (negative) more accurately, it has more difficulty predicting class 1 (positive).

Also, Figure 13.10 indicates that 11,982 were rightly classified as negative, and 6,220 data were rightly classified as positive using the random forest classifier. However, 48 were wrongly classified as positive, and 44 were wrongly classified as negative. Figure 13.14 is the CatBoost algorithm confusion matrix that displays 11,973 true negatives and 6233 data true positives. However, 31 data were classified as false positive, and 57 were false negative. From the various confusion matrices, the Logistic regression performed badly, followed by KNN, while the random forest performed best, followed

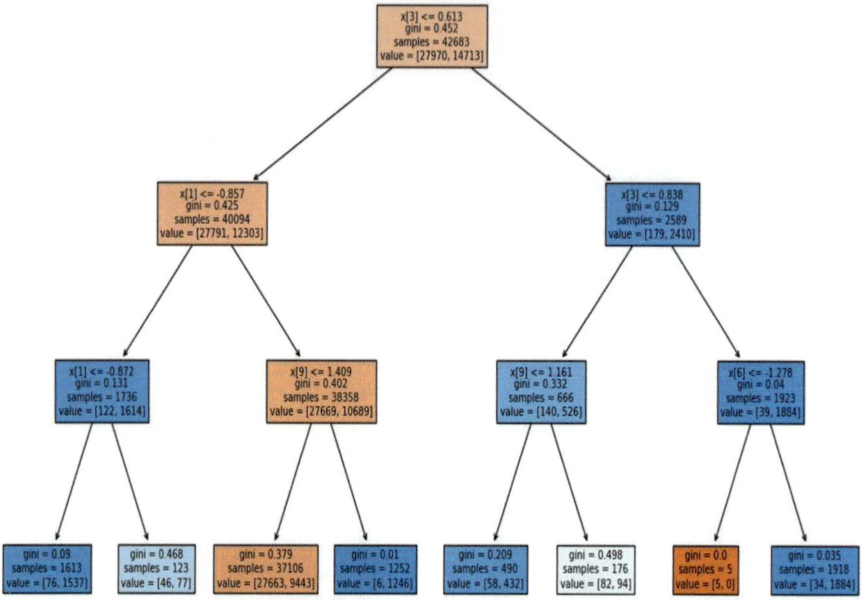

Figure 13.15 The classification tree used in the study.

by the CatBoost. Figure 13.15 is a classification map as observed from the results.

13.8 Lessons Learned

CPSs are systems that integrate the cyber-space with the physical environment to monitor physical processes in real time. They are designed to run in full isolation (or otherwise) and have been used in energy, healthcare, manufacturing, transportation, smart cities, etc. These systems optimize operations by altering physical contexts centered on digital computations. Examples of CPS include smart grids, self-driving cars, industrial robots, and other healthcare applications such as infusion pumps and pacemakers [1]. It was also noted that integrating physical and digital components in CPS has yielded enhanced effectiveness and efficiency, but these systems are still prone to different attacks. Because these systems interface with the internet and larger networks, they are susceptible to hacking. Therefore, it is important to develop suitable approaches that identify and prevent these attacks from occurring. It is also important to know that the computation of the attributes in a CPS environment by the contextual intrusion detection system incorporates physical and cyber data, thus facilitating the timely and accurate identification of threats in CPS [7]. Thus, in the event of a successful attack on a CPS, the failure is tragic, usually resulting in severe damage, power blackouts, system breakdown, interferences, etc. Hence, securing the CPS is critical, wherein intrusion detection plays a significant role in protection.

A summary of the lessons learned from this study is as follows:

1. CPS addresses the issue of securing the electronic parts of systems, processes, and operational enhancements. Fortification is sacrosanct; therefore, intrusion detection systems (IDS) are critical in providing security to these systems against intruders' access, malicious activities, and other related risks.

2. Intrusion detection in CPS has the important function of determining threats that need to be prevented from resulting in hazardous conditions or accident-prone conditions, consequently leading to loss of resources, either human or material.

3. Variations in sensor data and physical processes are also crucial to the confidentiality, accuracy, and security of the CPS.

4. Lastly, IDS in CPS is not only applicable to security and forensics; it could also be deployed in safety, disease detection, drug development, systemic variations, and other areas.

13.9 Future Direction of Cyber-physical Systems

CPS is very dynamic and unceasingly developing due to technological advancements, the perpetual smartness of hackers, increased system complexity, and the high demand for interconnectivity and autonomous systems. CPS is expected to be more intelligent, autonomous, and adaptive to the environment. As highlighted in Section 13.5, the future directions of CPSs should be in the following areas:

a. In-depth usage and application of top-notch technology should be embraced in fortifying subject matter such as artificial intelligence (AI) and machine learning with edge computing to enhance autonomy and intelligence overall.

b. Emphasis on the Industrial Internet of Things (IIoT), big data, blockchain technology, and other next-generation technologies should be promoted for enhanced security and resilience, human–machine collaboration, sustainability, and ethical considerations.

Indeed, machine learning models are numerous. No one is indispensable to others or ideal but very good with their respective peculiarities. In this study, nine were used for better and more reliable results, as one augments the other. They are not computationally intensive and have proven efficient and effective on similar classification problems. However, each one of these machine learning models, KNN, logistic regression, decision tree, random forest, XGBoost, lightGBM, AdaBoost, CatBoost, and naive Bayes exhibit some limitations, which are briefly reported below.

Even though KNN is adaptable and handles categorical features and numerical challenges, its limitations are not limited to the computational burden, slow speed, memory and storage concerns for large datasets, sensitivity to the choice of k and the distance metric, with susceptibility to the obscenity of dimensionality. It does not explain its predictions, which limits its interpretability and utility for some applications. Logistic regression requires large sample sizes and assumes linearity between the predicted and predictor variables, but it is unsuitable for evaluating a continuous outcome.

Decision trees are discriminatory toward the dominant class in classification tasks with unstable datasets, thus performing poorly in forecasting marginal classes. Convex loss function and scalability, time-consuming covetous algorithm, and the nonnecessity of multithreaded optimization are limitations of the XGBoost method. Working on big data slows down the time to train and cannot be easily executed with parallel computing. LightGBM is also slow. AdaBoost's limitation is more of overfitting and memory usage. Naïve Bayes often assumes independent predictors, which is not realistic in real-life situations.

13.10 Conclusion

Intrusion detection is an important aspect of the protection of CPS. Based on such considerations, it is possible to highlight the potential enhancement of organizations' CPSs if the distinctive challenges are addressed, and proper techniques are implemented. Given the growing complexity of these systems, comprehensive intrusion detection algorithms are necessary to protect CPS from developing cybersecurity threats. This study optimized safety and digital operations by evaluating multiple machine-learning techniques for detecting intrusions in a CPS. Nine machine learning models, namely XGBoost, LightGBM, AdaBoost, CatBoost, naive Bayes, k-nearest neighbors, logistic regression, decision tree, and random forest, have been investigated using the HAI security dataset in a case study of a power plant. The numerical outcomes demonstrate that random forest is the most successful model, outperforming CatBoost and XGBoost by a considerable margin and attaining over 99.31% accuracy, precision, sensitivity, F1-score, and AUC. These results highlight how crucial sophisticated detection techniques, such as behavior analysis and anomaly detection algorithms, are for reducing CPS vulnerabilities. Therefore, viable solutions for CPS security are provided by machine learning-driven intrusion detection systems. The study emphasizes how effective ensemble-based techniques like CatBoost and random forest are at identifying intricate attack patterns. To increase CPS resilience against new cyber threats, future research should examine other improvements, such as implementing systems for adaptive instruction and real-time monitoring.

References

[1] C. Alcaraz and J. Lopez, "A Cyber-Physical Systems-Based Checkpoint Model for Structural Controllability," *IEEE Systems Journal*, vol. 12, no. 4, pp. 3543–3554, Dec. 2018, doi: 10.1109/JSYST.2017.2740719.

[2] R. Mitchell and I.-R. Chen, "A survey of intrusion detection techniques for cyber-physical systems," *ACM Comput. Surv.*, vol. 46, no. 4, p. 55:1–55:29, Mar. 2014, doi: 10.1145/2542049.

[3] J. Chen, F. Zhang, and J. Sun, "Analysis of security in cyber-physical systems," *Sci. China Technol. Sci.*, vol. 60, no. 12, pp. 1975–1977, Dec. 2017, doi: 10.1007/s11431-017-9174-3.

[4] N. Cuppens-Boulahia, C. Lambrinoudakis, F. Cuppens, and S. Katsikas, Eds., *Security of Industrial Control Systems and Cyber-Physical Systems*, vol. 10166. in Lecture Notes in Computer Science, vol. 10166. Cham: Springer International Publishing, 2017. doi: 10.1007/978-3-319-61437-3.

[5] L. Bayou, D. Espes, N. Cuppens-Boulahia, and F. Cuppens, "WirelessHART NetSIM: A WirelessHART SCADA-Based Wireless Sensor Networks Simulator," in *Security of Industrial Control Systems and Cyber Physical Systems*, A. Bécue, N. Cuppens-Boulahia, F. Cuppens, S. Katsikas, and C. Lambrinoudakis, Eds., Cham: Springer International Publishing, 2016, pp. 63–78. doi: 10.1007/978-3-319-40385-4_5.

[6] R. (Raj) Rajkumar, I. Lee, L. Sha, and J. Stankovic, "Cyber-physical systems: the next computing revolution," in *Proceedings of the 47th Design Automation Conference*, in DAC '10. New York, NY, USA: Association for Computing Machinery, Jun. 2010, pp. 731–736. doi: 10.1145/1837274.1837461.

[7] R. Mahmud, R. Kotagiri, and R. Buyya, "Fog Computing: A Taxonomy, Survey and Future Directions," in *Internet of Everything: Algorithms,*

Methodologies, Technologies and Perspectives, B. Di Martino, K.-C. Li, L. T. Yang, and A. Esposito, Eds., Singapore: Springer, 2018, pp. 103–130. doi: 10.1007/978-981-10-5861-5_5.

[8] S. M. Othman, F. M. Ba-Alwi, N. T. Alsohybe, and A. Y. Al-Hashida, "Intrusion detection model using machine learning algorithm on Big Data environment," *J Big Data*, vol. 5, no. 1, p. 34, Sep. 2018, doi: 10.1186/s40537-018-0145-4.

[9] S. Chatzimiltis, M. Shojafar, M. B. Mashhadi, and R. Tafazolli, "A Collaborative Software Defined Network-Based Smart Grid Intrusion Detection System," *IEEE Open Journal of the Communications Society*, vol. 5, pp. 700–711, 2024, doi: 10.1109/OJCOMS.2024.3351088.

[10] K. Sadaf and J. Sultana, "Intrusion Detection Based on Autoencoder and Isolation Forest in Fog Computing," *IEEE Access*, vol. 8, pp. 167059–167068, 2020, doi: 10.1109/ACCESS.2020.3022855.

[11] M. Catillo, A. Pecchia, and U. Villano, "CPS-GUARD: Intrusion detection for cyber-physical systems and IoT devices using outlier-aware deep autoencoders," *Computers & Security*, vol. 129, p. 103210, Jun. 2023, doi: 10.1016/j.cose.2023.103210.

[12] S. Thakur, A. Chakraborty, R. De, N. Kumar, and R. Sarkar, "Intrusion detection in cyber-physical systems using a generic and domain specific deep autoencoder model," *Computers & Electrical Engineering*, vol. 91, p. 107044, May 2021, doi: 10.1016/j.compeleceng.2021.107044.

[13] O. Belarbi, T. Spyridopoulos, E. Anthi, I. Mavromatis, P. Carnelli, and A. Khan, *Federated Intrusion Detection System based on Deep Belief Networks*. 2023. doi: 10.48550/arXiv.2306.02715.

[14] R. Vinayakumar, M. Alazab, K. P. Soman, P. Poornachandran, A. Al-Nemrat, and S. Venkatraman, "Deep Learning Approach for Intelligent Intrusion Detection System," *IEEE Access*, vol. 7, pp. 41525–41550, 2019, doi: 10.1109/ACCESS.2019.2895334.

[15] Y. Xiao, C. Xing, T. Zhang, and Z. Zhao, "An Intrusion Detection Model Based on Feature Reduction and Convolutional Neural Networks," *IEEE Access*, vol. 7, pp. 42210–42219, 2019, doi: 10.1109/ACCESS.2019.2904620.

[16] Z. Wang, Y. Liu, D. He, and S. Chan, "Intrusion detection methods based on integrated deep learning model," *Computers & Security*, vol. 103, p. 102177, Apr. 2021, doi: 10.1016/j.cose.2021.102177.

[17] O. Belarbi, A. Khan, P. Carnelli, and T. Spyridopoulos, "An Intrusion Detection System based on Deep Belief Networks," vol. 13580, 2022, pp. 377–392. doi: 10.1007/978-3-031-17551-0_25.

[18] K. M. Ali, V. W. Samawi, and M. S. Al Rababaa, "The affect of fuzzification on neural networks intrusion detection system," in *2009 4th IEEE Conference on Industrial Electronics and Applications*, May 2009, pp. 1236–1241. doi: 10.1109/ICIEA.2009.5138399.

[19] R. A. R. Ashfaq, X.-Z. Wang, J. Z. Huang, H. Abbas, and Y.-L. He, "Fuzziness based semi-supervised learning approach for intrusion detection system," *Information Sciences*, vol. 378, pp. 484–497, Feb. 2017, doi: 10.1016/j.ins.2016.04.019.

[20] M. Sharma, H. Elmiligi, and F. Gebali, "A Novel Intrusion Detection System for RPL-Based Cyber–Physical Systems," *IEEE Can. J. Electr. Comput. Eng.*, vol. 44, no. 2, pp. 246–252, 2021, doi: 10.1109/ICJECE.2021.3053231.

[21] M. Attia, S. M. Senouci, H. Sedjelmaci, E.-H. Aglzim, and D. Chrenko, "An efficient Intrusion Detection System against cyber-physical attacks in the smart grid," *Computers & Electrical Engineering*, vol. 68, pp. 499–512, May 2018, doi: 10.1016/j.compeleceng.2018.05.006.

[22] M. Asif and Y. Al-Harthi, *Intrusion Detection System using Honey Token based Encrypted Pointers to Mitigate Cyber Threats for Critical Infrastructure Networks*. 2014. doi: 10.1109/SMC.2014.6974088.

[23] N. I. Mowla, N. H. Tran, I. Doh, and K. Chae, "AFRL: Adaptive federated reinforcement learning for intelligent jamming defense in FANET," *Journal of Communications and Networks*, vol. 22, no. 3, pp. 244–258, Jun. 2020, doi: 10.1109/JCN.2020.000015.

[24] G. Qawsar and K. Mustafa, "Hybrid Cyber-Attack Detection Model on Cyber-Physical Systems Using Machine Learning Techniques," in *International Conference on Data Analytics & Management*, Springer Nature Singapore, 2023, pp. 197–214.

[25] A. Thakkar and R. Lohiya, "Fusion of statistical importance for feature selection in Deep Neural Network-based Intrusion Detection System," *Information Fusion*, vol. 90, pp. 353–363, Feb. 2023, doi: 10.1016/j.inffus.2022.09.026.

[26] W. H. Aljuaid and S. S. Alshamrani, "A Deep Learning Approach for Intrusion Detection Systems in Cloud Computing Environments," *Applied Sciences*, vol. 14, no. 13, Art. no. 13, Jan. 2024, doi: 10.3390/app14135381.

[27] A. Biju and S. W. Franklin, "Evaluated bird swarm optimization based on deep belief network (EBSO-DBN) classification technique for IOT network intrusion detection," *Automatika*, Jan. 2024, Accessed: Sep. 23, 2024. [Online]. Available: https://www.tandfonline.com/doi/abs/10.1080/00051144.2023.2269646

[28] S. K. Gupta, M. Tripathi, and J. Grover, "Hybrid optimization and deep learning based intrusion detection system," *Computers and Electrical Engineering*, vol. 100, p. 107876, May 2022, doi: 10.1016/j.compeleceng.2022.107876.
[29] S. Siva Shankar, B. T. Hung, P. Chakrabarti, T. Chakrabarti, and G. Parasa, "A novel optimization based deep learning with artificial intelligence approach to detect intrusion attack in network system," *Educ Inf Technol*, vol. 29, no. 4, pp. 3859–3883, Mar. 2024, doi: 10.1007/s10639-023-11885-4.
[30] R. Chitrakar and C. Huang, "Selection of Candidate Support Vectors in incremental SVM for network intrusion detection," *Computers & Security*, vol. 45, pp. 231–241, Sep. 2014, doi: 10.1016/j.cose.2014.06.006.
[31] A. I. Gide and A. A. Mu'azu, "A Real-Time Intrusion Detection System for DoS/DDoS Attack Classification in IoT Networks Using KNN-Neural Network Hybrid Technique," *Babylonian Journal of Internet of Things*, vol. 2024, pp. 60–69, Jul. 2024, doi: 10.58496/BJIoT/2024/008.
[32] F. Zhao, M. Zhang, S. Zhou, and Q. Lou, "Detection of Network Security Traffic Anomalies Based on Machine Learning KNN Method," *Journal of Artificial Intelligence General science (JAIGS) ISSN:3006-4023*, vol. 1, no. 1, Art. no. 1, Jan. 2024, doi: 10.60087/jaigs.v1i1.213.
[33] F. Jemili, R. Meddeb, and O. Korbaa, "Intrusion detection based on ensemble learning for big data classification," *Cluster Comput*, vol. 27, no. 3, pp. 3771–3798, Jun. 2024, doi: 10.1007/s10586-023-04168-7.
[34] M. H. L. Louk and B. A. Tama, "Dual-IDS: A bagging-based gradient boosting decision tree model for network anomaly intrusion detection system," *Expert Systems with Applications*, vol. 213, p. 119030, Mar. 2023, doi: 10.1016/j.eswa.2022.119030.
[35] H. Mittal, A. K. Tripathi, A. C. Pandey, M. D. Alshehri, M. Saraswat, and R. Pal, "A new intrusion detection method for cyber–physical system in emerging industrial IoT," *Computer Communications*, vol. 190, pp. 24–35, Jun. 2022, doi: 10.1016/j.comcom.2022.04.004.
[36] K. Saraswat, M. Devi, D. Professor, and A. Guleria, "Decision Tree Based Algorithm for Intrusion Detection," *International Journal of Advanced Networking and Applications*, vol. 07, pp. 2828–2834, Jan. 2016.
[37] W.-H. Chen, S.-H. Hsu, and H.-P. Shen, "Application of SVM and ANN for intrusion detection," *Computers & Operations Research*, vol. 32, no. 10, pp. 2617–2634, Oct. 2005, doi: 10.1016/j.cor.2004.03.019.
[38] A. Iqbal and S. Aftab, "A Feed-Forward and Pattern Recognition ANN Model for Network Intrusion Detection," *International Journal*

of Computer Network and Information Security, vol. 11, pp. 19–25, Apr. 2019, doi: 10.5815/ijcnis.2019.04.03.

[39] S. Lakshmi Narayanan, M. Kasiselvanathan, K. B. Gurumoorthy, and V. Kiruthika, "Particle swarm optimization based artificial neural network (PSO-ANN) model for effective k-barrier count intrusion detection system in WSN," *Measurement: Sensors*, vol. 29, p. 100875, Oct. 2023, doi: 10.1016/j.measen.2023.100875.

[40] M. Azhar, S. Perveen, A. Iqbal, and B. Lee, "IDRandom-Forest: Advanced Random Forest for Real-Time Intrusion Detection," *IEEE Access*, vol. 12, pp. 113842–113854, 2024, doi: 10.1109/ACCESS.2024.3443408.

[41] M. Choubisa, R. Doshi, N. Khatri, and K. Kant Hiran, "A Simple and Robust Approach of Random Forest for Intrusion Detection System in Cyber Security," in *2022 International Conference on IoT and Blockchain Technology (ICIBT)*, May 2022, pp. 1–5. doi: 10.1109/ICIBT52874.2022.9807766.

[42] N. Farnaaz and M. A. Jabbar, "Random Forest Modeling for Network Intrusion Detection System," *Procedia Computer Science*, vol. 89, pp. 213–217, Jan. 2016, doi: 10.1016/j.procs.2016.06.047.

[43] A. Alsirhani, S. Sampalli, and P. Bodorik, "DDoS Detection System: Using a Set of Classification Algorithms Controlled by Fuzzy Logic System in Apache Spark," *IEEE Transactions on Network and Service Management*, vol. 16, no. 3, pp. 936–949, Sep. 2019, doi: 10.1109/TNSM.2019.2929425.

[44] C. Khammassi and S. Krichen, "A GA-LR wrapper approach for feature selection in network intrusion detection," *Computers & Security*, vol. 70, pp. 255–277, Sep. 2017, doi: 10.1016/j.cose.2017.06.005.

[45] O. A. Aldabash and M. F. Akay, "WS-AWRE: Intrusion Detection Using Optimized Whale Sine Feature Selection and Artificial Neural Network (ANN) Weighted Random Forest Classifier," *Applied Sciences*, vol. 14, no. 5, Art. no. 5, Jan. 2024, doi: 10.3390/app14052172.

[46] W. Al-Yaseen and Q. Abed, "Using a Grey Wolf Optimization and Multilayer Perceptron Algorithms for an Anomaly-Based Intrusion Detection System," *International Journal of Computing and Digital Systems*, vol. 16, no. 1, pp. 1553–1563, Mar. 2024, doi: 10.12785/ijcds/1601115.

[47] Y. K. Saheed and S. Misra, "A voting gray wolf optimizer-based ensemble learning models for intrusion detection in the Internet of Things," *Int. J. Inf. Secur.*, vol. 23, no. 3, pp. 1557–1581, Jun. 2024, doi: 10.1007/s10207-023-00803-x.

[48] N. O. Aljehane *et al.*, "Golden jackal optimization algorithm with deep learning assisted intrusion detection system for network security," *Alexandria Engineering Journal*, vol. 86, pp. 415–424, Jan. 2024, doi: 10.1016/j.aej.2023.11.078.

[49] A. V. Hanafi, A. Ghaffari, H. Rezaei, A. Valipour, and B. arasteh, "Intrusion detection in internet of things using improved binary golden jackal optimization algorithm and LSTM," *Cluster Comput*, vol. 27, no. 3, pp. 2673–2690, Jun. 2024, doi: 10.1007/s10586-023-04102-x.

[50] I. Ahmad, "Feature Selection Using Particle Swarm Optimization in Intrusion Detection," *International Journal of Distributed Sensor Networks*, vol. 11, no. 10, p. 806954, Oct. 2015, doi: 10.1155/2015/806954.

[51] S. M. H. Bamakan, B. Amiri, M. Mirzabagheri, and Y. Shi, "A New Intrusion Detection Approach Using PSO based Multiple Criteria Linear Programming," *Procedia Computer Science*, vol. 55, pp. 231–237, Jan. 2015, doi: 10.1016/j.procs.2015.07.040.

[52] N. Moustafa and J. Slay, "The evaluation of Network Anomaly Detection Systems: Statistical analysis of the UNSW-NB15 data set and the comparison with the KDD99 data set," *Information Security Journal: A Global Perspective*, Apr. 2016, Accessed: Sep. 23, 2024. [Online]. Available: https://www.tandfonline.com/doi/abs/10.1080/19393555.2015.1125974

[53] G. Andresini, A. Appice, N. D. Mauro, C. Loglisci, and D. Malerba, "Multi-Channel Deep Feature Learning for Intrusion Detection," *IEEE Access*, vol. 8, pp. 53346–53359, 2020, doi: 10.1109/ACCESS.2020.2980937.

[54] I. F. Kilincer, F. Ertam, and A. Sengur, "Machine learning methods for cyber security intrusion detection: Datasets and comparative study," *Computer Networks*, vol. 188, p. 107840, Apr. 2021, doi: 10.1016/j.comnet.2021.107840.

[55] National Science Foundation, "Cyber-Physical Systems (CPS)." Accessed: Sep. 11, 2024. [Online]. Available: https://new.nsf.gov/funding/opportunities/cps-cyber-physical-systems

[56] M. Raza, "Cyber-Physical Systems (CPS) Explained," Cyber-Physical Systems (CPS) Explained. Accessed: Sep. 09, 2024. [Online]. Available: https://docs.google.com/document/d/1m9k3WomC5pA_u56lwdkgSvpcUsIBqSsD6rfPrD5mTtU/edit

[57] H. S. Chase, U. A. Mughal, and M. Ismail, "Cyber-Physical Intrusion Detection System for Unmanned Aerial Vehicles," *IEEE Transactions on Intelligent Transportation Systems*, 2023.

[58] Wang, Haijun, Haitao Zhao, Jiao Zhang, Dongtang Ma, Jiaxun Li, and Jibo Wei, "Survey on unmanned aerial vehicle networks: A cyber

physical system perspective," *IEEE Communications Surveys & Tutorials*, vol. 22, no. 2, pp. 1027–1070, 2019.

[59] Y. Xinghuo and Y. Xue, "Smart grids: A cyber-physical systems perspective.," *Proceedings of the IEEE*, vol. 104, no. 5, Art. no. 5, 2016.

[60] Bhadani, U., "Smart Grids: A Cyber–Physical Systems Perspective.," *IRJET*, vol. 11, no. 6, Art. no. 6, 2024.

[61] P. J. Mosterman and J. Zander, "Industry 4.0 as a cyber-physical system study," *Software & Systems Modeling*, vol. 15, pp. 17–29., 2016.

[62] R. Mutaz, H. ElMoaqet, and M. AlFaouri., "Design of a smart factory based on cyber-physical systems and Internet of Things towards Industry 4.0," *Applied Sciences*, vol. 13, no. 4, p. 2156, 2023.

[63] A. A. Ali, M. Al-Maitah, and A. Alarifi, "Cyber-attack detection in healthcare using cyber-physical system and machine learning techniques.," *Soft Computing*, vol. 25, no. 18, pp. 12319–12332, 2021.

[64] T. Gennaro *et al.*, "An intelligent Medical Cyber–Physical System to support heart valve disease screening and diagnosis," *Expert Systems with Applications*, vol. 238, p. 121772, 2024.

[65] S. Han, M. Xie, H.-H. Chen, and Y. Ling, "Intrusion detection in cyber-physical systems: Techniques and challenges," *IEEE systems journal*, vol. 8, no. 4, Art. no. 4, 2014.

[66] Hossain-McKenzie Shamina *et al.*, "Towards the characterization of cyber-physical system interdependencies in the electric grid," presented at the IEEE Power and Energy Conference at Illinois (PECI), 2023, pp. 1–8.

[67] O. A. Ebere, I. Led, U. T. Ekene, D. G. Chijioke, and K. R. Ochuwa, "A Comprehensive Review of Intrusion Detection System Approach and Technique." International Journal of Advances in Engineering and Management," *IJAEM*, vol. 3, no. 12, pp. 70–81, 2021.

[68] C. Riccardo, F. Magri, S. Panzieri, and F. Pascucci, "Anomaly-based intrusion detection system for cyber-physical system security," presented at the 29th Mediterranean Conference on Control and Automation (MED), 2021, pp. 428–434.

[69] H. S. Ya, A. M. Davydenko, T. V. Matovka, and M. P. Prygara, "Tools for Analyzing Signature-Based Hardware Solutions for Cyber Security Systems," *Journal of Cyber Security and Mobility*, vol. 12, no. 3, pp. 339–366, 2023.

[70] K. Pratyush, D. Goswami, S. Chakraborty, A. Annaswamy, K. Lampka, and L. Thiele, "A hybrid approach to cyber-physical systems verification.," in *Proceedings of the 49th Annual Design Automation Conference,* 2012, pp. 688–696.

[71] J. K. Nazir and D. Yau, "Data driven physical modelling for intrusion detection in cyber physical systems," presented at the Proceedings of the Singapore Cyber-Security Conference (SG-CRC), 2016, pp. 43–47.

[72] S. Vyas and D. Bhargava, "Cyber-physical Systems for Healthcare," *Smart Health Systems, Singapore: Springer.*, pp. 71–86, 2021.

[73] F. Moradi, A. A. Sara, P. Bahman, M. Zahra, and S. Marjan, "CRYSTAL framework: Cybersecurity assurance for cyber-physical systems," *Journal of Logical and Algebraic Methods in Programming*, vol. 139, p. 100965, 2024.

[74] G. S. Karthick and V. Sumathi, "Cyber-Physical Systems: Foundations, Design Principles, Challenges, and Applications," *Contemporary Developments in Agricultural Cyber-Physical Systems*, pp. 1–22, 2023.

[75] P. H. J. Nardelli, *Cyber-physical Systems: Theory, Methodology, and Applications*. John Wiley & Sons, 2022.

[76] B. Manikandan, S. Priyadharshini, K. M. Hariram, P. Girija, and A. Sowmiya, "Development of Cyber Physical Based Manufacturing System Design," *IJARSCT*, vol. 4, no. 4, 2024.

[77] S. Rajendran, S. Shilpa, L. S. Priya, and N. Ramavenkateswaran, "Cyber-Physical System: Advances and Applications in Cyber Security," pp. 106–133, 2024, doi: 10.2174/9789815223286124010007.

[78] K. Muheden, M. Mariwan, and B. Noura, "Exploring the Landscape of Smart Cities: A Comprehensive Review of IoT and Cyber-Physical Systems," *The Indonesian Journal of Computer Science*, vol. 13, no. 2, pp. 3642–3656, 2024.

[79] S. Rudresha, R. G. Harsha, G. K. Kumar, S. Shruthi, and S. Kalpana, "A Cyber-Physical Systems Perspective on Smart Grids," *Futuristic Trends in Artificial Intelligence, Iterative International Publishers.*, pp. 28–48, 2024.

[80] R. Sharma, S. Parhi, and A. Shishodia, "Industry 4.0 Applications in Agriculture: Cyber-Physical Agricultural Systems (CPASs)," in *Advances in Mechanical Engineering*, V. R. Kalamkar and K. Monkova, Eds., Singapore: Springer, 2021, pp. 807–813. doi: 10.1007/978-981-15-3639-7_97.

[81] E. Mutua, "Cyber-Physical Systems and Their Role in Industry 4.0," *Journal of Technology and Systems*, vol. 6, no. 5, pp. 57–69, 2024, doi: https://doi.org/10.47941/jts.2149.

[82] P. Pishdad-Bozorgi, G. Xinghua, and D. R. Shelden, "Introduction to cyber-physical systems in the built environment," *Construction 4.0, Routledge*, pp. 23–41, 2020.

[83] M. I. Ghafoor *et al.*, "A review on enhancing cyber-physical system security using artificial intelligence.," *Journal of Applied and Emerging Sciences*, vol. 12, no. 2, pp. 210–218, 2023.

[84] Y. Junying, "Unstructured Big Data Analysis Algorithm for Grid CPS Based on Machine Learning," in *3rd International Conference on Mobile Networks and Wireless Communications (ICMNWC)*, 2023, pp. 1–6.

[85] D. Priyanka *et al.*, "An Intelligent Intrusion Detection System for Integrated Edge Computing CPS with Machine Learning," *International Research Journal of Modernization in Engineering Technology and Science.*, 2024.

[86] M. K. Habib and C. Chukwuemeka, "CPS: Role, characteristics, architectures and future potentials.," *Procedia Computer Science*, vol. 200, pp. 1347–1358, 2022.

[87] Y. Bobde *et al.*, "Enhancing Industrial IoT Network Security through Blockchain Integration," *Electronics*, vol. 13, no. 4, p. 687, 2024.

[88] H. Khan and D. Kaur, "CYBER-PHYSICAL SYSTEMS," *Machine Learning: An Art of Computer Thinking ,IIP Series*, vol. 3, pp. 213–229, 2024, doi: https://www.doi.org/10.58532/nbennurch188.

[89] R. Sindhu, S. P. Shilpa, L. S. Priya, and N. Ramavenkateswaran, "Cyber-Physical System," *Cyber Physical Systems-Advances and Applications*, p. 106, 2024.

[90] S. F. Mihalache, E. Pricop, and J. Fattahi, "Resilience enhancement of cyber-physical systems: A review.," *Power Systems Resilience: Modeling, Analysis and Practice*, pp. 269–287, 2019.

[91] B. J. Vries, "Materials: Towards a Circular Economy," *Sustainability Science, Cambridge University Press*, pp. 460–495, 2023.

[92] S. Thiede, "Environmental sustainability of cyber physical production systems," *Procedia CIRP*, vol. 69, pp. 644–649, 2018.

[93] A. N. Maksimović, V. R. Nikolić, D. V. Vidojević, M. D. Randjelović, S. M. Djukanović, and D. M. Randjelović, "Using Triple Modular Redundancy for Threshold Determination in DDOS Intrusion Detection Systems," *IEEE Access*, vol. 12, pp. 53785–53804, 2024, doi: 10.1109/ACCESS.2024.3384380.

[94] H.-K. Shin, W. Lee, J.-H. Yun, and H. Kim, "{HAI} 1.0: {HIL-based} Augmented {ICS} Security Dataset.," in *13Th USENIX workshop on cyber security experimentation and test (CSET 20)*, 2020, pp. 1–5.

14

Cyber-physical Systems: Strategies for Enhancing Availability, Recovery, and Auditing for Optimal Performance

Ilker Kara

Department of Computer Engineering, Faculty of Engineering, Çankırı Karatekin University, Turkey
Department of Medical Services and Techniques, Çankırı Karatekin University, Turkey

Email: karaikab@gmail.com

Abstract

There is a significant rise in data generation due to the large number of Internet of Things (IoT) devices available nowadays. Data integrity and reliability are key when those voices echo with information used by a wide range of applications, from smart cities to healthcare monitoring systems. On an abstract level, it is clear why traditional data cleaning and anomaly detection methods are an issue when dealing with IoT devices in resource-constrained environments. Accordingly, this research presents a fresh data cleaning and anomaly detection method: TinyCleanEDF. TinyCleanEDF employs a federated learning mechanism that moves beyond the conventional centralized data processing strategies at edge device levels for data cleaning and anomaly detection to tackle these issues. This framework allows users to do a collaborative learning model on edge when the data is federated without moving the data to a central server. This preserves the data privacy and reduces the overhead of transmitting these data. As a result, this work provides an interoperable and adaptable solution for many IoT applications such as home automation, industry 4.0, or environmental surveillance.

DOI: 10.1201/9788743801306-14

14.1 Introduction

IoT enables physical devices and everyday objects to connect to the internet to read, receive, and process data. The diversity of data generated has greatly increased as the use of IoT devices continues to grow rapidly. In fact, in 2020, it was assumed that there are more than 20 billion currently active IoT devices in the world; not excluding this figure is intended to keep growing in the future [1]. IoT technology supports a new paradigm of application opportunities in smart cities, health, industrial automation, and environmental surveillance [2]. However, this rapidly growing IoT device list has significant data accuracy, reliability, and trustworthiness issues.

Traditional data cleaning and anomaly detection methods are not directly applicable to IoT devices as these devices usually have energy-efficient operations, limited storage capacities, and reduced processing powers. Data cleaning refers to identifying and correcting (or removing) faulty, incomplete, or inconsistent records to maintain reliable information. In the IoT setting, this can manifest as sensor failures and exceptions, network latency, or unpredictable environmental behaviors [3]. Those mistakes can contaminate some of your data analysis results in the worst way: biasing accuracy. These errors can worsen the accuracy of the derived insights from Data Analytics. Thus, it is very important to clean the data appropriately and validate data to make IoT-based devices more reliable. In IoT systems, anomaly detection is a method to determine the abnormality of data events from the expected normal behavior. It is important in security vulnerability detection, system breakdown prevention, and IoT event anomaly detection [4]. The low resource constraints of the IoT (check our recent post on the subject) make it prohibitive to implement these algorithms locally while achieving real-time performance.

In this study, a new method, TinyCleanEDF, for data cleaning and anomaly detection in IoT devices has been proposed. TinyCleanEDF utilizes federated learning to work around the shortcomings of decentralized data processing mechanisms [5]. Considering the constraints of IoT devices, TinyCleanEDF supports data cleaning and anomaly detection. Therefore, this approach can be a good method for many IoT applications such as smart homes, industrial automation, and environmental monitoring.

14.1.1 Chapter contribution

This chapter presents TinyCleanEDF, a novel solution for data cleaning and anomaly detection for IoT [6-8]. In contrast to prior work, TinyCleanEDF uses federated learning to deal with constraints on IoT devices, such as low energy, storage, or computational power. The major contributions are:

- Decentralized data processing: TinyCleanEDF enables federated data processing, making model cleaning costly and reducing communication overheads.
- Domain-neutrality: the framework applies to various domains, such as smart homes, industrial automation, and environmental monitoring.
- Improving efficiency: TinyCleanEDF offers a scalable approach to enhance data reliability and system-level performance in IoT networks by maximizing the cost efficiency of limited device resources.

14.1.2 Chapter organization

This chapter is structured as follows:

- *14.1 Introduction*: this section provides background on IoT, particularly its upsurge, challenges, and the need for good data management.
- *14.1.1 Availability of CPS*: CPS availability can be described as the sufficiency in the ability of the system to run for a certain production time with no interruptions.
- *14.1.3 Availability of CPS*: availability in cyber-physical systems deals with the ability of a particular system to be fully operative in climes that are dangerous due to Atkins stresses like redundant equipment and fault-tolerant operational measures.
- *14.2 IoT and TinyCleanEDF*: TinyCleanEDF framework addressing demands of internet of things device resources constraints in the process of ensuring safety and confidentiality of information is introduced.
- *14.2.1 Disaster recovery*: The term disaster recovery as used here refers to a set of activities that are engaged in order to execute normal system operations in a short time after an unforeseen operational disruption.
- *14.3 Data cleaning in IoT systems*: Addressing the issues of why data cleaning is important, the benefits it has on the system performance, particularly within the IoT context and the challenges therein.
- *14.4 Anomaly detection in IoT systems*: an assessment of techniques employed in the organization of detection of anomalies, as well as their applications in the secure and stable running of IoT.

- *14.5 Conclusion*: highlights of the major findings in the study, including that of SlimCleanEDF and the possibilities and trends of the further development of TinyCleanEDF in IOT data management.

14.1.3 Availability of CPS

The term availability of cyber-physical systems (CPS) indicates their ability to operate in the required mode without interruption and continuity of services [9]. Availability is very important in areas like healthcare, industrial automation, and transport, as system unavailability may have great implications. The focus is on decreasing interruption and ensuring that the business remains operational even in the event of failure, such as hardware failure, software bugs, or outside interference [10].

CPS persistence depends on network stability, hardware availability, and effective resource management. With regard to these problems, various solutions are applied, including redundancy, fault management design, and predictive maintenance [10-12].

- *Redundancy*: The practice of adding backup components ensures that in the case of primary component failure, there will be no substantial downtime since the system can continue operation if the requirement needs one or many such components.
- *Fault tolerance*: Systems that are fault tolerant are able to detect and resolve the failure without external assistance, thus hampering technical operations is not an issue due to them not being interrupted.
- *Predictive maintenance*: Strain monitoring of system components is consistently performed so that strains leading to fatigue or malfunctioning of components can be recognized, which allows for repairs prior to equipment failure.

All these measures with regards to CPS performance enhancement lead to improvement in the CPS performance availability metrics being attained especially in the contexts that necessitate constant availability of services.

14.2 IoT and TinyCleanEDF

The Internet of Things (IoT) is a network of physical objects, devices, sensors, appliances, and other things that are configured such that they can connect to the Internet to collect, share, and analyze information with the aid of IoT Technologies [13]. This new technology allows different devices to communicate with each other and their controlled unit, thus becoming more intelligent, effective, and independent. The core aim of IoT is to make common devices smarter so that they are all connected to the internet and information can be transferred from one device to another [14].

Currently, IoT encompasses new features in almost all spheres and includes applications from smart homes and medicine to industrial processes and farming. For example, in smart homes, the functions of devices interconnected through IoT aid in energy efficiency, along with the improvement of lifestyle figures such as security systems and home automation. As in the case of the patient's home healthcare, in IoT, continuous data is gathered for the purpose of optimally managing and monitoring patients via remote means with the assistance of medical personnel.

In the industrial sector, IoT technology is primarily utilized to streamline manufacturing processes, anticipate machine maintenance needs, and boost overall efficiency. In agriculture, IoT is crucial in optimizing irrigation systems, enhancing crop yields, and monitoring environmental conditions. This technology goes beyond merely connecting devices to the internet; it provides solutions that enhance efficiency, safety, energy savings, and user experience, making it essential in today's world. As we look to the future, it is anticipated that the Internet of Things (IoT) will become increasingly ubiquitous, infiltrating numerous facets of everyday existence. TinyCleanEDF represents a specialized framework developed for data cleansing and anomaly detection designed for IoT devices. Its objective is to enhance data accuracy and reliability, particularly because it acknowledges the constraints imposed by the limited resources of these devices. Generally, IoT devices operate under various restrictions, including minimal energy consumption, constrained storage capacity, and reduced processing power. However, traditional data processing and anomaly detection methodologies are often ill-suited for the unique challenges presented by IoT environments. TinyCleanEDF addresses these obstacles by employing a federated learning approach, which enables data processing on distributed devices, thus eliminating the necessity to transfer the data to a central server.

The swift proliferation of IoT devices has led to the creation of vast quantities of data. However, guaranteeing the precision and dependability of this data is essential (because it underpins the validation of the outcomes generated by these devices). Traditional methods for data cleansing and anomaly detection often depend on centralized systems, which can introduce a range of risks pertaining to data security and privacy. TinyCleanEDF addresses these concerns by utilizing federated learning, thus facilitating local data processing and, consequently, protecting data privacy. This approach also enhances the efficiency of IoT devices by minimizing delays associated with data transmission and reducing energy consumption.

14.2.1 Disaster recovery

Disaster recovery is a careful plan designed to restore system functionality after unexpected interruptions (like hardware failures, cyberattacks, or natural disasters) [15]. This process is crucial for keeping systems strong, especially in important sectors where long downtimes could cause major issues, such as financial losses and safety risks. Many different strategies are used to improve recovery abilities. Regular backups of important data are kept in faraway places, ensuring that vital information can be reached if something goes wrong. However, copying data and services to various locations provides extra safety, helping operations continue smoothly even if the main system fails. Automated failover systems are also set up, which switch to backup systems without needing anyone to step in; this reduces downtime. Although these strategies greatly improve disaster recovery efforts, there are still challenges in putting them into action.

14.3 The Importance of Data Cleaning in IoT Systems

Data cleaning is essential in managing digital information [11]. It identifies and corrects faulty, incomplete, or inconsistent data (see Figure 14.1) [8]. In IoT systems, the accuracy and reliability of data directly influence the system's overall performance. IoT devices generate vast amounts of real-time data; however, the quality of services these systems offer depends on the quality of that data. Various factors, such as sensor failures, network delays, hardware malfunctions, and environmental conditions, can lead to errors in this data [7]. Although these errors can pose significant challenges during data processing, they must be addressed to ensure accurate analysis. This is crucial for the success of any IoT application [10].

IoT systems play a role in many fields (like smart cities, healthcare, industrial automation, and environmental monitoring) by providing accurate and dependable data [3-5]. However, inaccuracies in the data from these systems can negatively impact the quality of analyses and the overall performance of the system. For instance, in healthcare monitoring systems, incorrect data can lead to wrong diagnoses or treatments; this can be serious. However, in industrial automation, such inaccuracies may cause major disruptions in production. Because of this, it is essential to clean IoT data to enhance the reliability and efficiency of these systems. The success of IoT systems

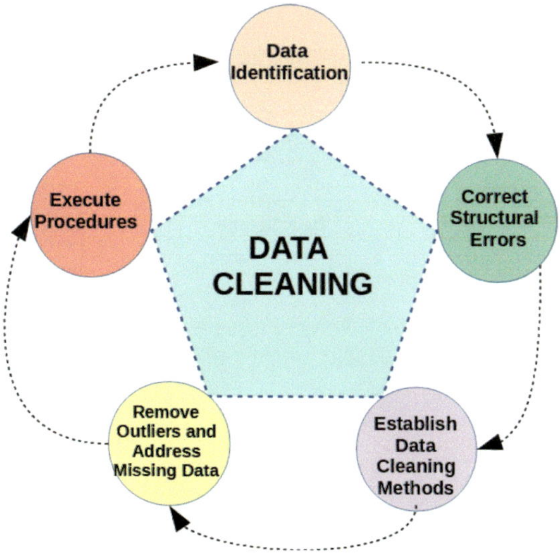

Figure 14.1 Data cleaning process.

heavily relies on effective data-cleaning processes. Traditional methods for data cleaning usually depend on centralized systems, which can raise various concerns about data security, privacy, and processing time. New strategies developed specifically for IoT systems aim to tackle these issues. Innovative techniques (like distributed data processing and federated learning) enable more efficient and reliable data cleaning in IoT environments [15].

Nonetheless, it (implementing data-cleaning processes in IoT systems) presents several challenges [4]. The limited energy capacity, low processing power, and restricted storage of IoT devices can hinder the effectiveness of these processes. Therefore, data cleaning methods must be tailored to IoT devices' limited resources. For instance, algorithms that prioritize energy efficiency and processing time can improve the performance of IoT devices and facilitate successful data cleaning processes (however, this is not always easy). Because of these limitations, developers must be creative; however, they can find ways to optimize performance [6]. Although it may seem difficult, it is crucial to address these issues (but) doing so can lead to significant improvements.

14.4 Anomaly Detection and Its Importance in IoT Systems

Anomaly detection is a method that spots deviations from typical behavior in datasets (see Figure 14.2) [12]. This technique plays a vital role in IoT systems

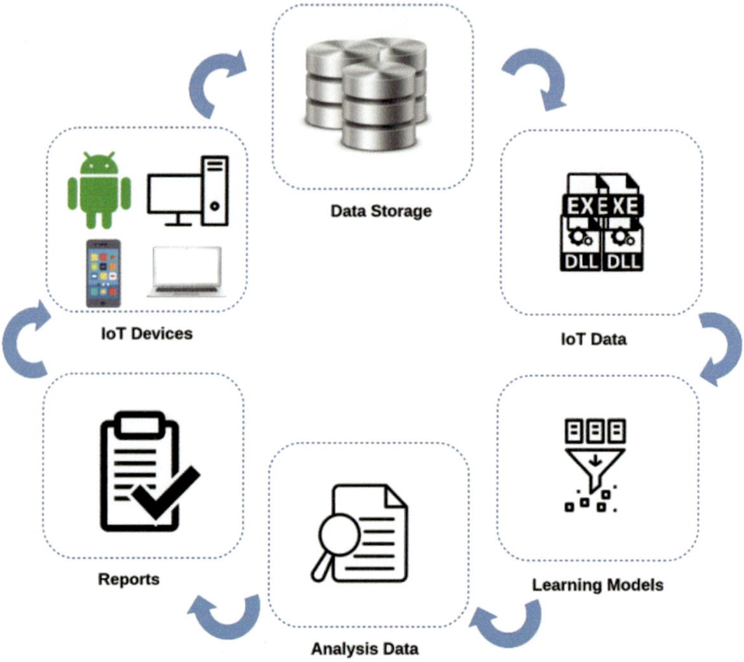

Figure 14.2 The process of anomaly detection in IoT systems.

by helping to identify security vulnerabilities, prevent system failures, and recognize unusual events. In an IoT setting, data flows continuously from various devices, making it crucial to analyze this information for systems to function effectively. Anomaly detection enables quick identification of unexpected changes or faults within the system. These deviations can arise from security breaches, hardware malfunctions, or external influences. However, catching these issues early can help avert more serious problems [11].

Because of the nature of IoT systems, these devices often face limitations in energy, processing power, and storage capacity. These constraints make it difficult to conduct anomaly detection on-site and in real time. Traditional methods for anomaly detection typically require substantial computational resources to analyze large datasets and execute complex algorithms. However, since IoT devices lack the necessary resources for such computation-heavy techniques, it becomes essential to create lighter and more energy-efficient algorithms. In this regard, modern strategies like federated learning can enhance the effectiveness of anomaly detection on IoT devices. Federated learning enables model training across distributed devices without the need to transfer data to a central server. This approach allows for local data processing (which safeguards data privacy) and minimizes communication costs. Furthermore, these methods improve overall system energy efficiency while facilitating real-time anomaly detection.

Anomaly detection is crucial (not only for security) but also for monitoring and enhancing the overall performance of IoT systems. For example, identifying anomalies in the production process in industrial IoT environments can help pinpoint potential failures that could result in significant expenses [12-14]. However, in healthcare monitoring systems, detecting abnormality in patient data can aid in identifying health issues that require immediate attention. This is important because early detection can save lives. Although it may seem complex, the benefits are clear.

14.5 Conclusion and Future Scope

IoT systems are quickly becoming one of the most dynamic sectors in modern technology (however). They face big challenges, especially regarding data management, security, and overall efficiency. The fast growth in the number (and) variety of IoT devices, along with technological advancements, has led to the creation of large amounts of data. Unfortunately, the reliability and accuracy of this data have become critical issues that affect the quality of services these systems can provide. Data cleaning and anomaly detection processes are important to ensure that IoT systems work securely and efficiently. It is crucial to identify and fix any faulty, incomplete, or inconsistent data that may happen. Neglecting to manage these errors properly can negatively impact data analysis accuracy and, in turn, the system's overall performance. Thus, using effective data-cleaning methods is essential for improving the reliability of IoT systems. The limited resources on IoT devices mean that these processes must be optimized. Factors like energy efficiency and processing time greatly influence how well data-cleaning algorithms work.

As IoT systems (which are growing rapidly) continue to expand, there is an urgent need to enhance data cleaning and anomaly detection processes. However, creating innovative solutions is essential. Some suggestions to tackle this challenge include (but are not limited to) improving algorithms and using machine learning techniques. Although these methods can be complex, they hold great potential. Effective cleaning and detection processes are necessary because data is crucial for IoT systems. This way, we ensure that the information we gather is accurate and reliable.

Given (the) limited resources of IoT devices, it is crucial to create lighter and more energy-efficient algorithms for data cleaning and anomaly detection. These algorithms should be tailored to fit the devices' limited energy capacity and processing power. Decentralized data processing methods hold significant promise for enhancing data privacy in IoT systems; however, they also cut down on processing time and energy use. Expanding the use of techniques like federated learning could provide substantial advantages in both the security and efficiency of IoT systems. Security vulnerabilities in IoT devices continue to pose a serious threat, especially regarding anomaly detection. Thus, it is vital to develop security-oriented anomaly detection methods and incorporate them into existing systems. Proactive security measures that identify threats early represent a crucial advancement because they help mitigate risks. Given the nature of IoT systems, data must be processed in real time. Therefore, implementing real-time anomaly detection and data cleaning processes will improve the reliability and efficiency of these systems. Such solutions are especially important in scenarios that require immediate action (although) they can be challenging to implement.

The rapid growth (1) in the number of IoT devices calls for scalable data management processes. Data cleaning and anomaly detection algorithms must be scalable to handle the increasing volume of data and the rising number of devices. This will be essential for the future success of IoT systems. However, data cleaning and anomaly detection processes are vital for the security, efficiency, and overall performance of IoT systems. Although future efforts in these areas will pave the way for greater acceptance of IoT technology, creating more dependable applications is crucial (2). Because of this, we must prioritize these processes to ensure a successful future.

References

[1] Malhotra, P., Singh, Y., Anand, P., Bangotra, D. K., Singh, P. K., Hong, W. C. (2021). Internet of things: Evolution, concerns and security challenges. *Sensors*, *21*(5), 1809.

[2] Gubbi, J., Buyya, R., Marusic, S., Palaniswami, M. (2013). Internet of Things (IoT): A vision, architectural elements, and future directions. *Future generation computer systems*, *29*(7), 1645–1660.

[3] Ding, X., Wang, H., Li, G., Li, H., Li, Y., Liu, Y. (2022). IoT data cleaning techniques: A survey. Intelligent and Converged Networks, 3(4), 325–339.

[4] Chandola, V., Banerjee, A., Kumar, V. (2009). Anomaly detection: A survey. *ACM computing surveys (CSUR)*, *41*(3), 1–58.

[5] McMahan, B., Moore, E., Ramage, D., Hampson, S., Arcas, B. A. (2017, April). Communication-efficient learning of deep networks from decentralized data. In *Artificial intelligence and statistics* (pp. 1273–1282). PMLR.

[6] Chu, X., Ilyas, I. F., Krishnan, S., Wang, J. (2016, June). Data cleaning: Overview and emerging challenges. In *Proceedings of the 2016 international conference on management of data* (pp. 2201–2206).

[7] Mohammed, A. F., Sultan, S. M., Lee, J., Lim, S. (2023). Deep-reinforcement-learning-based IoT sensor data cleaning framework for enhanced data analytics. *Sensors*, *23*(4), 1791.

[8] expressanalytics.com, https://www.expressanalytics.com/blog/growing-importance-of-data-cleaning/ (Access time, 6.10.2024)

[9] Singh, P. D., Singh, K. D. (2023). Security and privacy in fog/cloud-based IoT systems for AI and robotics. *EAI Endorsed Transactions on AI and Robotics*, *2*.

[10] Elsisi, M., Su, C. L., Ali, M. N. (2023). Design of reliable IoT systems with deep learning to support resilient demand side management in smart grids against adversarial attacks. *IEEE Transactions on Industry Applications*.

[11] Idrees, A. K., Abou Jaoude, C., Al-Qurabat, A. K. M. (2020, October). Data reduction and cleaning approach for energy-saving in wireless sensors networks of IoT. In *2020 16th international conference on wireless and mobile computing, networking and communications (WiMob)* (pp. 1–6). IEEE.

[12] Alghanmi, N., Alotaibi, R., Buhari, S. M. (2022). Machine learning approaches for anomaly detection in IoT: an overview and future research directions. Wireless Personal Communications, 122(3), 2309–2324.

[13] Mašková, M., Zorek, M., Pevný, T., Šmídl, V. (2024). Deep anomaly detection on set data: Survey and comparison. *Pattern Recognition*, 110381.

[14] Sater, R. A., Hamza, A. B. (2021). A federated learning approach to anomaly detection in smart buildings. *ACM Transactions on Internet of Things*, *2*(4), 1–23.

[15] Wei, J., Huan, L. (2024). Machine Learning-based Anomaly Detection for IoT Security: Challenges, Techniques, and Future Directions. *Asian American Research Letters Journal*, 1(2).

15

Legal Framework and Regulatory Policies for Cyber-physical Systems

Abubakar Aliyu[1], Emeka Ogbuju[1], Victoria Yemi-Peters[1], Agbotiname Lucky Imoize[2], Dauda Olorunkemi Isiaka[1], Godwin Sani[3] and Francisca Oladipo[4]

[1]Department of Computer Science, Faculty of Science, Federal University Lokoja, Nigeria
[2]Department of Electrical and Electronics Engineering, Faculty of Engineering, University of Lagos, Nigeria
[3]Directorate of Information and Communication Technology, Federal University Lokoja, Nigeria
[4]Department of Computer Science, Faculty of Computing and Applied Science, Thomas Adewumi University, Nigeria

Email: abubakar.aliyu@fulokoja.edu.ng; emeka.ogbuju@fulokoja.edu.ng; victoria.yemi-peters@fulokoja.edu.ng; aimoize@unilag.edu.ng; dauda.isiaka@fulokoja.edu.ng; godwin.sani@fulokoja.edu.ng; francisca.oladipo@tau.edu.ng

Abstract

Cyber-physical systems (CPS) integrate digital networks with physical processes and are essential to modern infrastructure such as electricity grids, healthcare, and transportation. As cyber-physical systems (CPS) expand, they encounter distinct security concerns necessitating robust legal frameworks and regulatory laws. This chapter analyses the significance of these frameworks in safeguarding cyber-physical systems (CPS) from cyber threats, maintaining resilience, and fostering innovation. We examine contemporary legislation, international standards, and treaties that govern CPS security, emphasizing the necessity for global collaboration. The chapter examines the difficulties of regulating rapidly advancing technology and the function

DOI: 10.1201/9788743801306-15

of governmental bodies. Industry best practices, certification processes such as the Common Criteria, and efficient incident response strategies are also examined. By focusing on these critical domains, the chapter offers significant insights and recommendations for regulators and organizations in protecting CPS in a progressively digital landscape.

15.1 Introduction

Cyber-physical systems (CPS) represent an emerging revolution in the integration of the physical and digital domains. These systems integrate computational components with physical processes and networked communication, serving essential functions in various sectors like healthcare, transportation, energy, manufacturing, and key national infrastructure [1]. Embedded networks that integrate cyber components (software, data processing, communication) with physical entities (sensors, actuators, and physical processes) in real time are transforming the management of smart buildings, smart grids, factories, smart cities, autonomous vehicles, industrial robotics, and medical devices [2]. The integration of physical and cyber domains fosters significant advancements in efficiency, innovation, and technology [3]. However, technology also presents considerable legal, regulatory, and ethical difficulties that necessitate a robust and adaptable legal framework [4].

As cyber-physical systems (CPS) become more interwoven into society [5], their ability to influence technological, social, economic, and environmental dimensions is essential [6]. The magnitude of possible injury and collateral damage to society also modifies risk exposure, including security vulnerabilities, privacy concerns, safety difficulties, and liability inquiries, all of which pose challenges to our current legal frameworks and regulatory approaches [7,8]. Consequently, governments, industry, and legal experts must create governance structures that can adeptly tackle the complexity, interconnection, and autonomy of CPS. This strategy ought to cultivate public trust and accountability from the grassroots level while also promoting innovation [9].

The legal and regulatory framework for cyber-physical systems (CPS) is fundamentally interdisciplinary, necessitating the integration of regulations about software, hardware, telecommunications, data protection, safety, and intellectual property [10]. Artificial intelligence (AI), machine learning, and the Internet of Things (IoT) are driving the rapid evolution of cyber-physical systems (CPS), necessitating the dynamic adaptation of rules to balance innovation and risk management [11]. Numerous cyber-physical systems (CPSs) are employed in critical sectors, and their failures or attacks can lead to significant harm, such as accidents involving autonomous vehicles [12], cyberattacks on industrial control systems, and malfunctions in healthcare devices. Consequently, regulatory policy must extend beyond functional safety to encompass stringent cybersecurity and privacy protections, enabling cyber-physical systems (CPS) to endure harmful assaults from both technical (e.g., cyberattacks) and nontechnical viewpoints [13].

The key to the regulation of CPS is several significant challenges. The complexity of cyber-physical systems (CPS), characterized by the integration of hardware and software components that interact in real time, necessitates a regulatory approach that is more comprehensive than that applied to conventional systems [14]. The diverse domains in which cyber-physical systems (CPS) function indicate that a uniform approach is neither practical nor advantageous [15]. Regulatory policies should be customized for individual industries to effectively address the distinct risks associated with cyber-physical systems (CPS) in sectors such as autonomous transportation, smart healthcare, and critical infrastructure [10]. The growing autonomy of numerous cyber-physical systems, particularly those incorporating artificial intelligence, introduces novel ethical and legal challenges concerning liability, accountability, and the necessity of human oversight. Cyber-physical systems (CPS) frequently depend on extensive datasets to operate effectively, especially those integrated with artificial intelligence systems that evolve and improve over time [15]. The dependence on data, much of which may be personal and sensitive, raises substantial issues related to data privacy, ownership, and adherence to international data protection regulations, including the European General Data Protection Regulation (GDPR) [16] and the US Health Insurance Portability and Accountability Act (HIPAA) [17]. Given that CPS systems often entail the collecting and processing of real-time data, maintaining adherence to these rules is a primary concern for both developers and operators.

Moreover, CPS generally function within highly interconnected ecosystems, indicating that a security compromise or failure in one system can propagate via linked systems, resulting in extensive disruption or damage [11]. The regulatory framework must integrate stringent cybersecurity mandates specifically designed to address the distinct vulnerabilities of cyber-physical systems (CPS), particularly within key infrastructure sectors like power grids, water systems, and transportation networks [14]. There is an increasing necessity for global collaboration and standardization in the regulation of CPS. Due to the worldwide nature of industries utilizing CPS, such as automotive, aerospace, and telecommunications, cross-border standardization of safety, security, and data protection requirements is important [18].

In the absence of such harmonization, corporations may encounter regulatory fragmentation, and consumers may face disparate degrees of protection based on their geographical location [19].

This chapter seeks to provide a comprehensive exploration of the legal and regulatory framework of cyber-physical systems broadly. This will examine the fundamental legal structures of CPS focusing on safety, accountability, confidentiality, and security, while also evaluating the reaction of regulatory bodies across various jurisdictions. This chapter will analyze the primary regulatory instruments relevant to sector-specific regulations, including the automotive, healthcare, and industrial sectors, from the viewpoints of cybersecurity and data protection law, as well as emerging global regulatory initiatives aimed at standardizing CPS governance. This chapter will emphasize the necessity for a sufficiently flexible legal framework to address technological advancements, while also being rigorous enough to mitigate the significant hazards associated with cyber-physical systems (CPS) that threaten social innovation.

15.1.1 Key contributions of the chapter

This chapter offers several important contributions to understanding how these systems are governed and protected in the modern world. These key contributions include the following.

1. The chapter explains why legal frameworks and regulations are critical for CPS, highlighting their role in ensuring security, stability, and compliance in industries that rely on these systems, such as energy, healthcare, and transportation.
2. A detailed exploration of current cybersecurity laws and regulations is provided, giving readers an understanding of how these legal structures address the unique challenges posed by CPS.
3. The chapter discusses international standards and guidelines, as well as treaties and agreements that help align global efforts in regulating and securing CPS. This promotes cross-border collaboration and consistency in dealing with cyber threats.
4. It addresses the difficulties regulators face in keeping pace with rapidly advancing CPS technology, providing insights into the gaps between innovation and legal enforcement.
5. The chapter identifies key government agencies responsible for regulating CPS, outlining their responsibilities and the strategies they employ to ensure compliance with cybersecurity standards.

6. It provides a summary of industry best practices that organizations can follow to meet regulatory requirements, helping them stay ahead of security risks while ensuring legal compliance.
7. The chapter covers certification processes such as the Common Criteria for IT Security Evaluation, showing how these frameworks help ensure CPS meets established security standards.
8. A structured approach to incident response and reporting is introduced, guiding organizations on how to prepare for, detect, and respond to security incidents effectively.
9. The chapter offers practical guidance for regulators, industry professionals, and policymakers on how to navigate the complex landscape of CPS governance, balancing innovation with security and compliance.

These contributions provide a holistic view of how CPS can be effectively regulated and secured, offering a roadmap for ensuring the safe and efficient operation of these systems in an increasingly interconnected world.

15.1.2 Chapter organization

This chapter is organized as follows: Section 15.1, introduction, presents cyber-physical systems (CPS) and their essential function in contemporary infrastructure, emphasizing the necessity for legal frameworks and regulatory regulations to protect these systems from cyber threats while promoting innovation. Section 15.2, related work, examines the existing literature and prior studies pertinent to CPS regulation. This section delineates the deficiencies in existing research, establishing a framework for the subsequent talks. Section 15.3, methodology, establishes the research techniques, data sources, and analytical tools employed to examine legal frameworks and regulatory policies about CPS. This guarantees a comprehensive comprehension of the methodology underlying the chapter's conclusions. Section 15.4, legal framework for cyber-physical systems, examines the current legal structures regulating CPS, demonstrating how these regulations tackle the distinct issues arising from the integration of physical and digital systems in essential industries. Section 15.5, regulatory policies for CPS, analyses essential regulatory policies, encompassing the functions of government agencies and international standards. We also examine industry best practices and the significance of certification for compliance. Section 15.6, emerging trends and challenges, addresses the rising difficulties in CPS regulation, including swift technical progress and the international scope of cybersecurity concerns. It underscores the necessity for flexible regulatory measures.

Section 15.7, lessons learned, encapsulates the principal insights from the chapter, highlighting the significance of adaptive legislative frameworks, global collaboration, and adherence to best practices for safeguarding CPS. Section 15.8, recommendations, provide pragmatic proposals for enhancing CPS regulation, fostering collaboration, and ensuring that legal frameworks evolve in tandem with technological advancements without obstructing innovation. Section 15.9, conclusion, summarizes the chapter by emphasizing the necessity for comprehensive legal and regulatory measures to safeguard CPS while maintaining a balance between security and innovation in the swiftly changing environment.

15.2 Related Work

This section offers a comprehensive analysis of the current literature about the legal framework and regulatory laws governing cyber-physical systems (CPS). The emphasis is on the varied issues and suggested solutions presented by multiple authors, emphasizing the interdisciplinary nature of CPS governance. The literature encompasses several essential domains, including privacy and data protection, cybersecurity, safety standards, liability issues, and ethical considerations, all of which are vital for the effective regulation of cyber-physical systems (CPS) across sectors such as healthcare, transportation, manufacturing, and critical infrastructure.

Table 15.1 encapsulates the contributions of 20 writers, outlining the emphasis of their research and the constraints of their findings. Each study examines concerns, such as data privacy issues (e.g., the effects of GDPR on CPS), cybersecurity risks in vital infrastructure, or the legal ramifications of autonomous systems in transportation. Nonetheless, despite advancements in these domains, several studies encounter constraints in breadth, frequently concentrating on individual sectors or theoretical frameworks without adequately addressing the wider, practical implementation issues across businesses. Table 15.1 systematically categorizes the literature, serving as a reference for comprehending the extent and deficiencies in the existing regulatory framework for CPS. Table 15.1 also summarizes the existing literature, including the conducted research and its associated limitations across diverse CPS areas.

15.2.1 Gaps analyzed

There is a comprehensive understanding of many components of CPS, and significant achievements in regulating certain parts; however, while much

Table 15.1 Summary of the related works.

Reference	Description of work done	Limitations of the work
[20]	Examined the legislative obstacles in the integration of cyber-physical systems in healthcare, emphasizing data privacy and security compliance.	Limited to healthcare and excluded critical infrastructure protection (CPS) in other essential sectors such as transportation or energy.
[21]	Analyzed the role of GDPR in protecting personal data in CPS, with an emphasis on IoT devices.	Lacked focus on AI-driven CPS and the evolving data protection concerns.
[2]	Explored liability issues in autonomous vehicles as CPS, suggesting new legal models to address accidents caused by system failures.	Focused mainly on the automotive sector and did not address broader CPS industries.
[22]	Investigated cybersecurity vulnerabilities in CPS used in smart grids, proposing enhanced network security protocols.	The narrow focus is on smart grids without considering cybersecurity challenges in other CPS domains like healthcare or industrial systems.
[23]	Evaluated the regulatory policies for CPS in critical infrastructure, emphasizing the need for international cooperation on cybersecurity standards.	Did not address liability or privacy concerns in CPS outside critical infrastructure.
[24]	Studied functional safety standards for CPS in manufacturing, particularly focusing on compliance with ISO standards.	There is a lack of discussion on the intersection of functional safety with cybersecurity and data privacy.
[25]	Proposed a framework for ethical AI in CPS, emphasizing bias prevention and transparency in decision-making systems.	The ethical framework was theoretical and lacked practical implementation strategies for regulatory compliance.
[26]	Discussed the role of intellectual property (IP) laws in protecting software and hardware innovations within CPS.	Focused solely on IP protection and did not consider security or safety concerns.
[27]	Provided an overview of international regulatory efforts in CPS.	The comparison was broad, without detailed sector-specific analysis.
[28,29]	Analyzed the legal challenges of cross-border data flows in CPS, particularly in cloud-connected IoT systems.	It did not address the complexities of ensuring cybersecurity in these cross-border systems.

(*Continued.*)

Table 15.1 *Continued*

Reference	Description of work done	Limitations of the work
[30]	Investigated the regulatory gaps in AI-driven CPS, emphasizing the need for real-time safety monitoring in autonomous systems.	The study focused on AI-driven CPS but lacked insight into non-AI-based CPS regulatory issues.
[31]	Explored the implications of emerging 5G networks on CPS, focusing on communication standards and regulatory challenges.	It is limited to communication technologies without discussing security or liability concerns in CPS.
[32]	Reviewed US legal frameworks for CPS in autonomous transportation, proposing new liability models for system malfunctions.	Focused only on the US legal system, not addressing international perspectives.
[33]	Studied the role of government regulations in ensuring the cybersecurity of industrial CPS, proposing stricter security protocols.	The focus was on government regulations, with little discussion on industry-led security standards.
[34]	Proposed a legal framework for managing the environmental impact of CPS in industrial sectors, especially energy consumption.	Concentrated on environmental impacts but overlooked cybersecurity and privacy issues.
[35]	Investigated CPS regulatory approaches in healthcare, focusing on FDA and MDR compliance for medical devices.	Narrowly focused on medical device regulation without addressing broader healthcare CPS concerns.
[36]	Analyzed data protection laws affecting CPS in smart cities, with emphasis on citizen privacy in smart infrastructure.	Did not cover cybersecurity risks or technical vulnerabilities in smart city CPS.
[13]	Proposed enhanced cybersecurity frameworks for CPS in defense sectors, focusing on advanced threat detection mechanisms.	Focused narrowly on defense, leaving out other critical infrastructure like transportation or energy.
[37]	Explored ethical implications of AI and machine learning in CPS, proposing regulatory guidelines to ensure fairness and transparency.	The ethical guidelines were theoretical and lacked practical regulatory strategies.
[38]	Evaluated liability and insurance frameworks for CPS in the context of autonomous maritime systems.	Specific to the maritime sector, with no discussion of CPS liability frameworks in other industries like healthcare or transportation.

work addresses the subject from a fragmented viewpoint concentrating on sectoral effects or concerns, broader consequences are frequently underexplored. The literature study identifies a notable gap, as the majority of studies focus on particular sectors (e.g., healthcare, autonomous vehicles, and transportation). This breadth, while valuable, neglects the broader uses of CPS across other sectors, including industry, smart cities, and critical infrastructure. It fails to elucidate the prevalent legislative solutions for interoperability, intersectoral communication, and the harmonization of safety and security standards.

There is limited examination of cross-cutting issues, such as cybersecurity, digital sovereignty, and data protection, particularly in relation to interconnected cyber-physical systems (CPS). There is a lack of extensive cross-disciplinary discourse regarding the problems and actionable measures necessary for attaining cybersecurity in highly interconnected and transnational CPS systems; yet, the necessity for such dialogue is evident and warrants further investigation. The GDPR seldom acknowledges the body of international cybersecurity law established in various contexts, and business compliance with AI-driven security governance remains largely unaffected by data privacy mandates. Moreover, numerous studies neglect to address the regulatory ramifications of future technologies like 5G networks and artificial intelligence, which increasingly constitute the foundation of cyber-physical systems. The liability frameworks in CPS are indeed a "literature-less field."

As CPSs increasingly depend on AI/ML for critical decision-making, existing regulatory frameworks must evolve to address the heightened complexity in assigning liability, particularly regarding the autonomy of these systems and the extent of human intervention, if any. The convergence of legal, ethical, and environmental challenges is a domain that has been largely overlooked in literature. This chapter will examine the characteristics and consequences of this gap as the world transitions toward enhanced sustainability and the development of green cyber-physical systems, alongside legislative frameworks that promote environmentally responsible practices while prioritizing safety and security. The necessity of composing a comprehensive chapter on the legal framework and regulatory policies for cyber-physical systems is clear given these deficiencies.

This study presents a comprehensive regulatory framework that considers the interdependence of cyber-physical systems (CPS) across several domains, including cross-border regulation while recognizing the importance of both practical compatibility and theoretical discourse as a crucial means to integrate disparate research components. This chapter may act as a shared reference to address the deficiency of sector-specific studies and could establish a robust basis that policymakers, companies, and academics require to navigate the intricate regulatory framework of CPS. This chapter will finish by offering a vital addition to the subject by addressing the constraints identified in the literature, including the absence of worldwide unification of cybersecurity standards, a comprehensive liability model for autonomy, and harmonization of rules within nations. It will also emphasize the dynamic character of CPS technologies, advocating for regulatory regulations that are sufficiently flexible and adaptive to keep up with swift technical progress while assuring safety, privacy, security, and accountability in CPS implementation across all sectors.

15.3 Methodology

This chapter employs a qualitative research methodology, considered to be the most suitable approach. This method is optimal as it facilitates a comprehensive examination of the rules and regulations essential for understanding the governance of CPS. Given that CPS encompasses a broad spectrum of legal, ethical, and technical concerns, a qualitative methodology offers the necessary flexibility to examine both existing frameworks and prospective requirements comprehensively. A primary element of this methodology is doctrinal legal research. This entails analyzing current legal documents, statutes, and regulations to evaluate their effectiveness in addressing the intricacies of CPS. For example, how do existing regulations address the data privacy challenges presented by cyber-physical systems (CPS), and how do they govern cybersecurity in critical infrastructure? Analyzing these documents allows for a comprehensive understanding of the current legal framework.

A crucial element is comparative legal analysis, which examines the legal frameworks of other countries or areas. CPS functions within a global framework, where each nation may possess distinct legislation regulating matters such as data protection or responsibility concerning autonomous systems. Through the comparison of different methodologies, the research can elucidate optimal practices and identify areas necessitating enhancement. For instance, Europe's GDPR may impose more stringent data protection restrictions than those in the United States, where regulations concerning autonomous vehicles may be better developed. This comparison aids in recognizing discrepancies and prospects for worldwide regulatory harmonization. Policy analysis is also significant in this research. It assesses the efficacy of existing legislation in mitigating risks related to CPS, including cybersecurity concerns and liability in autonomous systems. Policy analysis examines not only the existence of regulations but also their efficacy in practice. This might

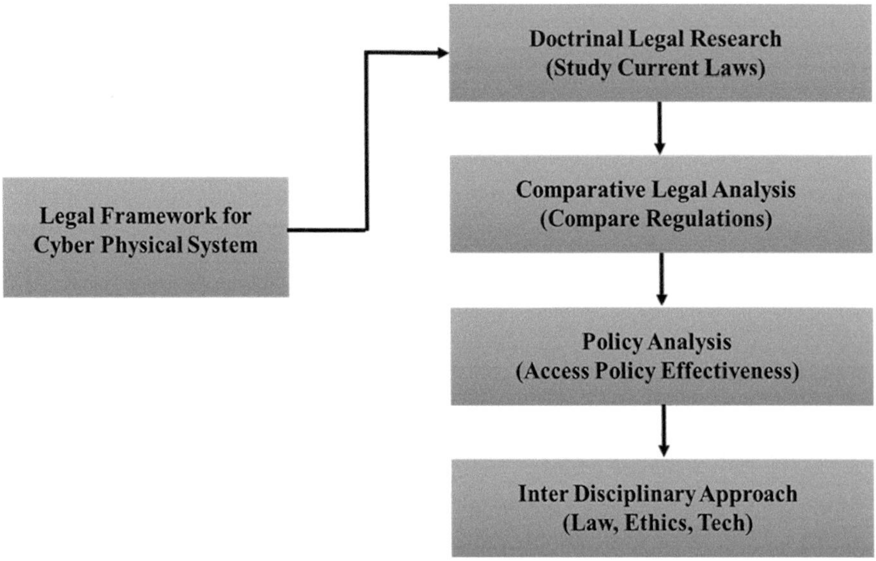

Figure 15.1 Review approach.

indicate whether existing regulations are obsolete or require adaptation to align with emerging technologies such as AI and 5G, which are essential to CPS. Ultimately, an interdisciplinary approach is essential.

CPS encompasses legal, ethical, technological, and sociological considerations. AI-driven cyber-physical systems provoke enquiries on transparency and bias, encompassing both legal and ethical concerns. By synthesizing insights from several fields, the research can provide more holistic solutions that tackle these complex difficulties. Figure 15.1 examines the regulation of CPS across diverse businesses through the subsequent steps. The steps are as follows:

1. *Doctrinal legal research:* this will involve studying the existing laws, regulations, and policies related to CPS, such as cybersecurity rules and data privacy laws. This helps understand the current legal landscape.

2. *Comparative legal analysis:* this compares how different countries handle CPS regulations. For example, how does the United States regulate autonomous vehicles compared to Europe? This gives insights into international differences and possible harmonization.

3. *Policy analysis:* this part evaluates how well current laws and policies work in practice. Are the regulations effective? Do they need updating as CPS technology evolves?

4. *Interdisciplinary approach:* since CPS involves law, ethics, and technology, an interdisciplinary approach ensures all perspectives are considered, particularly when dealing with issues like AI, data security, and liability.

In Figure 15.1, each stage is contingent upon the preceding one, culminating in the last step (interdisciplinary approach), which guarantees the simultaneous consideration of legal, ethical, and technical concerns. This methodology will facilitate the development of an exhaustive perspective on CPS regulations and policies, addressing deficiencies and suggesting new frameworks as necessary.

15.4 Legal Framework for Cyber-physical Systems

Cyber-physical systems (CPSs) are integral to modern technology, integrating physical processes with computational controls. These systems are prevalent throughout various industries, including healthcare, transportation, manufacturing, and energy. They oversee all aspects of self-driving vehicles [2], intelligent power grids [22], robotic surgical systems [40], and automated manufacturing facilities [41]. Due to their increasing significance and prevalence in daily life, it is essential to guarantee that CPS is safe, dependable, and secure. The legal foundation for CPS is crucial in this context. The legal framework for CPS comprises laws, regulations, and standards that dictate these systems' design, operation, and maintenance [42]. These regulations safeguard users, uphold privacy, assure safety, and designate accountability in the event of issues [14]. Without a robust legal framework, the dangers associated with CPS including cybersecurity threats, system malfunctions, and privacy violations – could inflict considerable damage on individuals and society [13]. As CPS technology advances, the corresponding regulations must also adapt [4]. The legal framework for cyber-physical systems (CPS) is continually evolving to accommodate technological advancements, focusing on cybersecurity, liability, and ethical issues [32]. Governments, international organizations, and companies are collaborating to establish norms and standards applicable across borders, as CPS systems frequently function on a worldwide scale [28].

This chapter will explore the significance of legal frameworks and regulatory policies for CPS. We will examine the various categories of laws and regulations, their protective functions for individuals and enterprises, and the difficulties associated with regulating rapidly evolving technology such as cyber-physical systems (CPS). Comprehending these legal frameworks is essential not only for engineers and developers but also for lawmakers, business executives, and consumers who depend on CPS in their everyday activities. The swift progression of cyber-physical systems (CPS) necessitates the establishment of comprehensive legal frameworks and regulations to guarantee their safe, secure, and responsible use. CPS influences numerous industries, including healthcare, transportation, and vital infrastructure, necessitating regulation of its design, operation, and maintenance. Table 15.2 delineates the principal justifications for the necessity of these frameworks, emphasizing aspects such as public safety, cybersecurity, privacy, liability, and international collaboration. These policies safeguard persons and industries while fostering innovation, equity, and ethical decision-making in CPS development. Table 15.2 outlines the fundamental reasons for the importance of legal frameworks and regulations in cyber-physical systems (CPS).

15.4.1 Existing laws and regulations related to cybersecurity

Considering the increasing integration of cyber-physical systems (CPS) into daily life and vital infrastructures, the demand for robust cybersecurity measures has heightened [1]. Cyber-physical systems (CPS), which govern a range of applications from autonomous vehicles to power grids [2], are vulnerable to cyberattacks that may disrupt critical services, jeopardize important information, or inflict physical damage [1]. In response to these concerns, numerous laws and regulations have been established worldwide to guarantee the protection and security of CPS [24]. Table 15.3 presents a summary of the main extant cybersecurity laws and regulations that regulate CPS. These frameworks, established by national governments and international organizations, delineate the criteria for the design, operation, and protection of CPS against cyber threats. Their objective is to protect both the systems and the data they manage, while also promoting proactive measures for organizations to defend against cyberattacks. This section will examine these regulations in further detail, emphasizing their applicability to CPS and their significance in safeguarding these systems within an increasingly linked environment. These laws and regulations guarantee that cyber-physical systems (CPS), whether utilized in vital infrastructure, healthcare, or consumer products, are constructed and upheld with robust security protocols. As cyber threats persistently evolve, numerous countries and international organizations are revising and augmenting these frameworks to ensure the security and resilience of cyber-physical systems (CPS).

Table 15.2 Benefits of legal frameworks and regulations for CPS.

Key aspect	Explanation
Ensuring public safety	Cyber-physical systems often operate in critical sectors such as healthcare, transportation, and infrastructure. Comprehensive legal frameworks ensure that these technologies adhere to safety standards to prevent accidents, injuries, or fatalities. Autonomous vehicles must comply with rigorous restrictions to ensure their safety on public roads.
Enhancing cybersecurity	Cyber-physical systems are vulnerable to cyberattacks because of their internet connectivity. Legislation and regulations establish protocols to safeguard these systems against hacking, malware, and other security infringements. These safeguards are vital for thwarting assaults on critical infrastructures such as smart grids or industrial control systems.
Protecting privacy	Many CPSs collect and process sensitive data, encompassing personal and health-related information. Regulations such as GDPR mandate the correct handling of data, safeguarding against misuse, and upholding individuals' privacy rights. CPS must adhere to data protection legislation to safeguard personal information.
Clarifying responsibility and liability	When a problem occurs in a CPS, it is crucial to identify the responsible party. Legal frameworks delineate liability for system failures, accidents, or security breaches. This is especially crucial in domains such as autonomous vehicles, where it may be ambiguous whether the user, manufacturer, or software developer bears responsibility.
Fostering consumer trust	People are more inclined to embrace new technology when they have confidence in the safety, security, and regulation of the systems. A definitive legal framework fosters confidence in CPS by guaranteeing that the systems adhere to safety and security norms, hence promoting broader use.
Promoting fair competition	Regulations establish an equitable environment for enterprises engaged in the development of cyber-physical systems (CPS). Regulations establish mandatory standards for all enterprises, preventing unfair competition and fostering innovation within a framework that safeguards both consumers and businesses.
Ensuring ethical decision-making	As cyber-physical systems (CPS) gain autonomy, they begin to make decisions independently of human intervention. Ethical laws guarantee that these systems render choices consistent with social norms, including fairness, openness, and the mitigation of bias, especially in sectors such as healthcare or criminal justice.

Key aspect	Explanation
Supporting innovation	Explicit restrictions enable companies to innovate without apprehension of legal repercussions. When enterprises comprehend the legal stipulations about safety, security, and privacy, they can concentrate on advancing innovative CPS technologies that extend limits while remaining compliant with the law.
Safeguarding critical infrastructure	CPS is progressively utilized in essential areas such as energy, water, and transportation. Legal frameworks safeguard these infrastructures against disruptions resulting from failures or assaults. This is particularly crucial for national security and public welfare.
Facilitating global cooperation	Child Protection Services frequently function transnationally, necessitating the establishment of international standards. Legal frameworks promote collaboration among nations, guaranteeing that systems established in one area can be securely and efficiently utilized in another. This global alignment is essential for managing the intricate, interrelated nature of CPS.

15.4.2 International standards and guidelines on legal framework and regulatory policies for cyber-physical systems

As cyber-physical systems (CPS) increasingly impact diverse global sectors, it is imperative to develop international standards and guidelines that offer a cohesive legal framework for their regulation [51]. These standards guarantee that CPS, irrespective of their development or deployment location, adhere to uniform safety, security, and operational criteria [14]. International collaboration is essential as cyber-physical systems frequently function transnationally, particularly in domains such as transportation, healthcare, and critical infrastructure [2]. The goal of these worldwide standards is to establish a unified regulatory framework that fosters innovation while ensuring public safety, data security, and system reliability. International entities like the International Organization for Standardization (ISO) and the International Electrotechnical Commission (IEC) have led the development of these rules [51]. Table 15.4 summarizes some significant international standards and guidelines pertinent to CPS. These international standards establish a thorough legal and regulatory framework for cyber-physical systems. By following these recommendations, companies may guarantee that their CPS comply

Table 15.3 Regulatory standard for CPS.

Regulation	Region	Description
General Data Protection Regulation (GDPR) [43]	European Union	Focuses on protecting personal data and privacy in the EU. It applies strict rules on how organizations, including CPS, handle and secure personal data.
NIST Cybersecurity Framework [1]	United States	Developed by the National Institute of Standards and Technology (NIST), this voluntary framework provides guidelines for improving cybersecurity in critical infrastructure and CPS.
California IoT Security Law [44]	California, United States	Requires manufacturers of IoT devices, including CPS, to equip them with reasonable security features to protect against unauthorized access and use.
Cybersecurity Information Sharing Act (CISA) [45]	United States	Encourages organizations to share cybersecurity threat information with the government to enhance collective defense against cyber threats.
Cybersecurity Law of the People's Republic of China [46]	China	Establishes rules for the protection of networks, especially critical information infrastructure, and enhances the monitoring and prevention of cyberattacks.
European Network and Information Security (NIS) Directive [47]	European Union	Aims to improve the cybersecurity of network and information systems across the EU, including those used in CPS, with obligations for operators to ensure security and report incidents.
Critical Infrastructure Protection (CIP) Standards [48]	North American Electric Reliability Corporation (NERC), United States and Canada	These standards set cybersecurity requirements for the protection of the electric grid, which involves CPS systems that control and manage critical infrastructure.
Digital Operational Resilience Act (DORA) [49]	European Union	Designed to ensure that financial institutions and their CPS systems are resilient to cyberattacks and maintain secure operations even under severe disruption.
Personal Information Protection Law (PIPL) [50]	China	Aims to protect personal information and holds organizations accountable for data breaches, especially in CPS systems handling sensitive data.
ISO/IEC 27001 [51]	International	An international standard providing requirements for establishing, implementing, maintaining, and continuously improving an information security management system (ISMS). CPS systems are often covered under these guidelines.

Table 15.4 Guidelines on the legal framework and regulatory policies for cyber-physical systems.

Guideline	Organization	Description
ISO/IEC 27001	ISO and IEC	An international standard that provides best practices for information security management systems (ISMS), is crucial for securing CPS environments.
IEC 61508	International Electrotechnical Commission (IEC)	A standard for functional safety of electrical, electronic, and programmable systems, ensuring CPS meets safety requirements in critical sectors.
ISO 26262	International Organization for Standardization (ISO)	Focuses on the functional safety of road vehicles, providing guidelines for the design and development of CPS in the automotive industry.
ISO/IEC 62443	IEC	Sets security guidelines for industrial automation and control systems, which are vital components of CPS used in manufacturing and other industries.
IEEE 1547	Institute of Electrical and Electronics Engineers (IEEE)	Establishes guidelines for the interconnection and interoperability of distributed energy resources (DER) with power systems, applicable to CPS in energy grids.
ITU-T Y.2060	International Telecommunication Union (ITU)	Provides a framework for the Internet of Things (IoT), which includes CPS, focusing on architecture and security requirements.
NIST Special Publication 800-53	National Institute of Standards and Technology (NIST), United States	A set of guidelines for securing information systems and CPS through controls that address privacy and cybersecurity risks.
ISO/IEC TR 29110	ISO and IEC	Guidelines for very small entities in software and systems engineering, including CPS, to improve development processes.
EN 50128	European Committee for Electrotechnical Standardization (CENELEC)	Focuses on railway applications, providing software and hardware standards for CPS in this sector to ensure safety and reliability.
ISO 13485	ISO	Specifies requirements for medical device CPS, ensuring they meet regulatory and safety standards across international markets.

with international safety, security, and operational standards, while also cultivating trust and reliability in the systems they develop and oversee. This global collaboration is essential for ensuring that CPS functions efficiently in an interconnected environment, where transnational systems and shared infrastructure necessitate uniform regulatory supervision.

15.4.3 International treaties and agreements governing cyber-physical systems (CPS)

As cyber-physical systems (CPS) rapidly influence global sectors such as transportation [2], healthcare [13], energy [52], and defense [53], the necessity for international treaties and agreements has become essential. These agreements aim to provide a collaborative and uniform legal framework regulating the deployment, security, and use of CPS across national boundaries [54]. CPS functions within a global framework, frequently necessitating collaboration among nations to tackle concerns like cybersecurity, data privacy, liability, and the protection of key infrastructure [47]. International treaties and agreements regulating CPS seek to set common norms, promote collaboration, and tackle the distinctive issues presented by these intricate systems. Through collaboration, nations can foster innovation, avert misuse, and guarantee that cyber-physical systems are safe, resilient, and compliant with international standards. Table 15.5 presents significant international treaties and agreements that impact the regulation of CPS.

International conventions and agreements are essential for tackling the difficulties presented by CPS on a worldwide scale. These agreements, as seen in Figure 15.2, facilitate

1. *Establish common rules:* these agreements create a shared legal framework that governs how CPS is regulated, ensuring consistency across countries.
2. *Enhance cybersecurity:* by addressing cyber threats and encouraging cooperation on incident response, these treaties protect CPS from cyberattacks and other malicious activities.
3. *Promote data privacy:* many CPS systems handle personal and sensitive data. International agreements help ensure that data is protected across borders.
4. *Coordinate cross-border use:* CPS systems often operate globally, and treaties facilitate cooperation between countries to ensure smooth and secure cross-border operations.

Table 15.5 International agreements governing CPS.

Treaty/agreement	Key participants	Description
Budapest Convention on Cybercrime (2001) [55]	Council of Europe, various nonmember states	The first international treaty focused on addressing cybercrime, it provides a legal framework for investigating and prosecuting cybercrimes that affect CPS systems.
Wassenaar Arrangement (1996) [56]	42 participating countries	A multilateral export control regime that includes controls on dual-use technologies, such as encryption and software used in CPS, to prevent their misuse in conflicts or cyberattacks.
Paris Call for Trust and Security in Cyberspace (2018) [57]	Over 75 countries, companies, and organizations	A voluntary agreement aimed at promoting peace and stability in cyberspace, it emphasizes the need for secure systems, including CPS, and cooperation to prevent cyberattacks.
United Nations Convention on the Use of Electronic Communications in International Contracts (2005) [58]	United Nations	This treaty promotes the use of electronic communications, which are essential for CPS, in international trade, ensuring legal recognition and security.
Tallinn Manual on the International Law Applicable to Cyber Warfare (2013/2017) [59]	NATO and legal scholars	Though not legally binding, this manual provides guidance on how international law applies to cyber operations, including attacks on CPS used in critical infrastructure during armed conflicts.
EU–US Privacy Shield Framework (2016) [60]	European Union, United States	Though invalidated in 2020, it set the stage for future agreements on data privacy and security, which are crucial for CPS that processes personal and sensitive data across borders.
Convention on Data Protection (Convention 108) [61]	Council of Europe	An international treaty that regulates the protection of personal data, ensuring that CPS handling sensitive information complies with privacy standards across multiple countries.
Oslo Manual on Science, Technology, and Innovation (2018) [62]	Organization for Economic Cooperation and Development (OECD)	Provides guidelines for evaluating technological innovation, including CPS, and encourages international collaboration to foster the development and regulation of emerging technologies.
North Atlantic Treaty Organization (NATO) Cyber Defense Pledge (2016) [63]	NATO member states	A commitment by NATO members to enhance their national defenses against cyberattacks, including those targeting CPS used in defense and national security systems.
Bilateral and Multilateral Cybersecurity Agreements[64]	Various countries	Countries like the United States, China, Russia, and members of the EU have signed bilateral and multilateral agreements focusing on cybersecurity cooperation, incident response, and cybercrime prevention, all of which are critical for protecting CPS.

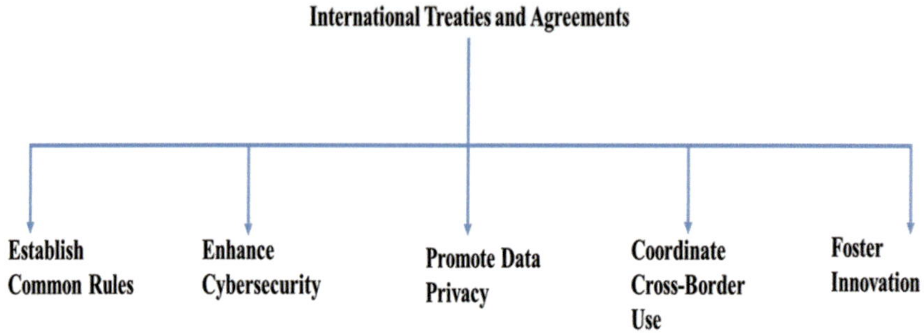

Figure 15.2 Benefits of international treaties and agreements.

5. *Foster innovation:* by creating a stable and cooperative regulatory environment, these agreements promote the development and adoption of CPS technologies while balancing the need for security and ethical use.

International treaties and agreements are essential for regulating the intricate, global dynamics of CPS. They facilitate the development, deployment, and use of these systems in a manner that is secure, ethical, and consistent with collective global interests.

15.4.4 Challenges in enforcing laws in the rapidly evolving technology landscape

The fast advancement of technology poses considerable issues in the enforcement of rules and regulations, particularly concerning cyber-physical systems (CPS) [65]. Cyber-physical systems frequently encompass advanced advances that exceed the capacity of current legal frameworks to adjust, resulting in regulatory and enforcement deficiencies [4]. This section delineates many key issues associated with law enforcement in the rapidly advancing technological environment. These obstacles are

1. *Lagging legal frameworks*
   Regulations and laws can require years for formulation and execution, but technological progress in cyber-physical systems occurs at a much accelerated pace. When rules are enacted, they may already be obsolete or inadequate to handle the latest advancements and concerns associated with CPS [66].

2. *Complexity of CPS*
   Cyber-physical systems amalgamate physical systems with digital control, resulting in intricate networks that are challenging to manage.

Conventional legal frameworks may be inadequate for addressing the hybrid characteristics of these systems, especially with cybersecurity, liability, and privacy concerns [67].

3. *Cross-border jurisdiction*
   Enforcing regulations consistently is a challenge because CPS frequently operates in numerous nations. Countries may possess disparate legislation, resulting in ambiguity over applicable laws. This may result in jurisdictional conflicts, particularly in instances of cross-border data transfer, cybersecurity infringements, or intellectual property transgressions [68].

4. *Cybersecurity threats and enforcement*
   Cyberattacks on critical infrastructure are increasing in complexity and occurrence, while law enforcement authorities find it challenging to adapt to these threats. Identifying attackers is frequently challenging, particularly when assaults stem from overseas companies or entail intricate cybercrime networks. The absence of universal cybersecurity standards impedes effective enforcement [13].

5. *Privacy concerns*
   CPS frequently manages substantial quantities of sensitive personal and financial information. As privacy requirements advance (e.g., GDPR), maintaining compliance becomes a hurdle. Numerous CPS systems gather and analyze data without explicit consent protocols, complicating the enforcement of privacy regulations, particularly as novel data kinds arise from sophisticated sensors and IoT devices [13].

6. *Liability issues*
   When a malfunction or cyberattack occurs in a CPS, establishing liability can be challenging. Is it the manufacturer, the software developer, or the end user? Legal frameworks frequently lack clarity in attributing culpability in certain instances, so hindering enforcement and the pursuit of damages or remedial remedies [69].

7. *Ethical and moral questions*
   As CPS gains increased autonomy, ethical and moral dilemmas emerge. How should the law govern CPS that makes life-and-death determinations, like autonomous automobiles or medical devices? Implementing laws that encompass ethical issues necessitates a balance between innovation and societal norms, a task that can be arduous in a swiftly evolving context [70].

8. *Rapid technological obsolescence*
   CPS technologies rapidly become antiquated; however, rules and regulations may still pertain to obsolete systems. The disparity between

technological advancement and regulatory procedures compels organizations to adhere to outdated legislation, resulting in compliance difficulties [71].

9. *Lack of technical expertise in law enforcement*
   The technological complexity of CPS necessitates specialized expertise for the efficient enforcement of regulations. Numerous law enforcement agencies and regulators may lack the requisite competence to comprehensively comprehend CPS technologies, hence complicating the investigation of breaches or the evaluation of compliance [72].

10. *Resistance to regulation*
    Organizations and innovators in the CPS sector frequently oppose new laws, perceiving them as impediments to innovation. This opposition can impede the enactment of essential legislation, complicating enforcement further. Achieving an equilibrium between promoting innovation and guaranteeing safety and security remains an ongoing problem for authorities [13].

The implementation of laws in the swiftly changing domain of CPS is beset by problems, including the necessity to update legal frameworks in accordance with technical progress and to tackle intricate matters such as cybersecurity, privacy, and cross-border jurisdiction. Confronting these difficulties necessitates cooperation among governments, companies, and international organizations to design adaptable and progressive policies that can align with technological advancements.

15.5 Regulatory Policies for Cyber-physical Systems (CPS)

Regulatory policies for cyber-physical technologies (CPS) are crucial to guarantee the safe, secure, and ethical operation of these advanced technologies [9]. Cyber-physical systems (CPSs) are embedded in essential industries including healthcare, energy, manufacturing, and transportation, rendering their regulation crucial for safeguarding public safety, data privacy, and national security. The principal regulatory regulations that oversee CPS and their role in mitigating the intricate risks and challenges linked to these systems include

1. *Safety regulations*
   CPS must comply with stringent safety regulations owing to their possible effects on human lives and infrastructure. Regulatory rules in industries like automotive (e.g., autonomous vehicles), healthcare (e.g.,

medical devices), and industrial automation prioritize the safe operation of CPS to prevent harm to users and the environment. These policies frequently require stringent testing, certification, and continuous monitoring. ISO 26262 for functional safety in automotive systems guarantees that cyber-physical systems in vehicles comply with safety standards to avert accidents and malfunctions [73].

2. *Cybersecurity regulations*
   As CPS systems become more susceptible to hackers, cybersecurity regulations are essential for their protection. Regulatory policies in this domain require secure software development methodologies, encryption protocols, and routine security updates to safeguard CPS against unauthorized access, data breaches, and various cyberattacks. The NIST Cybersecurity Framework offers standards for securing critical infrastructure cyber-physical systems, highlighting risk management and ongoing monitoring [1].

3. *Data privacy regulations*
   CPS often collects, handles, and disseminates substantial quantities of personal data, rendering data privacy a paramount concern. Regulatory policies mandate that CPS operators adhere to data protection laws, guaranteeing that sensitive information is acquired, stored, and disseminated in accordance with privacy requirements. This entails acquiring user consent, employing robust encryption, and guaranteeing data anonymization as required. The General Data Protection Regulation (GDPR) mandates stringent data protection rules throughout Europe, ensuring that CPS managing personal data adheres to privacy and security standards [13].

4. *Interoperability standards*
   Regulatory policies develop interoperability standards to ensure that CPS can communicate and interact efficiently across many platforms, systems, and sectors. These standards facilitate the seamless integration of CPS components, promoting innovation while guaranteeing compatibility across diverse technologies. IEC 61499 establishes interoperability standards for industrial automation systems, guaranteeing the efficient collaboration of CPS components from various manufacturers [74], [75].

5. *Liability and accountability policies*
   Determining culpability in cases of CPS failures, accidents, or cybersecurity breaches is a multifaceted subject. Regulatory policies delineate accountability in the event of a failure, specifying whether the

manufacturer, developer, or operator has responsibility. These policies elucidate legal responsibility, facilitating equitable dispute settlement and restitution for damages. Liability frameworks in autonomous vehicles provide accountability for accidents, identifying whether the responsibility is with the car manufacturer, the software developer, or the driver [2].

6. *Ethical and AI-related regulations*
   Considering the integration of artificial intelligence (AI) in several cyber-physical systems (CPSs), regulatory laws are progressively emphasizing ethical issues to guarantee that AI-driven CPSs render judgments equitably and openly. These policies tackle concerns related to prejudice, discrimination, and the responsibility of AI systems in essential decision-making processes. The EU's AI Act seeks to regulate high-risk AI applications in CPS, requiring transparency, explainability, and the absence of biases that may adversely affect individuals or society [11].

7. *Environmental and sustainability policies*
   CPS significantly influences businesses that affect the environment, like energy, transportation, and agriculture. Regulatory rules aim to ensure that cyber-physical systems (CPSs) are designed and run to reduce their environmental effect, fostering sustainability, energy efficiency, and responsible resource utilization. Environmental standards for CPS in smart networks emphasize enhancing energy efficiency and mitigating carbon emissions [6].

8. *Global regulatory alignment*
   As CPS functions internationally, regulatory rules are progressively emphasizing global alignment and collaboration. This guarantees that CPS complies with uniform standards and regulations irrespective of the country of development or deployment. International entities such as the ISO, IEC, and numerous regional regulatory agencies collaborate to standardize these protocols. The Wassenaar Arrangement regulates the export of dual-use technologies, including CPS components, to prevent the misuse of sensitive technologies [56].

9. *Sector-specific regulations*
   Various businesses possess distinct regulatory mandates for CPS. In the healthcare industry, medical cyber-physical systems (CPS) must adhere to rigorous standards to guarantee patient safety, whilst in manufacturing, CPS utilized in industrial automation must conform to operational

safety and cybersecurity regulations. FDA regulations in the United States oversee medical equipment, including CPS-based systems, to ensure compliance with safety and performance standards [76].

10. *Emerging technology policies*
    As CPS technology advances, legal frameworks must expand to encompass emergent domains such as the Internet of Things (IoT), autonomous systems, and smart cities. These regulations are perpetually revised to tackle emerging concerns, ranging from data sovereignty to ethical AI utilization, guaranteeing that CPS remains governed in a future-proof manner. Regulatory frameworks for smart cities emphasize that cyber-physical systems employed in public infrastructure comply with security, safety, and privacy criteria [77].

Regulatory rules for cyber-physical systems are crucial for mitigating the dangers and issues linked to these intricate and advancing technologies. These principles create explicit guidelines for safety, security, privacy, and accountability, ensuring that CPS functions to safeguard individuals, industries, and society while fostering innovation and worldwide collaboration.

15.5.1 Role of government agencies in regulating cyber-physical systems (CPS)

Government agencies are essential in regulating cyber-physical systems (CPS) to guarantee their safe, secure, and responsible utilization across diverse sectors, including healthcare, transportation, energy, and defense. These agencies are responsible for formulating and implementing policies that regulate CPS's operations, security, and ethical standards. Their participation aids in risk mitigation, national security preservation, consumer rights protection, and innovation promotion. The primary functions of government entities in regulating child protective services (CPS) are:

1. *Developing and enforcing regulations*
   Government agencies are tasked with formulating regulations that define the operational framework for CPS, guaranteeing compliance with safety, security, and privacy norms. These standards are applicable across several businesses and assist in alleviating hazards related to CPS, including system failures, data breaches, and cyberattacks. Enforcement is essential for ensuring compliance, and agencies frequently perform inspections, audits, and assessments to verify that CPS conforms to these regulations. The US Federal Aviation Administration

(FAA) governs the utilization of CPS in aviation, including drone systems and autopilot technology, to ensure compliance with stringent safety and operational regulations [78].

2. *Cybersecurity and risk management*
   Given the vulnerability of CPS to cyberattacks, governmental entities are pivotal in formulating cybersecurity norms and protocols. Agencies formulate rules that instruct industries on safeguarding critical infrastructure from hacking, data breaches, and cyber warfare. These rules often entail the implementation of cybersecurity frameworks, execution of risk assessments, and ongoing surveillance of CPS settings. The National Institute of Standards and Technology (NIST) in the United States offers a cybersecurity framework for critical infrastructure, including cyber-physical systems (CPS), to ensure robust protection against cyber threats [79].

3. *Protecting public safety*
   Numerous cyber-physical systems (CPSs) function in essential sectors such as healthcare, transportation, and energy, where public safety is of paramount importance. Government agencies guarantee that critical power systems adhere to safety standards to avert breakdowns that may jeopardize human life or disrupt vital services. This encompasses the regulation of autonomous vehicles, smart grids, and medical gadgets that depend on cyber-physical systems for their functionality. The Food and Drug Administration (FDA) in the United States regulates medical devices, including CPS-based systems, to ensure patient usage safety [80].

4. *Ensuring data privacy*
   CPS often collects and processes personal data, which poses issues about privacy and data protection. Government agencies implement data privacy regulations, guaranteeing that CPS operators manage personal information securely and legally. These regulations safeguard persons against unauthorized data acquisition, breaches, and exploitation. The European Data Protection Board (EDPB) enforces the General Data Protection Regulation (GDPR), ensuring that entities managing personal data adhere to rigorous privacy and security standards [60].

5. *Promoting innovation and standardization*
   Government agencies facilitate innovation by endorsing the establishment of standardized regulations that encourage competition while safeguarding public safety and security. They collaborate with industry

stakeholders to formulate laws that promote innovation while ensuring the safety, security, and reliability of new CPS technologies. The European Union Agency for Cybersecurity (ENISA) advocates for cybersecurity research and standards for cyber-physical systems (CPS) while striving to harmonize rules among EU member states, thereby fostering innovation within a secure framework [81].

6. *Coordinating international efforts*
   Given that CPS frequently functions transnationally, governmental bodies are tasked with collaborating with international organizations to provide uniform regulatory frameworks. This global coordination guarantees that CPS adheres to international safety, security, and operational standards, hence promoting cross-border collaboration and commerce. The International Telecommunication Union (ITU), a specialized organization of the United Nations, collaborates with governments globally to establish international standards for communication technologies, including CPS, to ensure global interoperability and security [82].

7. *Oversight of ethical and AI issues*
   Government agencies are increasingly assigned the responsibility of overseeing the ethical utilization of cyber-physical systems (CPS), particularly those that integrate artificial intelligence (AI) and machine learning. They formulate policies that guarantee equity, transparency, and accountability in the decision-making processes of CPS. These agencies also tackle issues such as bias, discrimination, and the ethical ramifications of autonomous CPS systems. For instance, the European Commission has proposed the EU's AI Act, designed to govern high-risk AI applications in cyber-physical systems (CPS), guaranteeing that AI systems employed in essential sectors such as healthcare and transportation are ethical and accountable [79].

8. *Ensuring sector-specific compliance*
   Various sectors possess distinct regulatory mandates for CPS, with government authorities supervising adherence within each industry. These organizations ensure that the CPS utilized in sectors including energy, manufacturing, and defense adhere to industry-specific safety, security, and operating standards. The US Department of Energy (DOE) oversees CPS utilized in smart grids and energy infrastructure, assuring compliance with criteria for energy efficiency, cybersecurity, and operational stability [83].

9. *Incident response and crisis management*
   In the event of a cyberattack, system malfunction, or other incidents involving critical public services (CPS), governmental institutions are tasked with coordinating responses and resolving emergencies. These agencies frequently conduct investigations, collaborate with industry partners, and offer assistance to alleviate the consequences of such occurrences. For instance, the Cybersecurity and Infrastructure Security Agency (CISA) in the United States orchestrates incident responses for critical infrastructure cyber-physical systems (CPS), collaborating with both public and commercial sectors to alleviate and recuperate from cyberattacks or system failures [84].
10. *Public awareness and education*
   Government agencies are crucial in informing the public and companies of CPS regulations, associated hazards, and optimal practices. By promoting awareness of cybersecurity, safety standards, and the ethical use of CPS, these entities facilitate improved preparedness for enterprises and individuals to function within the regulatory framework. CISA and ENISA consistently publish recommendations, principles, and best practices to improve cybersecurity awareness for cyber-physical systems (CPS) among the public and industries [85].

Government agencies play a vital role in regulating cyber-physical systems, guaranteeing that these intricate technologies function safely, securely, and ethically. By establishing legislative frameworks, enforcing cybersecurity measures, and fostering international collaboration, these authorities limit risks and safeguard public interests while promoting innovation and technological advancement.

15.5.2 Government agencies and their roles in regulating cyber-physical systems (CPS)

Several governmental entities globally are engaged in the regulation of cyber-physical systems (CPS) across diverse sectors. These agencies establish policies, enforce rules, and guarantee that CPS functions safely, securely, and by national and international standards. Table 15.6 delineates many principal government entities and their functions in governing child protective services (CPS).

Table 15.6 World regulatory agencies for CPS.

Agency	Country/region	Key roles in regulating CPS
National Institute of Standards and Technology (NIST) [79]	United States	a. Develops cybersecurity frameworks and standards for critical infrastructure, including CPS. b. Provides guidelines for securing CPS systems and managing risk.
Federal Aviation Administration (FAA) [85]	United States	a. Regulates CPS in aviation, such as drones and autopilot systems. b. Ensures compliance with safety and operational standards.
Food and Drug Administration (FDA) [86]	United States	a. Oversees medical devices that rely on CPS, ensuring they meet safety and performance requirements. b. Regulates cybersecurity for connected medical devices.
Cybersecurity and Infrastructure Security Agency (CISA) [84]	United States	a. This leads efforts to protect critical infrastructure CPS from cyberattacks. b. Coordinates incident response for CPS-related cybersecurity breaches.
Federal Communications Commission (FCC) [87]	United States	a. Regulates CPS-related technologies in telecommunications, such as IoT and 5G networks. b. Ensures secure communication systems for CPS.
European Union Agency for Cybersecurity (ENISA) [85]	European Union	a. Promotes cybersecurity standards for CPS across EU member states. b. Coordinates cybersecurity research and fosters cross-border cooperation on CPS security.
European Commission (EC) [88]	European Union	a. Develops regulations for CPS incorporating AI, especially regarding ethical concerns and accountability. b. Oversees regulatory policies for critical infrastructure CPS.
European Data Protection Board (EDPB) [89]	European Union	a. Enforces data protection regulations like GDPR, ensuring CPS that process personal data comply with privacy standards.
Information Commissioner's Office (ICO) [90]	United Kingdom	a. Enforces data privacy laws like GDPR for CPS that handle personal and sensitive data. b. Guides data protection best practices for CPS.
Health and Safety Executive (HSE) [91]	United Kingdom	a. Ensures CPS in industrial environments meet health and safety standards. b. Oversees safe integration of CPS into manufacturing and construction sectors.

(*Continued*)

Table 15.6 Continued.

Agency	Country/region	Key roles in regulating CPS
Ministry of Industry and Information Technology (MIIT) [92]	China	a. Develop policies for CPS, particularly in smart manufacturing and IoT. b. Regulates cybersecurity for CPS in telecommunications and industrial applications.
China National Internet Information Office (CNIIO) [93]	China	a. Oversees cybersecurity regulations for critical infrastructure CPS. b. Coordinates national policies on CPS data privacy and security.
Japan Ministry of Internal Affairs and Communications (MIC) [94]	Japan	a. Regulates communication technologies for CPS, such as 5G and IoT. b. Develop cybersecurity policies for critical infrastructure CPS.
Australian Cyber Security Centre (ACSC) [95]	Australia	a. Provides cybersecurity guidelines for protecting CPS. b. Coordinates incident response and risk management for critical infrastructure CPS.
Office of the Australian Information Commissioner (OAIC) [96]	Australia	a. Enforces data privacy laws related to CPS, ensuring compliance with data protection standards like the Privacy Act. b. Oversees data breach reporting and risk management for CPS.
National Cyber Security Centre (NCSC) [97]	United Kingdom	a. Provides cybersecurity guidelines and frameworks for critical infrastructure CPS. b. Coordinates national cybersecurity efforts for government and private sector CPS.
International Telecommunication Union (ITU) [98]	Global (United Nations)	a. Sets international standards for CPS in communication technologies. b. Promotes global cooperation on interoperability and cybersecurity for CPS.
International Organization for Standardization (ISO) [71]	Global	a. Develops international safety and interoperability standards for CPS. b. Provides guidelines for ensuring secure and reliable operation of CPS across industries.
International Electrotechnical Commission (IEC) [51]	Global	a. Creates standards for integrating CPS into energy and industrial systems. b. Promotes global standardization of CPS technologies in automation and smart grids.

15.5.3 Industry best practices for compliance with regulations for cyber-physical systems (CPS)

Industries must implement best practices to adhere to the intricate legal frameworks governing cyber-physical systems (CPS), ensuring safety, security, data privacy, and ethical operations [92]. These optimal practices assist businesses in fulfilling legal obligations while ensuring operational efficiency, fostering innovation, and safeguarding against hazards [1]. With technological advancements, firms utilizing cyber-physical systems (CPS) encounter increasing pressure to adhere to rules aimed at safeguarding safety, security, and privacy [4]. To ensure compliance, firms must implement effective procedures that adhere to legal standards while enhancing system functionality and resilience against attacks. Table 15.7 delineates clear and effective strategies that organizations can implement to comply with cybersecurity regulations, safeguard data, and uphold secure, dependable CPS operations. Table 15.7 encapsulates the fundamental industry best practices for ensuring adherence to regulations of cyber-physical systems (CPS). By following these rules, industries can enhance the protection of their CPS infrastructure and operations while remaining compliant with legal and ethical standards. Organizations must develop a comprehensive strategy to comply with the strict rules governing cyber-physical systems, encompassing cybersecurity best practices, data privacy protections, adherence to safety requirements, and proactive incident response strategies. By remaining cognisant of legislative modifications and cultivating a culture of compliance, industries may guarantee that their CPS activities are secure, ethical, and legally compliant, while simultaneously encouraging innovation and technical progress.

15.5.4 Impact of regulatory policies on innovation and development of CPS

Regulatory policies are essential in influencing the innovation and advancement of cyber–physical systems (CPS) [1]. Regulations are crucial for guaranteeing safety, security, and ethical practices; nevertheless, they may also impede innovation by introducing additional compliance requirements [13]. The effects of regulatory regulations on innovation and development are

a. *Encouraging safer and more secure systems*
   Regulations force organizations to prioritize safety and security in the design of CPS. By following stringent standards, developers construct

Table 15.7 Best practices for compliance with regulations for CPS.

Best practice	Description	Frameworks
Adopt cybersecurity frameworks	Implement established frameworks to protect CPS from cyber threats such as hacking and ransomware.	NIST Cybersecurity Framework
Conduct regular risk assessments	Perform security audits, penetration tests, and vulnerability scans to identify and mitigate risks in CPS systems.	Regular security audits, penetration tests
Ensure data privacy compliance	Implement measures to ensure compliance with data privacy laws (e.g., GDPR) for personal and sensitive data collected by CPS.	Encryption, anonymization, and access controls
Develop and enforce incident response plans	Create protocols to respond to cybersecurity breaches and system failures quickly, minimizing damage and complying with regulatory reporting requirements.	Incident response protocols, reporting breaches to authorities
Implement safety standards and certifications	Follow industry-specific safety standards to ensure that CPS is safe for users and critical infrastructures.	ISO 26262 for automotive CPS, IEC 60601 for medical devices
Promote interoperability and standardization	Adhere to interoperability standards to ensure seamless communication and operation across different CPS platforms and sectors.	IEC 61499 for industrial automation
Stay updated on regulatory changes	Track and adapt to updates in CPS regulations, cybersecurity standards, and data privacy laws.	Assign compliance teams to monitor regulatory updates
Engage in ethical AI practices	Ensure transparency, fairness, and accountability in AI systems used in CPS, addressing concerns such as bias and ethical decision-making.	Follow ethical AI guidelines like the EU's AI Act
Invest in training and awareness	Provide regular training on CPS cybersecurity protocols, regulatory requirements, and compliance best practices to reduce human error risks.	Employee cybersecurity and compliance training programs
Collaborate with regulatory authorities	Engage with regulatory bodies and industry associations to understand and comply with regulations while providing feedback for future policy development.	Participation in industry forums, regulatory consultations

more resilient systems capable of withstanding cyber assaults, hence assuring reliability in essential infrastructure such as healthcare, transportation, and manufacturing. This emphasis may result in advancements in secure system architectures and technology.

b. *Compliance costs and delays*
Compliance with regulations frequently necessitates further resources, effort, and financial investment. These expenses might impede the development process, particularly for smaller enterprises or startups. The necessity for numerous testing, certification, and reporting phases may postpone the introduction of new CPS technology, thus hindering innovation.

c. *Incentivizing innovation through standardization*
Regulatory regulations that promote interoperability and standardization stimulate innovation by establishing a unified framework for CPS development. Standards facilitate the smooth interoperability of diverse systems, enabling innovative ideas to integrate effortlessly with established infrastructure. This cultivates an atmosphere in which enterprises can innovate while ensuring compliance.

d. *Balancing privacy and data use*
Regulations such as GDPR limit the methods by which CPS can gather and utilize personal data, compelling companies to innovate in data privacy and protection. Although these regulations may restrict the use of specific data-driven technologies, they simultaneously foster innovation in encryption, anonymization, and data security protocols, guaranteeing that CPS can function efficiently without jeopardizing user privacy.

e. *Driving ethical development*
Regulations addressing ethical issues, particularly around the application of artificial intelligence (AI) in CPS, compel corporations to develop with responsibility. Regulations foster trust in CPS technologies by assuring openness, fairness, and accountability in AI-driven systems, hence promoting their wider implementation.

f. *Global regulatory differences*
Innovation in cyber-physical systems (CPS) can be influenced by varying regulatory norms across different locations. Companies may have difficulties in creating a product that adheres to regulations across many countries, resulting in elevated prices or the necessity to customize solutions for distinct markets. This can also stimulate innovation as

corporations create adaptive CPS systems capable of functioning across several legal environments.

Regulatory laws can prevent the advancement of CPS by imposing compliance obstacles; yet, they also promote safer, more ethical, and secure innovation. By adeptly maneuvering through these laws, organizations can advance CPS technology while assuring compliance with the requisite requirements.

15.5.5 Certification and assessment in cyber-physical systems (CPS)

Certification and evaluation are essential components in verifying that cyber-physical systems (CPS) comply with regulatory, safety, and security criteria. These methods offer a systematic method for organizations to demonstrate that their systems adhere to industry norms, thereby protecting both end-users and the wider infrastructure [28].

1. *Certification*
   Certification is a formal process in which CPS undergoes evaluation by accredited parties to verify compliance with set requirements. This may include certifications in cybersecurity, safety, performance, and interoperability, depending on the industry. Certifications assure customers, authorities, and organizations that the CPS adheres to established standards and operates safely and reliably.

   a. Examples of Certifications are
      i. ISO/IEC 27001
      ii. Certification for information security management, including aspects relevant to CPS
      iii. ISO 26262
      iv. Functional safety certification, especially for automotive CPS
      v. IEC 61508
      vi. Certification for the safety of electrical/electronic/programmable electronic systems, commonly applied in industrial CPS

2. *Assessment*
   Assessment involves a comprehensive review of CPS to verify compliance with regulatory requirements and performance standards. Assessments are frequently performed during development and post-deployment to evaluate system efficacy and safety. It is an ongoing process that encompasses security audits, risk assessments, and performance reviews. The fundamental categories of assessments include

- Risk assessment
  - Identifies potential vulnerabilities in CPS and evaluates the impact of possible threats.
- Safety assessment
  - Ensures that the CPS operates without endangering users, infrastructure, or the environment.
- Cybersecurity assessment
  - Focuses on identifying weaknesses in the system's security architecture and suggests improvements to protect against cyber threats.

3. *Benefits of certification and assessment*
   Some of the benefits of certification and assessment are
   - Trust and market access
     - Certification makes it easier to gain trust from consumers and partners, often being a requirement to enter certain markets.
   - Regulatory compliance
     - Certification helps businesses avoid penalties by ensuring they meet legal obligations in areas such as safety, security, and data privacy.
   - Risk Mitigation
     - Through continuous assessment, companies can identify and address potential risks early, reducing the chances of system failure or cyberattacks.

4. *Challenges*
   The major of certification and assessment in CPS are
   a. Costs and time.
   b. The certification process can be difficult and costly, especially for smaller enterprises or startups, as it necessitates adherence to stringent standards and the successful completion of numerous assessments.
   c. Keeping up with rapid changes.
   d. As CPS technology evolves, maintaining certification can be challenging. New threats and standards often require recertification, making it an ongoing effort to stay compliant.

5. *Emerging trends in certification and assessment*
   Emerging developments in certification and assessment in CPS include
   a. Automated compliance tools

b. As CPS grows increasingly intricate, organizations are employing automated technologies to evaluate compliance in real time, facilitating a swifter response to any deviations from established norms.

c. Continuous monitoring

d. Continuous assessment and monitoring, rather than one-time certifications, guarantee that CPS maintains compliance throughout its operational lifecycle.

Certification and assessment are essential processes that guarantee CPS are safe, secure, and consistent with industry norms. Although resource-intensive, they yield long-term advantages like trust, diminished risks, and facilitated market access, rendering them indispensable for enterprises engaged in the development and deployment of CPS.

15.5.6 Incident response and reporting in cyber-physical systems (CPS)

Incident response and reporting are essential for overseeing the security and stability of cyber-physical systems (CPS) [84]. These systems, integrating digital and physical elements, regulate critical infrastructure and services like power grids, healthcare apparatus, and manufacturing operations. Any incident, such as a cyberattack, system failure, or security breach, might yield substantial consequences. An effectively organized incident response plan facilitates the rapid identification, containment, and resolution of concerns, hence ensuring the ongoing safe operation of CPS and adherence to regulatory mandates. The phases of the incident response and reporting mechanism in CPS are illustrated in Figure 15.3.

The initial phase of any incident response strategy is preparation. This entails formulating a detailed response strategy that establishes the duties and responsibilities of each team member. Regular staff training guarantees that all personnel are equipped to respond appropriately in the case of an incident. An explicit plan mitigates ambiguity and accelerates the response procedure during incidents. Detection constitutes the subsequent pivotal phase. Continuous monitoring of systems for anomalous activity or security concerns enables businesses to identify possible incidents promptly. Timely identification of an issue minimizes potential damage. Automated detection techniques and real-time notifications can identify anomalies in CPS systems, including atypical traffic patterns or system failures. Upon detection

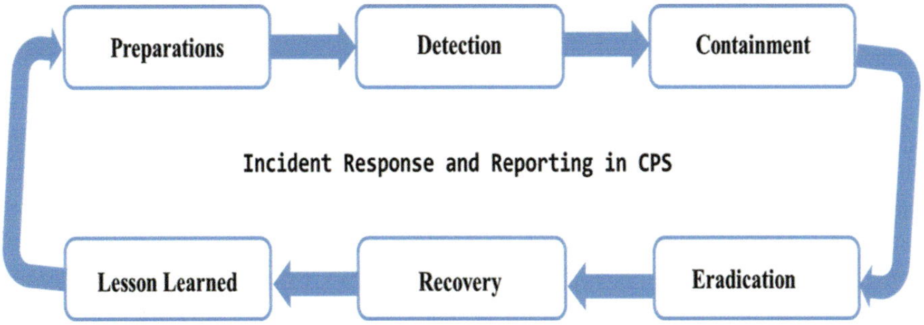

Figure 15.3 Incident response and reporting in cyber-physical systems.

of an incident, prompt containment is crucial to avert additional damage. Containment techniques may involve isolating impacted systems, obstructing hostile activities, or temporarily deactivating infected components. The objective is to contain the proliferation of the problem and mitigate its overall effect on the system. Upon containing the threat, the procedure advances to Eradication, wherein the root cause of the incident is located and eliminated. This may entail eliminating malware, rectifying vulnerabilities, or implementing system modifications to avert the recurrence of the situation. Eradication guarantees that the threat is completely neutralized and incapable of inflicting additional harm.

The Recovery phase emphasizes reinstating the CPS to standard operations. This entails restoring systems to operational status following confirmation of their security and functionality. Recovery encompasses the restoration of any lost or corrupted data and the reinstatement of systems to their pre-incident condition. Ultimately, lessons learned are a crucial component for enhancing future incident response initiatives. Subsequent to the resolution of the event, organizations had to perform a postincident evaluation to evaluate the failures and the management of the situation. This information can subsequently be utilized to enhance the incident response strategy, so augmenting the organization's preparedness for future occurrences. Reporting is essential throughout this procedure. Incidents must be notified to management and pertinent teams to guarantee transparency and coordinated response. Certain occurrences, such as data breaches or system failures, may necessitate reporting to regulatory bodies or affected stakeholders to adhere to legal obligations. Prompt and precise reporting fosters trust and guarantees that organizations fulfill their regulatory responsibilities. The incident response and reporting for CPS are organized into preparation, detection, containment, eradication, recovery, and postevent analysis. An effective and robust reaction plan guarantees that CPS can swiftly recuperate from disruptions, mitigating harm and averting future complications.

Figure 15.3 is a schematic representation that illustrates the fundamental phases of incident response and reporting for CPS. The picture progresses linearly from preparation to lessons learned, with reporting diverging at the conclusion. This streamlined process guarantees an effective response to problems, mitigating their effects on CPS systems and aiding in the prevention of future incidents. Table 15.4 is a concise overview of the processes in incident response and reporting for CPS. Table 15.8 establishes the phases of incident reaction and reporting in CPS, encapsulating essential actions and optimal procedures to guarantee proficient management of security occurrences. By adhering to these procedures, businesses can more effectively manage and alleviate the repercussions of accidents on their CPS infrastructure.

15.6 Emerging Trends and Challenges in Legal Framework and Regulatory Policies for Cyber-physical Systems

The rapid expansion of cyber-physical systems (CPS) in sectors like healthcare, transportation, manufacturing, and energy has presented novel legal and regulatory difficulties. These systems connect computing, networking, and physical processes, resulting in intricate and sophisticated systems that necessitate adaptive legal frameworks. Current trends indicate that governments and authorities are progressively prioritizing the resolution of privacy, security, and liability concerns, while simultaneously balancing innovation with societal implications. Nonetheless, numerous problems render the regulation of CPS a formidable undertaking.

An obvious trend is the heightened emphasis on security and privacy rules. Cyber-physical technologies (CPSs) are often incorporated with Internet of Things (IoT) technologies, rendering them susceptible to cyberattacks. Regulations such as the GDPR in Europe and the CCPA in the United States are being expanded to encompass CPS, thereby providing data protection and the resolution of privacy issues. A significant trend is the unification of global standards. Given that cyber-physical systems (CPS) frequently work across international boundaries, there is a necessity for uniform rules among countries, which is being addressed by entities like the ISO and IEC that are formulating globally acknowledged standards for CPS security and performance.

The proliferation of AI and machine learning in cyber-physical systems has introduced novel difficulties in accountability and transparency. AI systems in cyber-physical systems can autonomously make judgments,

Table 15.8 Incident response and reporting in CPS.

Incident response stage	Description	Best practices
Preparation	Develop and document an incident response plan, assign roles, and conduct training to ensure readiness for potential incidents.	• Create detailed incident response playbooks • Regularly train staff on procedures
Detection and identification	Continuously monitor CPS for unusual activity or system failures to quickly identify potential security incidents or threats.	• Implement continuous monitoring tools • Use automated alerts to notify the response team of potential incidents
Containment	Take immediate actions to contain the incident, such as isolating affected systems to prevent further damage.	• Use network segmentation to isolate compromised systems • Disable affected components temporarily
Eradication	Identify and eliminate the root cause of the incident to ensure the threat is fully neutralized and cannot recur.	• Conduct forensic analysis to find the root cause • Apply patches or security updates to close vulnerabilities
Recovery	Restore systems to normal operations after the incident, ensuring all vulnerabilities have been addressed and systems are fully operational.	• Test the system thoroughly before bringing it back online • Maintain accessible backups
Lessons learned	Conduct a postincident review to assess the response, identify improvements, and update the incident response plan accordingly.	• Hold postincident reviews with the response team • Document findings and update the response plan
Internal reporting	Report the incident internally to management and relevant teams to ensure transparency and timely action.	• Provide detailed incident reports • Ensure all stakeholders are informed of the incident and its impact
External reporting	Report the incident to regulatory authorities or affected stakeholders, especially in the case of data breaches or critical infrastructure disruptions.	• Follow industry-specific reporting requirements (e.g., GDPR and NERC-CIP) • Ensure timely reporting to avoid penalties or legal consequences
Challenges	Address the complexity of CPS incidents, coordination between different teams, and the potential real-time impact on physical processes.	• Ensure coordination between IT, engineering, and operations teams • Develop specialized incident response strategies for CPS real-time impact scenarios

prompting legal enquiries on accountability for those decisions. Policymakers are endeavoring to establish frameworks that consider the ethical and legal ramifications of AI-driven CPS. The notion of cybersecurity by design is increasingly being adopted, as regulators advocate for the incorporation of security elements directly into the design of cyber-physical systems (CPS), by frameworks such as the NIST Cybersecurity Framework. As cyber-physical systems (CPS) become increasingly integrated into vital infrastructure, there is a heightened focus on environmental and ethical considerations. Consumer product standards (CPS) are propelling progress in energy efficiency and automation, while regulatory policies are increasingly considering their environmental implications, assuring adherence to green energy standards and ethical labor practices.

Despite these advancements, the regulation of CPS is beset with obstacles. The primary concern is the regulatory delay. CPS technology advances swiftly, surpassing the establishment of legislative frameworks that tend to be reactive instead of proactive. This results in vulnerabilities in protection, especially for emerging technologies such as 5G and artificial intelligence. Likewise, attributing culpability and accountability poses challenges, particularly in autonomous systems with little human control. The topic of whether developers, users, or manufacturers should bear responsibility in the event of a failure remains unresolved. Reconciling the necessity for innovation with regulatory compliance presents a considerable hurdle. Excessive regulation can impede technological advancement, especially in sectors where swift innovation is essential for sustaining competitive advantages. Nonetheless, inadequate regulation may render users and systems susceptible to dangers. Cross-border legal challenges further complicate the regulatory framework, as CPS frequently operates across diverse legal jurisdictions with differing legislation, resulting in enforcement and consistency difficulties.

Cybersecurity is a key issue, as cyberattacks on critical infrastructure can result in significant repercussions, such as the disruption of energy grids, healthcare systems, or transportation networks. The necessity for robust security measures that safeguard against emerging threats is imperative. The emergence of CPS prompts ethical and human rights concerns. Concerns about data privacy, spying, and the displacement of human labor are driving regulators to guarantee that CPS advancements adhere to ethical norms. Interoperability and integration provide technical and regulatory obstacles. Given that CPS consists of numerous interconnected systems, guaranteeing their flawless operation across diverse platforms, vendors, and standards is intricate and necessitates unified policies to address compatibility while preserving security and performance. Table 15.9 encapsulates the principal

Table 15.9 Emerging trends.

Trend	Description
Security and privacy regulations	Focus on extending privacy laws like GDPR and CCPA to cover CPS systems, protecting user data.
Harmonization of international standards	Global standardization of regulations for CPS, led by ISO/IEC to ensure consistency.
AI and machine learning in CPS	The growing use of AI in CPS raises accountability and transparency concerns in legal frameworks.
Cybersecurity by design	Embedding security features into CPS from the design phase, following standards like NIST.
Environmental and ethical considerations	Regulations now include energy efficiency and labor ethics in CPS development and deployment.
Regulatory lag	Legal frameworks are slower to adapt to the rapidly evolving technology, leaving regulatory gaps.
Liability and accountability	Challenges in determining who is liable when autonomous CPS systems fail or cause harm.
Balancing innovation with regulation	Struggling to encourage innovation while maintaining sufficient regulation to ensure safety.
Cross-border legal challenges	Difficulty in enforcing uniform regulations for CPS that operate across different legal jurisdictions.
Cybersecurity and data integrity risks	Growing cyber threats to CPS systems require robust and evolving security measures.
Ethical and human rights considerations	CPS raises concerns about data privacy, surveillance, and worker displacement, needing ethical safeguards.
Interoperability and integration	Ensuring CPS systems from different vendors work together while maintaining security and reliability.

trends and issues confronting the establishment of legal frameworks and regulatory policies for CPS, underscoring the essential areas of concentration for regulators and industry participants.

15.7 Lessons Learned

This chapter highlights critical lessons for governments, industry, and regulators to guarantee the security, resilience, and compliance of cyber-physical systems (CPS). The principal lessons acquired are:

1. A strong legal framework is crucial for ensuring the security and safe operation of CPS. Legal structures provide the foundation for managing risks, setting clear guidelines for cybersecurity, and enforcing

compliance, especially for critical infrastructure sectors like energy, healthcare, and transportation.

2. CPS are unique because they combine digital and physical components, making them different from traditional IT systems. Regulations need to be designed specifically for CPS, taking into account the real-time physical impact of cyber threats and operational failures.

3. International treaties and agreements play a key role in regulating CPS, especially as threats to these systems are often global in nature. Cross-border cooperation and unified international standards help align efforts to protect CPS and respond to incidents in a coordinated manner.

4. One of the biggest challenges in regulating CPS is the rapid pace of technological innovation. Laws and regulations need to be flexible and adaptable, ensuring they can quickly respond to new technologies and emerging threats without stifling development.

5. Key government agencies are responsible for monitoring and enforcing CPS regulations. Their role is essential in ensuring compliance, assessing risks, and coordinating responses to incidents. However, these agencies need adequate resources and expertise to fulfill their responsibilities effectively.

6. Adopting industry best practices is critical for organizations to ensure that they meet regulatory requirements. By implementing security protocols, conducting regular assessments, and staying informed of the latest threats, organizations can better protect their CPS and avoid penalties.

7. Regulatory policies must strike a balance between ensuring security and allowing innovation. Overly restrictive regulations can stifle technological development, while a lack of regulation can lead to increased vulnerabilities in CPS. Policymakers must find the right balance to foster innovation while maintaining safety and security.

8. Effective incident response is vital for managing the risks associated with CPS. Organizations must have clear and well-practiced incident response plans that cover preparation, detection, containment, recovery, and reporting. These plans help minimize the impact of incidents and ensure a swift return to normal operations.

9. Certification mechanisms, like the Common Criteria for IT Security Evaluation, are essential for creating a standardized approach to

assessing and verifying CPS security. These assessments ensure that systems meet established security benchmarks, providing consistency and reliability.

10. Transparent reporting of incidents, both internally and externally, is necessary for accountability and regulatory compliance. Organizations must communicate effectively with internal teams, regulators, and the public when incidents occur, ensuring transparency and trust.

The chapter emphasizes the necessity of establishing flexible, globally harmonized, and industry-endorsed regulatory frameworks for CPS. It emphasizes the necessity of balancing security and innovation, while also underlining the importance of effective incident response and reporting in preserving CPS integrity. These lessons offer significant insights for enhancing the legal and regulatory framework for CPS.

15.8 Recommendations

This chapter offers several key recommendations to help stakeholders effectively manage and secure CPS.

1. Governments and regulatory authorities must persist in establishing and revising comprehensive legislative frameworks specifically designed to address the distinct requirements of CPS. These frameworks must encompass the integration of digital and physical elements, addressing both cybersecurity and the safety of physical operations.
2. International collaboration is crucial for the efficient regulation of CPS, due to the transnational characteristics of numerous cyber hazards. Countries ought to collaborate via treaties and accords to establish cohesive standards and practices for CPS security, assuring uniformity in responses to global threats.
3. Regulations must adapt to the swift progress of CPS technologies. Policymakers must prioritize adaptable regulatory frameworks that can be routinely modified to address changing technology and cyber dangers without hindering innovation.
4. Government agencies responsible for regulating CPS should be adequately resourced and given the necessary authority to enforce laws and standards. These agencies must have the expertise and tools to monitor compliance, assess risks, and respond to incidents efficiently.

5. Organizations managing CPS must use industry best practices for cybersecurity and regulatory adherence. This encompasses employing current security protocols, executing routine evaluations, and implementing personnel training to guarantee readiness for possible cyber events.
6. Regulatory authorities must combine the enforcement of rigorous security protocols with the promotion of an atmosphere conducive to innovation. Policies must facilitate research and development in cyber-physical systems technology while implementing sufficient protections to mitigate cyber risks.
7. Governments and industry regulators ought to advocate for the implementation of certification and assessment frameworks such as the Common Criteria for IT Security Evaluation. These guidelines ensure that CPS adheres to security standards, establishing a uniform bar for safety and reliability.
8. Organizations must establish comprehensive incident response plans specifically designed for their CPS contexts. These strategies must encompass preparedness, detection, containment, eradication, recovery, and lessons learned, ensuring that organizations can respond promptly and efficiently to any crises.
9. Transparent reporting of incidents is crucial for both internal and external stakeholders. Organizations should report incidents internally to ensure coordinated responses and externally to comply with legal obligations. Information sharing between industries can also enhance collective defenses against evolving threats.
10. Continuous training and awareness programs should be implemented across industries that rely on CPS. Employees at all levels need to be educated about potential threats, incident response procedures, and regulatory compliance to ensure that human error is minimized.

These recommendations seek to provide a strong and adaptable regulatory framework that ensures the secure and resilient functioning of CPS while promoting innovation and international collaboration.

15.9 Conclusion

This chapter has examined the essential function of legal frameworks and regulatory regulations in the security and management of cyber-physical systems (CPS). As cyber-physical systems (CPS) become increasingly integrated into critical sectors such as energy, healthcare, transportation, and manufacturing, the imperative to ensure their resilience and safety has reached unprecedented significance. The intricacy of these systems, which amalgamate digital and physical elements, necessitates a thorough and flexible regulatory framework. We have shown that well-organized legal frameworks are essential for tackling the specific cybersecurity concerns encountered by CPS, offering explicit instructions for protection, risk management, and compliance. International collaboration via treaties and standards is essential due to the global character of cyber threats. These coordinated initiatives foster a cohesive, international response to safeguard essential systems that surpass national boundaries. The chapter emphasized the necessity for rules to progress in accordance with technological changes. The swift advancement of CPS technology offers both benefits and challenges, necessitating regulatory regulations that are adaptable to new advancements while fostering progress. A crucial insight is the necessity of balancing security with innovation, ensuring that rules are neither excessively restrictive nor overly permissive. Government agencies are essential for monitoring, enforcing, and adjusting legislation, while industry best practices enable organizations to assure compliance and successfully minimize risks. Certification and assessment frameworks offer standardized metrics of security, guaranteeing that CPS adheres to defined norms for safety and reliability. Furthermore, we underscored the significance of incident reaction and reporting. Given that CPS are susceptible to many threats, the establishment of a clear and effective incident response plan is essential to mitigate damage and expedite the restoration of operations. Organizations must be equipped to manage security breaches in a manner that is systematic, transparent, and adheres to regulatory requirements. This chapter offers a guide for traversing the intricate legal and regulatory framework around CPS. It provides pragmatic insights and ideas for governments, regulators, and companies to collaborate in safeguarding these essential systems while promoting innovation. The future of CPS relies on a dynamic, worldwide strategy that harmonizes security with the swift advancement of technology, guaranteeing that the advantages of CPS may be completely attained without jeopardizing safety or security.

References

[1] Szczepaniuk, E. K., & Szczepaniuk, H. (2024). Cyber Regulatory policies Risk Management Framework for Cyber-physical Systems.

In *Emerging Trends for Securing Cyber Physical Systems and the Internet of Things* (pp. 114–134). CRC Press.

[2] de Oliveira, V. F., Matiolli, G., Júnior, C. J. B., Gaspar, R., & Lins, R. G. (2024). Digital Twin and Cyber-Physical System Integration in Commercial Vehicles: Latest Concepts, Challenges and Opportunities. *IEEE Transactions on Intelligent Vehicles.*

[3] Das, A., Bhale, P., & Adhikari, N. (2024). Cyber-Physical Systems and the Internet of Things: An Overview. *A Practical Guide on Security and Privacy in Cyber-Physical Systems: Foundations, Applications and Limitations*, 1–22.

[4] Lee, G., Epiphaniou, G., Al-Khateeb, H., & Maple, C. (2019). Security and privacy of things: Regulatory challenges and gaps for the secure integration of cyber-physical systems. In *Third International Congress on Information and Communication Technology: ICICT 2018, London* (pp. 1–12). Springer Singapore.

[5] Sztipanovits, J., Koutsoukos, X., Karsai, G., Sastry, S., Tomlin, C., Damm, W., ... & Köster, F. (2019). Science of design for societal-scale cyber-physical systems: challenges and opportunities. *Cyber-Physical Systems*, *5*(3), 145–172.

[6] Bhadani, U. (2024). Smart Grids: A Cyber–Physical Systems Perspective. *International Research Journal of Engineering and Technology (IRJET)*, *11*(06), 801.

[7] Tarr, A. A., Tarr, J. A., Thompson, M., & Wilkinson, D. (Eds.). (2023). The global insurance market and change: Emerging Technologies, Risks and Legal Challenges.

[8] Khargonekar, P. P., & Sampath, M. (2020). A framework for ethics in cyber-physical-human systems. *IFAC-PapersOnLine*, *53*(2), 17008–17015.

[9] Nabben, K., Wang, H., & Zargham, M. (2024). Decentralised Governance for Autonomous Cyber-Physical Systems. *arXiv preprint arXiv:2407.13566.*

[10] Polanec, K., Vereno, D., Fritzenwallner, E., & Neureiter, C. (2024). Integrating Legal Considerations into Model-Based Cyber-Physical-Systems Development. In *SMARTGREENS* (pp. 80–84).

[11] Radanliev, P., De Roure, D., Nicolescu, R., Huth, M., & Santos, O. (2022). Digital twins: artificial intelligence and the IoT cyber-physical systems in Industry 4.0. *International Journal of Intelligent Robotics and Applications*, *6*(1), 171–185.

[12] El-Kady, A. H., Halim, S., El-Halwagi, M. M., & Khan, F. (2023). Analysis of safety and security challenges and opportunities related to

cyber-physical systems. *Process Safety and Environmental Protection*, *173*, 384–413.

[13] Aliyu, A., Ogbuju, E., Imoize, A. L., Abari, O. J., Kunya, M. M., Sani, G., Salaudeen, F. A., & Oladipo, F. (2024). The ethics of cybersecurity in emerging healthcare systems. In *Cybersecurity in emerging healthcare systems* (pp. 363–400). The Institution of Engineering and Technology.

[14] Van Zomeren, M., Joiner, K., Sitnikova, E., & Qiao, L. (2023). Regulating Cyber-Physical Systems for Safety Consequences. In *Cybersecurity for Decision Makers* (pp. 169–198). CRC Press.

[15] Alvarez-Alvarado, M. S., Apolo-Tinoco, C., Ramirez-Prado, M. J., Alban-Chacón, F. E., Pico, N., Aviles-Cedeno, J., ... & Rengifo, J. (2024). Cyber-physical power systems: A comprehensive review about technologies drivers, standards, and future perspectives. *Computers and Electrical Engineering*, *116*, 109149.

[16] Weldert, J., Von Wedel, J. K., & Beul, C. (2019). A data privacy approach for cyber-physical systems. *Cyber Security: A Peer-Reviewed Journal*, *3*(1), 57–72.

[17] Jayashre, K., & Gummaraju, N. (2024). Integrating Cyber-Physical Systems for Enhanced Efficiency. *Technologies for Sustainable Healthcare Development*, 300.

[18] Damm, W., Hess, D., Schweda, M., Sztipanovits, J., Bengler, K., Biebl, B., ... & Veith, E. (2024). A Reference Architecture of Human Cyber-Physical Systems–Part I: Fundamental Concepts. *ACM Transactions on Cyber-Physical Systems*, *8*(1), 1–32.

[19] Chae, J., Lee, S., Jang, J., Hong, S., & Park, K. J. (2023). A survey and perspective on Industrial Cyber-Physical Systems (ICPS): from ICPS to AI-augmented ICPS. *IEEE Transactions on Industrial Cyber-Physical Systems*.

[20] Padmavathi, U., Harshitha, R. S., Jayashre, K., & Gummaraju, N. (2024). Integrating Cyber-Physical Systems for Enhanced Efficiency in Healthcare Solutions. In *Technologies for Sustainable Healthcare Development* (pp. 300–324). IGI Global.

[21] Baloyi, N., & Kotzé, P. (2018, September). A data privacy model based on internet of things and cyber-physical systems reference architectures. In *Proceedings of the Annual Conference of the South African Institute of Computer Scientists and Information Technologists* (pp. 258–268).

[22] Hasan, M. K., Habib, A. A., Shukur, Z., Ibrahim, F., Islam, S., & Razzaque, M. A. (2023). Review on cyber-physical and cyber-security system in smart grid: Standards, protocols, constraints, and recommendations. *Journal of network and computer applications*, *209*, 103540.

[23] Karabacak, B., Yildirim, S. O., & Baykal, N. (2016). Regulatory approaches for cyber security of critical infrastructures: The case of Turkey. *Computer Law & Security Review*, *32*(3), 526–539.

[24] Matta, G., Chlup, S., Shaaban, A. M., Schmittner, C., Pinzenöhler, A., Szalai, E., & Tauber, M. (2021). Risk management and standard compliance for cyber-physical systems of systems. *Infocommunications Journal*, *13*(2), 32–39.

[25] Radanliev, P., De Roure, D., Van Kleek, M., Santos, O., & Ani, U. (2021). Artificial intelligence in cyber physical systems. *AI & society*, *36*, 783–796.

[26] Yu, Z., Gao, H., Cong, X., Wu, N., & Song, H. H. (2023). A Survey on Cyber–Physical Systems Security. *IEEE Internet of Things Journal*, *10*(24), 21670–21686.

[27] Khargonekar, P. P., & Sampath, M. (2020). A framework for ethics in cyber-physical-human systems. *IFAC-PapersOnLine*, *53*(2), 17008–17015.

[28] Hossain, M. I., Steigner, D. T., Hussain, M. I., & Akther, A. (2024). Enhancing Data Integrity and Traceability in Industry Cyber Physical Systems (ICPS) through Blockchain Technology: A Comprehensive Approach. *arXiv preprint arXiv:2405.04837*.

[29] Zhao, Z., Zhang, M., Wu, W., Huang, G. Q., & Wang, L. (2024). Spatial-temporal traceability for cyber-physical industry 4.0 systems. *Journal of Manufacturing Systems*, *74*, 16–29.

[30] Mhapsekar, R. U., Umrani, M. I., Faizan, M., Ali, O., & Abraham, L. (2024). Building Trust in AI-Driven Decision Making for Cyber-Physical Systems (CPS): A Comprehensive Review. *arXiv preprint arXiv:2405.06347*.

[31] Puliafito, A., Tricomi, G., Zafeiropoulos, A., & Papavassiliou, S. (2021). Smart cities of the future as cyber physical systems: Challenges and enabling technologies. *Sensors*, *21*(10), 3349.

[32] Trentesaux, D., & Karnouskos, S. (2020). Ethical behaviour aspects of autonomous intelligent cyber-physical systems. In *Service Oriented, Holonic and Multi-agent Manufacturing Systems for Industry of the Future: Proceedings of SOHOMA 2019 9* (pp. 55–71). Springer International Publishing.

[33] Hamzah, M., Islam, M. M., Hassan, S., Akhtar, M. N., Ferdous, M. J., Jasser, M. B., & Mohamed, A. W. (2023). Distributed Control of Cyber Physical System on Various Domains: A Critical Review. *Systems*, *11*(4), 208.

[34] Sonntag, C., Engell, S., & Samad, T. (2020). Challenges and Potential for EU–US Collaboration at the Intersection of the Internet of Things

and Cyber-physical Systems. *ICT Policy, Research, and Innovation: Perspectives and Prospects for EU-US Collaboration*, 111–144.

[35] Gilbert, S. (2023). European regulation of digital respiratory healthcare. *Digital Respiratory Healthcare (ERS Monograph). Sheffield, European Respiratory Society*, 63–78.

[36] Sanwar, A. S. M. (2024). Explainable Artificial Intelligence into Cyber-Physical System Architecture of Smart Cities: Technologies, Challenges, and Opportunities. *J. Electrical Systems*, *20*(2), 2343–2362.

[37] Nayak, J., Naik, B., Vimal, S., & Favorskaya, M. (Eds.). (2024). *Machine Learning for Cyber Physical System: Advances and Challenges*. Springer Nature Switzerland, Imprint: Springer.

[38] Kouroupis, K., & Sotiropoulos, L. (2024). Cyber Challenges amid the Digital Revolution in Maritime Transport. *Juridical Tribune/Tribuna Juridica*, *14*(2).

[39] Javaid, M., Haleem, A., Singh, R. P., & Suman, R. (2023). An integrated outlook of Cyber–Physical Systems for Industry 4.0: Topical practices, architecture, and applications. *Green Technologies and Sustainability*, *1*(1), 100001.

[40] D'Auria, D., & Persia, F. (2017, August). A collaborative robotic cyber physical system for surgery applications. In *2017 IEEE International Conference on Information Reuse and Integration (IRI)* (pp. 79–83). IEEE.

[41] Ryalat, M., ElMoaqet, H., & AlFaouri, M. (2023). Design of a smart factory based on cyber-physical systems and Internet of Things towards Industry 4.0. *Applied Sciences*, *13*(4), 2156.

[42] Baloyi, N., & Kotzé, P. (2019). Guidelines for data privacy compliance: A focus on cyber-physical systems and internet of things. In *Proceedings of the South African Institute of Computer Scientists and Information Technologists 2019* (pp. 1–12).

[43] Zaguir, N. A., Magalhães, G. H., & Spinola, M. M. (2024). Challenges and enablers for GDPR compliance: systematic literature review and future research directions. *IEEE Access*.

[44] Ahmad, U., Zaib, H., & Qureshi, K. N. (2024). Cybersecurity Standards for AIoT Networks. In *Artificial Intelligence of Things (AIoT)* (pp. 179–197). CRC Press.

[45] Iqbal, S. (2024). Network Security Policies and Their Alignment with the Cybersecurity Information Sharing Act (CISA). *Network Security*, *2024*(8), 01–08.

[46] PIERȘINARU, A. M. (2024). Preliminary considerations on China's international cooperation in cyber security: legislation, competent

authorities, and challenges. *BULLETIN OF" CAROL I" NATIONAL DEFENCE UNIVERSITY, 13*(2), 121–141.

[47] Ruohonen, J. (2024, September). The Incoherency Risk in the EU's New Cyber Security Policies. In *Conference on e-Business, e-Services and e-Society* (pp. 284–295). Cham: Springer Nature Switzerland.

[48] Yigit, Y., Ferrag, M. A., Sarker, I. H., Maglaras, L. A., Chrysoulas, C., Moradpoor, N., & Janicke, H. (2024). Critical infrastructure protection: Generative ai, challenges, and opportunities. *arXiv preprint arXiv:2405.04874*.

[49] Buttigieg, C. P., & Zimmermann, B. B. (2024, June). The digital operational resilience act: challenges and some reflections on the adequacy of Europe's architecture for financial supervision. In *ERA Forum* (pp. 1–18). Berlin/Heidelberg: Springer Berlin Heidelberg.

[50] Zhang, L., & Kollnig, K. (2024). Theory and practice: the protection of children's personal information in China. *International Data Privacy Law, 14*(1), 37–52.

[51] Gichubi, P. M., Maake, B., & Chweya, R. (2024). Cybersecurity Framework for Kenyan Universities in Conformity with ISO/IEC 27001: 2022 Standard. *Open Access Library Journal, 11*(8), 1–16.

[52] Diaba, S. Y., Shafie-khah, M., & Elmusrati, M. (2024). Cyber-physical attack and the future energy systems: A review. *Energy Reports, 12*, 2914–2932.

[53] Helal, R., Seghiri, A., Belala, F., & Hameurlain, N. (2024, February). Towards a Formal Modeling Approach for Cyber-Physical Systems Requirements. In *Proceedings of the 2024 13th International Conference on Software and Computer Applications* (pp. 298–309).

[54] Jelinek, T., Bhave, A., Buchoud, N., Bühler, M. M., Glauner, P., Inderwildi, O., ... & Voss, A. (2024). International Collaboration: Mainstreaming Artificial Intelligence and Cyberphysical Systems for Carbon Neutrality. *IEEE Transactions on Industrial Cyber-Physical Systems*.

[55] Marcén, A. G. (2024). The Budapest Convention and the UN Cybercrime Convention negotiations. In *Global Cybersecurity and International Law* (pp. 174–192). Routledge.

[56] Preneel, B. (2024, June). The Encryption Debate: An Enduring Struggle. In *Proceedings of the Fourteenth ACM Conference on Data and Application Security and Privacy* (pp. 1–3).

[57] Paulus, A. (2024). Passivity. In *Building Bridges in Cyber Diplomacy: How Brazil Shaped Global Cyber Norms* (pp. 225–236). Cham: Springer Nature Switzerland.

[58] Herath, H. M. (2024, January). A Comparative Analysis of the Advantages and Disadvantages of the Implementation of United Nations Convention on Contracts for the Sale of Goods (CISG) by Sri Lanka and UK. In *A Comparative Analysis of the Advantages and Disadvantages of the Implementation of United Nations Convention on Contracts for the Sale of Goods (CISG) by Sri Lanka and UK (January 24, 2024).*

[59] Tsilonis, V. (2024). Cyber Warfare: International Criminal Law in the Digital Era. In *The Jurisdiction of the International Criminal Court* (pp. 315–339). Cham: Springer International Publishing.

[60] Batlle, S., & van Waeyenberge, A. (2024). EU–US Data Privacy Framework: A First Legal Assessment. *European Journal of Risk Regulation*, *15*(1), 191–200.

[61] Weippl, E., & Schrittwieser, S. (2024). Introduction to Security and Privacy. *Hannes Werthner· Carlo Ghezzi· Jeff Kramer· Julian Nida-Rümelin· Bashar Nuseibeh· Erich Prem·*, 397.

[62] Qian, X., & Zhang, Y. (2024). Science, technology, and innovation: the next frontier in Asia-Pacific's legal framework. *Asia Pacific Law Review*, *32*(1), 239–258.

[63] Kello, L. (2024). Digital Diplomacy and Cyber Defence. *The Oxford Handbook of Digital Diplomacy*, 121.

[64] Hassid, N., & Matania, E. (2024). A Global Regime for Cybersecurity and the Obstacles to Future Progress. *Global Governance: A Review of Multilateralism and International Organizations*, *30*(1), 13–40.

[65] Nweke, L. O., & Yayilgan, S. Y. (2024). Opportunities and Challenges of Using Artificial Intelligence in Securing Cyber-Physical Systems. *Artificial Intelligence for Security: Enhancing Protection in a Changing World*, 131–164.

[66] Gubbi, K. S., & Murthy, J. S. (2024). CloudSec Dynamics: Safeguarding Interconnected Realms–From Cyber-Physical Systems to Vehicular Networks in the Cloud Age. In *Cloud Security* (pp. 275–295). Chapman and Hall/CRC.

[67] Ahmad, I., Islam, Z. U., & Riaz, S. (2024, May). Complexity Analysis of Industrial Scale Cyber Physical Systems. In *2024 IEEE 7th International Conference on Industrial Cyber-Physical Systems (ICPS)* (pp. 1–6). IEEE.

[68] Ojo, B., Ogborigbo, J. C., & Okafor, M. O. (2024). Innovative solutions for critical infrastructure resilience against cyber-physical attacks. *World Journal of Advanced Research and Reviews*, *22*(3), 1651–1674.

[69] Kul, G., & Biringa, C. (2024). Forensics in Cyber-Physical Systems. In *A Practical Guide on Security and Privacy in Cyber-Physical Systems: Foundations, Applications and Limitations* (pp. 89–110).

[70] Kurkchi, Y. (2024, September). Towards Cyber-Physical-Ethical Systems. In *International Conference on the Quality of Information and Communications Technology* (pp. 419–426). Cham: Springer Nature Switzerland.

[71] Al-Ghuraybi, H. A., AlZain, M. A., & Soh, B. (2024). Ensuring authentication in Medical Cyber-Physical Systems: a comprehensive literature review of blockchain technology integration with machine learning. *Multimedia Tools and Applications*, *83*(12), 35673–35707.

[72] Bates, M. E., Campbell, E., & Lewinson, T. (2024). "Just Did The Best That I Could Do": CPS Social Workers' Perceptions of Self-Efficacy in Legal Aspects. *International Journal on Child Maltreatment: Research, Policy and Practice*, 1–17.

[73] Li, Y., Liu, W., Liu, Q., Zheng, X., Sun, K., & Huang, C. (2024). Complying with ISO 26262 and ISO/SAE 21434: A Safety and Security Co-Analysis Method for Intelligent Connected Vehicle. *Sensors*, *24*(6), 1848.

[74] Wilhelm, J., Niermann, D., Keiser, D., & Freitag, M. (2024). Towards Holistic Interoperability of Cyber-Physical Production Systems within RAMI 4.0. *Procedia Computer Science*, *232*, 946–955.

[75] Schlemitz, A., & Mezhuyev, V. (2024). Journal of Industrial Information Integration. *Journal of Industrial Information Integration*, *38*, 100578.

[76] Fraunhofer, I. K. S., Heidemann, L., Herd, B., Kelly, J., Mata, N., Tsai, W., ... & Zamanian, A. (2024). The European Artificial Intelligence Act.

[77] Hayashi, S., & Arai, K. (2024). Digital Society and Regulations: A Competition Policy Perspective. In *Digitalization and Competition Policy in Japan* (pp. 157–162). Singapore: Springer Nature Singapore.

[78] Kuleshov, Y. A., Nagpal, K., Ucpinar, K., Gadaginmath, A., Gadaginmath, S., O'Daniel, K., ... & Monangi, H. (2024). Cyber Attacks on Avionics Networks in Digital Twin Environment: Detection and Defense. In *AIAA SCITECH 2024 Forum* (p. 0277).

[79] Hätinen, M. (2024). Evolution of cybersecurity risk management standardization: Comparison of the NIST Cybersecurity Framework version 1.1 and 2.0.

[80] Neha, K., Ali, F., Kuwana, R. J., & Wakode, S. K. Regulations in the United States. In *Global Regulations of Medicinal, Pharmaceutical, and Food Products* (pp. 29–39). CRC Press.

[81] Ezeigweneme, C. A., Umoh, A. A., Ilojianya, V. I., & Adegbite, A. O. (2024). Review of telecommunication regulation and policy: comparative analysis USA and Africa. *Computer Science & IT Research Journal*, *5*(1), 81–99.

[82] Liu, H. (2024). Network and Communication Protocols in Cyber-Physical Systems. In *A Practical Guide on Security and Privacy in Cyber-Physical Systems: Foundations, Applications and Limitations* (pp. 25–88).

[83] Corbett, C., Weber, C. M., & Anderson, T. R. (2024, August). Smart Grid Cybersecurity in the Age of Artificial Intelligence. In *2024 Portland International Conference on Management of Engineering and Technology (PICMET)* (pp. 1–8). IEEE.

[84] Bountakas, P., Fysarakis, K., Kyriakakis, T., Karafotis, P., Aristeidis, S., Tasouli, M., ... & Illiashenko, O. (2024, July). SYNAPSE-An Integrated Cyber Security Risk & Resilience Management Platform, With Holistic Situational Awareness, Incident Response & Preparedness Capabilities: SYNAPSE. In *Proceedings of the 19th International Conference on Availability, Reliability and Security* (pp. 1–10).

[85] Wanyonyi Rodgers, M. (2024). Legal, Policy and Institutional Framework for Regulation of UAS in the United States of America (USA). In *The Law Regulating Unmanned Aircraft Systems in the United States, South Africa and Kenya: A Civil Aviation Perspective* (pp. 81–120). Cham: Springer Nature Switzerland.

[86] Goodwin, M. B., Whelan, A. M., & Gostin, L. O. (2024). Food and Drug Administration v Alliance for Hippocratic Medicine—A Cautious Win for Reproductive Health Care and FDA Authority. *JAMA*, *332*(6), 453–454.

[87] O'Shea, A. M., Mulligan, K., Carter, K. D., Haraldsson, B., Wray, C. M., Shahnazi, A., & Kaboli, P. J. (2024). Comparing Federal Communications Commission and Microsoft Estimates of Broadband Access for Mental Health Video Telemedicine Among Veterans: Retrospective Cohort Study. *Journal of medical Internet research*, *26*, e47100.

[88] Casarosa, F. (2024). European Health Data Space–Is the Proposed Certification System Effective against Cyber Threats?. *European Journal of Risk Regulation*, 1–11.

[89] Koulierakis, E. (2024). Certification as guidance for data protection by design. *International Review of Law, Computers & Technology*, *38*(2), 245–263.

[90] Li, Z., Yi, W., & Chen, J. (2024). Accuracy of training data and model outputs in Generative AI: CREATe Response to the Information Commissioner Office Consultation. *arXiv preprint arXiv:2407.13072*.

[91] Inayat, I., Farooq, M., & Inayat, Z. (2023). Safety and security risks management process for cyber-physical systems: A case study. *Journal of Software: Evolution and Process*, *35*(7), e2482.

[92] Chen, Q., & Li, C. (2024). The Green Paradox in NEV Manufacturing: Regulatory Impacts on Innovation from a Stakeholder Perspective. *Energies*, *17*(14), 3508.

[93] Shao, H. (2024). Research on Digital Literacy Survey and Promotion strategies of Rural E-commerce under the Perspective of Digital Economy——Taking Yiwu as an Example. *International Journal of Mathematics and Systems Science*, *6*(6).

[94] Seng, N. (2024). Cybersecurity Regulation—Types, Principles, and Country Deep Dives in Asia. *International Cybersecurity Law Review*, *5*(3), 387–411.

[95] Abeysooriya, Sasenka, Saeed Akhlaghpour, Ivano Bongiovanni, Dallas Dowsett, Joseph Grotowski, Mike Holm, Dan Kim et al. "Discussion Paper: 2023–2030 Australian Cyber Security Strategy." (2023): 1–31.

[96] Paltiel, M., Taylor, M., & Newson, A. (2023). Protection of genomic data and the Australian Privacy Act: when are genomic data 'personal information'?. *International Data Privacy Law*, *13*(1), 47–62.

[97] Tarka, M., Blankstein, M., & Schottel, P. (2023). Reply to: Empowering boards: How the National Cyber Security Centre Board (United Kingdom) toolkit is transforming cyber security governance. *Injury*, *54*(11).

[98] Solomon, Daniela, Margaret Phillips, Erin M. Rowley, and Chelsea Leachman. "10. Standards in Computer Science and Information Technology." (2023): 109–121.

16

Blockchain-based Security and Privacy Solutions for Cyber-physical Systems

Peace Busola Falola[1], Joseph Bamidele Awotunde[2], Abidemi Emmanuel Adeniyi[3] and Grace Oluwamayowa Ajiboye[4]

[1]Computer Science Unit, Distance Learning Center, University of Ibadan, Nigeria
[2]Department of Computer Science, Faculty of Communication and Information Sciences, University of Ilorin, Nigeria
[3]Department of Computer Science, College of Computing and Communication Studies, Bowen University, Nigeria
[4]Department of Computer Sciences, Precious Cornerstone University, Nigeria

Email: pb.falola@ui.edu.ng; awotunde.jb@unilorin.edu.ng; abidemi.adeniyi@bowen.edu.ng; ajiboyegrace@pcu.edu.ng

Abstract

Cyber-physical systems, predicted to become even more commonplace and spreading in the future, have seen unmatched success in integrating communication with the physical world. Applications of the physical environment around us may be managed and controlled using CPS. However, most conventional CPS-based solutions were created inside centralized systems, potentially compromising security, privacy, and trust (STP). The use of blockchain technology enables CPS. Block hashes and transaction validation techniques give data security and privacy. Blockchain is a tremendous tool for improving CPS because it provides a decentralized structure and capacity that increases security and transparency. Blockchain applications tend to improve CPS performance with the peer-to-peer (P2P) communication mechanism that guarantees data integrity and reduces the dangers that come with centralized. This chapter delves into the technical challenges of CPS

DOI: 10.1201/9788743801306-16

interoperability, scalability, and blockchain technology integration. Layer 2 methods and sharding innovations are offered to overcome the obstacles. A comprehensive analysis of how blockchain technology can alter CPS administration and security was conducted. By doing this, blockchain systems are guaranteed to remain robust and dependable for all foreseeable uses.

16.1 Introduction

Data transmission, computing, and physical process control in a methodical manner are incorporated into the multifaceted study areas of cyber-physical systems (CPS) [1]. CPS is defined as a network of embedded systems that communicates with physical input and output [2]. It is composed of several networked systems that agree to track and manage real-world IoT-related events and items [2]. It stands out because of the intricate process of connecting embedded cyber components with dynamic physical elements like human actions, mechanical components, and the surrounding environment [1]. The basic components of CPS are actuators, aggregators, and sensors. Furthermore, CPS systems possess environmental sensing capabilities, enabling them to manipulate and regulate the tangible world [2]. This is primarily due to their capacity and flexibility to employ real-time computing to alter the system(s) process(es) run-time [2]. Figure 16.1 displays various industries where cyber-physical systems (CPS) are applied, such as automotive, healthcare, manufacturing, and smart grids, showing the integration of physical processes with computational algorithms and networks [1][2].

These application domains benefit from the seamless integration of computational intelligence with physical processes. In power transmission systems, CPS enables real-time monitoring and control, enhancing the reliability and efficiency of electricity distribution networks [3]. Communication systems leverage CPS to optimize data transmission, ensuring robust and secure communication across devices, particularly in IoT environments. Autonomous systems, including drones, robotics, and autonomous vehicles, rely on CPS for real-time decision-making, safe navigation, and task execution without human intervention [4]. In military systems, CPS enhances situational awareness, supports autonomous operations, and improves the precision of defense technologies. Smart manufacturing benefits from CPS by integrating production processes with data analytics and real-time monitoring, leading to adaptive and efficient manufacturing systems. In smart grids, CPS allows for dynamic management of electricity distribution, supporting the integration of renewable energy and improving grid resilience [5]. Sophisticated driver assistance systems, vehicle-to-grid communication, and

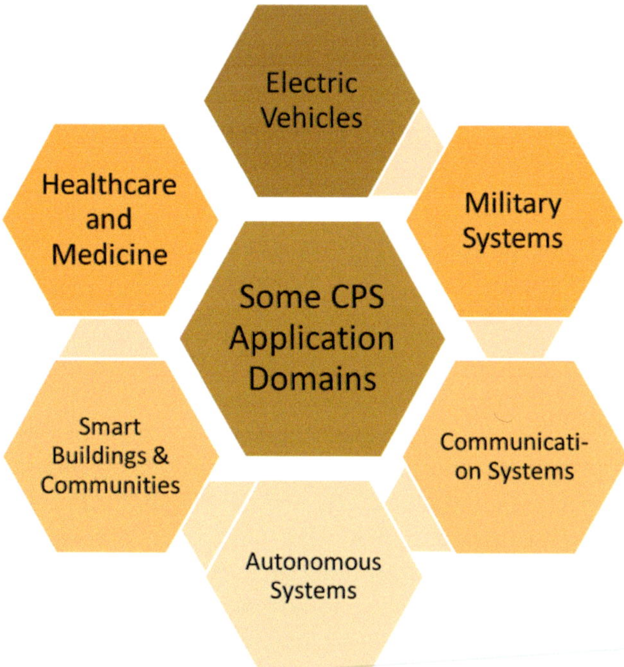

Figure 16.1 Some CPS application domains.

battery performance management are all made possible by CPS in electric cars (EVs) [6].

Healthcare and medicine are transformed by CPS through the development of smart medical devices, remote monitoring systems, and robotic surgery, enhancing patient outcomes with precise, data-driven care [7]. Smart homes are also transformed by CPS, which enables the incorporation of automation systems for energy management, security, and comfort. In smart buildings, CPS facilitates the dynamic adjustment of environmental controls, optimizing energy usage and creating more sustainable operations. At the community level, CPS supports the development of smart cities, where infrastructure systems such as transportation, utilities, and public safety are managed in real time, resulting in enhanced resource management, urban planning, and general quality of life. Across these diverse domains, CPS drives innovation, safety, and efficiency by closing the distance between the real and digital worlds. Table 16.1 has been used to identify, characterize, and discuss the basic features of CPSs.

Additionally, CPS may be used in supply chain management to facilitate manufacturing processes that are safe, economical, flexible, and

Table 16.1 CPS characteristics and their issues.

CPS characteristics	Issues
Distinct systems for development and target	It results in a multitude of design problems, as well as poor controllability and observability.
Narrowly targeted	One characteristic of embedded systems is that they are not multipurpose PCs.
Human–computer interaction (HCI) standards	A custom design was needed for the majority of CPS.
Utilizing actuators and sensors	In traditional systems, it is uncommon, but in CPS, it is widespread.

environmentally friendly. The design and management of CPS offer significant obstacles to several quality of service (QoS) challenges, including long-term viability, flexibility, safety, and dependability [1]. It is impossible to exaggerate the importance of cyber-physical systems in contemporary technology. They are crucial for solving security issues, fostering innovation, improving operational efficiency, and advancing sustainability. Their influence will probably increase as more industries use CPS, influencing how technology is used in many other fields in the future.

The current surge in cyberattacks, which mostly target vital systems, including those in the industrial, medical, and energy sectors, has raised serious concerns about security options [8]. Predictions based on tainted data surely lead to loss of life and money, even if the most recent industry infrastructures primarily rely on AI-driven maintenance [8]. Indeed, a weak data protection system might easily jeopardize the network's dependability and security [6]. A special blockchain-based framework is required, as evidenced by the inadequacies of trusted-certificate-driven or traditional cloud computing approaches. The security of CPSs is significantly affected by the intricacy of their objects, components, and communication systems [9].

Valid authentication and attestation are necessary for the cooperation of various sensors, actuators, and control systems. Different participants ask the controller to do different operations for different circumstances. Additional techniques (such as vibration, light, and electromagnetic) are used in addition to conventional communication ways to send information between various devices. Therefore, even a small mistake might result in highly privileged access or serious information exposure. For researchers, a more comprehensive knowledge of CPS security within a single framework can provide a broad perspective. As a result, we are able to identify

CPS's shortcomings and provide strong defenses against these kinds of assaults [9].

Cyber-physical systems (CPS) are susceptible to various security threats such as hardware- and software-based side-channel attacks, remote cyberattacks, and increased interconnectivity and dependencies between physical and cyber domains. This vulnerability is particularly evident in safety-critical applications, such as autonomous driving and healthcare [10]. Due to the vast amounts of data and interdependencies between the physical and digital worlds, existing software and hardware security methods can handle these threats in their respective domains; nevertheless, these strategies cannot be employed directly [10]. The limited memory, processing, and power capabilities of embedded devices are another important problem [9]. Numerous CPS devices are installed in physically inaccessible locations and do not receive routine maintenance. As a result, these devices with limited resources are unable to perform computing-intensive activities, which increases the difficulty of their security.

Common security mitigation is not provided in the majority of embedded devices. Therefore, intrusion detection, authentication procedures, and lightweight cryptographic techniques are essential to reduce computing costs and increase the longevity of these systems. Thus, intrusion detection, authentication procedures, and lightweight cryptographic techniques are required to lower computing costs and increase the longevity of these systems. Wearable technology is a common example, collecting people's everyday health, sports, and other data. However, many manufacturers and app developers do not prioritize security problems because of the limited battery and computing power. The security of users is at risk due to privacy challenges. Security protection becomes difficult because of the variability and limitations of CPS modules [9].

16.1.1 The key contributions of this chapter

The primary contribution of this work is to:

i. The chapter presents how the decentralized, immutable, and transparent architecture of data storage and transaction processing improves the security and trust of cyber-physical systems (CPS).

ii. This chapter also presents how several CPS components can interoperate with one another via blockchain, as blockchain offers a standardized framework for data exchange.

iii. The performance and scalability issues around integrating blockchain with CPS are discussed in his chapter.

16.1.2 Chapter organization

Section 16.2 presents the cyber-physical system (CPS) layers. Section 16.3 discusses challenges in cyber-physical systems security and privacy. Section 16.4 discusses the key components of blockchain. Section 16.5 discusses the application of blockchain in cyber-physical systems. Section 16.6 discusses the technical challenges and considerations. Section 16.7 discusses future trends and directions, and section 16.8 presents the conclusion.

16.2 Cyber-physical System (CPS) Layers

CPS systems are composed of several layers and components connected using various technologies and communication protocols. The CPS architecture consists of the perception, transmission, and application layers, all depicted in Figure 16.2.

16.2.1 Perception layer

The sensing or recognition layers are other names for the perception layer. It comprises several different devices, including RFID tags, aggregators, sensors, actuators, and global positioning systems (GPS). These devices collect data in real time to track, observe, and decipher external stimuli. Examples of such collected data, depending on the type of sensor, include location, heat, electricity consumption, biology, chemistry, and sound and light signals. These sensors generate real-time data in the local and wide network domains, which are then aggregated and analyzed by the application layer. Actuator security also depends on authorized sources to deliver error-free and secure feedback and control commands. End-to-end encryption at every layer is required to raise the security level. Complicated computations and significant memory requirements would, therefore, be added. In this case, it is vital to design lightweight security protocols that are both effective and consider the demands of security and the capabilities of the devices [2].

16.2.2 Transmission layer

It is also known as the network or transport layers. It is the second CPS layer. This layer transfers and analyzes data between the application and perception

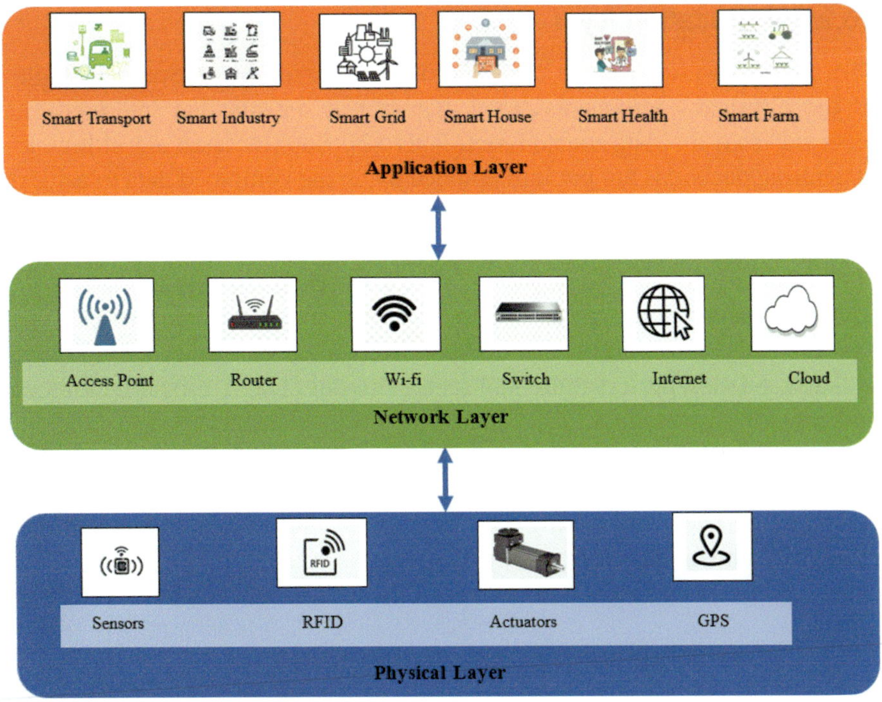

Figure 16.2 Cyber-physical system layers.

layers. Data transport and interaction over the Internet are facilitated via local area networks (LANs), Bluetooth, Wi-Fi, LTE, InfraRed (IR) ZigBee, and other technologies and communication protocols [2]. Many protocols, such as Internet Protocol version 6 (IPv6), are used to address the increasing number of devices connected to the internet [2]. This layer ensures that data is routed and delivered in addition to using cloud computing platforms, firewalls, switching and internet gateways, intrusion detection/prevention systems (IDS/IPS), and routing devices. To prevent malicious assaults and intrusions like malware, malicious code injection, distributed denial of service (DoS/DDoS), eavesdropping, and unauthorized access, data contents must be securely communicated before being outsourced. Imposing processor and power resource requirements is problematic, especially on devices with constrained resources. This is what causes these problems. Figure 16.2 depicts the hierarchical structure of CPS, showing different layers, such as the physical layer, network layer, data layer, and application layer, which facilitate the interaction between physical components and computational processes [2].

16.2.3 Application layer

The application layer is the third and most engaging layer. Some examples of the physical components are actuators and sensors that interpret data received from the data transmission layer [2]. Sophisticated algorithms for generating decisions are put into practice using the combined data to achieve this [2]. Furthermore, the application layer analyzes data from the perception layer to decide which automated actions should be triggered accurately [11]. Middleware, cloud computing, and data mining techniques manage the data at this layer. Some of the most well-known defensive strategies that prevent the leakage of information include anonymization, data masking (camouflage), privacy preservation, and secret sharing [12]. A robust multifactor authentication procedure is needed to stop unwanted access and privilege escalation [13]. Due to the high rise in the number of devices that are linked to the internet, which has created a huge amount of data, effective protection strategies are necessary for big data security to handle large volumes of data effectively and quickly [14].

16.3 Cyber-physical System Architecture

The CPS architecture, which starts with the sensors, gathers information from the real world [15]. Data such as temperature, velocity, pressure, and any other quantity important to the system's functioning are gathered. The embedded hardware further processes the data gathered by the sensors. The hardware mediates between the sensor and the remaining part of the CPS. Raw data is suitably prepared, filtered, and preprocessed if need be before being sent to the embedded hardware in the architecture. Embedded hardware manages real-time data perfectly in a CPS, and it is often tuned to low power consumption and efficiency [16]. The actuators are often linked to the embedded hardware. Actuators change the environment in response to the orders they receive, while sensors amass data from the environment around them [17]. This usually involves the handling of physical operations, adjusting equipment, or carrying out duties required by the system. The controller controls the actuator's actions, and the controller issues commands based on the processed data. Human operators monitor and make choices as needed in their interactions with the CPS [18]. The human operators take charge of advanced monitoring and decision-making procedures, which entail stepping in when the system encounters scenarios that need human intervention or when the automated processes require modifications.

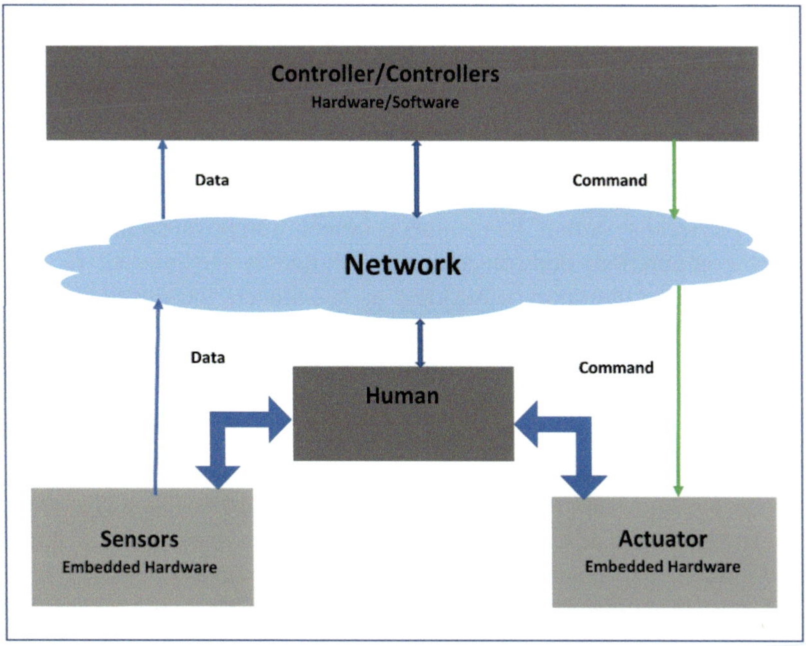

Figure 16.3 Cyber-physical system architecture.

Scenarios such as ensuring the surroundings are safe for the system to function require the involvement of the human operator. The central processing units are referred to as the controllers in CPS [19]. The central processing units obtain data from the sensors and use it for analysis to make judgments through embedded electronics. Based on the analysis, the controller instructs the actuators to change the physical environment. The controllers employ various algorithms, including artificial intelligence and control theory, to guarantee that the system performs optimally and achieves its objectives. CPS's components can communicate with one another because of the networks. The network connects the sensors, controls, actuators, and human operators, enabling the efficient exchange of information and commands across the system [20]. The network is responsible for every component of the CPS being in sync with one another, and they can respond instantly to environmental changes [21]. This is a crucial part that enables the integration of different CPS subsystems [15]. Figure 16.3 shows the data and command flow in the CPS architecture. Sensor data is sent to the embedded hardware and analyzed before sending it to the controllers. Commands are generated from the analysis and then given to the actuators to carry out certain tasks.

The network ensures the flow is constant and unbroken so that the CPS can operate efficiently.

16.4 Challenges in Cyber-physical Systems Security and Privacy

A cyber-physical system (CPS) connects objects and physical processes with sensing, computation, control, and networking via the internet [22]. This is important to contemporary business as it connects the physical and digital realms. The structures and functionality are always enhanced to meet the industry's constantly evolving demands. In the meantime, new security issues have emerged.

Unlike other networking systems, security services were not added to CPS system architecture, which allowed attackers to take advantage of several risks and vulnerabilities to carry out security attacks. This also resulted in the diverse nature of CPS devices, which are seen in several IoT domains and communicate via several technologies and protocols. A lot of vulnerabilities exist in the hardware and software used in CPS that attackers could use. Obsolete or poorly designed CPS hardware and software can birth some vulnerabilities. Furthermore, cybersecurity was not thought about in older groups of hardware, software, or network protocols [23].

As cyber-physical systems (CPS) are now common in vital systems, protecting assets from attacks is vital for ensuring security, safety, and credibility and preventing failure developments and loss reduction. Automated mode analysis of the CPS configuration is important to recognize and replace the most sensitive CPS component quickly. Scholars and practitioners are now focusing more on cyberattacks on industrial systems, as they are rising fast and posing serious risks [22-23].

16.4.1 Threats, vulnerabilities, and types of cyberattacks targeting cyber-physical systems

A comprehension of the dangers, weaknesses, and types of cyberattacks that are aimed at cyber-physical systems will assist in protecting the integration of digital and physical components. This section discusses the specific security challenges that cyber-physical systems encounter and points out the several ways that attackers can exploit the vulnerabilities in the system.

16.4.1.1 Threats

Cyber and physical dangers are two categories of CPS security risks. Cybersecurity is a multifaceted topic that may be seen from a variety of angles. For example, centered information necessitates safeguarding data flow throughout storage, transmission, and even processing phases [24]. A further viewpoint is orientated function, which demands that the cyber-physical elements be integrated into the CPS. Data availability, confidentiality, integrity, and accountability are all impacted by directed threats. These factors increase the likelihood of several problems with CPS systems [21]. The aforementioned problems render CPS systems vulnerable to wireless exploitation, which calls for an understanding of the system's architecture and takes use of its wireless capabilities to take over a system remotely, interfere with its functioning, and/or result in a collision or loss of control. Through the deployment of wireless jamming signals or waves of deauthentication, attackers can alter a device's intended actions and status, causing harm and depriving the device of system and device services [24].

Due to the limitations of traditional defenses, intelligence agencies conduct operations targeted at a country's industrial control system (ICS) and computational intelligence (CI) mostly through malware dissemination, compromising data confidentiality [10]. Unauthorized entry into CPS infrastructure by remote access can result in disruptions, monetary losses, blackouts, industrial data theft, and industrial espionage. Information disclosure happens when hackers breach confidentiality and privacy protections by deploying wireless hacking tools to intercept communication traffic [20]. To obtain sensitive information, attackers must obtain illegal access via physical or logical network breaches. This compromises user privacy. Hackers use weaknesses to listen in on private conversations, known as interception, which results in confidentiality and privacy violations. GPS exploitation is the act of hackers monitoring a device or car via GPS navigation systems, which exposes location privacy [25]. Software developers surreptitiously gather files and audit logs on devices to sell personal data without consent for marketing and commercial purposes.

Physical risks fall into three categories: loss, repair, and physical harm. System spoofing, denial of service, tracking, sabotage, and spoofing are just a few of the risks associated with CPS. Through the use of a hostile unknown source to disguise their identity as a legitimate business, an attacker can spoof sensors by sending false or misleading measurements to the control center. A person must either stop the communication process or intercept and redirect normal communication traffic to a malicious third party to carry out sabotage. For example, attackers might physically harm sensitive CPS components throughout the whole power system to induce a denial of service or other type of service disruption that could lead to a full or partial blackout [25]. Service disruption or denial of service occurs when an attacker physically tampers with a device to interfere with its functionality or change its configuration [24]. There may be disastrous results from this. Due to the physical exposure of CPS devices, tracking involves an attacker gaining access to a particular device, installing a malicious device, or following the legitimate ones [27].

16.4.1.2 Vulnerabilities

A security hole that may be used for industrial espionage (active assaults or reconnaissance) is called a vulnerability. Therefore, in order to decrease, mitigate, or even eradicate any risk, a vulnerability assessment encompasses both the discovery and analysis of the available CPS flaws, as well as the selection of relevant corrective and preventative activities [2].

There are three primary kinds of CPS vulnerabilities: management, platform, and network vulnerabilities. Network vulnerabilities encompass deficiencies in safeguarding protocols, in addition to compromised open wired and wireless communication and connections. These include attacks such as man-in-the-middle, replay, sniffing, spoofing, and communication-stack (network/transport/application layer) attacks, as well as back-doors, DoS/DDoS, packet manipulation, and eavesdropping [26]. Hardware, software, configuration, and database vulnerabilities are all considered platform vulnerabilities [27]. One area where management is vulnerable is in the absence of security rules, processes, and recommendations.

Numerous factors might lead to vulnerabilities. On the other hand, presumption and isolation, growing connection, and heterogeneity are the three primary sources of vulnerability. In most CPS designs, assumption and isolation are predicated on the "security by obscurity" trend [28]. This concentrates on creating a dependable and secure system and putting in place the required security services without assuming that systems are closed off from the outside world. As CPS systems are more linked these days, and manufacturers have enhanced CPS through the adoption and utilization of open networks and wireless technologies, increasing connectivity increases attack surfaces [28]. Before the internet shifted assaults to external ones in 2001, the majority of ICS attacks were centered on internal ones [29]. Heterogeneity in CPS systems refers to the integration of third-party components into CPS applications, which turns the system into a multivendor system with varying security vulnerabilities for each product [30].

Additionally, the utilization of USB devices, improper procedures, eavesdropping, employee suspicion, and uniformity are causes of CPS risks. Malware spreads via USB use, as demonstrated by the Stuxnet attack on Iranian power facilities. Bad programming practices include writing code that runs indefinitely or is readily altered by adversaries. Spying occurs when malware acquires covert access to CPS systems and stays hidden for years, allowing it to eavesdrop, steal, and collect private information [31]. As demonstrated by the Stuxnet worm assault on Iranian nuclear power plants, homogeneity refers to the vulnerability of comparable CPS types that, if attacked, can impact all devices nearby [28]. Employees with questionable motives may purposefully or unintentionally compromise CPS devices by altering or destroying code, or they may provide hackers remote access by unlocking restricted ports or connecting infected USB devices.

16.4.1.3 Types of cyberattacks

Cyber-physical systems (CPS) combine physical and computational components to create a dynamic interplay between the digital and physical domains. Cyberattackers find these systems to be appealing targets as they are used more often in vital infrastructures like electricity, transportation, and healthcare. The several kinds of cyberattacks in CPS are depicted in Figure 16.3. It is essential to comprehend the many kinds of cyberattacks that target CPS to create security plans that work.

Malware attacks: malware, which may take many different forms, such as viruses, ransomware, and spyware, continues to pose a great danger to CPS [32]. Critical system files may become unavailable until a ransom is paid due to ransomware, which might interfere with vital CPS functions [33]. Spyware can be used to get private data regarding user login credentials or system actions, which could result in additional vulnerability exploitation inside the CPS architecture [34]. Malware has become more sophisticated, and attacks are increasingly focusing on the particular operational technology employed in CPS, which results in both physical interruptions and data breaches.

Denial-of-service (DoS) attacks: attacks known as denial-of-service (DoS) and distributed denial-of-service (DDoS) overload CPS by sending an overwhelming amount of requests, which results in service disruptions [35]. A successful DDoS assault has the potential to disable control systems in vital infrastructures, such as power grids, resulting in extensive disruptions to service [36]. CPS are especially susceptible to these kinds of assaults because of their growing interconnectedness since a single point of failure may have a domino effect throughout the whole system.

Man-in-the-middle (MitM) attacks: MitM attacks entail the interception of communication within a CPS by an attacker [34]. This can provide hackers the ability to change data while it is being transmitted, which might result in the physical systems executing the wrong orders [37]. A smart grid system is an example of a system where an attacker can fake information about energy generation or consumption, which would affect the power supply's overall stability.

Advanced persistent threats (APTs): these are complicated and prolonged cyberattacks that target the theft of private data or interfere with the operations of CPS [38]. Several stages of assaults, such as initial penetration, lateral network movement, and data exfiltration, are the stages involved. APTs are regarded as being dangerous for vital infrastructures that have to continuously function because they might go unnoticed for a long time [38].

Supply chain attacks: to access the major system, supply chain attacks compromise software providers or third-party suppliers in the CPS supply chain [39]. After the compromised components are incorporated by injecting malicious code during manufacturing or software development, attackers exploit the loopholes in CPS [39]. This attack shows that supply chain security protocols are essential and that the current CPS is greatly linked.

Phishing and social engineering: phishing attacks entail deceiving users into giving their personal information or installing malicious software, and cyberattacks against CPS often start with this [40]. Social engineering techniques exploit human psychology by bypassing technical protections [41]. Successful phishing efforts result in credential theft, giving attackers illegal access to CPS and the capability to control operations.

16.4.2 The importance of robust security and privacy frameworks

CPS is an important component of healthcare, energy, transportation, and manufacturing industries. This buttresses the significance of high security and privacy standards in these systems. A broad range of cyberattacks and privacy violations are in CPS due to its complex and interconnected nature. It is essential to guarantee the security and privacy of CPS by ensuring the availability, integrity, and confidentiality of the systems and associated data [42]. High-security measures protect against misuse, data manipulation, and interruptions of services, and these have disastrous effects, particularly in industries that rely on vital infrastructure [40].

Also, privacy rules are essential to guard sensitive data that CPS collects and handles, including operational specifics, trade secrets, and personal health information [43]. A peril of data breaches, espionage, and mishandling of data can happen without enough privacy safeguards, all of which potentially erode public confidence and result in dire legal and financial consequences [44]. Robust privacy and security safeguards also advance CPS's dependability and resilience, and this allows them to operate successfully continuously in the face of intentional attacks or unfavorable circumstances [45]. Resiliency is important to reduce operational hiccups and guarantee service continuity, which is important for public safety and economic stability.

Moreover, comprehensive security and privacy frameworks make it easier to comply with industry standards and regulatory obligations, which are becoming increasingly strict as people become aware of cyber dangers [46]. By upholding these criteria, organizations can protect their legal stand and promote trust and confidence among investors and consumers. Furthermore, vigorous frameworks of security and privacy enable creativity and furnish a protected atmosphere for creating and implementing new technologies and apps in CPS.

16.5 Blockchain Technology: Basics and Beyond

Blockchain is a trailblazing technology impacting new society with its transparency, decentralization, and security aspects [47]. The open distributed ledger known as blockchain comprises a group of connected and related digital blocks [47].

The distributed and secure ledger known as blockchain makes storing and tracking resources simple without a centralized third-party authority [48]. A blockchain comprises a sequence of consecutive transaction blocks [49]. Blockchain is a peer-to-peer, distributed, decentralized, and tamper-proof technology that can trace and authenticate digital transactions [50]. Blockchain eliminates the requirement for a single trusted authority by enabling two parties to send and receive messages in a peer-to-peer network. It is demonstrably secure from an adversary attempting to misuse the plan and undermine the central controller [48]. Resources might be ethereal (like copyrights) or physical (like automobiles and money). Anything that has value may, in principle, use a blockchain network to reduce risks and safety dangers and the expense of monitoring connected to safety [48].

Conventional client/server systems have numerous administrators in charge and adhere to the client/server design [49]. On the other hand, every member of the blockchain network can govern the network [49]. Numerous computers are joined to form the blockchain technology network, and changes to a block require the approval of the whole network. Every computer in the blockchain network is referred to as a node, and every node holds a copy of the digital ledger. You may think of a block as a data container. Blockchain is a continually expanding network of linked, cryptographically secured blocks. A linear chain is used to store the records [32]. The blockchain uses linked list data structures and pointers to represent blocks. A linked list links the blocks together and sequentially organizes them. The location of the next block is indicated by pointers [49]. A set of protocols and consensus from each network member must validate new blocks.

Blockchain was initially exclusively used to record transactions involving virtual currencies, but it eventually began to be utilized for purposes other than payments and currency [47]. These applications include finance, supply chain management, healthcare, and government. Blockchain speeds up and reduces the cost of cross-border payments in the financial industry and enhances supply chain management's transparency and traceability, allowing buyers to verify an item's origin [51][52]. System interoperability and safe patient data management are advantageous to the healthcare industry [53]. Additionally, fractional ownership of assets is made possible by blockchain's tokenization capability, which encourages investments in sustainable projects and efforts. Blockchain technology represents a fundamental change in how data is maintained and transactions are carried out, not just a fad. Its decentralized structure, when paired with attributes like transparency and immutability, places it at the forefront of the development of digital interactions. As technology advances, its uses will probably grow, fostering efficiency and creativity across a wide range of industries while resolving the issues preventing its general acceptance at the moment [54].

16.5.1 Key components of blockchain

This part examines in depth and provides a detailed analysis of the fundamental components of blockchain technology that are necessary to comprehend its operations and uses (Figure 16.4).

16.5.1.1 Blocks

A blockchain's basic building pieces are called blocks, and they are made up of transaction data, metadata, and cryptographic hashes that bind the various components into a safe, unchangeable chain. A blockchain's blocks are made up of a collection of transactions, a hash – a special kind of identification, and the hash of the block before it. This arrangement creates a chain by joining the blocks in chronological sequence. A block becomes immutable after it is closed and added to the blockchain with transaction data included [55][56]. Block header and block body are the two components of every block [39]. This pursues better data integrity, security, and transparency [40]. Several industries, such as banking, energy, supply chain management, healthcare, and others, make use of the most reliable decentralized ledger [50].

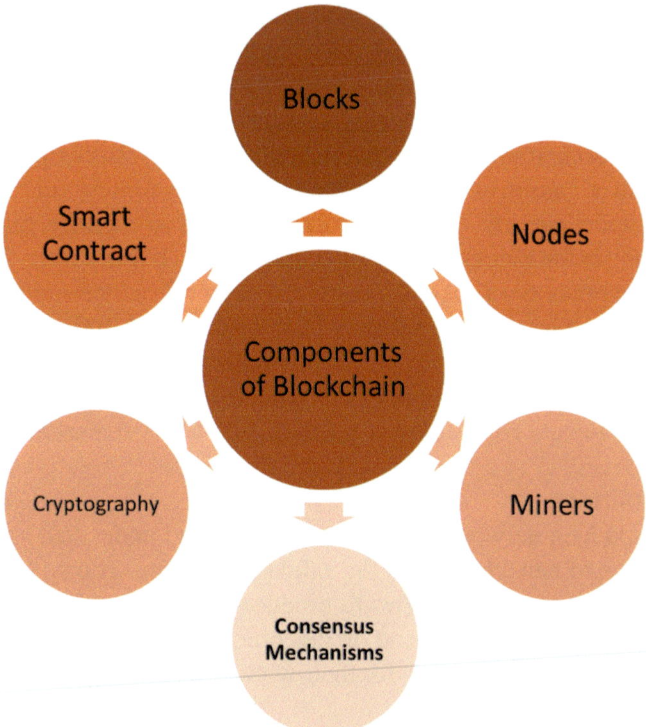

Figure 16.4 Key components of blockchain.

Mining, which includes figuring out a challenging cryptographic puzzle, births new blocks. Miners compete to add pending transactions to a new block and validate them. The new block is broadcast to the network by the first miner to solve the problem, and subsequent nodes confirm its authenticity [56]. A block is uploaded to the blockchain, and the miner is compensated for their work once confirmed. The SHA-256 method is used to create the block's hash, ensuring that changes to the block's contents cannot be made without recalculating the hash [55]. A key component of blockchain networks' functionality is the creation and validation of blocks, which maintains the distributed ledger's transparency and integrity. The wider use of blockchain technology will depend on resolving scalability issues and increasing block generation efficiency as the technology develops.

16.5.1.2 Nodes

Within blockchain transaction networks, the nodes are the unique addresses that participate in the network, and the edges are the actual asset transfers between these addresses [57]. A node is a single computer that takes part in the blockchain network. Every node keeps an exact replica of the whole blockchain and works along with other nodes to verify transactions and determine the current ledger state. Conversely, nodes in blockchain mining networks are computing entities that validate and add transactions to the ledger by using a consensus process, hence playing a critical role in preserving blockchain integrity [57]. The value assigned to an edge incident to a node is represented numerically by an edge weight. For instance, the number indicates the quantity of tokens transferred from one address to another in a blockchain token transaction network [57]. Lightweight and complete nodes are two types of nodes that exist. Lightweight nodes keep a portion of the blockchain and depend on full nodes to validate transactions, while full nodes maintain a complete copy of the blockchain and verify transactions [56].

16.5.1.3 Miners

Within blockchain networks, miners are specialized nodes that are essential to the creation of new blocks and the validation of transactions. Miners solve challenging mathematical puzzles to produce new blocks. The integrity and security of the blockchain depend on this procedure, which is called mining. Cryptocurrency rewards miners for their work, encouraging them to preserve the integrity of the network [56].

Usually, mining uses a consensus technique such as Proof of Work (PoW). Miners use a lot of computer power to solve difficult mathematical problems. This is essential to several consensus processes, especially Proof of Work (PoW). Miners are encouraged to donate their resources to the network by the benefits they receive from mining, usually in the form of bitcoin. Blockchain networks cannot function without miners because they supply the processing power to verify transactions and protect the ledger.

Despite being financially motivated, mining has several drawbacks, such as high energy costs, unstable markets, and governmental scrutiny. The function of miners and the mining procedure will probably change as blockchain technology develops further to meet these issues and preserve the network's integrity and decentralization.

16.5.1.4 Consensus mechanisms

Consensus mechanisms are protocols that ensure that all nodes in the network concur on the validity of transactions and the order in which they should be added to the blockchain. The distributed ledger is securely updated regularly using the consensus technique. State machine replication is an essential strategy to ensure that shared states exist and function by the predefined state transition rules. The state's execution will ultimately provide identical outputs since several copies share it in the network. As a result, replicas must communicate and use a consensus mechanism to reach a consensus on any changes to the state. Replicas use consensus to determine if a state is final [58]. Nevertheless, putting consensus into practice in a distributed system is challenging. A consensus mechanism is needed to preserve critical features like delay perseverance, partitioning throughout the network, adversity tolerance, and failure resilience. Additionally, it incorporates security protocols like message broadcasting or synchronization to control hostile nodes.

The maintenance of three essential characteristics that guarantee the effectiveness of the underlying network is the relevance of consensus in distributed ledgers, such as blockchain. In addition to maintaining consensus on a single global state for a distributed ledger, consensus ensures fault tolerance, safety, and liveness of the network. Consequently, these attributes may be used to assess consensus procedures. Safety may be preserved if the consensus process guarantees that every node will contribute to the same, consistent, and legitimate output. According to Lashkari and Musilek [58], liveness is the capacity of a consensus mechanism to focus nonfaulty nodes' contributions on creating value. To maintain a certain degree of fault tolerance, the consensus mechanism must recover from probable failures of contributing nodes [58]. The Proof of Work and Proof of Stake consensus procedures are widely used. Miners must solve cryptographic puzzles to implement Proof of Work (PoW) [56]. Depending on how many coins they own and are prepared to "stake" as collateral, validators can build new blocks using Proof of Stake (PoS) [46].

16.5.1.5 Cryptography

The foundation of blockchain security is cryptography. It guarantees data integrity preservation, identity verification, and transaction security. This method emphasizes the protection and safety of information. Every industry uses technology, and information security is essential. Because of its sensitive nature, blockchain security is protected against transactional activity by employing extra-advanced security algorithms and methods. Information sharing requires secrecy, integrity, nonrepudiation, and authentication, all cryptography supports. This guarantees data and information openness across the international network. Symmetric and asymmetric encryption techniques are used to link the data that is contained in a block. It has a very stringent tracking system that requires a key to remove or alter. The set of documents, which consists mostly of financial records, is secured using a public key, a private key, or a combination of the two. It is highly resistant to tampering [59]. This method significantly decreased the number of cash-driven interactions with every individual in the lengthy procedure of a financial institution. With a digital ledger like bitcoin or other cryptocurrency, it is a safe and secure method of transacting. An et al. [56] identified hash functions and public-key cryptography as important cryptographic approaches. Public-key cryptography uses both public and private keys for safe transactions. Each block in the chain is uniquely hashed using hash functions, which bind the blocks together safely and guarantee that any modifications to one will affect the hash, indicating tampering.

16.5.1.6 Smart contracts

Smart contracts are self-executing contracts that contain explicit coding encoding the terms of an agreement [60]. They operate automatically when specific conditions are met, eliminating the need for middlemen and lowering transaction costs. Smart contracts increase transaction automation and confidence, according to Khan et al. [61].

As blockchain technology has developed, smart contracts have become increasingly popular [62]. A smart contract is a state-of-the-art technical tool that may be used in a blockchain context to autonomously negotiate, execute, and enforce the conditions of a legally binding agreement. Smart contracts have several benefits over traditional contracts, such as less risk, cheaper service costs, fewer administrative costs, and more effective business processes. More significantly, smart contracts can potentially increase mutual trust when parties lack confidence in one another. It will change how businesses operate now in this way [62].

Smart contracts and distributed ledger technology (blockchain) offer various potential applications beyond the financial industry, such as supply chain management, processing insurance claims, and intellectual property enforcement. There is no indication that enterprises will stop using blockchain apps and smart contracts. However, in order for blockchain apps to satisfy strict requirements for security, scalability, and speed, they must be meticulously designed and put through a rigorous testing process. This is especially true when considering the nonstandard software life cycles utilized in creating smart contracts, which makes it challenging to update or correct bugs in apps that have already been deployed by releasing a new version of the software [62].

The design of smart contracts has its own distinct set of challenges since it differs greatly from more traditional kinds of software engineering. For instance, developers need to ensure code safety for smart contracts due to the immutability of blockchain and the sensitive nature of frequently managed digital information. They also need to be mindful of gas consumption because smart contracts are implemented using the gas mechanism in blockchain platforms like Ethereum. The specific constraints and features required by blockchain technology should be taken into account during the software development process and product lifecycle of smart contracts and blockchain-based applications. These changes in software products and processes must be recognized and examined to create a comprehensive body of knowledge based on blockchain software engineering [62].

16.5.2 Types of blockchain

Blockchains may be categorized into a variety of groups based on their distinct features and uses [47]. Blockchain technology is characterized by immutability, distributed computation, consensus, and authentication. Since blockchain technology is still in its early stages of development, different applications will call for various blockchain types. Blockchains that are public or permissionless are unmanageable. Reading and writing are available to everyone with a network connection. Additionally, only confirmed network members have access to permissioned or private ledgers. Each block is encrypted with a private key to prevent unauthorized access. Consortium blockchains are created by fusing public and private blockchains.

16.5.2.1 Public blockchains

A public blockchain network is entirely decentralized as anybody may join and take part in its administration [47]. A public blockchain is a decentralized, distributed system that enables any number of users to independently verify and exchange transaction data that takes place on the network. There is no separate management organization. Everyone can participate anonymously, and there are no constraints on authority. The basic technology of Bitcoin, a well-known cryptocurrency (also called virtual money) already in use worldwide, is now based on the public blockchain. Finance is, of course, actively investigating public blockchains. Distributed ledger technology is the core technology of public blockchains (DLT). Public blockchains may be beneficial for a variety of purposes, including crowdsourcing and transportation, in addition to financial activities like cryptocurrencies and international remittances. This is so that a public blockchain can enable the authentication process to be finished without the help of a trustworthy third party. Moreover, a public blockchain is an open network that everyone may join as a node and use to create transactions. It also provides excellent reliability and integrity through participant work verification. Despite these advantages, there is a disadvantage: processing and recording speeds may decrease if all participants' transaction data is shared and retained [63].

16.5.2.2 Private blockchains

Only invited members of a particular organization can join and administer private blockchains [47]. While a private and public blockchain is similar, a private blockchain restricts participation to those the service provider (business or organization) has authorized [63]. A centralized blockchain is known as a private blockchain. This kind uses a centralized blockchain architecture to improve security and transaction velocity. In contrast to a public blockchain, a single party manages the private kind autonomously. This kind of blockchain is exclusive to nodes validated by the network-created authentication mechanism. As a result, each participant has to have the necessary rights in order to access transactions. In a private blockchain, transactions may only be created by companies that accept legal responsibility; transaction histories and data can only be validated and authorized by entities that have been approved and vetted. Because only authorized nodes participate in private blockchains, block generation cycles and verification times are shortened. This eliminates the need for additional unapproved nodes' clearance and verification processes. However, compared to public blockchains, the dependability of private blockchains is restricted as its users are dependent on the service provider [63].

16.5.2.3 Consortium blockchain

The consortium blockchain, sometimes called the "federated blockchain," sits between the public and private blockchains regarding management and rights. A consortium blockchain is one in which users are limited to those who have been preapproved or who satisfy certain requirements, including businesses and organizations. Users in this specific form of blockchain are assigned different levels of authority. For instance, certain participants could have access to all or a portion of the transaction data, while others would be able to add new blocks to their accounts and conduct transactions [63-65]. This blockchain is semicentralized and composed of many joint entities, such as companies or organizations. Participation in this type of blockchain is limited to authorized user computers or nodes, much like private blockchains [64].

16.5.3 Blockchain as a security and privacy tool

The protection of people's personal information is becoming an urgent issue of utmost importance as the world grows more linked and dependent on CPSs.

Blockchain technology has demonstrated its capacity to get over these problems by offering a transparent and decentralized platform for safe data management. The prevalence of CPS in domains such as healthcare, transportation, and energy shows the need for high security and privacy protocols. By providing a decentralized and safe technology platform for data communication and exchange, the integration of blockchain technology with CPS shows good promise for resolving these issues. However, creating a private and secure protocol for blockchain-integrated CPSs is a challenging task that requires in-depth knowledge of CPS intricacies, as well as blockchain technology [64].

Immutability, privacy, and security are a few advantages of blockchain technology. When we talk about security, we imply that a transaction posted to the blockchain will ensure the availability, integrity, and secrecy of the data involved (if needed). The data's secrecy can be preserved if the transaction originator encrypts it. Blockchain protects the data's availability and integrity because, once a transaction is included in a deep enough block, it is nearly impossible to change without being discovered. Blockchain provides data far greater safety; that is, in addition to protecting the availability and integrity of the data itself, it also ensures that the context in which a transaction takes place is predetermined and cannot be changed by anybody due to the chain structure. The term "immutability" is also used to emphasize this unique security feature that goes beyond conventional security. Blockchain technology provides further privacy protection beyond the secrecy aspect, which may be ensured by encrypting the transaction's data if desired. Blockchains provide pseudo-anonymous protection to the user initiating transactions, particularly those systems that employ the UTXO approach for maintaining cryptocurrency balances, such as IOTA and Bitcoin [65].

16.6 Application of Blockchain in Cyber-physical Systems

Blockchain technology is a key advancement in raising the security and effectiveness of CPS. Because CPS include physical and computational components, they are vulnerable to many cyberattacks. Blockchain in CPS addresses these challenges by providing a decentralized, immutable, and transparent data management and transaction processing architecture. Blockchain adapts to various applications because of its qualities, such as decentralization, pseudonymity, transparency, democratization, immutability, auditability, fault tolerance, and security [47]. The availability of application development frameworks (ADFs) is another important factor in the success of blockchain technology. Table 16.2 displays CPS applications and blockchain solutions. Table 16.2 presents a comprehensive analysis of blockchain technology's

Table 16.2 CPS applications and blockchain solutions.

Applications	Challenges	Proposed solutions	Lessons
Smart homes, smart cities	Secrecy, flexibility, volume of data, and dependability of data sources	Blockchain that is lightweight and scalable, public key infrastructure for entity identification, and timestamp obfuscation	The blockchain data model had to be modified, each block had to be connected to a distinct entity, and access control had to be implemented.
Supply chains	Traceability, agreement, flexibility, secrecy, data trust, absence of automation, and lack of detail	Blockchain architecture with a multitiered consortium, sharding, access control, transaction language, reputation and integrity module, incentives and sanctions, and smart contracts	The implementation of access control methods and numerous chains is necessary to ensure the privacy of business transactions while maintaining openness for tracking.
Connected and autonomous vehicles	Liability attribution, centralization, safety, and confidentiality	Permissioned blockchain architecture for liability attribution, blockchain for automobile safety and confidentiality	Mobility is a crucial concern for blockchain-based automotive designs.
Distributed energy trading	Centralization, reliance on middlemen, and contract compliance	Smart contracts, several trestles brokers, and a distributed marketplace	Solution needed safeguards against malevolent actions.
IoT data markets	Blockchain overheads, a reliable third party, and a lack of confidentiality	SPB: decentralized trading with atomic meta transactions, private authentication, and private backbone routing	Solution addressed routing, storage, and meter authentication using a number of interconnected systems.
Other applications	Erroneous sensor data, malevolent nodes, amount of data, and overhead in block validation	Distributed consensus, lightweight block creation, adaptive block validation, and data trust and gateway reputation systems	The solution must take into account the blockchain nodes' and sensor data's dependability in order to achieve end-to-end trust.

role in addressing various challenges within CPS applications, including areas like smart homes, smart cities, supply chains, connected vehicles, distributed energy trading, and IoT data markets. In examining each application area, specific challenges were identified, such as issues with data secrecy, the centralization of systems, and the necessity of establishing trust in data sources [47].

Blockchain-based solutions specifically tailored to each context's unique needs were proposed to address these challenges. For example, lightweight blockchain models are suggested to enhance efficiency; smart contracts are employed to ensure automated and secure transactions, and decentralized trading systems are introduced to reduce reliance on centralized authorities. It also reflects on the lessons from implementing these blockchain technologies in various CPS settings. These insights are crucial as they shed light on the practical challenges and adjustments required when integrating blockchain into these complex environments. For instance, there may be a need to modify blockchain models to better suit the application, implement robust access control mechanisms, and address issues related to mobility and the trustworthiness of data. This discussion underscores the importance of a nuanced approach when applying blockchain in diverse CPS contexts, recognizing that while blockchain holds great promise, its deployment must be carefully aligned with the specific demands of each application.

16.6.1 Smart homes, smart cities

Every home has an increasing number of networked devices. These devices are utilized in homes to improve everyday duties and give residents a more enjoyable existence. These gadgets are intelligent since they may also judge based on information gathered and received. In the context of a smart community and metropolis, data gathered from smart homes becomes significant information on a bigger scale. A smart city encompasses more than just smart houses; it includes cars, service providers, and government agencies. As Table 16.2 illustrates, managing data and entities in this context brings new opportunities and problems. The use of blockchain technology facilitates interoperability between various CPS components. Since CPS frequently consists of several systems and devices from different manufacturers, blockchain can offer a consistent data exchange and communication platform. Interoperability is crucial in smart cities, where several systems, like energy distribution, traffic control, and public safety, must function flawlessly. These systems can communicate data more effectively and securely thanks to blockchain, which improves overall operational effectiveness [66].

16.6.2 Supply chains

Globalization, ongoing innovation for increased efficiency and integration, and customer expectations all influence the intricate and interrelated structure of today's supply chains, which transcend territorial borders. Although historical supply chain management systems worked well for straightforward supply networks, they are not well-suited to handle the difficulties that arise in contemporary supply chains. The promising technology known as blockchain can revolutionize supply chains by addressing these significant problems [66].

In supply chain management, blockchain enhances traceability and accountability. By tracking every transaction and the movement of commodities on a blockchain, all parties involved may follow things from the point of origin to the delivery point. This ability is especially useful in businesses like the food and pharmaceutical ones, where compliance and safety are essential. Blockchain-enabled real-time product tracking allows for quick reactions to safety alerts and recalls, protecting businesses and customers.

16.6.3 Connected and autonomous vehicles

New possibilities for traffic management, road safety, and innovative vehicular services like car sharing or electric vehicle charging arise as cars become more autonomous and networked. There are additional difficulties associated with this fast growth in autonomy and connection, which are outlined in Table 16.2

16.6.4 Distributed energy trading

With the rapid expansion of renewable energy from solar, wind, and hydropower, the energy ecosystem is changing from a basic model of producers and consumers to prosumers who can generate and consume energy. Energy trading, in which prosumers may sell their extra energy to other prosumers or consumers, has emerged due to this change. Dedeoglu et al. [66] investigated how blockchain technology may facilitate peer-to-peer energy trade. Increasing security and trust is one of the main uses of blockchain in CPS. Conventional CPS frequently depends on centralized systems open to intrusions such as data manipulation and unlawful access. By dispersing data among several nodes, blockchain's decentralized architecture reduces these dangers and makes it more difficult for attackers to alter data without the network's approval. Blockchain, for example, may securely record energy transactions in smart grid applications, guaranteeing data integrity and enabling independent verification of transactions by all network participants.

16.6.5 IoT data markets

IoT presents a significant opportunity to transform society by unlocking and releasing a universe of data that has, until now, either remained uncollected or mainly unused. IoT data streams are becoming increasingly common in many application domains, such as smart cities, healthcare, personal fitness, and on-site energy optimization. For example, in a public transportation network, the transportation authority and taxi companies may benefit from the density of individual trip card swipes at certain transit stations over time in order to optimize fleet scheduling. As a result, a whole new business model called a "data marketplace" is beginning to take form, enabling data providers to offer interested purchasers their IoT data [66].

16.6.6 Other applications

A layered architecture was presented by Dedeoglu et al. [66] and may be used in a range of CPS applications (e.g., healthcare, industrial IoT, and social media analysis) where physical observations are kept on blockchains. Dedeoglu et al. [66] examined indoor target localization as a use-case scenario for a smart construction application in which Internet of Things (IoT) sensors gather data from the building site to monitor the project at every stage. Subsequently, gateway nodes receive the sensor data and record it on a blockchain.

Blockchain is essential to guaranteeing data integrity and transparency in CPS. By employing cryptographic hashing, blockchain ensures that once data is captured, it cannot be changed covertly. This capability is very helpful in industries like healthcare, where patient data must be kept private and unmodified. With blockchain, medical information is shared securely with authorized parties while all records of interactions are kept. Investors benefit from this transparency as it allows them to confirm the accuracy of the data.

16.7 Technical Challenges and Considerations

Blockchain in CPS is not without challenges, even with its benefits. Challenges such as energy consumption, scalability, and regulatory compliance must be resolved to ensure broad usage. For example, in resource-constrained situations, the energy-intensive nature of various blockchain consensus algorithms, such as Proof of Work, poses questions as regards sustainability. In the future, research and development will focus on building effective consensus algorithms and investigating hybrid models that integrate the advantages of blockchain technology with other fields like artificial intelligence and the Internet of Things. This section discusses some of the challenges and potential fixes.

16.7.1 Scalability and performance issues

The two main technological obstacles to integrating blockchain in cyber-physical systems are scalability and performance. Blockchain technology has built-in limits that relate to transaction volume and speed, particularly in its more popular variants (like Bitcoin and Ethereum). Due to the consensus processes, traditional blockchain handle a certain number of transactions per second, which can cause bottlenecks when the volume of transactions grows. This is a trouble for CPS applications where high transaction throughput and real-time data processing are important.

New consensus algorithms like Proof of Stake (PoS) and delegated Proof of Stake (dPoS), which aim to outperform the conventional Proof of Work (PoW), are examples of potential remedies and current research in blockchain scalability [67]. To manage transactions off the major blockchain and reduce congestion plus advance speed, layer 2 solutions such as Ethereum's plasma and Bitcoin's lighting network are created to advance speed [68]. Sharding divides the blockchain into segments that are small and easy to manage; this is another interesting technique to be checked to advance scalability [69].

16.7.2 Interoperability between different blockchain systems

Integrating interoperability for several blockchains is a major challenge; CPS often uses a broad range of systems and devices that can use several blockchain designs, and this can cause issues with data exchange and good functioning. Several systems incorporated into CPS can be vulnerable due to the absence of standards among blockchain platforms, making data sharing and process automation very difficult. Blockchain interoperability is therefore created to overcome these obstacles, new protocols, and standards [70]. The goal of projects like the cosmos and the interledger protocol (ILP) is to provide frameworks that allow various blockchains to interact and do business with one another [70]. A common standard that can link different blockchain systems, enabling more seamless and effective communication inside CPS, is the goal of these protocols [61]. Cross-chain technology potentially answers interoperability problems, enabling the movement of value and data between various blockchains [72].

16.7.3 Security and privacy

In CPS, where sensitive data is often sent between networked devices, security and privacy are paramount [43]. Because blockchain technology is decentralized and less likely to have single points of failure, it can improve security [73]. Data security and tamper-proofing are guaranteed by the application of cryptographic techniques, such as block hash generation and transaction validation [74]. Access control and private key management are still difficult, though. By restricting access to authorized parties, consortium blockchains where a preselected set of companies controls the consensus process can enhance security [74]. Furthermore, to safeguard sensitive data while still permitting essential data exchange, privacy-enhancing methods, including encryption, secure multiparty computing, and zero-knowledge proofs, are being investigated [76]. Furthermore, new consensus algorithms like the Proof of Improved Participant (PoP) model [77] are being developed to improve blockchain network security and trustworthiness by confirming the integrity of transactions and detecting bad actors. These developments are necessary to guarantee that CPS can function safely where user privacy and data integrity are crucial.

16.7.4 Data integrity and availability

Data availability and integrity are essential for CPS to operate efficiently. A truthful history of transactions is maintained by the blockchain's immutable ledger, which guarantees that once data is recorded, it cannot be changed or removed [78]. This aspect is especially crucial for applications where accurate data is needed to make decisions, such as smart grids, driverless cars, and healthcare systems [79]. However, problems with data availability may also arise, particularly when an enormous amount of data is taking place on the network or when nodes malfunction. To ensure data integrity and persistent accessibility, robust systems for data replication and distribution over the network are important. Sharding can improve data availability and access speed, which breaks the blockchain into smaller portions that are easy to manage [64]. But, the combination of blockchain and other technologies like cloud and edge computing can be better with the availability of data [80]. With the use of distributed storage solutions, CPS can ensure that data is easily available and safe for authorized users, which helps decision-making in real time.

16.7.5 Latency and real-time processing

Latency and real-time processing are important in CPS applications that require quick data processing. Traditional blockchain systems may cause delays, making it more difficult to satisfy real-time needs because of their consensus processes [81]. For instance, unacceptably long latency in applications such as industrial automation or autonomous driving might result from the time required to reach a consensus and ascertain transactions. Layer 2 scaling solutions to process transactions off-chain to speed them up are being considered to address latency problems [82]. Hybrid blockchain designs (public and private blockchains) can also maximize transaction speeds while preserving the security and decentralization benefits. Also, consensus algorithms such as Proof of Stake (PoS) and delegated Proof of Stake (dPoS) should be built to reduce latency and offer real-time processing capabilities [83]. These developments are crucial to ensure CPS can function well in settings where rapid reactions to data inputs are important.

16.8 Future Trends, Lessons Learned, and Research Directions

Blockchain is being integrated into CPS to improve interconnected systems' security, privacy, and operational efficiency. Among the industries where CPS is expanding and evolving include supply chains, energy, healthcare, smart cities, and others. Blockchain technology's decentralized, transparent, and irreversible characteristics provide a solid basis for addressing the issues these systems will unavoidably encounter. However, the process of integrating blockchain into CPS has also produced several new trends, research directions, and lessons learned that are crucial for guiding future work in the field.

Prospective developments in blockchain-enabled CPS center on surmounting present constraints and augmenting the broader usability of blockchain technology in many fields. Blockchain technology is expected to be able to manage the increasing needs of CPS thanks to innovations like sharding, layer 2 solutions, and the integration of blockchain with AI and ML. These innovations are positioned to address scalability and performance challenges. Furthermore, it is anticipated that developing decentralized identity management systems and quantum-resistant cryptography approaches would strengthen these systems' interoperability and security, guaranteeing their resilience in the face of new technical difficulties.

The use of blockchain technology in CPS provides significant insights into the practical considerations that must be made for implementation to be successful. The lesson learned is to buttress the need to adjust data models to ascertain mobility in automobile designs and implement powerful access control measures to tailor blockchain models to the exact needs of any CPS application. The insights obtained from industries present how important it is to balance efficiency, openness, and privacy – especially in settings where data quality and trust are critical.

The need to address open issues and investigate fresh approaches to better the integration of blockchain into CPS will shape the research paths in this area. The expansion of blockchain's role in enabling real-time decision-making in CPS, the investigation of socioeconomic and regulatory ramifications, and the creation of standardized protocols for blockchain interoperability are some of the main areas of study. The future of blockchain-integrated CPS will be greatly formed by these research initiatives as they advance, ensuring that these systems are safe, effective, and flexible enough to meet changing societal demands.

16.8.1 Future trends

Future trends targeted at improving the usefulness and efficiency of blockchain technology are expected to greatly influence its application in cyber-physical systems. Innovations like sharding and layer 2 solutions are the trigger to these developments. When transactions are performed simultaneously, sharding, which splits the blockchain into smaller, more manageable portions called shards, can highly boost scalability [84]. Off-chain transactions are possible with layer 2 technologies such as Bitcoin Lightning Network and Ethereum Plasma Network, which reduces overcrowding and boosts transaction efficiency [85]. The performance restrictions that forbid blockchain from being extensively employed in CPS applications must be solved as these progresses are vital.

The potential of CPS is anticipated to be transformed by combining blockchain technology with artificial intelligence (AI) and machine learning (ML) fields. Due to AI, ML, and blockchain, CPS can handle large volumes of data, forecast, and adapt to new information in real time, ensuring this data is securely managed and open [86]. As a result of these technological improvements, CPS has become very intelligent and automatic, requiring less involvement to make choices. Blockchain assures that the data used in these studies is dependable and impermeable to tampering, while AI can evaluate traffic patterns in smart cities to enhance flow.

Blockchain technology with edge computing is another thrilling development. Edge computing reduces latency and bandwidth consumption, especially for time-sensitive applications [87]. When paired with blockchain, edge computing provides more speedy, localized processing and decentralized data management. Applications that require making decisions in real time, including industrial automation and driverless cars, rely on this connection.

16.8.2 Lessons learned

The knowledge acquired gives valued standpoints on the pragmatic obstacles and vital modifications that come up during the integration of blockchain technology into diverse cyber-physical systems (CPS) applications. These lessons show the need to use blockchain models, the importance of implementing strong access control mechanisms, and the need to deal with mobility-related concerns, especially in automobile design.

The blockchain data architecture has to be adjusted for smart cities and houses to manage data dependability, adaptability, and secrecy. To ensure all blocks are linked to a unique entity, access control is needed. Multiple chains and access control mechanisms have to be implemented in supply chains to protect the confidentiality of business transactions and ensure transparency for tracking purposes. These two requirements highlight the need to balance traceability and privacy. The lesson in the context of connected and autonomous automobiles is that movement is important, and this ensures blockchain-based automotive designs can consider the dynamic nature of these systems. Integrating blockchain technology into distributed energy trading shows the need for protective measures against malicious acts, underlining the essence of security in decentralized settings. The solution addresses routing, storage, and meter authentication for IoT data markets. This highlights the necessity of a strong system to achieve overheads and preserve secrecy [88].

Finally, additional applications that involve malicious nodes and inaccurate sensor data show that taking sensor data reliability and blockchain node reliability into account is important to achieve end-to-end trust. These lessons show how important it is to integrate blockchain in diverse CPS scenarios with a nuanced and application-specific strategy, ensuring that the promise of technology is realized while satisfying the exact requirements of each application.

16.8.3 Research directions

Vital new paths for study are raised by the incorporation of blockchain technology into CPS, most especially in the fields of security and privacy. The progress of quantum-resistant encryption is one of the important fields. The development of quantum computing technologies greatly threatens the encryption techniques employed in blockchain systems [89]. Research is therefore becoming important to ensure the security of blockchain-integrated CPS against future technological breakthroughs. This research depends on the lasting success of blockchain as a safe solution for CPS, specifically in industries like national security, healthcare, and banking.

Decentralized identity management systems are becoming increasingly important as a research topic in the evolving field of CPS. Conventional identity management systems depend on centralized authority and can be targets of cyberattacks and single points of failure. Blockchain offers a decentralized method so that devices and people can handle their credentials and identities apart from a centralized organization [90].

Another important area of research is the socioeconomic and legal implications of integrating blockchain technology into CPS. As blockchain is becoming common, it is essential to think about how it will impact society, specifically in terms of privacy, data ownership, and access to technology. Future research could look into how blockchain technology can be used to ensure the benefits of CPS are shared fairly and prevent new socioeconomic gaps from emerging. Laws governing the use of blockchain and CPS technologies will also need to quickly adapt to protect people's rights and ensure that the moral implications of automation and data management are properly addressed.

16.9 Conclusion

This chapter has covered the potential of blockchain technology to improve CPS security and privacy. CPS can reduce the risks of using traditional centralized systems, such as data modification and unlawful access, because of blockchain technology's decentralized, immutable, and transparent design. The application of blockchain in CPS gives significant advantages to several industries, such as supply chain management, smart grids, healthcare, and smart cities, by guaranteeing data integrity, transparency, and increased operational efficiency. The chapter also emphasized how blockchain technology can help with CPS's specific issues, such as scalability, interoperability, and real-time processing. Blockchain technology presents sharding and layer 2 solutions as ways to solve drawbacks, increasing its scalability and efficiency for CPS applications. The development of quantum-resistant cryptography techniques and decentralized identity management systems enhances CPS's security and resilience against arising technical threats. Blockchain technology and CPS are expected to boost innovation and improve operational efficiency, which will pave the way for future breakthroughs in several sectors. Blockchain technology will ensure CPS's secure and ethical implementation across several industries, specifically in data protection and automated decision-making. Research and development will be further guided by the lessons learned from the present blockchain integration in CPS, and this ensures that these systems remain adaptable, safe, and dependable despite rapidly advancing technology. Finally, blockchain technology with CPS creates a revolutionary method that controls and safeguards lined systems. This can greatly impact the direction of technology and its practical uses.

References

[1] Yu, B., Zhou, J., & Hu, S. (2020). Cyber-physical systems: An overview. Big data analytics for cyber-physical systems, 1–11.

[2] Yaacoub, J. P. A., Salman, O., Noura, H. N., Kaaniche, N., Chehab, A., & Malli, M. (2020). Cyber-physical systems security: Limitations, issues and future trends. *Microprocessors and microsystems*, *77*, 103201.

[3] Ravikumar, G., Hyder, B., & Govindarasu, M. (2020). Hardware-in-the-loop cps security architecture for der monitoring and control applications. In *2020 IEEE Texas Power and Energy Conference (TPEC)* (pp. 1–5). IEEE.

[4] Sobana, S., Prabha, S. K., Seerangurayar, T., & Sudha, S. (2022). Securing future autonomous applications using cyber-physical systems and the Internet of Things. In Handbook of Research of Internet of Things and Cyber-Physical Systems (pp. 81–148). Apple Academic Press.

[5] Wang, Q., Zhang, G., & Wen, F. (2021). A survey on policies, modelling and security of cyber-physical systems in smart grids. *Energy Conversion and Economics*, *2*(4), 197–211.

[6] Elma, O., Cali, U., & Kuzlu, M. (2022). An overview of bidirectional electric vehicles charging system as a Vehicle to Anything (V2X) under Cyber–Physical Power System (CPPS). *Energy Reports*, *8*, 25–32.

[7] Gawali, P. P., Mahalle, P. N., & Sule, B. (2024). Integration of Cyber-Physical Systems in Medicine: A Comprehensive Study. *Recent Trends in Artificial Intelligence & It's Applications*, *3*(1), 29–36.

[8] Rahman, Z., Khalil, I., Yi, X., & Atiquzzaman, M. (2021). Blockchain-based security framework for a critical industry 4.0 cyber-physical system. *IEEE Communications Magazine*, *59*(5), 128–134.

[9] Wang, Z., Xie, W., Wang, B., Tao, J., & Wang, E. (2021). A survey on recent advanced research of CPS security. *Applied Sciences*, *11*(9), 3751.

[10] Khalid, F., Rehman, S., & Shafique, M. (2020). Overview of security for smart cyber-physical systems. *Security of Cyber-Physical Systems: Vulnerability and Impact*, 5–24.

[11] Bengler, K., Damm, W., Luedtke, A., Jochem, R., Austel, B., Biebl, B., ... & Veith, E. (2024). A References Architecture for Human Cyber Physical Systems, Part II: Fundamental Design Principles for Human-CPS Interaction. *ACM Transactions on Cyber-Physical Systems*, *8*(1), 1–27.

[12] Majeed, A., Khan, S., & Hwang, S. O. (2022). A comprehensive analysis of privacy-preserving solutions developed for online social networks. *Electronics*, *11*(13), 1931.

[13] Mostafa, A. M., Ezz, M., Elbashir, M. K., Alruily, M., Hamouda, E., Alsarhani, M., & Said, W. (2023). Strengthening cloud security: an innovative multi-factor multi-layer authentication framework for cloud user authentication. *Applied Sciences*, *13*(19), 10871.

[14] Chen, C. P., & Zhang, C. Y. (2014). Data-intensive applications, challenges, techniques and technologies: A survey on Big Data. *Information sciences*, *275*, 314–347.

[15] Maleh, Y., Lakkineni, S., Tawalbeh, L. A., & AbdEl-Latif, A. A. (2022). Blockchain for cyber-physical systems: Challenges and applications. *Advances in blockchain technology for cyber physical systems*, 11–59.

[16] Alvarez-Alvarado, M. S., Apolo-Tinoco, C., Ramirez-Prado, M. J., Alban-Chacón, F. E., Pico, N., Aviles-Cedeno, J., ... & Rengifo, J. (2024). Cyber-physical power systems: A comprehensive review about technologies drivers, standards, and future perspectives. *Computers and Electrical Engineering*, *116*, 109149.

[17] dos Santos, B. J., Leão, T. F., Silva, M. B., da Silva, E. D., & Bock, E. G. P. (2024). Embedded Cyber-physical System for Physiological Control of Ventricular Assist Devices. *Journal of Electronics and Electrical Engineering*, 148–165.

[18] Serôdio, C., Mestre, P., Cabral, J., Gomes, M., & Branco, F. (2024). Software and Architecture Orchestration for Process Control in Industry 4.0 Enabled by Cyber-Physical Systems Technologies. *Applied Sciences*, *14*(5), 2160.

[19] Noor, M. M., Selamat, A., Husain, N. A., & Krejcar, O. (2024). Security and Safety in Cyber-Physical System (CPS): An Inclusive Threat Model.

Journal of Advanced Research in Applied Sciences and Engineering Technology, *40*(2), 176–202.

[20] Etezadi, H., & Eshkabilov, S. (2024). A Comprehensive Overview of Control Algorithms, Sensors, Actuators, and Communication Tools of Autonomous All-Terrain Vehicles in Agriculture. *Agriculture*, *14*(2), 163.

[21] Salam, A. (2024). IoT in Cyber-Physical Systems. In *Internet of Things for Sustainable Community Development: Wireless Communications, Sensing, and Systems* (pp. 349–364). Cham: Springer International Publishing.

[22] Duo, W., Zhou, M., & Abusorrah, A. (2022). A survey of cyber attacks on cyber physical systems: Recent advances and challenges. *IEEE/CAA Journal of Automatica Sinica*, *9*(5), 784–800.

[23] Northern, B., Burks, T., Hatcher, M., Rogers, M., & Ulybyshev, D. (2021). Vercasm-cps: Vulnerability analysis and cyber risk assessment for cyber-physical systems. *Information*, *12*(10), 408.

[24] Singh, C. (2024). Security Issues in Cyber-physical System. In *Emerging Trends for Securing Cyber Physical Systems and the Internet of Things* (pp. 41–57). CRC Press.

[25] Bradbury, M., Taylor, P., Atmaca, U. I., Maple, C., & Griffiths, N. (2020). Privacy challenges with protecting live vehicular location context. *IEEE Access*, *8*, 207465–207484.

[26] Pundir, A., Singh, S., Kumar, M., Bafila, A., & Saxena, G. J. (2022). Cyber-physical systems enabled transport networks in smart cities: Challenges and enabling technologies of the new mobility era. *IEEE Access*, *10*, 16350–16364.

[27] Aslan, Ö., Aktuğ, S. S., Ozkan-Okay, M., Yilmaz, A. A., & Akin, E. (2023). A comprehensive review of cyber security vulnerabilities, threats, attacks, and solutions. *Electronics*, *12*(6), 1333.

[28] Kayan, H., Nunes, M., Rana, O., Burnap, P., & Perera, C. (2022). Cybersecurity of industrial cyber-physical systems: A review. *ACM Computing Surveys (CSUR)*, *54*(11s), 1–35.

[29] Miller, T., Staves, A., Maesschalck, S., Sturdee, M., & Green, B. (2021). Looking back to look forward: Lessons learnt from cyber-attacks on industrial control systems. *International Journal of Critical Infrastructure Protection*, *35*, 100464.

[30] Awotunde, J. B., Oguns, Y. J., Amuda, K. A., Nigar, N., Adeleke, T. A., Olagunju, K. M., & Ajagbe, S. A. (2023). Cyber-physical systems security: analysis, opportunities, challenges, and future prospects. *Blockchain for Cybersecurity in Cyber-Physical Systems*, 21–46.

[31] Sharma, C. (2023). Security and Privacy Aspects of Cyber Physical Systems. In *Cyber Physical Systems* (pp. 53–66). Chapman and Hall/CRC.

[32] Rao, S. M., & Jain, A. (2024). Advances in Malware Analysis and Detection in Cloud Computing Environments: A Review. *International Journal of Safety & Security Engineering*, *14*(1)

[33] Malik, M. I., Ibrahim, A., Hannay, P., & Sikos, L. F. (2023). Developing resilient cyber-physical systems: a review of state-of-the-art malware detection approaches, gaps, and future directions. *Computers*, *12*(4), 79

[34] Amin, M., El-Sousy, F. F., Aziz, G. A. A., Gaber, K., & Mohammed, O. A. (2021). CPS attacks mitigation approaches on power electronic systems with security challenges for smart grid applications: A review. *Ieee Access*, *9*, 38571–38601.

[35] Singh, J., & Jyoti, N. (2022). A Comprehensive Review: Detection and Mitigation Solutions of DDoS Attacks in CPS. *Security and Resilience of Cyber Physical Systems*, 61–80.

[36] Vähäkainu, P., Lehto, M., & Kariluoto, A. (2022). Cyberattacks Against Critical Infrastructure Facilities and Corresponding Countermeasures. In *Cyber Security: Critical Infrastructure Protection* (pp. 255–292). Cham: Springer International Publishing.

[37] Wlazlo, P., Sahu, A., Mao, Z., Huang, H., Goulart, A., Davis, K., & Zonouz, S. (2021). Man-in-the-middle attacks and defence in a power system cyber-physical testbed. *IET Cyber-Physical Systems: Theory & Applications*, *6*(3), 164–177.

[38] Cortés, J. E. R. (2022). Analysis and design of security mechanisms in the context of Advanced Persistent Threats against critical infrastructures. *Unpublished Ph. D. thesis, University of Malaga, Spain.*

[39] Sobb, T., Turnbull, B., & Moustafa, N. (2020). Supply chain 4.0: A survey of cyber security challenges, solutions and future directions. *Electronics*, *9*(11), 1864.

[40] Sheikh, Z. A., Singh, Y., Singh, P. K., & Ghafoor, K. Z. (2022). Intelligent and secure framework for critical infrastructure (CPS): Current trends, challenges, and future scope. *Computer Communications*, *193*, 302–331.

[41] Siddiqi, M. A., Pak, W., & Siddiqi, M. A. (2022). A study on the psychology of social engineering-based cyberattacks and existing countermeasures. *Applied Sciences*, *12*(12), 6042.

[42] Keshk, M., Turnbull, B., Sitnikova, E., Vatsalan, D., & Moustafa, N. (2021). Privacy-preserving schemes for safeguarding heterogeneous data sources in cyber-physical systems. *IEEE Access*, *9*, 55077–55097.

[43] Ali, A., Al-Rimy, B. A. S., Almazroi, A. A., Alsubaei, F. S., Almazroi, A. A., & Saeed, F. (2023). Securing secrets in cyber-physical systems: A cutting-edge privacy approach with consortium blockchain. *Sensors*, *23*(16), 7162.

[44] Telo, J. (2021). Privacy and cybersecurity concerns in Smart governance systems in developing countries. *Tensorgate Journal of Sustainable Technology and Infrastructure for Developing Countries*, *4*(1), 1–13.

[45] Colabianchi, S., Costantino, F., Di Gravio, G., Nonino, F., & Patriarca, R. (2021). Discussing resilience in the context of cyber physical systems. *Computers & Industrial Engineering*, *160*, 107534.

[46] Mullet, V., Sondi, P., & Ramat, E. (2021). A review of cybersecurity guidelines for manufacturing factories in industry 4.0. *IEEE Access*, *9*, 23235–23263.

[47] Bhutta, M. N. M., Khwaja, A. A., Nadeem, A., Ahmad, H. F., Khan, M. K., Hanif, M. A., Alshamari M.& Cao, Y. (2021). A survey on blockchain technology: Evolution, architecture and security. *IEEE Access*, *9*, 61048–61073.

[48] Ramasamy, L. K., KP, F. K., Imoize, A. L., Ogbebor, J. O., Kadry, S., & Rho, S. (2021). Blockchain-based wireless sensor networks for malicious node detection: A survey. *IEEE Access*, *9*, 128765–128785.

[49] Komalavalli, C., Saxena, D., & Laroiya, C. (2020). Overview of blockchain technology concepts. In *Handbook of research on blockchain technology* (pp. 349–371). Academic Press.

[50] Jena, A. K., & Dash, S. P. (2021). Blockchain technology: introduction, applications, challenges. In *Blockchain Technology: Applications and Challenges*. Cham: Springer International Publishing. (pp. 1–11).

[51] Deng, Q. (2020, March). Application analysis on blockchain technology in cross-border payment. In *5th International Conference on Financial Innovation and Economic Development (ICFIED 2020)* (pp. 287–295). Atlantis Press.

[52] Kshetri, N. (2021). Blockchain and sustainable supply chain management in developing countries. *International Journal of Information Management*, *60*, 102376.

[53] Zaabar, B., Cheikhrouhou, O., Jamil, F., Ammi, M., & Abid, M. (2021). HealthBlock: A secure blockchain-based healthcare data management system. *Computer Networks*, *200*, 108500.

[54] Gupta, A., Gupta, R., & Choudhary, S. (2024). Blockchain Technology for Sustainable Investment: A Comprehensive Review and Future Prospects. *Harnessing Blockchain-Digital Twin Fusion for Sustainable Investments*, 329–362.

[55] De Novi, G., Sofia, N., Vasiliu-Feltes, I., Zang, C. Y., & Ricotta, F. (2023). Blockchain Technology Predictions 2024: Transformations in Healthcare, Patient Identity, and Public Health. *Blockchain in Healthcare Today*, *6*.

[56] An, M., Fan, Q., Yu, H., An, B., Wu, N., Zhao, H., ... & Zhao, B. (2023). Blockchain technology research and application: A literature review and future trends. *Journal of Data Science and Intelligent Systems*.

[57] Zhu, J., Khan, A., & Akcora, C. G. (2024). Data depth and core-based trend detection on blockchain transaction networks. *Frontiers in Blockchain*, *7*, 1342956.

[58] Lashkari, B., & Musilek, P. (2021). A comprehensive review of blockchain consensus mechanisms. *IEEE Access*, *9*, 43620–43652.

[59] Onifade, M., Adebisi, J. A., & Zvarivadza, T. (2024). Recent advances in blockchain technology: Prospects, applications, and constraints in the minerals industry. *International Journal of Mining, Reclamation and Environment*, 1–37.

[60] Madir, J. (2020). Smart Contracts-Self-Executing Contracts of the Future? *Int'l. In-House Counsel J.*, *13*, 1.

[61] Khan, S. N., Loukil, F., Ghedira-Guegan, C., Benkhelifa, E., & Bani-Hani, A. (2021). Blockchain smart contracts: Applications, challenges, and future trends. *Peer-to-peer Networking and Applications*, *14*, 2901–2925.

[62] Taherdoost, H. (2023). Smart contracts in blockchain technology: A critical review. *Information*, *14*(2), 117.

[63] Kim, J. W. (2020). Blockchain technology and its applications: Case studies. *Journal of System and Management Sciences*, *10*(1), 83–93.

[64] Ali, A., Joseph, N., & Nadaf, T. A. (2023b). Blockchain Segmentation: An Industrial Solution for Large Scale Data. In *International Conference on Soft Computing and its Engineering Applications* (pp. 180–192). Cham: Springer Nature Switzerland.

[65] Zhao, W., Jiang, C., Gao, H., Yang, S., & Luo, X. (2020). Blockchain-enabled cyber–physical systems: A review. *IEEE Internet of Things Journal*, *8*(6), 4023–4034.

[66] Dedeoglu, V., Jurdak, R., Putra, G. D., Dorri, A., & Kanhere, S. S. (2019). A trust architecture for blockchain in IoT. In *Proceedings of the 16th EAI international conference on mobile and ubiquitous systems: computing, networking and services* (pp. 190–199).

[67] Fahim, S., Rahman, S. K., & Mahmood, S. (2023). Blockchain: A comparative study of consensus algorithms PoW, PoS, PoA, PoV. *Int. J. Math. Sci. Comput*, *3*, 46–57.

[68] Sguanci, C., Spatafora, R., & Vergani, A. M. (2021). Layer 2 blockchain scaling: A survey. *arXiv preprint arXiv:2107.10881.*

[69] Hashim, F., Shuaib, K., & Zaki, N. (2022). Sharding for scalable blockchain networks. *SN Computer Science*, *4*(1), 2.

[70] Belchior, R., Vasconcelos, A., Guerreiro, S., & Correia, M. (2021). A survey on blockchain interoperability: Past, present, and future trends. *Acm Computing Surveys (CSUR)*, *54*(8), 1–41.

[71] Jahid, A., Alsharif, M. H., & Hall, T. J. (2023). The convergence of Blockchain, IoT and 6G: potential, opportunities, challenges and research roadmap. *Journal of Network and Computer Applications*, *217*, 103677.

[72] Puneeth, R. P., & Parthasarathy, G. (2023). Seamless Data Exchange: Advancing Healthcare with Cross-Chain Interoperability in Blockchain for Electronic Health Records. *International Journal of Advanced Computer Science and Applications*, *14*(10).

[73] Singh, S., Hosen, A. S., & Yoon, B. (2021). Blockchain security attacks, challenges, and solutions for the future distributed iot network. *Ieee Access*, *9*, 13938–13959.

[74] Dong, S., Abbas, K., Li, M., & Kamruzzaman, J. (2023). Blockchain technology and application: an overview. *PeerJ Computer Science*, *9*, e1705.

[75] Awotunde, J. B., Farhaoui, Y., Imoize, A. L., Folorunso, S. O., & Adeniyi, A. E. (2023, November). An Enhanced Internet of Medical Things Data Communication Based on Blockchain and Cryptography for Smart Healthcare Applications. In *The International Conference on Artificial Intelligence and Smart Environment* (pp. 305–313). Cham: Springer Nature Switzerland.

[76] Khalid, M. I., Ahmed, M., & Kim, J. (2023). Enhancing data protection in dynamic consent management systems: formalizing privacy and security definitions with differential privacy, decentralization, and Zero-Knowledge proofs. *Sensors*, *23*(17), 7604.

[77] Hussein, Z., Salama, M. A., & El-Rahman, S. A. (2023). Evolution of blockchain consensus algorithms: a review on the latest milestones of blockchain consensus algorithms. *Cybersecurity*, *6*(1), 30.

[78] Falola, P. B., Awotunde, J. B., Adeniyi, A. E., Jimoh, R. G., Adebayo, A. O., Olatunji, E. K., & Imoize, A. L. (2024). Artificial intelligence and blockchain enabling data access authorization in telehealth systems. *Artificial Intelligence and Blockchain Technology in Modern Telehealth Systems*, 119.

[79] Gadekallu, T. R., Pham, Q. V., Nguyen, D. C., Maddikunta, P. K. R., Deepa, N., Prabadevi, B., ... & Hwang, W. J. (2021). Blockchain for edge

of things: Applications, opportunities, and challenges. *IEEE Internet of Things Journal*, *9*(2), 964–988.

[80] Xue, H., Chen, D., Zhang, N., Dai, H. N., & Yu, K. (2023). Integration of blockchain and edge computing in internet of things: A survey. *Future Generation Computer Systems*, *144*, 307–326.

[81] Cai, W., Jiang, W., Xie, K., Zhu, Y., Liu, Y., & Shen, T. (2020). Dynamic reputation–based consensus mechanism: Real-time transactions for energy blockchain. International Journal of Distributed Sensor Networks, 16(3), 1550147720907335.

[82] Yusoff, M. N. B., & Abd Ali, S. M. (2024). Bitcoin Layer Two Scaling Solutions: Lightening Payment Channels Network Comprehensive Review, Mechanisms, Challenges, Open Issues and Future Research Directions. *Iraqi Journal For Computer Science and Mathematics*, *5*(1), 25–59.

[83] Venkatesan, K., & Rahayu, S. B. (2024). Blockchain security enhancement: an approach towards hybrid consensus algorithms and machine learning techniques. *Scientific Reports*, *14*(1), 1149.

[84] Dhulavvagol, P. M., Totad, S. G., & Pratheek, P. (2023). Enhancing Transaction Scalability of Blockchain Network Using Sharding Technique. In *International Conference on Soft Computing for Security Applications* (pp. 253–269). Singapore: Springer Nature Singapore.

[85] Rebello, G. A. F., Camilo, G. F., de Souza, L. A. C., Potop-Butucaru, M., de Amorim, M. D., Campista, M. E. M., & Costa, L. H. M. (2024). A survey on blockchain scalability: From hardware to layer-two protocols. *IEEE Communications Surveys & Tutorials*.

[86] Biswas, A., Mondal, K. K., & Guha Roy, D. (2023). A study of smart evolution on ai-based cyber-physical system using blockchain techniques. In *AI models for blockchain-based intelligent networks in IoT systems: Concepts, methodologies, tools, and applications* (pp. 327–346). Cham: Springer International Publishing.

[87] Nigam, S., & Karyakarte, M. S. (2023). Edge Computing: A Paradigm Shift for Delay-Sensitive AI Application. In *AI, IoT, Big Data and Cloud Computing for Industry 4.0* (pp. 65–89). Cham: Springer International Publishing.

[88] Dedeoglu, V., Dorri, A., Jurdak, R., Michelin, R. A., Lunardi, R. C., Kanhere, S. S., & Zorzo, A. F. (2020). A journey in applying blockchain for cyberphysical systems. In *2020 International Conference on COMmunication Systems & NETworkS (COMSNETS)* (pp. 383–390). IEEE.

[89] Cherbal, S., Zier, A., Hebal, S., Louail, L., & Annane, B. (2024). Security in the internet of things: a review on approaches based on blockchain, machine learning, cryptography, and quantum computing. *The Journal of Supercomputing*, *80*(3), 3738–3816.

[90] Hosseini, S. M., Ferreira, J., & Bartolomeu, P. C. (2023). Blockchain-based decentralized identification in iot: An overview of existing frameworks and their limitations. *Electronics*, *12*(6), 1283.

17

Privacy-utility Trade-offs in IoT Networks: A Comparative Analysis of Differential Privacy Mechanisms for Sensor Data Aggregation

Oleksandr Kuznetsov[1], Oleksii Smirnov[2], Tatyana Kuznetsova[3], Aigul Shaikhanova[4] and Igor Svatowsky[3]

[1]Department of Theoretical and Applied Sciences, eCampus University, Italy
[2]Department of Cyber Security and Software, Central Ukrainian National Technical University, Ukraine
[3]Department of Information and Communication Systems Security, V. N. Karazin Kharkiv National University, Ukraine
[4]Department of Information Security, L.N. Gumilyov Eurasian National University, Republic of Kazakhstan

Email: oleksandr.kuznetsov@uniecampus.it; dr.SmirnovOA@gmail.com; kuznetsova.tatiana17@gmail.com; shaikhanova_ak@enu.kz; i.svatowsky@karazin.ua

Abstract

The rapid growth of Internet of Things (IoT) networks has heightened concerns about data privacy in sensor-based systems. This chapter offers a thorough empirical evaluation of differential privacy mechanisms for IoT data aggregation, emphasizing the essential balance between preserving privacy and maintaining data utility. We analyze four privacy mechanisms – Laplace, Gaussian, Exponential, and Stochastic – across various sensor types and aggregation functions in a large-scale network consisting of 1000 nodes. Our experimental framework takes into account real-world sensor data characteristics, including temperature (18–28 °C), humidity (30%–70%), and

DOI: 10.1201/9788743801306-17

energy consumption (0–1000 W) measurements. Through rigorous statistical analysis, we demonstrate that the Stochastic mechanism delivers superior performance, achieving a mean relative error of 0.001304 for mean aggregation, and significantly outperforms traditional approaches. Our findings indicate that the effectiveness of these mechanisms is strongly linked to both data characteristics and aggregation functions, with wide-ranging measurements posing greater challenges for privacy preservation. We provide empirical evidence that effective privacy preservation in IoT networks necessitates a context-aware approach, taking into consideration the relationship between mechanism selection, data characteristics, and aggregation methods. These results lay the groundwork for implementing differential privacy in IoT systems while ensuring optimal trade-offs between utility and privacy.

17.1 Introduction

Internet of Things networking has brought about a complete revolution in the way data can be gathered and monitored across various environmental, industrial, and automation domains [1], [2]. Such networks consist of thousands of interconnected sensors generating huge streams of data for enabling complex analytics and decision-making [3]. However, such an unprecedented scale of data gathering is greatly risky to privacy, particularly with sensitive information derivable from aggregated sensor measurements [4], [5].

The imperative for privacy preservation in IoT networks has grown increasingly critical as these systems become more pervasive in sensitive applications, from healthcare monitoring to smart infrastructure [6], [7]. Traditional privacy approaches often fail to provide rigorous guarantees while maintaining data utility, particularly in the context of continuous data collection and real-time aggregation [5]. While differential privacy offers a promising theoretical framework [8], [9], its practical implementation in IoT contexts presents unique challenges that remain inadequately addressed in the current literature [4].

The complexity of privacy preservation in IoT networks stems from several factors [10], [11]: the heterogeneous nature of sensor data, the requirement for real-time processing, and the need to maintain utility for diverse aggregation operations. Previous studies have primarily focused on theoretical aspects or limited experimental evaluations, leaving a significant gap between theoretical guarantees and practical implementation requirements. Our work addresses this gap through a comprehensive empirical investigation of privacy mechanism performance across realistic IoT scenarios.

Among various frameworks that can help address these challenges, differential privacy has emerged as one of the most promising ones, providing mathematical guarantees on the protection of individual data points while ensuring the utility of aggregate statistics [9], [12]. While the theoretical aspects of differential privacy are well understood, its practical implementation in IoT networks poses unique challenges due to continuous data collection, resource constraints at sensor nodes, and diverse aggregation requirements.

17.1.1 Chapter contributions

This paper investigates the relative performance of different differential privacy mechanisms in IoT sensor networks, with particular emphasis on their effectiveness at balancing privacy guarantees and data utility. We explore four popular privacy mechanisms, including Laplace, Gaussian, Exponential, and Stochastic, under different sensor data types and aggregation functions. Our work offers several key contributions:

- First, we present a comprehensive experimental evaluation of privacy mechanisms in a realistic IoT setting, with respect to multiple sensor types, namely temperature, humidity, and energy consumption, as well as common aggregation functions-mean and sum.
- Second, we introduce a novel analytical framework for assessing the privacy-utility trade-offs across different mechanism parameters and data characteristics.
- Third, we provide empirical evidence to show that the Stochastic mechanism significantly outperforms existing mechanisms in utility with strong privacy guarantees.

It also shows significant divergences in mechanism performance within different scenarios. The mean aggregation performs the best with the lowest average relative error using the Stochastic mechanism at 0.001304, while traditional mechanisms like the Gaussian mechanism have considerably higher averages at 0.004802. Our analysis strengthens these findings and shows that both the type of sensor data and the type of intended aggregation function must be taken into careful consideration while choosing an appropriate privacy mechanism since performance characteristics change significantly along these two dimensions.

These findings have important implications for the design and implementation of privacy-preserving IoT systems. They provide practical guidance to system architects and developers in the selection of appropriate privacy mechanisms, considering specific application requirements and data characteristics.

17.1.2 Chapter organization

The rest of this chapter is organized as follows. Section 17.2 provides the background and reviews related work about differential privacy and IoT privacy protection. Section 17.3 describes our system model and problem formulation. Sections 17.4 and 17.5 describe our experimental methodology and implementation framework. Section 17.6 presents and analyzes our experimental results. Finally, Sections 17.7 and 17.8 conclude this chapter and discuss future research directions.

We undertake a broad analysis of IoT network mechanisms that apply privacy to bring differential privacy closer to practical deployment in real systems while inspiring future research on this crucial topic.

17.2 Background and Related Work

17.2.1 Differential privacy in IoT networks

Differential privacy, as initially defined by Dwork [8], has come to be one of the milestones in the privacy-preserving analysis of data. While applied to IoT networks, differential privacy provides a formal framework of protection for individual sensor measurements and enables meaningful statistical data analysis. A basic guarantee of differential privacy ensures that the presence or absence of any particular sensor reading has a quantifiably limited effect on the results of analysis [13].

The now widely popular concept of differential privacy gained the serious, sound mathematical formulation by Dwork and Roth through an approach that defined this concept in terms of neighboring datasets and probabilistic upper bounds on query answers [9], [14]:

- for any two datasets X and X' that differ in no more than one record, a mechanism M is said to provide (ϵ,δ) -differential privacy if for any set S of possible output

$$P[M(X) \in S] \leq e^{\epsilon} P[M(X') \in S] + \delta. \tag{17.1}$$

This definition has been particularly relevant for IoT networks, whereby the continuous collection and aggregation of data in such networks present unique challenges to privacy [15], [16].

17.2.2 Privacy-preserving mechanisms

In practice, several mechanisms for differential privacy have been designed targeting these various settings. The Laplace mechanism introduced in the paper by Dwork et al. [14] adds noise, drawn from a Laplace distribution calibrated on the sensitivity of the query function, whereas the Gaussian mechanism [13] develops a different paradigm, most applicable for (,) -differential privacy.

Wang and Guan [17] recently considered adaptive differential privacy mechanisms, which adaptively adjust the privacy parameters in accordance with data characteristics and utility requirements. Their work points out an important direction toward context-aware privacy protection in a federated learning environment.

17.2.3 IoT data aggregation and privacy

The challenge of maintaining privacy in IoT data aggregation has been the subject of considerable attention. Along this line, McSherry and Talwar [18] proposed a relationship of differential privacy with mechanism design and shed light on how the guarantees of privacy are maintained through the process of data aggregations.

Recently, Liu et al. [16] have presented personalized differential privacy schemes for federated learning that can achieve different levels of protection with utility. Their work is especially relevant to IoT networks where different sensors may have different privacy requirements.

17.2.4 Privacy-utility trade-offs

A fundamental challenge in implementing differential privacy is how to manage the trade-off between privacy and utility. Dwork considered this trade-off in several settings, illustrating how the privacy budget $\in$ directly impacts the accuracy of query results [9].

Very recent work of Zhao et al. [19] introduced some new ways of optimally managing this trade-off by using techniques of alternative minimization. It is expected to provide profound insights into the balancing between the requirements of privacy and the need for the effective analysis of data in IoT networks.

17.2.5 Current challenges and future directions

Applications of differential privacy in IoT networks face a number of challenges in practical usage. Huang et al. [20] identified issues about privacy budget auditing and verification with complex network settings. Besides, Jiao et al. [21] have presented some visual analysis approaches for formulating privacy schemes, which can help to fix some practical challenges of implementing differential privacy in real-world scenarios.

Recent works, such as that by Garg and Torra [22], indeed consider hybrid approaches that combine different techniques for privacy preservation with the aim of achieving better utility while still maintaining strong privacy guarantees.

17.2.6 Enhanced mechanisms for the protection of privacy

From then on, the mechanisms for privacy protection evolved and began to take more sophisticated approaches toward IoT environments. Dwork and Roth [23], [24] formalized a number of basic mechanisms beyond simple addition of Laplace noise, together with composition theorems, that allowed analysis of the privacy guarantees under a set of multiple queries

$$\epsilon_{\text{total}} = \sum_{i=1}^{k} \epsilon_{\text{i}}. \tag{17.2}$$

This composition property is particularly crucial in IoT networks where several aggregation operations happen continuously.

17.2.7 Real-time data processing and privacy

Indeed, it does introduce new challenges for IoT to be covered for real-time data streams with differential privacy as was originally introduced by Dwork [14], and very recently, new mechanisms were introduced by Wang et al. [15] dealing with continuous data releases with the guarantee of privacy using adaptive mechanisms

$$M_{\text{t}}(X) = f(X) + Noise\left(\frac{\Delta f}{\epsilon_{\text{t}}}\right), \tag{17.3}$$

where $\in_{\text{t}}$ denotes some time-varying privacy budget that is adapted to a context or requirements at hand.

17.2.8 Privacy in distributed systems

IoT networks inherently operate in distributed environments, making the preservation of privacy particularly difficult. Wu et al. [12] address the challenge by proposing dynamic differential privacy approaches with consideration to network topology and data distribution patterns. Their work comes up with a framework that will balance both local and global privacy requirements

$$L(\theta) = \sum_{i=1}^{n} \alpha_i L_i(\theta) + \lambda R(\theta), \tag{17.4}$$

where $L_i(\theta)$ are local loss functions and $R(\theta)$ is a regularization term that includes privacy constraints.

17.2.9 Upcoming trends and future directions

Recent advances in differential privacy for IoT systems point to some encouraging directions:

1. Adaptive privacy mechanisms: Liu et al. [16] have demonstrated the feasibility of context-aware privacy protection where privacy parameters vary with data sensitivity and application requirements.
2. Hybrid approaches: actually, works from Garg and Torra [22] review how differential privacy can be combined with other techniques in the literature on privacy in order to increase its utility while keeping strong guarantees about privacy.
3. Optimization frameworks: Zhao et al. [19] have developed new optimization approaches for privacy-utility trade-offs

$$\min_{,} \mathbb{E}_{x,y}[L(h_{,}(x), y)] + \lambda\Phi(\theta), \tag{17.5}$$

where $\Phi(\theta)$ represents privacy constraints incorporated into the optimization objective.

17.2.10 Implementation metrics and evaluation

Privacy-preserving mechanisms should be assessed while considering several metrics when performing privacy assessments in IoT contexts. Indeed, according to the most recent studies, such as the work of Jiao et al. [21], this would provide well-established frameworks for assessing the effectiveness of both privacy guarantees and utility preservation:

Utility of M is given by

$$\text{Utility}(M) = \mathbb{E}[| M(X) - f(X) |]. \tag{17.6}$$

It provides a measure to quantify the amount of accuracy loss that protection mechanisms may introduce for privacy.

17.2.11 Practical considerations

Following are some of the practical challenges while implementing differential privacy in real-world IoT systems:

1. Resource constraints: IoT devices are typically limited by small computational resources; hence, this restricts the complexity of the privacy mechanisms that can be deployed.
2. Overhead due to communication: privacy-preserving protocols tend to introduce much more communication requirements, which could seriously impair network efficiency.
3. Scalability: privacy mechanisms should scale well with network size and data volume, as pointed out by Huang et al. [20].

These challenges have brought about constant research in efficient implementation strategies and optimized algorithms that would guarantee privacy in resource-constrained environments.

This overview on differential privacy in IoT networks will reveal both the huge progress that has been achieved in the last years and what is still to be identified as open challenges, a fact that has driven study in this field. Finally, the integration of these various approaches and considerations will pave the way for practicality in the development of preservation techniques in IoT systems that are necessary to meet the ever-present demands of real-world applications.

17.3 System Model and Problem Formulation

In this section, we present a formal framework for evaluating differential privacy mechanisms in IoT networks. Our model captures the essential characteristics of sensor networks while providing a rigorous mathematical foundation for privacy analysis. We first describe the network architecture and data collection process, then formalize the privacy requirements and optimization objectives that guide our experimental evaluation.

17.3.1 Network model

Consider a typical IoT sensing network consisting of N sensor nodes, distributed over a large area under monitoring. Each node $i \in 1,\ldots, N$ periodically collects measurements from multiple sensor types, including temperature, humidity, and energy consumption. The network operates over a time horizon T, with measurements collected at discrete time intervals $t \in 1,\ldots, T$.

The measurement from the sensor node i for sensor type j at time t is denoted as $x_{ij}(t)$. Every sensor type operates within its own measurement space, a valid range

$$x_{i,j}(t) \in [L_j, U_j], \tag{17.7}$$

where, L_j and U_j denote, for each sensor type j, lower and upper bounds, respectively. In our configuration of the experiment, these bounds take values as:

- Temperature: $x_{i,1}(t) \in [18°C, 28°C]$;
- Rel. humidity: $x_{i,2}(t) \in [30\%, 70\%]$;
- Energy consumption: $x_{i,3}(t) \in [0W, 1000W]$.

The complete state of the network at time t may be represented by the matrix $X(t) \in \mathbb{R}^{N \times J}$, where J is the number of sensor types

$$X(t) = x_{i,j}(t) \mid i \in 1,.,N, j \in 1,.,J. \tag{17.8}$$

17.3.2 Data collection and aggregation

In practice, this network periodically aggregates the measurements that were collected, using the function f: for a given sensor type J and a time window t, the aggregation function computes

$$y_j(t) = f(x_{i,j}(t) \mid i \in 1,.,N). \tag{17.9}$$

In particular, we consider two basic aggregation functions of primary importance in IoT applications:

1. Mean aggregation

$$f_{\text{mean}}(X) = \frac{1}{N}\sum_{i=1}^{N} x_i. \tag{17.10}$$

This function provides average measurements across the network, which is important to monitor typical conditions and identify trends.

2. Summing

$$f_{\text{sum}}(X) = \sum_{i=1}^{N} x_i. \tag{17.11}$$

Sum aggregation is particularly important for cumulative measurements, such as total energy consumption.

The temporal aspect of data collection introduces an added complexity due to the fact that measurements can be temporally correlated

$$\mathrm{Corr}(x_{\mathrm{i,j}}(t), x_{\mathrm{i,j}}(t+\tau)) \neq 0, \tag{17.12}$$

where τ represents a time lag between measurements.

17.3.3 Privacy requirements

The system must provide (ϵ,δ)-differential privacy, meaning it should be impossible to determine with significant probability from the aggregation result whether any sensor reading is in or out. Formally, for any two neighboring datasets, X and X', that differ by at most one element and for any set of possible outcomes S

$$P[M(X) \in S] \leq e^{\epsilon} P[M(X') \in S] + \delta, \tag{17.13}$$

where M is the privacy mechanism and $\epsilon > 0$ is the privacy budget that controls the privacy-utility trade-off. The parameter δ denotes the probability of privacy failure, with $\delta \in (0,1)$.

The privacy guarantee should hold for any possible query $q \in Q$ where Q is a set of allowable queries on the dataset. In our context

$$Q = f_{\mathrm{mean}}, f_{\mathrm{sum}} \times 1,\ldots,J. \tag{17.14}$$

17.3.4 Sensitivity analysis

The sensitivity of our aggregation functions determines the scale of noise required for privacy preservation. For an aggregation function f, the global sensitivity is defined as

$$\Delta f = \max_{\mathrm{X,X'}} |f(X) - f(X')|. \tag{17.15}$$

For our specific aggregation functions, we obtain the following sensitivities:

1. Aggregate via mean

$$\Delta f_{\mathrm{mean,j}} = \frac{U_{\mathrm{j}} - L_{\mathrm{j}}}{N}. \tag{17.16}$$

2. Sum aggregation

$$\Delta f_{\mathrm{sum,j}} = U_{\mathrm{j}} - L_{\mathrm{j}}. \tag{17.17}$$

The sensitivity bounds directly affect the magnitude of the noise to be added for privacy preservation

$$M(X) = f(X) + \text{Noise}(\Delta f, \epsilon, \delta). \tag{17.18}$$

17.3.5 Problem formulation

Given a system model with privacy requirements, we present a few different mechanisms (*M*) that will suit the definition of (ϵ,δ)-differential privacy while ensuring minimum errors in aggregated results. Formally, given a certain mechanism *M*, we define performance by the relative error defined below

$$E(M,f,j) = \mathbb{E}\left[\frac{|M(f(X_j)) - f(X_j)|}{|f(X_j)|}\right]. \tag{17.19}$$

The optimization problem can be cast as

$$\min_{M} \max_{f,j} E(M,f,j), \tag{17.20}$$

subject to:

1. (ϵ,δ)-differential privacy constraints: $P[M(X) \in S] \leq e^{\epsilon} P[M(X') \in S] + \delta, \forall X, X', S$;
2. Privacy budget constraints: $\epsilon \in [0.1, 10]$;
3. Privacy failure probability constraints: $\delta \in 0.001, 0.01, 0.1$;
4. Domain constraints: $x_{i,j}(t) \in [L_j, U_j], \forall i, j, t$.

This formulation captures the fundamental challenge of finding privacy mechanisms that provide robust performance across different aggregation functions and sensor types while maintaining strong privacy guarantees. The multiobjective nature of the problem, combining privacy preservation with utility maximization, makes it particularly challenging in the context of IoT networks where data characteristics and aggregation requirements can vary significantly.

17.4 Experimental Methodology

This section presents our comprehensive approach to evaluating differential privacy mechanisms in IoT networks through systematic experimentation.

We detail our experimental setup, implementation choices, and evaluation framework, designed to provide reproducible and statistically significant results. Our methodology encompasses both the technical aspects of privacy mechanism implementation and the practical considerations of IoT deployment scenarios.

17.4.1 Network model and data generation

The experiment emulates a large-scale IoT network with 1000 sensor nodes spread over the monitoring area. Each node samples data at fixed intervals of 300 seconds over a period of 24 hours, collecting 288 samples per node. This sampling frequency is chosen because it provides a good trade-off between the granularity of data collection and computational feasibility while allowing for sufficient temporal resolution for meaningful analysis.

For each sensor node, we generate synthetic data for three kinds of different measurements:

1. Temperature: between 18 and 28 °C, to model indoor environmental monitoring.
2. The relative humidity values between 30% and 70% are representative of typical indoor conditions.
3. Energy consumption measurements from 0 to 1000 W, simulating device power monitoring.

The data generation process is designed to incorporate both deterministic and stochastic components. The base signal for each sensor type is periodic and follows the model given by

$$s(t) = A + B\sin(2\pi t\ /\ T + \phi) + n(t), \qquad (17.21)$$

where A is the mean value, B is the amplitude of daily changes, T is 24-hour period, ϕ is a random phase shift, and additive noise $n(t)$ in a normal distribution $\mathcal{N}(0,\sigma^2)$ with a given $\sigma = 0.1$ modeling the measurement variations in real applications.

17.4.2 Privacy mechanisms

We consider four different differential privacy mechanisms that provide a different privacy guarantee and perturbation characteristics:

Laplace mechanism
The Laplace mechanism adds noise drawn from a Laplace distribution whose scale parameter is calibrated to the sensitivity Δf and privacy budget ϵ:

$$M(x) = f(x) + \text{Lap}(\Delta f \; / \; \epsilon), \tag{17.22}$$

where $f(x)$ is the query function and Δf is its sensitivity.

Gaussian mechanism
For (ϵ,δ)-differential privacy the Gaussian mechanism adds normally distributed noise with a standard deviation of

$$\sigma = \frac{\Delta f}{\epsilon}\sqrt{2\ln(1.25 \; / \; \delta)}. \tag{17.23}$$

Exponential mechanism
This mechanism samples from a probability distribution exponentially weighted by a utility function

$$P(r) \propto \exp\left(\frac{\epsilon u(x,r)}{2\Delta u}\right), \tag{17.24}$$

where Δu is the sensitivity of the utility function.

Stochastic rounding mechanism
This mechanism implements discrete noise through controlled randomized rounding

$$M(x) = f(x) + \text{round}(U[-s,s]), \tag{17.25}$$

where $s = \Delta f / \varepsilon$ and rounding probability is proportional to the fractional part.

17.4.3 Sensitivity analysis

The sensitivity calculation is central to the calibration of noise addition. For each aggregation function and data type, we calculate the global sensitivity as follows:

For mean aggregation

$$\Delta f_{\text{mean}} = \frac{R}{n}. \tag{17.26}$$

For sum aggregation

$$\Delta f_{\text{sum}} = R \times n, \tag{17.27}$$

where R is the range of possible values for each sensor type and n is the number of nodes.

17.4.4 Evaluation framework

Experimental evaluation studies the following parameter space:

- Privacy budget $\epsilon \in \{0.1, 0.5, 1.0, 2.0, 5.0, 10.0\}$;
- Relaxation parameter $\delta \in \{0.001, 0.01, 0.1\}$.

For each parameter combination, we evaluate four aggregation functions: mean, sum, maximum, and minimum. The performance assessment utilizes several metrics:

The relative error

$$E_{\text{r}} = \left| \frac{f(x) - M(x)}{f(x)} \right|. \tag{17.28}$$

The absolute error

$$E_{\text{a}} = \left| f(x) - M(x) \right|, \tag{17.29}$$

where $f(x)$ is the true query result and $M(x)$ is the private result.

The experimental procedure will systematically investigate all combinations of the following:

- Privacy mechanisms;
- Privacy parameters: (ϵ, δ);
- Aggregate functions;
- Sensor types.
- Time windows.

Each experiment is repeated several times with different random seeds for statistical significance. The results are analyzed in terms of both average performance and distribution characteristics to provide a comprehensive understanding of the privacy-utility trade-offs in different scenarios.

17.4.5 Statistical analysis

Analysis of the results makes use of both the parametric and nonparametric methods in order to come up with strong conclusions. We compute the 1000 times of bootstrapped resamplings to calculate our confidence intervals. In order for the test of whether this mechanism has significant differences concerning a certain paired sample, under this circumstance where multiple comparisons would be carried out, the Wilcoxon signed-rank test along with the Bonferroni method is used as we verify for significance.

It looks into average performance metrics but also analyzes the full distribution of errors regarding possible worst-case scenarios and outliers that may affect practical deployment. This allows substantial insight into the strengths and limitations that each privacy mechanism presents, within diverse operational contexts, in a very fine-grained way.

17.5 Implementation Framework

The implementation of privacy-preserving mechanisms in IoT networks requires careful consideration of both theoretical guarantees and practical constraints. In this section, we present our software framework for implementing and evaluating different privacy mechanisms. Our implementation emphasizes modularity, extensibility, and reproducibility while maintaining computational efficiency for large-scale experiments (https://colab.research.google.com/drive/1qevNI5j3GD3ga1_aD2NmkiiI9BTpgd5v).

17.5.1 Software architecture

The implementation follows a modular architecture with a clear separation of concerns, implemented in Python 3.10. Core components interact using well-defined interfaces, which enable modifications or extensions to each module independently from the rest. The core architecture is divided into four primary layers: configuration management, data generation, privacy mechanism implementation, and analysis.

The foundational configuration classes establish the experimental parameters:

```
python
class NetworkConfig:
    def __init__(self, network_size: int, sampling_interval: int,
        simulation_duration: int):
```

```
        """
        Args:
            network_size: Number of IoT nodes
            sampling_interval: Data collection frequency in seconds
            simulation_duration: Total simulation time in hours
        """
        self.network_size = network_size
        self.sampling_interval = sampling_interval
        self.simulation_duration = simulation_duration
```

This structured approach ensures that the parameters are kept the same across all experiments.

17.5.2 Data generation and management

The data generation module implements the theoretical model described in Section 17.3, where mathematical formulations are interpreted as computational procedures. The class DataManager generates and manages the synthetic sensor data:

```
Python
class DataManager:
    def __init__(self, network_config: NetworkConfig,
                 sensor_config: SensorConfig):
        self.network_config = network_config
        self.sensor_config = sensor_config
        self._initialize_data_structures()

    def generate_data(self) -> pd.DataFrame:
        timestamps = self._generate_timestamps()
        data = {}

    for device_id in range(self.network_config.network_size):
        for sensor_type in self.sensor_config.sensor_types:
            data.update(self._generate_sensor_readings(
                device_id, sensor_type, timestamps))

    return pd.DataFrame(data)
```

The implementation uses vectorized operations via NumPy arrays, which have much better computational efficiency especially if one needs to build massive synthetic data.

17.5.3 Implementation of the mechanism of privacy

The privacy mechanisms are implemented through an abstract base class that defines the common interface:

```
python
class NoiseGenerator(ABC):
    """"Abstract base class for privacy mechanisms""""

    def __init__(self, epsilon: float, delta: float = 0.0):
        self.epsilon = epsilon
        self.delta = delta

    @abstractmethod
    def generate_noise(self, sensitivity: float, size: int = 1) -> np.ndarray:
        """"Generate noise according to privacy mechanism""""
        pass
```

Each concrete mechanism implementation extends this base class, which guarantees the coherence of the behavior and interface:

```
Python
class LaplaceMechanism(NoiseGenerator):
    def generate_noise(self, sensitivity: float, size: int = 1) -> np.ndarray:
        scale = sensitivity / self.epsilon
        return np.random.laplace(0, scale, size)
```

It also has a careful treatment of numerical precision and stability, especially important in the Gaussian and Exponential mechanisms, where overflow or underflow may affect the results.

17.5.4 Experimental execution engine

The ExperimentRunner class orchestrates the running of experiments over the parameter space:

Python
```
class ExperimentRunner:
    def __init__(self):
        self.epsilons = [0.1, 0.5, 1.0, 2.0, 5.0, 10.0]
        self.deltas = [0.001, 0.01, 0.1]
        self.noise_types = [“laplace,” “gaussian,” “exponential,” “stochastic”]
        self.aggregation_methods = [“mean,” “sum,” “max,” “min”]
        self.sensor_types = [“temperature,” “humidity,” “energy”]

        self._initialize_configurations()
```

The execution engine provides advanced error handling and logging to ensure experimental validity:

Python
Copy
```
    def run_experiments(self) -> pd.DataFrame:
        data = self.data_manager.generate_data()
        results = []

        total_experiments = self._calculate_total_experiments()

        for params in self._parameter_combinations():
            try:
                result = self._run_single_experiment(params, data)
                if result:
                    results.append(result)
            except Exception as e:
                self._log_experiment_error(params, e)
                continue

    return pd.DataFrame(results)
```

17.5.5 Framework for the analysis and visualization

The analytical framework offers extensive tools to consider in analyzing experimental results:

Python
```
class Analyzer:
```

```
def __init__(self, results: pd.DataFrame):
    self.results = results
    self._initialize_plotting_style()

def plot_privacy_utility_tradeoff(self, delta: float = None):
    data = self._filter_results(delta)
    grouped_data = self._compute_statistics(data)

    self._create_tradeoff_plot(grouped_data)
```

Visualization components use Matplotlib and Seaborn to create publication-quality figures, with careful attention to color schemes, font sizes, and layout for maximum readability.

17.5.6 Error analysis and statistical processing

The framework implements robust error analysis and statistical processing:

```
Python
def compute_metrics(self, true_values: np.ndarray,
                    noisy_values: np.ndarray) -> Dict:
    """Compute comprehensive error metrics"""
    relative_error = np.abs(true_values - noisy_values) / np.abs(true_values)
    absolute_error = np.abs(true_values - noisy_values)

    return {
        "mean_relative_error": float(np.mean(relative_error)),
        "std_relative_error": float(np.std(relative_error)),
        "median_relative_error": float(np.median(relative_error)),
        "max_relative_error": float(np.max(relative_error)),
        "mean_absolute_error": float(np.mean(absolute_error))
    }
```

17.5.7 Extensibility to framework

The implementation is designed to support easy extension through:

1. Abstract base classes to implement new privacy mechanisms
2. Configurable data generation models

3. Pluggable analysis components
4. Customizable visualization templates

This modular design will enable other future researchers to build upon our work by adding new mechanisms or modifying some components in the framework while retaining the structural integrity and experimental rigor of the framework.

17.6 Results and Analysis

This section presents a detailed analysis of our experimental results, examining the performance of different privacy mechanisms across various scenarios and configurations. We provide both quantitative metrics and qualitative insights into the behavior of privacy mechanisms under different conditions. Our analysis focuses on three key aspects: statistical performance evaluation, privacy-utility trade-off analysis, and practical implications for IoT deployments.

17.6.1 Statistical performance analysis

This section presents a comprehensive analysis of our experimental results comparing four differential privacy mechanisms: Laplace, Gaussian, Exponential, and Stochastic. The analysis includes various aggregation functions and types of sensor data in the IoT network environment.

Table 17.1 summarizes the error rates using different privacy mechanisms and aggregation functions. The results indicate a huge variation in mechanism performance even for simple statistical operations.

Among the two aggregation functions, Stochastic is doing the best: 0.001304 for mean aggregation and 0.003112 for sum aggregation, which is a very huge improvement from the traditional approaches. This is far better when compared to the Gaussian mechanism, whose mean relative errors are 0.004802 and 0.026053 for the mean and sum aggregations, respectively.

The Laplace mechanism is performing really well for mean aggregation, with an average relative error of 0.001813, and hence is a very reliable alternative to the Stochastic mechanism. The Exponential mechanism maintains moderate performance levels with mean relative errors of 0.003429 for mean aggregation and 0.008239 for sum aggregation.

Table 17.2 summarizes various mechanisms' performance for different types of sensors, highlighting several key patterns in error distribution and mechanism sensitivity to data characteristics.

Table 17.1 Error rates by privacy mechanism and aggregation function.

Noise_type	Aggregation	Count	Mean	Std	Min	Max
Exponential	Mean	54	0.003429	0.010293	0.000002	0.063437
Exponential	Sum	54	0.008239	0.020984	0.000010	0.117148
Gaussian	Mean	54	0.004802	0.011266	0.000000	0.064484
Gaussian	Sum	54	0.026053	0.064714	0.000149	0.311216
Laplace	Mean	54	0.001813	0.003332	0.000002	0.016260
Laplace	Sum	54	0.011200	0.039619	0.000001	0.278362
Stochastic	Mean	54	0.001304	0.003193	0.000000	0.020004
Stochastic	Sum	54	0.003112	0.010308	0.000000	0.069459

Note: In Tables 17.1–17.3, the "count" column represents the number of experimental trials conducted for each combination of parameters. For example, in Table 17.1, each mechanism-aggregation pair shows a count of 54, which is derived from the product of our experimental parameters: 6 epsilon values × 3 delta values × 3 sensor types = 54 trials. Similarly, in Table 17.2, the count of 36 for each mechanism-sensor type combination results from 6 epsilon values × 3 delta values × 2 aggregation methods = 36 trials. These counts ensure statistical significance in our analysis and demonstrate the comprehensive nature of our experimental evaluation across the parameter space. The consistency in these counts across different combinations validates the completeness of our experimental design, with each parameter combination being thoroughly tested. This systematic approach allows us to draw statistically sound conclusions about the relative performance of different privacy mechanisms under various conditions.

Table 17.2 Error rates by privacy mechanism and sensor type.

Noise_type	Sensor_type	Count	Mean	Std	Min	Max
Exponential	Energy	36	0.009719	0.022787	0.000054	0.117148
Exponential	Humidity	36	0.005671	0.016776	0.000002	0.097777
Exponential	Temperature	36	0.002113	0.003820	0.000010	0.017673
Gaussian	Energy	36	0.032197	0.074024	0.000079	0.311216
Gaussian	Humidity	36	0.010057	0.029553	0.000000	0.176307
Gaussian	Temperature	36	0.004028	0.008768	0.000027	0.038164
Laplace	Energy	36	0.014711	0.047992	0.000017	0.278362
Laplace	Humidity	36	0.002329	0.004969	0.000002	0.026567
Laplace	Temperature	36	0.002478	0.005468	0.000001	0.030576
Stochastic	Energy	36	0.003757	0.011961	0.000000	0.069459
Stochastic	Humidity	36	0.001860	0.004944	0.000000	0.027776
Stochastic	Temperature	36	0.001008	0.002697	0.000000	0.015093

From the sensor-specific performance analysis, it can be gathered that the most difficult energy consumption measurements with wider value ranges, 0–1000 W, challenge all mechanisms. Gaussian is especially sensitive to this range, whereas the stochastic mechanism maintains much better performance for the same type of data, with a mean relative error of 0.003757 for energy data.

Table 17.3 Error rates by aggregation function and sensor type.

Aggregation	Sensor_type	Count	Mean	Std	Min	Max
Mean	Energy	72	0.005822	0.012877	0.0	0.064484
Mean	Humidity	72	0.001544	0.003274	0.0	0.020804
Mean	Temperature	72	0.001145	0.002310	0.0	0.011375
Sum	Energy	72	0.024370	0.063647	0.0	0.311216
Sum	Humidity	72	0.008415	0.024097	0.0	0.176307
Sum	Temperature	72	0.003668	0.007565	0.0	0.038164

The temperature data, accordingly, provides the most stable outcome in all three mechanisms while having its smallest range at 18–28 °C. It may present the best result for the Stochastic mechanism when the mean of the relative error is 0.001008, while that is almost correct behind the Laplace mechanism at 0.002478.

Table 17.3 investigates the relationship between aggregation functions and data types, which gives important practical implementation guidance.

The result obviously proves the effect of the type of data on aggregation performance: for any kind of sensor, mean aggregation is better than sum aggregation. For example, when performing the mean aggregation, the average error for the energy consumption data is 0.005822, while the sum aggregation has an error as high as 0.024370. Similar happenings are with humidity and temperature data; in this case, temperature measurements gave the best overall results where the error in the case of mean aggregation was as low as 0.001145.

The significance of these results has been confirmed through the rigorous hypothesis testing. We confirm, using the Wilcoxon signed-rank test with Bonferroni correction for multiple comparisons, that the performance differences between mechanisms are statistically significant at $p < 0.01$. Also, two-way ANOVA testing confirms the impact of data types and aggregation methods at $p < 0.01$.

17.6.2 Visualization analysis and performance trends

The following sections offer a graphical analysis that gives deeper insights into the behavior and performance characteristics of different privacy mechanisms across various experimental conditions.

Privacy-utility trade-off analysis

Figure 17.1 presents the privacy-utility trade-off curves for three different δ values (0.001, 0.01, and 0.1), illustrating how the relative error changes with increasing privacy budget (ϵ).

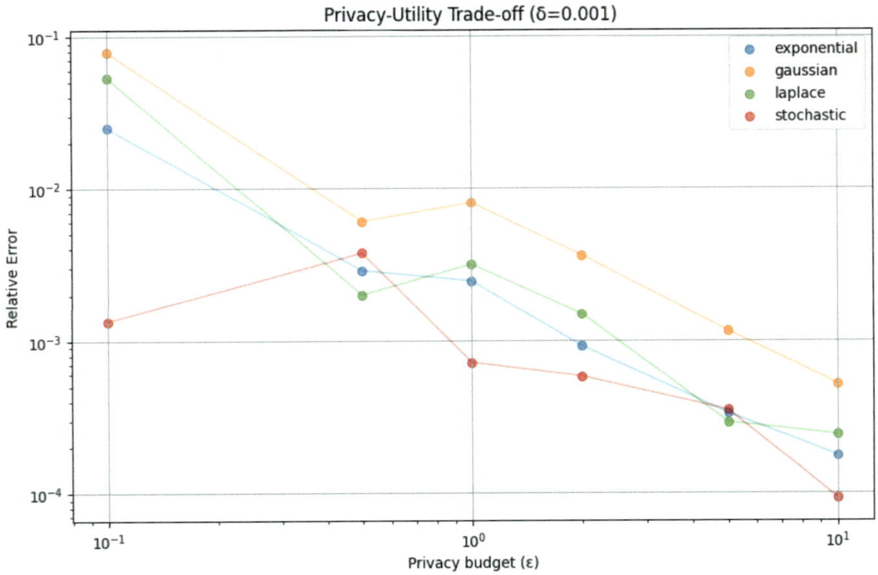

(a)

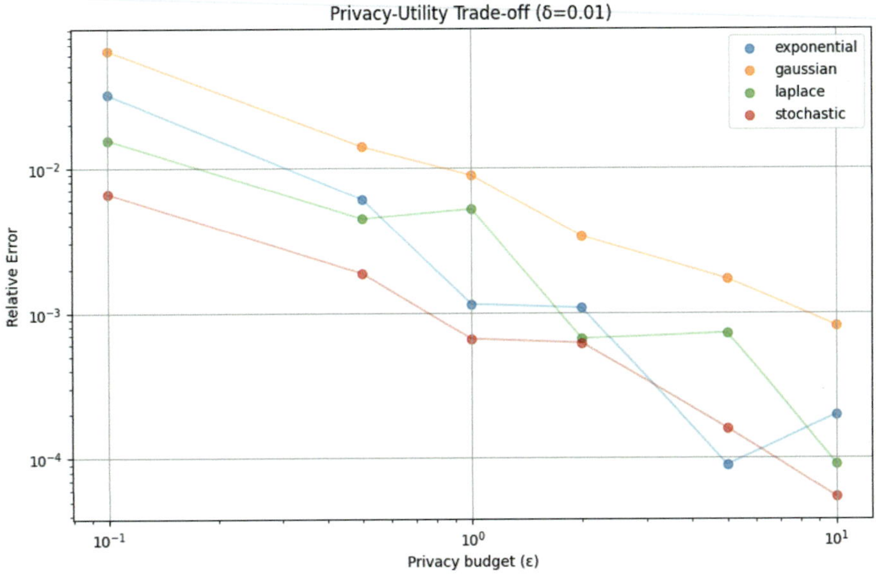

(b)

Figure 17.1 Privacy-utility trade-off curves showing the relative error versus the privacy budget (ϵ) for various differential privacy mechanisms: (a) δ = 0.001, (b) δ = 0.01, and (c) δ = 0.1.

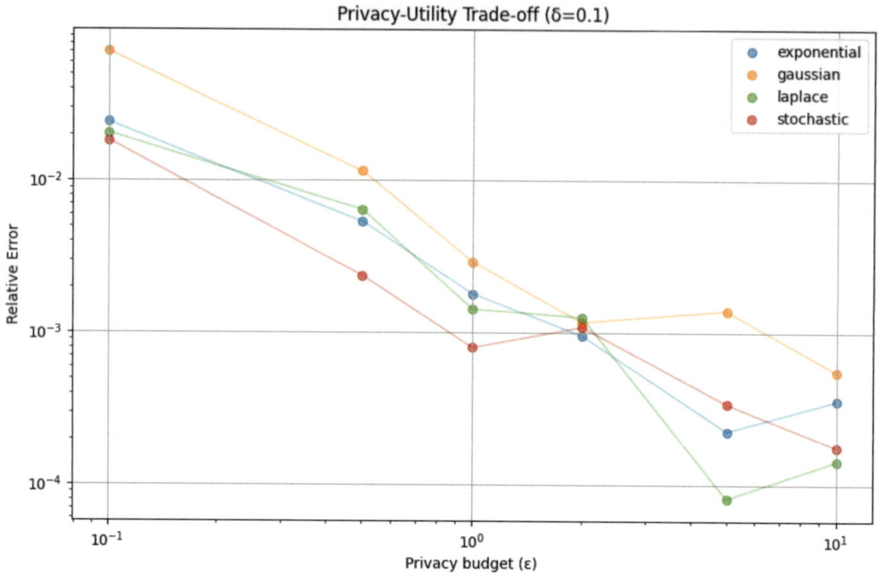

(c)

Figure 17.1 Privacy-utility trade-off curves showing the relative error versus the privacy budget (ϵ) for various differential privacy mechanisms: (a) $\delta = 0.001$, (b) $\delta = 0.01$, and (c) $\delta = 0.1$.

Note: Privacy-utility trade-off curves demonstrate the relationship between privacy budget (ϵ) and relative error for different differential privacy mechanisms. Results are shown for three δ values: (a) $\delta = 0.001$, demonstrating high privacy requirements; (b) $\delta = 0.01$, representing moderate privacy requirements; and (c) $\delta = 0.1$, showing relaxed privacy constraints. The x-axis (privacy budget ϵ, log scale) ranges from 0.1 to 10, where smaller values indicate stronger privacy guarantees. The y-axis (relative error, log scale) shows the accuracy loss, with lower values indicating better utility preservation.

A number of interesting patterns can be seen from the trade-off curves. For example, for $\delta = 0.001$, the Gaussian mechanism starts off with the highest error rate at $\epsilon = 0.1$ but sees very consistent improvement as the privacy budget increases. Meanwhile, the Stochastic mechanism performs reasonably well across all budgets, being especially effective in the high privacy regime $\epsilon < 1$.

It has been observed that both mechanisms of Laplace and Exponential have shown the same decaying pattern. Thus, an error rate reduces more swiftly in a range of the moderate privacy budget $1 < \epsilon < 5$.

As δ increases to 0.01 and 0.1, we see a general increase in utility across all mechanisms, though the relative ordering of mechanism performance

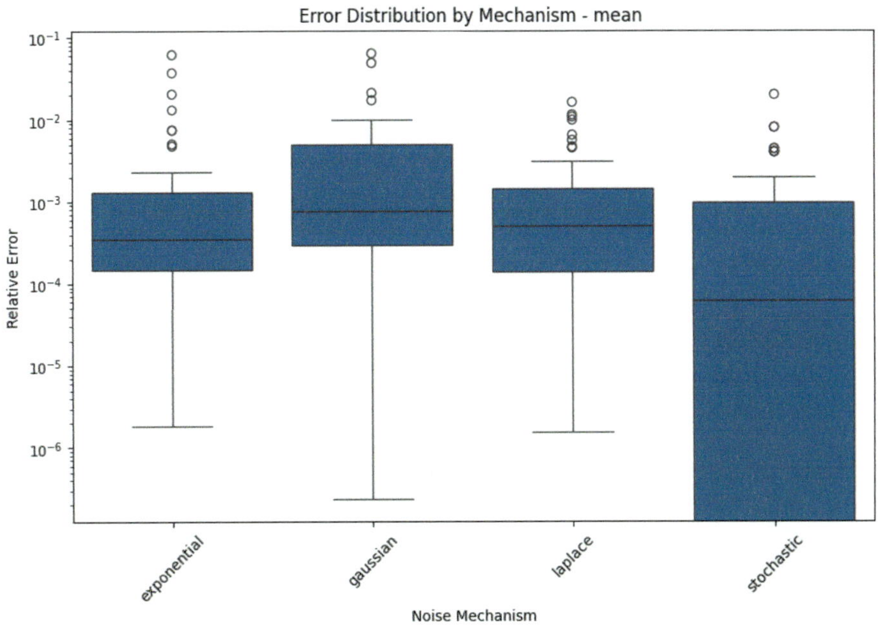

Figure 17.2 Error distribution by the mechanism for mean aggregation; quartiles, median, and outliers.

Note: Error distribution for mean aggregation across different privacy mechanisms. Box plots show the quartiles (box), median (horizontal line), whiskers (extending to 1.5× interquartile range), and outliers (points) of relative errors. The y-axis uses a logarithmic scale to better visualize error variations across different orders of magnitude. Lower median values and smaller boxes indicate better and more consistent performance.

remains largely consistent. For larger values of δ, the stochastic mechanism's relative advantage is more pronounced, especially in the high privacy regime.

Error distribution analysis

Figure 17.2 presents the error distribution for average aggregation concerning the considered mechanisms to provide insights into the stability and reliability of each.

Distribution analysis hence reveals that the smallest median error is achieved through the Stochastic mechanism because it exhibits the most stable behavior, given its low interquartile range. The Gaussian mechanism follows to display competitive median behavior; however, it develops the highest variance, often leads to outliers, and also tends to yield outliers within the upper range.

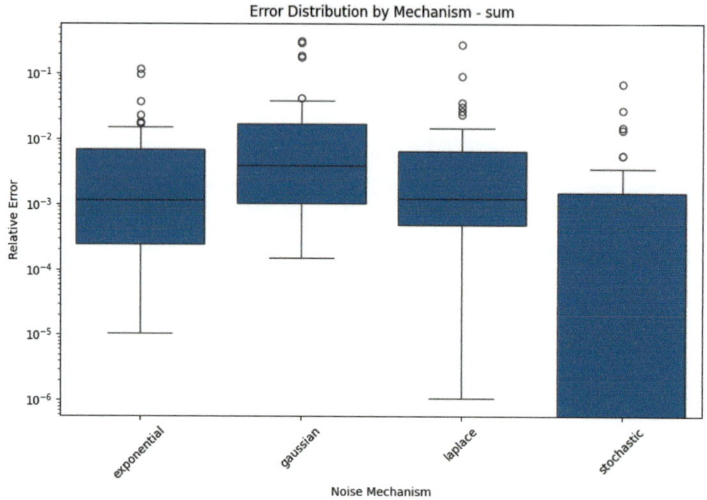

Figure 17.3 Error distribution of mechanisms for the sum aggregation, box plot of quartiles median, and outliers.

Note: Error distribution for sum aggregation across privacy mechanisms, showing the increased challenge of preserving privacy for summation operations. Box plot elements are defined as in Figure 17.2, with the *y*-axis again using a logarithmic scale. Note the generally higher error values compared to mean aggregation, particularly evident in the outliers.

Figure 17.3 extends this analysis to sum aggregation, demonstrating critical mechanism behavior differences across different aggregation functions.

From this figure, in general, error distributions are large when compared to the average aggregation results; all of the mechanisms in sum aggregations cause a higher frequency in outliers. This trend is noticeable in the case of Gaussian mechanisms; it may have given an indication that sum queries pose the task tougher from the point of view of privacy protection.

Data type sensitivity analysis

Figures 17.4–17.6 illustrate the performance of mechanisms for various types of sensors that may be useful in some practical implementations.

If all mechanisms are considered in terms of their distribution across data types, an unmistakable relation between value range and magnitude of error obviously emerges. The narrow-range temperature data shows the densest distributions for the three mechanisms at hand, whereas energy consumption is the widest, especially due to the Gaussian mechanism. In turn, for the Stochastic mechanism, very similar results across all the investigated data types are obtained. That would hint at a larger robustness of this type of mechanism against variations of the range in which different values spread.

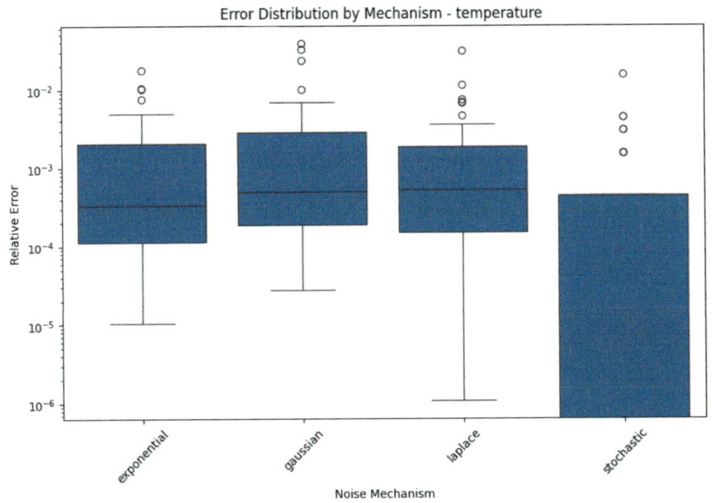

Figure 17.4 Distribution of the errors in the temperature measurements within the range 18–28 °C.

Note: Error distribution for temperature measurements (18–28 °C range), demonstrating mechanism performance for narrow-range data. The relatively small data range results in more concentrated error distributions across all mechanisms. Box plots show relative errors on a logarithmic scale, with outliers indicating worst-case privacy leakage scenarios.

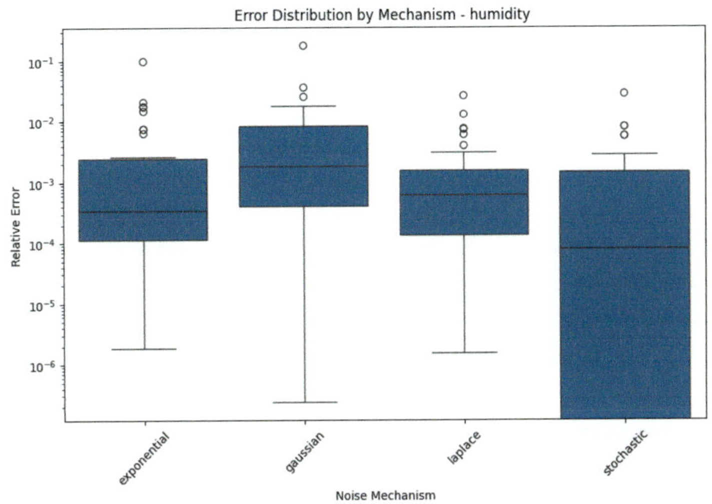

Figure 17.5 Distribution of the error in the humidity measurements (30%–70%).

Note: Error distribution for humidity measurements (30%–70% range), showing mechanism performance for medium-range data. The increased data range compared to temperature measurements results in larger error distributions, particularly evident in the Gaussian mechanism's performance.

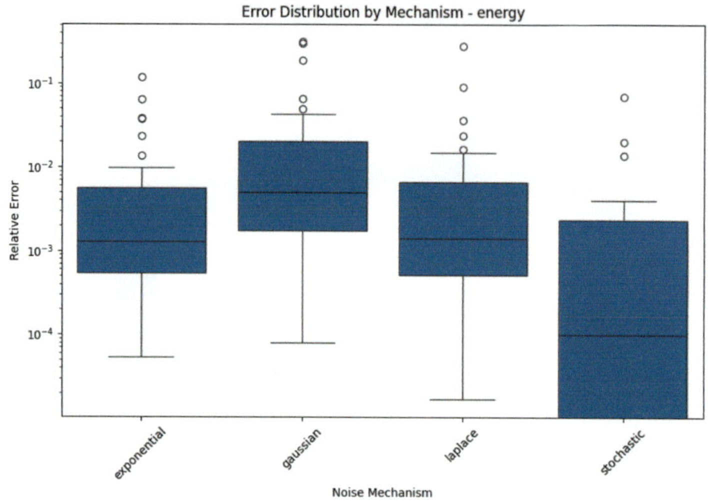

Figure 17.6 Distribution of error for energy consumption in the range 0–1000 W.

Note: Error distribution for energy consumption measurements (0–1000 W range), illustrating mechanism performance for wide-range data. The large data range presents the greatest challenge for privacy preservation, especially visible in the increased number and magnitude of outliers across all mechanisms.

These plots are supportive of the statistical tests in Section 17.6.1, and hence, provide clear evidence of the superiority of the Stochastic mechanism across most of the experimental conditions. At the same time, this analysis shows that when it comes to selecting a privacy mechanism for a practical application, both the type of data and the aggregation function need to be taken into consideration.

Finally, consistency among numerical results and visual analysis further strengthens our conclusions on the relative performance of different privacy mechanisms, hence giving useful guidelines for practitioners during the implementation of differential privacy in IoT environments.

17.7 Discussion and Future Research Directions

Building on our experimental results and analysis, this section explores the broader implications of our findings and identifies promising directions for future research. We discuss both theoretical insights and practical considerations that emerge from our study while highlighting remaining challenges and opportunities in the field of privacy-preserving IoT systems.

17.7.1 Key findings discussion

Our comprehensive analysis of various differential privacy mechanisms in IoT networks drew several key insights beyond the immediate results of our experiments. First, since in various scenarios, the Stochastic mechanism performs stronger, the results hint at a certain fundamental advantage in noise generation-especially for continuous streams of IoT data. The strength here is most evident for the aggregation operations of mean, for which the relative error turns out to be 0.001304 for the same Stochastic mechanism, and it indeed outperformed other methods approached.

The relationship between data range and the performance of the privacy mechanism becomes important. Energy consumption measurements, for their wider range of 0–1000 W, always pose a greater challenge in preserving privacy compared to temperature data in the range of 18–28 °C. Indeed, this pattern is persistent across all mechanisms tested: error rates for energy are typically 3–4 times higher than for temperature. For example, the Gaussian mechanism is highly sensitive to the range of data, whose error rate increases drastically when the measurements have a wide range.

The large differences in mechanism performance across various aggregation functions call into question the one-size-fits-all approach so often taken in privacy-preserving systems. Mean aggregation performs consistently better than sum aggregation, with error rates usually 2–3 times lower. This difference in performance becomes more pronounced for smaller values of ϵ, indicating that the choice of aggregation function becomes increasingly important in high-privacy settings.

17.7.2 Implications: theoretical and practical

These results provide a significant contribution to both the theoretical understanding and practical implementation of privacy-preserving IoT systems. Theoretically, our results call for reconsideration of the traditional exclusive focus on continuous noise distributions. The exceptional performance of the Stochastic mechanism suggests that in IoT contexts, discrete bounded noise distributions may offer some basic advantages.

Practical implications are also very serious: the system architects have to consider the integration of dynamic mechanism selection so that for different aggregation functions and data types, different privacy approaches can be applied. Further, this strong dependence of the mechanism's performance on data range may suggest that strategies of data preprocessing and normalization could turn out to be very helpful in privacy preservation.

17.7.3 Future research directions

Our current study provides a number of insights that point to some promising directions for future research. In particular, one of the most important avenues is the development of adaptive privacy mechanisms, which can automatically adjust their parameters based on real-time data characteristics and network conditions and provide significant improvements in both privacy protection and data utility.

Such deserves deep investigation into hybrid mechanisms for privacy. The mechanisms join various techniques, depending on different contexts, and allow leveraging both strengths while both weaknesses of each method considered are mitigated. Thus, a hybrid system involving the stochastic mechanism for execution according to mean aggregation on narrow data and modified Laplace mechanisms for sum operations in terms of wide data is suitable.

Resource-aware privacy is another fundamental direction of research, especially with regard to IoT environments. Future research work will develop privacy mechanisms specifically optimized for resource-constrained devices, considering computational and energy constraints. This covers efficient techniques of noise generation and optimized protocol design in battery-powered devices.

Therefore, much attention should be directed at how to handle privacy budgets within continuous data collection scenarios. Most of the existing solutions for managing and budgeting privacy do not scale properly in a long-lived IoT deployment. Novel approaches, such as reusing and dynamic allocation of the privacy budget, can enable it to work out the inefficiencies and limit them, keeping strong guarantees on privacy.

17.7.4 Theoretical foundations and extensions

The theoretical foundations of differential privacy in IoT contexts are not yet fully developed. New composition theorems are needed to deal with continuous data release scenarios more effectively. The relation between data characteristics and optimal privacy parameters needs to be characterized formally. Besides, the development of tighter utility bounds for various mechanism combinations may provide useful guidelines for system design.

Such partial information scenarios would be great, where the adversary may have some background knowledge regarding data distribution, to extend the theoretical work on. This allows for more refined privacy mechanisms that adapt to realistic threat models while sustaining utility.

17.7.5 Path forward

The evolution of privacy-preserving IoT systems has remained and is going to be challenging and opportunistic. Future research should focus on closing the gap between theoretical guarantees and practical implementation requirements: development of holistic frameworks for mechanism selection and configuration, large-scale validation studies in production environments, and novel approaches to privacy preservation able to adapt to emerging IoT applications and threats.

These results from our current study set the stage for future investigations by putting into perspective what has been accomplished and what remains to be done in this very important area of research. With the growth and development of IoT networks, there is a corresponding increase in the importance of effective mechanisms for privacy preservation as a factor in responsible deployments.

This brings us to a promising juncture now in this field, a great potential for developing some sophisticated context-aware methods in privacy preservation that can able to meet the growing needs of the current IoT applications while strong guarantees about privacy ensured.

17.8 Conclusion

This study provides comprehensive insights into the practical implementation of differential privacy mechanisms in IoT networks. Through systematic experimentation and rigorous analysis, we have demonstrated the relative effectiveness of different privacy mechanisms and identified key factors that influence their performance. Our findings have significant implications for both the theoretical understanding and practical deployment of privacy-preserving IoT systems.

The comprehensive review of the IoT network's differential privacy mechanisms provides significant insight into the practical implementation of the privacy-preserving data aggregation system. The experimental results have shown that the Stochastic mechanism consistently outperforms traditional approaches, achieving superior privacy-utility trade-offs across various scenarios and data types. This indicates that privacy mechanisms depend not only on the data characteristics but also on the applied aggregation functions: wide-range measurements, like energy consumption data, are more challenging to handle by privacy preservation methods than narrow-range temperature data. Also, the mean aggregation is steadily performing better than the sum aggregation; thus, query design is to be included in the privacy preservation strategy. These results have important implications for the design and deployment of privacy-preserving IoT systems. Choices between privacy mechanisms should be informed by careful consideration of data characteristics, aggregation requirements, and application-specific privacy needs. The strong performance of the Stochastic mechanism suggests that discrete, bounded noise distributions may provide fundamental advantages in IoT contexts. Our work contributes to the area by providing real-world application empirical evidence about mechanism selection and by developing a framework for evaluating the privacy-utility trade-off. Results show that an effective solution to privacy preservation in IoT networks calls for a fine-grained approach, considering the interplay among mechanism selection, data characteristics, and aggregation functions. The role of effective mechanisms of privacy preservation is growing fast due to ever-increasing and evolving IoT networks. Our research can form the basis for future work in this critical area since it has tried to bring forth practical considerations that one needs to make for implementing differential privacy in real-world IoT systems.

References

[1] G. Aceto, V. Persico, and A. Pescapé, "Industry 4.0 and Health: Internet of Things, Big Data, and Cloud Computing for Healthcare 4.0," *Journal of Industrial Information Integration*, vol. 18, p. 100129, Jun. 2020, doi: 10.1016/j.jii.2020.100129.

[2] S. F. Ahmed *et al.*, "Industrial Internet of Things enabled technologies, challenges, and future directions," *Computers and Electrical Engineering*, vol. 110, p. 108847, Sep. 2023, doi: 10.1016/j.compeleceng.2023.108847.

[3] B. Kaur *et al.*, "Internet of Things (IoT) security dataset evolution: Challenges and future directions," *Internet of Things*, vol. 22, p. 100780, Jul. 2023, doi: 10.1016/j.iot.2023.100780.

[4] S. Aroua *et al.*, "Security and PrIvacy foR the Internet of Things: an overview of the project," in *2019 IEEE International Conference on Systems, Man and Cybernetics (SMC)*, Oct. 2019, pp. 3993–3998. doi: 10.1109/SMC.2019.8914221.

[5] B. Cremonezi, A. B. Vieira, J. Nacif, E. F. Silva, and M. Nogueira, "Identity management for Internet of Things: Concepts, challenges and opportunities," *Computer Communications*, May 2024, doi: 10.1016/j.comcom.2024.05.014.

[6] S. Banerjee *et al.*, "A Provably Secure and Lightweight Anonymous User Authenticated Session Key Exchange Scheme for Internet of

Things Deployment," *IEEE Internet of Things Journal*, vol. 6, no. 5, pp. 8739–8752, Oct. 2019, doi: 10.1109/JIOT.2019.2923373.

[7] S. Dhar, A. Khare, A. D. Dwivedi, and R. Singh, "Securing IoT devices: A novel approach using blockchain and quantum cryptography," *Internet of Things*, vol. 25, p. 101019, Apr. 2024, doi: 10.1016/j.iot.2023.101019.

[8] C. Dwork, "Differential Privacy," in *Automata, Languages and Programming*, M. Bugliesi, B. Preneel, V. Sassone, and I. Wegener, Eds., Berlin, Heidelberg: Springer, 2006, pp. 1–12. doi: 10.1007/11787006_1.

[9] C. Dwork, "Differential Privacy in New Settings," in *Proceedings of the 2010 Annual ACM-SIAM Symposium on Discrete Algorithms (SODA)*, in Proceedings. , Society for Industrial and Applied Mathematics, 2010, pp. 174–183. doi: 10.1137/1.9781611973075.16.

[10] O. Kuznetsov, E. Frontoni, N. Kryvinska, S. Volodymyr, and T. Smirnova, "Harnessing edge computing for real-time cybersecurity in healthcare systems," in *Cybersecurity in Emerging Healthcare Systems*, IET Digital Library, 2024, pp. 471–508. doi: 10.1049/PBHE064E_ch16.

[11] O. Kuznetsov, E. Frontoni, N. Kryvinska, D. Prokopovych-Tkachenko, and B. Khruskov, "Adaptive cybersecurity: AI-driven threat intelligence in healthcare systems," in *Cybersecurity in Emerging Healthcare Systems*, IET Digital Library, 2024, pp. 75–106. doi: 10.1049/PBHE064E_ch3.

[12] Z. Wu, X. Gao, Y. Qian, Y. Hao, and M. Chen, "Dynamic differential privacy-based dataset condensation," *Neurocomputing*, vol. 608, p. 128394, Dec. 2024, doi: 10.1016/j.neucom.2024.128394.

[13] C. Dwork, F. McSherry, K. Nissim, and A. Smith, "Calibrating Noise to Sensitivity in Private Data Analysis," in *Theory of Cryptography*, S. Halevi and T. Rabin, Eds., Berlin, Heidelberg: Springer, 2006, pp. 265–284. doi: 10.1007/11681878_14.

[14] C. Dwork, "Differential Privacy: A Survey of Results," in *Theory and Applications of Models of Computation*, M. Agrawal, D. Du, Z. Duan, and A. Li, Eds., Berlin, Heidelberg: Springer, 2008, pp. 1–19. doi: 10.1007/978-3-540-79228-4_1.

[15] J. Wang, Z. Zhang, J. Tian, and H. Li, "Local differential privacy federated learning based on heterogeneous data multi-privacy mechanism," *Computer Networks*, vol. 254, p. 110822, Dec. 2024, doi: 10.1016/j.comnet.2024.110822.

[16] X. Liu, J. Wang, X. Xiong, and H. Sun, "Federated learning data protection scheme based on personalized differential privacy in psychological evaluation," *Neurocomputing*, vol. 611, p. 128653, Jan. 2025, doi: 10.1016/j.neucom.2024.128653.

[17] D. Wang and S. Guan, "FedFR-ADP: Adaptive differential privacy with feedback regulation for robust model performance in federated learning," *Information Fusion*, vol. 116, p. 102796, Apr. 2025, doi: 10.1016/j.inffus.2024.102796.

[18] F. McSherry and K. Talwar, "Mechanism design via differential privacy," presented at the Proceedings - Annual IEEE Symposium on Foundations of Computer Science, FOCS, 2007, pp. 94–103. doi: 10.1109/FOCS.2007.4389483.

[19] P. Zhao, K. Zhang, H. Zhang, and H. Chen, "Alternating minimization differential privacy protection algorithm for the novel dual-mode learning tasks model," *Expert Systems with Applications*, vol. 259, p. 125279, Jan. 2025, doi: 10.1016/j.eswa.2024.125279.

[20] W. Huang *et al.*, "Auditing privacy budget of differentially private neural network models," *Neurocomputing*, vol. 614, p. 128756, Jan. 2025, doi: 10.1016/j.neucom.2024.128756.

[21] S. Jiao *et al.*, "DPKnob: A visual analysis approach to risk-aware formulation of differential privacy schemes for data query scenarios," *Visual Informatics*, vol. 8, no. 3, pp. 42–52, Sep. 2024, doi: 10.1016/j.visinf.2024.09.002.

[22] S. Garg and V. Torra, "Privacy in manifolds: Combining k-anonymity with differential privacy on Fréchet means," *Computers & Security*, vol. 144, p. 103983, Sep. 2024, doi: 10.1016/j.cose.2024.103983.

[23] C. Dwork and A. Roth, "An adaptive approach to real-time aggregate monitoring with differential privacy," *Foundations and Trends®in Theoretical Computer Science*, vol. 9, no. 3–4, p. 211, 2014.

[24] C. Dwork and A. Roth, "The Algorithmic Foundations of Differential Privacy," *TCS*, vol. 9, no. 3–4, pp. 211–407, Aug. 2014, doi: 10.1561/0400000042.

18

Enhancing Cyber-physical Systems Through Artificial Intelligence and Machine Learning

Cristian Randieri[1], Nicola Delmonte[2], Marco Simonazzi[2] and Claudio Tomazzoli[3]

[1]Department of Theoretical and Applied Sciences, eCampus University, Italy
[2]Department of Engineering and Architecture, University of Parma, Italy
[3]Department of Computer Science, University of Verona, Italy

Email: cristian.randieri@uniecampus.it; nicola.delmonte@unipr.it; marco.simonazzi@unipr.it; claudio.tomazzoli@univr.it

Abstract

Today, more than ever before, cyber-physical systems (CPSs) are used for a wide number of human activities thanks to the synergy of computational algorithms and physical processes to create increasingly robust, efficient, and adaptable systems. However, this integration process introduces new vulnerabilities and challenges in cybersecurity mainly due to the intrinsic nature of their cyber and physical components and relative interconnectivity. Thanks to the advent of artificial intelligence (AI) and machine learning (ML), the world of CPSs is revolutionizing, allowing for advanced automation, decision-making, and adaptability capabilities. The primary purpose of this chapter is to explore the integration of AI and ML in improving CPS by addressing their most critical challenges regarding system performance optimization and autonomy of operations. Starting from some key concepts of AI and ML, their applications in CPSs are discussed. The aim is to demonstrate

DOI: 10.1201/9788743801306-18

their practical implications through detailed case studies, providing a framework to connect theoretical advances with real-world applications. This work offers extremely valuable insights into the design and implementation of brilliant CPSs, supporting all those who want to propose further innovations in today's highly strategic sectors, such as energy and healthcare.

18.1 Introduction

Today, more than ever in modern applications, cyber-physical systems (CPS) represent an integration, which in many aspects can be considered critical, of computational algorithms and physical processes [1–4]. These systems, which can range from minor and closed systems such as an artificial pancreas to large, complex, and interconnected systems such as a regional energy grid, have seen a dramatic increase in their reliance on technological developments such as low-cost sensing, powerful embedded system hardware, and widely deployed communication networks. However, the emergent nature of these systems also introduces new security threats, as the integration of cyber and physical components and the interaction between them [4] can lead to vulnerabilities and risks that must be addressed.

Over time, these systems have become increasingly widespread in various contexts, allowing the spread of new applications in most strategic and critical sectors, such as IT [5–7], manufacturing [8], healthcare [9], transportation [10], and energy [11]. Their diffusion has received a significant boost also thanks to the advent of artificial intelligence (AI) [12] and machine learning (ML) [13] that revolutionize some aspects of CPS, giving them further capabilities in further contexts in terms of automation, decision-making processes, and adaptability. As is well known, artificial intelligence (AI) represents a broad domain that includes multiple techniques and models specifically designed to imitate human intelligence. While CPS has countless advantages, such as enhanced physical system capabilities, increased reliability, and greater efficiency, integrating cyber and physical components introduces new security opportunities and challenges that must be addressed [14].

Cyber-physical systems are vulnerable to a wide range of security threats [15] due to their heterogeneity of components, lack of perimeter protection, the longevity of their systems, and strict constraints on their resources. Attacks on CPS can seriously compromise sensitive user data [16], the availability and reliability of critical resources, and user safety, potentially leading to monetary losses. Various techniques have been developed to mitigate these risks, such as data encryption, authentication, firewalls, cryptography, and digital watermarking, typically deployed to protect the cyber layer of CPS [17].

However, these approaches primarily focus on the cyber domain and do not adequately address security threats that can simultaneously target CPS's cyber and physical aspects. Therefore, new approaches providing a comprehensive and integrated security framework that addresses the unique security challenges posed by CPS are needed. These capabilities include reasoning, learning, and problem-solving according to a decision-making process [18].

ML is characterized as a subset of AI, which focuses on developing algorithms that allow systems to learn from the information in data and improve their performance over time without using classic explicit programming techniques. The main key concepts that concern AI and ML include:

- Supervised learning: It is a training technique for models that use labeled datasets to predict results on data that the model has never seen before. In the specific context of CPS, this approach is typically used for applications that concern predictive maintenance [19], a discipline in which systems learn to predict the occurrence of new anomalies or system failures by making predictions that arise from an analysis of historical data of the various physical process measurements that come from various sensors.
- Unsupervised learning: Unlike the previous one, this type of learning allows identifying patterns and structures starting from datasets that do not have predefined labels. Unsupervised learning is beneficial in CPS when there are problems related to the grouping of similar operating states or in the case in which it is necessary to detect anomalies in the behavior of the specific system, for example, in the anomaly detection in environment sensors [20];
- Reinforcement learning: This type of learning approach is considered a midpoint between the supervised and supervised ones because it enables systems to learn by interacting with their surrounding environment, gradually optimizing the model for specific objectives. In the context of CPS, this type of learning is typically applied to the control systems of autonomous vehicles [21] or robotic arms [22], where the essential peculiarity is to have continuous feedback capable of providing new information to the systems in order to improve the related decision-making processes in time and over time.
- Deep learning: It is a particularly consolidated technique that, by exploiting multi-layer neural networks, can manage and model highly nonlinear and complex information in the data. In the context of CPS, this deep learning technique is typically used whenever there are particularly

advanced tasks such as image recognition in quality control processes [23], speech recognition in the context of human–machine interfaces, and in the field of fault diagnosis that are particularly complex;

- Transfer learning: Similar to the typical human context of transfer learning, this method uses the specific knowledge acquired in a particular domain to improve learning in a second related domain. For example, in the context of predicting cyberattacks in CPS [24], it is possible to handle different issues using similar systems that share the same operational characteristics, thus allowing for a reduction in training times and data requirements.

Now consolidated in AI-based applications, these concepts find multiple direct applications in the context of CPS systems through fundamental approaches that exploit AI and ML [25].

One example concerns data-based analysis, in which AI and ML allow CPS systems to examine a large amount of data from various sensors. Information will be extracted and used in operational optimization processes. These technologies transform raw data into knowledge to fuel continuous improvement in this context.

Another area refers to adaptive systems that, by leveraging the capabilities of AI and ML models, can ensure that their behavior is modified based on conditions characterized by high variability. In this context, learning from collected data allows CPS to have a greater capacity to adapt to new scenarios. For example, in smart grids, ML algorithms have demonstrated a remarkable ability to optimize power usage using real-world data dynamically [26].

Another pervasive aspect concerns predictive and prescriptive analysis in which AI models have proven to be valid allies in helping the future states of CPSs prediction [27], not only in the case of failures but also in suggesting optimal actions to mitigate any risks or optimize performance. All this allows preventive and timely intervention on the equipment and offers targeted recommendations to deal with complex situations as efficiently and effectively as possible.

Enabling autonomous operations is also a benefit that deserves to be mentioned. In this context, thanks to ML, CPSs can perform complex activities almost autonomously, i.e., with minimal human intervention. There are several emblematic examples, such as drones capable of autonomously delivering packages [28] or monitoring particular critical areas, managing to adapt in real-time to the operating conditions that are gradually proposed.

Finally, another key element often requested from the market for CPS is the ability to manage the real-time decision-making process by instantly analyzing incoming data flows and responding promptly to situations that evolve dynamically [29]. This ability is particularly relevant in all applications involving autonomous driving, in which decisions must be taken in milliseconds or emergency response systems characterized by a high capacity for speed and efficiency to minimize risks as much as possible while maximizing benefits. This chapter's primary objective is to explore how AI and ML can improve CPS by making them more intelligent to obtain more dynamic and efficient system performances.

18.1.1 Contribution of the chapter

This chapter is essential for those interested in exploring the cutting-edge integration of AI and machine learning in CPS, where the power of machine learning to provide predictions about future data and perform accurate classifications is employed to enhance the capabilities of CPS. The goal is to provide a step-by-step exploration of current challenges and solutions in this field, offering the reader a logical framework for connecting fundamental technologies with real-world applications. Through three case studies, we aim to highlight the practical and innovative potential of AI and ML in CPS, demonstrating their practical implications across multiple domains while providing valuable insights to enhance the design and implementation of intelligent CPS.

18.1.2 Chapter organization

This chapter is organized into five main sections. This section introduced the research problem, objectives, and scope, highlighting the context of this manuscript. The role of AI in CPS is highlighted in Section 18.2, which also identifies research needs and looks at the developments in CPS and AI/ML approaches. The technological evolution of AI/ML into CPS is the main topic of Section 18.3. Results from some case studies are analyzed in Section 18.4, which also describes how AI/ML affects system flexibility, decision-making, and energy efficiency. The results are summarized, their implications discussed, and future research directions for developing CPS through AI/ML breakthroughs are suggested in Section 18.5, which closes the chapter.

18.2 Role of AI

Cyber-physical systems (CPS) integrate computational and physical processes with artificial intelligence playing a key role in driving their development.

The integration of AI into CPS enables the development of intelligent, adaptive, and autonomous systems that enhance decision-making capabilities, optimize real-time operations, and create innovative solutions across industries, as detailed in recent publications [30–33].

AI integrates real-time data analytics and machine learning algorithms to improve CPS's decision-making processes. For instance, AI-powered CPS systems in the construction sector employ sophisticated automation and predictive analytics to manage resources better and forecast environmental effects like air pollution. ML state-of-the-art algorithms can provide creative solutions for infrastructure optimization and material quality evaluation [30]. Furthermore, introducing real-time data analytics into CPS facilitates swift decision-making under dynamic conditions, a goal that can be achieved thanks to the hybrid edge-cloud computing paradigm [31], where latency is dramatically reduced. Empowering edge devices with AI capabilities allows the process of data closer to its source so that real-time responses in CPS are possible.

AI delivers real value when dealing with the important topic of energy harvesting and sustainability in CPS. When CPS is equipped with AI capabilities [32], energy efficiency in IoT networks is boosted.

CPS attains greater sustainability and operational efficiency by optimizing energy harvesting using AI algorithms that combine data from several sensors. These solutions enhance situational awareness and adaptive energy management in IoT-enabled CPS situations.

Another transformative area of CPS application is Industry 5.0, where human–robot collaboration, enabled by AI, plays a key role. Collaborative robots (cobots) that rely on AI-driven CPS can interoperate with seamless interaction with human workers [33].

In addition to prioritizing automation, these systems enhance human capabilities by strongly emphasizing accuracy, safety, and flexibility. In line with the goals of Industry 5.0, cobots are a prime example of the transition from automation-centric systems to more human-centred design philosophies. Industry 5.0 builds on the ideas of Industry 4.0 by emphasizing collaborative intelligence, sustainability, and human-centric methods.

While Industry 4.0 revolutionized production with automation and cyber-physical systems (CPS), Industry 5.0 emphasizes symbiosis between humans and machines, integrating AI to create intelligent, adaptive, and socially aware systems [33–35].

Cobots are used in Industry 5.0 to improve the collaboration between machine accuracy and human innovation. AI-powered cobots can carry out intricate manufacturing operations with accuracy, freeing human operators to concentrate on innovation and supervision [33]. These cobots are powered by AI algorithms that analyze real-time data to optimize task allocation and adapt to changing production requirements.

Integrating CPS with advanced AI capabilities enables real-time decision-making while prioritizing sustainability. Varadarajan et al. [34] highlight how Industry 5.0 facilitates using digital twins and edge AI to monitor, simulate, and optimize energy consumption and waste reduction processes. This is particularly important in industries where resource efficiency and environmental impact are critical considerations.

The applications of Industry 5.0 extend beyond manufacturing to healthcare, agriculture, and logistics. For example, cobots in healthcare environments support surgical precision and personalized patient care [34].

Creative farming solutions that optimize crop yields and monitor environmental parameters using CPS and AI further demonstrate the paradigm's disruptive potential.

AI is key in improving CPS security by tackling issues with secure communication, anomaly detection, and intrusion detection.

CPS, which integrates computational and physical processes, relies on AI to identify threats, respond to anomalies, and ensure data security [36–39].

Intrusion detection systems (IDS) form the backbone of CPS security. AI-powered IDS leverage machine learning and deep learning to detect malicious activities and unauthorized access. Feature extraction and classification can empower intrusion detection frameworks to identify malware in embedded CPS devices [37]. Similarly, AI and cognitive computing can enhance IDS for industrial CPS, emphasizing real-time detection with minimal computational overhead [38].

Anomaly detection is critical for identifying deviations from normal system behavior. For instance, multimodal fusion techniques can detect anomalies in CPS networks, integrating data from diverse sources for more accurate detection [36]. Entropy-based anomaly detection methods that quantify irregularities in CPS operations can enable early threat identification and mitigation [36].

AI also strengthens secure communication protocols within CPS. Generative models and advanced cryptographic methods ensure data integrity during transmission. A recent work emphasized dispersion entropy and secure transmission methods to safeguard communication in industrial CPS, mitigating risks such as eavesdropping and data breaches [39].

18.3 AI Evolution

The technological evolution of computer systems, both in terms of hardware and software, is increasingly facilitating the implementation of the system-of-systems envisaged for the next generation of Society 5.0. This concept represents an advanced vision of society, in which the physical and digital worlds are perfectly integrated to improve the quality of life [40]. At the heart of this ongoing transformation, there are cyber-physical spaces, which merge physical components with digital infrastructures and artificial intelligence.

Since Society 5.0 targets the entire human society, its implementation requires collaboration among experts from various sectors. For example, this includes professionals in engineering, economics, social sciences, industrial engineering, agronomy, medicine, biology, and chemistry, as well as policymakers. This list is not exhaustive because Society 5.0 is human-centric without specifying specific sectors as happens for Industry, Agriculture, and Healthcare 4.0 which are now evolving toward their 5.0 version.

The concept of artificial intelligence emerged alongside the birth of computers based on theories of computability, formulated with the contribution of Alan Turing for developing the machine that bears his name in 1936 [41]. Shortly after, in 1937 Claude Shannon, in his master's thesis at the Massachusetts Institute of Technology, showed how Boolean algebra and binary operations could be implemented with electronic circuits [42]. This marked the beginning of digital innovation in telecommunication networks.

In 1943, McCulloch and Pitts published what is considered the first work related to artificial intelligence [43]. For many years following this, progress in scientific research about the AI was slow. However, in the past decade, thanks to the advancements in computer technology, the number of scientific publications in the fields of artificial intelligence, machine learning, and deep learning has shown a rather important growth.

To illustrate the growth of scientific research on artificial intelligence, one can analyze databases like Web of Science, Scopus, and Google Scholar. For example, searching for terms such as "Artificial intelligence," "Supervised machine learning," "Unsupervised machine learning," "Deep learning," or, finally, "Digital twin" in article titles, abstracts, and keywords on Scopus reveals a remarkable trend in the number of publications related to these technologies over the years. As can be seen from the Figure 18.1, recent years have seen a growth that is more than exponential in scientific publications where the term AI has been written in the title, or the abstract and the keywords. In 2024, the number of this kind of publications is little bit lower than 90,000. When we examine the different types of ML and deep learning (DL), focusing on the same research on Scopus over the same time period, it's evident that deep learning stands out as the most dominant (Figure 18.2). In 2024, it achieved a record number of publications totaling 123,000, far exceeding the others. To better appreciate the differences between them, Figure 18.3 shows the detail of ML techniques in the last decade.

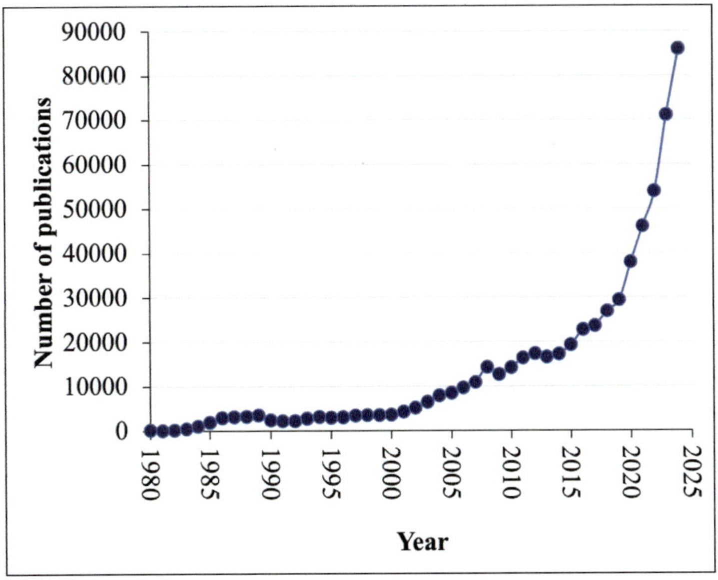

Figure 18.1 Number of scientific publications related to the AI recorded in Scopus from 1980 to 2024.

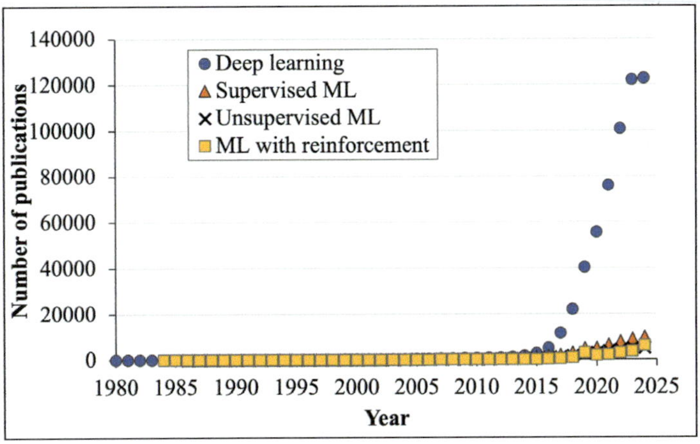

Figure 18.2 Number of scientific publications related to the DL and ML techniques recorded in Scopus from 1980 to 2024.

18.3.1 Digital twins

In a cyber-physical system of Society 5.0, learning techniques are typically linked to so-called digital twins. A digital twin (DT) is a virtual representation, created through a digital model, of a physical system, or a real process. This digital model allows the simulation of the system, or the process by

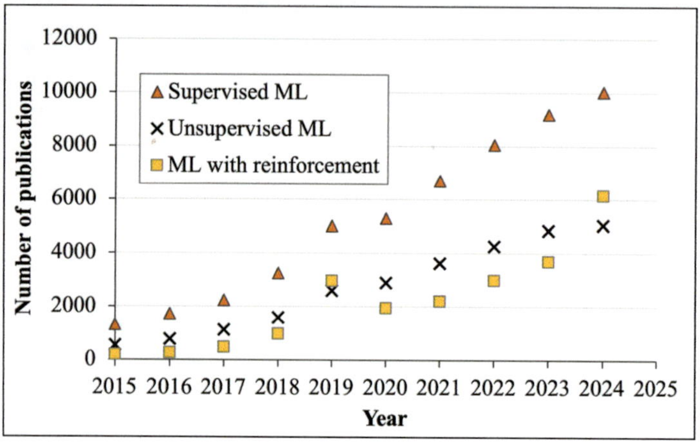

Figure 18.3 Number of scientific publications related to ML techniques recorded in Scopus from 2015 to 2024.

mimicking its behavior. Thus, by applying artificial intelligence algorithms to it, it is possible to monitor, analyze, and optimize the system/process in real time more effectively.

In summary, DTs are useful for real-time monitoring, predictive analysis, offline optimization, and as an aid to decision-making.

For real-time monitoring, a DT allows the visualization of the current state of a system in a synthetic way considering only the parameters of interest. This allows us to quickly identify any anomalies or inefficiencies of what the DT models are representing.

Since machine learning techniques can be applied to a DT just like on what it represents, in many cases the use of this digital model allows for predictive analysis to be carried out to foresee potential failures or to identify critical points in the life cycle of a system more promptly and effectively.

Virtuality provides a safe space to test changes and improvements without interfering with the real system. This allows you to optimize systems and processes with reduced time and costs.

Instead, for decision-making, simulations of the virtual model allow you to make informed decisions of various types, for maintenance, asset management, or future design.

The literature offers several examples of DT applications [44–48]. Even in this case, technological evolution has had a strong acceleration in the last 10 years, as shown in the Figure 18.4 that can be obtained from the analysis of the data extracted from Scopus with a search for the term "Digital Twin" in the titles, abstracts, and keywords of the scientific publications in its database.

In the following section, some case studies will be presented as examples of ML and DL techniques application to digital twins of different physical systems.

18.4 Case Studies

This section highlights several case studies that exemplify the application of learning techniques to DTs and the implementation of ML techniques on a real system equipped with sensors. The first case is a reference to demonstrate how the application of AI can be used to make a smart grid more efficient with a DT obtained by merging virtual models obtained with different numerical techniques. The second case shows the application of neural networks to a DT of a nano grid created with MATLAB/Simulink to optimize the management of the batteries of a fleet of industrial autonomous guided vehicles. The last example, instead, describes the results obtained from the application of ML modeling of gait and posture invariants in a wearable system equipped with different sensors.

18.4.1 Smart grids. AI models for demand forecasting and fault prediction

CASE 1 – Cyber-physical systems and digital twins for building energy management: the case of the Rinascimento III District in Rome

The first research case study examines digital ICT-based energy management strategies applied to a residential district in Rome called Rione Rinascimento III [49]. This district, consisting of 16 eight-floor buildings, is the most significant Italian residential implementation of a geothermal source heat pump (GSHP) system, currently the largest in Europe. It houses approximately 900 apartment units with 2500 residents.

This work investigates the potential for integrating DT models with AI systems, focusing on a practical application to implement the developed methodology. The case study involves creating an efficient DT model for the residential district, aiming to improve energy efficiency and identify cost-effective solutions to reduce both energy consumption and expenses.

Sensors link the physical and digital models, tracking and transmitting electrical power information for lighting, HVAC systems, and smart plugs used by devices such as computers, TVs, and washing machines.

AI systems empower DT to gain predictive abilities, learning from past events to enhance outcomes and making independent decisions based on analysis without human input. The AI system optimizes energy consumption and production performance, adjusting to the environment to achieve set goals.

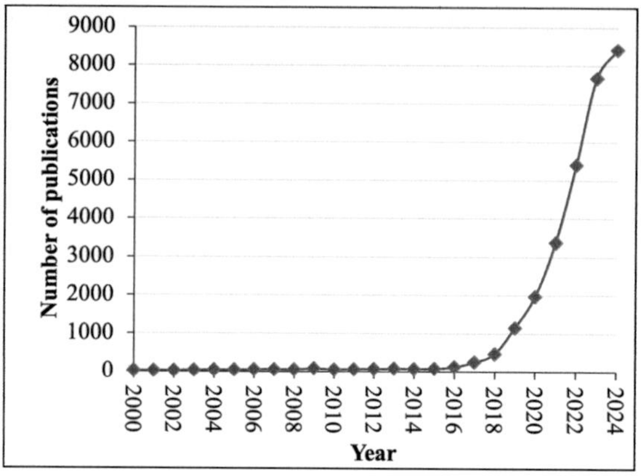

Figure 18.4 The publications rate of digital twin by year from 2000 to 2024 (source Scopus).

The system gathers data from sensors and uses reasoning systems to create specific actions, optimizing energy use. It combines information from IFC-BIM and CityGML-GIS models, continuously feeding them with real-time data. A large part of the energy for the complex is self-generated from renewable geothermal sources.

This application leverages BIM and GIS to enhance energy management. It focuses on the technical parameters of the building envelope, thermal zones, individual rooms, HVAC systems, and related equipment. Additionally, it incorporates localization data, climate information, and boundary conditions sourced from the BIM system. Figure 18.5 provides an overall view of the BIM model.

The primary objective of the DT-based methodology is to utilize data models in various simulation and monitoring processes. This approach integrates information from BIM, GIS, IoT, and other sources into a three-dimensional model aligned with the system in near real-time.

Shaping a BIM-based methodology allows for assessing the building system's energy performance and supporting decision-making processes. The DT mirrors the energy properties of the building's structure and technical systems, including renewable energy elements. Figure 18.6 schematizes how data flow and processing are designed for the realization of the DT.

Building energy model (BEM)

To develop a building energy model (BEM), each element of the information model was associated with the corresponding products in the BEM software, which was integrated with the BIM data, defining various thermal zones and boundary conditions.

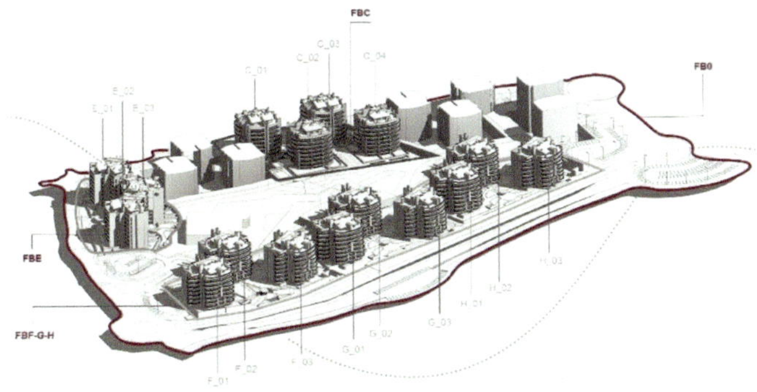

Figure 18.5 Overall view of the Rione Rinascimento III 3D model.

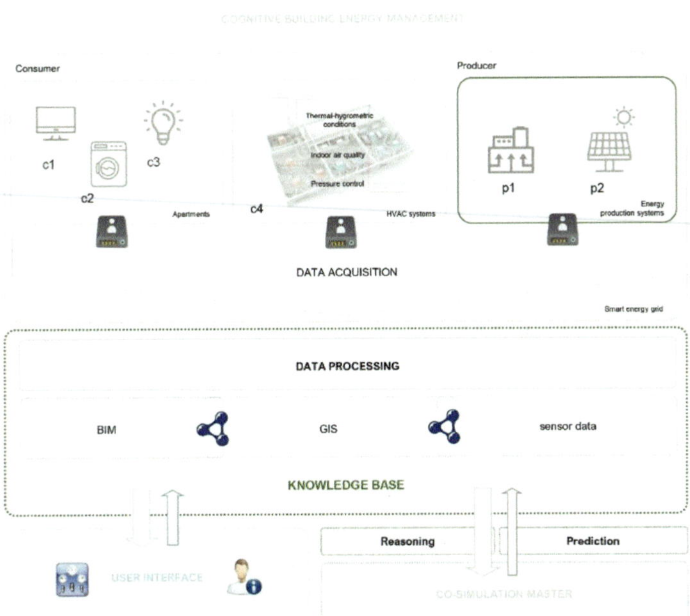

Figure 18.6 Data processing and flow applied in the DT for energy optimization.

The energy model was validated to comply with Italian regulation DLgs. 30 May 2008, which states that the deviation between estimated and actual consumption values must not exceed 5% on average.

In the pilot project, the building complex is powered by the largest European residential geothermal plant with a ground source heat pump (GSHP) system (COP of 3.8 in winter and 5.5 in summer), equipped with

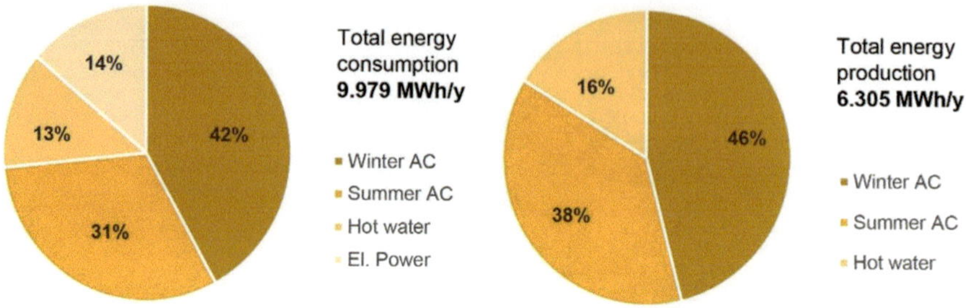

Figure 18.7 Total energy consumption and RES production quotas of the Rinascimento district.

200 vertical geoprobes, each 150 meters deep. The total energy consumption of the Rinascimento district is categorized into four main areas: winter air conditioning, summer air conditioning, hot water, and electric power supply. Renewable energy sources, particularly the geothermal plant, generate approximately 6305 MWh/year out of the 9979 MWh/year consumed, covering 63% of the total primary energy requirement. The total energy consumption and renewable energy source (RES) production of the Rinascimento district are illustrated in Figure 18.7.

The energy assessment was conducted on a single building of approximately 3648 m², using the Revit Suite from Mc4 Software and BIM data for dynamic simulation of the building's behavior, supported by a modular section of the geothermal plant. This building was selected for energy modeling and real-time monitoring because it is the only one fully occupied by residents who consented to the installation of sensing devices for the digital twin (DT) configuration.

The DT model aimed to simulate an increase in RES production to achieve the goal of transforming the district into a near-zero energy district (nZED). The energy simulations included the installation of photovoltaic panels for electricity generation and solar collectors for domestic hot water production.

Specifically, the model incorporated 312 kWp of monocrystalline photovoltaic modules on the building fa¸cade, capable of producing 276.000 kWh/year of electricity, and an area with 405 high-efficiency flat-plate solar collectors, generating 410.000 kWh/year. The simulation results indicated that 6991 MWh/year of energy would be produced from RES (geothermal and solar), covering about 70% of the district's energy consumption through the RES microgrid.

The findings focused on the building, outlining various thermal zones based on usage, occupancy times, HVAC types, external envelope features,

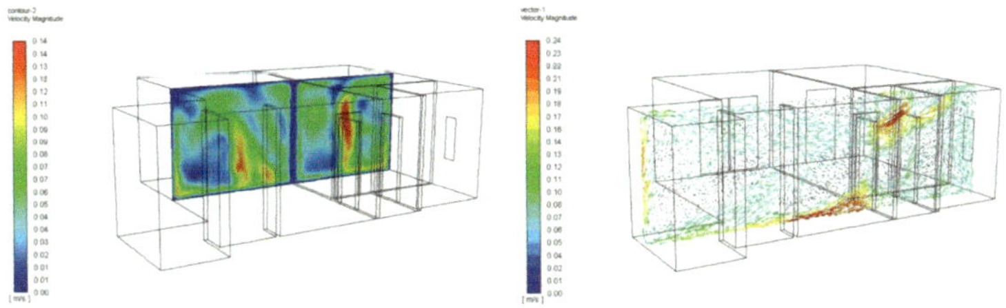

Figure 18.8 CFD simulation analysis: temperature gradient and air velocity vectors.

and sun exposure. On a more detailed level, the analysis highlighted indoor environmental quality, including thermal-hygrometric conditions. The BIM model was upgraded with HVAC systems to perform computational fluid dynamics (CFD) analysis [50].

The standard k-ϵ model was chosen for its computational efficiency and quick iteration time (under 300 iterations), as well as the lack of high-pressure gradients in the rooms. The input conditions were: an average outdoor air temperature of 5 °C, a radiant floor water temperature of 40 °C, an underfloor heating surface temperature ranging from 24 °C to 29 °C, a discrete ordinates radiative model, and a 1-second time-step.

Four control probes were temporarily installed in the center of each room in a typical apartment, positioned 1.5 m above the ground, matching the height of the DT temperature and humidity monitors in all apartment rooms. Fluid dynamics analyses (Figure 18.8) were derived from the BIM model to examine temperature gradients and convective airflows in rooms, driven by the operation of radiant floors in winter heating mode. These analyses aimed to evaluate comfort parameters and explore data interoperability from the BIM model to CFD analysis.

Machine learning for energy efficiency optimization

This study utilizes a machine learning approach to optimize energy-efficiency models using AI while maintaining normal comfort and living conditions. Energy data, comprising time series of power consumption or production, are collected from real sensors over specific periods. Each sensor transmits data via its own API and is situated near energy loads or power sources. This decentralized data collection presents an analytical challenge, requiring a cost-effective IT infrastructure to ensure reliable data processing. The operational concept of the developed infrastructure is illustrated in Figure 18.9.

Each apartment is equipped with monitoring sensors to track the energy consumption of every device, enabling the formulation of control solutions for overall energy requirements. The substantial data generated by these

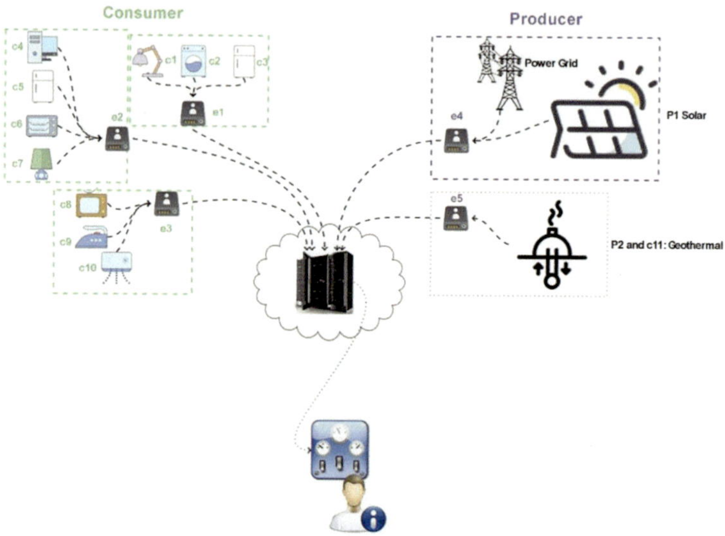

Figure 18.9 Operative concept of the developed infrastructure.

sensors necessitates significant computational resources for effective analysis. To minimize installation costs, the optimal solution involves centralizing data acquisition in a data center or service.

This architecture requires a local system to interconnect IoT sensors and actuators over a geographical network (such as the Internet), perform local computations, and buffer data during connection outages.

This approach leverages ubiquitous and pervasive computing [51] techniques to address the computational challenges of centralized intelligence.

The most peripheral component of the infrastructure is a subsystem that handles various transmission protocols and time frames, outputting synchronized power consumption or production data from smart metered devices. It also receives instructions on how to control the devices. It must be located near the sensor networks to minimize transmission issues and monitor the local environment even without communication with the central control system.

The peripheral nodes are connected to the centralized control system through proxy nodes. Each proxy also manages bandwidth and network reliability issues. The central unit stores and processes data operates, builds digital simulation models, and sends commands back to the proxies.

This logical infrastructure involves equipping a series of inexpensive small computers or systems on chips (SoCs) with both the sensor and proxy nodes. These computers are connected to a high-performance server in a data center, which runs the central control system software.

Once data is stored in the central control system, it can be analyzed to create digital numerical models that simulate and optimize the main parameters of the smart energy grid. The data is formatted uniformly as {location, date-time, object, value}.

For a single location, ML techniques and rule-based methods, such as association rule learning, can identify which devices are active at specific times. However, not all locations can be treated the same due to varying uses (home, office, mixed-use) and layouts. By grouping locations based on similarities, AI can automate the process of assigning each location to the most appropriate cluster. This requires using a clustering ML technique to automatically form groups of similar apartments for mathematical representation. Energy consumers and producers are grouped by type to create a feature vector for each unit. Using the K-means clustering technique, we automatically identified groups of energy-similar apartments. After an observation period, a sample from each homogeneous group was selected to extract behavioral rules applicable to the entire group.

By analyzing the configuration of each location at a given time, we can compare any apartment "A_i" with a reference sample "A_s." For example, an association rule might state: "A_t time t_k, compare device type d_j in apartment i ($dA_{i,j}$) with the corresponding device type in the reference apartment (dA_{sj}). If they are in similar states, do nothing; otherwise, switch the device on or off to match the reference state.

An association rule in a smart grid might look like:

$$\text{“}\mathit{TheSolarPanelIsOn} \rightarrow \mathit{TheWashingMachineIsOn}.\text{”}$$

We utilized the Apriori Algorithm to mine frequent item sets for Boolean association rules, identifying item frequencies and extending them to larger sets based on their dataset occurrences. However, automated systems can fail if digital representation does not align with reality. Over time, smart plugs may be connected to different devices, impacting model accuracy.

To maintain an up-to-date digital model, AI techniques convert a device's power absorption curve into a sequence of characters, or "energy words," using text analysis methods. The Naïve Bayes classifier then identifies the type of each load, detecting mismatches between the digital model and actual network connections. This approach generated a dictionary of over 60,000 energy words, with most appearing fewer than three times. We set this threshold to avoid dimensional issues. The predictive model, developed using

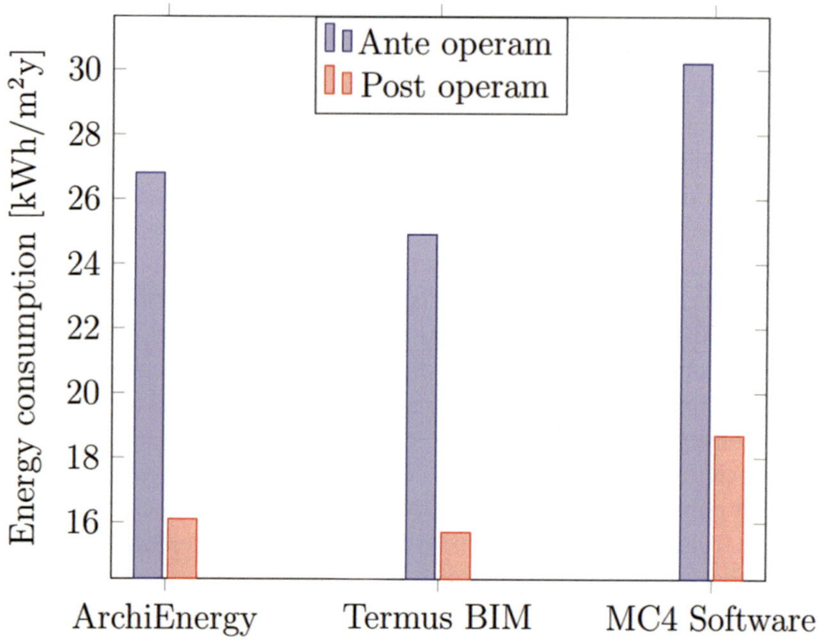

Figure 18.10 Comparison of energy diagnosis results obtained with three different software packages.

the Naïve Bayes classifier, was validated with a 66% train, 33% test split, and a 10-fold cross-validation technique.

Main results of case study 1

Thanks to the implementation of renewable energy systems, the geothermal power plant provides heating and domestic hot water to all buildings during winter. Solar collectors supplement this system, while the photovoltaic system powers the external lighting around the buildings. In the summer, solar collectors meet 100% of the domestic hot water needs, and the geothermal power plant is used only for cooling via an absorber. The photovoltaic system continues to power the entire lighting system.

An energy assessment of a single building using the BIM model through Mc4 software's Revit Suite improved from an A2 energy class (26.8 kWh/m^2y) to an A4 class (16.1 kWh/m^2y). The calculation was repeated with two other numerical simulation tools to further validate the results: (1) Termus BIM, based on the BIM model, and (2) ArchiEnergy, developed by Sapienza University of Rome. Results are shown in Figure 18.10.

The outcomes and deviation values were compared with other energy evaluations of similar building systems. The analysis revealed that the diagnoses made using the energy software produced comparable results, with a maximum deviation of 12%. The discrepancy between the two BIM-based tools, Mc4 Suite for Revit and Termus BIM, was 5%.

Fluid dynamics analysis in certain rooms of an apartment validated sensor data, showing no discomfort from the radiant floor setup. Significant air movement was noted, driven by the temperature difference between the floor and the surrounding environment. Convective currents impacted all areas, but the temperature gradient complied with regulations, and air speeds stayed low, within the comfort range.

The internal temperature in each area was initially 5 °C (equal to the external temperature) and reached the comfort temperature of 20 °C in about 1900 seconds (just over 30 minutes). An intelligent energy management model, an automatic ML system, was implemented to modulate loads based on expected energy self-production. Predictive meteorological data from the European Copernicus earth observation system were used [52].

The energy-smart-grid system, equipped with solar collectors and photovoltaic panels, required guidelines to prioritize energy production and consumption:

- *Production*: Electricity from solar sources, being cost-free, is supplied first to the distribution network, followed by energy from the geothermal power plant (which requires electricity for circulation pumps). As a last resort, energy from the public electrical grid or gas can be utilized.
- *Consumption*: Priority is given to the lighting system, followed by the electromotive force circuit. If there is an energy shortage, air conditioning systems can be adjusted by modifying the optimal temperature by up to 2 °C.

The AI system increased the overall energy efficiency by more than 10%, reducing the building complex's dependence on electricity and gas distribution networks to a maximum of 20% of the total energy consumed. The energy load forecasting and management system was applied in a single apartment through two phases: (a) developing a method to categorize plants based on energy efficiency outcomes and (b) measuring, assessing, and analyzing the consumption data of the chosen plant.

The DT facilitated the assessment of smart-grid implementation effects. Specifically, Figure 18.11 illustrates the decreased energy consumption and the relatively lower CO_2 emissions as analyzed by the Mc4 Suite for Revit.

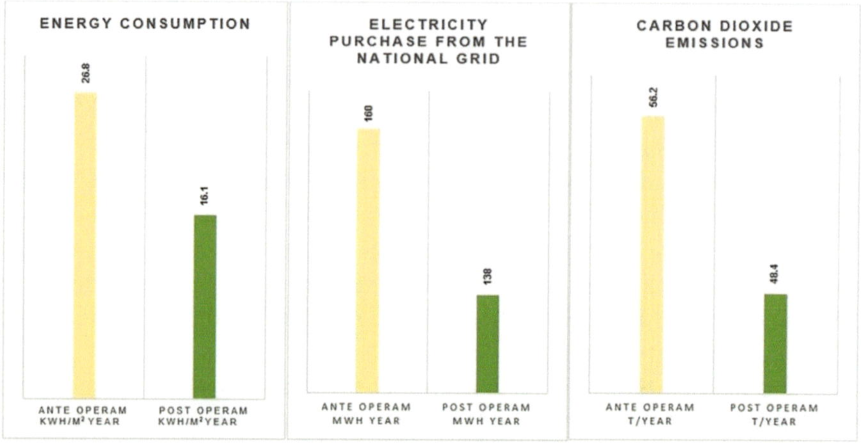

Figure 18.11 Comprehensive view of the smart-grid DT implementation effects.

The system considered the inevitable changes in apartment usage and energy load variations over time. An algorithm was used to identify devices at each power outlet by analyzing the hourly current absorption trend. Energy sensors were applied, and data were collected in a central system. Submetering identified the largest single load in the apartment and each room, simplifying energy-saving strategies by targeting the most consuming items and effectively contributing to overall energy savings.

CASE 2 – Design of the grid architecture and size for electric vehicle fleets in industrial environments through neural networks

The widespread adoption of autonomous EVs with batteries, such as electric forklifts in industrial settings necessitates careful design of power supply and battery recharging systems. The increasing availability of RES, like PV systems, enhances the autonomy of industrial plants from the PG and lowers management costs. However, the variables involved in optimal electric energy production, storage, and usage management are becoming more complex.

Based on workload and management algorithms, these vehicles can autonomously connect to one or more charging stations. Numerous studies address trajectory tracking and planning for scheduling work cycles of forklift groups [53–55]. However, designing a fleet of autonomous vehicles powered by renewable energy sources (RES) is complex, particularly when optimizing for the economic, technological, and environmental sustainability of the PV plant, storage capacity, number of vehicles, and overall battery size. Adding a backup battery to recharge vehicles in case of RES power supply failure could be advantageous, but there are no definitive formulas, equations, or mathematical models available for system sizing [56].

This case study aims to develop simulation models to help designers identify the optimal specifications for various components, including the size of the PV plant, the number of vehicles, the battery capacity for each vehicle, and the number of charging stations [57]. A simulation model in MATLAB/ Simulink is designed to describe the behavior of a typical industrial scenario. As depicted in Figure 18.12, the model includes:

- the power supply system utilizing renewable energy sources (RES);
- the charging system, including models of charging stations and electric vehicles;
- the scheduling and control algorithm.

The operation of the EVs is determined by a model of the onboard battery, paired with a finite state machine (FSM) that controls the vehicle's functions based on the job schedule. The battery model scales a single cell to reach the required nominal voltage and capacity, with each cell's voltage characteristics empirically estimated as described by authors in [57]. To simplify implementation, each vehicle contains the logic for both its job schedule and charging process, with the appropriate algorithm selected based on scheduler commands. The FSM has three states: *off*, *charging*, and *working*.

The system controller oversees the fleet's overall status and the availability of charging stations, assigning new tasks to vehicles. During each simulation cycle, the algorithm checks for vehicles that have completed their tasks and are available. If a charging station is free, the first available vehicle is assigned for charging. The algorithm then randomly selects an available vehicle with a safe SoC for a new task.

Vehicle charging power is primarily supplied by a PV plant and an auxiliary Battery Energy Storage System (BESS)

EV battery modeling enhanced by ML state of health estimation

To enhance the framework's capabilities and make more sophisticated estimations state of health (SoH) prediction algorithms are included in the EVs' battery models. Two different levels of complexity have been explored:

1. a first-order prediction considering only the charge/discharge cycle history of the EV's battery,
2. a more sophisticated one based on the electrochemical impedance spectroscopy (EIS) technique [58, 59].

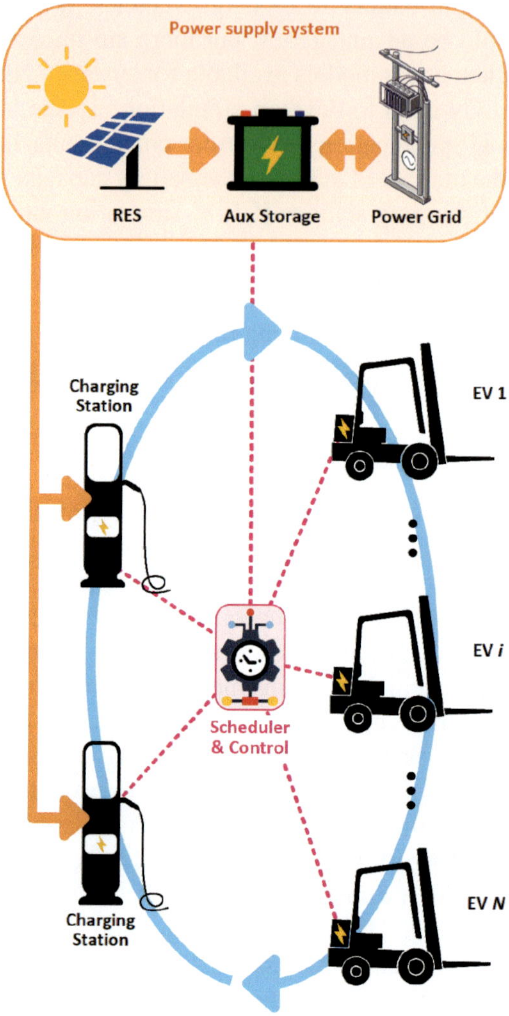

Figure 18.12 Diagram of the simulation model [57].

In the first case, we collected SoH data versus recharging cycles for 26 batteries, creating a dataset of 220 samples. The SoH trajectory varied for each battery based on its history.

Experiments were conducted using MATLAB, employing sigmoidal feed-forward neural networks (FNN) with varying neurons and hidden layers, trained using the Levenberg–Marquardt algorithm with regularization. Datasets were partitioned into training, validation, and testing sets

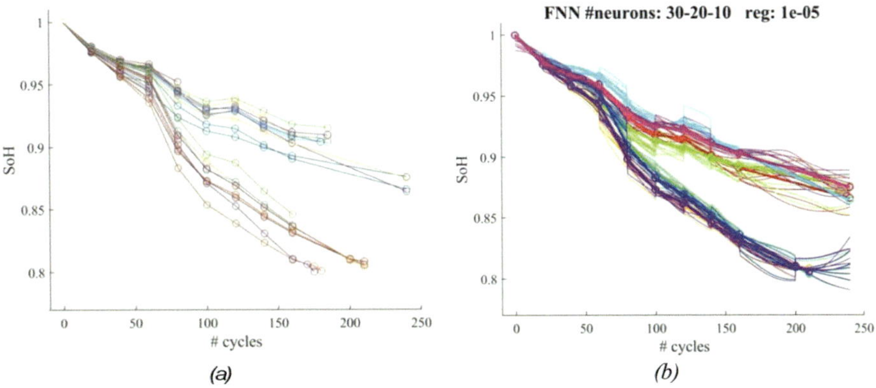

Figure 18.13 Training results for the FNN in the case of battery charge/discharge cycle history: (a) the training dataset (different batteries are depicted using different colors), (b) the FNN models approximating the batteries SoH [57].

(60%-20%-20%), and each experiment was repeated 10 times. In the first case, we collected SoH data versus recharging cycles for 26 batteries, creating a dataset of 220 samples. The SoH trajectory varied for each battery based on its history.

In Figure 18.13, the functions approximated by the trained models are reported. Finally, Figure 18.14 displays the histogram and regression of one of the trained models (the statistics for the other models are similar and have been excluded for clarity). The majority of the approximations lie within an error range of [–0.05, 0.05].

Hardware-in-the-loop prototype and framework results

A hardware-in-the-loop (HIL) test bench (Figure 18.15) is designed for a single EV charging at one station to validate the simulation model. The setup includes a variable DC generator with PV emulator capability, an auxiliary battery acting as a DC bus, and multiple DC/DC buck converters. A HIL-specialized simulator oversees key electrical parameters and produces PWM control signals to operate the converters, replicating the electric vehicle's power consumption during operations.

The simulation framework allows parametric scenario simulations to find the optimum size for PV and BESS to minimize the total operating cost (for cost estimation details, see [57]).

Figure 18.16 presents results from a 1-year simulation of EVs operating 24 hours a day. By evaluating different PV/BESS size combinations, a cost surface is generated, and the most cost-effective configuration is identified.

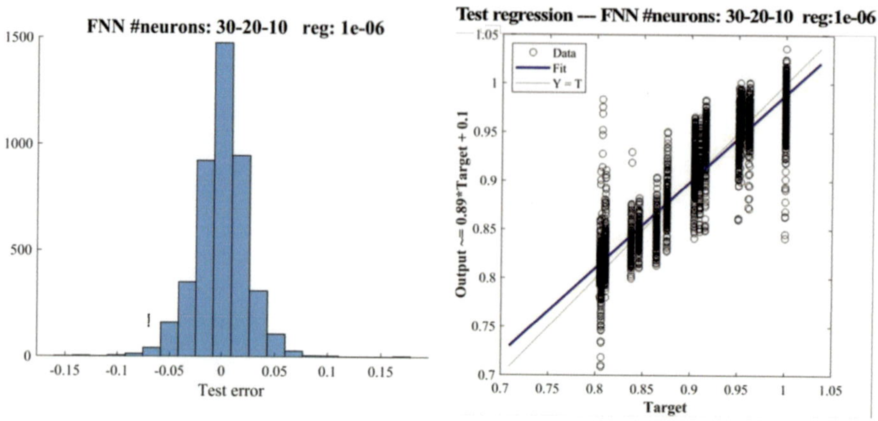

(a) (b)

Figure 18.14 Histogram (a) and regression curve (b) of one of the trained models in the case of the EIS dataset [57].

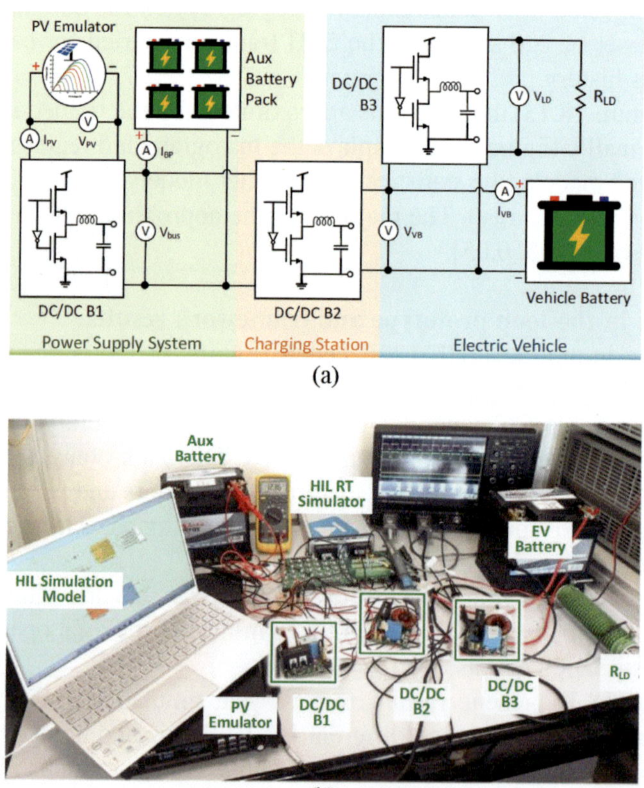

(a)

(b)

Figure 18.15 Test bench: (a) Block diagram; (b) picture of the system made for testing [57].

18.4.2 Healthcare CPS

CASE 3 – Posture and gait evaluation through wearable technologies and machine learning

In medicine and sports science, assessing posture is essential for correcting gait and posture [60]. Although there are advanced tools for measuring the efficiency and stability of the postural system, they often face challenges such as accessibility, cost, size, intrusiveness, usability, and lengthy setup times.

Various instruments have been used to detect musculoskeletal activation in sports and rehabilitative medicine, with electromyography (EMG) being the primary method. However, EMGs are not commonly used alongside accelerometers for predicting and customizing measures to analyze body motion. This is due to the limited research on musculoskeletal responses to a wide range of stimuli that can identify thresholds for the ideal postural system status. As a result, there is a lack of affordable technology for these measurements.

In the past decade, the rise of the Internet of Things (IoT) has led to the integration of embedded sensors into personal devices like smartphones and smartwatches. Sensors are also embedded into clothing and other everyday objects, becoming a key research focus due to their importance in healthcare, interactive gaming, sports, and general monitoring systems in both controlled and uncontrolled environments [61–63].

The project presented in this case study [64] aims to address the main limitations of postural detection systems by investigating the assembly and use of wearable devices to provide feedback for enhancing gait and posture. This approach could benefit sports performance and the rehabilitation of motor impairments caused by neurodegenerative diseases, aging, or injuries. Three potential application scenarios are developed with input from psychiatric medicine professionals and sports training experts.

1. Diagnostic evaluation:
   - Context: Psychiatric medical practice.
   - Use case: A patient with postural instability due to trauma or neurodegenerative disorder undergoes diagnostic evaluation.
   - Process: The patient performs exercises while wearing a sensor-equipped jacket that interacts with a cloud-based application. The system measures reaction times and other variables, helping medical personnel assess progress.

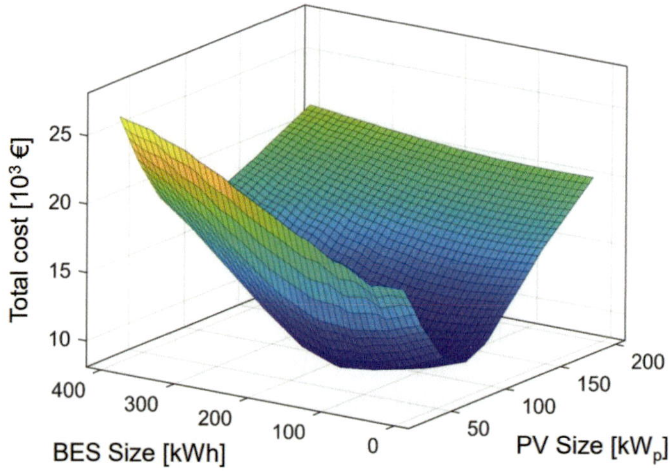

Figure 18.16 Cost surface resulting from a 1-year simulation scenario of EVs operating 24 hours a day [57].

2. Sport performance benchmarking:
    - Context: Athletic training.
    - Use case: An athlete trains for an event, monitored by a coach.
    - Process: The athlete wears a sensor-equipped jacket during training. Performance is benchmarked against predefined standards, allowing the coach to track progress and identify areas for improvement.
3. Rehabilitation follow-up:
    - Context: Post-traumatic rehabilitation.
    - Use case: A patient follows a rehabilitation program.
    - Process: The patient performs exercises while wearing the jacket. Performance is compared to benchmarks set during the diagnostic phase, helping track recovery and adjust the rehabilitation plan as needed.

These scenarios illustrate how the technology can be applied in different contexts to enhance diagnostic evaluation, athletic training, and rehabilitation follow-up. For this purpose, a gait and posture smart jacket (GPSJack) is designed as a low-cost inertial sensor-based system working inside the gait and posture smart environment (GPSEnv) [64]. The GSPJack/GPSEnv framework architecture will enable medical and sports staff to perform the following actions:

- register a GPSJack/GPSEnv administrator;
- initiate the setup of a GPSJack/GPSEnv;
- register a new user;
- define the profile of a registered user;
- delete a profile;
- conduct a base test for a registered user;
- register a new exercise;
- register a new benchmark for an existing exercise;
- assign a benchmark for a specific exercise to a user;
- execute an exercise;
- register a sequence of exercises as a training path;
- associate benchmark values with a training path;
- assign benchmark values for a training path to a user;
- visualize the progress of a single test over a period;
- visualize progress relative to a given benchmark.

Architecture of the system

Figure 18.17 shows the GPSJack/GPSEnv architecture. It is composed of several modules:

- User interface. Enables users to input "environments" and displays all data/results generated by the ML module.
- Configurator. Accepts a set of environments as input and produces a set of feasible "exercises" for the trainer, based on user input and ML algorithms.
- Trainer. Utilizes the exercises to determine optimal paths, specifying which exercises should be performed and in which environment.
- Evaluator. Evaluates data and automatically compares it with benchmarks.

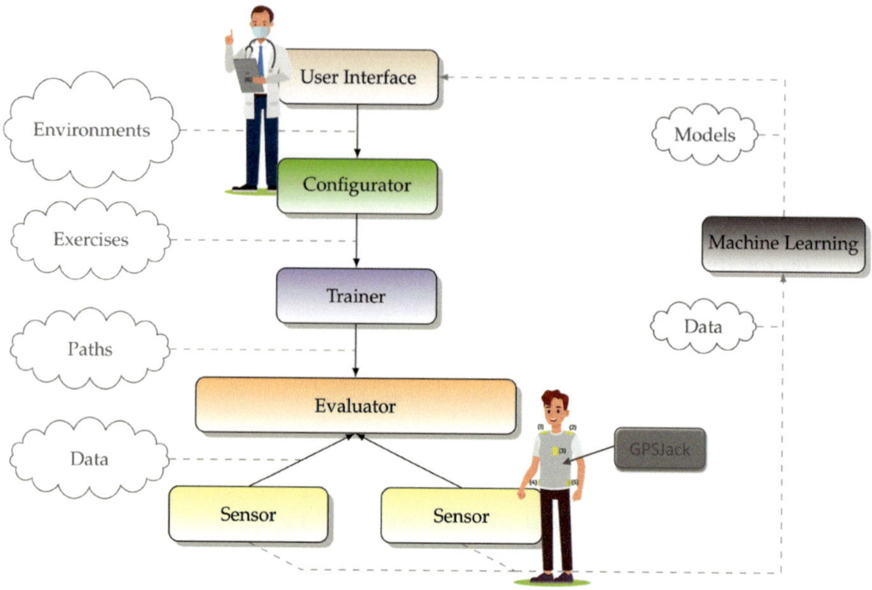

Figure 18.17 Diagram of the GPSJack/GPSEnv system architecture.

- Sensor. Manages wearable sensors, collecting and normalizing data.
- ML. Collects data and generates models.

The user interface produces a structured sequence of "environments," which serve as inputs for the configurator. The configurator constantly processes these inputs and, at designated intervals, employs models from the ML module to generate a set of viable "exercises." These exercises are provided to the trainer, who develops chains of exercises, or "paths," for patients or athletes to follow. The trainer's work allows for different paths at different times. Data collected by the sensor module is sent to the evaluator for storage, visualization, and comparison with benchmarks. This data is also used to develop potential "paths" and exercises, which are suggested to the user. The ML module acts as a feedback generator for the entire system, continuously enhancing performance.

- A four-step method is designed to accomplish system requirements:
- identification of the motor tasks;
- overview and structure of the data acquisition systems that make up the GPSEnv/GPSJack;

- collected data analysis;
- ML modeling of consistent patterns in gait and posture.

The motor tasks are designed to challenge postural stability and require anticipation of sudden disturbances. These tasks help train and measure essential motor skills like adaptation, compensation, and anticipation. A typical trial involves three main steps:

- Rotation: The participant stands on an unstable board, holding a heavy ball, and rotates their torso to specific angles while maintaining balance.
- Ball drop: The participant drops the ball quickly, with anticipatory postural adjustments captured and analyzed.
- Recovery: After losing balance from the ball drop, the participant regains balance as quickly as possible.
- Different experimental conditions are tested to evaluate deviations from standard measurements, involving various populations from elite athletes to individuals with neuromuscular diseases. The data collected helps in assessing and improving postural control.

GPSEnv performs gait and posture analyses using three main instruments:

1. Force platform: Measures forces in three orthogonal directions and the center of pressure (COP) migration. The AMTI Biomechanics Force Platform (model BP900900) is used, featuring high sensitivity, low crosstalk, and excellent repeatability, making it ideal for research and clinical studies.
2. Surface electromyography (EMG): Records the activity of sixteen postural muscles on both sides of the body using electrocardiographic electrodes (Figure 18.18(a)). The EMG system collects and amplifies signals at a sampling rate of 1000 Hz.
3. Motion capture cameras: Five retro-reflective markers (Figure 18.18(b)) are attached to the subject's body to record position, velocity, and acceleration at a sampling rate of 200 Hz using eight motion capture cameras and Vicon Nexus 2.6 software.

The GPSJack prototype uses the nRF52840 SoC, which supports multiple communication protocols and features low energy consumption. It interfaces with various sensors, such as accelerometers, gyroscopes, and magnetometers. The Nordic Thingy 52 IoT Sensors kit is used for initial testing,

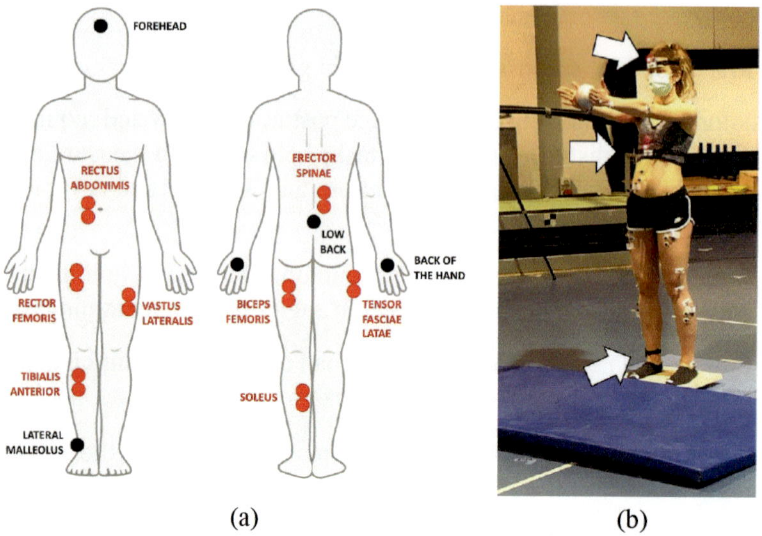

Figure 18.18 GPSEnv apparatus: (a) location of EMG electrodes (*red*) and (b) retro-reflective markers (*black*).

with future plans to develop dedicated data collection nodes based on the nRF52840 SoC.

Key features of the GPSJack system [65] include dimensions of 5 cm × 5 cm × 1.5 cm, 47 g weight, a 9-axis motion-tracking sensors, up to 200 Hz sampling frequency, rechargeable Li-Po battery (1440 mAh), Bluetooth Low Energy (BLE), low cost of $ 38. The GPSJack system supports of up to 11 nodes that communicate with a tablet or single-board computer. It can operate for over 48 hours at a sampling frequency of 200 Hz.

Data processing, analysis and results

Data processing steps for the collected data (Figure 18.19) include:

- Data cleaning: Reduces noise and handles missing or corrupted data using interpolation and low-pass filtering techniques.
- Feature extraction: Represents time-series data as a set of features in the time and frequency domains, using tools like the TSFEL library.
- Preprocessing of features: Normalizes data to ensure all variables equally influence the model and uses feature selection techniques to improve recognition accuracy.

Following the experimental design described earlier, we collected data from 12 male participants, whose physical characteristics are listed in Table 18.1.

Table 18.1 Subjects physical characteristics.

Subject	Age [Years]	Height [cm]	Weight [kg]
22	24	182	72.6
23	24	183	61.1
24	22	186	97.7
25	28	176	65.1
26	28	172	69.7
28	23	170	64.7
29	24	174	69.0
30	28	176	78,0
31	25	187	86.9
32	23	189	78.1
33	23	176	66.9
34	19	175	72.8
Min	19	170	61.1
Max	28	189	97.7
Avg	24.76	178.65	73.71
Std	2.78	6.15	9.97

Each participant completed 84 data collection sessions, involving seven tasks (no rotation, and rotations of 30°, 60°, or 90° to the left and right) under two conditions (stable/unstable) with six repetitions each. These sessions included five movement phases: rotate, in position, APAs, drop, and recover. The collected data were categorized into three datasets based on the technology used: force platform, EMGs, and acceleration data, as summarized in Table 18.2. Each dataset type (A, B, and C) underwent the data-processing pipeline outlined in Figure 18.19. The data were segmented into 150 ms windows, representing the APA movement phase, and used to train three machine learning models. The models' performance in recognizing the movement phases was evaluated using accuracy (A), precision (P), F1-score ($F1$), and recall (R), calculated as follows:

$$A = \frac{tp + tn}{tp + tn + fp + fn} \qquad P = \frac{tp}{tp + fp}$$

$$F1 = 2 \times \frac{P \times R}{P + R} \qquad R = \frac{tp}{tp + fp}$$

Table 18.2 Summary of the three analyzed datasets individually, also using a 5-fold cross-validation.

Dataset ID	Time [ms]	Force Platform (#1)	EMG's (#10)	Acceleration (#9)	Sampling Freq. [Hz]
A	✓	✓	✓		1000
B	✓			✓	200
C	✓	✓	✓	✓	200

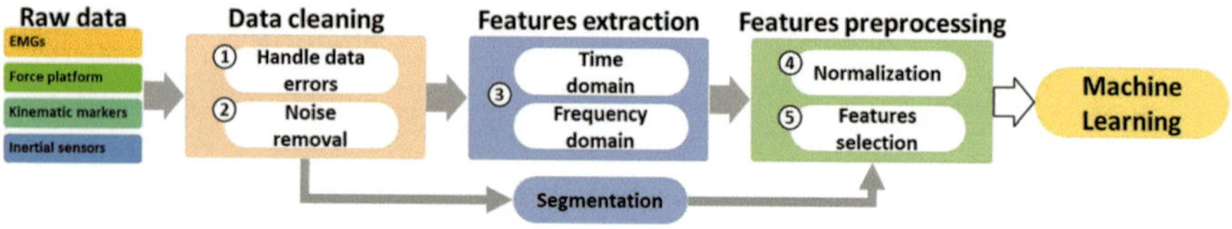

Figure 18.19 Data processing steps.

where t_p represents the number of true positives, n represents the number of true negatives, f_n represents the number of false negatives, and f_p represents the number of false positives.

Tables 18.3 and 18.4 present the preliminary analysis results. Table 18.3 shows the average results for datasets A, B, and C across all subjects using a 5-fold cross-validation. Table 18.4 details the results for each subject.

The random forest model outperformed across all datasets and data-treatment types. Combining datasets A (EMGs and Force Platform) and B (acceleration values) significantly enhanced performance compared to using them individually. The F1-score rose by 12.2% from dataset A to C and by 39.9% from dataset B to C, underscoring the importance of acceleration data. The random forest model achieved F1 scores of 88.2% and 89.6% in the segmentation and feature representation modes, respectively.

When models were trained and tested on individual subjects, performance varied. The random forest model consistently excelled (F1 score >91.6%) in both segmentation and feature representation modes, with an average 5% higher F1 score than when training and testing on all subjects' data. Combining datasets A and B again showed significant improvements, with F1-score increases of 7.3% from dataset A to C and 31.1% from dataset B to C.

The GPSJack system's performance was assessed for RAM, storage, CPU, battery usage, and data loss using a Samsung Galaxy Tab A7. The setup connected three Nordic Thingy 52 devices to the tablet for three hours at sampling rates of 50 Hz, 100 Hz, and 200 Hz. The system functioned efficiently across different configurations with no data loss and minimal resource

Table 18.3 Average results for segmentation and feature-extraction data representation across all 12 subjects.

	Segmentation												Feature Extraction											
	A				B				C				A				B				C			
Model	A	P	R	F1	A	P	R	F1	A	P	R	F1	A	P	R	F1	A	P	R	F1	A	P	R	F1
k-NN	58.1	56.2	58.1	55.2	47.4	45.0	47.4	44.0	57.3	55.5	57.3	54.4	42.7	39.4	42.7	40.2	38.9	36.8	38.9	35.8	71.4	67.7	71.4	69.2
RF	77.7	80.2	77.7	76.0	54.5	55.3	54.5	48.3	88.8	89.3	88.8	88.2	84.0	84.8	84.0	83.5	63.0	68.6	63.0	59.5	89.9	90.2	89.9	89.6
LDA	49.2	48.9	49.2	47.3	42.5	64.7	42.5	25.7	49.5	49.2	49.5	48.4	36.8	34.6	34.5	31.45	61.3	67.6	61.3	56.9	65.1	67.4	65.0	63.6

Table 18.4 Results on segmentation and feature extraction data representation for each subject.

		Segmentation												Feature Extraction											
		A				B				C				A				B				C			
Subject	Model	A	P	R	F1	A	P	R	F1	A	P	R	F1	A	P	R	F1	A	P	R	F1	A	P	R	F1
P22	k-NN	56.8	55.6	56.8	54.4	40.0	42.1	40.0	39.0	56.5	55.3	56.5	54.2	39.4	37.4	39.4	37.7	34.5	31.9	34.5	32.6	44.5	60.5	44.5	48.9
	RF	83.6	84.8	83.6	82.7	54.1	55.9	54.1	49.2	84.9	85.7	84.9	84.1	83.6	84.8	83.6	83.0	61.5	63.3	61.5	59.4	83.9	85.1	83.9	83.2
	LDA	59.5	59.5	59.5	59.4	32.1	30.8	32.1	31.2	54.8	56.4	54.8	55.5	39.3	76.0	39.3	40.0	3.0	8.3	3.0	0.4	44.5	60.5	44.5	48.9
P23	k-NN	66.7	67.3	66.7	64.3	42.1	42.8	42.1	37.4	65.8	63.5	65.8	63.0	49.1	46.8	49.1	47.8	37.8	34.7	37.8	35.0	82.9	81.4	82.8	80.3
	RF	86.1	87.7	86.1	85.6	48.9	47.9	48.9	43.5	99.8	99.8	99.8	99.8	87.6	88.0	87.6	87.2	62.4	64.9	62.4	60.3	100	100	100	100
	LDA	61.1	61.9	61.1	61.4	37.8	33.7	37.8	33.4	98.6	98.7	98.6	98.6	30.5	0.1	3.1	0.01	3.6	12.9	3.6	1.2	97.4	97.5	97.4	97.4
P24	k-NN	63.7	64.0	63.7	62.6	46.1	43.9	46.1	41.0	64.4	63.7	64.4	63.1	46.1	44.2	46.1	44.9	40.9	38.0	40.9	37.2	65.8	61.6	65.8	63.5
	RF	89.4	90.8	89.4	88.8	56.2	60.6	56.2	49.8	88.1	89.6	88.1	87.3	91.4	91.7	91.4	91.1	65.3	70.5	65.3	62.3	92.1	92.3	92.1	91.7
	LDA	59.7	60.8	59.7	60.0	35.0	32.3	35.0	33.8	52.8	57.2	52.8	54.5	58.2	66.6	58.2	57.1	30.0	34.4	30.0	15.0	61.8	64.3	61.8	62.9
P25	k-NN	63.3	62.8	63.3	60.9	49.5	50.9	49.5	46.5	63.4	63.0	63.4	61.1	48.0	45.4	48.0	46.4	37.6	37.6	37.6	34.9	68.3	65.0	68.3	66.2
	RF	85.0	85.6	85.2	84.7	55.9	63.4	55.9	52.1	90.1	90.3	90.1	89.7	86.1	85.9	86.1	85.8	65.2	72.3	65.2	62.4	90.1	90.0	90.1	89.7
	LDA	55.9	56.1	55.9	55.7	37.5	35.2	37.5	35.6	54.1	54.4	54.1	54.1	20.0	7.8	20.0	10.5	3.7	11.6	3.7	1.9	40.0	46.4	40.0	31.8
P26	k-NN	65.0	64.1	65.0	62.3	48.1	46.4	48.1	43.1	65.0	64.1	65.0	62.3	49.7	46.7	49.7	47.5	37.3	32.9	37.3	34.2	80.4	76.9	80.4	77.7
	RF	86.3	86.5	86.3	85.9	58.7	61.5	58.7	52.7	99.8	99.8	99.8	99.8	88.4	88.3	88.4	88.1	65.3	65.2	65.3	60.8	100	100	100	100
	LDA	57.9	58.6	57.9	58.2	41.7	38.7	41.7	38.6	98.3	98.4	98.3	98.3	41.3	25.7	41.3	31.0	31.4	11.2	31.4	15.8	98.3	98.4	98.3	98.3
P28	k-NN	65.5	64.3	65.5	62.8	46.7	46.2	46.7	41.7	65.5	64.3	65.6	62.8	52.3	49.5	52.3	50.2	38.7	33.6	38.7	35.0	64.0	60.7	64.1	62.2
	RF	84.2	85.4	84.2	83.1	56.7	60.7	56.7	49.7	85.8	86.5	85.8	84.8	86.1	86.8	86.1	85.4	63.4	67.1	63.4	59.0	85.5	86.1	85.5	84.8
	LDA	58.8	59.3	58.8	59.0	46.7	41.4	46.7	39.1	53.6	56.2	53.5	54.5	56.6	62.7	56.6	60.6	3.4	17.9	3.4	0.6	50.8	57.0	50.1	52.5

(*Continued*)

Table 18.4 Continued.

P29	k-NN	61.0	60.1	61.0	58.1	46.8	47.5	46.8	42.7	61.1	60.6	61.1	58.4	49.0	46.0	49.0	46.7	39.6	37.9	39.6	36.5	69.4	65.4	69.4	67.0
	RF	85.0	87.0	85.0	84.3	59.3	59.5	59.3	51.4	84.8	86.5	84.8	84.0	86.1	87.4	86.1	85.6	65.1	68.4	65.1	58.9	87.8	88.8	87.8	87.3
	LDA	61.7	61.3	61.7	61.3	39.0	35.1	39.0	35.9	54.6	57.4	54.6	55.4	59.9	65.6	59.9	61.5	46.9	22.9	46.9	30.5	49.2	54.9	49.2	50.3
P30	k-NN	59.2	62.0	59.2	55.9	51.4	54.5	51.4	43.5	59.7	59.3	59.7	56.5	42.6	39.8	42.6	40.4	37.9	34.9	37.9	34.6	77.8	75.3	77.8	74.2
	RF	84.6	85.8	84.6	83.6	61.8	65.0	61.8	57.2	99.8	99.8	99.8	99.8	86.4	87.1	86.4	85.9	69.9	72.8	69.9	67.3	99.8	99.8	99.8	99.8
	LDA	53.4	55.3	53.4	54.1	41.1	38.3	41.1	38.9	99.0	99.0	99.0	99.0	11.9	45.4	11.9	13.4	30.1	17.5	30.1	14.9	98.7	98.8	98.7	98.8
P31	k-NN	58.2	55.4	58.2	54.8	45.8	44.3	45.8	38.3	55.6	52.6	55.6	52.5	42.9	39.8	42.9	39.4	38.9	37.1	38.9	35.7	77.8	72.7	78.8	74.4
	RF	81.2	83.1	81.2	80.2	53.7	59.6	53.6	47.5	99.8	99.8	99.8	99.8	86.4	87.3	86.4	85.8	62.0	67.2	62.0	58.9	99.9	99.9	99.9	99.9
	LDA	59.8	60.0	59.8	59.7	44.1	41.1	44.1	40.4	98.9	98.9	98.9	98.9	65.3	66.1	65.3	65.3	16.8	66.1	16.8	20.5	98.4	98.4	98.4	98.4
P32	k-NN	68.3	67.8	68.3	65.1	30.7	36.8	30.7	30.2	68.3	67.8	68.3	65.0	56.3	53.7	56.3	54.3	41.0	37.5	41.1	38.2	71.2	67.5	71.2	68.7
	RF	87.2	87.3	87.2	86.1	58.5	63.6	58.5	53.2	89.3	87.0	89.3	87.9	88.3	87.5	88.3	87.5	67.4	66.1	67.4	64.4	88.6	87.9	88.6	87.9
	LDA	56.8	56.7	56.8	56.7	42.3	37.5	42.3	37.9	53.6	55.5	53.6	54.4	15.3	3.9	15.3	06.2	18.6	20.3	18.6	7.0	42.2	25.4	42.2	28.8
P33	k-NN	69.2	65.5	69.2	66.5	45.0	46.1	45.0	43.4	69.4	65.3	69.4	66.7	53.2	49.0	53.2	50.3	38.1	35.0	38.1	34.8	70.4	66.5	70.4	67.7
	RF	89.8	90.3	89.8	89.2	53.9	54.8	53.9	48.2	92.0	92.5	92.0	91.3	91.4	91.2	91.4	90.9	63.9	64.7	63.9	59.6	93.8	94.0	93.8	93.2
	LDA	60.0	60.3	60.0	60.1	38.9	37.7	38.9	37.3	54.2	56.4	54.2	55.0	14.3	45.8	14.3	18.3	3.3	35.1	3.3	0.8	50.0	57.6	50.0	46.9
P34	k-NN	73.4	73.3	73.4	71.6	52.8	51.4	52.8	45.6	73.9	73.9	73.9	72.0	57.6	54.1	57.7	55.6	40.5	36.4	40.5	37.2	76.4	73.0	76.4	74.5
	RF	91.6	91.8	91.6	91.3	58.8	67.9	58.8	52.1	93.8	94.1	93.8	93.4	91.7	91.6	91.6	91.5	66.2	70.1	66.2	60.5	92.4	92.3	92.4	92.2
	LDA	63.3	63.5	63.3	63.4	43.1	37.6	43.1	39.0	57.7	58.9	57.7	58.2	28.8	9.1	28.8	13.4	28.9	26.8	28.9	13.7	49.5	49.2	49.5	48.4
k-NN	Min	56.8	55.4	56.8	54.4	30.7	36.8	30.7	30.2	55.6	52.6	55.6	52.5	39.4	37.4	39.4	37.7	34.5	31.9	34.5	32.6	44.5	60.5	44.5	48.9
	Max	69.2	67.8	69.2	66.5	51.4	54.5	51.4	46.5	69.4	67.8	69.4	66.7	56.3	53.7	56.3	54.3	41	38	41.1	38.2	82.9	81.4	82.8	80.3
	Avg	63.4	62.6	63.4	60.7	44.7	45.6	44.7	40.6	63.2	61.8	63.2	60.5	48.1	45.3	48.1	46.0	38.4	35.6	38.4	35.3	70.2	68.5	70.3	68.3
RF	Min	81.2	83.1	81.2	80.2	48.9	47.9	48.9	43.5	84.8	85.7	84.8	84.0	83.6	84.8	83.6	83	61.5	63.3	61.5	58.9	83.9	85.1	83.9	83.2
	Max	89.4	90.8	89.4	88.8	61.8	65	61.8	57.2	99.8	99.8	99.8	99.8	91.4	91.7	91.4	91.1	69.9	72.8	69.9	67.3	100	100	100	100
	Avg	85.3	86.4	85.3	84.5	56.4	59.8	56.4	50.6	92.2	92.5	92.2	91.7	87.0	87.5	87.0	86.5	64.8	67.8	64.8	61.4	92.8	93.0	92.8	92.4
LDA	Min	53.4	55.3	53.4	54.1	32.1	30.8	32.1	31.2	52.8	54.4	52.8	54.1	11.9	0.1	3.1	0.01	3.0	8.3	3.0	0.4	40.0	25.4	40.0	28.8
	Max	61.7	61.9	61.7	61.4	46.7	41.4	46.7	40.4	99.0	99.0	99.0	99.0	65.3	76.0	65.3	65.3	46.9	66.1	46.9	30.5	98.7	98.8	98.7	98.8
	Avg	58.5	59.0	58.5	58.6	39.7	36.4	39.7	36.5	71.8	73.2	71.8	72.3	39.8	42.0	37.1	34.6	18.8	22.3	18.8	10.8	68.1	70.2	68.1	66.8

consumption. The battery allowed for nearly 8 hours of data collection, and the Nordic Thingy 52 could run for over 48 hours at 200 Hz.

18.5 Conclusions

Artificial intelligence, with the evolution of machine learning techniques and digital modeling, is profoundly transforming the landscape of cyber-physical systems. It brings tangible benefits to everyone, addresses challenging goals, and opens new horizons for the future. This concluding section summarizes the main contributions of AI to CPS, indicating the issues that are still unsolved and future scenarios.

The most important benefits that AI can bring to CPS are: (i) operational efficiency, i.e., the optimized use of resources in real-time to improve productivity by reducing waste; (ii) the management of complex systems (with ML, it is possible to analyze large amounts of data collected with distributed sensor networks to manage complex systems even in critical situations proactively); (iii) scalability, thanks to advanced techniques such as federated learning; (iv) autonomy, as it enables CPS to make decisions independently (a very useful feature when operations must be carried out in dangerous or remote environments); (v) security and privacy that can be improved with more effective data protection and more timely intrusion detection and threat response. Scalability, complexity, security, and privacy are already tangible benefits. Still, some open challenges remain for them, such as integration into systems with non-linear interactions and rigid time constraints rather than resistance to specific attacks, also conducted with increasingly sophisticated techniques. Additionally, there are concerns about the reliability of critical CPSs, such as defense and security, healthcare and medical, and aviation systems, or smart grids and nuclear power plants, where ensuring continuous and correct operation is essential.

Finally, the use of AI in CPSs is the subject of ethical discussions. Questions of fairness, transparency, and accountability are still open in order to avoid discrimination and ensure responsible use of the technology presented here.

There are many prospects for the future.

As a first example, we can mention the growing data processing on edge devices to meet the needs of some types of applications that require very low latency, such as autonomous vehicles and advanced robots. Another topic of interest is federated learning for decentralized systems, as collaborating between devices to train models without sharing sensitive data enables more secure and privacy-friendly CPSs.

In the future, CPSs that can detect faults and repair them autonomously will also be developed. This will increase the resilience of systems by reducing downtimes.

In the context of Society 5.0, much of the focus in future developments will be on human–machine collaboration, for a more harmonious integration between people and CPSs.

However, for this to be successful, regulatory and technical frameworks must be developed to ensure the responsible use of AI. This will ensure fair, transparent, and trustworthy systems.

In short, today, there is a clear evolutionary trend, with AI as the driving force, toward increasingly autonomous, resilient, and collaborative systems.

References

[1] F. J. Furrer. Safe and secure system architectures for cyber-physical systems. *Informatik-Spektrum*, 46:96–107, 2023.

[2] M. Repetto, D. Striccoli, G. Piro, A. Carrega, G. Boggia, and R. Bolla. An autonomous cybersecurity framework for next-generation digital service chains. *Journal of Network and Systems Management*, 29, 2021.

[3] J. A. Stankovic, J. W. Sturges, and J. Eisenberg. A 21st century cyber-physical systems education. *Computer*, 50:82–89, 2017.

[4] N. B. Akhuseyinoglu and J. Joshi. A constraint and risk-aware approach to attribute-based access control for cyber-physical systems. *Computers & Security*, 96:101802, 2020.

[5] C. Pimsarn, T. Boongoen, N. Iam-On, N. Naik, and L. Yang. Strengthening intrusion detection system for adversarial attacks: improved handling of imbalance classification problem. *Complex & Intelligent Systems*, 8:4863–4878, 2022.

[6] M. Warkentin and R. Willison. Behavioral and policy issues in information systems security: the insider threat. *European Journal of Information Systems*, 18:101–120, 2009.

[7] M. Trend. The fragility of industrial iot's data backbone. Technical report, Trend Micro, 2018. Available at: https://documents.trendmicro.com/assets/white_papers/wp-the-fragility-of-industrial-IoTs-data-backbone.pdf.

[8] X. Cui. Cyber-physical system (cps) architecture for real-time water sustainability management in manufacturing industry. *Procedia CIRP*, 100:337–342, 2021.

[9] TA Shaikh, T Rasool, and P Verma. Machine intelligence and medical cyber-physical system architectures for smart healthcare: Taxonomy, challenges, opportunities, and possible solutions. *Artificial Intelligence in Medicine*, 146:102692, 2023.

[10] A. Pundir, S. Singh, M. Kumar, A. Bafila, and G. J. Saxena. Cyberphysical systems enabled transport networks in smart cities: Challenges and enabling technologies of the new mobility era. *IEEE Access*, 10:16350–16364, 2022.

[11] I. Onyeji, M. Bazilian, and C. Bronk. Cyber security and critical energy infrastructure. *The Electricity Journal*, 27:52–60, 2014.

[12] P Radanliev, D De Roure, M Van Kleek, and O Santos. Artificial intelligence in cyber physical systems. *AI & Society*, 36:783–800, 2021.

[13] F. O. Olowononi, D. B. Rawat, and C. Liu. Resilient machine learning for networked cyber physical systems: A survey for machine learning security to securing machine learning for cps. *IEEE Communications Surveys & Tutorials*, 23:524–552, 2021.

[14] AH El-Kady, S Halim, MM El-Halwagi, and F Khan. Analysis of safety and security challenges and opportunities related to cyber-physical systems. *Process Safety and Environmental Protection*, 170:209–223, 2023.

[15] H Harkat, LM Camarinha-Matos, and J Goes. Cyber-physical systems security: A systematic review. *Computers & Industrial Engineering*, 184:109891, 2024.

[16] Z. Yu, H. Gao, X. Cong, N. Wu, and H. H. Song. A survey on cyber–physical systems security. *IEEE Internet of Things Journal*, 10:21670–21686, 2023.

[17] Y Zhang, M Fei, D Du, and Y Hu. Security state assessment in cyber-physical systems post-dos attack based on cyber layer partitioning. *IEEE Transactions on Industrial Informatics*, 20:15–27, 2024.

[18] S Abad´ıa, O Avila, and V Goepp. Towards a framework for intelligent cyber-physical system (icps) design. In *International Conference on Business Process Management*, pages 235–247. Springer, 2023.

[19] E. Gultekin and M. S. Aktas. Predictive analytics in iot and cps: Enhancing industrial machinery reliability through sensor data-driven remaining useful life estimation. In *2023 IEEE International Conference on Big Data (BigData)*, pages 2456–2465. IEEE, 2023.

[20] Y. T. Acquaah and R. Kaushik. Normal-only anomaly detection in environmental sensors in cps: A comprehensive review. *IEEE Access*, 2024.

[21] N. E. Fard, R. R. Selmic, and K. Khorasani. A review of techniques and policies on cybersecurity using artificial intelligence and reinforcement learning algorithms. *IEEE Technology and Society Magazine*, 42:57–68, 2023.

[22] E Modrakowski, N Braun, M Hajnorouzi, and A Eich. Architecture for digital twin-based reinforcement learning optimization of cyber-physical systems. In *International Conference on Software and Systems Modeling*, pages 235–251. Springer, 2023.

[23] A Arora and R Gupta. Snrlm: a cyber-physical based stepwise noise removal and learning model for automated quality assurance. *International Journal of Information Technology*, pages 1–15, 2024.

[24] AA Nour, A Mehbodniya, JL Webber, and A Bostani. Optimizing intrusion detection in industrial cyber-physical systems through transfer learning approaches. *Computers and Electrical Engineering*, 108:108929, 2023.

[25] O Niggemann, B Zimmering, and H Steude. Machine learning for cyber- physical systems. In *Cyber-Physical Systems: Core Technologies and Applications*, pages 309–325. Springer, 2023.

[26] BVS Krishna, S Pauline, and S Sivakumar. Enhanced efficiency in smart grid energy systems through advanced ai-based thermal modeling. *Thermal Science and Engineering Progress*, 47:102765, 2024.

[27] J. Chae, S. Lee, J. Jang, S. Hong, and K. J. Park. A survey and perspective on industrial cyber-physical systems (icps): From icps to aiaugmented icps. *IEEE Transactions on Industrial Cyber-Physical Systems*, 1:257–272, 2023.

[28] A Heidari, N Jafari Navimipour, and M Unal. Machine learning applications in internet-of-drones: Systematic review, recent deployments, and open issues. *ACM Computing Surveys*, 56:1–32, 2023.

[29] CL Hu, L Wang, ML Chen, and C Pei. A real-time interactive decision-making and control framework for complex cyber-physical-human systems. *Annual Reviews in Control*, 59:100938, 2024.

[30] EZ Gill, D Cardone, and A Amelio. Revolutionizing the construction industry by cutting edge artificial intelligence approaches: A review. *Frontiers in Artificial Intelligence*, pages 1–15, 2024.

[31] V Kuwar, V Sonwaney, and S Upreti. *Real-Time Data Analytics and Decision Making in Cyber-Physical Systems*, chapter 2, pages 25–47. IGI Global, 2025.

[32] A Vaseashta. On the material considerations for energy harvesting in iots. *Materials Science and Condensed Matter Physics*, pages 342–362, 2024.

[33] S Lipsa and RK Dash. *Cobots as an Enabling Technique for Industry 5.0: A Conceptual Framework*, chapter 2, pages 23–45. Wiley Online Library, 2025.

[34] MN Varadarajan, C Viji, and N Rajkumar. *Industry 5.0 and the AI/ML Era: Revolutionizing Manufacturing*, chapter 9, pages 95–117. Taylor & Francis, 2025.

[35] R Rathee, M Singh, and M Yadav. *Embracing Industry 5.0: Evolution, Applications, and Strategies in the Era of Human AI Collaboration*, chapter 3, pages 51–72. IGI Global, 2025.

[36] A. Ahmed. Advancements in anomaly detection: A review of machine learning applications in cyber-physical system networks. *Research Square*, pages 1–28, 2024.

[37] A. Albasir and K. Naik. Toward improving the security of iot and cps devices: An ai approach. *Digital Threats: Research and Practice*, pages 12–34, 2023.

[38] S. Islam, D. Javeed, and P. Kumar. Generative ai and cognitive computing-driven intrusion detection system in industrial cps. *Cognitive Computing*, pages 112–134, 2024.

[39] M. Adil and A. Hassan. Ng-icps: Next generation industrial-cps, security threats in the era of artificial intelligence, open challenges with future research directions. *IEEE Internet of Things*, pages 645–672, 2024.

[40] Masaaki Nagahara. A research project of society 5.0 in kitakyushu, japan. In *2019 IEEE Conference on Control Technology and Applications (CCTA)*, pages 803–804, 2019.

[41] A. M. Turing. On computable numbers, with an application to the entscheidungsproblem. *Proceedings of the London Mathematical Society*, s2-42(1):230–265, 1936.

[42] Claude Elwood Shannon. A symbolic analysis of relay and switching circuits. Master's thesis, Massachusetts Institute of Technology, August 1937. Available at http://hdl.handle.net/1721.1/11173.

[43] Warren S. McCulloch and Walter Pitts. A logical calculus of the ideas immanent in nervous activity. *The bulletin of mathematical biophysics*, 5, 1943.

[44] Rakiba Rayhana, Ling Bai, Gaozhi Xiao, Min Liao, and Zheng Liu. Digital twin models: Functions, challenges, and industry applications. *IEEE Journal of Radio Frequency Identification*, 8:282–321, 2024.

[45] Sabrina Manickam, Laasya Yarlagadda, Shynu Padinjappurathu Gopalan, and Chiranji Lal Chowdhary. Unlocking the potential of digital twins: A comprehensive review of concepts, frameworks, and industrial applications. *IEEE Access*, 11:135147–135158, 2023.

[46] Honghai Wu, Pengwei Ji, Huahong Ma, and Ling Xing. A comprehensive review of digital twin from the perspective of total process: Data, models, networks and applications. *Sensors*, 23(19), 2023.

[47] Angira Sharma, Edward Kosasih, Jie Zhang, Alexandra Brintrup, and Anisoara Calinescu. Digital twins: State of the art theory and practice, challenges, and open research questions. *Journal of Industrial Information Integration*, 30:100383, 2022.

[48] Rasha F. El-Agamy, Hanaa A. Sayed, Arwa M. AL Akhatatneh, Mansourah Aljohani, and Mostafa Elhosseini. Comprehensive analysis of digital twins in smart cities: a 4200-paper bibliometric study. *Artificial Intelligence Review*, 57(154), 2024.

[49] Sofia Agostinelli, Fabrizio Cumo, Giambattista Guidi, and Claudio Tomazzoli. Cyber-physical systems improving building energy management: Digital twin and artificial intelligence. *ENERGIES*, 14:1–27, 2021. Articolo in rivista.

[50] Helen H.L. Kwok, Jack C.P. Cheng, Alison T.Y. Li, Jimmy C.K. Tong, and Alexis K.H. Lau. Multi-zone indoor cfd under limited information: An approach coupling solar analysis and bim for improved accuracy. *Journal of Cleaner Production*, 244:118912, 2020.

[51] Claudio Tomazzoli, Simone Scannapieco, and Matteo Cristani. Internet of things and artificial intelligence enable energy efficiency. *JOURNAL OF AMBIENT INTELLIGENCE AND HUMANIZED COMPUTING*, 2020.

[52] Lars Gidhagen, Jonas Olsson, Jorge H. Amorim, Christian Asker, Danijel Belusic, Ana C. Carvalho, Magnuz Engardt, Yeshewatesfa Hundecha, Heiner K¨ornich, Petter Lind, David Lindstedt, Esbj¨orn Olsson, J¨orgen Rosberg, David Segersson, and Lena Stro¨mba¨ck. Towards climate services for european cities: Lessons learnt from the copernicus project urban sis. *Urban Climate*, 31:100549, 2020.

[53] Mohammad Mohammadpour, Sousso Kelouwani, Marc-Andr´e Gaudreau, Lotfi Zeghmi, Ali Amamou, Hossein Bahmanabadi, Bilel Allani, and Massinissa Graba. Energy-efficient motion planning of an autonomous forklift using deep neural networks and kinetic model. *Expert Systems with Applications*, 237:121623, 2024.

[54] Marcin Witczak, Bogdan Lipiec, Marcin Mrugalski, Lothar Seybold, and Zbigniew Banaszak. Fuzzy modelling and robust fault-tolerant scheduling of cooperating forklifts. In *2020 IEEE International Conference on Fuzzy Systems (FUZZ-IEEE)*, pages 1–10, 2020.

[55] Yizhen Sun, Junyou Yang, Zihan Zhang, and Yu Shu. An optimization based high-precision flexible online trajectory planner for forklifts. *Actuators*, 12(4), 2023.

[56] S. Jayashree and K. Malarvizhi. Methodologies for optimal sizing of battery energy storage in microgrids: A comprehensive review. In *2020 International Conference on Computer Communication and Informatics (ICCCI)*, pages 1–5, 2020.

[57] Paolo Cova, Nicola Delmonte, Stefano Ferrari, Massimo Lazzaroni, Roberto Menozzi, Danilo Santoro, and Marco Simonazzi. Electrical

vehicle fleet management for industrial environment with battery soh prediction through neural networks. In *Proceedings 2023 IEEE International Conference on Metrology for eXtended Reality, Artificial Intelligence and Neural Engineering (MetroXRAINE)*, pages 323–328. IEEE, 2023.

[58] Hassan Shabbir, William Dunford, and Tina Shoa. State of health estimation of li-ion batteries using electrochemical impedance spectroscopy. In *2017 IEEE Transportation Electrification Conference and Expo (ITEC)*, pages 108–112, 2017.

[59] Marvin Messing, Tina Shoa, and Saeid Habibi. Estimating battery state of health using electrochemical impedance spectroscopy and the relaxation effect. *Journal of Energy Storage*, 43:103210, 2021.

[60] Luca Petrigna, Ewan Thomas, Ambra Gentile, Antonio Paoli, Simona Pajaujiene, Antonio Palma, and Antonino Bianco. The evaluation of dual-task conditions on static postural control in the older adults: a systematic review and meta-analysis protocol. *Systematic Reviews*, 8(1):188, Jul 2019.

[61] Florenc Demrozi, Graziano Pravadelli, Azra Bihorac, and Parisa Rashidi. Human activity recognition using inertial, physiological and environmental sensors: A comprehensive survey. *IEEE Access*, 8:210816–210836, 2020.

[62] Florenc Demrozi, Graziano Pravadelli, Patrick J Tighe, Azra Bihorac, and Parisa Rashidi. Joint distribution and transitions of pain and activity in critically ill patients. In *2020 42nd Annual International Conference of the IEEE Engineering in Medicine & Biology Society (EMBC)*, pages 4534–4538, 2020.

[63] Val Mikos, Chun-Huat Heng, Arthur Tay, Shih-Cheng Yen, Nicole Shuang Yu Chia, Karen Mui Ling Koh, Dawn May Leng Tan, and Wing Lok Au. A wearable, patient-adaptive freezing of gait detection system for biofeedback cueing in parkinson's disease. *IEEE Transactions on Biomedical Circuits and Systems*, 13(3):503–515, 2019.

[64] Paola Cesari, Matteo Cristani, Florenc Demrozi, Francesco Pascucci, Pietro Maria Picotti, Graziano Pravadelli, Claudio Tomazzoli, Cristian Turetta, Tewabe Chekole Workneh, and Luca Zenti. Towards posture and gait evaluation through wearable-based biofeedback technologies. *Electronics*, 12(3), 2023.

[65] Cristian Turetta, Florenc Demrozi, and Graziano Pravadelli. A freely available system for human activity recognition based on a low-cost body area network. In *2022 IEEE 46th Annual Computers, Software, and Applications Conference (COMPSAC)*, pages 395–400, 2022.

19

Case Studies on the Security and Privacy of Cyber-physical Systems

Adetola AbdulFattah Sogbesan and Uche M. Mbanaso

Centre for Cyberspace Studies, Nasarawa State University, Nigeria

Email: tolasogbesan@ieee.org; u.m.mbanaso@nsuk.edu.ng

Abstract

Integrating physical processes with network digital technologies in cyber-physical systems (CPS) has raised fundamental concerns regarding privacy, security, safety, and trust (PSST). These issues have become increasingly critical as CPS grows in complexity and deployment. This chapter provides a unique and in-depth analysis of privacy, security, safety, and trust in CPS from the perspectives of selected use cases. The vulnerability, threat, and risk landscapes may vary from one physical domain to another, which strongly makes a case for analysing privacy in the context of the application domain. We examined each use case's constrained environment and the vulnerability, threat, and risks. This underscores the urgency and importance of a comprehensive understanding of PSST for cyber-physical systems (CPS) stakeholders. This understanding can significantly aid in informed decision-making and CPS's practical design, development, and deployment. The chapter emphasizes the necessity of implementing robust PSST measures to foster the creation of secure and privacy-preserving CPS, guaranteeing these intricate systems' dependability and credibility.

19.1 Introduction

Cyber-physical systems (CPS) represent integrated systems that merge computation, networking, and physical processes, allowing for the control of physical operations, automation, smart experiences, and real-time monitoring [1].

DOI: 10.1201/9788743801306-19

These systems are found in various application domains, including smart grids, autonomous vehicles, transportation, healthcare, etc., enhancing efficiency and automation by leveraging technologies such as sensors, actuators, artificial intelligence, machine learning, and deep learning [2] [3] [4]. The potential of these systems is immense, promising a future of unprecedented efficiency and innovation [5]. The seamless integration of cyber and physical components introduces unique challenges, particularly concerning PSST, as these systems are susceptible to cyber threats, which can turn off essential services or even cause human harm [2] [5]. However, with the suitable measures in place, the potential of CPS to revolutionize our world is inspiring.

The CPS introduces the intersection of technologies in computing abstractions that account for computational and physical dynamics, thereby raising the complexity and sophistication of these emerging modern systems [3] [5]. Besides the inherent technological flaws and the CPS's increasing integration into critical infrastructure and everyday applications exacerbating PSST, cybersecurity threat actors have multiple malicious opportunities to harm systems and humans. Notably, the cybersecurity vulnerability landscape of CPS is characterized by risks at the device, network, human, and organizational levels. Therefore, it should be recognized that the vulnerability landscape of cyber-physical systems (CPS) is a complex and rapidly evolving area due to the interconnected nature of these systems and their integration with the physical world. These integrations introduce combined effects to critical infrastructure, making it a prime target for cyberattacks [6] [7] [8]. In the current context, it is imperative to examine several crucial facets of the vulnerability landscape for cyber-physical systems (CPS):

i. Physical-layer vulnerabilities: The fact that CPS depends massively on sensors to interact with the physical environment can result in *sensor tampering*. This implies the potential for malicious parties to tamper with these sensors, which can result in feeding erroneous data to the system, which can cause inappropriate actions [8]. For instance, interfered temperature sensors in healthcare systems may cause diagnosis or analysis of a patient's condition. Furthermore, attackers can hijack actuators (components responsible for the control of physical operations) to interrupt normal functions, such as stopping the administering of drugs or manipulating the speed of automated processes [9] [10].

ii. Network-layer vulnerabilities: CPS systems exchange enormous amounts of data, sometimes across unsecured or poorly secured channels, which can result in data-in-transit attacks. Consequently, it creates the opportunity for man-in-the-middle (MITM) attacks, where malicious actors can intercept, manipulate, or eavesdrop on transit data. In addition, CPS systems can be overwhelmed with traffic denial of service (DoS) or (DDoS), thereby disrupting critical services such as transport management systems, healthcare systems, or other critical infrastructure [6] [11]. More specifically, a malicious party can gain a foothold in a CPS and move laterally across the network, potentially gaining access to more vital systems.

iii. Device-layer vulnerabilities: The cyber components depend on firmware, which may be outdated. This unpatched firmware and software can make these components susceptible to known vulnerability issues. CPS components characteristically depend on communication protocols, such as Modbus, controller area network (CAN), or Zigbee, to interact with the physical objects, which lack robust built-in security features and can result in interception or manipulation [12]. In addition, CPS devices habitually use default credentials or weak authentication methods, which are susceptible to malicious exploits or to gain unauthorized access.

iv. Supply chain risks: In some cases, there is the potential for indiscriminate or targeted pre-installed backdoors in CPS components or devices, which can be introduced at some point in the supply chain. This can lead to adversaries exploiting the backdoors to gain unauthorized access. Similarly, forged components or hardware with obscured malicious attributes (such as hardware trojans) can compromise a CPS's integrity, resulting in significant security and safety risks.

v. Human factor vulnerabilities: Insider threats have emerged as one of the potent ways of compromising technological systems. Personnel or contractors with authorized access to CPS can pose a risk resulting from negligence or malicious intent. This threat may lead to data breaches, sabotage, or cyber-physical attacks. Furthermore, lack of awareness or training may negatively impact CPS operators without adequate cybersecurity training, resulting in poor procedures such as misusing credentials, becoming victim to phishing attacks, or disregarding security processes.

vi. Legacy systems: Most critical infrastructure technologies were not designed and implemented with cybersecurity in mind. They often needed fundamental security and safety features, which raised enormous concerns. This leaves legacy systems more susceptible to cyber threats and retrofitting them with basic security measures can prove costly and complicated.

vii. Cloud computing platforms: To a certain extent, cyber-physical systems (CPS) depend on cloud platforms for data storage and processing, necessitating remote monitoring and management. This introduces a new layer of potential cyberattack vectors, such as cloud misconfigurations, insecure remote access tools, API vulnerabilities, etc.

viii. Artificial intelligence (AI)/machine learning (ML)/deep learning (DL) security issues: AI/ML/DL is becoming increasingly dependent on algorithms for automation and decision-making. Malicious actors can create adversarial inputs to deceive ML models into making erroneous decisions, particularly in autonomous vehicle navigation or predictive maintenance systems. Tampering with the data used to train CPS systems can significantly result in biased or faulty decision-making processes in safety-critical applications.

ix. Regulatory and compliance issues: The cybersecurity standards for cyber-physical systems (CPS) are usually fragmented across various industries, such as the National Institute of Standards and Technology (NIST), the International Electrotechnical Commission (IEC), and the International Standards Organisation (ISO). This fragmentation makes it challenging for organizations to meet all the requirements, potentially resulting in security gaps. Furthermore, regulatory bodies may still need to fully develop their standards in specific industries, such as emerging ones like intelligent cities, leaving significant vulnerabilities unaddressed.

19.1.1 Chapter contribution

This chapter examines the concepts of privacy, security, safety, and trust (PSST) within cyber-physical systems (CPS), drawing insights from applicable use cases. Use cases are introduced and scrutinized within constraints, highlighting the operational environment's vulnerabilities, threats, and risks. This analysis expounds the critical need for a comprehensive understanding of the interrelated dimensions of PSST, which is essential for stakeholders involved in the development and management of CPS. The findings underscore the significance of a well-rounded understanding of PSST, as it is pivotal in guiding stakeholders toward making informed decisions regarding CPS's design, development, and implementation. By recognizing the unique challenges and risks associated with each use case, stakeholders can better navigate the complexities of these systems, ensuring that they are functional, secure, and trustworthy.

The chapter further stresses the imperative of establishing robust PSST frameworks to facilitate the development of secure and privacy-conscious cyber-physical systems. The insights provided herein contribute to the ongoing discourse on CPS, encouraging a shift toward more resilient and trustworthy designs that can withstand the evolving landscape of threats and vulnerabilities.

19.1.2 Chapter organization

The chapter is structured as follows: Section one introduces the chapter, focusing on CPS's vulnerability landscape and security issues. Section 19.2 covers the background and related works. Section 19.3 deeply delves into CPS's privacy, security, safety, and trust (PSST) issues. Section 19.4 explores CPS in the context of PSST, highlighting the intersections, complexities, and challenges. Section 19.5 provides valuable discussions on the case studies. Finally, Section 19.6 serves as the conclusion with future research directions.

19.2 Background and Related Works

The diversity of cyber-physical systems (CPS) devices contributes to a wide range of challenges in privacy, security, safety, and trust (PSST). The wide variety of these devices amplifies the scope of cyber threats, as billions of constantly evolving interconnected objects create numerous potentials cyber-attack vectors. Consequently, the increased flow of sensitive data through CPS devices in inadequately secured or unsecured environments heightens the risk of breaches in the realm of PSST. The context and environments of the deployment of CPS are vastly different, implying that one-size-fit security policies cannot be applied to all. This exacerbates PSST remediation, which is more complicated and requires a comprehensive and different approach to securing the ecosystem. The challenges outlined have a profound impact on the complete realization of the potential of CPS in contemporary society. The increasing complexity and demand of addressing these challenges pose significant difficulties for government entities, organizations, and individuals.

Thoroughly exploring the CPS attack surfaces is crucial for strengthening the foundation of the problem space and enabling a comprehensive understanding of it. Figure 19.1 depicts the CPS's cyberattack surfaces, which refer to the various points in the system where adversaries can attempt to compromise or exploit CPS, which are layers of opportunities for malicious actors.

The intricate interplay of cyber-physical systems makes them susceptible to various cyber and physical attacks. Physical components like

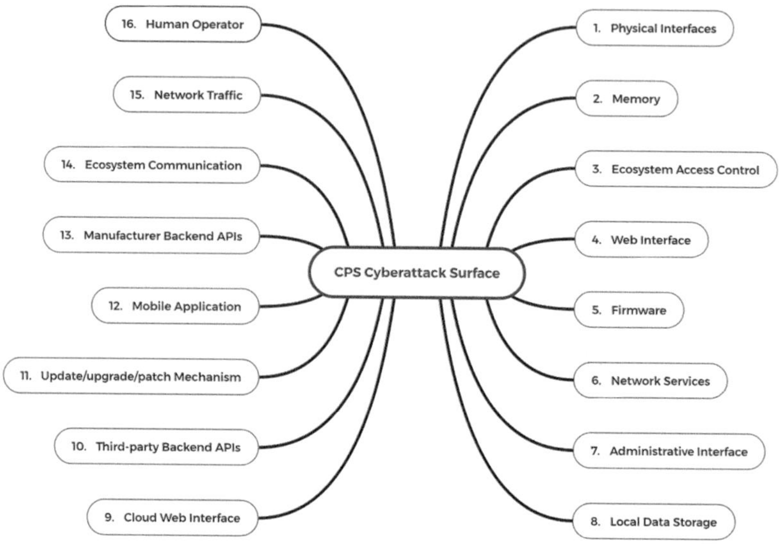

Figure 19.1 CPS cyberattack surface.

sensors gather data from the environment and are susceptible to spoofing, data manipulation, or sensor disruption, which can lead to denial-of-service attacks. Similarly, actuators execute physical actions based on system instructions, potentially resulting in hazardous outcomes such as faulty brakes in an automated vehicle or incorrect robotic movements in a factory. In the communication layer, wired and wireless networks present the attack surface, allowing data transmitted between components to be compromised based on eavesdropping, interception, or modification if inappropriately secured. Wireless communications (e.g., in smart grids or autonomous vehicles) are particularly vulnerable to jamming, man-in-the-middle (MitM), and replay attacks. Equally, protocol vulnerabilities, such as unencrypted communication or weak authentication, can be exploited by malicious actors to intercept or modify information.

In general, every software system has inherent vulnerabilities. In the case of CPS, the firmware running on hardware components is a potential target for attackers seeking to disrupt operations or gain control of the system. Operating systems and middleware software, which manage the interaction between physical and cyber components, can be vulnerable to attacks such as buffer overflows, privilege escalation, and other exploits. Additionally, software updates, upgrades, and patches can introduce new vulnerabilities that malicious actors can exploit to introduce malware. Supervisory control and data acquisition (SCADA) is a critical component of cyber-physical systems (CPS) and is commonly employed to monitor and regulate vital infrastructure such as power grids and water systems. SCADA systems are susceptible to compromise, potentially enabling malicious entities to manipulate physical operations or instigate extensive disruption [13] [14]. Similarly, it is essential to note that programmable logic controllers (PLCs), responsible for controlling machinery and processes, are susceptible to compromise through malware, leading to potential physical damage or operational disruptions [15] [16].

Malicious parties can focus on human interface and management systems, including human–machine interfaces (HMIs) for overseeing or controlling CPS. Their objective could be to illicitly gain entry to system controls or mislead operators into making incorrect judgments. Similarly, inadequate or compromised authentication mechanisms (such as weak passwords or stolen credentials) can lead to unauthorized access to CPS control systems. Social engineering, which involves exploiting human factors, such as phishing or spear-phishing, can be used by adversaries to obtain credentials or access that can be used to manipulate the system.

Furthermore, most CPSs use cloud computing services for storage, processing, or analytics. This platform presents yet another attack vector that adversaries can exploit, especially when they are inappropriately secured (e.g., vulnerable APIs and insecure configurations). The remote monitoring of CPS presents a vulnerability attack surface, which can be compromised, primarily when inadequate secure channels are used to gain access and attackers control the physical system. Adversaries can introduce hardware trojans into hardware components during the supply phases and can later be triggered to cause system failures or leak sensitive information. Similarly, the reliance on cyber-physical systems (CPS) on third-party software or components can introduce substantial vulnerabilities. Vulnerabilities present in third-party software libraries or hardware may serve as potential entry points for attackers, thus posing significant security risks to CPS.

When improperly secured, CPS's physical environment or location can create a vulnerable point, leading to physical tampering, manipulation, damage, or turning off critical components like sensors, PLCs, etc. In addition, there is the potential for side-channel attacks, which involve obtaining information based on physical phenomena such as power consumption or electromagnetic emissions without directly interfering with the system. Emerging technologies have the potential to expand vulnerability surfaces, leading to the exposure of underlying vulnerabilities such as insecure devices and weak encryption. Similarly, the advent of next-generation mobile networks, offering high speed and low latency, can enhance the connectivity of cyber-physical systems (CPS). However, this also results in an expanded attack surface, particularly by introducing new networking protocols and hardware.

Integrating artificial intelligence (AI) into CPS introduces asymmetric and symmetric characteristics. While AI can enhance PSST, it can also be a potent tool for the adversary to advance its goals [17]. The trade-off between privacy and detection performance is explored, suggesting that privacy-preserving mechanisms can inadvertently degrade system performance, necessitating careful optimization [18]. Thus, the pressing need for a multidisciplinary approach is underscored, advocating collaboration among researchers and industry stakeholders to develop comprehensive solutions that address the evolving landscape of threats in CPS [19].

Safeguarding these systems necessitates a multifaceted strategy that encompasses the security of physical components, communication channels, software, control systems, and user interfaces while also addressing emerging risks posed by emerging technologies.

19.3 The CPS PSST Use Cases and Cyber Threats

CPS facilitates smarter, more efficient, and responsive physical processes by integrating computation, networking, and bodily systems. It has diverse applications across different sectors, each presenting unique PSST challenges. This section aims to explore these challenges across various use cases.

19.3.1 Potential use cases

i. **Autonomous vehicle**
   A self-driving vehicle has sensors and computing capabilities to interact with its surroundings in real time, allowing it to navigate and make operational decisions without human involvement [20]. The system utilizes various sensor technologies, including GPS, radar, light detection and ranging (LIDAR), and cameras, integrated with sophisticated algorithms to control speed, steering, and braking [21] [22]. Additionally, it establishes communication with other vehicles and current infrastructure to navigate its environment effectively. Autonomous cars use vehicle-to-vehicle (V2V) and vehicle-to-infrastructure (V2I) communication to navigate their environs, creating another stack of attack surfaces [23]. Consequently, based on the established vulnerability, threat, and risk landscapes, autonomous vehicles have several attack points

from the physical to the software stacks and the sensors and actuators [8] [16]. As a data-centric machine, manipulating or poisoning the dataset used for training or a fresh dataset for decision-making can cause fatality far beyond anticipated [24] [25]. From the PSST perspective, autonomous vehicles present critical risk factors that must be continuously addressed.

ii. Healthcare and medical technologies

Implementing cyber-physical systems (CPS) in healthcare settings encounters similar challenges but also presents unique scenarios with the potential to lead to more severe consequences. CPS is revolutionizing healthcare by advancing smart medical devices, robotic surgery, and patient monitoring systems. In addition, they are utilizing wearable devices for remote patient monitoring that track vitals in real-time, as well as implementing robotic surgery systems for minimally invasive procedures. Smart prosthetics and implants are being developed to adapt to the wearer's needs and integrate electronic health records (EHRs) with physical monitoring devices. Notwithstanding, healthcare facilities typically function within different security domains, highlighting the importance of trust in partnerships and collaborations [26]. For instance, when an ambulance equipped with CPS transports a patient from one hospital to another, a seamless transfer is expected without encountering any issues. To facilitate collaboration between the CPS in the hospital and the ambulance CPS, it's essential to establish a series of security protocols and access controls. By implementing these measures, the two systems from different autonomous security domains can work together to deliver healthcare services effectively. However, implementing suits of security protocols in such situations introduces a fresh and crucial challenge regarding latency and, consequently, can be detrimental to patients. On the other hand, weak implementation of security measures is also highly risky, as adversaries or rogue ambulances equipped with CPS can cause cascaded effects. This argues that PSST should be treated with cryptographic solid services based on the environmental context instead of generic PSST solutions.

iii. Smart city

The idea of "smart cities" leverages cyber-physical systems (CPS) to effectively oversee infrastructure, resources, and services such as transportation, waste management, and utilities [27] [28]. This includes intelligent traffic management systems that can adjust traffic lights in response to real-time data and innovative waste management solutions that utilize sensors to detect when bins reach capacity. Similarly, intelligent street lighting is designed to adapt following the time of day or motion detection. Furthermore, it involves integrating public safety systems such as surveillance cameras and emergency response mechanisms. Notwithstanding that, an intelligent city contributes to an improved quality of life for citizens by minimizing energy consumption and resource wastage and enhancing public safety and the efficiency of city services, it raises enormous concerns regarding PSST. Adversaries can hack into smart city infrastructure with weak security control measures to gain unauthorized access to components or disrupt services. Again, every stack of CPS deployment to the smart city concept is prone to cyberattacks.

iv. **Industrial automation and manufacturing**
In Industry 4.0, cyber-physical systems (CPS) play a central role, revolutionizing manufacturing by interconnecting machines, robots, and control systems to enable more autonomous and adaptable production processes. This encompasses using autonomous robots for assembly and material handling, predictive maintenance leveraging sensor data to detect equipment issues, real-time process monitoring and optimization through digital twins, and seamless supply chain data integration for efficient production planning. However, industrial automation and manufacturing face significant cyber threats like other CPS deployments due to inherent and emerging vulnerabilities [29] [30]. In the supply chain context, trojans or backdoors can be introduced into CPS components. These malicious modifications can induce erratic system behavior or are specifically designed to harm technical infrastructures, human safety, or the environment. Such vulnerabilities underscore the critical need for robust security measures within the supply chain to safeguard against potential threats.

19.3.2 CPS cyber threat landscape

The CPS provides critical services and functions and supports contemporary society's digital infrastructure and various industrial sectors. The integration enhances operational efficiency and facilitates the seamless interaction between physical and digital environments, thereby contributing to the overall robustness of modern societal frameworks. However, these systems are increasingly becoming the target of cyberattacks. It is widely acknowledged that cyber threats to CPS can lead to significant consequences such as PSST risks, economic damage, human harm, and operational disruptions. In this section, we examine the various threats that potentially pose grave risks.

i. **Denial of service (DoS) threat**
The threat of DoS and its variant DDoS involves flooding CPS networks with excessive traffic, leading to system overload and potential unresponsiveness. As a result, critical services and functions may become unavailable, disrupting the core services and functions of the CPS and posing a risk to human lives [31]. This can be a case within the V2V in autonomous cars, resulting in cascaded or escalating effects involving many vehicles and fatalities.

ii. **Malware and ransomware threat**
Malicious software can infiltrate CPS components, disrupting or rendering them non-functional [32]. For example, ransomware can immobilize critical CPS components like sensors, industrial robots, or manufacturing systems until a ransom is paid. This can lead to interruptions in production lines or the disturbance of vital services such as power generation and transportation.

iii. **Data integrity threat**
The CPS is data-centric and depends on real-time data for decision-making and physical control of environmental processes. This implies that if a malicious party compromises the integrity of the data by tampering with it or injecting false data, the system can make erroneous decisions, potentially resulting in physical damage or harm [33] [34]. For instance, manipulating sensor data in a chemical plant could precipitate hazardous reactions or equipment failure, which can be harmful.

iv. **Insider threat**
Employees or contractors may intentionally or unintentionally compromise the security of the CPS system. Malicious insiders have the potential to exploit system weaknesses, manipulate operations, steal data, or install malware [9] [16] [35]. Additionally, negligent insiders may inadvertently create vulnerabilities by failing to adhere to PSST protocols.

v. **Unauthorised access and control**
Adversaries have the potential to exploit vulnerabilities in CPS networks, allowing them to gain unauthorized access and exert control over physical systems. Once infiltrated, they can manipulate system functions, deactivate alarms, or even assume control of devices such as drones, robotic arms, or autonomous vehicles. Such actions could lead to accidents, sabotage, or data theft [9] [33].

vi. **Supply chain threat**
Cyber-physical systems often rely on hardware and software provided by third-party vendors. Adversaries may focus on these suppliers during the design, production, and implementation stages to insert malicious code or hardware backdoors. Once these compromised components are incorporated into a CPS, they can be used to execute further cyberattacks or gain unauthorized access.

vii. **Firmware and software exploit threat**
CPS components, including industrial control systems (ICS), frequently operate on embedded software or firmware. These components can be challenging to patch and may harbor vulnerabilities that adversaries can exploit to take control of the physical system or manipulate its behavior. For instance, outdated firmware in a power grid control system could be targeted by adversaries to cause outages.

viii. **Physical tampering and sabotage**
Unauthorized individuals with physical access to CPS components can manipulate sensors, control units, or communication systems. This physical tampering can disrupt the system's normal operations or lead to hazardous malfunctions. For instance, interference with the sensors in an autonomous vehicle could result in accidents.

ix. **Man-in-the-middle (MitM) threat**
In a man-in-the-middle (MitM) attack, an unauthorized party intercepts communication between different CPS components, allowing them to manipulate or modify the exchanged data. This can cause the system to perform incorrect actions, such as activating security gates, disabling alarms, or adjusting operational settings.

x. **Remote code execution (RCE)**
Remote code execution vulnerabilities enable malicious actors to execute unauthorized code on a targeted system. In the realm of CPS, this can empower attackers to remotely seize control of a device or process, resulting in potentially hazardous malfunctions or operational sabotage. RCE can pose a significant threat to industries such as manufacturing and healthcare.

xi. **AI and machine learning exploits**
Systems using AI and machine learning for decision-making can be susceptible to attacks on the algorithms they rely on. Adversarial attacks involve feeding manipulated data into machine learning models, which can result in incorrect predictions or decisions. This vulnerability

is particularly concerning in autonomous systems such as self-driving cars, where adversarial attacks could lead to the vehicle misinterpreting road conditions and causing accidents.

xii. **Zero-day vulnerability threat**
Zero-day vulnerabilities, previously undiscovered security flaws exploited by malicious actors, pose a significant threat before a patch or fix is released. Cyber-physical systems (CPS) often have lengthy lifecycles. They may experience delays in receiving security updates, rendering them particularly susceptible to zero-day exploits that potentially compromise critical physical processes [16].

xiii. **Command injection threat**
Command injection attacks involve inputting malicious commands into a vulnerable system interface. In the context of cyber-physical systems (CPS), this attack could involve sending harmful instructions to programmable logic controllers (PLCs) in industrial settings or directly to autonomous machines. Unauthorized access can lead to detrimental actions, equipment damage, or safety hazards, posing significant risks within industrial and autonomous environments.

xiv. **Spoofing and replay threat**
Spoofing attacks occur when unauthorized users impersonate legitimate devices or users within the CPS network, gaining unauthorized access or manipulating communications. In replay attacks, hackers capture and retransmit valid data packets to the system to initiate unauthorized actions, such as restarting a machine or unlocking a facility door.

xv. **Cross-site scripting (XSS) and SQL injection threat**
Exploiting software components in cyber-physical systems (CPS) is a common target for attacks, particularly those linked to web-based control interfaces. For instance, SQL injection attacks enable assailants to tamper with databases that house critical operational data. In contrast, cross-site scripting (XSS) attacks can insert malevolent scripts into web-based control panels.

19.4 Exploration of PSST Case Studies

Cyber-physical systems (CPS) are sophisticated integrations of computational elements and physical processes. Due to their inherently interconnected architecture, they engender distinct challenges regarding privacy, security, safety, and trust (PSST). The following case studies illustrate significant

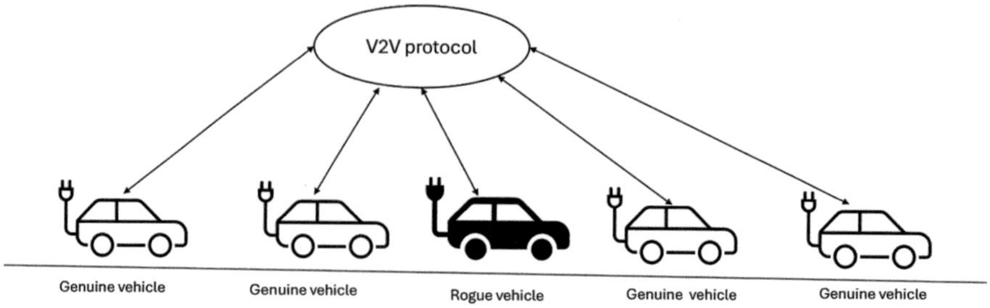

Figure 19.2 Autonomous vehicles in V2V scenario.

PSST issues pertinent to CPS and comprehensively analyze these critical dimensions.

19.4.1 Autonomous vehicles

Scenario: A self-driving car communicates with other vehicles using a vehicle-to-vehicle (V2V) protocol. However, a rogue vehicle could exploit this protocol to identify cars with weak security measures.

Concern: An adversary can deploy a rogue autonomous vehicle that leverages V2V vulnerabilities to disrupt or cause harm to opponents' cars using known attack techniques such as DDoS, MitM, session hijacking, etc. Figure 19.2 illustrates how an adversary can deploy a rogue autonomous vehicle to disrupt or degrade an opponent's car. In this instance, the rogue vehicle can use known techniques to scan for vulnerabilities that can be exploited. It can launch attacks complementary to its objectives or mission upon discovering vulnerabilities. Compromising any of these vulnerable vehicles could allow for collecting data on passenger locations, preferences, and driving habits, potentially causing damage. The gathered information may expose personal habits and behaviors, such as the times passengers arrive home or leave. This situation breaches privacy and undermines security, safety, and trust, complicating efforts to secure CPS.

19.4.2 Smart healthcare systems

Scenario: Smart healthcare devices deployed to patients can monitor and track their vital signs and activities, but hackers can also compromise them.

Concern: Unauthorized access to sensitive health information could seriously affect patients and even cause fatality. Figure 19.3 illustrates a typical case

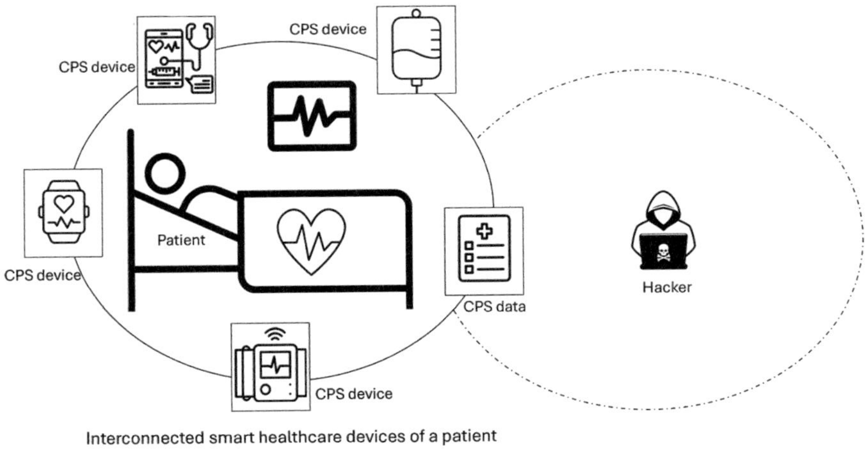

Figure 19.3 Patient smart healthcare network.

study of a potential breach of PSST, whereby a hacker within the CPS network can use known techniques to scan for vulnerabilities that can be exploited. It can initiate attacks based on identified vulnerabilities that align with its objectives or mission. Compromising a particular patient can allow for collecting vital health information, e.g., type of illness, prescriptions, medication locations, preferences, and habits, potentially affecting the patient. The collected data may reveal sensitive personal health issues and behaviors and can lead to prescription modifications, vital signs, and other related information. Such circumstances represent a violation of privacy and can compromise security, safety, and trust. Consequently, this situation complicates the assurance of confidentiality, integrity, availability, authenticity, and trust in CPS.

19.5 Discussion

Cyber-physical systems' intricate nature and interconnectedness expose them to a broad spectrum of cyber and physical attacks. Protecting these systems necessitates a comprehensive approach that safeguards physical components, communication channels, software, control systems, and user interfaces while addressing potential risks arising from new technologies. The growing dependence on interconnected digital systems and IoT devices to oversee urban infrastructure has elevated concerns about cyber threats to smart cities. These threats can impact various aspects of city management, from public transportation to energy grids, with potentially severe consequences. Mitigating and containing cyberattacks against CPS requires a risk-aware

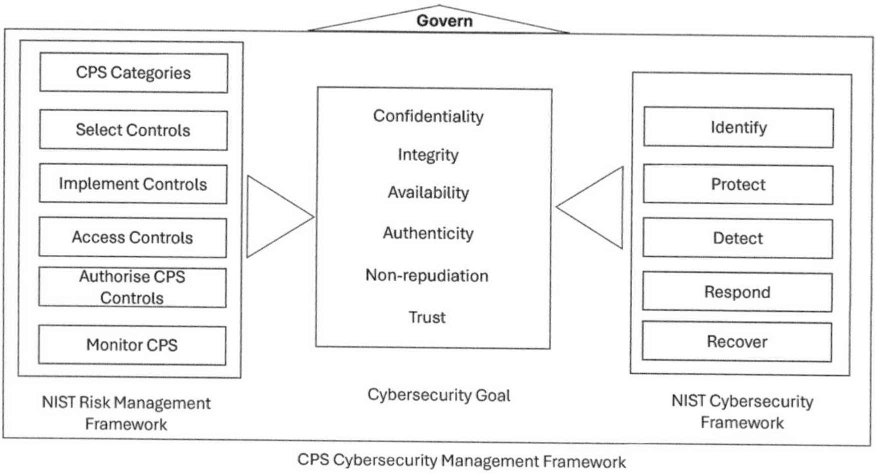

Figure 19.4 CPS cybersecurity management framework.

and defense-in-depth approach based on understanding the requirements of cybersecurity goals. This requires extensive risk assessment and understanding of PSST requirements contextually.

Moreover, advancing and implementing CPS in our modern society raises significant ethical considerations. These issues encompass their impact on privacy, safety, security, and trust (PSST), potential societal repercussions, and the imperative for governmental bodies, institutions, and individuals to confront and tackle these ethical concerns. The formulation of regulatory frameworks for CPS entails significant difficulties and complexities, particularly considering CPS's escalating intricacy and regulatory demands. Addressing these challenges is crucial for ensuring CPS's PSST and promoting their responsible use. Understanding the various attack surfaces in CPS and discussing potential vulnerabilities in components such as sensors, controllers, communication networks, and actuators is crucial. This demands thorough contextual risk management based on real-world use cases of CPS attacks and their implications for critical functions and services. Risk management should focus on strategies to strengthen the PSST of CPS, including the role of security controls such as encryption, authentication, and access control in mitigating potential cyberattacks. Figure 19.4 depicts the mapping of cybersecurity goals, the NIST Cybersecurity Framework (CF), and the NIST Risk Management Framework (RMF) to the cybersecurity management framework.

Based on the NIST Cybersecurity Framework (NIST CF) [36], the first step is identifying all the CPS devices or components in each security domain through thorough inventorying and categorizing them to align with the risk management framework. To safeguard CPS against present and forthcoming cyber threats, conducting a comprehensive risk assessment rooted in the six cybersecurity objectives is essential. This will help identify suitable and proportional security measures to be implemented in the system. Subsequently, the NIST CF pillars of detect, respond, and recover should be strategically integrated within the premise of PSST. This integration can furnish the metrics essential for evaluating the cybersecurity of the CPS. Following a thorough risk assessment, the remaining elements of the NIST RMF can be implemented to continually enhance the cybersecurity of the CPS. This approach enables the exploration of securing legacy CPS and developing solutions for integrating cybersecurity measures into the environment. Consequently, the CPS framework necessitates comprehensive risk assessments and the rigorous implementation of robust security controls. It also emphasizes the importance of continuous updates and timely patching of vulnerabilities to mitigate the opportunities available to adversarial entities.

19.6 Conclusion

This chapter has examined privacy, security, safety, and trust as critical elements of safeguarding and preserving CPS to ensure public safety and the physical infrastructure. The complexity and interconnection of cyber-physical systems make CPS vulnerable to a wide range of cyber threats from both the cyber and physical domains. Cyber threats to CPS are a significant concern due to the increasing reliance on interconnected digital systems and IoT (Internet of Things) devices to manage essential urban infrastructure. The CPS ecosystem's various vulnerability and threat landscapes have been comprehensibly discussed based on real-world use cases. The potential consequences of a successful cyberattack on CPS systems such as transportation, smart cities, energy, and healthcare have been explored. Protecting these systems necessitates a multifaceted strategy, which involves securing physical components, communication channels, software, control systems, and user interfaces while mitigating emerging technological threats. The chapter concludes by proposing the CPS cybersecurity management framework that can help stakeholders to provision PSST based on risk prioritization and appropriate application of security measures and controls. In forthcoming research, the cybersecurity vulnerability landscape of cyber-physical systems (CPS) is expected to undergo significant expansion, characterized by risks that permeate multiple levels – including the device, network, human, and organizational dimensions. This multifaceted risk environment necessitates a comprehensive understanding of the interdependencies and interactions among these layers to mitigate potential threats effectively. It requires a thorough understanding of the interplay between technological components, human factors, and structures governing security practices. The direct oversight of physical processes requires the implementation of stringent security protocols, as such measures are essential to mitigate potentially severe financial, operational, and safety-related repercussions. Thus, further research in improving the layers of PSST is necessary for exploring the integration of AI and cybersecurity measures for automating PSST security controls, particularly in scenarios involving transaction parties across multiple security or untrusted domains.

References

[1] C. Ruben, J. Heynssens, I. Burke, A. Mahafujul and B. and Cambou, "Enhancing cyber-physical systems (CPS) robustness through sensor-pair health indicator," in SPIE Defense + Commercial Sensing, 2024.

[2] A. Kumari and A. Sharma, "Cyber-Physical Systems - Advances and Applications," Bentham Science Publishers, 2024.

[3] H. Khan and D. Kaur, "Cyber Physical Systems," in Machine Learning: An Art of Computer Thinking, IIP Books, 2024.

[4] R. U. Mhapsekar, M. I. Umrani, M. Faizan, O. Ali and L. & Abraham, "Building Trust in AI-Driven Decision Making for Cyber-Physical Systems (CPS): A Comprehensive Review.," arXiv preprint, 2024.

[5] S. Rudresha, H. R. Gopinath, K. G. R. Kiran and S. Shruthi, "A cyber-physical systems perspective on smart grids.," in Futuristic Trends in Artificial Intelligence, vol. 3, IIP Series, 2024.

[6] M. D. Kumar, K. M. Bhabendu and C. Sangay, Security Issues and Challenges in Deploying a CPS Using WSN., Springer, 2024, pp. 24 – 46.

[7] M. Malik, A. Ibrahim, P. Hannay and L. Sikos, "Developing Resilient Cyber-Physical Systems: A Review of State-of-the-Art Malware Detection Approaches, Gaps, and Future Directions.," 2023.

[8] M. W. Gelber, A. Wyatt, A. Al Habbal and R. H. and Klenke, "Functional Monitor Models and Detection Methods for Sensor Data Variance of a Real-Time Cyber-Physical System," in AIAA SCITECH, 2024.

[9] F. Alghamdi and A. Alghamdi, "Navigating the Privacy and Cybersecurity Risks of Smart Homes.," in 1 Conference: 2023 24th International Arab Conference on Information Technology (ACIT), 2023.

[10] G. Solorzano, A. Gutiérrez and A. Gordillo, "Data Security Threats On Smart Devices At Home," Ajman, UAE, 2023.

[11] N. Mishra and A. Yadav, "Privacy and Security Control Approach for DDoS Attacks in Cyber-Physical Systems using Deep Learning," in 2nd International Conference for Innovation in Technology, Bangalore, India., 2023.
[12] D. Trancă, A. Pălăcean, A. Mihu and D. and Rosner, "ZigBee based wireless modbus aggregator for intelligent industrial facilities," Belgrade, Serbia, 2017.
[13] M. K. Gulzar Q, "An analytical survey of cyber-physical systems in water treatment and distribution: Security challenges, intrusion detection, and future directions.," Security and Privacy. , no. e440., 2024.
[14] N. Ortiz, M. Rosso, E. Zambon, J. den Hartog and A. A. and Cardenas, "From Power to Water: Dissecting SCADA Networks Across Different Critical Infrastructures. In Passive and Active Measurement:," Berling, Heidelberg, 2024.
[15] A. Patil, A. Shinde and S. Banerjee, Stuxnet-Tool for Zero-Day Attack. Handbook of Research on Cybercrime and Information Privacy., 2021, pp. 650 – 676.
[16] G. Mazzarolo and A. D. & Jurcut, Insider threats in Cyber Security: The enemy within the gates., arXiv preprint, 2019.
[17] A. Bandi, "A Taxonomy of AI Techniques for Security and Privacy in Cyber-Physical Systems.," 2023.
[18] L. Wu, H. Wang, K. Liu, L. Zhao and Y. Xia, "Privacy and security trade-off in cyber-physical systems: An information theory-based framework.," no. 34, 2024.
[19] M. Sharma, "Enhancing Security and Privacy in Cyber-Physical Systems: Challenges and Solutions.," 2024.
[20] P. Joe Prathap, M. Kumar, K. Kiran, M. V. Sai Praneeth, L. Beevi and W. Dani, "Advancements in Autonomous Vehicle Object Detection and Tracking Systems.," in IEEE, 2024.
[21] H. Wang, L. Zhou, R. Jing, Z. He and R. Xiao, "An overview of the development of key technologies in autonomous driving technology.," 2024.
[22] T. Ying, "Analysis on key technologies of autonomous vehicle sensing system.," 2024.
[23] J. Sun, "A Comprehensive Overview of the Current State of Development in Autonomous Vehicle Driving.," 2024.
[24] S. Bak and S. and Sheikhi, "Coverage-guided State Space Exploration of Autonomous Cyber-Physical Systems," in IEEE 9th International Conference on Space Mission Challenges for Information Technology (SMC-IT), Pasadena, CA, USA., 2023.

[25] T. M. Islam, A. Sheakh, A. N. Jui, O. Sharif and Z. M. Hasa, "A review of cyber-attacks on sensors and perception systems in autonomous vehicle," Journal of Economy and Technology, vol. 1, pp. 242–258, 2023.
[26] Y. Bao, W. Qiu and X. & Cheng, "Privacy-preserving and fine-grained data sharing for resource-constrained healthcare CPS devices.," Expert Systems, vol. 40, no. 6, 2023.
[27] K. Meroua, Z. Abdella and N. Zerroug, "Review of Technics Used In Smart House," in International Conference on Electrical Engineering and Automatic Control (ICEEAC), 2024.
[28] B. Farooq, "Privacy and Security Issues in Smart Homes in an IoT Environment.," in Book Chapter 17: Internet of Things Vulnerabilities and Recovery Strategies (1st ed.)., Auerbach Publications., 2024.
[29] U. Izuazu, V. Ihekoronye, D.-S. Kim and J. M. Lee, "Securing Critical Infrastructure: A Denoising Data-Driven Approach for Intrusion Detection in ICS Network," in International Conference on Artificial Intelligence in Information and Communication (ICAIIC), 2024.
[30] A. Pinto, L. Herrera, Y. Donoso and J. Gutierrez, "Survey on Intrusion Detection Systems Based on Machine Learning Techniques for the Protection of Critical Infrastructure.," vol. 5, no. 23, 2023.
[31] K. Veerabudren and V. Ramsurrun, "Cyber Resilience in Autonomous Vehicles: Defending Against Emerging Threats.," vol. 33, pp. 22–31, 2024.
[32] Y. Li, A. M. Mandalari and I. Straw, "Who let the smart toaster hack the house? An investigation into the security vulnerabilities of consumer IoT devices.," arXiv, 2023.
[33] A. Alhammad, M. Yusof and D. and Jambari, "A Review of Cyber Threats to Medical Devices Integration with Electronic Medical Records," in International Conference on Cyber Resilience (ICCR), Dubai, United Arab Emirates, 2022.
[34] A. &. S. I. Kumar, "Enhancing Data Privacy of IoT Healthcare with Keylogger Attack Mitigation.," in 4th International Conference for Emerging Technology (INCET), 2023.
[35] I. Zaheera, A. Zuraida, Z. Nurul, N. Hashim, M. Esuwary, R. & Ahmad and P. Puvanasvaran, "Conceptual Model of Risk Assessment for Insider Threats Detection.," in 1st International Conference on Electrical, Control and Instrumentation Engineering (ICECIE), 2019.
[36] NIST, " The NIST Cybersecurity Framework (CSF) 2.0," NIST, 2024. [Online]. Available: https://doi.org/10.6028/NIST.CSWP.29. [Accessed 10 October 2024].

20

Recent Advances and the Future of Cyber-physical Systems

Agbotiname Lucky Imoize[1], Kinzah Noor[2], Hasnain Ahmad[3] and Mercy Oka Ebute[4]

[1]Department of Electrical and Electronics Engineering, Faculty of Engineering, University of Lagos, Nigeria
[2]Office of Research Innovation and Commercialization, University of Management and Technology, Pakistan
[3]Department of Computer Science, COMSATS University, Pakistan
[4]Department of Accounting, Anderson School of Management, University of New Mexico, USA

Email: aimoize@unilag.edu.ng; kinzah.noor@umt.edu.pk; sp22-bcs-140@cuilahore.edu.pk; mercyebute02@gmail.com

Abstract

Cyber-physical systems (CPS) integrate computational and physical processes seamlessly, offering transformative potential across various domains. However, the development and implementation of CPS face numerous challenges. This chapter aims to provide a comprehensive understanding of this multidisciplinary field by first outlining the fundamental characteristics of CPS. It then presents recent advancements across key components, including system modeling, communication, and control; finally, several standard applications are highlighted to demonstrate the practical potential and impact of CPS in real-world scenarios.

20.1 Introduction

The Industrial Internet of Things (IIoT) has emerged as a cornerstone of Industry 4.0, integrating smart computing and network technologies into

DOI: 10.1201/9788743801306-20

industrial processes to enhance intelligence, safety, efficiency, and productivity. Unlike consumer IoT, IIoT requires specialized devices, advanced network protocols, and stringent command-and-control mechanisms. This chapter provides an in-depth analysis of IIoT, focusing on its architecture, key applications such as factory and process automation, and core system components: control, networking, and computing. Two comprehensive three-dimensional frameworks exploring technologies like 5G, machine-to-machine (M2M) communication, and cloud-edge platforms are proposed to address networking and computing challenges. Finally, critical research directions are highlighted, including the integration of machine learning to advance IIoT systems. CPSs and IoT are rapidly advancing as traditional and mobile devices evolve into intelligent systems and smart devices. These technologies facilitate the development of cyber–physical–social systems (CPSSs), which integrate human-centric factors, offering significant opportunities and complex challenges. This chapter comprehensively reviews recent research on CPSSs, focusing on their evolution, architectural frameworks, applications, standards, real-world case studies, and enabling technologies. The proposed virtualization architecture and integrated caching, computing, and networking framework also demonstrate notable performance enhancements through simulations. Finally, critical research challenges and potential solutions are thoroughly examined.

A notable outcome of Industry 4.0 is the development of cyber-physical systems (CPS), which play a crucial role by seamlessly integrating the physical and digital realms, enabling real-time data processing and enhanced interactivity [1]. More specifically, a CPS allows a virtual system to function as a monitor for a physical system, enabling data collected from the physical world to be analyzed within the virtual environment. This capability supports informed decision-making that can influence the behavior and trajectory of the physical system. Consequently, a CPS facilitates comprehensive system optimization, real-time monitoring, and seamless information integration, sharing, and collaboration [2]. CPSs are utilized across a wide range of modern industries, including smart grids, healthcare, aviation, digital manufacturing, and robotics [3].

The rapid growth of modern industry has heightened the need for CPS integration to bridge gaps across networks, technologies, tools, and devices. However, the complexity of integrating diverse systems creates an exposed framework that adversaries can exploit, raising significant security concerns. Cyberattacks are common, potentially leading to malfunctions or reduced system performance. CPS security relies on three foundational pillars: confidentiality, integrity, and availability [4]. The research [5] provides a comprehensive analysis of IoT from the perspective of CPS, with a particular focus on computation, networking, and control. Control systems are pivotal in managing numerous industrial devices, including sensors, actuators, and equipment, within the IoT ecosystem. In industrial systems, advanced networking technologies enable the seamless and timely exchange of data and control signals, facilitating a wide range of distributed tasks. The computational platforms integrated into IoT systems support efficient and reliable real-time data collection, storage, and analysis, ensuring optimal system performance [6].

In contrast to centralized cloud computing, edge computing is a distributed paradigm that allocates computing, storage, networking, and control resources between cloud servers and terminal devices. Bringing cloud capabilities closer to the network edge reduces latency and minimizes bandwidth usage. While several challenges remain, integrating edge or edge-cloud computing into CPS design is essential for reducing service latency. During this integration, issues such as energy consumption, security, privacy, and reliability must also be addressed. The research [7] centers on optimizing IoT performance and emphasizes the enhancement of CPS quality of service (QoS). Despite certain similarities [8], CPS and IoT are developed based on distinct foundational principles. CPS is characterized by intricate coordination and feedback control mechanisms that integrate the physical and virtual components, positioning them as a type of distributed system. In contrast, IoT is often described as the "Internet" – a networking architecture that links diverse networks to facilitate resource sharing and data processing [9].

A key example of a CPS is the supervisory control and data acquisition system, which is used in critical infrastructures like the smart grid and industrial control systems (ICS). Other examples include wearable and implantable medical devices and small control systems in modern cars to improve fuel efficiency and safety. ICS are used in industries such as nuclear plants, water systems, and irrigation. These systems often involve programmable logic controllers (PLCs) and microprocessors designed to operate in harsh environments [10]. PLCs connect to the physical world through sensors and actuators and can communicate via wired or wireless networks, often linking to control centers for monitoring and operation.

The smart grid represents the next evolution of power grids. It comprises two key components: power applications, which encompass the generation, transmission, and distribution of electricity, and supporting infrastructure, which consists of intelligent systems that leverage hardware, software, and communication networks to monitor and control these operations [11]. Medical devices have evolved to advance healthcare by integrating physical and digital technologies. The focus is on cyber-enabled devices that directly impact patients, such as wearable technologies and implanted medical devices. These devices are often equipped with wireless communication capabilities, enabling them to interact with programmers, other devices, remote healthcare providers, or smartphones [12]. Smart cars are fuel-efficient, eco-friendly, and equipped with advanced safety, entertainment, and comfort features. These innovations rely on 50–70 interconnected electronic control units, which oversee functions such as engine emission control, braking systems, and comfort features like cruise control and window operations.

Researchers are increasingly emphasizing the interplay between networks and human society as advancements in traditional embedded information systems progress. This connection underscores the intricate relationship between the physical world and networked systems [13]. The concept of cyber–physical–social systems (CPSSs) has emerged as a groundbreaking paradigm, integrating the domains of physical systems, computation, and human resources. These systems enable seamless interaction across the physical, social, and digital realms [14]. CPSSs facilitate supervisory control, parallel execution, and self-synchronization across multiple dimensions, including physical entities, information flows, cognitive processes, and societal dynamics [15]. This integration offers a robust framework for designing and developing intelligent environments that support effective command and control structures, ultimately fostering innovation and smarter systems.

In CPSSs, humans are not merely service users but can also act as service providers, a dual role that sets them apart from their counterparts in conventional CPSs. For effective integration, CPSSs must account for individual capabilities before involving them in the loop. This requires understanding the decisions individuals are likely to make and their ability to perform assigned tasks in specific scenarios successfully. Achieving this level of integration presents significant challenges, particularly in accurately modeling and predicting human behavior and capabilities.

The primary challenge in further integrating the social dimension into CPSS lies in the fundamental differences between human behavior and computer operations. Unlike computers, humans often approach tasks in diverse and unpredictable ways and may sometimes choose to deviate from predefined rules without prior notice. While humans may appear less reliable than computers in terms of consistency, they excel in adaptability, creativity, and problem-solving in dynamic environments. As a result, CPSS designers must carefully consider these unique human attributes during the system's development and optimization. This ensures seamless interaction and communication among humans, computers, and devices, fostering harmonious physical, computational, and social integration.

20.1.1 Key contributions of the chapter

The following are the significant contributions of this chapter:

i. This chapter comprehensively explores cyber-physical systems (CPSs), shedding light on their defining characteristics, advancements, and integration into various domains. CPS represents the convergence of physical processes with computational and communication technologies, enabling real-time monitoring, control, and optimization of complex systems. By detailing the core elements of CPS, including system modeling, communication frameworks, and control strategies, this chapter emphasizes how these technologies have revolutionized fields such as smart manufacturing, healthcare, and smart environment. These insights aim to provide researchers and practitioners with a solid foundation for understanding the potential and challenges of CPS in an increasingly interconnected world.

ii. This chapter examines the transformative role of the Industrial Internet of Things (IIoT) within the framework of Industry 4.0, the ongoing industrial revolution marked by automation, interconnectivity, and data exchange. The IIoT leverages advanced sensor technologies, edge computing, and robust communication protocols to seamlessly integrate machines, systems, and humans in manufacturing environments. This contribution reviews IIoT architectures, emphasizing key components such as smart devices, cloud platforms, and cybersecurity mechanisms essential for ensuring reliable and efficient operations. This chapter highlights real-world implementations and challenges. It offers a nuanced perspective on how IIoT reshapes traditional industries, fostering smarter, more adaptive, and sustainable manufacturing systems.

iii. This chapter surveys the evolution of CPS into cyber–physical–social systems (CPSS), a paradigm that integrates social networks and human interactions into the technological fabric. CPSS builds on CPS by incorporating human-centric applications, creating systems that are intelligent, automated, socially aware, and user-centric. This contribution delves into the architectures underpinning CPSS, highlighting the interplay between physical entities, cyber components, and social elements. Applications in smart cities, healthcare, and e-commerce are discussed to showcase the added value of integrating human dynamics. This chapter underscores the potential of CPSS to enhance decision-making, user engagement, and system adaptability. The insights provided aim to inspire future research and practical developments in bridging the gap between technology and society.

20.1.2 Chapter organization

Section 20.2 delves into a comprehensive review of the existing literature on cyber-physical systems (CPSs), emphasizing their evolution and transformative potential in the Internet of Things (IoT) context. Section 20.3 presents an in-depth analysis of CPS models, including control systems, architectural frameworks, and the progression from traditional CPS to the more integrated cyber–physical–social systems (CPSS). This section highlights the intricate interplay of architecture and real-world applications within CPSSs. Section 20.4 explores emerging insights and cutting-edge advancements in CPS and CPSS research, offering a critical examination of their future trajectories and untapped research avenues, with a particular focus on innovative applications. Finally, Section 20.5 provides a forward-looking conclusion, proposing key directions for future research and development within the realm of CPS and CPSS.

20.2 Related Work

While no universally accepted definition of CPS exists, it can be broadly described as systems designed to monitor and control the physical world. CPS is considered the next generation of embedded control systems due to its foundation as a networked embedded system. Moreover, systems that integrate networks of sensors and actuators are also classified as CPS [16]. CPSs are characterized by their reliance on IT systems, enabling seamless incorporation into real-world applications. This integration stems from advancements in information and communication technologies (ICT), which enhance interactions with physical processes. These definitions highlight the significant interplay between the virtual and physical environments, underscoring the critical role of CPS in bridging the gap between the two domains. Unlike traditional CPSs, CPSSs incorporate humans as a fundamental component of the system. CPSSs emphasize the consideration of human factors during operation through intelligent human–computer interaction, seamlessly integrating the "human" element into the supervision and decision-making processes of the framework [17].

Furthermore, the integration of machine learning across IoT systems enhances their capability for intelligent decision-making and predictive analysis. However, the rapid data growth has hindered the widespread implementation of CPS applications. The significant distance and limited bandwidth between terminal devices and remote cloud servers often lead to unacceptable communication delays despite cloud computing's powerful computational capabilities. Alternatively, the system's QoS in terms of service latency can be significantly improved by utilizing edge-computing or edge-cloud computing solutions [18].

Manufacturing and automation systems that utilize industrial equipment to execute specialized production and automation tasks are collectively called physical systems. Current research efforts in this domain focus on comprehending IoT systems comprehensively, addressing specific IoT-related challenges, and leveraging advanced IoT methodologies. For instance, the research [19] conducted a case study on a large-scale petrochemical plant, highlighting critical research challenges and difficulties associated with data management in IIoT environments. The research [20] addressed a specific challenge in IIoT by employing auction-based mechanisms to tackle the problem of computing resource allocation. Similarly, research [21] explored trust-related issues in resource allocation, providing valuable insights into this critical aspect. Moreover, several studies have leveraged advanced communication technologies, such as software-defined networking (SDN) and 5G, to enhance IIoT capabilities [22].

The field of CPS security presents numerous complex and unresolved challenges. Broadly, current CPS security approaches can be categorized into two perspectives: control theory, information security, and systems. While information security techniques effectively safeguard the software layer of computer control systems, they often fail to leverage the physical models inherent to CPSs. Consequently, such techniques are unable to predict a physical response of the system to attacks or provide adequate defenses against them. On the other hand, methods rooted in system and control theory, such as secure estimation, attack detection, and resilient control, are more adept at addressing cyberattacks that target physical systems. These techniques enable systems to detect and mitigate attacks while maintaining operational stability. In research [23], recent advancements in CPS security are reviewed from a system and control perspective and highlight several promising directions.

Cyber–physical security encompasses two critical components: passive and active security. Passive security focuses on preventing unauthorized access through encryption and stringent network controls. In contrast, active security emphasizes the recovery of CPS after attacks, utilizing strategies such as connection failover and attacker isolation to ensure resilience. While passive security has garnered significant attention in traditional cybersecurity research, active security, which integrates network resilience with the dynamic nature of physical systems, remains underexplored and warrants further investigation [24]. The existing network-focused surveys [25] primarily address analysis, detection, and prevention mechanisms for conventional IT security challenges within the IoT domain. However, these surveys are limited in their ability to represent the real-time physical behaviors associated with cyber–physical attacks comprehensively. Threats to CPS and resilient design techniques are reviewed in [26]. The research examines the effects of attacks, compares numerical examples with traditional anomaly detectors, and assesses anomaly detection methods employing physics, networks, and machine learning. It also examines resilient CPS designs in control theory, network management, and data-driven technologies and discusses attack detection developments.

The research [27] comprehensively reviews the latest cyberattack advancements targeting CPS. It begins by examining common system models employed in the analysis of complex systems, with a particular focus on time-driven and event-driven methodologies. Specifically, in-depth analysis of availability and integrity attacks from both attacker and defender perspectives, emphasizing the alignment of offensive and defensive strategies across various system architectures. In contrast, research [28] adopts a holistic approach, leveraging control theory to analyze cyber–physical attacks and detect anomalies in real time. Notably, a breakdown in social infrastructure CPS can lead to catastrophic consequences, including severe personal injuries, equipment damage, and substantial financial losses. For example, the 2015 BlackEnergy attack exploited an unprotected network to target the Ukrainian power grid, resulting in a severe blackout and highlighting the critical need for robust cybersecurity measures in CPS. The research [29] reviews the requirements a CPS must meet to address future challenges, focusing on understanding and reinforcing the resilience of CPS. It explores healthcare, energy, and transportation applications, emphasizing IoT's growing importance in CPS. It identifies a critical gap in multi-layered security measures and underscores the need for integrated systems to strengthen CPS security. Table 20.1 describes the previous work and future directions in CPS.

20.3 CPS System Model

Modeling and validating CPS pose significant challenges due to the complex interaction dynamics among their integrated components. Traditional

Table 20.1 Related work and future direction in CPS.

Research focus	Methodology	Key findings	Identified gaps	Research contribution	Future directions
Assessment of cyberattack modeling and CPS	Comprehensive evaluation of attack models and CPS frameworks	Highlighted key vulnerabilities and attack vectors in CPS	Limited focus on emerging threats, including quantum-based and AI-driven attacks	Advances cyberattack modeling by AI for adaptive threat mitigation & integrating real-time detection mechanisms	Explores attack modeling for emerging technologies, focusing on AI-driven threats and quantum-enabled cyberattacks
Exploring strategic placement of edge servers to minimize response times in mobile edge-cloud computing	Optimization strategies for edge server placement to minimize response time	Proposed effective positioning strategies that significantly reduced average response time	Failed to account for dynamic variations in workload and network conditions	Enhances response times in dynamic environments by employing real-time adaptive placement algorithms	Develop adaptive placement algorithms for systems capable of withstanding faults and handling dynamic workloads
Formalization of CPSS: comprehensive literature review	A comprehensive survey of the literature on CPSS frameworks and their formalization	Emphasized the interdisciplinary nature of CPS, IoT, and social systems, identifying various CPSS models	Lack of integrated frameworks that account for social factors and systemic impacts	Develops integrated CPSS architecture that incorporates real-time social component feedback to enhance system resilience	Proposes a comprehensive CPSS architecture that integrates social feedback and real-time data to enable adaptive system behavior
Analysis of cyberattacks on CPS: recent developments and ongoing challenges	Survey on cyberattacks directed at CPS, examination of current patterns, and mitigation strategies	Examined various types of CPS attacks and identified new threats	Insufficient investigation of adaptive defense tactics against new threats	Proposes an integrated defense system that combines adaptive countermeasures for emerging cyberattacks with AI-based anomaly detection	Examine AI-powered, adaptable defenses against changing CPS threats
In-depth analysis of threats and attacks targeting smart devices and sensor-based applications	Thorough analysis of smart device vulnerabilities and threats based on sensors	Classification of the impact of various sensor-based attacks on IoT platforms	Limited focus on mitigation strategies for multi-sensor environment	Proposes adaptive multi-sensor anomaly detection system for diverse smart device configuration	Develops robust, context-aware defenses for multi-sensor IoT systems

(*Continued*)

Table 20.1 *Continued*

Research focus	Methodology	Key findings	Identified gaps	Research contribution	Future directions
Cyberattack trends and defenses for industrial control systems	Examining and evaluating the patterns of cyberattacks against ICS	Examined several cyberattack techniques aimed at ICS and defenses put in place	Insufficient attention to new attack methods, like cyberattacks driven by AI	Incorporates cutting-edge AI-driven methods for ICS intrusion detection and mitigation	Examine ICS defense measures based on AI and machine learning
Study of safe and robust CPS using systems science	Conceptual model for robust and safe CPS	Suggested using systems science to ensure security and create robust CPS	Insufficient investigation of real-time threat adaption	Proposes paradigm for real-time, dynamic adaptation to enhance the resilience of CPS against threats	Create flexible frameworks for CPS's real-time threat identification and mitigation
Overview of cyber–physical network security: from dangers to resilient architecture	Analysis of network security issues and robust design strategies for CPS	Examined various network security risks and robust design techniques for CPS	Insufficient attention on scalable solutions for extensive CPS networks	Proposes a multi-layered, interconnected security framework that uses adaptive strategies to enhance resilience in large-scale CPS	Create multi-layered, scalable security frameworks for extensive CPS
Recent developments in CPS: trends, applications, and challenges	Examining CPS uses in industrial, energy, healthcare, and automobiles	Discuss future smart infrastructure, machine learning for CPS security, and IoT integration	Insufficient attention is given to multi-layered security frameworks for scalable and evolving CPS systems	Increased IoT in smart grids and autonomous vehicles	AI-driven real-time adaptive defenses and enhanced data encryption techniques
Next-generation resilient CPS	Review of resilience requirements for CPS, focusing on security and adaptation to future challenges	Focused on enhancing the resilience of CPS by addressing network and system vulnerabilities	Lack of practical implementation for resilience strategies in large-scale CPS	Provides framework for resilient CPS, focusing on system-level security and scalability	Research into scalable resilience models for critical infrastructure CPS

modeling and verification approaches, typically confined to a single discipline, are no longer adequate to address the intricate interdependencies inherent in CPS. To enable meaningful advancements in this field, it is imperative first to reconcile the dynamics of the physical and virtual domains within a unified system model [30].

20.3.1 Hybrid system model

Physical processes in modeling techniques are often represented using continuous models. In contrast, communication and control software are typically implemented with discrete execution semantics, creating a fundamental challenge in bridging these two paradigms. Designing and validating CPS models becomes particularly complex due to the intrinsic concurrency between software behavior and the physical world it interacts with. As illustrated in Figure 20.1, the model of physical processes is distinct and operates independently from the cyber domain. A closed-loop hybrid software model is developed to address this, integrating communication, physical, and cyber components, enabling a cohesive framework for CPS design and analysis.

Model-driven engineering (MDE), supported by knowledge bases, plays a pivotal role in software design. The MDE approach is considered essential for modeling CPS [31]. For example, the Ptolemy Project at UC Berkeley aims to tackle the challenges associated with CPS modeling. As depicted in Figure 20.2, Ptolemy II employs actor-oriented modeling, enabling the representation of multiple domains (models of computation) within a unified design environment. In this framework, input ports trigger actors, executing internal logic and generating events through output ports. Actors can be programmed to implement various computational models, reflecting either real-world phenomena or control systems. Additionally, actors can be organized in a nested structure, where one actor contains another (modal model). Other modeling languages for CPS, such as ExCHARON, CPSHCML, and even direct mathematical models, provide similar capabilities for modeling complex CPS behaviors.

Advancements in hybrid dynamics for CPS focus on stability, safety, and integration. Hybrid models assess smart grid performance, address multicast routing challenges in energy systems, and enable online model checking for medical CPS by predicting short-term human parameters. The Simplex architecture ensures safety in large-scale CPS by combining high-performance unverified logic with verified controllers. Additionally, hybrid models unify time for components, aiding synchronization in systems like

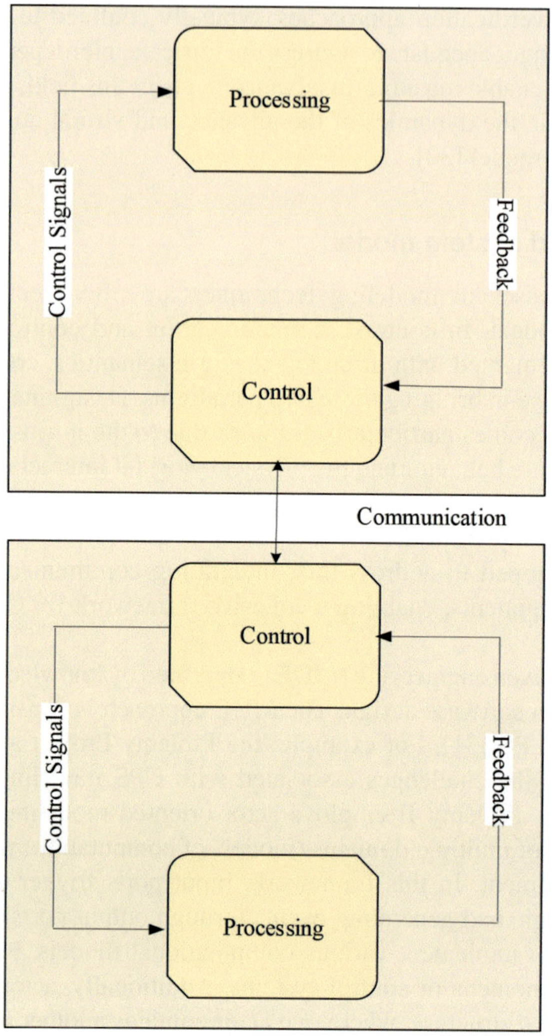

Figure 20.1 Closed-loop framework in CPS.

underwater sensor networks. These approaches enhance CPS design and reliability across diverse applications.

20.3.2 Architectures

This section delves into the architecture of IIoT, with a particular focus on edge computing and its interaction with cloud systems. It highlights the

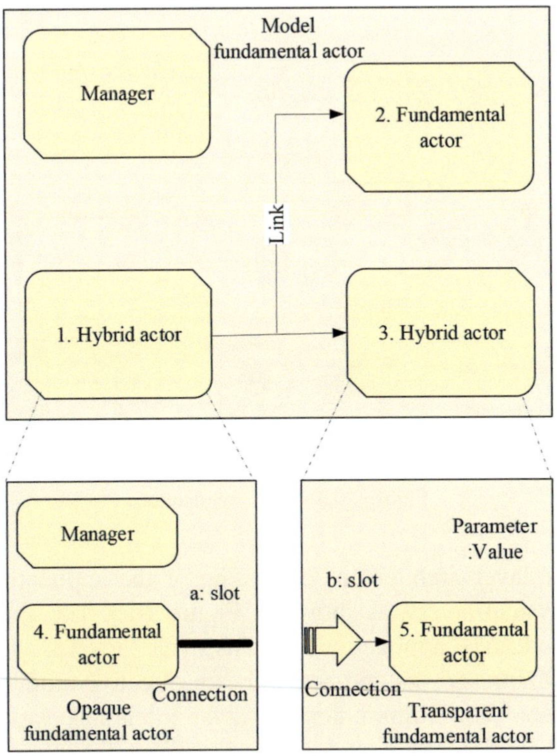

Figure 20.2 Modeling CPS with Ptolemy II.

seamless operational synergy between edge and cloud layers while exploring various architectural frameworks that enhance system efficiency and responsiveness.

20.3.2.1 IoT architecture

IoT, IIoT, and Industrial CPS (ICPS) are interconnected yet distinct concepts. IoT focuses on connecting numerous physical devices for monitoring and control, primarily in consumer-oriented systems such as smart grids or transportation networks, creating a smart, connected world. In contrast, IIoT extends IoT to industrial applications by interconnecting intelligent devices with management platforms to enhance operational efficiency and productivity. ICPS, on the other hand, is designed specifically for manufacturing and industrial production, integrating cyber and physical systems to create smart factories. Within ICPS, IIoT plays a critical role by enabling communication layers that connect industrial devices like machines and monitors, supporting efficient manufacturing processes through seamless interconnectivity. IIoT

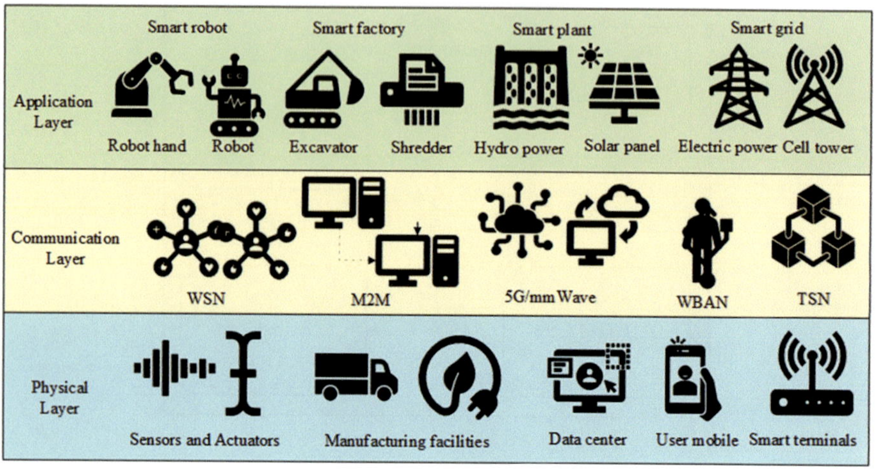

Figure 20.3 IIoT architecture.

follows a three-layer architecture consisting of the application, communication, and physical layers, as shown in Figure 20.3. The application layer encompasses industrial applications such as smart factories, plants, and supply chains, utilizing sensors and actuators for effective monitoring, control, and management. The communication layer integrates various networks, including WSANs, 5G, M2M, and SDN, to facilitate the interconnection of a large number of sensors and actuators. Finally, the physical layer comprises widely deployed devices such as sensors, actuators, manufacturing equipment, and other objects related to industrial automation.

Figure 20.4 illustrates the IIoT system from a CPS perspective, emphasizing its integration with industrial applications, such as process automation (PA) and factory automation (FA), within the physical system (left). These applications align with the manufacturing lifecycle, which comprises stages such as preparation, production, transportation, usage, and recycling. Each lifecycle phase generates substantial data volumes from various tools and devices. Control, networking, and computing systems play a pivotal role in ensuring seamless integration and connectivity between components and physical systems. These systems enable real-time monitoring and control, enhancing the efficiency and effectiveness of physical system operations.

20.3.2.2 Architectures of edge computing and edge-cloud computing

In contrast to centralized cloud computing, edge computing significantly reduces latency by positioning servers closer to end devices, often colocated with base stations, as shown in Figure 20.5. This proximity enables distributed

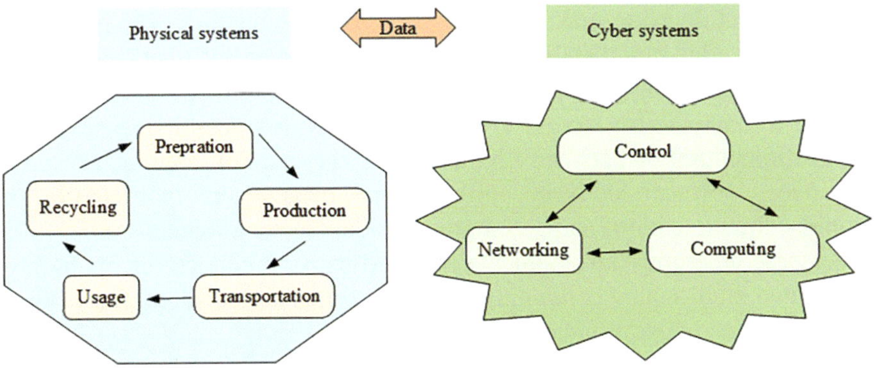

Figure 20.4 IIoT from a CPS perspective.

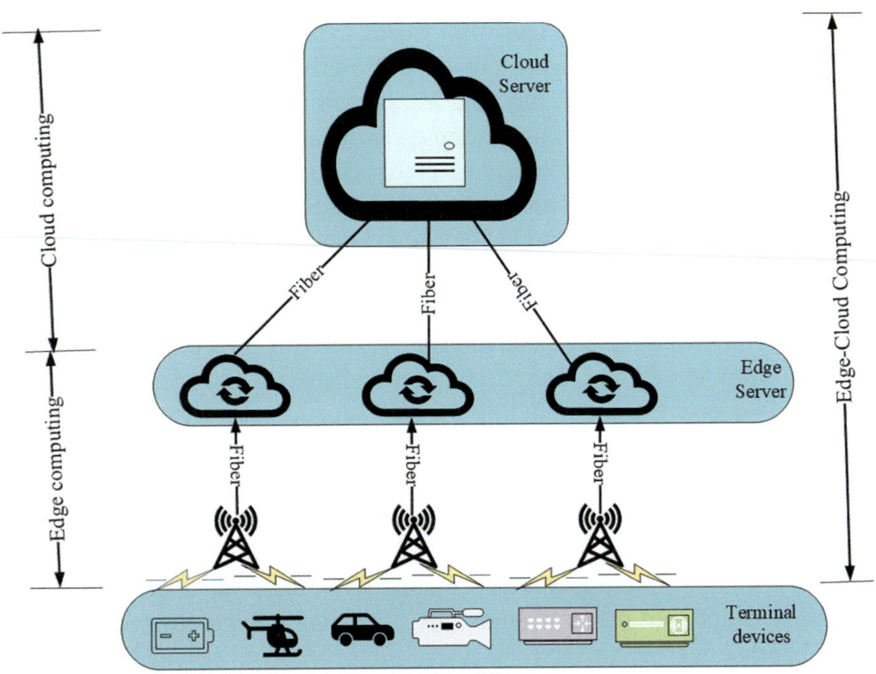

Figure 20.5 Edge computing and edge-cloud computing architecture.

networking, control, computation, and storage capabilities. However, edge servers are insufficient for handling global operations due to their limited processing power and localized decision-making scope. To address these limitations, edge-cloud computing integrates the strengths of both cloud and edge resources. Complex, resource-intensive tasks can be partially processed at the edge and offloaded to cloud servers, leveraging high computational power, global decision-making capabilities, and low latency. The evolution of edge and edge-cloud environments is further driven by advancements in cloud-native technologies. Container-based microservices enhance flexibility and interoperability across diverse infrastructures, facilitating seamless application migration between edge and cloud servers. This approach ensures continuous software delivery and efficient management, particularly in mobile communications and automotive systems sectors. Recent studies [32] underscore emerging developments in cloud-native architectures, including distributed multi-tenant computing and optimized network slicing, reshaping the edge-cloud integration landscape.

20.3.2.3 Edge and edge-cloud computing enhanced CPS architecture

Sensors capture data from the physical world, cyberspace processes this data, and actuators execute commands, forming the seamless integration of virtual information processing with physical infrastructure in CPS. Edge and edge-cloud computing are increasingly adopted to enhance CPS efficiency, reduce latency, and enable distributed data processing. Examples include industrial platforms such as Advantech's WISE-PaaS and Schneider Electric's EcoStruxure IT. The research [33] developed an edge-cloud CPS framework to mitigate mosquito-borne diseases, as shown in Figure 20.6. These solutions leverage the Asset Administration Shell (AAS) standards and the RAMI 4.0 reference architecture to facilitate industry 4.0 initiatives by ensuring interoperability, seamless data exchange, and comprehensive lifecycle management of digital assets. Edge computing further supports digital twin concepts by enabling local or cloud-based AAS implementations for intelligent and non-intelligent assets. As demonstrated by collaborations such as Ericsson and Comau for edge-integrated smart factories and the deployment of DJI M210 drones for power line and infrastructure inspections, industrial adoption is expanding. In the realm of vehicular CPS, edge servers like Siemens Roadside Units and Zotac Magnus are advancing vehicle-to-infrastructure (V2I) interactions, enhancing road safety and operational efficiency.

Table 20.2 illustrates the evolution of IoT architectures through the integration of edge and cloud computing, highlighting advancements in security, scalability, reliability, and latency reduction within CPS.

20.3.3 CPS communication

Domain-specific communication technologies in CPS use wired and wireless protocols and proprietary and open technologies. TCP/IP is used in

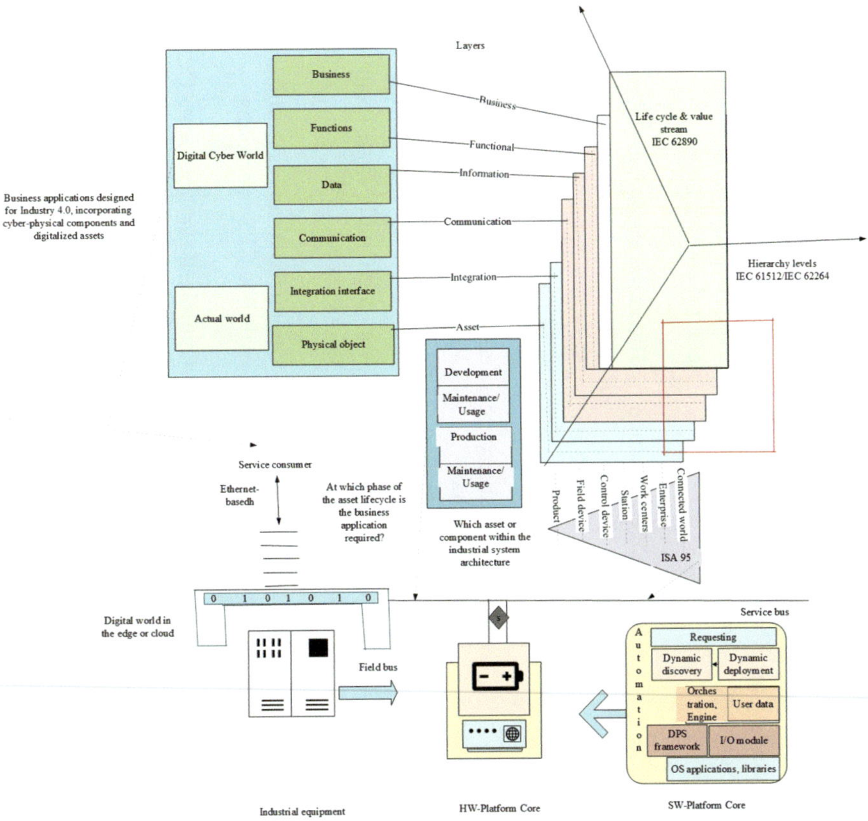

Figure 20.6 Asset and AAS in industry 4.0 edge-cloud architecture.

conjunction with automation protocols (like Modbus and DNP3) and control center connectivity protocols (like ICCP) in ICS. Control centers in smart grids employ ICCP, whereas field devices use DNP3, IEC 61850, and Modbus. ZigBee and other wireless protocols are frequently used by smart meters for data transfer and diagnostics. Wireless communication plays an important role in medical devices. Wearables employ body area networks (BANs) with Bluetooth and ZigBee for monitoring [34], whereas IMDs use medical implant communication service (MICS) for updates. Vehicle-to-vehicle (V2V), V2I, and in-vehicle networks with approximately 70 oecus are all examples of communication in smart automobiles. CAN (soft real-time, like ABS), FlexRay (hard real-time, like brakes), and LIN (low-speed) are essential protocols, and MOST (entertainment). Many vehicles also support Bluetooth and cellular connectivity.

Table 20.2 Evolution of IoT architectures within CPS.

Feature	IoT architecture	Edge computing architecture	Edge-cloud computing architecture	Edge and edge-cloud enhanced CPS architecture
Characterization	System of linked devices sending information via the internet	Distributes processing to devices that are close to data sources	Combines edge devices with cloud infrastructure	Combines edge, cloud, and CPS to provide distributed, real-time control and sensing
Data processing location	Centralized cloud	Decentralized edge devices/nodes	Hybrid edge and cloud	Hierarchical edge, cloud, and CPS layers
Latency	High	Low local processing	Moderate, depends on task distribution	Very low, optimized for real-time CPS operations
Scalability	High dependent on cloud resources	Limited to edge device capabilities	High, leverages both edge and cloud resources	High combines the scalability of edge, cloud, and CPS
Reliability	Vulnerable to network outages	High, local processing reduces dependency on connectivity	High edge reduces load, cloud provides redundancy	Very high, distributed control with fault-tolerant mechanisms
Security	Moderate, cloud-focused security	High, local data handling reduces the attack surface	High, edge devices provide initial security, and the cloud enhances it	Very high, multi-layer security protocols for CPS
Energy efficiency	Moderate dependent on cloud	High, local processing reduces transmission energy	Moderate to high, depending on balance between edge and cloud	Optimized for energy-efficient real-time CPS operations
Data volume handling	High data transfer to the cloud	Limited by local processing capabilities	Balanced between edge and cloud	Optimized for large-scale CPS networks
Example technologies	MQTT, CoAP, RESTful APIs	Fog nodes, multi-access edge computing (MEC)	AWS IoT Greengrass, Azure IoT Edge	Digital twins, ORAN, NTNs
Applications	Smart homes, wearables, industrial monitoring	Real-time data analytics, autonomous vehicles	Smart cities, healthcare monitoring, IIoT	Critical infrastructure, autonomous systems, smart grids

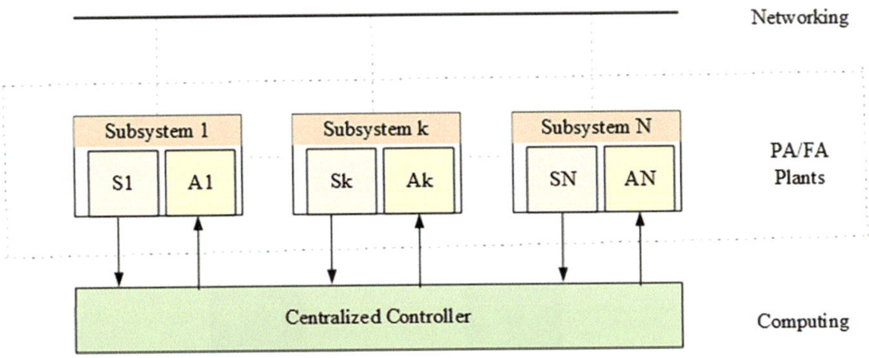

Figure 20.7 Centralized controller.

20.3.4 Control systems in IIoT

In IIoT environments, control systems are crucial in managing critical infrastructures, such as oil and gas distribution, electricity generation, and manufacturing processes. The three primary types of control systems – centralized, decentralized, and hierarchical – each employ distinct structural approaches to system management and control [35].

20.3.4.1 Centralized control

Figure 20.7 shows a centralized control system, a central controller overseeing and managing multiple subsystems, each equipped with sensors (S) and actuators (A). A notable example of this system is Supervisory Control and Data Acquisition (SCADA), shown in Figure 20.8, which has been widely implemented in large-scale infrastructures such as electricity, gas, oil, and water distribution networks. SCADA enhances connectivity and interoperability for industrial applications by integrating with IoT technologies, including 5G, Wi-Fi, and SDN. However, integrating IoT into SCADA systems introduces new vulnerabilities, particularly in data integrity, privacy, and communication security. Various solutions, such as encryption and authentication mechanisms, have been proposed [36].

20.3.4.2 Decentralized control

Figure 20.9 shows decentralized control systems, such as distributed control systems (DCSs), which employ individual controllers within subsystems to manage localized operations. DCS is commonly implemented in industrial environments where multiple controllers work in coordination, including manufacturing plants, oil refineries, and power generation facilities [37]. In

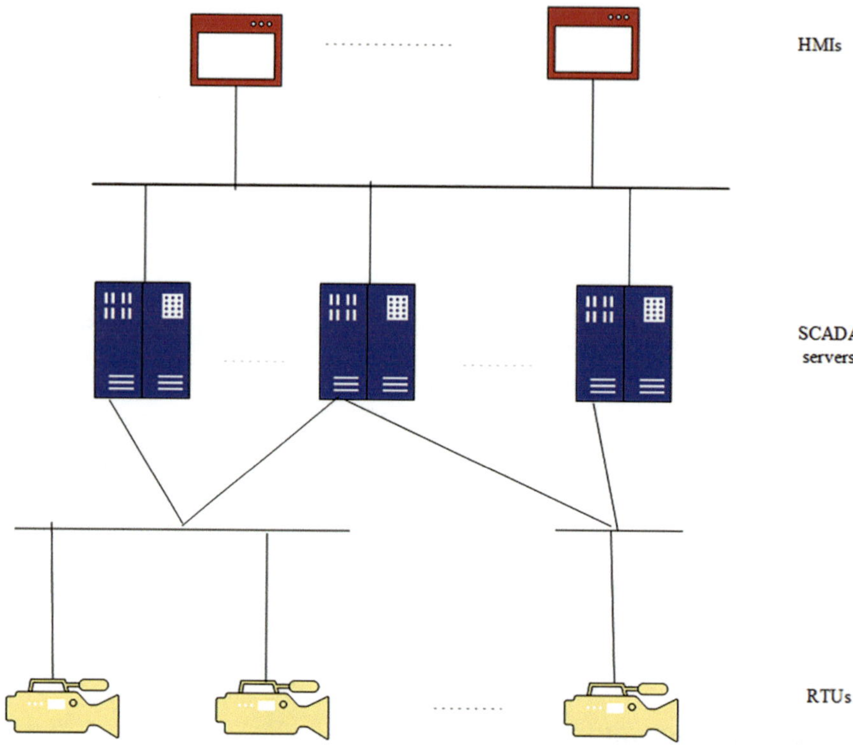

Figure 20.8 SCADA architecture overview.

these systems, PLCs provide precise regulatory control for specific tasks. The integration of radio technologies, such as RFID, enhances data acquisition, system flexibility, and overall performance, resulting in improved responsiveness and operational efficiency.

20.3.4.3 Hierarchical control

The hierarchical control shown in Figure 20.10 combines local and supervisory control to manage large-scale and complex systems. Lower-level controllers directly interact with subsystems, while higher-level controllers oversee and coordinate these subsystems. A typical example is of integrating SCADA and DCS systems in power generation, where DCS handles plant operations, and SCADA provides higher-level coordination [38]. The seamless integration of SCADA and DCS improves system efficiency and scalability, particularly in complex industrial environments like power plants or food production. PLCs often serve as key components in these integrated systems, providing control and communication between the control center

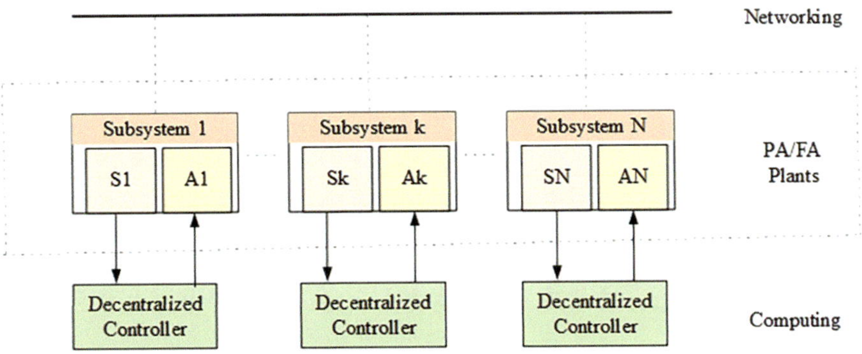

Figure 20.9 Decentralized controller.

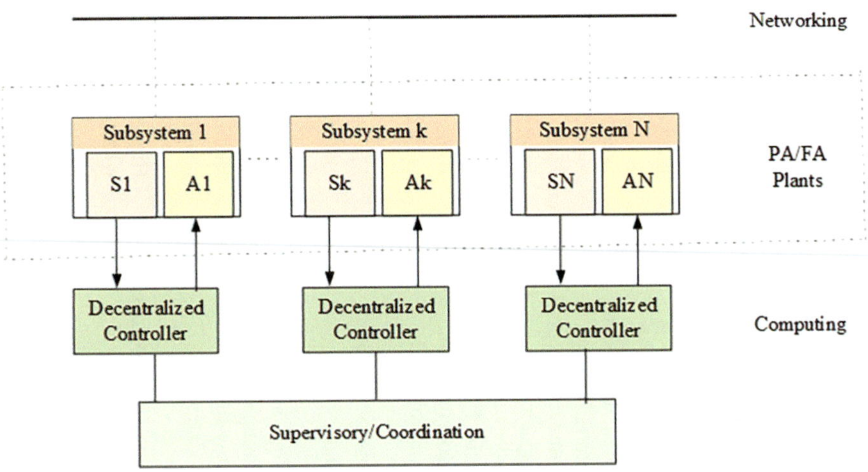

Figure 20.10 Hierarchical control.

and end devices. These control systems, through their integration and the use of advanced communication technologies, are fundamental to the operation of modern industrial applications. However, their vulnerability to security risks necessitates ongoing research into secure and efficient operation solutions.

Table 20.3 contrasts the key characteristics of IIoT control system architectures, including hierarchical, decentralized, and centralized control models. Each architecture seeks to optimize system performance by distributing control, data processing, and decision-making across different system levels. This comparison highlights their unique scalability, responsiveness, and system complexity approaches.

Table 20.3 Control systems in IoT.

Feature	IIoT control systems	Centralized control	Decentralized control	Hierarchical control
Characterization	IoT-integrated control systems enable real-time industrial automation	A single central controller manages the entire system	Several controllers, each in charge of a certain subsystem	Central and local control units are combined in multi-level control
Architecture	Distributed and connected through IoT platforms	Centralized and cloud-reliant	Decentralized, with independent control nodes	Layered structure with local, regional, and central controllers
Latency	Low, enabling near-real-time responses	High, due to data centralization	Low, as processing is localized	Moderate, depending on communication between layers
Scalability	Highly scalable through IoT-based connections	Limited by central controller capacity	High, due to the independent nature of control nodes	Moderate to high, depending on system hierarchy depth
Reliability	High, with redundancy through multiple IoT nodes	Low, vulnerable to central point failure	High, with minimal impact from isolated node failures	Very high due to redundancy at multiple levels
Security	High, leveraging IoT security protocols and edge computing	Moderate, prone to a single point of attack	High, as localized systems reduce attack surfaces	Very high, with multi-layered security measures
Complexity	High, due to IoT device integration and network dependencies	Low, with simpler control logic	Moderate coordination among decentralized units	High coordination between hierarchical layers is complex
Communication overhead	Moderate, with efficient IoT protocols (MQTT, CoAP)	High, as all data flows through a central point	Low, since communication is mostly local	Moderate, with inter-layer communication
Flexibility	Very high, adaptable to dynamic industrial processes	Low changes require central updates	High, with adaptable local controllers	Moderate, balancing central policies with local adjustments
Fault tolerance	High, with self-healing and redundancy in IoT nodes	Low, single point of failure	High faults are contained within subsystems	Very high, with fallback mechanisms at different levels
Applications	Smart factories, predictive maintenance, autonomous systems	Traditional manufacturing, legacy systems	Distributed energy systems, modular production lines	Smart grids, large-scale industrial automation, smart cities

20.3.5 Evolution from CPSs to CPSSs

The integration of human and social dynamics into CPSs led to the emergence of CPSSs in 2010. This integration seeks to enhance coordination among the physical environment, cyberspace, and human resources, with the goal of making businesses and industries more innovative and more productive. Over the years, CPS research [39] has yielded innovative solutions, and CPSSs – also known as enhanced living environments (ELEs) – have garnered significant attention for their role in facilitating human engagement. In CPSSs, humans participate in two primary roles: as service providers, contributing through sensing and actuation, and as consumers, accessing the services. Citizen actuation involves the use of actuators to take action based on collected data, while citizen sensing relies on sensors operated by citizens to gather and report data [40].

Research [41] indicates that these features can significantly enhance energy efficiency, with citizen actuation shown to reduce energy consumption by up to 24%. Additionally, two critical components of CPSSs are crowdsourcing and crowdsensing. Crowdsensing leverages mobile devices to expand data collection and sensing coverage at a lower cost compared to traditional sensor networks, while crowdsourcing taps into the collective intelligence of groups to obtain services and ideas. These methods are supported by platforms like CARDAP, which offer scalable, energy-efficient data analytics to enhance processing and resource utilization. Understanding human behavior, particularly in the context of service provision, is crucial for the effective design of CPSSs. Key considerations include task management, user identification, human accessibility, and the dynamic nature of human interactions.

Assigning tasks can be challenging due to the unpredictable nature of human behavior and the variability of performance over time. However, a human behavior model can help by aligning tasks with qualifications of users and capabilities. Moreover, analyzing user-related data, such as access duration and task completion quality, further supports this process by encouraging active participation. By categorizing users based on performance, offering incentives for top performers, and sanctions for underperformers, CPSSs foster greater engagement. Ultimately, incorporating human input, enhancing system adaptability, and ensuring effective management through motivated participation significantly improves the overall functionality of CPSSs. The feedback loop between citizen sensing and actuation, shown in Figure 20.11, begins with data acquisition, where state data is gathered and processed. Next is information retrieval, where users interpret insights via visual tools like graphs and alerts. In the third phase, user feedback refines the system based

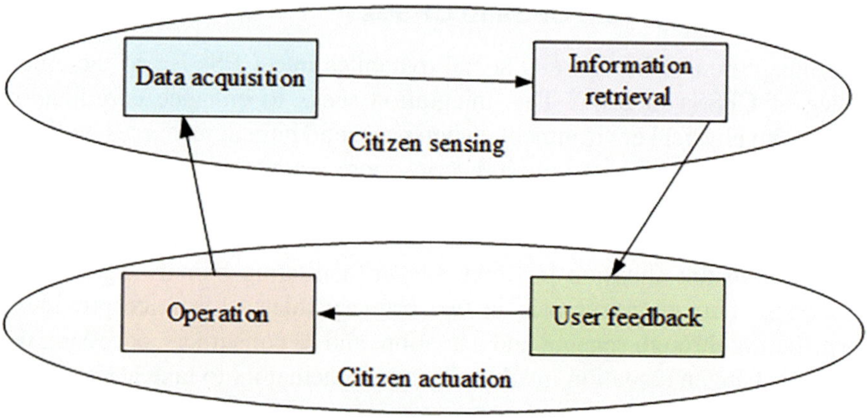

Figure 20.11 Citizen sensing and actuation feedback loop.

on user input. Finally, users take operation, influencing the system and triggering a new feedback loop for continuous improvement.

20.3.6 Applications

Figure 20.12 presents a conceptual vision of CPSS. Unlike traditional design paradigms that exclude human elements from the system loop, contradicting the widely embraced user-centered design philosophy, CPSSs aim to integrate human participation. This integration fosters the continuous enhancement of environmental intelligence through innovative social applications such as citizen actuation and citizen sensing. CPSSs have transformative potential across various domains, including transportation, industry, agriculture, environmental sustainability, energy, and healthcare. This section will provide real-world case studies, highlight relevant standards, and review the current state of research on CPSS applications. A comprehensive analysis of recent advancements reveals the vast market potential of CPSSs in driving intelligence across diverse application areas.

20.3.6.1 Transportation

Integrating automobiles with pedestrians, other vehicles, and infrastructure CPSSs can be effectively developed to enhance smart traffic management. These connections facilitate real-time environmental data collection and analysis by supporting semi-autonomous and autonomous driving. Intelligent transportation spaces integrate pedestrians, vehicles, roadside infrastructure, and traffic management centers to promote traffic safety and sustainability.

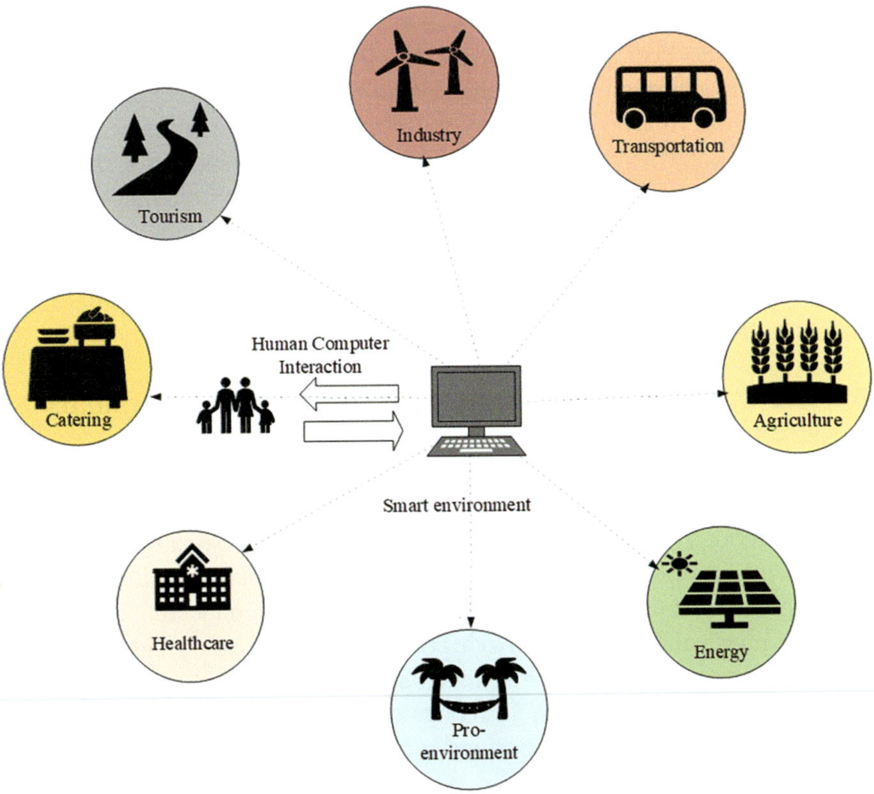

Figure 20.12 Applications of CPSSs across key sectors.

CPSS-based intelligent transportation systems (ITSs) enable smart parking and communication-driven traffic control innovations. The authors in [42] explore the architecture, applications, traffic data characteristics, and operational mechanisms of ITS, emphasizing its multifaceted approach to improving urban mobility. Furthermore, society is viewed as an active participant in sensing, computing, communication, control, and management, highlighting the crucial role of human involvement in ITS operations. This paradigm, referred to as transportation 5.0, envisions the future of ITS as a collaborative, human-centric system aimed at fostering safer and more sustainable transportation networks.

An important application of CPSSs in transportation is the development of intelligent vehicles with varying levels of automation, from continuous driver monitoring to full driver disengagement for specified periods. However, fully autonomous driving faces challenges in complex, dynamic environments, limiting reliability. A cloud-based CPSS framework for parallel driving has been proposed to address this, enhancing connected autonomous driving through secure vehicle-driver-information interactions using parallel testing, machine learning, and reinforcement learning techniques. Traffic signals are also crucial in CPSS-driven smart transportation. Research [43] introduces a self-configuring traffic signal control system that combines signal controllers with a centralized configuration center, dynamically adjusting to social traffic dynamics. Experimental results confirm its feasibility, offering significant improvements in traffic management for future intelligent transportation networks.

20.3.6.2 Intelligent manufacturing and smart factory systems

In social manufacturing and smart factories, CPSSs collect manufacturing data from connected facilities to optimize production through data analysis, enabling dynamic configuration and adaptation to consumer behavior and business models. Social manufacturing focuses on personalized products and services for prosumers, addressing business models, architecture, and challenges. Smart factories similarly integrate CPSSs, connecting cyber control with physical factories via NodeTrix-based visualization. Smart factory operation management also presents CPSS-based manufacturing modes for mutually beneficial outcomes. To reduce data latency, the in-line data deduplication file system improves performance by decoupling unique data blocks and fingerprint indices [44].

20.3.6.3 Ecology and sustainable development

CPSSs can significantly contribute to sustainable development and environmental preservation. For example, a CPSS-based agricultural management system reduces labor and fertilizer waste, promoting sustainable production. In contrast, a smart hydroponic farming system monitors variables such as temperature and humidity for adaptive system control. To address challenges such as population shifts and climate change, CPSSs are employed in river basins to develop smart water grids that integrate data collection, decision support, and automated responses [45].

20.3.6.4 Energy allocation

Smart grids are used in cities for smart energy distribution, which provides user-aware power to residences, workplaces, and other applications. In order to optimize energy distribution, the system gathers and examines regional data. The consumer-centered energy system (CCES), as suggested in [46], integrates power grids, communications, computation, and consumer interactions to achieve effective energy coordination through smart grid and electric car integration. Furthermore, CPSSs improve gasoline distribution; in public petrol stations, CPSS-based inventory control raises customer satisfaction and sustainability.

20.3.6.5 Healthcare

CPSSs enable smart personal healthcare by utilizing sensors placed on the body or within medical facilities to monitor health conditions and detect potential issues. This real-time data allows healthcare professionals to prescribe appropriate treatments and offer informed advice. Furthermore, CPSSs support advanced systems, such as bionic limbs and robotic surgery, through the integration of customized medical devices. The research [47] has expanded the application of CPSSs in e-healthcare, notably through the use of green CPSS frameworks designed to manage infectious diseases. These frameworks analyze social factors to predict and prevent outbreaks, offering a proactive approach to public health. Moreover, CPSS-driven smart recommender systems enhance personalized healthcare. These systems leverage sophisticated algorithms to match patients with doctors based on performance metrics and personal preferences, addressing the common challenge of selecting the most suitable physician. By considering a patient's symptoms and medical history, these systems significantly improve the accuracy and effectiveness of healthcare recommendations, thereby optimizing patient outcomes.

20.3.6.6 Hospitality and tourism

Smart recommendation systems [48] are applied in fields like catering and tourism. A group-centric recommender system for personalized smart computing in CPSSs includes group discovery, preference modeling, and rating revision. Smart culinary systems, incorporating GPS, cloud computing, and social media, can recommend restaurants and provide location-based services for tourists. Similarly, cultural heritage spaces use recommendation systems to suggest museums and attractions. To reduce contextual complexity, the dynamic social structure of things (DSSoT) framework helps users navigate unfamiliar places. It classifies social objects and smart services to meet the short-term goals of users. In geological services, a novel modeling method based on cyber–physical–social thinking (CPST) evaluates geological hazards in dynamic environments. Smart evacuation systems are essential in crowded places like restaurants. A framework for artificial evacuation systems simulates evacuation processes and uses CPSS-based computational experiments to guide real-time evacuations.

Table 20.4 presents the diverse applications of CPSSs across various industries, including energy, tourism, healthcare, and transportation.

Table 20.4 Overview of CPSS applications across various domains.

Application area	Description	Key components	Impact
Transportation	Autonomous driving, intelligent traffic management, and effective public transportation are all made possible by CPSSs	Cloud platforms for data analysis, sensors for data collecting, vehicle-to-everything (V2X) connection, and AI algorithms for traffic optimization	Decreases traffic, improves road safety, and makes autonomous and semi-automated driving possible
Intelligent manufacturing and smart factory systems	By combining IoT devices, data analytics, and human feedback for dynamic manufacturing processes, CPSSs in smart factories maximize production	IoT devices for real-time monitoring, cloud computing for data processing, human–machine interfaces for adaptive control, AI for predictive analytics	Enhances productivity, cuts waste, and modifies production to meet consumer tastes and market demands
Ecology and sustainable development	Through pollution prevention, water management, and intelligent agriculture systems, CPSSs help to preserve environment	Social features for citizen input, automation systems for adaptive responses, data analytics for resource optimization, and sensors for environmental monitoring	Encourages effective environmental management, trash reduction, and resource conservation
Energy allocation	By combining electric vehicles, renewable energy sources, and user-centric energy management, CPSSs make smart energy distribution networks possible	Electric vehicle integration for energy storage, smart grids for optimizing energy flow, and consumer-centric systems for individualized energy use	Increases power system dependability, encourages use of renewable energy, and boosts energy efficiency
Healthcare	Provide individualized and preventive care; CPSSs integrate wearable sensors, smart medical devices, and remote monitoring	Cloud platforms for data sharing, wearable sensors for health monitoring, robotics and AI for surgery and diagnostics, remote monitoring systems for telemedicine	It enhances patient care, aids in early diagnosis, and makes robotic surgery and telehealth services possible
Hospitality and tourism	CPSSs in hospitality and tourism provide personalized experiences through smart recommendation systems for dining, lodging, and activities	GPS for location tracking, cloud computing for real-time data, recommender engines for personalized suggestions, social media integration for user feedback	Increases the effectiveness of service delivery and improves client happiness by providing customized experiences

Each sector leverages the integration of sensors, data analytics, and user engagement within CPSSs to enhance efficiency and sustainability. The table outlines key components and impacts, demonstrating how CPSSs drive innovation, optimize processes, and elevate overall system performance.

20.4 Recent Trends, Future Research Directions, and Lessons Learned

This section delves into the critical insights and emerging trends shaping the advancements in CPS and their evolution into CPSS. By integrating cutting-edge technologies such as artificial intelligence and edge computing, CPS has demonstrated transformative potential in domains like healthcare, smart grids, autonomous systems, and industrial automation. The transition to CPSS, characterized by the inclusion of human and social dimensions, has further broadened the scope of applications, enabling systems to become more user-centric, adaptive, and socially aware. This discussion highlights the technological innovations and challenges, such as ensuring security and ethical considerations in complex, interconnected environments. Moreover, the section identifies promising areas for future research, including the development of resilient architectures, enhanced human–machine interaction, and sustainable practices. These advancements and directions underscore the significant potential of CPS and CPSS to drive innovation and address pressing societal needs.

20.4.1 Recent trends

CPS is evolving rapidly with advancements in various technologies. The integration of AI and machine learning has enabled real-time data processing, predictive analytics, and autonomous decision-making, improving the efficiency of applications like smart factories and autonomous vehicles. Edge and cloud computing are being adopted to address latency and bandwidth limitations, bringing computation closer to data sources for faster responses. The rise of digital twins has provided virtual representations of physical systems, offering real-time monitoring, simulation, and predictive maintenance to enhance system reliability. Furthermore, the proliferation of IoT and the rollout of 5G networks have boosted connectivity, enabling seamless interaction between devices and supporting complex, low-latency applications.

Security has become a critical focus area, with innovations such as blockchain, zero-trust architectures, and physical-layer security emerging to protect CPS from evolving cyber threats. Human-centric and collaborative systems are also gaining prominence by incorporating user preferences, behaviors, and social contexts, fostering more intuitive and efficient interactions in domains like healthcare and smart cities. Additionally, sustainability is a growing priority, with CPS solutions increasingly designed to optimize energy consumption and integrate renewable energy sources. These trends collectively showcase how CPS is adapting to meet the demands of modern applications while addressing challenges in efficiency and security.

20.4.2 Research directions

CPSSs present challenges and opportunities requiring innovative research to achieve optimization, sustainability, and robust system performance. One critical area is energy management, as many connected devices, such as sensors and actuators, are energy-constrained. Research can focus on designing energy-efficient protocols that balance energy consumption with other performance indicators, leveraging renewable energy sources, and exploring radio energy harvesting methods. While renewable energy integration requires additional infrastructure, radio energy harvesting offers a space-efficient alternative, albeit with challenges like random fluctuations in energy availability. Intelligent caching and computing are also vital for advancing CPSSs. Optimizing caching involves addressing dynamic user preferences, content diversity, and data characteristics, where machine learning can predict content popularity and user mobility for smarter decisions. In computing, CPSSs must process vast amounts of data in real time while filtering out noise. Intelligent computing, supported by machine learning, can streamline this process and enable predictive analytics. Collaborative computing, which uses nearby servers for distributed tasks, can further enhance efficiency in handling big data.

Resource coordination and security are additional pressing issues. Distributed multi-resource deployment can address scalability challenges in large-scale CPSSs by utilizing algorithms like the alternating direction method of multipliers to reduce computational complexity. Security and privacy are equally critical, with CPSSs requiring robust solutions to prevent side-channel attacks and safeguard user data. Techniques like physical layer security and differential privacy models can provide enhanced protection while supporting real-time big data analysis. Lastly, cross-layer and cross-system design must evolve to accommodate the heterogeneous nature of CPSSs, ensuring compatibility and performance optimization across diverse intelligent and functional systems.

20.4.3 Lesson learned

The transition from CPS to CPSS introduces a new dimension of complexity by integrating social elements into the cyber–physical framework. This integration emphasizes balancing technological advancements with human-centric considerations, such as user preferences, dynamic behaviors, and collaborative interactions. The lesson learned highlights the need for collaborative approaches and advanced technologies to address the dynamic demands of CPSSs effectively.

Lesson 1: Toward an advanced modeling paradigm for CPS design and validation

Current modeling approaches fail to address the diverse and complex requirements of CPS fully. In the past, system description languages were sufficient for designing entire systems. However, due to the increasing complexity and diversity of CPS, these languages now fall short of capturing critical physical details, such as the geographical locations of networked components. This limitation highlights the need for a specialized modeling language tailored for CPS development. For instance, Ptolemy II provides a certain level of encapsulation and abstraction, which somewhat supports CPS design. Nevertheless, it does not adequately address the needs of all application domains. An ideal modeling language for CPS would seamlessly integrate event-driven computation and communication with real-time control mechanisms. Moreover, it should balance abstract representation and detailed physical and cyber information, ensuring comprehensive system coverage while maintaining manageability. The new modeling paradigm must enable designers to effectively develop, verify, and validate CPS. It should address both physical and cyber dimensions to ensure high levels of reliability and adaptability, even in complex real-world applications. Such an approach would mark a significant step toward creating dependable, reconfigurable, and holistic CPS models that meet the stringent demands of modern systems.

Lesson 2: Impact of CPS, Industry 4.0, and IoT proliferation

Traditional centralized data centers have long served as the backbone of cloud services. However, they increasingly fall short of meeting the QoS demands for applications requiring computationally intensive and latency-sensitive data processing. This shortcoming emphasizes the necessity of transitioning toward more dynamic and distributed cloud models to accommodate modern CPS requirements. The proliferation of CPS, Industry 4.0, and IoT technologies has led to an exponential increase in data generated at the edge of networks. The adoption of 5G and beyond will further amplify this trend by enabling a vast number of interconnected IoT devices in CPS applications. Organizations are turning to edge computing and edge-cloud computing paradigms in response to this data explosion. These approaches decentralize data processing by extending computational and storage resources closer to end-users through scaled-down data centers positioned at the network edge.

Technologically, edge servers, functioning as microdata centers, bring analytics and AI closer to the end-users and processes they serve. By eliminating the need to transfer massive CPS data to centralized data centers, edge computing reduces latency, enhances resiliency, optimizes bandwidth usage, and lowers costs. Leading industrial automation and digitalization firms like Schneider Electric APC, Advantech, and Siemens are integrating edge intelligence and advanced data analytics into their platforms. This enables real-time data collection, storage, and processing at the network edge, empowering businesses with immediate insights and facilitating smarter decision-making. The evolution toward edge-centric architectures is a pivotal step in addressing the demands of modern CPS applications. It meets the real-time processing and reliability needs of these systems and enables the effective deployment of intelligent, supervised digitalized solutions across diverse domains. This lesson underscores the strategic importance of edge computing in shaping the future of CPS.

Lesson 3: Energy efficiency, reliability, and challenges in edge computing for CPS

Although instrumental in supporting CPS requiring real-time responsiveness and high reliability, edge computing and edge-cloud computing inherently exhibit greater energy consumption than traditional cloud computing when processing identical applications. This increased energy demand is a consequence of the distributed nature of computational resources within edge paradigms, which prioritize reduced service latency over energy efficiency. Despite these trade-offs, edge computing is indispensable for latency-sensitive CPS applications, whereas cloud computing remains a more energy-efficient alternative for scenarios that can tolerate transient failures and less stringent latency requirements. As CPS scales up, the reliability of edge and edge-cloud computing systems tends to diminish significantly. This degradation arises from the dependence on the coordinated operation of numerous interconnected components in large-scale systems. The failure of even a single component can substantially increase the risk of erroneous outputs. Moreover, CPS subsystems' intrinsic heterogeneity and tightly coupled nature introduce challenges in establishing a universal authentication protocol for edge computing-assisted applications. Instead, bespoke authentication mechanisms are essential to facilitate secure and efficient user handovers, particularly in the context of advanced communication networks.

Lesson 4: Next-generation communication solutions for enhancing real-time CPS performance

The limited bandwidth of current communication systems further constrains the performance of real-time CPS applications supported by edge or edge-cloud computing. However, the advent of next-generation communication technologies, such as 5G and 6G, promises to alleviate these limitations. These technologies offer a pathway to enhanced bandwidth, reduced latency, and improved system reliability, creating new opportunities for the seamless integration of edge computing into CPS. Future research should focus on effectively leveraging these advanced communication technologies to address the challenges inherent in edge computing. Integrating next-generation communication solutions with edge and edge-cloud paradigms will unlock the full potential of real-time CPS applications, ensuring higher energy efficiency, reliability, and security in increasingly complex and dynamic environments.

Lesson 5: Advancing ICS with self-awareness, diagnosis, and healing

ICSs, categorized as centralized, distributed, or hierarchical, are undergoing transformative advancements through the integration of IIoT technologies. A critical mission within IIoT is enabling self-awareness, self-diagnosis, and self-healing in these systems. Self-awareness allows control systems to monitor industrial operations' health and production quality. Self-diagnosis and self-healing capabilities ensure that faults and failures are promptly detected, classified, and addressed with appropriate corrective actions, significantly enhancing system reliability and resilience. Despite these advancements, achieving such capabilities presents challenges, particularly in managing the significant overhead associated with data collection, processing, analysis, and transmission. Large-scale industrial systems generate massive volumes of data during continuous monitoring, necessitating high-capacity computing resources, such as cloud computing, for timely analysis and processing. These time-sensitive operations are vital to maintaining the efficiency and functionality of industrial systems under multidimensional disturbances. Predictive learning algorithms, including supervised, unsupervised, semi-supervised, and reinforcement learning, are crucial for extracting valuable insights from big industrial data. These methods can uncover hidden patterns and correlations, aiding control systems in making informed decisions. This lesson emphasizes the need for advanced computational strategies and predictive analytics to enable self-awareness, diagnosis, and healing in industrial control systems. These innovations are essential for efficient management, effective resource utilization, and timely maintenance in the dynamic industrial landscape.

Lesson 6: Improving performance and resilience in ICS
Achieving the performance objectives of ICS, such as efficient management, effective utilization, and timely maintenance, requires seamless coordination across all stages of the manufacturing lifecycle – preparation, production, transportation, utilization, and recycling. Information exchange between these stages enhances efficiency by balancing demand and supply, while full utilization of production resources minimizes waste and maximizes productivity. Timely maintenance ensures the health of critical infrastructure, mitigating risks and preventing potential damage. Key enablers for these objectives include visualization, virtualization, and interoperability, which provide better infrastructure insights and assist operators in making optimal decisions. However, the complexity of managing diverse devices and configurations in industrial environments increases the challenges of observability and controllability. To address these challenges, resilience emerges as a critical property of ICS. Resilience entails the ability of a system to withstand and recover from disturbances, including malfunctions, physical component failures, and cyberattacks. It can be measured by the reaction time of the system and its ability to maintain functionality during and after disturbances. These lessons highlight the importance of integrating advanced resilience assessment and response mechanisms into ICS. By understanding disturbances and developing appropriate preventive and reactive strategies, industrial systems can achieve greater reliability, adaptability, and functionality in dynamic and challenging environments.

Lesson 7: Leveraging CPSSs for intelligent community development
The integration of both contemporary methods and the natural resources of the local population drives the development of an intelligent environment. To enhance smart surroundings, it is essential to incorporate both "things" and "humans." By applying advanced technologies, individuals can benefit from intelligent services while contributing to the advancement of business intelligence. As CPSs continue to evolve, CPSSs emerge as a crucial strategy for fostering a smarter environment. CPSSs collect and analyze data from individuals, offering users increased awareness and engagement.

Lesson 8: Promoting CPSS integration of standards and applications
To promote CPSSs and simplify their implementation, designing the system's different parts – physical, cyber, social, physical–cyber, and cyber–social – separately allows existing standards and proposals to be applied more straightforwardly. However, operating these parts as a whole requires

standards to be integrated and harmonized. Current real-world case studies of CPSSs are often confined to a single research area, which limits their applicability across diverse fields due to varied application and business requirements. The challenge lies in modifying main standards to implement efficient interfaces among existing proposals, which impacts whether CPSSs can be commercialized. Despite these challenges, the theoretical developments of CPSSs demonstrate significant potential across various sectors, including transportation, industry, agriculture, environment, energy, healthcare, catering, and tourism. As the IoT evolves, the market for CPSSs will expand, offering new momentum for the global economy. The future of CPSSs involves designing a comprehensive platform and business model that integrates relevant technologies and human behavior patterns. This will enable long-term development by achieving multi-win scenarios for hardware or software manufacturers, network operators, system integrators, and service providers. Advances in CPSSs will enhance adaptability, capability, resiliency, scalability, safety, security, and usability, surpassing today's simple embedded systems. The mature foundation of CPSs provides an effective channel for implementing CPSSs, which benefit from taking humans as part of the system, forming a closed loop that makes smart environments even smarter.

20.5 Conclusions and Future Scope

This chapter reviews the design and application of CPS, focusing on an integrated system approach rather than treating cyber and physical components separately. It outlines the requirements of CPS components and highlights current advancements. The chapter also surveys the IIoT, covering its architecture, applications, and ongoing research in control, communication, and computing systems, emphasizing cloud and edge computing. Additionally, it explores the evolution of CPSs into CPSSs, discussing key research, standards, and real-world case studies. A virtualized CPSS architecture is proposed, incorporating wireless network virtualization and an integrated framework for caching, computing, and networking, optimized through a four-dimensional approach.

The next generation of CPS must be scalable and maintain reliable performance in dynamic environments. Industry 4.0 exemplifies this evolution, integrating cloud computing, big data, and the IoT to enable seamless communication between cyber and physical domains. To support future CPS, new software architectures are needed to manage resources, ensure security, and offer application-independent services. Additionally, advances in software-defined networking are essential for accommodating diverse applications on a unified platform. This chapter addresses challenges in IIoT computing systems, such as the seamless integration of computing resources, and identifies key research needs in control, networking, and machine learning integration. It explores the techniques and networks required to advance CPSSs, focusing on hyper-connectivity, hyper-intelligence, and hyper-automation. Key research challenges and possible solutions for future exploration are highlighted, emphasizing proactive efforts from the wireless community. The chapter provides an overview of CPSS architecture and applications, outlining future research directions for the development of the smart world.

References

[1] Y. Lu, "Cyber physical system (CPS)-based industry 4.0: A survey," Journal of Industrial Integration and Management, vol. 2, no. 3, p. 1750014, Sep. 2017, doi: 10.1142/S2424862217500142.

[2] G. Wu, J. Sun, and J. Chen, "A survey on the security of cyber-physical systems," Control Theory and Technology, vol. 14, no. 1, pp. 2–10, Feb. 2016, doi: 10.1007/s11768-016-5123-9.

[3] L. P. Chang, T. W. Kuo, C. Gill, and J. Nakazawa, "Introduction to the special issue on real-time, embedded and cyber-physical systems," ACM Transactions on Embedded Computing Systems, vol. 13, no. 5S, p. 155, Nov. 2014, doi: 10.1145/2660488.

[4] A. Humayed, J. Q. Lin, F. J. Li, and B. Luo, "Cyber-physical systems security — A survey," IEEE Internet Things Journal, vol. 4, no. 6, pp. 1802–1831, Dec. 2017, doi: 10.1109/JIOT.2017.2703172.

[5] M. Wollschlaeger, T. Sauter, and J. Jasperneite, "The future of industrial communication: Automation networks in the era of the Internet of Things and Industry 4.0," IEEE Industrial Electronics Magazine, vol. 11, no. 1, pp. 17–27, Mar. 2017, doi: 10.1109/MIE.2017.2649104.

[6] F.-H. Tseng, M.-S. Tsai, C.-W. Tseng, Y.-T. Yang, C.-C. Liu, and L.-D. Chou, "A lightweight autoscaling mechanism for fog computing in industrial applications," IEEE Transactions on Industrial Informatics, vol. 14, no. 10, pp. 4529–4537, Oct. 2018, doi: 10.1109/TII.2018.2799230.

[7] J. Ren, D. Zhang, S. He, Y. Zhang, and T. Li, "A survey on end-edge-cloud orchestrated network computing paradigms," ACM Computing Surveys, vol. 52, no. 6, pp. 1–36, Oct.2019, doi: 10.1145/3362031.

[8] V. Tsiatsis, K. Stamatis, J. Höller, D. Boyle, and C. Mulligan, Internet of Things: Technologies and Applications for a New Age of

Intelligence. New York, NY, USA: Academic, Nov.2018, doi: 10.1016/C2017-0-00369-5.

[9] J. Lin, W. Yu, N. Zhang, X. Yang, H. Zhang, and W. Zhao, “A survey on Internet of Things: Architecture, enabling technologies, security and privacy, and applications,” IEEE Internet Things Journal, vol. 4, no. 5, pp. 1125–1142, Oct. 2017, doi: 10.1109/JIOT.2017.2683200.

[10] E. A. Lee and S. A. Seshia, Introduction to Embedded Systems: A Cyber-Physical Systems Approach. Berkeley, CA, USA: Lee & Seshia, 2011.

[11] P. McDaniel and S. McLaughlin, “Security and privacy challenges in the smart grid,” IEEE Security & Privacy, vol. 7, no. 3, pp. 75–77, May/Jun. 2009, doi: 10.1109/MSP.2009.76.

[12] M. Rushanan, A. D. Rubin, D. F. Kune, and C. M. Swanson, “SoK: Security and privacy in implantable medical devices and body area networks,” in Proceedings of the IEEE Symposium Security Privacy (SP), Berkeley, CA, USA, 2014, pp. 524–539, doi: 10.1109/SP.2014.40.

[13] S. K. Sowe, E. Simmon, K. Zettsu, F. de Vaulx, and I. Bojanova, “Cyber-physical-human systems: Putting people in the loop,” IT Professional, vol. 18, no. 1, pp. 10–13, Jan./Feb. 2016, doi: 10.1109/MITP.2016.14.

[14] X. Zheng, Z. Cai, J. Yu, C. Wang, and Y. Li, “Follow but no track: Privacy preserved profile publishing in cyber-physical social systems,” IEEE Internet Things Journal, vol. 4, no. 6, pp. 1868–1878, Dec. 2017, doi: 10.1109/JIOT.2017.2679483.

[15] J. Liu, D.-S. Yang, D. Wen, W.-M. Zhang, and W. Mao, “Cyber-physical-social systems for command and control,” IEEE Intelligent Systems, vol. 26, no. 4, pp. 92–96, Jul./Aug. 2011, doi: 10.1109/MIS.2011.69.

[16] H. F. Fan, M. Ni, L. L. Zhao, and M. L. Li, “Review of cyber physical system and cyber attack modeling,” in Proceedings of the 12th IEEE PES Asia-Pacific Power and Energy Engineering Conference, Nanjing, China, 2020, pp. 1–5, doi: 10.1109/APPEEC48164.2020.9220505.

[17] B. A. Yilma, H. Panetto, and Y. Naudet, “Systemic formalisation of Cyber-Physical-Social System (CPSS): A systematic literature review,” arXiv, Apr. 2021, doi: 10.48550/arXiv.2104.05710.

[18] K. Cao, L. Li, Y. Cui, T. Wei, and S. Hu, “Exploring placement of heterogeneous edge servers for response time minimization in mobile edge-cloud computing,” IEEE Transactions on Industrial Informatics, vol. 17, no. 1, pp. 494–503, Jan. 2021, doi: 10.1109/TII.2020.2975897.

[19] L. Shu, M. Mukherjee, M. Pecht, N. Crespi, and S. N. Han, “Challenges and research issues of data management in IoT for large-scale

petrochemical plants," IEEE Systems Journal, vol. 12, no. 3, pp. 2509–2523, Sep. 2017, doi: 10.1109/JSYST.2017.2700268.

[20] W. Sun, J. Liu, Y. Yue, and H. Zhang, "Double auction-based resource allocation for mobile edge computing in industrial Internet of Things," IEEE Transactions on Industrial Informatics, vol. 14, no. 10, pp. 4692–4701, Oct. 2018, doi: 10.1109/TII.2018.2855746.

[21] S. Jeong, W. Na, J. Kim, and S. Cho, "Internet of Things for smart manufacturing system: Trust issues in resource allocation," IEEE Internet of Things Journal, Mar. 2018, doi: 10.1109/JIOT.2018.2814063.

[22] P. Duan, Y. Jia, L. Liang, J. Rodriguez, K. M. S. Huq, and G. Li, "Space-reserved cooperative caching in 5G heterogeneous networks for industrial IoT," IEEE Transactions on Industrial Informatics, vol. 14, no. 6, pp. 2715–2724, Jun. 2018, doi: 10.1109/TII.2018.2794615.

[23] A. A. Cardenas, S. Amin, Z. Lin, Y.-L. Huang, C.-Y. Huang, and S. Sastry, "Attacks against process control systems: Risk assessment, detection, and response," in Proceedings of the 6th ACM Symposium Information Computer and Communications Security, Hong Kong, 2011, pp. 355–366, doi: 10.1145/1966913.1966959.

[24] X. D. Koutsoukos, "Systems science of secure and resilient cyber-physical systems," Computer, vol. 53, no. 3, pp. 57–61,Mar. 2020, doi: 10.1109/MC.2020.2966109.

[25] A. K. Sikder, G. Petracca, H. Aksu, T. Jaeger, and A. S. Uluagac, "A survey on sensor-based threats and attacks to smart devices and applications," IEEE Communications Surveys & Tutorials, vol. 23, no. 2, pp. 1125–1159, Mar. 2021, doi: 10.1109/COMST.2021.3064507.

[26] S. Kim, K.-J. Park, and C. Lu, "A Survey on Network Security for Cyber–Physical Systems: From Threats to Resilient Design," IEEE Communications Surveys & Tutorials, vol. 24, no. 3, pp. 1325–1349, Sep. 2022, doi: 10.1109/COMST.2022.3187531.

[27] W. Duo, M. Zhou, and A. Abusorrah, "A Survey of Cyber Attacks on Cyber Physical Systems: Recent Advances and Challenges," IEEE/CAA Journal of Automatica Sinica, vol. 9, no. 5, pp. 1051–1063, May 2022, doi: 10.1109/JAS.2022.105548.

[28] T. Alladi, V. Chamola, and S. Zeadally, "Industrial control systems: Cyberattack trends and countermeasures," Computer Communication, vol. 155, pp. 1–8, Apr. 2020, doi: 10.1016/j.comcom.2020.03.007.

[29] S. Rani, S. Aman Kataria, S. Kumar, and V. Karar, "A new generation cyber-physical system: A comprehensive review from security perspective," Computers & Security, vol. 104095, 2024. doi: 10.1016/j.cose.2024.104095.

[30] X. Guan, B. Yang, C. Chen, W. Dai, and Y. Wang, “A comprehensive overview of cyber-physical systems: From perspective of feedback system,” IEEE/CAA Journal of Automatica Sinica, vol. 3, no. 1, pp. 1–14, Jan. 2016, doi: 10.1109/JAS.2016.7389672.

[31] M. A. Wehrmeister, C. E. Pereira, and F. J. Rammig, “Aspect-oriented model-driven engineering for embedded systems applied to automation systems,” IEEE Transactions on Industrial Informatics, vol. 9, no. 4, pp. 2373–2386, Nov. 2013, doi: 10.1109/TII.2012.2236545.

[32] R. Bruschi, F. Davoli, P. Lago, and J. F. Pajo, “A multi-clustering approach to scale distributed tenant networks for mobile edge computing,” IEEE Journal on Selected Areas in Communications, vol. 37, no. 3, pp. 499–514, Mar. 2019, doi: 10.1109/JSAC.2019.2894236.

[33] S. Sood and I. Mahajan, “Fog-cloud based cyber-physical system for distinguishing, detecting and preventing mosquito borne diseases,” Future Generation Computer Systems, vol. 88, pp. 764–775, 2018, doi: 10.1016/j.future.2018.01.008.

[34] M. S. Hajar, M. O. Al-Kadri, and H. K. Kalutarage, “A survey on wireless body area networks: architecture, security challenges and research opportunities,” Computers and Security, vol. 104, no. C, pp. 102211, May. 2021, doi: 10.1016/j.cose.2021.102211.

[35] R. Scattolini, “Architectures for distributed and hierarchical model predictive control—A review,” Journal of Process Control, vol. 19, no. 5, pp. 723–731, May. 2009, doi:10.1016/j.jprocont.2009.02.003.

[36] T. C. Yang, “Networked control system: A brief survey,” IEE Proceedings- Control Theory and Applications, vol. 153, no. 4, pp. 403–412, Jul. 2006, doi: 10.1049/ip-cta:20050178.

[37] K. A. Stouffer, V. Y. Pillitteri, S. Lightman, M. Abrams, and A. Hahn, “Guide to industrial control systems (ICS) security,” NIST, Gaithersburg, MD, USA, Tech. Rep. 800-82 Rev 2, 2015,doi:10.6028/NIST.SP.800-82r2 T.

[38] F. Alhebshi, H. Alnabilsi, J. Alzebaidi, A. Bensenouci, T. Brahimi, and M.-A. Bensenouci, “Monitoring the operation of transmission line in a smart grid system through IoT,” in Proceedings of the IEEE 15th Learning Technology Conference (LT), Feb. 2018, pp. 139–146, doi:10.1109/LT.2018.8368498.

[39] J. J. Zhang, F.-Y. Wang, X. Wang, G. Xiong, F. Zhu, L. Yisheng, J. Hou, S. Han, Y. Yuan, Q. Lu, and Y. Lee, “Cyber-Physical-Social Systems: The State of the Art and Perspectives,” IEEE Transactions Computational Social Systems, vol. 5, no. 3, pp. 829–840, Sep. 2018, doi: 10.1109/TCSS.2018.2861224.

[40] X. Wang, L. T. Yang, J. Feng, X. Chen, and M. J. Deen, "A tensor-based big service framework for enhanced living environments," IEEE Cloud Computing, vol. 3, no. 6, pp. 36–43, Nov./Dec. 2016, doi: 10.1109/MCC.2016.130.

[41] D. N. Crowley, E. Curry, and J. G. Breslin, "Citizen actuation for smart environments," IEEE Consumer Electronics Magazine, vol. 5, no. 3, pp. 90–94, Jul. 2016, doi: 10.1109/MCE.2016.2556918.

[42] Y. Zhou, Y. Deng, L. T. Yang, R. Yang, and L. Si, "LDFS: A low latency in-line data deduplication file system," IEEE Access, vol. 6, pp. 15743–15753, 2018, doi: 10.1109/ACCESS.2018.2800763.

[43] H. Ramadhan, D. Oktaria, and I. G. B. B. Nugraha, "Road traffic signal control using cyber physical social system," in Proceedings of the International Conference Information Technology Systems Innovation (ICITSI), Bandung, Indonesia, Oct. 2017, pp. 223–227, doi: 10.1109/ICITSI.2017.8267947.

[44] F. Zhang, M. Liu, and W. Shen, "Operation modes of smart factory for high-end equipment manufacturing in the Internet and big data era," in Proceedings of the IEEE International Conference Systems, Man, Cybernetics (SMC), Banff, AB, Canada, Oct. 2017, pp. 152–157, doi: 10.1109/SMC.2017.8122594.

[45] M. Kang, X.-R. Fan, J. Hua, H. Wang, X. Wang, and F.-Y. Wang, "Managing traditional solar greenhouse with CPSS: A just-for-fit philosophy," IEEE Transactions Cybernetics, vol. 48, no. 12, pp. 3371–3380, Dec. 2018, doi: 10.1109/TCYB.2018.2858264.

[46] X. Cheng, R. Zhang, and L. Yang, "Consumer-centered energy system for electric vehicles and the smart grid," IEEE Intelligent Systems, vol. 31, no. 3, pp. 97–101, May/Jun. 2016, doi: 10.1109/MIS.2016.52.

[47] Q. Xu, Z. S. Su, and Y. Shui, "Green social CPS based e-healthcare systems to control the spread of infectious diseases," in proceedings of the IEEE International Conference on Communications (ICC), Kansas City, MO, USA, May 2018, pp. 1–5, doi: 10.1109/ICC.2018.8422421.

[48] Y. Zhang, "GroRec: A group-centric intelligent recommender system integrating social, mobile and big data technologies," IEEE Transactions on Services Computing, vol. 9, no. 5, pp. 786–795, Sep./Oct. 2016, doi: 10.1109/TSC.2016.2592520.

Index

C

W

Z

About the Editors

Agbotiname Lucky Imoize (senior member, IEEE) received a BEng degree (Hons) in Electrical and Electronics Engineering from Ambrose Alli University, Nigeria, in 2008 and an MSc degree in Electrical and Electronics Engineering from the University of Lagos, Nigeria, in 2012. He is a lecturer in the Department of Electrical and Electronics Engineering at the University of Lagos, Nigeria. Before joining the University of Lagos, he was a lecturer at Bells University of Technology, Nigeria. He has been a research scholar at the Ruhr University Bochum, Germany, under the sponsorship of the Nigerian Petroleum Technology Development Fund (PTDF) and the German Academic Exchange Service (DAAD) through the Nigerian–German Postgraduate Program. He was awarded the Fulbright fellowship as a visiting research scholar at the Wireless@VT Laboratory, Bradley Department of Electrical and Computer Engineering, Virginia Tech., United States, where he worked under the supervision of Prof. R. Michael Buehrer from 2017 to 2018. He worked as a core network products manager at ZTE, Nigeria, and as a network switching subsystem engineer at Globacom, Nigeria. His research interests cover the fields of 6G wireless communication, wireless security systems, holographic metasurfaces, and artificial intelligence. He is the vice chair of the IEEE Communication Society Nigeria chapter. He is a registered engineer with the Council for the Regulation of Engineering in Nigeria and a member of the Nigerian Society of Engineers.

Webert Montlouis (Fellow, IEEE) is a chief scientist at Johns Hopkins University, where he shares his time between the Applied Physics Laboratory (APL) and the Electrical and Computer Engineering Department. He received his PhD degree in electrical engineering from Northeastern University, Boston, MA, United States. His research interests are communications, adaptive signal processing, robust tracking and localization, algorithm development, system-on-chip implementation of DSP algorithms, networking, and antenna array signal processing. He has previously worked for the System Architecture, Design, and Integration Directorate, a division of the Raytheon Company in Boston, MA, where he was cochair of the Radio Communication Propagation and Atmospheric Physics Technical Interest Group. At Raytheon, he was developing system architecture, concept of operations, algorithm development, and performance analysis for phased array radar systems. He has also worked as a technical consultant for consulting firms specializing in developing ASIC and FPGA for communication systems. He is a fellow of the IEEE and a member of the IEEE Signal Processing Society and the IEEE Communications Society.

Segun I. Popoola is a senior lecturer in the School of Computing and Information Science at Anglia Ruskin University, United Kingdom. He received the BTech degree in Electronic and Electrical Engineering from the Ladoke Akintola University of Technology in 2014, the MEng degree in Information and Communication Engineering from the Department of Electrical and Information Engineering, Covenant University, in 2018, and the PhD degree in Cyber Security and Artificial Intelligence from the Department of Engineering, Faculty of Science and Engineering, Manchester Metropolitan University, Manchester, United Kingdom in 2022. His PhD thesis on federated deep learning for botnet attack detection in IoT networks was a product of an academic-industry partnership project jointly funded by the Department of Engineering at Manchester Metropolitan University and a cyber security company, Cyraatek Ltd United Kingdom. He is a lecturer in the Department of Computing and Mathematics at Manchester Metropolitan University, United Kingdom. In June 2022, he was endorsed as a Global Exceptional Talent by The Royal Society. His research interests include wireless communications, deep learning, federated learning, cyber security, the Internet of Things, and smart critical infrastructure. He is a registered engineer with the Council for the Regulation of Engineering in Nigeria (COREN) and a member of IEEE. He has published over 100 research papers in reputable journals and conference proceedings, including IEEE Transactions on Consumer Electronics, IEEE Internet of Things Journal, IEEE Access, and IEEE Vehicular Technology Conference.

Mohammad Hammoudeh is the Saudi Aramco cybersecurity chair professor at King Fahd University of Petroleum and Minerals. His research interests are quantum communication technologies, quantum-safe protection methods, and quantum risk assessment in IT and OT systems. He has hands-on experience in working with quantum hardware and algorithms. Mohammad developed practical ways of thinking when evaluating the real applications of new technology, such as digital twins and blockchains. Mohammad Hammoudeh received the BSc degree in Computer Communications from Arts Sciences and Technology University, Beirut, Lebanon, in 2004, the MSc degree in Advanced Distributed Systems from the University of Leicester, Leicester, United Kingdom, in 2006, the postgraduate certificate in academic practice from Manchester Metropolitan University, Manchester, United Kingdom, in 2011, and the PhD degree in Computer Science from the University of Wolverhampton, Wolverhampton, United Kingdom, in 2008. He is the Saudi Aramco chair professor of cyber security with the Information and Computer Science Department, King Fahd University of Petroleum and Minerals, Dhahran, Saudi Arabia. His research interests include the applications of zero trust security to internet-connected critical national infrastructures, blockchains, the Internet of Things/cyber-physical systems, and other complex, highly decentralized systems. Hammoudeh is the founder and coeditor-in-chief of ACM's journal Distributed Ledger Technology: Research and Practice.

For Product Safety Concerns and Information please contact our EU representative GPSR@taylorandfrancis.com Taylor & Francis Verlag GmbH, Kaufingerstraße 24, 80331 München, Germany